America's Problems

America's Problems

Social Issues and Public Policy

Elliott Currie and Jerome H. Skolnick • UNIVERSITY OF CALIFORNIA, BERKELEY

LITTLE, BROWN AND COMPANY • BOSTON • TORONTO

Library of Congress Cataloging in Publication Data

Currie, Elliott.
    America's problems.

    1. United States — Social conditions — 1980 —   .
2. United States — Social policy — 1980 —   . I. Skolnick,
Jerome H.   II. Title.
HN65.C88   1984   306′.0973   83-24814
ISBN 0-316-16534-4

Library of Congress Catalog Card Number 83-24814

ISBN 0-316-16534-4

9 8 7 6 5 4 3 2 1

HAL

Published simultaneously in Canada
by Little, Brown & Company (Canada) Limited

Printed in the United States of America

Produced by Ron Newcomer & Associates

Acknowledgments
    "Bay Area Firms Loaded with Cash" by Timothy Gartner appearing in the San
Francisco *Chronicle,* January, 16, 1981. © 1981 by San Francisco *Chronicle.* Reprinted
with permission.
    Excerpts from Patrick Derr et al., "Worker/Public Protection: the Double
Standard" and David Burmaster, "The New Pollution: Groundwater
Contamination," reprinted with permission of *Environment,* a publication of the
Helen Dwight Reid Educational Foundation.
    Pages 6 and 281: "Allentown." Words and music by Billy Joel. Copyright © 1981,
1982 by Billy Joel Songs (BMI). Administered by Blackwood Music, Inc., 49 East
52nd Street, New York, New York 10022.

Preface

This book is a social problems text for the 1980s, a decade that may prove to be a turning point in American social thought and policy. After years of pessimism and fashionable despair about social problems, the 1980s bring a growing demand for fresh insights, new perspectives, and a renewed will to change and to experiment.

In the years after World War II, the American mood was strongly optimistic. Americans believed in an indefinite future of affluence and expansion, and their optimism was reflected in social theory and public policy. Yet the early 1980s found many Americans expressing anxiety about the present and despair about the future. Their anxiety and confusion have generated a politics of narrow self-interest that seems increasingly to dominate social and political life.

These developments suggested the themes of a new text on social problems. More than ever, we saw a place for a book that would interpret the forces underlying contemporary changes in American society and American attitudes, and do so in a way that was accessible and interesting to students. We have tried to write a textbook for people who don't like textbooks — one that achieves depth without being stuffy and formal, that teaches without being pedantic, that is up-to-date and timely while staying in touch with the best traditions of social science.

As does our reader, *Crisis in American Institutions*, *America's Problems* assumes that particular problems must be understood in the context of broader social and economic structures and forces that shape them. Too often the literature still treats social problems in isolation from each other and from larger social processes. As a consequence, most texts on social problems, even if they have moved beyond the traditionally narrow focus on personal deviance and disorganization, seem awkwardly fragmented. They often appear to be a hodgepodge of disconnected concerns; they seldom make an effort to provide students with an overall sense of the master forces of their society, and of how these forces affect social and personal life.

Our book's organization addresses these shortcomings. It covers the traditional categories within the field — from family problems to crime and poverty — but consistently focuses on them through the lens of fundamental structures and processes of American society.

Specifically, *America's Problems* is divided into two closely related parts. The first, "Systems and Structures," deals with what we regard as some of the most important of the broad structural features of American society — basic aspects of our social organization that profoundly shape other social problems and the social policies we have devised to cope with them. Chapters 2 and 3 focus on the structure and operation of the *economy* as such a central social institution, while Chapters 4, 5, and 6 address different facets of the social and economic *inequalities* that pervade American life.

Chapter 2 sketches the contours of the American economic system, with particular emphasis on the concentration of economic power in large private corporations and on its relationship to another concentration of power, the government. Much recent social policy has been based on the assertion that government has become an overpowering, all-pervasive force that has slowly crippled the operation of what would otherwise be a model of competitive free enterprise. In Chapter 2, we argue that the relationship between business and government is considerably more complicated than this, and that traditional conceptions of free enterprise bear little relation to the reality of contemporary economic institutions in America. This analysis provides the background for our discussion, in Chapter 3, of the dimensions of the recent crisis of the American economy and of several common explanations for it. We do not pretend that the multiple roots of the economic crisis can be adequately understood in such a brief space, or that a single chapter can substitute for a long and careful study of economic problems. Our aim is the more modest one of sorting through some of the current debates about our economic troubles in order to separate rhetoric from reality.

The following three chapters (Chapters 4, 5, and 6) address the continuing inequalities of class, race, and gender in the United States. All three chapters share a common theme. During the 1970s, some social scientists and policymakers began to argue that these inequalities were on the verge of disappearing, for all practical purposes, from American life. Others argued, on a somewhat different tack, that government antidiscrimination and antipoverty programs had "gone too far" in trying to eliminate social inequalities, and that social stability and economic growth had suffered as a result. These chapters confront such arguments with evidence on continuing patterns of disadvantage by race, class, and gender. In all three chapters, we focus primarily on the broad material aspects of inequality: jobs, income, wealth, and the risk of poverty.

Other aspects of inequality in America are considered in the chapters in Part II, "Institutions and Impacts." These chapters view several areas of social concern through the lenses provided by the larger structural and systemic issues we addressed in Part I. We focus on six areas: the family, work, health, energy and the environment, crime and justice, and national security. Without applying the straightjacket of a rigid theoretical system, we have emphasized the many ways in which the specific troubles of particular institutions are linked, in often rough but nonetheless predictable ways, with the broader structural issues of inequality and the distinctive arrangements of economic priorities in America.

Our concluding chapter, "Social Issues and Public Policy," draws together some of the themes raised throughout the book — not simply to summarize what we've said before, but to help understand some of the possibilities for social change in America. An effective treatment of social problems should not be static; though it cannot predict the future, it should offer some guide to understanding developments on the leading edge of social action and social policy.

The book's organization, then, stresses the linkages in American society between public and private, social and personal, structure and symptom. In addition, two emphases further distinguish *America's Problems* from other texts in the field.

First, though we do not grind axes or indulge in narrow polemic, *America's Problems* (like *Crisis in American Institutions*) does not pretend to be value-neutral. Its approach consistently stresses the values of democracy, equality, and personal fulfillment. In an age where these values are under renewed attack, we feel this is a vital part of our task as social scientists and as educators.

Second, though we stress the *social* nature of social problems — the idea that personal problems are deeply influenced by larger social processes — we view people not as passive objects of social forces, but as active participants who shape those processes as well as being shaped by them.

In emphasizing these themes, we affirm what we feel is the most powerful and valuable tradition in social problems writing. It is the tradition of C. Wright Mills' insistence on the value of the "sociological imagination," and the tradition of E. A. Ross' conception of a "civic sociology" that not only analyzes and describes social issues, but helps prepare students for a more aware and more principled participation in public life.

A book of this size and scope is necessarily a collective effort, whose quality depends enormously on the effort and dedication of the many people who help create it. Rod Watanabe, Chief of Staff at the Center for the Study of Law and Society, helped see the project through from beginning to end with his customary skill and patience. Susan Senger's skills, insight, and good spirits were indispensable in helping us turn out a finished manuscript under very demanding time constraints. Much of the original work on the manuscript was ably done by Christina Miller, Ingrid Barclay, and Margo Cisneros. We were also blessed with an unusually capable group of researchers: special thanks to Jennifer Hammett, Michael Peltz, and Laurie Rubinow for their initiative and creativity.

Finally, a project of this kind makes heavy demands, both direct and subtle, on family and friends who have to endure the book's intrusion into their lives. We are especially grateful to Rachael Peltz and Arlene Skolnick for the good advice, indispensable personal support, and consistent encouragement that ultimately made this book possible.

Elliott Currie
Jerome H. Skolnick
Center for the Study of Law and Society
Berkeley, California

Contents

Part I: Systems and Structures

**Chapter 6:
Social
Inequality III:
Gender
192**

Part II: Impacts and Institutions

**Chapter 9:
Health:
Gains and Losses**
323

1

Introduction: Thinking about Social Problems

Twenty-five years ago, the sociologist C. Wright Mills wrote that "ours is a time of uneasiness and indifference" — a time, Mills thought, stricken by the vague feeling that "all is somehow not right" (1959, p. 11). Today, we still feel that all is "somehow not right," but the national mood has shifted from uneasiness to alarm, from indifference to resignation. For many of us, the past few years have brought a gnawing sense that things are out of control — from our neighborhood streets to our foreign policy, from the most distant workings of the international economy to the most intimate aspects of our family lives.

Opinion polls show that many Americans feel that their children's lives will be worse than their own. "American confidence," one social critic notes, "has fallen to a low ebb. Those who recently dreamed of world power now despair of governing the city of New York" (Lasch, 1978, p. xiii). Another writes that "my reading of the present is that it is not so much progress that is to be achieved but, if lucky, catastrophe that is to be avoided" (Gouldner, 1979, p. 34); and one of the most popular country songs of 1982 plaintively asks "are the good times really over for good?" (Haggard, 1982).

By now, terms like "age of scarcity" or "age of decline" (Lasch, 1978; Blumberg, 1980) have become common shorthand for our times; and those coming of age in the 1980s may scarcely remember that these bleak visions haven't always dominated the American scene. The post–World War II age in which the authors grew up was full of optimism about American society and its possibilities. In the 1960s that sense of possibility fostered a great deal of creative social experimentation and helped bring about important

1

advances for minorities, the poor, and others left out of the American main-stream. Both the optimism and the influence of the social policies that flowed from it are easy to exaggerate, of course; nostalgia for a more hopeful time blurs the problems of the past and makes the differences with the present seem more stark than they really are.

But the differences are real ones. Rarely in American history have so many people felt so much doubt about the present and fear for the future. In a society that, at the time Mills wrote, was believed to have conquered most of the major technological and material problems of human civilization, many people today feel vague but genuine fears for their survival and that of future generations. In the midst of what used to be described as a society of abundance, we live with the nagging worry that we may be unable to make ends meet, to enjoy a home of our own, or to achieve a good job. We watch helplessly as the products of our advanced technology hover over us as agents of destruction — as deadly chemicals seep into middle-class lawns and the threat of nuclear catastrophe hangs over America (and the world) like a lowering cloud. In a society that was supposed to have banished serious economic problems years ago, respected financial experts talk seriously about the possibility of a worldwide economic collapse (Rowen, 1983). Almost thirty years after the birth of the civil rights move-ment, America's urban ghettos are still impoverished, and some of the steps toward equality minorities achieved in the 1950s and 1960s are being halted or even reversed.

All of this has generated considerable alienation and resignation, perhaps best illustrated by the striking withdrawal of great numbers of Americans from political participation in recent years. Only about a third of the Ameri-can people, as of mid 1983, describe themselves as satisfied with the way things are going in the United States. But many of the dissatisfied also feel that there is little they can do about it, at least through the usual political process. By the end of the 1970s, only a little more than half of Americans surveyed believed that voting had any effect on what the government does today (*Business Week*, May 14, 1979, p. 14); a smaller percentage of the elec-torate voted in the 1980 presidential election than in any election since 1924. Younger people, in particular, seem even less convinced than most of their elders that much good can come from voting — or from any other form of political or social involvement (see, generally, Burnham, 1983).

Social scientists and other "experts" often seem as confused and disori-ented as everyone else. Sociologists who, in the 1950s and 1960s, focused on the concerns of an affluent society seem to have lost their bearings in an age characterized by what the sociologist Paul Blumberg calls a "revolution of falling expectations" (1980, p. 253). Honest economists confess their inabil-ity to predict the course of the economy — next year or even next month. Political scientists have trouble fitting their usual categories to a society in which so many people have opted out of the political process altogether.

The anti-war movement challenged complacency about America's military role.

New Problems, Old Solutions

The past several years, then, have been filled with the sense that, in many ways, American society simply no longer seems to work as it did in more hopeful times; or, more accurately, that problems and contradictions that were often hidden before are now, like an untreated illness, both more serious and more visible. And the malaise and confusion this brings are compounded by the growing awareness that old ways of dealing with many of these problems can no longer be relied on. In other words, not only are America's problems more urgent and pressing today, but some of the by-now traditional tools of social policy that served us reasonably well in the past now seem shopworn. Three broad changes, in particular, may be singled out: the limits to economic expansion, the crisis of the welfare state, and the failure of technological solutions.

The Limits to Economic Expansion

Probably the most telling of these changes is that, for the first time in American history, we are faced with truly constricted economic prospects; not just a period of slower-than-normal growth, or a temporary downturn in the economy, but the apparent closing-off of economic options we had come to expect and to depend on — and on which we had based a whole way of life.

American society began with what seemed like limitless lands and natural resources. The pattern that began with the exploitation of the American frontier continued, especially after World War II, as American businesses increasingly expanded overseas in search of new resources and new markets. Only recently have we begun to understand how much of our peculiarly American brand of prosperity has depended on that capacity for expansion, first throughout the country and then throughout the world. The expansion was not, of course, entirely a blessing — either for Americans or for the rest of the world. But it did allow us to postpone reckoning with some fundamental issues: the limits of natural resources, the distribution of income and wealth, and the need for planning and coordinating the economy.

As the political theorist Alan Wolfe has written, "economic growth offered a smooth and potentially harmonious future," leading to "a whole new approach to government, one that would not so much exercise political power to make choices as it would manage expansion and empire to avoid choice" (1981, p. 10). It seems clear now that this approach to the "management" of America's problems is running out of time. For a variety of reasons, we are no longer able to roam the rest of the planet at will, mining its human and natural resources to fuel the engines of an ever-expanding economic growth. Some of the reasons are political, some economic, and some ecological.

On the political level, the most obvious example is the oil-producing countries' seizure of greater control over the most crucial resource of all for the energy-guzzling economies of the industrial world — an event that has had profound and far-reaching consequences for every industrialized country. But the rise of OPEC is only the tip of the iceberg. The "underdeveloped" countries' assertion of greater control over their own destinies is one of the key political facts of our time. Many countries that were once considered passive subjects of American policy are now charting a much more independent course.

At the same time, American dominance has been challenged on the economic level; first, by other industrial countries, especially Japan and West Germany, which, after starting from rock bottom at the end of World War

II, are now often "winning" in competition with the United States in several key industries; and now by a number of Third World countries, such as South Korea, Taiwan, and Brazil. Thus, the terms of international economic competition have shifted in basic and perhaps irrevocable ways.

Even more fundamentally, we have discovered that our traditional pattern of economic growth is deeply constrained by the limits of what the authors of the Global 2000 report, a major study of world ecological trends, call the "carrying capacity of the planet." "If present trends continue," that report argues, "the world in 2000 will be more crowded, more polluted, less stable ecologically, and more vulnerable to disruption . . . barring revolutionary advances in technology, life for most people on earth will be more precarious in 2000 than it is now — unless the nations of the world act decisively to alter current trends" (Council on Environmental Quality, 1980, p. 1).

American "affluence," too often based on a heedless disregard of the limits of the natural environment, has been increasingly revealed as unstable and self-destructive. Specific catastrophes — like the mounting problem of toxic wastes or the threatened shortages of some nonrenewable energy sources — are only symptoms of a larger contradiction between our style of economic growth and the integrity of the natural ecology on which growth ultimately depends.

These developments have, in a dramatically brief time, altered the terms of debate about social problems in America. They have created a whole new set of questions and sharpened the urgency of more familiar ones.

Perhaps the most obvious expressions of these changes in recent years have been economic. The American economy has always had its ups and downs. As we'll see in Chapter 3, the consequences of economic instability have often been severe, even in the more prosperous decades of the 1940s, 1950s, and 1960s. In the 1980s, however, there are added concerns of an even deeper kind. As the decade began, large parts of America's former industrial heartland, the Northeast and Midwest, were laid waste: factories were bolted and shuttered — and the disturbing question was whether some of these stricken industries and regions would *ever* recover to levels approaching those of 10 to 20 years before. Greater numbers of people were unemployed than at any time since the 1930s — but, worse, it was unclear whether even renewed economic growth would put all of them back to work in an age of sophisticated robots and computer-guided machinery.

More subtly, the economic crises of the 1970s and 1980s seem to have eroded the future prospects of entire generations of Americans. Even a college education, or, increasingly, even a postgraduate education, no longer guarantees a reasonably rewarding job or the kind of living standards that were taken for granted in earlier years. (Though not always, as Figure 1-1 suggests.)

One of the benefits of the age of economic expansion, for many Americans, was the belief in the possibility of getting ahead, of moving up the

Figure 1-1

Feiffer cartoon

ladder of social and economic opportunity. It goes without saying that the realistic chances for upward mobility were always much more limited than our homegrown mythology assumed, especially for minorities and women. But though America was never the land of boundless opportunity many of us were taught it was, there is reason to fear that, with the shrinking prospects for growth, it may become even less so in the future. A popular song from 1982, Billy Joel's "Allentown," captures the mood of this change in expectations:

> Every child had a pretty good shot
> To get at least as far as their old man got;
> But something happened on the way to that place;
> They threw an American flag in our face.
> [Copyright © 1981, 1982 by Billy Joel Songs (BMI)]

The impact of limited growth has been especially harsh for minorities and the poor. An expanding economy could find some room for those with talent or luck to rise. It could lift some of the poor out of poverty and open some doors for minorities and women, all without greatly limiting anyone else's chances. As we'll see in later chapters, most of the recent successes in the struggle for equality — the reduction of poverty and the narrowing of disparities in income and jobs for minorities and women — took place in the expansionary 1960s; they slowed, stopped, or even reversed in the 1970s.

Today, there is a widespread sense that a significant social advance for any one group must happen at the expense of others — that we have become, in the economist Lester Thurow's phrase, a "zero-sum" society (1980). This theme runs like a red thread through much of our social policy. We see it in attacks against equal-opportunity programs, in often-successful campaigns to dismantle social services, and, more generally, in a concerted attack on the policies and programs of the welfare state.

Some of the attack on the welfare state reflects a crisis in the welfare state itself, a loss of belief in its capacity to serve as a primary means of dealing with America's problems.

Given the current social concern with the dangers of "big government," it is easy to forget that the package of government policies and programs that have come to be called the welfare state is fairly new to the United States. Until the 1930s, the American economy was mainly run on the principles of laissez-faire: the idea that an economy powered by the drive for private profit and free from government intervention would produce constantly rising levels of prosperity while preserving political freedom and social choice. (That some intervention by government to aid private interests has always been a part of our history, as we'll see in Chapter 2, did not detract much from the intensity of this belief.) Then came the Great Depression, which brought growing acceptance of the idea that the private-profit economy would work much better with certain kinds of government intervention — indeed, that it might not work at all if left to its own devices.

That idea led to two profound developments in American social policy. One was a commitment to at least a minimal level of intervention by the government in managing the economy itself, in order to avert the possibility of another severe depression. The other was a commitment to a system of public services and benefits that would provide a basic cushion for those most at risk in the private-profit economy: the old, the sick, and the involuntarily unemployed. That commitment grew in the 1960s' era of activist government, both through an expansion of the amount of money spent on conventional welfare programs and through the creation of newer, more innovative programs in areas like job training, compensatory education, and community health care. But today, both parts of the welfare state's approach to economic and social problems have come under increasing criticism.

The reasons are not hard to find. We have only to look at the troubling legacy: a mixed economy that seems prone to periodic stagnation and declining productivity growth; a public welfare system that is both costly and degrading to its recipients; an "urban renewal" program that blasted inner cities into craters and destroyed more low-income housing than it built; and a public school system that turns out illiterates and threatens us with what a national commission in 1983 called a "tide of mediocrity" (National Commission on Excellence in Education, 1983, p. 2). The positive results of other social programs on which we once placed great hopes are often hard to see at first glance, and some seem disappointingly small even on hard analysis. The neo-conservative social critic Irving Kristol puts his finger on the source of popular frustration and discontent with those programs: "The question is, *where has all the money gone?* The skyrocketing costs of the welfare state seem way out of line with its modest (if indubitable) benefits" (1979, p. 231).

Much of the criticism of the welfare state's tendency to "throw money at problems" misleadingly exaggerates the amount of money we *did* spend, and some of the "failure" of social programs is the result of their not being taken seriously from the start. Moreover, some important programs have been extremely successful, in ways that the criticism often ignores. But the ineffectiveness and cost of some programs, especially when coupled with the fiscal strains of a declining economy, dealt a severe blow to faith in the government as a provider of solutions to crippling social problems.

It isn't surprising, therefore, that in the 1970s and 1980s the attack on the welfare state — through tax cuts, reductions in spending on public services, and the elimination of some social programs — increased in vigor and intensity. So, more broadly, did a rejection of the whole idea of government intervention in American life. But, for the most part, this has been a *negative* vision — one that rejects the role of government without offering plausible alternative approaches to the problems that government intervention tried to solve. The result is a kind of vacuum that helps account for much of the drift and confusion that seem to infect public policy and social theory in America today.

The Failure of Technological Solutions

A third theme underlying our current sense that we have lost the capacity to deal with social problems is the increasingly apparent failure of modern science and technology to deliver what we (somewhat naively) expected from them. The tendency to believe that technical solutions can ultimately be found for virtually every social problem (from drug addiction to cancer to dwindling energy resources) has been particularly strong in the United States, a country that traditionally prided itself on its technical know-how and its pragmatic approach to problems. Like economic growth, technological progress has often served as a surrogate for decision making about social problems; but, also like economic growth, it is no longer capable of performing this function as it once did.

Energy is a good example. In the 1950s and 1960s, the apparent promise of unlimited energy supplies through splitting the atom was one reason for America's heedless approach to energy conservation and for our ostrich-like avoidance of the need to develop effective *social* policies governing energy use. But today questions of both safety and economics have badly crippled the promise of nuclear power: What was once regarded as a quick-fix solution to the world's energy problems now seems more like a costly and dangerous albatross around society's neck.

But the changing fortunes of nuclear energy are only the most dramatic example of the failures and dilemmas of modern technology in its American social setting. Thus, as with energy, Americans have often looked to technology as a cure-all for problems of disease and ill-health; and, indeed, some medical technologies have worked wonders in the fight against disease. But other technologies are increasingly implicated in *causing* disease, particularly cancer and other diseases associated with exposure to industrial chemicals in the workplace and the environment.

OPEC's decisions to raise oil prices helped bring a world-wide energy crisis in the 1970s.

Modern, highly sophisticated microelectronic technologies also promise great increases in economic productivity and, perhaps, the elimination of some of the most menial and stifling kinds of work. But they also threaten us with massive structural unemployment and the destruction of the economic base of entire communities, paradoxically impoverishing American society as they enrich it.

Finally, there is the frightening evidence that technologies we once accepted, enthusiastically and unreflectively, as the engines of our unprecedented economic growth, are also deeply (and perhaps irreversibly) harmful to the natural environment. Acid rain, contaminated groundwaters, and the ever-increasing dimensions of the toxic waste problem signal the end of an age in which we could take the economic benefits of productive technology for granted while ignoring its social and environmental costs.

The problem is not that technology in general is harmful in some abstract sense, as some critics were inclined to argue during the 1960s. It is rather that technological innovation without some social means of controlling its pace and evaluating its larger costs has not only failed to solve America's problems, but has often fostered new — and even more threatening — ones. Clearly, we can no longer depend on technical innovation to avoid crucial choices about our priorities in energy policy, environmental health, and employment and industrial growth.

Approaches to Social Problems

Every age has its dominant ways of thinking about social problems. In the generally complacent 1950s, American writing on social problems typically celebrated the achievements of the "affluent" society uncritically and regarded serious departures from its norms and values as expressions of personal pathology or extremism. In the 1960s, the era of John F. Kennedy's New Frontier and Lyndon Johnson's Great Society, both social science and public policy grew more activist and energetic. America launched a War on Poverty and created a host of new social agencies to address issues ranging from delinquency prevention to community mental health to environmental protection. Legislation like the Civil Rights Act of 1964 and the Occupational Health and Safety Act of 1970 created new rights and entitlements for minorities, workers, and women. Somewhat similar developments took place in the more intimate spheres of personal and family life, and those changes were reflected in both social science and public policy. Many of these changes were consequences of the growing women's movement, which challenged long-entrenched norms governing the roles of women and men at home and on the job. Meanwhile, especially because of the tragedy of the Vietnam War, the military establishment — and its role in helping achieve the global power of the United States — came under unprecedented scrutiny as a social problem in its own right.

The overlapping crises of the 1970s brought these changes into question. In their place, another, quite different, perspective on social problems and social policy gathered momentum and rose to a dominant position in public life in the early 1980s. Though it has many variants, this perspective also presents several consistent themes.

The Retreat from Intervention One of the most important themes is the idea that many of America's problems are the unanticipated results of the very social programs that the welfare state created to deal with them. In this view, not only did those programs fail to achieve their goals but, in Irving Kristol's words, "in many respects they made matters worse" (1979, p. 221). The chief problem, from this perspective, was that the welfare state, especially in its activist 1960s variant, raised expectations it could not fulfill, creating "incessant turbulence within the body politic."

Many social critics would agree, for example, that the expansion of the welfare system and other programs for the disadvantaged had failed to eliminate poverty by the 1970s. But this perspective further argues that such programs actually *caused* poverty — along with a host of other social pathologies, including rising crime, family breakup, drug addiction, and illegitimacy — by removing the incentive to work and weakening the bonds of low-income families. By the early 1980s, it had become almost an article of faith among many writers on social policy that "the troubling behavior and conditions of the disadvantaged is due to the social programs on which many are dependent" (Mead, 1982, p. 22). That is, this perspective sees many of America's social problems, from crime to economic stagnation, largely as the result of the unruly growth of the welfare state — a growth that has sapped the fiscal capacities of the economy and simultaneously created a climate of self-indulgence and moral decline. "Government benefits," wrote one impassioned critic in 1982, "have begun to unhinge the civilities on which society depends for its coherence and energy" (Mead, 1982, p. 31).

This view became standard fare in less academic circles during the 1970s and early 1980s. A 1980 article in *Time*, for example, captured this mood, laying much of the blame for America's economic troubles on the unfortunate attitudes that American prosperity itself had created:

> Capitalism created the affluent society, but the more prosperity the public enjoyed, the more it wanted. If hard work, talent and savings no longer provided the affluence, the public demanded it from government . . . In short, people today ask things from capitalism that no system can deliver. (*Time*, 1980, p. 44)

An editorial in *Fortune* added the voice of an important segment of America's business community, attributing "America's ills" primarily to "the fact that Americans want just about everything, without considering or fully understanding the cost." The big questions for social policy, the editorial declared, involved whether American democracy could "restrain the excessive demands made on the society"; and, more specifically, "the drift toward the welfare state and egalitarianism" (Grunwald, 1981, p. 72). According to *Fortune* and many other observers in government, the media, and the universities, the disastrous effects of this drift toward excessive government and an overzealous concern for equality were compounded by the less tangible, but nonetheless destructive, effects of the "permissive excesses" of the 1960s and 1970s (Grunwald, 1981, p. 73).

That corrosive loss of traditional moral standards, in turn, was frequently held responsible for aggravating social problems ranging from the erosion of authority and stability in the family (Kramer, 1983) to the weakening of America's military and economic position in the international arena (Podhoretz, 1980). From this perspective, the decline of American power and influence in the wider world was only partly to be explained by the increasing aggression of the Soviet Union and the growth of anti-American sentiments and actions, especially in the Third World. Another part of the explanation, as the critic Peter Steinfels notes, pointed to a failure of nerve within American society itself (1980, p. 78) — a failure that led Americans to play down the foreign threats to American prosperity and security and to flinch at confronting the need to build up our military capacity in the face of those threats. "If Americans want to be a power in the world," *Fortune* intoned, "we will have to pay for it" (Grunwald, 1981, p. 73).

During the early 1980s, these themes — the critique of government in general and the welfare state in particular, the threat of excessive egalitarianism, and the loss of moral and military power at home and abroad — began to influence the practice of social policy to an extraordinary extent. The speed at which these themes became translated into political reality may be unprecedented in American history, particularly the rapid growth of the peacetime military budget and the simultaneous dismantling of a variety of the domestic social and environmental programs of the 1960s and 1970s.

New Realities, New Doubts

The political successes of this approach to social problems and public policy may be understandable in the light of the fears and frustrations that have run through American life in the past decade. To many, this vision is appealing in its apparent simplicity, its ability to offer what seem to be clear and direct solutions in an age when social, economic, and political forces seem both deeply threatening and often incomprehensible. And its frequent appeal to the simpler virtues of a less complex society of unfettered markets, traditional families, and American "strength" resonates with basic values that lie deep within the American cultural tradition, including those of individual liberty, self-reliance, and mistrust of government power.

But despite these appeals, and despite their political successes, this approach has met with mounting criticism and challenge. Part of the reason is that, in practice, it has presented a number of striking inconsistencies. It is a vision that calls for reducing government spending — for social programs, but not for defense. It calls for curtailing government regulation of business — but often has no qualms in calling for more government regulation of our private lives. It calls for limiting the concentration of power in big government — but not necessarily for limiting the concentration of power in big corporations. It calls for "putting America back to work" — but also calls for deliberately increasing unemployment to help fight inflation.

By the middle of the decade, these inconsistencies were joined by the apparent failure of this political vision to accomplish what it had promised. Despite considerable success in reducing government regulation and taxation of business, the state of the economy remained precarious and uncertain; and even when the economy appeared to be undergoing a "recovery," unemployment seemed stuck at disturbingly high levels. Despite substantial reductions in the social programs that were said to be the main cause of poverty and social pathology, there were many more, not fewer, Americans below the poverty line as the 1980s progressed. And despite an unprecedented shift of public spending toward the military, there were no signs of either an improvement in America's sense of national security in a threatening world or in the quality and efficiency of America's huge but clumsy military apparatus.

One result of these contradictions is that in the mid-1980s America's thinking about social problems is once again in ferment. There is a clear sense that old answers — and even some not-so-old ones — are no longer very helpful, but there is no strong consensus around *new* ones. Instead, there is a deep and wide-ranging debate about the roots of America's problems — and about what kinds of social policies we should create in response to them.

Our Perspective

Our purpose in this book is to help give you some of the tools you will need to become effective participants in this debate. The chapters that follow are short on definitive answers, long on describing what we feel are some of the most important *questions* and some of the best ways of going about *looking* for the answers.

In pursuit of that goal, we have emphasized bringing the most recent, most sophisticated social scientific research to bear on the issues raised in contemporary debates over social problems and public policy. We also explain how to understand and interpret some of the common statistics and data sources on which so much of these debates depend: crime and unemployment rates, for example, or measures of poverty and the distribution of income. These are crucial tools for the analysis of social issues, and understanding how to use them is a necessary first step in thinking about social problems, regardless of the moral or political questions they raise.

Nevertheless, we want to make some of our own assumptions and preconceptions clear at the beginning. All books about social problems rest, in part, on deeply personal values. Some of those values reflect broad social and political convictions, which frequently translate into decisions about what constitutes a "social problem" in the first place. Others concern the authors' sense of the "possible" — their visceral feelings about how much of society's ills can usefully be addressed by social action at all. Still others have to do with more mundane issues, including the style of a book's presentation and the way it fits into past traditions of research and scholarship.

Values and Biases

In the past, as we noted in an earlier book (Skolnick and Currie, 1982), social scientists often tried to avoid confronting (and explaining) the judgments that lay behind their own approaches to the study of social problems. They were likely to make a sharp (and misleading) distinction between a "scientific" versus a "value-laden" approach to society, and spent a good deal of effort in trying to convince readers that they possessed the key to an "objective" or "value-free" study of social problems. The fallacy in such a position was pointed out many years ago by the Swedish social scientist, Gunnar Myrdal, with a directness that is hard to improve upon. "Every study of a social problem," Myrdal wrote, "however limited in scope, is and must be determined by valuations. A 'disinterested' social science has never existed and, for logical reasons, can never exist." But, Myrdal argued, the value premises that underlay most social science were "generally hidden," left "implicit and vague" (1969, p. 54).

For Myrdal, as for us, there is an important difference between values, in this sense, and the personal or political biases that often distort social research and analysis. *Values* are both inevitable and necessary; a social science *without* any values or moral foundations would be not only incomprehensible but — if it could exist — morally repugnant. *Biases,* on the other hand, are the result of values that are unacknowledged and left to work their way into the analysis of social issues by the back door. As Myrdal continued, the only way to avoid such biases, and to achieve the kind of objectivity that *is* possible in social science, is to "expose the valuations to full light," and to make them "conscious, specific, and explicit" (1969, pp. 55–56).

Particularly in a book with two authors of somewhat different backgrounds and interests, it would be too much to try to discuss our own "valuations" in great detail. But some of our more general, shared assumptions are reasonably well expressed by a list of social values offered by the political theorists Norman Furniss and Timothy Tilton as those underlying what they call the "social welfare state"; the list includes "equality, freedom, democracy, solidarity, security, and economic efficiency" (1979, p. 28). These are broad values, and we recognize that there are many constraints on achieving them — and even many difficulties in precisely *defining* them. A good part of policy-related social science, in fact, is about locating these constraints and clarifying these definitions. But this book's roots in these basic values should be quite clear at the beginning and will become more apparent in the chapters that follow.

Social Theory and Social Policy

We are less clear about what to call ourselves, which may disappoint some who care about political or academic labels. Both of us tend to be somewhat distrustful of such labels; those looking for the name of our "theoretical system" won't find it here. But some clues about our inclinations toward both social action and social science are relevant. Both of us have been participants in a number of activist movements and causes in the past two decades. Both of us also tend to be a little impatient with the abstractions of what C. Wright Mills called "grand theory," and to look early on for the more concrete, practical implications of social theories for public policy.

This leaning helps explain why *America's Problems,* unlike some other books on social problems, is so strongly concerned with issues of social *policy.* Contrary to some recent currents in social science, we believe that the tools of social science ought to help inform decisions about social policy; even more importantly, we also believe it's *possible* for social science to do so. Nowadays, it has become all too fashionable in some quarters to denigrate the use of the tools of reason and analysis to affect the course of social life. We don't share that pessimism, or the often self-serving quietude it induces. We think that much can be done to build a society that is more equal, more supportive, more respectful of personal liberties and differences, less insecure, less dangerous. At the same time, we believe that doing so will require the best intellectual efforts we can muster and the most skillful use of the analytical tools available to us.

For us, this means using tools from whatever academic disciplines will help. Both of us were trained as sociologists, but, like many others in our field whose interests center on social policy issues, we regard that training as a starting point, and we tend to be impatient with the somewhat artificial boundaries of traditional academic disciplines. (As the growth of interdisciplinary programs in social science and public policy indicates, those boundaries are increasingly being regarded as flexible ones.) *America's Problems* thus draws on the methods and findings of political scientists, social psychologists, specialists in public health and environmental science, and many others. And it pays particular attention to economic issues, some of which have traditionally been considered as the "territory" of professional economists.

Disciplines and Boundaries

In placing such strong emphasis on the economy and its troubles, we are departing, to some extent, from the usual organization of books on social problems. Many conventional treatments of social problems have either ignored the problems of economic life altogether or have touched only on isolated aspects, such as poverty or the economic aspects of racial discrimination. But we feel that this traditional neglect is increasingly damaging. For one thing, the problems of unemployment, industrial decline, and economic stagnation are among the first priorities on the national agenda today, at all points on the political spectrum, and opinion polls consistently reveal that most Americans regard them as the most pressing troubles in their own lives. Another even more important reason for our emphasis on economic issues is simply that the way we organize our economic activity has a deep and wide-ranging effect on the rest of our social and personal lives. We will not understand issues like racial inequality, the welfare system, the problem of youth unemployment, or even the state of the family without viewing them in the context of broader economic trends and priorities.

At the same time, we believe that it is important to understand that the economy is not simply an abstraction made up of costs and benefits, supply and demand, and the other technical concerns of the modern economics profession, but a *social* institution, and, like other social institutions, one that is itself profoundly shaped by the clash and struggle of competing social groups: business and labor, affluent and poor, taxpayers and bureaucrats.

There is another sense, too, in which this book remains distinctly sociological. Two broad themes, which we believe are basic to the best traditions of sociology, underlie the approach we've taken to social problems throughout.

The first is what we would call the *importance of the social* in thinking about social problems. The other is the importance of reconnecting — in C. Wright Mills's phrase — the realm of private troubles with that of public issues. What do we mean by this?

The Importance of the Social

By the importance of the social, we mean that we will not be able to understand social problems if we see them as simply the result of the accumulation of millions of individual, personal choices. Mills's description of the quality he termed the *sociological imagination* is still the best expression of this principle.

> The first fruit of the sociological imagination is the idea that the individual can understand his own experience and gauge his own fate only by locating himself within his period, that he can know his own chances in life only by becoming aware of those of all individuals in his circumstances. In many ways it is a terrible lesson — in many ways a magnificent one. (Mills, 1959, p. 5)

Taking a social view of social problems means that we begin with the recognition that, as individuals, we are enmeshed in a complex network of social and economic relations that limit our range of choices and shape fundamentally our prospects for health or illness, wealth or poverty, emotional satisfaction or misery. Moreover, that network is not a world of timeless abstractions but a concrete society with its own peculiar history, its own unique way of organizing the production and allocation of goods and services, and its own priorities about the use of natural and human resources. Living in America is not the same as living in China or Nigeria; living in the corporate America of the late twentieth century is not the same as living in the society of small entrepreneurs that was nineteenth-century America. The social critic Paul Goodman (1970, p. x) once wrote of these surrounding social and technological conditions that "the way they lay out the streets is the way we must walk" — a metaphor that is particularly appropriate in an age that often seems to regard humans as if they were small computing machines, calculating their courses of action in isolation from community, history, or tradition.

Within that specific social, economic, and historical framework, moreover, we do not confront the world as an assortment of individual atoms but as members of particular social classes; sex, race, and age groups; and a multitude of other collectivities, of ethnicity, region, religion, and many more. We will not understand social problems until we understand how those memberships shape and filter the impact of social and economic forces on individuals.

Consider unemployment, by any account one of the most devastating social problems of the 1980s. To many economists, whether an individual has a job or not is simply a matter of a transaction in the labor market, a result of individual choices by employers on the one hand and potential employees on the other. To some politicians, many taxpayers, and some of those fortunate enough to be still employed, it is a matter of individual merit or motivation: "People who really want to work can always find a job." Both perspectives, of course, may have a kernel of truth in them. But neither tells us why *some* societies, or *some* regions, have much greater unemployment

The threat of nuclear accident hovers in the background of American life.

than others; neither tells us anything about why *some* groups suffer much more joblessness than others.

The idea that social problems must be understood within a specific socioeconomic and group context has an important corollary: it is that social problems are, in the broadest sense, political and ethical problems. For social groups do not confront each other in a vacuum, but in a setting often involving power and conflict, domination and subordination. Decisions about what we should consider social problems at all — much less how we should deal with them once we have defined them as problems — involve often bitter and sometimes deadly struggles over social resources. The form that social problems take, therefore, is not the inevitable result of blind social forces but rather the outcome of continuous conflict and negotiation between competing groups.

What the American sociologist Willard Waller said more than 40 years ago remains true: Very often, social problems "are not solved because people do not want to solve them" (1936, p. 928). What Waller means is that often a social problem that profoundly injures some people may have considerable *benefits* for others. Unemployment is a problem for those who lose their jobs — and for their families and communities — but not necessarily for employers, who may benefit because the scarcity of work brings a widespread fear of joblessness that allows them to maintain low wages, benefits, and poor working conditions for those still on the job.

As the economist Robert Lekachman puts it:

> Unemployment is as universally deplored as it is privately welcomed by conservative politicians and corporate employers . . . The brutal fact is that unemployment at "moderate" 7 or 8 percent rates . . . confers many benefits upon the prosperous and truly affluent. If everyone were employed, extraordinarily high wages would have to be paid to toilers in restaurant kitchens, laundries, filling stations, and other unpleasant work environments. Whenever decent employment at living wages is available, it is exceedingly difficult to coax young men and women into our volunteer armed services. . . . Unemployment calms unions and moderates wage demands. Threats to shut down or shift mills and assembly plants coerce workers into acceptance of wage freezes or actual wage cuts and unfavorable revisions of work rules. When men and women fear for their jobs, they work harder and gripe less. (Lekachman, 1982, p. 200)

This same point is illustrated, even more straightforwardly, in the candid remarks of the president of a large grocery-store chain in 1980:

> We cannot run good stores when unemployment by government standards is below 5 percent. . . . Productivity even for you and me is better when two or three people are waiting at the door for our jobs. (Davis, 1980, p. 11)

Social problems, then, are often problems for some groups and not for others; and even when they are universally considered to be problems, they are often the by-product of social and economic processes that are difficult to change precisely because some groups have a stake in maintaining them. Few people really profit from street crime; but to the extent that street crime is, in part, a reflection of unemployment, inequality, and the disruption of communities by economic dislocation, it is a by-product of arrangements that are not only profitable for some groups but are an integral part of our traditional pattern of economic development.

Our first principle in looking at social problems, then, is that they cannot be understood outside of the specific social and economic structures in which they occur — and that they are unlikely to be effectively addressed without confronting those structures themselves.

Private and Public: Bridging the Gap
The second principle is closely related. It is that the social-scientific analysis of social problems should help to bridge the gap between what Mills called "private troubles and public issues." In other words, it should help individuals understand the connections between their personal anxieties, fears, and

frustrations and the larger social forces that often give rise to them — between their hopes for themselves and their families and the obstacles in the larger society that often frustrate them.

Think about unemployment once again. Losing a job is experienced, on the personal level, as a private tragedy and a nagging worry, as feelings of self-blame and inadequacy, as the catalyst for the disintegration of a family. In the United States, these private feelings are often confirmed and aggravated by a political culture that views unemployment as mainly a problem of individual bad luck or personal failure. One of the most important functions of social science is to move us beyond that narrowly personal level by illuminating the connections between the private tragedy of job loss and the driving forces of an economy that predictably puts millions of Americans out of work each year.

We believe that the need for that kind of social science is especially critical today. Too often both our popular culture and our official institutions enforce the idea that we have only ourselves to blame for our troubles. This idea is then used as a justification for dismantling or failing to develop the most basic *social* provisions for the care and support of individuals in need. At the same time, we are encouraged to believe that we must look *inward* for our own security and gratification, relying on our individual wits and nerve to "make it" in a harsh and competitive society. Or, as an ad for a new business magazine starkly puts it: "Tomorrow only the fit will survive. And only the *very* fit will flourish" (*Venture*, 1980, p. 54).

That kind of message can only feed confusion, cynicism, and despair. But a social science that insists on connecting our private lives to the play of larger social forces helps open up another, less passive, way of perceiving social issues. By locating private problems in their social setting, such a social science can help demonstrate that individuals are not alone in confronting the social forces that shape their lives for better or worse — and, by extension, that they are not powerless to change them.

Summary

This chapter has described some of the trends in thinking about social problems in America in recent years, examined some social changes that may underlie those trends, and outlined our own approach to the study of social problems.

The optimism that characterized scholarly and public thinking about social problems up through the 1960s changed to a more pessimistic approach in later years.

This shift is partly the result of several trends that have changed American society in fundamental ways. These include: new limits on economic expansion; the apparent inability of the welfare state and/or technical innovation to cope with American social problems, and the tendency for technology to generate problems of its own.

These trends helped pave the way for widespread criticism of government intervention, of "excessive" concern for social equality, and of the "neglect" of America's international military role. But social policies based on these criticisms have proved no better at resolving America's problems. Thus, the debates over the nature and solution of America's problems in the 1980s continue.

Our own approach to those debates emphasizes that the values that guide a discussion of social problems should be made explicit. We believe that the study of social problems cannot provide all the answers, but should give students the tools to provide their own; that those tools can and should be drawn from a variety of academic disciplines; and that an effective approach to social problems should emphasize their *social* nature and stress the connections between personal experience and larger social forces.

For Further Reading

Burnham, Walter Dean. *The Current Crisis in American Politics*. New York: Oxford University Press, 1983.

Harrington, Michael. *Decade of Decision: The Crisis of the American System*. New York: Simon & Schuster, 1980.

Mills, C. Wright. *The Sociological Imagination*. New York: Oxford University Press, 1959.

Skolnick, Jerome H., and Elliott Currie. *Crisis in American Institutions*, 5th ed. Boston: Little, Brown, 1982.

Steinfels, Peter. *The Neoconservatives*. New York: Simon & Schuster, 1980.

Wolfe, Alan. *America's Impasse: The Rise and Fall of the Politics of Growth*. New York: Pantheon, 1981.

Part I

Systems
and
Structures

2

Economy and Society: Business, Government, and Labor

In the 1980s, much of the debate over America's social problems revolves, in one way or another, around the relations between business and government, between the private sector and the public, between the welfare state and the system of "free enterprise." The intensity of this debate is a reflection of important changes in American life during the past few decades.

The ideal of the free enterprise system — a multitude of small, independent entrepreneurs depending on hard work and initiative to compete successfully in a market system largely free of interference by government — is deeply embedded in our culture. In the popular vision that idealized system is contrasted with others based on "planning" or "government control" or what some economists call the principle of "command": it is a system in which individuals, in the economist Milton Friedman's (1980) phrase, are "free to choose," constrained in their actions only by the discipline of the market itself. In many ways, this is an appealing vision and, with qualifications that we'll describe later, one that bears some resemblance to the American reality in the past.

But, aside from occasional bursts of national nostalgia, it is generally understood that this vision, in its pure form, no longer corresponds to American reality. On the one hand, even the hardiest believers in the free enterprise ideal acknowledge that private enterprise in the United States is no longer adequately described as a collection of small individual or family businesses: The reality of General Motors does not fit comfortably in a vision based on the corner grocery store. On the other hand, especially since the Great Depression and World War II, the government has taken on a crucial, and complex, role in American economic and social life.

To an important extent, current controversies over economic issues (and many other social problems as well) are about the balance that has resulted from these changes. One view, increasingly popular in the past several years, is that the growth of government has gotten out of hand, threatening to overpower a fragile, besieged private enterprise system. From this perspective, both economic and social life in America are increasingly dictated by the decisions of coercive and distant bureaucrats (especially in the federal government) rather than by the natural and beneficial choices of the free market. Thus, government is Goliath, private business David. Government is bureaucratic, the private sector is free; and the results of growing control by government are grim and pervasive. The growth of government has, in this view, been responsible for most of the problems of the American economy in recent years: inflation, loss of international competitiveness, stagnation, and unemployment. As Milton Friedman, surveying a deeply troubled economy in 1983, argued, "There is nothing wrong with the American economy that a dose of good government wouldn't cure. By that, I mean a dose of smaller government" (in *U.S. News and World Report*, 1983, p. 67). And the president of the United States told a responsive audience in 1983 that many of America's problems are due to the fact that "government has intervened in areas where it is neither competent, nor needed, nor wanted by the mass of Americans" (quoted in *San Francisco Chronicle*, May 10, 1983).

Controversy over the balance between government and private interests shapes almost every facet of public policy in the United States today, whether the specific issue is regulation of business, the distribution of income, the problems of the welfare system, the best ways of dealing with race or sex discrimination, or a host of others. In this chapter, we will begin with a profile of the dimensions of private power in America, focusing on the size and concentration of economic resources in the large corporations. We will then consider the parallel issue of the trends in the government's size and role in the economy, especially in comparison with the role of the public sector in other industrial societies. Finally, we will look briefly at some of the ways in which government and business have historically been interconnected in the United States. As we'll see, the relations between private business and government are more complex than the nostalgic vision of threatened free enterprise assumes, and the balance between them appears considerably different than much conventional wisdom suggests.

The Dimensions of Private Power

It takes only a few statistics to show how far we have come from the society of small independent producers envisioned by the traditional conception of free enterprise. Let's consider, first of all, the sheer size of the largest American corporations and the magnitude of their growth in recent years.

Corporate size has traditionally been measured from a variety of angles: most often by the dollar volume of their sales in a given year, the dollar value of their total assets, or the number of their employees. The different measures give somewhat different pictures of corporate size and influence, but all illustrate that big business in America is very big indeed. Each year the business magazine *Fortune* publishes a list of the 500 largest industrial corporations in the United States. In 1982, the Fortune 500 had combined sales of almost $1.7 *trillion (Fortune*, 1983, p. 246). When the list was first published (for the year 1954), the corporation at the bottom of the list had roughly $50 million in sales, or about $180 million in 1982 dollars. By 1982, the bottom company had sales of about $424 million — an increase of over 135 percent, even adjusting for inflation *(Fortune*, 1980, p. 89; 1983, p. 246).

As Figure 2-1 demonstrates, several of the largest American corporations have sales that rank them among the world's largest economies.

A similar picture emerges when we consider corporate assets. In 1982, the Fortune 500 had total assets of about $1.3 *trillion*. If we broaden the focus to include corporations other than industrial (defined as those mainly involved in manufacturing or mining), the assets of the big corporations loom even larger. Many of the largest in terms of assets are banks, and the very largest (in 1982, before it was broken up by an antitrust decision) was another nonindustrial corporation — the telephone company (AT&T), which held assets of over $148 billion in 1982. The top 500 corporations together held a mammoth $3.8 trillion — or about $800 billion more than the entire American gross national product *(Forbes*, 1983, p. 247).

Figures on this scale are difficult to comprehend in ordinary terms. But a historical comparison may be helpful. By the late 1970s, the two largest American industrial corporations, Exxon and General Motors, together had greater sales (even adjusted for inflation) than *all manufacturing corporations combined* at the turn of the century (Mueller, 1977, p. 444).

The trends in numbers of people employed by the largest corporations are somewhat different. A substantial part of the American labor force is employed by the biggest firms; in 1982, the 500 largest industrials employed 14.4 million people, while slightly over 800 of all (including nonindustrial) corporations accounted for almost 22 million, or better than 1 in 5 of employed Americans in the civilian labor force *(Forbes*, 1983, p. 307; *Fortune*, 1983, p. 247). The telephone company alone employed only slightly fewer people than the total population of Detroit; General Motors only slightly fewer than the population of San Francisco.

But, as Figure 2-2 illustrates, the *growth* in the number of people working for the biggest corporations has been much less dramatic than the growth in size (or in profits). After a period of substantial growth in the mid-to-late 1960s, employment in the largest industrial corporations leveled off, and it declined in the early 1980s *(Fortune*, 1983, p. 227).

But it is not simply the *size* of America's giant corporations that is at issue. What has most concerned observers of the American economic system since before the turn of the century is the problem of economic *concentration* —

Measuring Economic Concentration

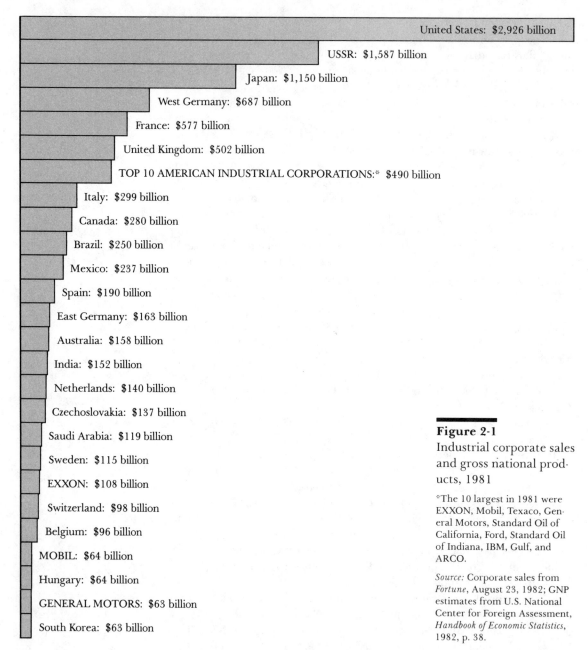

United States: $2,926 billion

USSR: $1,587 billion

Japan: $1,150 billion

West Germany: $687 billion

France: $577 billion

United Kingdom: $502 billion

TOP 10 AMERICAN INDUSTRIAL CORPORATIONS:* $490 billion

Italy: $299 billion

Canada: $280 billion

Brazil: $250 billion

Mexico: $237 billion

Spain: $190 billion

East Germany: $163 billion

Australia: $158 billion

India: $152 billion

Netherlands: $140 billion

Czechoslovakia: $137 billion

Saudi Arabia: $119 billion

Sweden: $115 billion

EXXON: $108 billion

Switzerland: $98 billion

Belgium: $96 billion

MOBIL: $64 billion

Hungary: $64 billion

GENERAL MOTORS: $63 billion

South Korea: $63 billion

Figure 2-1
Industrial corporate sales and gross national products, 1981

*The 10 largest in 1981 were EXXON, Mobil, Texaco, General Motors, Standard Oil of California, Ford, Standard Oil of Indiana, IBM, Gulf, and ARCO.

Source: Corporate sales from *Fortune,* August 23, 1982; GNP estimates from U.S. National Center for Foreign Assessment, *Handbook of Economic Statistics,* 1982, p. 38.

the degree to which a relatively small number of corporations control a disproportionate share of the country's economic resources.

The concentration of corporate power is not a new trend. It was already well on its way (and, by some measures, may even have reached a peak) in the last years of the nineteenth century, which saw the rise of giant corpo-

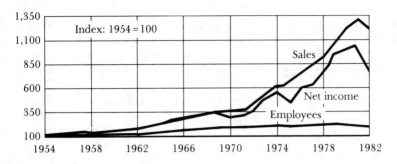

Figure 2-2

Growth in sales, profits, and employment of the 500 largest American corporations, 1954–1982

Source: Fortune, May 2, 1983, p. 227. Reprinted with permission.

rate "trusts" in banking, railroads, steel, and many other industries (Herman, 1981, pp. 191–193). This growing concentration led to the creation of our system of antitrust laws, designed to curb some of the more glaring excesses of private power. But, despite those laws, corporate concentration increased substantially by the 1930s, causing President Franklin D. Roosevelt to declare that

> Among us today, a concentration of private power without equal in history is growing. This concentration is seriously impairing the economic effectiveness of private enterprise as a way of providing employment for labor and capital and as a way of assuring a more equitable distribution of income and earnings among the people of the nation as a whole. (U.S. House Committee on Small Business, p. 37)

In at least one sense, Roosevelt's fears about growing private power have been confirmed; economic concentration has increased in the years since he sounded that alarm. At the end of the Great Depression, in 1941, the largest 100 manufacturing firms held just over 39 percent of all manufacturing assets; 40 years later, as Table 2-1 shows, their share had risen to about 47 percent.

This table and our preceding discussion are based on a measure of economic power called the *aggregate concentration ratio* — the share of total corporate assets (or, sometimes, total sales, value of output, profits, or employment) held by a small number of companies. As Table 2-1 shows, the largest 200 manufacturing firms — which represent less than one-tenth of 1 percent of all such firms in the United States — now hold *three-fifths* of all

Table 2-1

Largest manufacturing corporations*—percent share of assets held, 1950–1981

Corporation Ranking	1950	1955	1960	1965	1970	1975	1980	1981
100 largest	39.7	44.3	46.4	46.5	48.5	45.0	46.7	46.8
200 largest	47.7	53.1	56.3	56.7	60.4	57.5	59.7	60.0

*Prior to 1970, excludes newspapers. Data prior to 1975 not strictly comparable with later years.
Source: Statistical Abstract of the United States, 1982–83 (Washington, D.C.: Government Printing Office, 1983) p. 535.

Year of company ranking and company ranking	Number of Companies									
	1977	1972	1970	1967	1966	1963	1962	1958	1954	1947
1977										
Among 50 largest	50	43	41	39	38	34	36	32	30	23
Among 51st to 100th largest	—	7	9	9	8	9	7	8	12	10
Among 101st to 200th largest	—	—	—	1	2	4	4	6	1	10
Net among 200 largest	—	—	—	1	2	3	3	4	7	7
1947										
Among 50 largest	26	25	24	24	25	30	29	34	35	50
Among 51st to 100th largest	13	13	13	17	18	16	16	12	12	—
Among 101st to 200th largest	5	6	8	5	4	3	5	4	3	—
Net among 200 largest	8	4	5	4	3	1	—	—	—	—

Source: Adapted from U.S. Bureau of the Census, *Concentration Ratios in Manufacturing* (Washington, D.C.: Government Printing Office, 1981), p. 8.

Table 2-2

Changes in ranking of the 50 largest identical companies, 1977 and earlier years

manufacturing assets. Moreover, this share increased markedly — by about one-fourth — during the 1950s and 1960s, though it reached an apparent plateau thereafter.

This pattern of concentration is repeated, though somewhat less dramatically, for other measures of economic activity, including employment, value of goods produced, and investment. Thus, in 1977, the 200 largest manufacturing companies accounted for about 44 percent of the value added (that is, the value of new goods and services produced) by American manufacturing industry, 33 percent of its employees, and 49 percent of new capital spending. The 50 largest manufacturing companies alone accounted for about one-fourth of total value added, almost one-fifth of employees, and over one-fourth of new capital expenditures (U.S. Bureau of the Census, 1981a, p. 9).

The usefulness of aggregate concentration ratios in measuring economic power has been the subject of considerable debate. One issue is that simply describing the shares of economic activity that a small group of companies hold at any given point doesn't tell us whether those companies are the *same* ones over the years. Obviously, if the top 50, 100, or 200 corporations are entirely different ones every few years, our assessment of the significance of economic concentration would be different than if the same corporations dominated the economy year after year. Table 2-2 helps sort this out. It shows the proportion of companies among the 50 largest in the late 1940s that remained in the top 50 to 200 30 years later; and, viewing the question from the other direction, the proportion in the top 50 in 1977 that were also among the largest 30 years before.

Table 2-2 shows considerable movement over the years, but also substantial continuity. Thus, of the 50 largest companies in 1947, about half were still among the 50 largest in 1977, and another fourth were in the group of 100 largest. Only 8 of the 50 were not among the largest 200 companies in 1977. Similarly, of the 50 largest firms in 1977, just 7 were not among the 200 largest firms 30 years earlier.

Another difficulty with the aggregate concentration measure is that it tends to obscure the fact that a high proportion of the truly giant corporations are concentrated in just a few major industries. Among the 50 largest industrial companies in 1982, for example, 17 were oil companies, 6 were in chemicals, 5 in aerospace, 4 in electronics/appliances, and 3 each in autos, food, and photographic equipment (*Fortune*, 1983, pp. 228–229). Moreover, to the extent that aggregate concentration increased during the 1970s, most of the increase was accounted for by rises in two industries — oil and chemicals — alone (Bock, 1979, pp. 532–533).

Though the aggregate concentration ratio clearly gives us a rough portrait of the overall distribution of private economic power, if we want to know how much an industry — or the sale of some particular product — is dominated by a small group of companies, we need to use a measure that economists call *market concentration*.

Market concentration is a measure of the amount of sales in a given industry or product category (rather than in the economy as a whole) accounted for by a small number of companies. Data on market concentration are gathered periodically by the Census Bureau and are usually presented as the shares of sales accounted for by four, eight, and twenty firms.

The meaning of market concentration can be illuminated by considering the way a small number of corporations influences the daily morning routine most of us follow. The alarm clock you wearily turn off in the morning was probably made by one of the four companies that account for 84 percent of all clocks and watches sold in the United States. Four other companies make 90 percent of the linoleum you walk on as you go to open the kitchen refrigerator, which in turn was almost certainly sold by one of the four companies that sell 82 percent of American refrigerators. If you have cereal for breakfast, it is highly likely that it comes from one of the four corporations that produce four-fifths of breakfast cereals or from one of three companies that produce three-fourths of cold cereals. Four companies provide two-thirds of the coffee you may drink (two companies sell three-fourths of all instant coffee), and another four sell two-thirds of the sugar you may put in it.

If you smoke a cigarette with your coffee, there is an 88 percent chance that it was made by one of four tobacco companies. And the car you drive (if it is American made), as well as over nine out of ten other cars produced in America, was made by one of four companies, as are three-quarters of the tires they ride upon.

Is market concentration increasing? Again, the question has been the subject of considerable debate. The answer is made more difficult by the lack of

The "Beer Wars": A Closeup of Economic Concentration

Beer is an integral part of the American economy — a $9 billion a year industry in 1980. Americans over the age of 18 consume an average of about 35 gallons of beer annually, a total of more than 186 million barrels in 1982.

Serious beer drinkers are aware that beer has changed in the past several years. There are fewer independent brands to choose from, though there are many new labels and new kinds of brew, such as the light beers. To many drinkers, the different beers seem to taste more and more alike. And beer, like nearly everything else, costs more than it used to. Behind these differences lies a drastic reorganization of the beer industry that has had even deeper consequences for those who work in the industry itself. For the beer business, once a classic example of small, family-based enterprises, has become an arena in which a handful of giant, aggressive corporations are battling tooth and nail for shares of the national beer market. In the process literally thousands of independent businesses have been wiped out, along with tens of thousands of good, skilled jobs and a part of the economic base of many communities. The beer industry, in short, is a kind of microcosm of the wider trend toward concentration in the American economy and of some of its social impacts.

The beer industry in the United States grew during the nineteenth century, largely through the efforts of European (especially German) immigrants who brought with them long-established, sometimes centuries-old brewing skills. The small breweries they built catered mainly to local markets, and they took great pride in producing a small (by current standards) number of barrels of high-quality, distinctive beer. In 1880, there were 2,741 independent breweries in the United States.

But the industry began to change rapidly by the early part of this century. By 1935 there were 750 brewers; by 1967, 125; and by 1979, only 40. The process is continuing so rapidly that beer industry experts expect as few as 5 or 6 main brewers to survive within the next few years. In 1982 the two biggest brewers alone, Anheuser-Busch and Miller, were estimated to share about 54 percent of the market — up from 43 percent just four years earlier.

What lies behind this transformation?

The growth of concentration in the beer industry escalated after World War II. Before then, most brewers sold their beer locally, or at most regionally. A handful were so-called national brewers: Anheuser-Busch (makers of Budweiser and Michelob), Schlitz, Pabst, and Miller. During the 1950s, these national companies began moving aggressively to conquer local and regional beer markets, followed by some of the larger and more powerful regional brewers (like Coors, Falstaff, and Lone Star). From the 1940s to the early 1960s, an average of 16 beer firms each year went out of business; about 9 each year in the 1960s and early 1970s. Close to 90 others were bought out by bigger brewers from 1958 to 1975.

The big brewers were able to wipe out the smaller, localized ones partly because they could afford to build much bigger and more cost-effective breweries.

Similarly, the bigger companies could save labor costs by building new, highly automated breweries, and by building them mainly in the South, where labor costs were low, rather than in the highly unionized Midwest and Northeast where most of the industry had traditionally been located. In the old Schlitz main brewery in Milwaukee, the brewhouse (the heart of the beermaking operation) employed 24 workers per shift. The company's new brewhouses in its automated southern plants (now owned by the Stroh corporation, which bought Schlitz in 1982) are run by only two workers.

The new cost-effective breweries also require enormous capital investment that the smaller firms could not manage. As late as 1960 there were 229 working breweries in the United States, by 1981, just 92.

The biggest brewers were also able to outspend their competitors on advertising and promotion. Like so many of today's consumer products, there are really very few noticeable differences among different brands of beer. What makes growth in market shares possible is the ability to sell the beer's *image* — to develop what in the corporate world is called brand-name capital. Big brewers, to gain a greater share of the market or avoid losing what they have, must make their brand names so well known that customers reach for them almost automatically. The main way of accomplishing this is through massive ad campaigns (beer, wine, and liquor ads account for about 8 percent of all magazine advertising); another is to develop new ways of packaging beer. These strategies require enormous amounts of money. As far back as 1946, the beer industry was already spending $50 million a year on advertising; by 1977, largely because of the mushrooming use of costly TV advertising, the top five companies alone spent about a quarter of a *billion* dollars on advertising. Obviously, only the largest corporations can afford to compete at this level.

The most striking example of these trends has been the battle by what is now the number two brewer in the country, Miller, for dominance in the industry. Always one of the major national brewers, Miller began an ambitious effort to become number one in the early 1970s, when it was purchased by the Philip Morris Company, makers of Marlboro cigarettes and Virginia Slims. (Philip Morris, in turn, bought Miller from yet another giant conglomerate, the agribusiness corporation W. R. Grace.)

Philip Morris changed the terms on which the "wars" among the beer companies were fought. Through aggressive marketing and a promotion of its cigarettes (the "Marlboro Man," "You've Come a Long Way, Baby"), it had built an empire with assets, in 1977, of more than $4 billion, and it sold 160 brands of cigarettes in 170 countries. It had also begun to diversify into several other industries and real estate ventures. As a huge conglomerate, Philip Morris could afford to sink enormous resources into its Miller subsidiary for promotion and new plant capacity. It launched the trend to light beers with an ad campaign for its Lite brand that ultimately cost hundreds of millions of dollars. It attacked the market for high-priced premium beers by buying the right to use the name and label of Lowenbrau, the old, established German beer, in the United States. (American beer drinkers can no longer buy the real Lowenbrau in this country; Miller's variety is another beer altogether, made through a different — and cheaper — process, though costing the same.) To launch its Lowenbrau against other competitors' premium beers, Miller spent more than $11 million on ads, in 1977 alone — this for a beer that, by 1982, accounted for less than 1 percent of the country's beer sales.

The strategy of flooding the market with massive advertising worked well for Miller. During the mid-1970s, the company's share of the beer market grew by 30 percent a year; by 1982, Miller controlled 22 percent of the domestic beer market.

Obviously, only a company backed by massive corporate assets could have pulled off this kind of victory in the beer wars. Miller itself actually lost hundreds of millions of dollars during the first years of its campaign because of its huge expenditures, but it had a virtually inexhaustible fund of cash in its parent corporation.

The rapid concentration of the brewing industry has led to great profits for the winners in the battle of the beers. During the mid-1970s, corporate profit rates were six times as high for beer companies with more than $50 million in assets than for those with less. But what about the costs? Some argue that concentration has brought greater efficiency to brewing, resulting in many benefits to the consumer. And it is true that brewing has become, in bare economic terms, more cost-effective. But these potential benefits have not been passed on to the consumer.

Beer is considerably more expensive today than it was before the surge in industry concentration during the 1970s. Increasingly, the price you pay for a six-pack has little to do with what it actually costs to produce it. The light beers, to take the most obvious example, generally cost the consumer more than regular beers, though they cost considerably less to make; premium beers cost roughly 10 percent more than regular beers at the store, but they cost the same to produce.

What the consumer pays for is the price of the packaging and advertising that go into creating the beer's brand image. In 1977, about 35 percent of the wholesale price of a bottle of

Lowenbrau went to pay for advertising designed to convince consumers that Lowenbrau was still a "special" beer, despite the fact that it was no longer imported.

There have been larger *social* costs as well. Growing concentration has been accompanied by declining jobs, as smaller, labor-intensive breweries are replaced by the big, automated ones. Between 1965 and 1980, the number of brewery industry workers in the United States dropped from about 60,000 to 43,000 — though production went up from 108 to 193 million barrels. These jobs have traditionally been highly skilled and well-paid ones. The workers who lose them are typically middle-aged or older, with few other job prospects. (In the mid-1970s, workers at one New York brewery, Rheingold, which had been passed through several conglomerate owners, including the Chock-Full-O-Nuts coffee chain, chained themselves to their machines to protest the closing of their plant.).

The rapid destruction of so many of the smaller breweries has brought substantial economic problems for many communities, especially in the Northeast and Midwest. In a deeper sense, the rapid shakeout of the industry has sped the decline of a whole way of life, a change summed up in the testimony of a brewery association official before a Senate committee investigating the changes in the industry:

> Brewers are a wonderful lot. A brewery was a family affair; small salaries and dividends have always been the rule. Profits were poured back into making the brewery a better place in which to brew their fine beer. Brewers take pride in their product; if product trouble ensues, it is a matter of real and sustained grief, and to witness, as I have, the demise of small brewers — my friends — has not been an easy thing to face. The very thought of ending a family brewery was a source of grief. Fathers and grandfathers before them had always been able to keep the brewery going. What is the matter with me that I cannot do as well? (U.S. Congress, Senate, Committee on the Judiciary, 1978, p. 72)

Sources: Beverage Industry, 1982; *Business Week*, November 7, 1977; Keithan, 1979; Maslow, 1979; Morrison, 1982; *Newsweek*, September 4, 1978; *Time*, May 21, 1979; U.S. Congress, Senate, Committee on the Judiciary, 1978, p. 72.

good data for earlier years and the practical difficulties of defining changing products and industries with sufficient precision to make reliable comparisons possible. On the whole, the evidence is that the *average* degree of concentration has increased in American industry since World War II, though there is some dispute over its magnitude. But such an average may obscure more than it reveals, since it conceals important differences between different industries. Note in Table 2-3 how different the production of many goods has become from the classical image of a market system made up of a multitude of small entrepreneurs. At the top of the scale, a few products — cars, razor blades, spark plugs — are, for all practical purposes, produced entirely by four (or fewer) companies. (The table even minimizes the degree of concentration in these markets, by presenting the data only in terms of four or more companies; sometimes a huge market share is held by just one or two.) Many of these highly concentrated industries have been so for some time, at least since the 1950s or early 1960s. Others have shown very rapid increases in concentration in recent years: electronic calculators, washing machines, refrigerators and freezers, cotton fabrics, radios, and TVs, among others. At the same time, other industries have clearly followed a different path. The computer industry is the most obvious example of a rapid decrease in concentration, at least during the 1970s; the production of records, metal cans, and glass has also grown significantly less concentrated.

Some important industries are not highly concentrated by this measure, and show few signs of becoming so in the near future. These include furniture, publishing, parts of the plastics industry, and some parts of the clothing industry (though other parts are undergoing rapid concentration). The oil industry is something of an anomaly here; though it contained 12 of the 20 largest American corporations in 1982, its level of concentration is relatively low according to the 4 or 8 company measure, though 20 companies do control four-fifths of production.

All this suggests that the American economy is best understood (at least for rough purposes) as containing two somewhat distinct sectors, one highly concentrated and the other characterized by a large number of smaller producers where no one producer controls a very large share of the market.

Both the aggregate and market concentration measures, as striking as they often appear, actually understate the degree of concentration of private sector power in the American economy, for a number of reasons.

Mergers and the Role of "Conglomerate" Corporations

One is the increasing importance of so-called conglomerate corporations — businesses that operate in several unrelated industries and markets at once and whose power eludes measures that focus on concentration in specific industries.

Conglomerates are the most recent variant of the long process through which corporations have grown ever larger by acquiring, or merging with, other firms. Historically, economists have distinguished three types of mergers, all of which, in different ways, represent increasing economic concentration. The first, *horizontal mergers,* involves the acquisition of one company by another doing the same kind of business. Much of the earliest spurt of concentration in the American economy, in the nineteenth century, was horizontal, as when many smaller steel companies merged to form the giant U.S. Steel Corporation.

In the second type, the *vertical merger,* a company in one industry acquires another in a related, but different industry, as when a steel company buys a coal mine or a soup firm buys a company that makes cans. The third type, *conglomerate mergers,* involves the acquisition of wholly unrelated companies, as when Mobil Oil buys Montgomery Ward, or International Telephone and Telegraph acquires the company that makes Wonder Bread.

This last kind of merger is increasingly the dominant form in the American economy. Between 1950 and 1970, one in five of the *largest* American corporations was swallowed up by another corporation. In 1978, there were more than 2,000 mergers of this kind, with a total value of $34 billion (a value only slightly less than the gross national product of Hungary). Eighty of the companies acquired were worth more than $100 million each (*Time,* 1979, p. 63). In 1982, the two largest acquisitions alone — those of Mara-

Table 2-3
Examples of market
concentration

Selected products and years	Shares of largest companies, percentages		
	4 companies	8 companies	20 companies
Passenger cars			
1977	99+		
1954	98		
Spark plugs			
1977	99+		
1963	96		
Razor blades and razors			
1977	99		
1954	99		
Chewing gum			
1977	93		
1963	81		
Light bulbs			
1977	89		
1958	90		
Cigarettes			
1977	88	100	
1958	80	99	
Electronic calculators			
1977	88	97	
1972	68	97	
Washing machines			
1977	85	99	
1958	68	90	
Copper			
1977	84	99	
1972	83	99	
Watches and clocks			
1977	84		
1958	82		
Flat glass			
1977	82	93	
1958	90	96	
Household refrigerator/ freezers			
1977	82	97	
1958	65	85	
Household detergents			
1977	80		
1972	84		
Tractors			
1977	80	99	
1958	72	96	

Selected products and years	Shares of largest companies, percentages		
	4 companies	8 companies	20 companies
Fine cotton fabrics			
1977	78	98	
1958	40	59	
Tires (auto)			
1977	76	94	
1958	74	90	
Home and car radios			
1977	75	90	
1963	51	74	
Military aircraft			
1977	75	93	
1958	61	86	
Sanitary tissue			
1977	70		
1954	37		
Televisions			
1977	70	93	
1958	55	81	
Men's and boys' underwear			
1977	66		
1958	31		
Motorcycles and bicycles			
1977	62		
1963	47		
Roasted coffee			
1977	62		
1958	46		
Phonograph records and tapes			
1977	60	75	
1963	68	74	
Metal cans			
1977	56		
1958	80		
Electronic computers			
1977	49	67	
1972	75	86	
Semiconductors			
1977	41	60	
1958	46	64	

Table 2-3
(*continued*)

Selected products and years	Shares of largest companies, percentages		
	4 companies	8 companies	20 companies
Boys' suits			
1977	41		
1958	18		
Men's suits			
1977	33		
1958	15		
Petroleum refinery products			
1977	30	53	81
1958	31	54	81
Canned fruit and vegetables			
1977	19		
1963	24		
Book publishing			
1977	16		
1958	16		
Wood furniture			
1977	14		
1972	14		
Miscellaneous plastics			
1977	7		
1972	8		

Source: Adapted from U.S. Bureau of the Census, *Concentration Ratios in Manufacturing, 1977 Census of Manufacturers* (Washington, D.C.: Government Printing Office, May 1981), table 9.

thon Oil by U.S. Steel and of Cities Service Oil by Occidental Petroleum — added up to $10 billion. The top fifteen mergers and acquisitions involved about $26 billion (Steyer, 1983, pp. 48–50).

A measure of market concentration in a particular industry obviously cannot give the whole picture when a corporation holds a leading position in several industries at once. It cannot adequately measure the resources and influence of such corporations as Gulf and Western, for example, which grew from a small manufacturing company in the 1940s with 500 employees to gain control of more than 100 other companies together employing more than 100,000 workers, and which is now involved in a bewildering variety of enterprises. Gulf and Western, as the head of the U.S. Federal Trade Commission noted in the late 1970s, "owns Madison Square Garden, grows sugar cane in the Dominican Republic, produces movies for Paramount Pictures, publishes books under Simon and Schuster, makes cigars, weaves clothing, manufactures pulp, rolls steel and lends money, to name a few of its businesses" (Pertschuk, 1980, p. 362).

The rise of the conglomerate is only one reason why the structure of the modern American economy is even more concentrated than the official statistics suggest. Another reason is that a variety of interconnections bind the largest corporations together in crucial ways. As Edward Herman notes, "Corporate power depends not only on the resources and market control of individual companies, but also on the extent to which companies coordinate their behavior and activities" (1981, p. 194). Studies of American industry have come to different conclusions about the significance of these connections in influencing business decisions and overriding competition between corporations. But no one doubts that corporations are linked together in many ways, including everything from the common schooling, background, and club membership of corporate executives (Domhoff, 1970, 1974) to informal discussions over drinks or on the golf course, to more formal, institutional links between firms.

Among the latter, probably the most important is the *interlocking directorate* — the somewhat cumbersome term for the tendency for large corporations to have the same people sit on their boards of directors. In a *direct interlock,* a single director sits on the boards of two supposedly separate corporations. In an *indirect interlock,* two corporations' directors meet through sitting on the board of a third corporation. Direct interlocks, in particular, tend to create close working ties, mutual interest, and channels of communications that bind corporations together in ways that cast doubt on the conventional picture of independent, competitive enterprises.

A 1978 Senate study of interlocks among the largest 130 American corporations (which together controlled over a trillion dollars in assets) found the following (U.S. Congress, Senate, Committee on Government Affairs, 1978, p. 457):

- The 130 corporations shared a total of 530 direct and more than 12,000 indirect interlocks.
- Indirect interlocks often took place between companies that were, formally, competitors. Thus, both AT&T and I.B.M. — officially heavy competitors in communications equipment — had directors who sat together on the board of Citicorp, a bank that lent to both companies and was a customer of their products.
- The top 13 corporations alone had 249 direct and over 5,500 indirect interlocks with other corporations. AT&T alone interlocked with 93 of the 130 top corporations.
- The major oil companies were all tightly interlocked with each other, as were the major auto companies. Exxon had 21 indirect interlocks

The Corporate Network

with other oil majors; General Motors had 6 interlocks with the two other "big three" auto companies (Ford and Chrysler) through mutual directors on the boards of major banks.

Major banks play an important role in these intercorporate linkages, partly through interlocks with other corporations (including other financial ones) and partly through the ownership of influential amounts of corporate stock. In 1975, for example, Morgan Guaranty Trust of New York had a total of 43 interlocks with 35 of the 250 largest American corporations; the bank also held 2 percent or more of the stock in 32 corporations (Herman, 1981, pp. 224–225). (Though 2 percent may appear small, most analysts agree that ownership of very small percentages of a company's stock is now usually sufficient to strongly influence its operation.)

The Role of the "Internationalization" of the Economy

One further limitation of the usual measures of economic concentration deserves mention: The measures do not encompass either the growing role of American corporations overseas since World War II or, the other side of the coin, the increasing role (especially since the 1970s) of foreign corporations in the American economy. These two developments (both of which will be treated in more detail in Chapter 3) distort the conventional measures of corporate power, in opposite directions.

Thus, our usual measures of corporate shares in the domestic economy ignore the fact that a substantial number of corporations now do much of their business in foreign countries. Between 1970 and 1981 alone, American private direct investment in foreign countries grew from about $76 billion to about $227 billion (*Economic Report of the President*, 1983, p. 281). A growing number of the largest American corporations (and many smaller ones as well) now draw a substantial proportion (even a majority) of their income from foreign sales, and foreign workers are a substantial fraction of their total work force. The Ford Motor Company is still headquartered in Michigan, but it builds Fords and Ford components in countries as diverse as Brazil, Germany, and Spain, and supplies the livelihoods of thousands of workers there. In 1980, fully 55 percent of Ford's worldwide production took place in foreign countries; 30 percent of General Motors' employees are foreign (United Nations, 1983, pp. 41, 203). Understanding only the domestic role of these corporations, therefore, obscures the influence they exert throughout the world's economy.

At the same time, however, as a glance along any American street reveals, the same measures of corporate power also ignore the growing role of foreign businesses in the American economy. As Japanese cars (to take only one of the more obvious examples) gained an increasing share of the American auto market in the 1970s, measures of the American auto companies' share of domestic production obviously became less useful guides to the shape of the automobile market as a whole in this country. Increasingly, consumers in the past few decades have been faced with fewer choices among American-made cars, and the signs are that this trend, if anything, may increase. On the other hand, consumers gained many more choices among Japanese, German, French, Italian, Swedish, and British cars; and a similar process has taken place in many other industries. In assessing the concentration of private power in the American economy, therefore, it's important to keep in mind that at least some effects are modified by the fact that our economy is not a closed, impermeable system but (increasingly) part of a constantly shifting balance of resources and power in a *world* economic system.

The Two Economies

The other side of the increasing power of the largest corporations is the relatively shrinking share of economic activity accounted for by *small* businesses. In focusing on the growth of the large corporation, we have so far ignored the other end of what the economist John Kenneth Galbraith (1973) has called a "bimodal" economy. This sector contains millions of small businesses, often with only a handful of employees, which must scramble for a diminishing share of the economic pie.

The lopsided character of business enterprise in America becomes apparent when we look at tax returns. More than 2.5 million active corporations filed income tax returns with the Internal Revenue Service in 1979; almost 1.5 million of them reported assets of less than $100,000. Just 2.7 percent reported assets of more than $250 million (*Statistical Abstract of the U.S., 1982–83*, pp. 536, 543).

Students of the structure of American industry have developed a variety of ways of characterizing this split between (in Galbraith's 1973 phrase) the "planning" versus the "market" sector. Some distinguish between the "monopoly" versus the "competitive" sector, or, more simply, between "primary" and "secondary" sectors of the economy. But whatever terms are used, the trend is the same. The traditional conception of free enterprise — the competition of many small, independent businesses — applies, where it applies at all, to only *part* of our economy. The other part is, more and more, a center of concentrated power that bears virtually no resemblance to the nostalgic conception of small enterprise. This division has many consequences, some of which we'll examine in later chapters. The nature and quality of work, for example, as well as the level of earnings on the job, vary

The image of the small business no longer fits the reality of America's corporate economy. America's urban skylines reflect the dominance of the large corporation.

considerably between these sectors of the economy. So, too, do the risks of unemployment and poverty. And the different distribution of minorities and women in the two sectors has much to do with their differing life chances, as we'll see in Chapters 5 and 6.

The displacement of much small-scale production by large corporate enterprise, as the political scientist Charles Lindblom puts it, "constitutes a revolution" — a revolution "never much agitated, never even much resisted," and for which "no flags were raised" — but one that has "transformed our lives" (1977, p. 95). What are the consequences of this growth of private power for social and economic life in America? We will be addressing that question, in one way or another, throughout many of the chapters of this book. But first we need to look at two other aspects of the distribution of economic power in America. For it is not size or concentration alone that defines the contours of corporate power in American life, or that distinguishes the United States from other industrial societies, many of which, in fact, have as great or greater levels of concentration among a few giant firms. Even more important is the question of how that power stacks up against two other, potentially counterbalancing sources of social and economic influence: government and labor. As we've noted, there has been much criticism of the overpowering effects of "big government" on the economy and society as a whole in recent years, and a similar criticism of the overbearing role of "big labor." To round out our preliminary picture of the basic institutions of the American economy, therefore, let's look at some key facts about the relative place of government and, secondarily, of labor, in the American system.

How Big Is "Big Government"?

In an article ominously titled "Big Government: Democracy's Deadly Creation," the economist Allan Meltzer (1980) puts forward a view of the role of government in the American economy that has become widely shared. "Whether measured by the share of income taken by taxes or by the portion of the labor force employed," Meltzer says, "government has grown relentlessly." Is this an accurate assessment?

It is certainly true that the government plays a much greater role in the economy than it did in the past. But both the *size* and the *functions* of government in the American economy turn out to be considerably different, on close examination, than this perspective assumes.

Let's consider first the evidence of government *employment.* At first glance, the government appears as a very large employer, indeed; in 1981 government at all levels (federal, state, and local) employed almost 16 million people — 16 percent of all Americans employed in the civilian labor force. Two facts, however, qualify this picture.

Trends in Government Employment

First, the overwhelming majority of government employees work for state and local government. Less than one in five works for the federal government. The frequent references to the federal government as a giant, overweening bureaucracy seem less compelling in the light of the fact that it employs less than one-fifth as many people as the Fortune 500 manufacturing corporations. Measured by number of employees, the biggest "bureaucracy" in the United States in the early 1980s was not a government agency but a private corporation, AT&T, which employed even more people than the Department of Defense. AT&T has since been broken into smaller companies, but General Motors ranked not far behind, and several other private corporations, including Ford, IBM, General Electric, and Sears, Roebuck, are larger bureaucracies than any single federal agency other than Defense and the Postal Service (*Forbes*, 1983, p. 307).

Second, we need to examine the kind of work most government employees in fact *do.* Again, the conventional image is one of legions of faceless bureaucrats wielding inordinate power over economic decisions. But the reality is quite different. At the federal level, government employment is overwhelmingly dominated by civilian employees of the Department of Defense, who constituted more than 1 million (more than a third) of the 2.9 million federal workers in 1981. Adding together the Defense Department workers with the next largest category by far, the 665,000 postal workers, accounts for well over half of all federal civilian employment. Another roughly 250,000 work in health care. In state and local government, the work force is dominated by teachers and health care workers: More than half of local government employees work in education.

Sepp Seitz/Woodfin Camp & Associates

Most of the growth in government employment have been in education and health care.

Still another perspective on the growth of government-as-employer is provided by the trend of government employment over time. Viewed in raw figures, this growth has been substantial. Government employment more than doubled between 1955 and 1981. But, once again, the overall trend masks crucial distinctions. Of 8.5 million new government workers during that period, roughly 8 million went to work for state and local government. Federal government employment has grown relatively little since the 1950s, and has actually *declined* since 1970. Even during the late 1960s — the era often characterized as one in which federal programs and spending spun wildly out of control — federal employment grew at the unremarkable pace of 2.2 percent a year.

One result is that state and local government (and especially the latter) have taken a growing share of all government employment. Though it's often said that the growth of the federal government has meant that more and more power is concentrated in distant, unresponsive bureaucracies, the actual trend is in the opposite direction, at least in the case of government employment. The federal presence in American life has been increasingly overshadowed by the growth of more *localized* levels of government. In 1955, 68 percent of government workers were employed at the state and local levels; by 1981, 82 percent were. And even there the rise in government employment peaked during the late 1960s and slowed thereafter, showing some decline by the early 1980s (see Table 2-4).

So far we have ignored an important qualifying factor — the growth in the American population. Statistics on the growth of government seem more impressive than they really are if they are taken out of the context of a growing population whose needs the government must serve. In fact, when measured against the growth of the population as a whole, federal government employment has *fallen* substantially since 1950. More precisely, most of the post–World War II era falls into two periods: between 1950 and 1970, when per capita federal employment remained virtually unchanged, and after 1970, when it fell considerably. Thus, in 1950 there were 71 civilians for each civilian employed by the federal government; in 1970, 70; and in 1981, 79 (*Statistical Abstract of the U.S., 1982–83*, pp. 6, 303).

Government employment, however, is just one of many indicators of the government's size and influence. The levels of taxing and spending by government are another.

The "relentless" growth in government's share of income through taxation is often cited, along with the growth in employment, as a sign that the government has taken an ominously increasing role in American life.

Evaluating this claim is complicated because of the many kinds of taxation at the different levels of American government and because of the variety of benchmarks against which their impact can be measured. One of the most common ways of measuring the significance of the government tax burden is to view it as a proportion of economic activity as a whole. Table 2-5 presents the level of national and local taxes as well as Social Security contributions for the United States and a number of other countries.

Two things are immediately apparent. First, taxes as a proportion of the gross domestic product (the GDP is the value of all goods and services produced by the domestic economy in a given year; it is the same as the gross national product, but minus goods and services produced abroad) have remained remarkably stable in the United States in recent years: there was *no* significant increase in the government's role, measured in this way, during the decade of the 1970s. Second, even more strikingly, the relative level of taxes is *greater* in almost every country represented than in the United States. Indeed, Table 2-5 shows that every advanced industrial society except Japan gathers a higher share of taxes than the United States; only the less-developed of the European countries (Spain, Portugal, and Greece) tax

Government Spending and Taxes

Table 2-4
Trends in government employment, 1950–1981

Level of government	1950	1955	1960	1965	1970	1975	1980	1981
Employees (1,000)								
Total	**6,402**	**7,432**	**8,808**	**10,589**	**13,028**	**14,973**	**16,213**	**15,968**
Federal (civilian)	2,117	2,378	2,421	2,588	2,881	2,890	2,898	2,865
State and local	4,285	5,054	6,387	8,001	10,147	12,084	13,315	13,103
Percent of total	66.9	68.0	72.5	75.6	77.9	80.7	82.1	82.1
State	1,057	1,250	1,527	2,028	2,755	3,271	3,753	3,726
Local	3,228	3,804	4,860	5,973	7,392	8,813	9,562	9,377
Average annual percent change								
Employees, total	**−.5**	**3.0**	**3.5**	**3.8**	**4.2**	**2.4**	**1.5**	**−1.5**
Federal	−8.9	2.4	.4	1.3	2.2	.6	1.0	−1.2
State and local	6.1	3.4	4.8	4.6	4.9	2.9	1.6	−1.6

Source: Adapted from *Statistical Abstract of the United States, 1982–83* (Washington, D.C.: Government Printing Office, 1983), p. 303.

Table 2-5
Tax revenues as percent
of gross domestic
product, 1970 and 1980

| | Years | |
Country	1970	1980
United States	30.1	30.7
Australia	25.4	30.9
Austria	35.7	41.3
Belgium	36.0	44.7
Canada	32.0	32.9
Denmark	40.4	45.7
Finland	32.2	35.3
France	35.6	42.6
Greece	24.3	26.5
Italy	27.9	32.4
Japan	19.7	26.1
Netherlands	39.9	46.2
New Zealand	26.6	31.7
Norway	39.2	47.3
Portugal	23.2	29.8
Spain	17.2	29.8
Sweden	40.7	49.6
Switzerland	23.8	30.8
United Kingdom	37.5	36.1
West Germany	32.8	37.4

Source: Statistical Abstract of the United States, 1982–83 (Washington, D.C.: Government Printing Office, 1983), p. 870.

less. In some cases (Belgium, Denmark, the Netherlands, Norway, and Sweden), the tax burden is roughly 50 percent higher than in the United States. Moreover, Japan, the major exception to this rule, turns out on closer inspection to be less an exception than it seems at first blush since — like many other countries in the table — its tax burden as a proportion of its gross domestic product has increased rapidly in recent years, while ours has stabilized.

What is true of taxes — the government's main source of income — is also true of government *spending*. As Figure 2-3 demonstrates, the United States falls, once again, near the very *bottom* of the advanced industrial societies in the proportion of economic activity accounted for by public spending. As with taxes, Japan is the only comparable country on the list with a lower proportion of government outlays. (Though the figure doesn't show this, the only reason our government expenditures are slightly higher than Japan's is our much higher spending on *defense*. When it comes to spending on *nondefense* programs, the United States' proportion is even smaller than Japan's. The same point, of course, should also be kept in mind in understanding Japan's lower taxes.)

Even these rather dramatic comparisons, however, fail to express the differences between the government's role in the United States and in most other advanced societies. It is not merely the *amount* of government spending that differs among industrial societies, for example, but also the *kind* of government spending. In most other advanced industrial countries, the government takes a far more active, productive role in the overall economy than it does in the United States. In many countries substantial sectors of the economy are owned and operated as *public* enterprises rather than as private ones. These public enterprises range from coal and steel (in several European countries) to automobiles (such as France's Renault, Germany's Volks-

Public and Private Enterprise

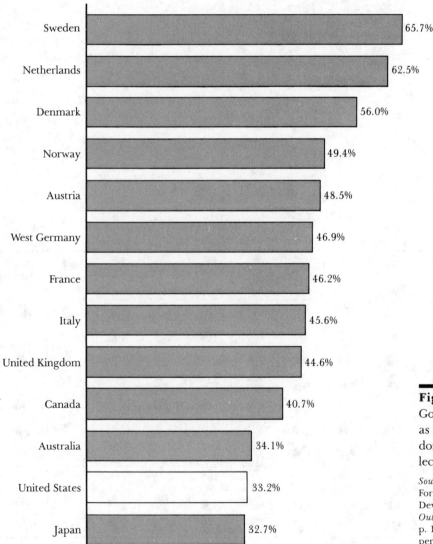

Figure 2-3
Government expenditures as a percentage of gross domestic product, selected countries, 1980

Source: Data from Organization For Economic Cooperation and Development, *OECD Economic Outlook*, Paris, December 1982, p. 161. Reprinted with permission.

wagen, and Italy's Alfa Romeo) to a substantial part of oil, gas, and other energy production (as in Italy) (see Figure 2-4). In a number of countries, an important part of the banking industry is publicly or partially publicly owned as well, as are many national airlines and railway systems. (In the United States, probably the best-known example is the major public utility, the Tennessee Valley Authority, TVA.) As this implies, many of these public enterprises are very large ones, integral to their national economies and, in fact, major contenders on the list of the most important *world* enterprises. Italy's public energy conglomerate, ENI, was the world's tenth largest industrial corporation in 1981; Compagnie Francaise des Petroles, the French public oil company, was seventeenth, Renault thirtieth, among the world's industrial firms (*Fortune*, 1982, p. 181).

The *importance* of public enterprise in other countries is suggested by Table 2-6, which is based on a recent analysis from the Organization for Economic Cooperation and Development (OECD). Table 2-6 shows the shares of overall investment accounted for by public enterprises, as well as the share of national employment.

Once again, the comparative differences are striking. It is not just that the United States has a smaller sector of public enterprise; its public enter-

Figure 2-4
Shares of public ownership in selected sectors in selected countries, 1978

Source: Adapted from William Shepherd and Clair Wilcox, *Public Policies Toward Business*, 6th ed. (Homewood, Ill.: Irwin, 1979), p. 410. Reprinted with permission.

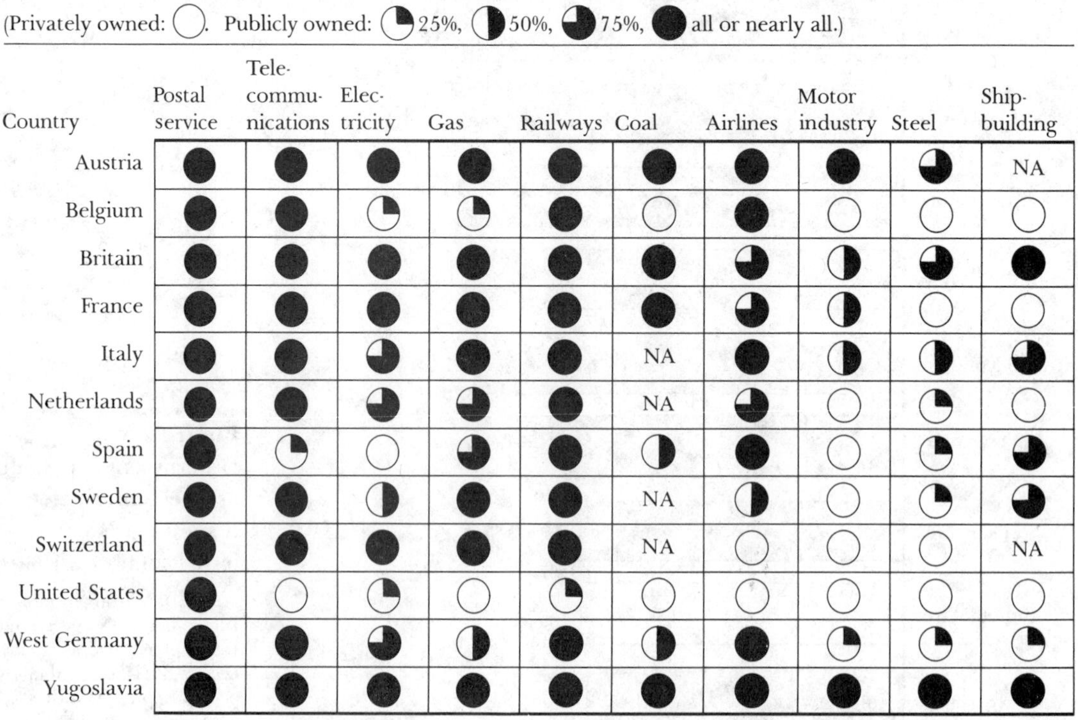

(Privately owned: ○. Publicly owned: ◔25%, ◑50%, ◕75%, ●all or nearly all.)

Country	Postal service	Telecommunications	Electricity	Gas	Railways	Coal	Airlines	Motor industry	Steel	Shipbuilding
Austria	●	●	●	●	●	●	●	●	◕	NA
Belgium	●	●	◔	◔	●	○	●	○	○	○
Britain	●	●	●	●	●	●	◕	◑	◕	●
France	●	●	●	●	●	●	◕	◑	○	○
Italy	●	●	◔	●	●	NA	●	◑	◑	◕
Netherlands	●	●	◔	◕	●	NA	◕	○	○	○
Spain	●	◔	○	◔	●	◑	●	○	◔	◕
Sweden	●	●	◑	●	●	NA	◑	○	◕	◕
Switzerland	●	●	●	●	●	NA	○	○	○	NA
United States	●	○	◔	○	◔	○	○	○	○	○
West Germany	●	●	◕	◑	●	◑	●	◔	◔	◔
Yugoslavia	●	●	●	●	●	●	●	●	●	●

Country	Investment	Employment
Australia	4.5	NA
Austria	5.3	12.4
Belgium	3.3	5.2
Canada	3.7	4.5
France	2.5	4.4
Ireland	3.6	5.7
Italy	3.3	6.4
Japan	3.8	NA
Netherlands	2.9	NA
Norway	6.5	4.2
Sweden	3.5	8.0
United Kingdom	3.5	8.2
United States	0.9	1.6
West Germany	2.7	7.9

Table 2-6
Share of public enterprises in total investment and employment, 1975–1978/9

Note: NA means not available.

Source: Leila Pathirane and Derek W. Blades, "Defining and Measuring the Public Sector: Some International Comparisons," *Review of Income and Wealth*, series 28, no. 3, September 1982, pp. 268–273. Reprinted with permission of the International Association for Research in Income and Wealth and the authors.

prise sector isn't even in the same ball park as the others. In terms of shares of investment, the foreign countries nearest to our level of public-sector enterprise invest close to three times what we do in such enterprises, and the difference in shares of employment is often equally great. Countries like Sweden and West Germany employ almost 1 in 12 of their labor force in public enterprises, and Austria almost 1 in 8. In the United States, the figure is 1 in *60*.

Simply knowing that an enterprise is officially public rather than private tells us little about its priorities or its mode of operation in practice. But these sharp differences in both the size and the function of the public sector do help illustrate, once more, how thoroughly *private* the American economy is in comparison to the economies of other countries. This is true not only of the role of government employment, revenue, and spending in general but, perhaps even more decisively, in terms of the location of control over economic *investment*. In the United States, where not only virtually all industrial production but also virtually all banking and finance are under *private* auspices, decisions about what kinds of investment should be undertaken and financed, more than in most comparable societies, are overwhelmingly made by private actors for private purposes.

This difference, it should be emphasized, goes beyond the somewhat clumsy categories of capitalism versus socialism: None of the countries we've just compared with the United States is socialist since, in all of them, *most* production still remains in private hands — though some are governed by Socialist political parties. All of this variation in the role of the public sector is within the spectrum of the world's "mixed" economies. Chapter 3 touches on some of the ways in which government planning in these other countries has affected the growth and performance of their economies in recent years. For now, it's important to stress that — contrary to the image often promoted in the United States — a strong role for government in the economy doesn't necessarily translate into the grim, totalitarian rigidities often associated with some of the countries of Eastern Europe. In varying degrees, it is a fundamental development common to most of the world's advanced industrial nations.

How Big Is "Big Labor"?

"Big labor" is frequently classified with "big business" and "big government" as the third member of a three-cornered system of shared power in the American economy. Big labor and big business are both regarded as interest groups that contend with each other for social and economic influence, and the implication is that they join that battle with roughly equivalent resources (Lindblom, 1977, p. 193). This conception is partly responsible for the general public's dim view of labor unions, which have recently been ranked very low in opinion polls measuring public support for various institutions. Along with government and business, labor is often seen as yet another powerful but unresponsive giant bureaucracy.

The reality of labor's current position in the United States is quite different, however. To begin with, unions now enroll a relatively small — and declining — proportion of the American labor force. From a little less than 25 percent of the total labor force in 1955, union members became slightly less than 20 percent by the end of the 1970s. In some states, especially in the South, the proportion of workers in unions is considerably smaller, below 10 percent, for example, in both North and South Carolina (*Statistical Abstract of the U.S., 1982–83*, pp. 407–410). The labor movement has had great difficulty organizing workers in many of the fast growing parts of the economy, such as the data processing and computer industries, fast-food restaurants and other retail sales industries, and banking and finance, among others. Of about 36 million new jobs in the American economy added during the 1960s and 1970s, only about 2 million have been organized by unions (Chernow, 1981, p. 20).

At the same time, the unions' traditional base of strength in the blue-collar manufacturing industries has eroded badly. During the 1970s, the labor movement made significant membership gains, especially in some service industries and in state and local government. But, from 1970 to 1978, it lost over a million members in manufacturing industries and more

During the 1980s, the balance of power may be shifting away from unions.

than 300,000 in the food industry alone (*Statistical Abstract of the U.S., 1982–83*, p. 410). Another estimated 300,000 members of the United Auto Workers have lost unionized jobs over the past several years (Meyer, 1981, p. 67). Recession-level unemployment, automation, and the movement of production jobs overseas or to nonunion areas of the Sun Belt have all taken their toll on union membership in these industries.

But declining membership is only one facet of labor's present difficult position. Unions have been relatively unsuccessful in winning the right to represent workers through elections in recent years. In 1934, unions won 94 percent of those representation elections; they won 61 percent of them in 1966, but just 45 percent in 1979. And the threat of a strike as a weapon in the struggle with employers has been weakened in a number of ways in addition to the loss of membership and representation.

For one thing, automation in many industries has meant that, in a pinch, companies can often keep up close to their usual level of production with only supervisory employees on the job. And this is likely to become an even more telling problem for unions as workplace automation becomes still more sophisticated; as an article in *Fortune* puts it, "Robots don't strike" (Meyer, 1981, p. 67). For another, the rise of the conglomerate corporation has also hurt unions' ability to pose a threat to management since, in order to keep up with a company's diversification, labor must coordinate different unions across a variety of industries in order to make a coherent effect on a company's policy. A similar dilemma has resulted from the increasingly multinational character of many American corporations. A company that does half of its production overseas can easily shift even more of it abroad in the event of labor problems at home, and labor has not yet been able to create the international organizations that could match the corporations' mobility.

The result of these trends is that, as *Fortune* declared in 1981, "a historic

How Big Is "Big Labor"?   **49**

shift appears to be looming in the balance of power between labor and management" (Meyer, 1981, p. 66). What makes this shift especially painful for labor is that unions have traditionally occupied a distinctly subordinate position in relation to business in the United States, as compared with most other advanced industrial countries. Some of that disparity is revealed by membership figures; while American unions now comprise about 20 percent of the labor force, the proportion of organized workers is about 40 percent in Germany and Spain, 45 percent in Italy, 50 percent in Britain, and an astonishing 90 percent in Sweden (Hayward, 1980, p. 4). These differences translate into a much greater political role for labor in most European countries — a role that has profoundly affected the social fabric of those countries in many ways: tougher occupational health and safety laws, higher and more easily available social welfare benefits, regulations governing plant closings and retraining policies, and many others. In the United States, business's discretion to lay off workers, to shut down factories and stores, and to determine the levels of toxic chemicals in the workplace — to name only a few key issues of labor policy — is much greater than it is in most comparable societies. And if "big labor" shrinks further, this imbalance could become even more telling.

Government Support for Private Enterprise

Though the public sector of the American economy is relatively small by comparison with that of other countries, the government's role in economic life in the United States is by no means insignificant. On the contrary, government intervention in the service of economic goals has been an important feature of America's development since well before the Civil War. Moreover, that intervention has not been uniformly hostile to business interests; indeed, government support of various kinds has been actively — and successfully — sought by private enterprises from the country's beginnings (Herman, 1981, chap. 5).

The great system of canals that opened up settlement beyond the East Coast in the early nineteenth century was largely underwritten by public funds; as much as 80 percent of the investment came from the government (DuBoff, 1980, p. 397). In the later part of the century, the government continued this tradition with extensive support for the development of the railroads that provided the transportation arteries for both America's westward expansion and the post–Civil War industrial revolution. Private railroad companies received grants of valuable land (often bearing coal, copper, and other mineral wealth) totaling more than 180 million acres. Other subsidies and tax exemptions, from local and state as well as the federal government, brought public support to the private railroad industry to an estimated $1.3 billion during the nineteenth century. Following World War II, the federal government provided a bonanza to private business by selling more than $15 billion worth of war-related assets to private industry at less than a third of their cost (Shepherd and Wilcox, 1979, p. 568).

Today, that tradition of government aid has blossomed into a complex, often confusing array of publicly funded supports for private enterprise. Some of them are direct and tangible, others indirect and difficult to estimate with any precision. In Chapter 4 we will consider how they affect the distribution of income and wealth in the United States. But it is helpful to look at them briefly now as well, for this network of subsidies and protections should profoundly affect the way we think about the relations between business and government. Taken together, they amount to what may be called a hidden welfare system for private business. They include:

- *Bailouts:* These are probably the most obvious examples of government support of private business. They include subsidies and guaranteed loans to enable failing companies to remain afloat. The largest and best known of these, the $1.2 billion federal loan to stave off the collapse of the Chrysler Corporation in the early 1980s, is only the most striking example of government's frequent commitment to providing a safety net for badly managed corporations.

- *Direct subsidies:* Another relatively straightforward part of the system of public assistance to business is the payment of direct subsidies to benefit certain key industries. Two of the most important consumers of public funds have traditionally been the energy industries and agriculture. As we'll see in Chapter 10, the private energy industry has benefited from an estimated $250 *billion* in direct government subsidies since the end of World War I, of which half has gone to the oil industry alone. The much younger nuclear power industry, by the mid-1970s, accounted for about 8 percent of that historical total and is now thoroughly dependent on continuing federal subsidies for its economic survival. The federal government has paid for most of the research that built the industry, has helped pay for the construction of nuclear power plants, and has subsidized the cost of insurance against nuclear accidents.

    Federal subsidies to agriculture amount to a rich mixture of policies, many of them dating from the Great Depression. A number of crops are protected by "target" prices, meaning that government will pay farmers the difference between the price their crop brings on the market and a preestablished price. The government also supports agricultural prices by buying surplus farm products (including sugar, cotton,

Sometimes, corporations (like individuals) need government help to survive.

and wheat) that would otherwise be unsold on the market. And the government also provides a number of other direct services that promote private agriculture with public funds. Nearly four-fifths of all water used in the United States is for cropland irrigation, most of it in the West. An estimated 90 percent of the cost of irrigation systems has been borne by the government (Shepherd and Wilcox, 1979, p. 578), and by far the biggest beneficiaries have been large, corporate farms (Harrington, 1980, p. 75).

- *Trade restrictions:*   Despite much rhetorical support for the idea of free trade, many industries have sought — and won — extensive government protection against competition from foreign producers. Liquors, motorcycles, some fabrics, clothing, machinery, sporting goods, musical instruments, and appliances, among numerous others, are protected by import tariffs that artificially raise the prices of foreign goods for American consumers. Foreign-built ships are restricted from operating in certain American waters. The steel industry is protected by a system of so-called trigger pricing that automatically regulates the cost of imported steel. The value of these government-enforced restrictions has ranged from about 5 percent to close to 50 percent of the cost of the particular product.

- *Tax expenditures:*   In addition to outright subsidies and payments, the government also supports private industry through exemptions from taxes. As chapter 4 shows, such tax expenditures are widespread throughout the American economy, and some benefit individuals and groups other than private businesses. But the financial support such tax breaks provide to business is staggering. In fiscal year 1982, the federal government gave the oil and gas industry tax credits for exploration and development that, if calculated as direct government spending, amounted to almost $3.3 billion. Tax credits for business investment generally amounted to more than $19 billion. Another $2.9 billion went to business through the device of "domestic international sales corporations," which provide special tax treatment for income earned overseas (U.S. Office of Management and Budget, 1983, pp. G-26, G-27).

- *Shields against competition:*   We've already seen that government trade restrictions help protect many American industries against foreign competition. The risks of domestic competition are also mitigated by the government in a variety of ways. The most important example is defense production. Military production is a giant sector of the American economy, supplying a significant proportion of the total sales of a number of the largest American corporations as well as many smaller ones. But the bulk of defense contracting is done in ways that bear no resemblance to the model of free enterprise. Government defense planners typically establish close working relations with a small number of familiar, established companies; little genuinely competitive bidding for military contracts occurs. One comprehensive review estimates that about two-thirds of military purchases "occur under conditions with virtually no competition at all" (Shepherd and Wilcox, 1979, p. 559).

- *Absorbing "externalities":* A more subtle kind of government aid for private business may be the most important of all, though its dollar costs are virtually impossible to measure. Many of the social and ecological problems that are created in the course of doing business are enormously costly — but they do not appear as costs on the balance sheets of private industry. In economists' language, these costs are called *externalities*. But the fact that they are "external" to the firms themselves doesn't mean that no one ultimately pays for them. In both direct and subtle ways, they are typically paid by the public — often appearing, somewhat paradoxically, as perverse costs of "big government." Two of the most important examples are industrial pollution and unemployment due to layoffs and business shutdowns. In both cases private business decisions create conditions that demand a response; in both cases much of the response — the disposal of toxic wastes, the payment of public assistance benefits — falls on the shoulders of government agencies and is paid for by the general public through taxes. To the extent that this public subsidization takes place, as Barry Commoner notes with regard to pollution, "the enterprise, though free, is not wholly private" (1971, p. 267).

Whatever one may believe about the appropriateness of these various public supports for business, the important point is that they are deeply enmeshed in our economic system. Private industry is aided and cushioned by a complex system of publicly funded "welfare," which substantially diminishes the risks of private enterprise and spreads the true costs of doing business throughout society as a whole. Whether the cost involved is that of drilling an oil well, cleaning up a toxic chemical spill, or paying for the inefficiency of a new weapons system, business relies heavily, in one way or another, on that system of public welfare. And this not only affects our understanding of the true meaning of government spending but has important consequences for many aspects of American life — from the distribution of income to the state of national security.

A Privatized Economy

In the 1950s and 1960s, many social scientists believed that the world's advanced societies were coming more and more to resemble each other. Common technological and political trends, it was argued, were leading to an increasing convergence among what were variously called the "new industrial states" or, slightly later, the "postindustrial societies" (see, for example, Galbraith, 1967; Bell, 1971). In some important respects these predictions have been borne out. The industrial societies of Europe, North America, and Japan are all characterized by the growth of large corporate bureaucracies alongside of their more traditional sectors of small enterprise and also by the increasing role of government in economic life. But, at the same time, these predictions unduly minimized the persistence of important differences among the industrial societies — particularly in the realm of the relative influence of private versus public power, which, in turn, is closely bound up with the relative strength of business versus labor.

In the United States, as we've seen, the private economy is no longer wholly understandable in the terms traditionally applied to the competitive market system. Instead, it is characterized by an extraordinary — and in some respects still increasing — concentration of private economic power in a relatively few very large corporations. But this in itself is not what distinguishes the United States from other countries within the advanced capitalist world. What *is* strikingly different is the relative balance of resources and power among government, private business, and labor. Even among the world's mixed economies, the United States stands out as uniquely dominated by *private* power, with a relatively miniscule public sector and a generally small, historically weak labor movement.

This obviously casts considerable doubt on the argument that many of America's problems are primarily the result of the growth of government at the expense of business, of the public sector as opposed to the private. Indeed, whatever one may believe about the moral or philosophical issues involved, it is difficult to comprehend American social problems and the public policies addressing them without viewing them through the lens of the underdevelopment of *public* institutions and programs in the United States, relative to other, comparable societies. These issues have been raised most urgently in recent years in reference to the problems of the American economy itself, to which we now turn.

Summary

This chapter has described some dimensions of the institutions of business, government, and labor in America, and some of the relationships among them.

Though the American economy is often regarded as a system of small enterprises competing together in a free market, it is increasingly dominated by a relatively small number of large, often interconnected corporations wielding great economic influence.

The American government — especially the federal government — is sometimes seen as a giant, all-powerful bureaucracy overwhelming private business. But by a variety of measures, including government spending, taxation, and the role of public enterprise, government has a *smaller* role in America than in almost any other advanced industrial society. The role of the *federal* government hasn't grown in recent years. The growth that *has* taken place in government in the past decade has been at the state and local level, mainly in the provision of basic services like schooling and health care. With the exception of the Department of Defense, America's largest bureaucracies are private, not governmental, ones.

Government and "free enterprise" are often thought to be opposing forces in American society. But the federal government provides an elaborate network of special supports and subsidies that constitute a kind of "hidden welfare system" for private business. That system includes bailouts of troubled corporations, public subsidies for agriculture and other industries, special tax reductions, and protection against foreign competition.

The other "partner" in the American economic system — labor — is neither as large nor as powerful as is often believed. The organized labor movement is at a low point, and changes in the economy itself, including automation and the decline of traditional blue-collar industries, may make labor's influence even more precarious.

Because of the relatively small roles of government and labor, our economic and social policies are influenced to an unusually high degree (as compared to other advanced societies) by the interests of private business.

For Further Reading

Carnoy, Martin, and Derek Shearer. *Economic Democracy: The Challenge of the 1980's*. White Plains, N.Y.: Sharpe, 1980.

Galbraith, John Kenneth. *Economics and the Public Purpose*. Boston: Houghton Mifflin, 1973.

Herman, Edward S. *Corporate Control, Corporate Power*. 2nd ed. New York: Cambridge University Press, 1981.

Lindblom, Charles E. *Politics and Markets: The World's Political-Economic Systems*. New York: Basic Books, 1977.

Scherer, Frederick M. *Industrial Market Structure and Economic Performance*, 2nd ed. Chicago: Rand McNally, 1980.

Shepherd, William G., and Clair Wilcox. *Public Policies toward Business*, 6th ed. Homewood, Ill.: Richard D. Irwin, 1979.

3

The End of Affluence?
Social Aspects of
Economic Decline

Throughout most of the past decade, the threat of economic insecurity has touched almost every corner of American life. The specifics of what we have come to call an economic crisis have varied in important ways in recent years. In particular, the relative balance between the two great scourges of the modern American economy, unemployment and inflation, has shifted with often bewildering speed. But beneath the confusing variation in the dry statistics on unemployment, lost production, and changing price levels lie some continuing harsh realities that affect most Americans in one way or another — shrinking chances for a decent job, housing prices so high that an adequate home may seem forever out of reach, having to take on a second job just to pay the bills, the closing of factories and the sudden, devastating collapse of long-established businesses.

It wasn't always this way. For most of the period from World War II to the 1970s, constant economic growth was virtually taken for granted in the United States. Social theorists celebrated the coming of what John Kenneth Galbraith (1957) called the "affluent society"; some went so far as to argue that America's prosperity was a sign that most of the fundamental economic problems of the past had been essentially solved (Bell, 1965). No one denied that we still had problems — poverty, inadequate housing, urban decay — but these were often regarded as unfortunate leftovers from the less affluent past. Continued economic growth would, in the economic metaphor of the time, "trickle down" to the poor and the less prosperous areas of the country. What growth failed to accomplish could be provided by antipoverty or urban renewal programs. Even critics of American society during the 1950s and 1960s usually took its affluence for granted; they leveled most of their criticism at what they regarded as America's cultural sterility and loss of meaning and purpose, not at its failure to grow and produce in material terms (see, for example, Riesman, 1955; Goodman, 1960; Marcuse, 1964).

These expectations of continued growth were based on what was at least a partial reality. A unique combination of factors had put the United States in the enviable position of being the dominant economic power in the world, and that power was translated into rising standards of living at home. *Business Week* put this postwar development succinctly in a 1980 article on the "Shrinking Standard of Living":

> For three decades after the end of World War II, Americans enjoyed an ever-rising standard of living; each successive year, with few exceptions, found people working less and earning more. It became not only two chickens in every pot, but two cars in every garage for most Americans, not to mention the radios, TV sets, hi-fi's, blenders, wall ovens, and trash compactors. (1980c, p. 73)

The profusion of consumer goods wasn't, of course, the only fruit of postwar economic growth. Even more important for the way most Americans lived and thought were other benefits: the feeling that hard work would bring solid rewards — economic security and the good life — for one's children if not for oneself, and the opening of possibilities for social and economic advancement for many people who had been denied them.

But the crippling recessions and mounting inflation of the 1970s ended the era of largely unbroken economic growth, jolting the country awake from the "American dream." As *Business Week* concluded, "The American credo that each generation can look forward to a more comfortable life than its predecessor has been shattered" (1980c, p. 72).

In the 1980s, this rude awakening has led to fundamental changes in the concerns that animate both social science and social policy in the United States. Rather than describing the still-unresolved social problems of affluence, much recent social research has been directed to the causes and consequences of economic decline, and the political agenda has been dominated by competing strategies of economic "revitalization." Though there is little disagreement about the seriousness of America's economic troubles, there is great disagreement about their causes and cures.

As we've already noted, the problems of the American economy have often been blamed on the role of government — along with the excessive expectations of workers, environmentalists, and the poor. Logically enough, these views have resulted in (sometimes successful) demands to "free" the economy from government regulation, to reduce spending on certain social programs, and to tolerate (or encourage) high levels of unemployment in the name of "fighting inflation." And, on the premise that the economy has performed poorly in large part because business has been denied enough resources and incentives to produce, recent public policy has included a wide array of tax benefits and other measures designed to stimulate renewed private investment and growth.

Yet by the early 1980s, other voices began to argue that the troubles of the economy were due less to the restrictive influences of government and labor than to the failure to use effectively the human and material resources the American economy does possess. From this point of view, the crisis has been not simply an economic but a social and political one, and one that involves the organizational and social shortcomings of business at least as much as the encroachment of government.

Whatever the outcome of the debate among these perspectives in the immediate future, the issues it raises will remain fundamental concerns for years to come. This chapter explores some of them. The first section examines the dimensions of recession, inflation, and the stalemated standard of living in recent years, with particular attention to the changing balance of economic power and performance between the United States and a number of foreign countries. Disagreements over economic policy often involve differing judgments about the social and personal costs of alternative strategies of dealing with economic problems, so another section of the chapter addresses what social scientists know about the human costs of recession and unemployment. Finally, the last part of the chapter critically examines several popular explanations for the problems of America's economy in the light of the best evidence available to us.

The End of Affluence?

The phenomenon loosely called the economic crisis is actually a combination of several different trends in the American economy (and the economies of most other countries of the world) over the past decade or so. Americans feel the crisis in the higher risk of losing a job (or failing to land one in the first place); in higher bills for food, energy, and housing; and in the decline in the vitality and prosperity of local communities. In ways that are less immediate and personal, the economic crisis appears in national economic statistics as slower rates of growth and industrial production and as a decline in the economic performance of the United States as compared to some foreign countries. Let's look at several of these trends in turn.

Slower Growth

The state of a country's economy can be measured in a variety of ways, each carrying somewhat different implications. But by virtually all measures, the American economy ran into serious, stubborn problems during

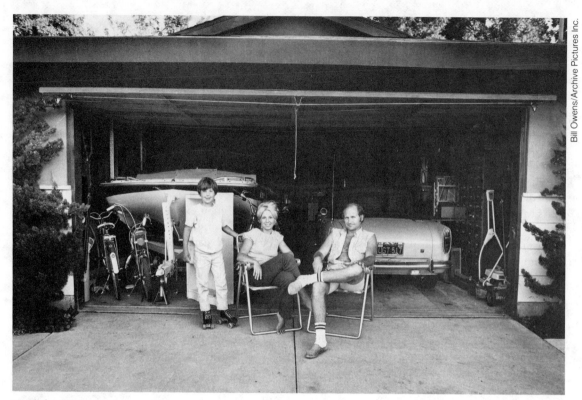

Until the 1970s, many Americans took material abundance for granted.

the 1970s and 1980s. The most basic indicator of this is the slowing of the pace of economic growth.

Economic growth is usually measured by the rate of increase in gross national product (GNP) or its close relation, gross domestic product (GDP) — the two being very similar measures, often used interchangeably to count the dollar value of all goods and services the economy produces each year. Table 3·1 shows growth rates in GDP for the United States and several other countries since 1950. Two trends are clearly apparent: The rate of economic growth in the United States peaked during the 1960s and slowed during the 1970s, and American economic growth has been relatively weak by comparison with many other countries. Our rate of growth for the entire 30-year period is lower than any other country in the table except the United Kingdom. Adjusting the rates to account for changes in population gives us figures for GDP per capita, also shown in Table 3·1. Measured in this way, the relatively slow growth of the American economy is even clearer. Per capita GDP grew more than twice as fast in West Germany and Italy and more than three times as fast in Japan — and even slightly faster in Britain. And though all these countries experienced slower growth in the 1970s, most still fared better than the United States during the worldwide recession of those years.

As a result, despite the fact that the Western European countries and Japan faced many of the same economic trials as the United States did (like rising prices for oil), their living standards — to the extent that these standards are measurable by per capita GDP — increased relative to ours, often rapidly. Of course, comparing these measures across different countries is difficult and controversial, partly because of fluctuations in the money exchange rates among countries and partly because of problems in determining what money will buy (its purchasing power) in different economies. But is is clear that as late as the beginning of the 1970s, America's GNP per capita was the highest of any industrial country. By 1975, by most accounts, we had been surpassed by two industrial countries, Sweden and Switzerland. And by 1981 the list also included, at a minimum, Denmark, France, Norway, and West Germany (U.S. National Center for Foreign Assessment, 1982, p. 40; *Statistical Abstract of the U.S., 1982–83*, p. 868). Whatever the exact measure used, there is no dispute over the broad shift in America's relative position. In 1970, the West German and Danish GDP per capita were only about two-thirds that of the United States'; those of Norway and France about two-fifths. And Japan's per capita GDP, which had reached at least three-fourths of the American level by the start of the 1980s, was only about two-fifths of it in 1970 (Reich and Magaziner, 1982, p. 13).

The relative stagnation of the American economy is actually understated by these figures, however. During the 1970s an extraordinary proportion of Americans entered the labor force — at a rate significantly higher than that

Country	1950–80	1950–60	1960–70	1970–80
United States, total	3.3	3.1	3.9	3.0
Per capita	2.0	1.3	2.6	2.0
Canada, total	4.6	4.6	5.2	4.0
Per capita	2.7	1.9	3.4	2.8
France, total	4.6	4.6	5.6	3.6
Per capita	3.7	3.6	4.5	3.1
Italy, total	4.8	5.5	5.7	3.1
Per capita	4.1	4.8	5.0	2.5
Japan, total	7.8	8.0	10.6	4.9
Per capita	6.6	6.9	9.5	3.6
United Kingdom, total	2.5	2.8	2.8	1.9
Per capita	2.1	2.4	2.3	1.8
West Germany, total	5.1	8.0	4.7	2.8
Per capita	4.3	6.4	3.8	2.7

Table 3-1
Annual percentage growth rates in gross domestic product, 1950–1980

Source: Adapted from *Statistical Abstract of the United States, 1982–83* (Washington, D.C.: Government Printing Office, 1983), p. 421.

of most other industrial countries. Other things being equal, that comparatively higher rate of increased work ought to have translated into comparatively higher output for the United States. But, as Figure 3-1 illustrates, other things were *not* equal. In both the manufacturing and nonmanufacturing sectors of the economy, America's growth in output was the lowest of all the countries in the chart except the United Kingdom. A more telling measure combines both trends into a figure for GDP per employed person (Table 3-2). This statistic can serve as a rough but revealing measure of the productive use an economy is making of its work force. As Table 3-2 shows, by this measure the American economy has done very badly indeed. Our growth in GDP per worker averaged *less than a fourth* that of some European countries, such as France, West Germany, and the Netherlands; less than a fifth that of Japan; and only a little more than a third that of Great Britain — a country often considered to be a particularly bad example of economic stagnation.

Figure 3-1

Output growth in major industrial countries, 1964–1980

Source: U.S. National Center for Foreign Assessment, *Handbook of Economic Statistics* (1982), p. 20.

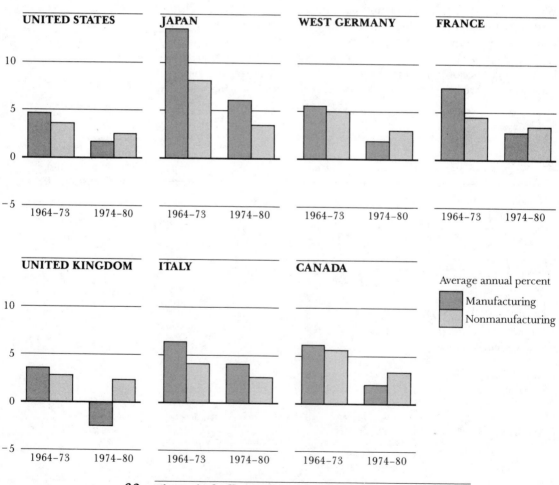

Areas and countries	GDP
Asia	
Singapore	3.0
Japan	4.2
Korea	5.9
Europe	
United Kingdom	2.1
Belgium	3.0
Netherlands	3.3
France	3.4
West Germany	3.4
North America	
United States	0.8
Canada	1.1

Table 3-2
Growth of gross domestic product per employed person, 1970–1979

Source: Adapted from Bruce R. Scott, "Can Industry Survive the Welfare State?" *Harvard Business Review* (September/October 1982, pp. 78–79). Copyright © 1982 by the President and Fellows of Harvard College; all rights reserved. Reprinted by permission of *Harvard Business Review.*

Deepening Recession

Economic instability — the ups and downs of what economists call the *business cycle* — is not new to the American economy. But the experience of the 1980s and late 1970s has been especially troubling, both because of the severity of the economic slump and the disturbing evidence that the economy's tendency toward recession and stagnation has been deepening over time.

As Figure 3-2 shows, the level of unemployment during the 1981–1982 recession was considerably higher than in any of the other seven recessions since World War II. (In fact, unemployment in the early 1980s was higher than at any time since the Great Depression of the 1930s.) Moreover, the *declines* in unemployment after each recession have left us with progressively higher jobless rates even in the peak of the business cycle (shown by the size of the lower portions of the bars in Figure 3-2).

The same ominous pattern appears if we consider data on the loss of American jobs in specific industries. The economic crisis has not struck uniformly across all sectors of the economy but has hit some key industries much more than others. And the evidence suggests that many (though not all) of these hard-hit industries are undergoing long-term losses in employment that are considerably more devastating than those experienced in 1974–1975, the worst of the previous postwar recessions. The auto industry has been the most discussed of these industries but, as Table 3-3 shows, it is only one of many. Between 1979 and 1982 alone, the primary metal industries (iron and steel, copper, and so on) lost well over a *third* of their employment; transportation equipment (autos, aircraft, shipbuilding, and railroads) lost almost a *fourth;* and several other industries lost a *fifth or more* of their

The End of Affluence?   **63**

Percent

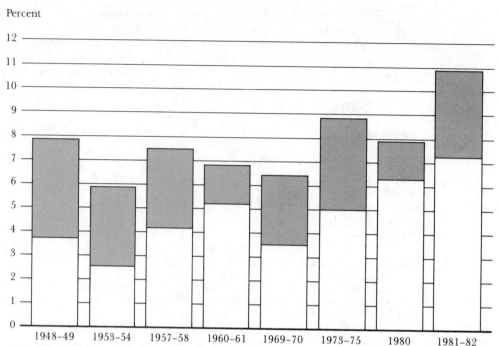

Note: The shaded area of each bar in the chart indicates the peak and trough of unemployment during each period.

Figure 3-2

Unemployment rates during the eight postwar recessions

Source: Michael A. Urquhart and Marillyn A. Hewson, "Unemployment Continued to Rise in 1982 as Recession Deepened," *Monthly Labor Review,* February 1983, p. 4. Reprinted with permission.

total work force. During 1982 alone, the American machinery industry lost 400,000 jobs, the primary metal industries 260,000, and the transportation equipment industry 180,000 — a loss that brought the latter industry to its lowest job level since 1962. These three industries, together with the fabricated metal industries, suffered the loss of over a *million* jobs in 1982 (Urquhart and Hewson, 1983, p. 5).

What is true of jobs is also true for indicators of the extent to which the economy is using its overall productive capacity. For manufacturing industries, this is usually calculated by a measure called the *capacity utilization rate.* In 1982, that rate fell to less than 70 percent — its lowest level since before World War II. Even more troubling, however, is that the capacity utilization rate reached its highest level (about 91 percent) in 1966 and has never risen as high again. As Figure 3-3 illustrates, the *average* level of capacity utilization fell steadily and significantly after the late 1960s. In the early 1980s, on average, a quarter of our industrial capacity was simply not being used.

Two further factors make these declines in employment and production especially troubling for the future. One is that there is every indication that, because of increasing automation, many of the job losses of the past decade will not be recovered even if the economy as a whole undergoes a healthy revival. The second is that the process of what the economists Barry Bluestone and Bennett Harrison (1982) call *deindustrialization* has by no means been limited to the older traditional industrial regions of the northeast and

Industry	Percent Decline		
	1981–82	1979–82	1973–75
Durable goods			
Primary metal industries	29.4	35.8	15.5
Machinery, except electrical	17.5	17.6	10.3
Transportation equipment	15.7	23.0	13.2
Fabricated metal products	15.6	21.3	15.2
Stone, clay, and glass products	14.7	22.8	15.3
Lumber and wood products	12.5	21.6	22.7
Miscellaneous manufacturing	11.0	17.1	13.7
Furniture and fixtures	9.0	14.1	21.3
Electric and electronic equipment	8.4	9.8	17.9
Instruments and related products	6.7	6.7	9.8
Nondurable goods			
Leather and leather goods	15.1	19.8	17.8
Tobacco manufactures	14.1	15.3	7.6
Textile mill products	13.8	19.7	19.3
Apparel and other textile products	10.3	16.0	18.1
Rubber and miscellaneous plastic products	10.0	15.2	16.7
Paper and allied products	6.5	8.6	12.4
Petroleum and coal products	5.1	5.1	5.1
Chemicals and allied products	5.0	5.6	6.3
Food and kindred products	3.5	6.3	5.2
Printing and publishing	1.0	1.0	3.9

Table 3-3
Employment decline in manufacturing industries, selected periods, 1973–1982

Source: Michael A. Urquhart and Marillyn A. Hewson, "Unemployment Continued to Rise in 1982 as Recession Deepened," *Monthly Labor Review*, February 1983, p. 7. Reprinted with permission.

northcentral states. The economic crisis *has* had an uneven geographic impact. At the height of the recession in 1982, state unemployment rates ranged from less than 5 percent in Oklahoma and South Dakota to over 15 percent in Michigan and West Virginia. In the 1970s it became popular to contrast the economic troubles of the northern "Frost Belt" with the growth and prosperity of the Sun Belt of the South and West. But almost half of all American jobs lost as the result of the closing or relocation of plants during the 1970s were in the Sun Belt states (Bluestone and Harrison, 1982, p. 9). On both counts, it seems clear that what is happening is much more than simply another trough in the familiar economic cycle from which we will effectively recover, and also much more than just the relative stagnation of

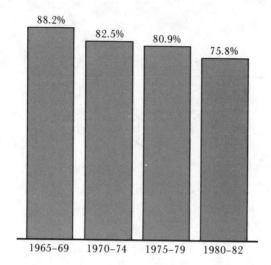

Figure 3-3

Capacity utilization rates in manufacturing industries, annual averages, in percentages

Source: Adapted from *Economic Report of the President* (Washington, D.C.: Government Printing Office, 1983), p. 213.

88.2% 82.5% 80.9% 75.8%

1965–69   1970–74   1975–79   1980–82

some regions as opposed to others. The evidence suggests that the basic shape of the American economy is undergoing important changes — in the kinds of things we will produce and in the number and kinds of workers who will be needed to produce them.

More Stubborn Inflation

Another ominous trend involves the problem of *inflation* — and, more specifically, of the changing relation between inflation and unemployment. Like the business cycle, inflation is not a new phenomenon in the American economy. As Figure 3-4 shows, prices have almost never *fallen* since 1950, and the rate of inflation rose over 6 percent as far back as the early 1950s. But the trend from the 1970s onward shows two disturbing tendencies. First, the inflation rate increased very dramatically for many years; it reached an average of 13.5 percent in 1980, nearly twice as high as it had ever been since the end of World War II. Second, and even more important, in the 1970s very high rates of inflation began to coexist with high levels of unemployment, creating the phenomenon that became known by the unlovely term *stagflation.* Previously, the relationship between the two had generally fit the pattern of what economists call a "trade-off" between inflation and unemployment. Unemployment was relatively high in the early 1960s, for example, and inflation was relatively low. Lower unemployment during the late 1960s was associated with higher inflation. But, as Figure 3-4 shows, both inflation and unemployment reached high peaks in the recessions of the 1970s.

The hand-in-hand rise in these two sources of economic insecurity is illustrated by a rough measure known as the *discomfort index* (Figure 3-5). Since the index is simply the sum of the national unemployment rate and the national inflation rate, it doesn't really measure people's subjective experience of economic hardships. But it does show clearly that the terms of the

The End of Affluence? Social Aspects of Economic Decline

Percent

Figure 3-4

Trends in inflation and unemployment

Source: Adapted from U.S. Congressional Budget Office, *The Outlook for Economic Recovery,* Part 1 (Washington, D.C.: Government Printing Office, February 1983), p. 16.

so-called inflation-unemployment trade-off have shifted considerably. The traditionally expected balance between them — evident to some extent in the 1960s — obviously broke down in the 1970s. In the first three years of the 1980s, the average discomfort index was almost three times as high as it was in the early 1960s.

Figure 3-5 conceals the fact that the rate of inflation did decline in the early 1980s — from a high of over 13 percent in 1980 to about 6 percent in 1982. But this was accomplished only by a dramatic slowdown of the economy that gave 1982 the worst rate of unemployment since the Great Depression — accomplished only, as the Nobel economist Wassily Leontieff puts it, by "beating the economy into the ground" (1982, p. 33). As a result,

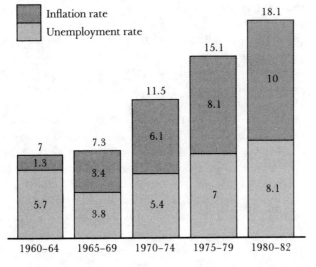

Figure 3-5

Discomfort index (combined rates of inflation and unemployment), annual averages

Source: Data from *Economic Report of the President* (Washington, D.C.: Government Printing Office, 1983), pp. 199, 225.

these policies leave the discomfort index at a level that is still more than twice its average during the 1960s. The trade-off between unemployment and inflation, in other words, apparently still exists — but it now takes a much more drastic level of joblessness to make a dent in the inflation rate.

Rising International Competition

Other troubling long-term economic changes show up if we consider the comparative position of the United States in the world market. America's economy is increasingly being integrated into the larger international economy, and one further statistic helps illustrate this point: As Robert Reich points out, 70 percent of all American-made goods now compete with foreign-made ones, either within the United States or outside it (1983a, p. 44). And though most countries have faced severe economic problems in recent years, the relative position of the United States in that competition has weakened. Moreover, America's role in the world market is not only *smaller* than it once was, but also *different* in important ways.

As the 1980s began, *Business Week* declared that, relative to the economies of the rest of the world, the United States was "in steep decline." We were, the magazine lamented, "entering the decade of the 1980s as a wounded, demoralized colossus" (1980a, p. 1). This is something of an exaggeration; in most respects, the United States remains the dominant economic power in the world. But the overall message is on target, for there have been important changes in the relative success of different economies — changes that are at once both a cause and a consequence of America's troubles.

The most obvious of these shifts is the increasing dependence of the American economy on imported oil. In 1965, fuels were only about 10 percent of all American imports; by 1980, they accounted for over a third (*Statistical Abstract of the U.S., 1982–83*, p. 840). America's balance of trade in oil and gas (the excess of what we import over what we export) was less than a billion dollars in 1960; by the end of the 1970s it had risen to over thirty-three billion dollars annually (Reich and Magaziner, 1982, p. 73). As we will see in Chapter 10, this change has had momentous implications for American life. But paralleling it is another shift of almost equal importance. Not only has the United States become a massive importer of basic fuels, it has also become an importer of many crucial *manufactured* goods. At the beginning of the 1960s, only 4 percent of the cars we bought were imported. By 1981, more than 25 percent were. In 1960 we imported about 3 percent of our machine tools; by 1981, 27 percent. We imported less than 6 percent of consumer electronic products (such as radios, TVs, stereos, and calculators) in 1960; just two decades later, 45 percent of calculators and over 50 percent of other consumer electronics were imported (*Business Week*, 1980a, p. 60; Reich, 1983, pp. 44–45). As late as 1965, the United States imported only $63 million dollars worth of semiconductors, transistors, and electronic parts. By 1981, the total was almost $4 *billion* (*Statistical Abstract of the U.S., 1982–83*, p. 842).

The face of unemployment in the 1980s: an American worker scours the want ads.

These shifts translate into changing shares of the world market for industrial goods — changes in favor of Japan, Western Europe, and (increasingly) some countries of the Third World. During the 1960s and 1970s, the American share of the world market for passenger cars and industrial machinery fell by about a third each; the share of agricultural machinery by two-fifths, and of telecommunications equipment by half (Reich, 1983, p. 45).

The growing presence in America of Japanese cars and electronics products is by now obvious and familiar. In 1981 we imported $38 billion worth of goods from Japan (about $633 for every American family), while we shipped only $22 billion worth in the other direction (*Statistical Abstract of the U.S., 1982–83*, pp. 838, 43). But a substantial and growing part of the change in the composition of the world's industrial economy involves the increasing shares of some fast-growing Third World countries. Consider the steel industry — once one of the foundations of America's international economic power. In 1950 the United States produced almost half (47 percent) of the world's raw steel; by 1981 it produced just 15 percent. Japanese steel production (in a country with half our population) surpassed that of the United States by 1980. In the last half of the 1970s, Japanese steel production increased slightly, American production dropped significantly, and *Korean* production nearly tripled (*Statistical Abstract of the U.S., 1982–83*, p. 875).

Two important consequences flow from this increasingly successful international competition. The first is that assuring growth and prosperity in the American economy — and hence in Americans' standard of living — will henceforth be more difficult than it was in the past. The other is that the very nature of the American economy may be shifting in fundamental ways, as many kinds of industrial production are increasingly being ceded to Japan, Europe, and the industrializing Third World. Given these recent trends, one observer argues, we are in danger of becoming "a nation of extractors, assemblers, and retailers — relatively poor by the standards of the industrial world" (Reich, 1983b, p. 102).

A Shrinking Standard of Living?

Thus, since the 1970s, the United States has suffered slower growth, deeper recessions, more stubborn inflation, and a shrinking role in the world economy. Though it would be hard to find many who disagree with that description, there is some controversy over how these economic changes have actually affected the way Americans live. On the one hand, some argue that recession and high unemployment have had a less painful impact on personal well-being than is usually assumed (we will take up this question in the following section). Others argue more specifically that the effects of inflation on American living standards, as revealed by statistics on personal and family income, have been exaggerated. Is this true?

Like so many debates about social problems, the answers depend on what exactly is being measured. Let's look first at the trends in family incomes over the past several years.

Measured simply in dollars, American families seem, at first glance, to have done well even during the age of stagflation. Family income rose steadily, with few setbacks, even during the recession years of the 1970s and early 1980s. The median family income in 1960 was only $5,620. By 1970 it had nearly doubled to $9,867, and by 1981 it had more than doubled again, to $22,388 (*Statistical Abstract of the U.S., 1983*, p. 432).

But these figures do not take into account the changing value of the dollar; they are not adjusted for inflation. The figures are in what economists call *current dollars*. If we measure family income instead in *constant dollars* — adjusted by how much the dollars can buy — the picture is very different, as Table 3-4 shows. Thus, measured by what it would have bought in 1981 dollars, the median family income in the United States was more than $17,000 in 1960; by 1970 it was more than $23,000, but by 1981 it was only a little more than $22,000 — lower than at the start of the 1970s.

Measured by average family income, then, American families were poorer as the 1980s began than they were in 1973. Some writers dispute the meaning of these figures, however. The economist Lester Thurow, for example, has argued that (as of the late 1970s) the American standard of living had not declined at all. According to Thurow (and some other commentators), the more accurate measure of living standards is *real per capita disposable income* — the nation's total personal income after taxes and corrected for population growth and inflation. During the 1970s, real per capita disposable income rose — by 28 percent, for example, between 1969 and 1979 (Heilbroner and Thurow, 1981, p. 21) — leading Thurow to ask, "Why, then, are we in the middle of a period of national economic masochism where it is widely believed that the American standard of living is collapsing?" (Thurow, 1980, p. 48).

Part of the problem with this argument is simply that it was premature. Things became considerably worse for American families, on average, in the early 1980s as declining production and rising unemployment slowed the growth of real per capita disposable income to a virtual halt. Between 1979 and 1982, real per capita disposable income rose by only $32 — indicating that if the American standard of living was not necessarily "collapsing," it was certainly stagnating (*Economic Report of the President*, 1983, p. 191). But two other problems with this argument are even more telling.

First, it tells us nothing about who, exactly, has received this income. We will discuss this question more fully in later chapters, where we will examine trends in poverty and the distribution of income in recent years. But we may anticipate that discussion by noting that the early 1980s were marked by extraordinary increases in the proportion of the American population living in poverty, and by an increase in the overall *inequality* of incomes. Thurow, along with other writers, argues that since the size of the overall economic "pie" has increased, even if slowly, then someone must be getting the rewards. But it seems increasingly clear that even the slim pickings from the slowed economy of the late 1970s and early 1980s were being distributed unequally; stagflation created both its winners and its losers (Currie, Dunn, and Fogarty, 1982; Osborne, 1983).

Second, a purely economic argument like Thurow's ignores the fact that beneath the bare figures on changes in personal incomes lies one of the most important social changes of our time: the great increase in the number of people who have entered the labor force. This phenomenon is even more

Table 3-4

Trends in median family income (in constant 1981 dollars)

Year	Income
1960	$17,259
1965	20,054
1970	23,111
1973	24,663
1975	23,183
1980	23,204
1981	22,388

Source: Data from *Economic Report of the President* (Washington, D.C.: Government Printing Office, 1983), p. 194.

important in understanding the trends in family income. The only reason why average measures of family income have not shown clearer declines in recent years is that more and more Americans have gone to work.

The most striking aspect of this trend is the rising proportion of dual-earner families. As we will observe in more detail in Chapter 6, there are more of these families mainly because of the rising participation of women in the paid labor force. On average, *only* those families that have been able to put two (or more) earners to work have avoided declines in their standard of living, as Table 3-5 shows. From the 1950s to 1970, all kinds of families enjoyed an average rise in income. But during the 1970s, only married couples with a wife in the paid labor force increased their income (and then only slightly). Single heads of families (of both sexes) saw their real incomes decline, as did married couples in which the wife did *not* work in the paid labor force. Another bit of evidence drives the same point home. If we look at what individuals earned during this period (instead of at overall *family* income), we discover that men and women who worked year-round, full time in 1981 made less money, in real terms, than in *1969 (Economic Report of the President*, 1983, p. 194). If the *total* personal income of Americans rose during the stagflation of the 1970s and 1980s, then, it did so largely because a great many more hours of labor were being put into creating it.

Another factor must be taken into account when assessing the recent course of our standard of living. The argument that living standards have not declined as a result of rising prices ignores the fact that some prices have risen faster than others — and Figure 3-6 shows that, on the whole, the ones that have risen the fastest are necessities — housing, health care, and, especially, energy.

Table 3-5
Median family income by family type and labor-force participation (in constant 1980 dollars), selected years, 1955–1980

The overall cost of living has increased too, but not as fast, while some less necessary expenses, like entertainment, have risen much more slowly. The result of this change is that families must now spend a bigger proportion of their income on basic necessities than they did 15 or 20 years ago and thus have less income left over to spend on anything else. This amounts to a kind of hidden tax that is obscured by conventional statistics on trends

Family type	1955	1960	1965	1970	1975	1980
Married-couple families	14,153	16,341	19,143	22,316	22,762	23,141
Wife in paid labor force	17,301	19,199	22,546	26,051	26,390	26,879
Wife not in paid labor force	13,312	15,359	17,514	19,744	19,524	18,972
Male householder, no wife present	12,894	13,523	17,015	19,124	19,896	17,519
Female householder, no husband present	7,604	8,258	9,232	10,808	10,478	10,408

Source: Adapted from *Statistical Abstract of the United States, 1982–83* (Washington, D.C.: Government Printing Office, 1983), p. 434.

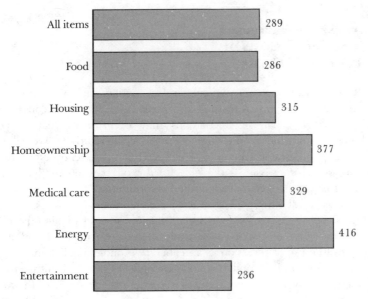

All items	289
Food	286
Housing	315
Homeownership	377
Medical care	329
Energy	416
Entertainment	236

Figure 3-6

The rising cost of necessities (changes in the consumer price index, selected items, 1967–1982)

Source: Data from *Economic Report of the President* (Washington, D.C.: Government Printing Office, 1983), p. 221.

Note: 1967 is used as the base year for the consumer price index; that is, it is given the index number 100.

in family income. Economists have developed a measure of *discretionary income* — all income left over after paying for taxes and necessities — that helps illuminate this important, often neglected dimension of the standard of living. Discretionary income per worker fell by 16 percent between 1973 and 1979 alone (*Business Week*, 1980c, p. 73).

But statistics on income alone do not tell the whole story. The living standard of a family — or a country — is ultimately made up of much more than income. It includes the risk of unemployment, the availability of public services, the quality of the natural environment, and the risks of crime and disease, among other things. Many of these will be taken up later in this book. But one recent attempt to put dollar values on some of these other aspects of America's living standard deserves mention. According to the economist Horace Brock (1983), an accurate assessment of economic well-being would have to adjust the usual statistics of income downward by adding some other important measures of long-run economic prospects. These include the increased chance of being unemployed, the economic impact of the deterioration of the nation's physical capital (such as roads and bridges) and of the quality of education, and the future costs of paying for obligations for Social Security and health care. The "risk premium" for the increased chance of unemployment, in Brock's calculation, for example, would knock about $660 off the income of a full-time, married male worker in 1982. Adding up all these usually uncounted liabilities and the effects of inflation, Brock calculates that American workers actually suffered a 17 percent decline in average income between 1972 and 1982.

The Social Costs of Economic Crisis

Recession, high unemployment, and economic stagnation have, then, become all too common features of American life. There is considerable evidence that, whatever fluctuations may occur from year to year, the longer-term trends in the economy are deeply disturbing. We will look in a moment at some common explanations for those trends. Now we need to consider another issue — the *human impact* of recession and high unemployment on the lives of individuals and communities.*

This is not simply an abstract, academic issue — it is a crucial one for social policy. As we've seen, many economists and public officials believe that, because of the so-called trade-off between inflation and unemployment, the use of recession as a deliberate economic policy may be justified as a tool for fighting inflation and generally restoring a healthy efficiency to the economy. Indeed, encouraging recession has been one of the most common themes of economic policy in recent years, in the United States as well as in some other countries (notably Great Britain).

Policies designed to slow the economy have typically been rationalized partly on the ground that, though painful, they are a necessary "medicine" for sick economies; and partly, too, by the argument that their impact on individuals, families, and communities is much less painful than it may have been in the past because of increased unemployment insurance and other benefits for those out of work (Feldstein, 1973, 1978). Similarly, it is often assumed that workers who lose their jobs through economic slowdown can always pick up new ones when the economy recovers. This notion of painless unemployment helps make policies that throw great numbers of people out of work more publicly acceptable, especially when their presumably low costs are balanced against the hoped-for benefits of lower inflation and an efficient "shaking-out" of the economy. But how does this argument square with the evidence?

Not well. It is probably true that the impact of unemployment is not as devastating as it was in the 1930s, but social science research backs up what many of us know already from personal experience — for most who lose their jobs, unemployment is still extremely painful. Many social and personal problems are aggravated by job loss; worse, unemployment often causes a kind of chain reaction in the lives of the jobless, a vicious cycle with harsh consequences not only for the unemployed but for society as a whole.

---

*This section draws on materials prepared for the U.S. National Advisory Council on Economic Opportunity by Elliott Currie and published as "The Human Costs of Unemployment — 1981," in Arthur I. Blaustein, ed., *The American Promise: Equal Justice and Economic Opportunity* (New Brunswick, N.J.: Transaction Books, 1982).

Much of the argument for the relative painlessness of recession rests on the assumption that, because of the benefits of the "welfare state," unemployment no longer brings significant losses in income. This argument sidesteps the emotional and psychological losses that are not measurable in economic terms. But it also misreads the *economic* situation of the unemployed. We will consider this issue at greater length in Chapter 8, but a few points will help provide some perspective now. In 1981, the average weekly unemployment benefit was $106.54: on an annual basis, about $3,700 *less* than the federal poverty line for a family of four (*Economic Report of the President*, 1983, p. 204; *Statistical Abstract of the U.S., 1982–83*, p. 440). Furthermore, fewer than half of the unemployed even collect unemployment benefits at all, and, in the course of the long-term recessions of the 1970s and 1980s, increasing proportions of those who *did* collect benefits exhausted them without ever finding new jobs. In a special survey taken during the recession in 1976, the U.S. Bureau of Labor Statistics found that, of the unemployed workers they sampled, only a little over 33 percent had received income from unemployment insurance in the previous month, only 13 percent had received food stamps, and only 12 percent had received welfare payments. As many as 5 percent of the sample reported that they had no income at all (Rosenfield, 1977, pp. 42–43).

Data from a University of Michigan sample of 5,000 American families (Hill and Corcoran, 1979) show how drastic the income losses from unemployment can be. According to this survey, male family heads who lost their jobs in 1976 lost, on the average, about a fourth of their normal disposable income — even after unemployment benefits and foregone taxes were included. These losses are typically made up by cutting back on spending, sometimes dramatically. The Bureau of Labor Statistics survey found that 7 out of 10 unemployed workers were meeting living costs by cutting back on spending for food, transportation, and clothes; over 1 in 10 had been forced to move to cheaper housing; and over a fourth had had to borrow money to stay afloat (Rosenfield, 1977, pp. 42–43). A New York State study found that 16 percent of workers idled by plant closings were eating less, about a third were buying fewer clothes, and one in seven had cut spending on medical care. Workers who exhaust unemployment benefits, moreover, may be forced to sell cars and other assets in order to qualify for other kinds of welfare relief (Bluestone and Harrison, 1982, p. 62).

Though it is frequently argued that these economic losses, even at worst, are only short-term ones — since most of the unemployed soon find new jobs — the evidence suggests otherwise. A number of studies of workers laid off as a result of plant closings, for example, show that it often takes years for them to recover lost earning levels, and some (particularly women and older workers) may *never* find work of comparable pay and benefits. One study found that among a group of laid-off auto workers, the jobs they had two years later paid an average of 43 percent less than the ones they lost (Bluestone and Harrison, 1982, pp. 11–12; Rayman and Bluestone, 1982).

Economic Deprivation

Mental Illness

The *noneconomic* losses from high unemployment are sometimes more subtle, but they are equally well documented. The connection between job loss and mental health problems, from loss of self-esteem and depression to psychosis and suicide, is well established in social research.

Some of the most influential research linking mental illness to the state of the economy has been done by the sociologist M. Harvey Brenner (1973a, b, 1976). In one study (1973b), Brenner looked at the historical relations between economic cycles and the rate of admissions to psychiatric hospitals in Massachusetts from the mid-nineteenth century to the 1960s. Brenner found that the admission rate was closely related to changes in the level of employment in manufacturing industries. In a more recent study (1976), Brenner examined mental hospital admissions from the 1940s through the 1960s and concluded that every increase in the national unemployment rate had a precisely measurable impact on the number of people undergoing psychiatric hospitalization. A 1 percentage point increase (say, from 7 to 8 percent) in the unemployment rate, in Brenner's calculation, could be expected to raise psychiatric admissions by 3.4 percent.

The changing world economy: U.S. and Japanese automakers sign an agreement to produce cars jointly in California . . .

Rick Browne/Picture Group

Other researchers have argued that these increases may be the result of factors other than the stresses of unemployment. During periods of economic stress, the usual family and community resources for dealing with the mentally ill may be lost or weakened, forcing more of the burden of care onto public institutions (Catalano, Dooley, and Jackson, 1981). Likewise, a higher level of admissions to mental hospitals could simply mean that more hospital beds are being created to accommodate the mentally ill. But one recent study that does take into account changing hospital capacities confirms that, for people of working age, the rate of admission to psychiatric hospitals is "decisively influenced by the extant level of economic distress" (Marshall and Funch, 1979, p. 243). It seems most likely that high unemployment causes *both* an increase in the kinds of stresses that can bring on psychiatric symptoms *and* a weakening of the ability of family and community agencies to provide help.

Other studies have used interviews and psychological tests to trace the link between the loss of a job and the development of various psychological symptoms. One study of the mental well-being of 80 families after the hus-

while American industries feel the pinch of foreign competition.

Rick Browne/Picture Group

band lost his job found much higher levels of psychiatric symptoms among these husbands as compared with a control group who were not unemployed. If and when they were reemployed, the study found, the formerly unemployed men actually felt *better* than those in the control group (Liem and Rayman, 1982, pp. 118–119).

A number of studies have shown that the direct effects of unemployment on mental health are compounded by the fact that job loss often leads to other stressful crises — like divorce or having to move from a community — which in turn are often associated with greater risks of mental illness (Catalano and Dooley, 1977). In addition, recession simultaneously diminishes (through cuts in the funds and staff of mental health and family counseling agencies) the community resources available to help individuals cope with these problems.

Probably the most drastic effect of high unemployment — and one of the best established — is its impact on the suicide rate. As one study puts it, "Unemployment rates tend to be the most important and stable predictor of short- and long-term variations in suicide rates examined across time" (Vigderhous and Fishman, 1978, p. 239). Brenner concluded that each 1 percent increase in the national unemployment rate would raise the suicide rate by about 4 percent, and that the suicide rate was indeed so closely related to changes in unemployment levels that it was one of the most reliable of all indicators of the state of the economy (1976, p. 29).

Physical Health

Research has also established strong links — sometimes surprising ones — between unemployment and the risk of disease. Brenner (1976) concluded that cardiovascular disease (heart disease and stroke), cirrhosis of the liver, and kidney disease, were among the most frequent and devastating consequences of high rates of unemployment. The 1.4 percent increase in the national jobless rate in 1970, he calculated, was responsible for over 25,000 deaths from these diseases during the following five years. Brenner attributed the rise in deaths from liver disease to increased alcohol consumption brought on by unemployment — another example of the chain-reaction effect of recession on individual well-being.

Even more striking evidence of the pervasive effects of job loss on health has been found by researchers who tested the health status of workers who lost their jobs. In a series of studies during the 1970s, for example, Stanislav Kasl, Susan Gore, and Sidney Cobb found a number of symptoms, including high blood pressure, as well as more subtle medical indicators of physical stress (including abnormally high levels of cholesterol and uric acid) among men who lost industrial jobs in the Midwest. And many of these symptoms appeared as soon as the men learned that their jobs were in jeopardy, even before they had actually lost them (Cobb, 1974; Kasl, Gore, and Cobb, 1975).

Another illustration of the chain-reaction effect of job loss is the association between infant mortality and the rate of unemployment. Some research suggests that two somewhat distinct processes are at work, one responsible for higher death rates of very young infants and another for older ones. The adverse impact of unemployment on the mother's health — through poor nutrition; high levels of stress; or increased use of alcohol, tobacco, or sedatives — is probably responsible for much of the increase in early infant deaths. The increase in deaths among slightly older infants more likely results from longer-acting environmental stresses that come from lowered income — such as impaired ability to provide or purchase adequate medical care and increased risk of accidents and preventable infections (Brenner, 1973a).

Family Stress, Child Abuse, and Crime

Recent research confirms that "economic uncertainty brought on by unemployment and marginal employment is a principal reason why family relations deteriorate" (Furstenberg, 1974, p. 354). The wives of unemployed workers in the 80-family study described above were found to be significantly more depressed, anxious, and unhappy about their family relationships after their husband's job loss; a few months after that loss, their families became much less cohesive and more conflict-ridden than the families of employed workers (Liem and Rayman, 1982). A survey of unemployed workers in the Boston area in the late 1970s (Schlozman and Verba, 1978) found that unemployment benefits (which some commentators argue have eliminated the pain of unemployment) did not alleviate the family tensions that rose predictably as the length of time without work increased. As we'll see in greater detail in Chapter 7, family violence — both between husbands and wives and between parents and their children — has also been closely linked with economic insecurity. [According to one recent estimate (Riegle, 1982), reported child abuse and neglect cases rose by 36 percent in the Detroit area from mid-1981 to mid-1982.]

A number of studies have also linked rising unemployment with increasing crime rates. Higher rates of unemployment have been found to be associated with substantial increases in admissions to state and federal prisons (Brenner, 1976; Yeager, 1979). The relationship between joblessness and crime often turns out to be complex; we will return to it in more detail in Chapter 11.

What these findings do make abundantly clear is that economic policies cannot be adequately understood or evaluated in economic terms alone. We have said before, and will have many occasions to say again, that the economy is a *social* institution. What we decide to do with it — to slow it down, heat it up, or shake it out — has consequences that ripple out through all the other institutions that affect personal well-being: the family, the local community, the agencies of social support and intervention. A responsible approach to economic policy must take these consequences into consideration.

Explaining Economic Decline

These, then, are some of the dimensions and consequences of America's economic problems in the 1980s. What are the *causes?*

There has been no lack of explanations. As traditional economic policies appear less and less capable of coping effectively with industrial decline, unemployment, and a shrinking standard of living, explanations that blame these problems on the misguided practices of the past have become increasingly popular. The ones we will consider here have much in common. They often focus on the excessive role of government in the economy, or the unfair demands and inadequate performance of American workers. Many of them, as a consequence, lead to policies designed to "get the economy moving again" by restricting the scope of government and/or tilting the balance of economic rewards more toward private business and away from workers, consumers, and environmental concerns.

As we will see, however, these issues are rarely as simple as is often assumed. Let's consider five of the factors that are most often held to be at the root of the problems of the economy: too much government spending, excessive taxes, a shortage of capital for business, high wages, and the decline of the "work ethic."

What Unemployment Really Costs

Everyone laments the rise of unemployment during periods of recession and slow economic growth. But government programs to put the unemployed back to work are often condemned as too costly. This attitude carries a hidden assumption — that no substantial economic costs are incurred by the public as a result of government's *failure* to create new jobs for the unemployed. But that assumption is misleading. Some of the social costs of maintaining unnecessary unemployment are difficult to express in economic terms, but others can be measured accurately.

The most immediate and the largest of the costs of unemployment is the cost of lost production. When workers do not work, the economy does not produce goods and services. According to an early 1980s estimate by the U.S. Bureau of Economic Analysis, each 1 percentage-point increase in the national unemployment rate, over a year's time, reduces the gross national product by $68 billion (Bluestone and Harrison, 1982, p. 11).

On top of the lost production is the tax revenue lost as the income of both workers and employers declines. According to an estimate by the director of the U.S. Congressional Budget Office in 1982, each 1 percentage-point increase in unemployment costs the federal government between $20 and $30 billion in revenues per year (Rivlin, 1982, p. 3). [Note that this does not include losses in state or local revenues; one study estimated that each $10,000-per-year job lost in Massachusetts costs the state over $1,300 in lost local and state taxes (Bluestone and Harrison, 1982, p. 73).]

Unemployment involves not only lost government *revenues,* but also increased government *spending.* Indeed, a substantial part of the growth in domestic government spending in recent years has been for income support for the unemployed. In 1982, each one-point rise in unemployment caused an estimated increase of $3 to $4 billion in unemployment insurance outlays, and another $1 billion for other forms of social welfare. To these expenses may be added an estimated $2 to $5 bil-

It's often argued that, as government has become ever larger, its spending (especially on social programs) has drained funds from more productive private investment and put a brake on economic growth. Is this charge accurate?

We've already had a clue to one important problem with this argument. If government spending in itself were a major cause of economic stagnation, we would expect economic performance to be predictably worse in countries with relatively high levels of government spending. But, as we saw in Chapter 2, the United States actually spends much *less,* proportionately, on government than almost all other advanced industrial societies — including many that have consistently outperformed the United States by most economic measures for years.

Table 3-6 shows that West Germany's government spending (exclusive of defense) was 60 percent higher than the United States' in the late 1970s, while its average unemployment rate was less than half that of the United States'. Sweden, with an extraordinarily low jobless rate (about 2 percent through the late 1970s and early 1980s) spent more than *twice* what the American government spent. Measured in another way, by growth in GDP per worker, the German economy outperformed the American by over four to one during the 1970s, as did the Dutch economy — with a rate of government domestic spending second only to the Swedish and twice that of the United States.

Too Much Government Spending?

lion in interest costs resulting from higher government budget deficits (Rivlin, 1982, p. 3).

Adding up even the lower of these estimates gives $94 billion for each one-point of increase in unemployment. If that cost were spread out evenly among American households, it would amount to $1,150 per household in 1981. Recall, though, that this amount is what *each* percentage-point increase in unemployment costs. In 1981, the American unemployment rate averaged 7.6 percent, or about 5 percentage points higher than the Swedish rate of 2.5 percent. Our failure to reduce unemployment to Sweden's level, therefore, cost each American household an average of about $5,750 — to about 30 percent of the median household income in 1981. In other words, the average household pays an extraordinarily high "tax" to maintain a high rate of unemployment. Some of that "tax" actually does consist of increased tax payments for income support; some of it is, of course, less tangible — income not earned because of the slowed economy and public services not enjoyed because the govern-

ment is taking in less tax revenue and can afford fewer public expenditures.

These estimates are conservative; they count only the most obvious costs associated with unemployment. They do not take into account the costs of higher rates of imprisonment or of psychiatric hospitalization, for example, though both have been clearly linked to increases in unemployment. Nevertheless, adding up these figures produces estimates of the cumulative costs of our failure to achieve full employment that are almost too enormous to be readily comprehensible. One former chair of the president's Council of Economic Advisors estimates that in the years from 1953 to 1980, the failure to operate the economy at full employment cost over $8 *trillion* (in 1979 dollars) in lost production — and more than $2 trillion in lost federal, state, and local tax revenues (Keyserling, 1981, p. 227).

Table 3-6
Government spending
and economic
performance

Country	Government spending (excluding defense) as proportion of GDP, 1978 (%)	Average annual unemployment rate, 1975–81 (%)	Growth rate in GDP per worker, 1970–79 (%)
United States	26.3	7.1	0.8
Japan	28.0	2.1	4.2
France	40.1	5.6	3.4
West Germany	42.2	3.4	3.4
Netherlands	51.4	NA	3.3
Sweden	56.5	2.0	NA

Note: NA means not available.
Source: Government spending data from Ira C. Magaziner and Robert B. Reich, *Minding America's Business* (New York: Harcourt, Brace, Jovanovich, 1982), p. 43. Unemployment rates calculated from *Statistical Abstract of the United States, 1982–83* (Washington, D.C.: Government Printing Office, 1983), p. 873. GDP growth rates from Bruce R. Scott, "Can Industry Survive the Welfare State?" *Harvard Business Review* (September/October 1982, p. 78).

The same pattern holds if we compare another measure of government's role — the size of the public sector — with economic performance. We've seen in Chapter 2 that the United States has the lowest level of public ownership of enterprises among advanced industrial societies. Austria, with one of the highest levels, achieved some of the lowest unemployment rates of any industrial society during the late 1970s and early 1980s, while also keeping inflation well below American levels.

The argument about the negative effects of government spending is sometimes phrased in terms of government *deficits* (the amount the government spends over what it takes in through taxes and other sources of revenue). Some argue that large deficits mean that government must borrow so much to pay its obligations that not enough funds are available for private business investment: Government's borrowing "crowds out" borrowing by the private sector, which is starved for capital as a result. More generally, an unbalanced budget is taken as a sign that a spendthrift government is wasting scarce capital that would otherwise be spent for productive investment. Balancing the budget, in this view, is a necessary first step to economic prosperity. We will look in a moment at the issue of whether American business is starved for capital — and whether shifting more resources to the private sector will lead to productive investment. For the moment, let's point out some more general difficulties with the notion that deficits are inherently bad for the economy.

One of the difficulties is that, historically, no clear relationship has existed between the level of the deficit and the performance of the economy; high deficits have been coupled with strong economic growth as often as not. The United States emerged from World War II with one of the most unbalanced budgets in history as a result of massive war spending — and promptly entered a long period of unparalleled economic prosperity and growth.

An even more telling statistic is that the government's total outstanding debt (the amount it has borrowed and not repaid) has *fallen* considerably, as a proportion of gross national product, since the 1960s and, indeed, since the end of World War II. When the war ended in 1945, the government's debt was greater than the total GNP; about 120 percent of it, in fact. By 1960 the debt was about 58 percent of GNP; by 1970, about 40 percent; and about 35 percent as the 1980s began (*Statistical Abstract of the U.S., 1982–83*, p. 246).

The experience of other countries also casts doubt on the belief that it's necessarily bad for a government to spend more than it takes in. As with government spending in general, the excess of spending over revenues has generally been *greater* in many countries that have outperformed the United States economically (*Business Week*, 1982a, p. 91). Figure 3-7 shows that West

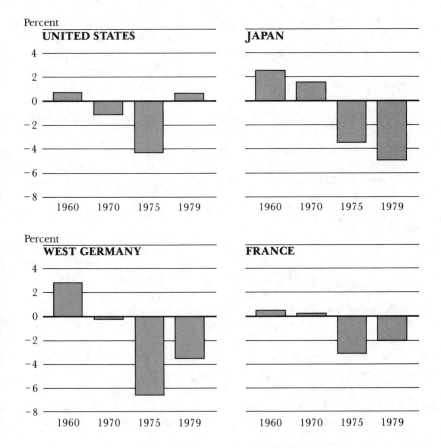

Figure 3-7
Government surpluses and deficits as a percentage of GNP

Source: Adapted from U.S. National Foreign Assessment Center, *Handbook of Economic Indicators* (Washington, D.C.: Government Printing Office, 1982), p. 13.

German deficits are typically higher than ours, and so, recently, have been the Japanese.

Why doesn't deficit spending hurt these economies? Ultimately, the problem with this argument is that it fails to acknowledge what most families and most businesses know from experience: Spending more than you have is not always an unproductive or irresponsible thing to do. What counts is the *purpose* of the spending. It's generally felt that borrowing money to buy or improve a house is an intelligent long-term economic decision for a family, assuming that it's within their means to make the payments on what they borrow. Innovative businesses borrow money from banks in order to start up, expand, or invest in new plants or equipment. Is there some reason why the same principle shouldn't apply to government?

Whether the borrower is a family, a government, or a business, the real issue is whether the money borrowed is invested in productive ways. We feel one way when a family borrows to help send a child to college, another way when they ignore the child's education and borrow to buy a pleasure boat or a luxury car.

And here, in fact, there are reasons for concern about the nature of government spending in America. But the concerns have less to do with the *amount* of government spending than with its *direction*. We will consider one aspect of this problem later, in Chapter 12, when we examine the growth and impact of government spending for defense. But another problem needs mentioning here. To an important extent, what we have created in America in recent years has been what the economist Jeff Faux (1983) calls a *passive deficit*. Government has had to spend more to cushion the consequences of high unemployment, while its revenues have simultaneously been reduced by unemployment, slow growth, and public policies that have cut taxes on businesses and affluent individuals. That is, large deficits have been a *result* of the slowdown of the economy rather than a cause of it. An active deficit would reflect more positive uses of government spending (especially direct efforts by the government to create jobs) rather than simply paying the costs (in income supports and lost revenues) of a stalled private economy.

Excessive Taxes? Just as government spending is often blamed for the problems of the economy, so too are the taxes that make that spending possible. Critics argue that the use of the tax system to further the American quest for a more egalitarian distribution of income has deeply hurt the economy. Because corporations and wealthy individuals must pay so much to the government, it's argued, their incentive to invest and produce is weakened. In this view, economic prosperity can only be assured by keeping taxes low — at least for businesses and for those with substantial amounts of money to save and invest (Wanniski, 1979; Gilder, 1981).

We will look more closely at the effects of taxes on inequality in America in Chapter 4. But we need to point out several facts that make this a less than satisfactory explanation of the poor performance of the American economy.

For one thing, like the case against government spending, this argument runs up against a basic paradox: How can *excessive* taxes be a primary cause of America's economic problems when our taxes are much *less* heavy than those of most of our successful economic competitors? In Chapter 2 we saw that the general level of taxation is higher in almost every advanced industrial society than in the United States, and that our overall tax rates as a proportion of GDP remained stable through the 1970s while those of many other industrial societies (including Japan) *increased*. Now consider how these differences affect rates of economic growth. Taxes account for half again the share of economic activity in the Netherlands as in the United States, but the Dutch growth rate in GDP per employed person was four times higher than ours during the 1970s. West German taxes took a 22 percent greater share of the GDP than did American taxes, while the West German growth rate was also more than four times ours. If we consider only taxes on corporations, a recent article in the *Wall Street Journal* points out that the corporate tax rate in Japan is the highest in the world (Nukazawa, 1983, p. 29). Meanwhile, the Japanese growth rate per worker was more than five times the American rate during the 1970s.

A second difficulty with the view that high taxes cause economic stagnation is a historical one. During the recent years of economic slump, the share that corporate taxes have contributed to the government's coffers has *fallen* sharply. In 1960, corporate income taxes accounted for about 20 percent of government tax revenues; in 1970, about 16 percent; and in 1980, less than 14 percent. What took up the slack in the other direction? Mainly the individual income taxes which all earners pay. Revenues from individual income taxes were 38 percent of total tax revenues in 1960, and almost 50 percent in 1980 (*Statistical Abstract of the U.S., 1982–83*, p. 277). Over the years, wage earners have been paying a greater share of taxes, corporations a smaller share. The declining tax on corporate incomes should have spurred a surge of productive investment during the 1970s; it did not. Similarly, extensive cuts in taxes for business and wealthy individuals during the early 1980s had no clearly discernable effect on economic growth or unemployment.

We have, in fact, been fairly steadily *decreasing* the relative tax burden we place on corporations and the affluent. Why hasn't this had the hoped-for effect?

The answers are complicated, and we can only touch on them here; other aspects will be taken up in later chapters. It seems clear that the failure of these policies to generate productive growth and jobs involves both the failure of businesses and wealthy individuals to invest their considerable tax savings in productive ways — and the failure of the investments they *do* make to create much employment. Cutting taxes for wealthy individuals is at least as likely to lead to unproductive investment in luxury goods or real estate speculation as it is to more productive uses. And, as we'll see next, much (though certainly not all) corporate investment has followed a similarly unproductive path in recent years. We'll examine in Chapter 8 why, in a modern, highly automated economy, even more productive, growth-generating investment will not necessarily create many new *jobs*. One statistic may help illustrate this problem now. According to a 1981 analysis by Citizens for Tax Justice, about 80 percent of all the tax savings from the business tax reductions in the Reagan administration's "Program for Economic Recovery" went to 1,700 large corporations. But those corporations had generated only *4 percent* of all new jobs during the last 20 years (Lekachman, 1982, p. 71).

A Shortage of Capital?

American business frequently describes itself as being starved for sufficient capital for investment. Without investment, of course, the economy slows down and workers lose their jobs. As we've seen, the criticism of excessive government spending and high business taxes is based largely on the argument that they drain funds from productive business to unproductive social uses. We've seen some of the limitations of those arguments. Now let's look more closely at the broader question: Is a shortage of capital a compelling explanation for the recent problems of the American economy?

A first difficulty is that the rate of investment has *not*, in fact, declined in the American economy. In early 1982 the United States was investing a higher proportion of its gross national product in plants and equipment than it had since 1928. Investment in manufacturing industries, where America's economic problems have been most dramatic, increased even more than in the economy as a whole in the 1960s and 1970s (Reich, 1983, p. 44).

Other evidence makes the point more concretely. A *Business Week* article in 1980 described the "dilemma" of one company, Standard Oil of Ohio, which had brought in so much cash from its Alaskan oil operations that it was "swimming in money" and facing the unusual problem of finding places to "invest a mountain of cash." Unable to find ways of reinvesting more than $2.4 billion of extra cash in the oil business itself, Sohio was looking for other industries to buy into — including coal, chemicals, genetic engineering, and information processing (1980b, pp. 60–61). A similar picture appears in a 1981 article in a San Francisco paper entitled "Bay Area Firms Loaded with Cash." The cash-heavy corporations included Kaiser Steel, which held a "hoard" of over a quarter-billion dollars; Natomas Corporation, with hundreds of millions in cash from Indonesian oil profits, busily "looking for natural resource properties" to buy; and Standard Oil of California, with cash reserves of $3.4 billion. The article examined the uses to which these massive funds were put:

> Do they reinvest in new capital projects? Well, there's no big hurry when there's double-digit returns on commercial paper (18.5 percent), govern-

ment securities (14–15 percent), . . . and Eurodollars (18.8 percent). Or, the companies can simply put their money in a bank in a certificate of deposit that pays 14.5–18.5 percent, depending on how long they want to tie it up.

Those are safe, guaranteed returns — tough to match when compared to the uncertainties and risks of investing in a refinery, a coal mine, or a savings and loan. (Gartner, 1981)

Nor did corporations, on the whole, seem to have much trouble finding banks willing to lend them substantial funds in the early 1980s. According to a 1982 *Business Week* survey of 875 of the country's largest corporations, these companies had managed to increase their total debt by more than 15 percent — or about $73 billion — over the preceding 18 months. The oil companies alone borrowed more than $17 billion in that period, the chemical companies, $7.5 billion. IBM alone accounted for much of the $2.4 billion borrowed by the computer and office equipment industry (*Business Week*, 1982b, p. 52).

Quite a few American companies, then, either held or borrowed vast sums of money in the slump of the early 1980s. What did they do with the money? The steel industry — one of the biggest losers in international competition — illustrates the answer. Faced with stiff competition from Japanese and European steelmakers in the 1970s, the American steel companies demanded government protection, including trade restrictions on the import of foreign steel. This protection amounted to a massive government subsidy to the steel industry, justified on the ground that it would help give the industry breathing room to enable it to modernize and meet the challenge of the more efficient foreign competitors. Instead, most of the large steel corporations began shifting their assets out of steel production (and its related industries) and into other, more immediately profitable lines of business. Often the steel companies "disinvested" in plants and subsidiaries that were actually *profitable* ones. As *Fortune* noted in 1981, for example, the U.S. Steel Corporation sold a profitable cement division to the West Germans, instead of investing in the new technology that would have made it more competitive. What did the company do with the cash it didn't invest in its steel (or cement) divisions? According to *Fortune*, it shopped for "selective acquisitions." The company appeared "to have several hundred million dollars to shop around with," and the potential shopping list included companies in transportation, chemicals, and perhaps a mortgage or credit company. Meanwhile plans to build a new, technically advanced steel plant in Ohio had been shelved "indefinitely" (Kirkland, 1981a, p. 30). Another corporation, National Steel, planned to acquire three savings and loan companies with a combined value of almost $7 billion (Reich, 1983, p. 99).

The steel industry is by no means the only example of this trend. One of the distinguishing features of the American economy in recent years is that many corporations have used their resources to invest in something *other* than new productive capacity. A study of more than 400 of the largest American corporations discovered that during the 1970s they invested in the expansion of only *one in seven* of the plants they owned at the beginning of the decade (Bluestone and Harrison, 1982, p. 41).

In place of expansion and modernization, a substantial part of the business done by many major corporations has involved the *acquisition* of other, already existing firms. The dollar value of the 50 largest of these transactions in 1982 was about $48 billion and about $50 billion the year before. The bankers and other financial intermediaries who handled these 50 biggest "deals" themselves earned almost a quarter of a *billion* dollars (Steyer, 1983, p. 48).

We have touched on this trend already when examining the rise of the conglomerate corporation. What concerns us here is the trend's social and economic impact. There is some debate over whether these conglomerate acquisitions necessarily result in lowered efficiency and performance (Scherer, 1980; Siegfried, 1980; Brozen, 1982). But what *is* clear is that, on the whole, the main result of this trend has been to shift economic resources from one formal, "paper" ownership to another, without creating new jobs or productive capacity (Reich, 1983, p. 55). As Robert Reich puts it, the result is the growth of a "symbolic economy" that doesn't enlarge the total economic "pie," but merely rearranges its "slices" (1983, p. 52). It is an economy in which enormous resources of both capital and human ingenuity are devoted to complicated financial transactions that may be lucrative for some of the parties involved, but that add no new goods to the economy and divert resources that could otherwise be used to upgrade our industrial capacity and efficiency.

What is the reason for this tendency to substitute paper shuffling for productive investment? Some observers argue that behind this trend lies an often-noted difference in the *attitudes* of American and Japanese or Western European managements (Hayes and Abernathy, 1980). According to this view, American management is inclined to aim for maximum *short-term* profit, while many European or Japanese managers emphasize *long-term* efficiency and competitiveness. Japanese businesses, for example, typically target their expected profits at lower levels than do their American counterparts. Where some American steel companies rapidly abandoned operations that brought in less than 20 percent profits, for example (Kirkland, 1981a, p. 30), Japanese steel companies were content with profits averaging well below 10 percent. Japanese steel companies during the 1960s and 1970s shifted much more of their investment into long-term improvements in technology rather than to outside acquisitions or cheaper, "quick-fix" investments in expanding capacity using existing, less efficient technology (Reich and Magaziner, 1982, Chapter 13). The resulting long-term loss in the competitive position of American steel has been replicated in many other industries as well.

Excessive wages and benefits for workers are often blamed for both inflation and the slowdown of the economy. In this view, wages push up the prices of everything from energy to housing, and the rising demands of workers have cut deeply into business profits and, consequently, into business' capacity to invest and produce. Is this true?

High Wages?

Figure 3-8 illustrates the central problem with this argument. It shows two different measures of earnings: *Spendable weekly earnings* are a worker's average earnings minus taxes, while *compensation per employee-hour* includes other forms of on-the-job benefits in addition to cash wages. Measured in current dollars (not adjusted for inflation), both rose somewhat in the 1970s and early 1980s. But in constant dollars (adjusted for inflation), the picture is very different; since the early 1970s, workers' earnings have fallen behind the cost of living.

In June 1982, the average American worker was making about $32 a week *less* (when corrected for inflation) than his or her counterpart 10 years earlier, and about the same as the average worker in *1960* (*Statistical Abstract*

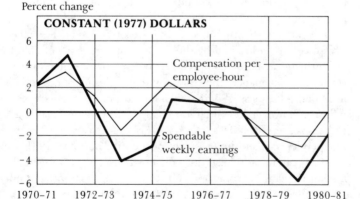

Figure 3-8

Annual percent changes in earnings and compensation, 1970–1981

Source: Statistical Abstract of the United States, 1982–83 (Washington, D.C.: Government Printing Office, 1983), p. 373.

of the U.S., 1982–83, p. 401). It is sometimes argued that such average figures are misleading because they ignore a number of important changes in the American work force, such as the increase in part-time workers and the growing proportion of women and youth. We will examine the impact of some of these changes in Chapter 8. But for now we should note that the slowdown in earnings has affected workers across the board. Measured by the consumer price index, the cost of living rose 134 percent between 1970 and 1981. The average weekly earnings of *full-time* workers rose just 122 percent, leaving them well behind in the race to keep up with inflation. Men who worked full-time did do better than women, but their earnings (which rose 129 percent) also fell behind the rise in the cost of living (*Statistical Abstract of the U.S., 1982–83*, pp. 404, *xxiv*).

None of this means that there are no overpaid workers. But pinpointing workers' high wages as a *general* explanation of the larger problems of the economy fits badly with the evidence. Most workers have done poorly over the past decade.

Other evidence supports this point. Business paid 19 cents of every sales dollar for labor costs in 1980, the lowest level in 26 years (Oswald, 1982, p. 44). Moreover, earnings and benefits for workers have increased faster — sometimes *much* faster — in some of the countries that are our most effective competitors in the world economy. In the crucial manufacturing industries (where we have suffered the most from international competition), hourly compensation for American workers rose an average of about 154 percent between 1970 and 1981; in West Germany, compensation rose 374 percent; and in Japan, 518 percent (*Economic Report of the President*, 1983, p. 287).

Interestingly, critics who blame workers' wages for inflation often ignore the important and well-documented role of the large corporation. We've seen that the American economy no longer fits the model of pure competitive capitalism in which many small firms compete with one another. One result of the concentration of economic power among a smaller number of large corporations is a profound change in the ability of the normal forces of the economic market to affect the prices of goods and services.

In a genuinely competitive system, according to traditional economic theory, prices are restrained by the threat that higher prices will drive consumers into the arms of competitors. Where many sellers are vying for the consumer's allegiance, the company that raises its prices too high will price itself out of business. Where only a few corporations effectively dominate an industry, however, the situation changes. In economic language, these corporations are now able to *administer* prices — to set them with considerable independence from the pressures of the market (Case, 1981, Chapter 2).

Most often, administering prices doesn't involve actual agreements among the large corporations not to undercut each other's prices; such direct "price fixing" is illegal. Instead, the usual pattern is one of "price leadership," in which a tacit understanding exists that if one company raises its prices, the others will follow. This ensures that competition through prices is diminished in the concentrated industries. The effect on the consumer is that prices in such industries (which, as we've seen, include most of the important ones in the economy) rarely go down and almost always *go up,* short of a really dramatic slowdown in the economy. This is one key reason why prices have often continued to rise even during recessions, creating the double-edged problem of stagflation. Economists estimate that the annual cost to consumers of such "monopoly pricing" may run to about 3 percent of gross national product, or about $90 billion in 1982 (Scherer, 1980, p. 117).

A somewhat similar argument blames the economy's troubles on workers' *attitudes.* In the 1960s and 1970s, the argument runs, the traditional "work ethic" that animated older generations of American workers was increasingly replaced by an ethos of "rights without responsibilities," especially among younger workers (O'Toole, 1981). More generally, the rise of the welfare state is often said to have created profound "disincentives to work" (Scott, 1982) and to have fostered the desire to get something for nothing. What is the evidence for this view?

The Decline of the "Work Ethic"?

Again, no one would deny that the description applies in *some* cases. But two problems immediately arise. One is that there is simply no evidence that work has ceased to be a central social value for Americans of *any* age (see Chapter 8). The other is that the image of a population grown increasingly lazy as a result of the largesse of the welfare state fits badly with the fact that a greater proportion of people have gone to work in recent years than ever before in American history. What economists call the *labor-force participation rate* (the proportion of the population either at work or looking for work) rose from about 59 percent through the 1960s to an all-time high of 64 percent in 1982 (*Economic Report of the President*, 1983, p. 196).

The fact that more people are in the labor force, of course, doesn't mean that they're working *harder,* and critics often point to statistics on declining rates of productivity in America as evidence that the quality of workers' effort is going down. But this represents a misunderstanding of the meaning of productivity as an economic concept. The misunderstanding is not surprising since productivity is a very tricky concept, indeed.

Productivity is defined as the level of output of some good or service per hour of work put in to produce it. It's often said that, measured in this way, productivity has been falling dramatically in the United States. This isn't the case. Between 1970 and 1982, output per hour in American industry fell in only three years (1974, 1979, and 1980); in 1982 it was higher than ever before in American history. But it was only a tiny fraction higher than it had been in 1977 and 1978 — and this suggests the real problem. Though productivity has generally risen, the *rate* at which it has done so has been quite low in recent years. During the first three years of the 1980s, for example, output per hour increased by just 0.5 percent a year, on average. The annual average in the late 1970s was 1.5 percent; in the first half of the 1970s, about 1.6 percent; and in the late 1960s, almost 2.5 percent (*Economic Report of the President*, 1983, p. 209). Something has obviously happened to the rate of productivity growth in America. But what?

Recall that the usual measure of productivity is output per hour of work. Many things can affect that ratio; how hard individual workers work is one of them, but it is not the only one, or even necessarily a very important one. The amount of output — production — workers can turn out in a modern, technologically advanced economy also depends on such things as the level of technology (the quality of the tools and techniques of work), the intrinsic technical difficulty of the job at hand, the changing mix of goods and services being produced throughout the economy as a whole, the ways in which workers are trained and organized to do the work, and the other social goals we may choose to implement in the process of producing goods and services.

Some of the decline in rates of productivity, for example, reflects the reduced pace of technological changes that shifted workers out of what had been a low-productivity sector of the economy (agriculture) into higher-productivity manufacturing. The shift away from agriculture has been one of the most profound changes in the nature of work in America (see Chapter 8). In terms of productivity statistics, for many years it meant both rapidly rising productivity in agriculture, as fewer workers were needed for the same level of output, and an overall rise in the productivity of the economy as a greater proportion of workers moved into manufacturing. But this transformation is now largely complete, and so it no longer pushes up our rates of productivity (Thurow, 1981).

A similar though somewhat later change has shifted workers from manufacturing industries, where productivity is relatively high, to the so-called service industries (including white-collar industries like finance and health care) in which it has traditionally been lower. There is some dispute over how much this shift has lowered overall productivity, but there is wide agreement that it bears *some* responsibility.

Productivity in some parts of the economy is declining simply because of inevitable changes that make production more difficult and costly in terms of workers' effort. A good example is energy; as the supply of domestic oil reserves runs down, extracting what remains has become more difficult and expensive, resulting in a lower measured output per hour worked. Recession also lowers the rate of productivity by idling some of the most productive workers in the economy first. When a factory closes down, high-productivity production workers are laid off faster than lower-productivity central office workers. The same principle applies to the economy as a whole; the recent recessions have struck manufacturing industries hardest, so that the workers who have been idled are disproportionately those whose average output is statistically the highest. Recession, then, is a *cause* of low productivity, not just a *consequence* of it.

Productivity also involves the effectiveness with which the skills and potentials of the economy's human resources are put to use. And though it is difficult to pin down the elusive decline of the work ethic, it is increasingly clear from recent research that the ways in which we organize our human capital may have much to do with the faltering performance of the American economy, particularly when compared to other countries. Most workers in Japan, West Germany, or Scandinavia enjoy both considerably greater security of employment and much greater participation in the workplace than their American counterparts, as shown in Table 3-7.

In the United States, for example, firms are not required to provide workers any advance notice of plant shutdowns, while the European countries and Japan require from one to six months notice by law. The foreign countries listed in the table all guarantee worker benefits if a company goes out of business; the United States provides none. The European countries and Japan *mandate* extensive leaves for illness and childbirth. Perhaps more strikingly, most of the other countries — either by law or (as in Japan) by established industry policy — provide for at least some degree of worker representation in the management of their companies.

Many other differences do not appear in the table. For example, Japanese corporations typically grant workers considerable authority to make day-to-day decisions in the workplace (Cole, 1979; Thurow, 1981, p. 4), a practice also followed in some European countries. The Japanese system of so-called lifetime employment has become well known. In some Japanese industries, company policy strives as much as possible to keep workers productively employed throughout their life cycle, despite changes in technology or in the demand for particular products. On the other hand, the lifetime employment system is not uniformly adopted throughout the Japanese economy, and, in general, it would be mistaken to overstate the concern of Japanese employers for the well-being of their workers (Junkerman, 1982; Kamata, 1982). But the contrast between that approach and the typical American practice, in which business firms accept little or no responsibility for the security and continuity of their workers' jobs, is an important one.

Many European countries also tackle the problem of job insecurity more positively than the United States, though in somewhat different ways than the Japanese. Most have extensive training and retraining programs, often government run, that help ensure that workers are not simply cut adrift by changes in technology, business relocations, or failures. As Robert Reich notes, "Alone of all Western industrial nations the United States lacks any retraining program available to the majority of its labor force" (1983, p. 102). Most other advanced industrial countries also provide much higher and more easily available income supports for unemployed workers.

In the United States, programs and benefits to promote job security have traditionally been viewed as unwarranted government meddling in private

Table 3-7
Rights of workers in large companies in selected industrialized countries

Rights	West Germany	France	Japan	United Kingdom	Netherlands	Sweden	United States
Average period of notice for shutdown	2–6 months by law	1–3 months by law	1 month by law 6 months by custom	3 months by law	2–6 months by law	6 months + by law	None
Worker representation in management	⅓–½ of board members from workers	Consultation with workers' council on decisions affecting work rules	No law, but ⅔ of companies have board members who are active in unions	None	Consultation with workers' council on all major management decisions	2 members on board; consultation on all major management decisions	None
Paid leaves							
Sickness (not including disability insurance)	6 weeks full pay and 4 weeks 75% pay	50% of earnings up to 36 months after brief waiting period	80% of wages indefinitely	Average 50% for 6 months	80% of pay for 1 year	6 months at full pay	None
Maternity or paternity	6 months after birth and 6 weeks before birth with monthly allowance and guarantee against dismissal	4 months at 90% pay with monthly nursing allowance and guarantee against dismissal	No law, but 3 months' paid leave is widely adhered to	6 weeks at 90% salary	3 months full pay	9 months full pay shared between parents	None
Employee rights on employer insolvency	First priority is 68% average pay for 1 year to all workers	Guaranteed income maintenance allowances varying by age and seniority	Full wage for 2 years; 80% of 3 months' salary guaranteed by the state	Guaranteed 1 weekday for every year of service	80% of all wages for 6 months guaranteed, then 75% for additional time to a maximum of 2 years	90% of wages for 6 months to 2 years	None

Source: Adapted from Ira C. Magaziner and Robert B. Reich, *Minding America's Business* (New York: Law & Business, Inc./Harcourt, Brace, Jovanovich, 1982), p. 144. Reprinted with permission.

matters. We have also tended to believe that workers should fend for themselves if their employer moves or if they lose their jobs for any other reason. But much research (O'Toole, 1981; Reich and Magaziner, 1982) suggests that this attitude has disruptive consequences for the economy. It wastes the skills of workers and potential workers and makes it difficult for them to develop a long-term identification with their work or a sense of its meaning and purpose. In many American industries, this is aggravated by extraordinary inequalities in wages and benefits (relative to many other countries) among different groups of workers and between workers and management. We will return to look at some consequences of this unusual degree of inequality in Chapter 4. For now, note that it is precisely those countries that have invested *most* in the care and training of their human resources (such as Sweden or Japan) that have also chalked up the best records of economic performance in recent years.

Before leaving the question of the productivity of American workers, we need to touch on one final issue: the impact of government *regulations* on productivity. We will save most of our discussion of the impact of regulation for Chapters 9 and 10 since, as we'll see, so much of the debate about regulation centers on antipollution and health and safety measures. But the effect of such regulations on productivity raises the important issue of the limits of the concept of productivity itself as a guide for social policy. Thus, it's widely agreed that the passage of the Coal Mine Safety Act in 1969 — one of the first federal efforts to enforce safety standards in an industry — caused output per hour in the coal industry to decline. Measured productivity in coal mining declined over 4 percent in the early 1970s. But death rates on the job were also cut by two-thirds. In other words, in the abstract, statistical arguments about productivity (as in so many other seemingly "technical" questions of social policy), fundamental choices about social and economic *goals* are at issue. The question is not simply how much coal we produce per hour of miners' labor, but also *how* we produce it, and with what social costs.

Conclusion: The Economic Crisis as a Social Problem

In the 1950s and 1960s, the study of economic problems was usually left to professional economists. One likely reason why other social scientists generally ignored the economy is simply that it seemed to work so well that its problems could safely be left to the technical experts. All this has changed, of course, because of the awareness of the depth of our economic problems in the 1970s and 1980s. The state of the economy has come to be seen (even by many economists) as an issue too important and too many-faceted to be encompassed by the tools of conventional economic analysis alone. It is increasingly understood that the abstraction we call the economy is part of a larger society, and that it is deeply affected by that society's institutions — just as these institutions are themselves affected by what happens in the economy.

Much recent controversy over economic policy, as we saw in Chapter 2, concerns the nature of this relationship between the economy and the larger society — especially the institution of government. Many common explanations of the troubles of the American economy suggest, in one way or an-

Some Economic Vocabulary

Like other social science disciplines, economics contains a language all its own. That language can be mystifying and frustrating to the uninitiated. Here are a few basic definitions that may help:

Anti-trust: legislation aimed at reducing or eliminating monopoly in business. The earliest in the United States, the Sherman Antitrust Act of 1890, was designed to combat the giant combinations of companies *(trusts)* in oil, steel, and other key industries.

Business cycle: the more-or-less regular alternation in the economy from recession to prosperity and back. The high periods are often called *peaks, upswings,* or *expansions;* the low points are variously called *contractions, troughs, downturns,* or some similar term. The movement out of a downturn is most often called a *recovery.*

Capital: often used to describe money available for investment, but it more generally means the sum of all the funds, tools, and equipment used to produce goods and services.

Capital-intensive: an industry or production process that uses a large amount of capital relative to the amount of labor. Likewise, *labor-intensive* refers to processes that use relatively large numbers of workers in proportion to the amount of capital invested. Thus, the oil industry, with enormous plants and equipment but relatively few workers, is highly capital-intensive; restaurants are labor-intensive.

Competition: the condition in which rival sellers of goods and services vie for buyers and profits at each other's expense.

Concentration: the degree of control of an industry, a particular market, or the economy as a whole exercised by a relatively small number of firms. Concentration is measured by *concentration ratios* or *market shares.*

Conglomerate: a corporation that does business in several different markets at once. Conglomerates are typically created by the *merger* of formerly separate firms.

Constant dollars: a measure of purchasing power that adjusts the buying power of the dollar to account for inflation. It is calculated by dividing *current dollars* by some measure of changes in their value, such as the consumer price index.

Consumer price index (CPI): a measure of changes in the prices of goods and services, calculated monthly by the U.S. Bureau of Labor Statistics. It is a rough measure of changes in the cost of living and is usually presented both for all items produced and for several key items, including food, energy, housing, and medical care.

Deficit: generally, an excess of debts over assets or income; in this book, used to describe an excess of government spending over government revenues.

Depression: an extreme downturn in the economy, characterized by very high unemployment and low levels of production and growth. There is no hard-and-fast line between depression and a

other, that efforts at social control of the economy through government intervention are the heart of the problem. But things are not so simple. The American economy is actually one of the least taxed and least regulated among advanced industrial societies; it spends among the least on government; and it has the smallest and least active public sector. It seems apparent that the decline in our economic situation relative to some other industrial countries has less to do with a general, government-induced lack of resources for private enterprise than with a systematic misuse of the resources that are available. And this again is a social and organizational issue,

severe recession: The depression of the 1930s, ending only with World War II, was the worst in recent American history.

Disposable income: personal income minus taxes, therefore available to be consumed or invested.

Gross national product (GNP): the money value of the total production of goods and services, usually measured over a year. *Gross domestic product (GDP)* is GNP minus income from investments and possessions owned outside the country. GNP (or GDP) *per capita* divides this sum by the population; it is often used as a very rough indicator of a country's economic well-being.

Human capital: the sum of skills, abilities, and knowledge possessed by individuals. The income individuals earn in the labor market is sometimes described as the *returns* to human capital.

Inflation: an increase in the prices of goods and services, often measured by rises in the consumer price index (see definition above).

Labor force and labor-force participation rate: the total number of people over age 14 who are either at work or unemployed but willing to work. The *labor-force participation rate* (LFPR) is the proportion of a given population in the labor force as defined.

Market share: the proportion of sales in a particular industry, or for a particular product, enjoyed by one or more firms; a common measure of economic concentration (see definition above).

Market system: technically, the exchange relations of buying and selling goods and services for profit; loosely used to describe the economy of the United States and other countries with relatively little government intervention in the private economy compared to those with relatively more.

Mixed economy: an economy combining substantial private control of economic activity with substantial government intervention in certain areas, particularly the provision of social welfare.

Monopoly: technically, the condition in which a single firm dominates an entire market; more loosely, one in which a relatively small number of firms exert great influence in particular markets or in the economy as a whole. (Economists often use the more precise term *oligopoly* for the latter condition.)

Multinational corporation: a corporation that derives a substantial part of its income from producing (as opposed to merely selling) goods overseas.

Productivity: the amount of some product produced by a worker per some unit of time; often measured as workers' *output per hour.*

Recession: a mild version of depression; a downturn in the business cycle.

Stagflation: the combination of inflation with recession or economic stagnation. Coined to describe the unprecedented coexistence of the two in the American economy during the 1970s.

Transfers or transfer payments: payments not made in return for some service performed, as opposed to *earnings;* usually used to describe government payments to the needy, such as Social Security and public assistance.

not just a technical, economic one. It involves the relative social and cultural values we place on the pursuit of private gain and on other social goals, on the broader social responsibilities of management, and on the care and welfare of our human and environmental resources. So far we have only begun to touch on these issues. They will reappear again and again throughout this book. In the next three chapters we will focus on some of their most important and pervasive aspects — the patterns of social inequality in America.

Summary

This chapter has examined the problems of the American economy in recent years. Though the specific expression of those problems changes rapidly, several disturbing long-term trends seem clear: slower growth compared to earlier periods and to other industrial countries; deeper recessions over the years, leaving ever-greater numbers of people unemployed; more stubborn inflation requiring more drastic recessions and higher unemployment to bring it within bounds; and growing international competition leading to a loss of our uniquely commanding position in the world economy.

Though it has often been argued that recession and unemployment are less painful than in the past, the evidence shows that they still cause increased family disruption, mental and physical illness, suicide, and crime, in addition to staggering economic costs in lost production and government revenues.

Common explanations for the economy's troubles include excessive government spending and taxation, a shortage of capital for business investment, excessive wages for American workers, and the decline of the work ethic. But none of these explanations stands up well to the evidence. Government spending is lower in the United States than in most countries with more successful economies. American taxes are among the lowest of industrial societies, and taxes on *business* specifically have fallen sharply. Many businesses do not lack capital to invest, but have frequently invested what they have in unproductive ways. Workers' wages have generally fallen in recent years relative to the cost of living. And there is no evidence that American workers are less motivated than in the past or that poor attitudes have much to do with America's problems of productivity.

The uncertain performance of the economy, especially in comparison with other countries, seems better explained as partly the result of the misuse of human and natural resources. That misuse often results from choosing short-term gains over long-term economic and social health.

For Further Reading

Alperovitz, Gar. "The New Inflation." *Annals of the American Academy of Political and Social Science* 456 (July 1981).

Blaustein, Arthur I. *The American Promise; Equal Justice and Economic Opportunity.* New Brunswick, N.J.: Transaction Books, 1982.

Bluestone, Barry, and Bennett Harrison. *The Deindustrialization of America.* New York: Basic Books, 1982.

Cole, Robert. *Work, Mobility and Participation; A Comparative Study of American and Japanese Industry.* Berkeley: University of California Press, 1979.

Heilbroner, Robert, and Lester Thurow. *Five Economic Challenges.* Englewood Cliffs, N.J.: Prentice-Hall, 1981.

Reich, Robert B. "The Next American Frontier." *Atlantic*, March/April, 1983.

Thurow, Lester. *The Zero-Sum Society.* New York: Penguin Books, 1980.

4

Social Inequality I:
Wealth and Poverty

The ideal of material equality has always been an ambivalent one for Americans. At least in principle, we feel that equality is an important social value. But we also tolerate enormous discrepancies in living standards and extremes of wealth and poverty.

In the 1950s and 1960s, when the American economy was expanding rapidly and the overall standard of living was rising, social scientists often argued that sharp social cleavages were on the verge of disappearing. The coming of affluence, they believed, would gradually eliminate differences among classes and income groups and would reduce poverty to a minor problem, confined to a relative handful of maladjusted people.

Unfortunately, that prognosis was based on very slim evidence. And, as we entered the gloomier age of limits in the 1970s and 1980s, a different concern began to be voiced. Instead of celebrating the imminent end of inequality in America, we heard that we had already achieved "too much equality — or, in the words of one theorist, that we had achieved "all the equality we could afford" (Browning, 1976, p. 76). In this view, the growth of the welfare state, funneling ever-increasing amounts of government benefits to the poor, was threatening to tip the balance too far toward egalitarianism, stifling individual initiative and sapping sources of funds for productive economic growth.

The ideal of equality, in other words, is now often qualified by the assertions that the level of economic equality we already have is more than enough and that excessive devotion to that ideal bears a large part of the blame for the problems of the economy. These beliefs are often marshalled in support of policies designed to shift more social and economic rewards upward, to the wealthy and to corporate business, while correspondingly limiting the government's generosity to lower-income groups and urging most middle-income working people to tighten their belts.

In this chapter we'll examine the evidence of just how much economic equality has, in fact, been achieved — and how much the extremes of wealth and poverty have been affected by government policies and the growth of the economy. Our focus for now will be on the more quantifiable differences in income, earnings, and wealth. These are, of course, only some of the ways in which inequality makes itself felt in society. Inequality is not only a matter of differences in income or assets but also of the differing pleasures — and dangers — of work, the quality of education and health care, and much more. The pervasive effects of economic inequality are a guiding theme throughout this book. But, for now, we will focus on the more specific issue of inequality in the distribution of income and wealth. Has it changed? If so, what factors lie behind these changes — and what further changes can we expect in the future?

First, we'll consider what the evidence tells us about trends in inequality in the distribution of income and wealth in the United States — the ways in which the American "pie" has been divided since World War II. Then we'll examine the most troubling aspect of that distribution, the depth and persistence of poverty in America. This leads us into a discussion of the modern welfare system and some of its effects on poverty and inequality, and, finally, to a look at some of the ways in which a lesser-known, hidden welfare system for the affluent tends to counterbalance the effects of the better-known welfare system for the poor.

The Distribution of Income

In economic language, *income* means money derived from any of several different sources, including earnings, Social Security benefits, and welfare payments. Not all sources of income are counted, however, in government statistics, and this has important consequences for the way income distribution is measured. For example, income from capital gains (income derived from the increased value of business or other property) is not counted in most income statistics, which means that the statistics tend to underestimate the income of those more affluent people who are more likely to be property owners. And, of course, much income is never reported (usually in order to foil the tax collector) and therefore never appears in official statistics.

Poor people underreport welfare payments; blue-collar workers, professional people, and casual workers fail to report extra work done "under the table"; and wealthy people hide the extent of their unearned income. Who under-reports the most is obviously hard to determine, but it's important to keep in mind that this is one reason why income statistics must be treated with caution.

The most common way of measuring the distribution of income is to divide the population into fifths, rank the fifths from highest (richest) to lowest (poorest), and determine how large a percentage of the nation's total personal income each fifth receives. (This approach measures income *before* taxes; we will look at the effect of taxation on income distribution shortly.) As Figure 4-1 and Table 4-1 show, these income shares have remained highly unequal in the United States since World War II. The highest fifth of American families has enjoyed over two-fifths of all income; the lowest fifth, only about one-twentieth. The top fifth, in other words, has consistently had about eight times the share of the bottom fifth.

Focusing on the top fifth, however, minimizes the concentration of income at the top of the scale since the top fifth includes many people who aren't wealthy — everyone, in fact, with a family income above about $37,000 a year in 1981. The picture is sharper if we look instead at the share of the top 5 percent of American families — those making more than about $59,000 in 1981. Those families received more than 15 percent of the total income — a proportion that, again, has not changed significantly since World War II. Their share is roughly the same as that of the bottom two-fifths — 40 percent of the population — combined.

Although the figure and table show a remarkable consistency in American income distribution over a period of 35 years, a closer look reveals some

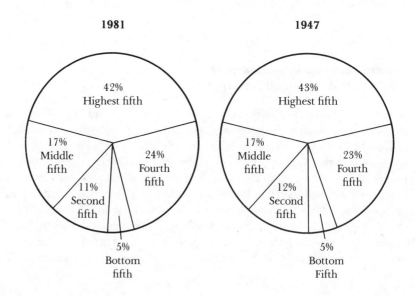

Figure 4-1
Slicing the American pie: shares of total income by fifths of the population, 1981 and 1947

Source: Data from U.S. Bureau of the Census, *Current Population Reports*, series P-60, no. 137, Washington, D.C., April 1983, p. 47.

distinct changes over time. The share of the bottom (poorest) fifth of the population rose during the decade of the 1960s, for instance, while that of the top fifth fell. Though the percentages are small, the shift is significant, particularly for the lowest fifth, whose income share rose by about 17 percent during that decade. This change is also expressed in the decrease in the size of the other measure in Table 4-1, the *index of income concentration*. This figure (technically called the *Gini index*) measures the overall degree of inequality throughout the entire income distribution. The higher the value of the Gini, the greater the inequality of incomes. The Gini dropped somewhat during the early 1950s and again in the mid to later 1960s, indicating a noticeable (though hardly overwhelming) trend toward equality during those years.

Now note, however, what seems to have happened in more recent years. The share of the poorest fifth has fallen to its early 1960s levels and that of the upper fifth has grown beyond its 1960s levels. The Gini index, similarly, shows the greatest degree of overall income inequality in two decades. If these figures are to be believed, there has been a fairly clear reversal of the trend toward greater income equality that peaked in the late 1960s. But *can* we believe the statistics?

Like most official statistics, these have been criticized as inaccurate and misleading. Some critics argue that the official statistics exaggerate income inequality; others argue that they understate it.

Are Income Statistics Misleading?

One of the most important criticisms is that the official income statistics fail to take into account changes in the broader society that may have a powerful effect on the distribution of income. In particular, the changing *age* structure of American society, in this argument, means that simple comparisons of income over time are misleading. Other things being equal, older people (and very young people) have smaller incomes than people in the prime working ages, since a much smaller proportion of the former work for a regular salary or wage or, if they do, are either on their way out of the labor force or just getting started. Since the aged are now a larger proportion of the American population, and often live alone rather than in a household with other wage-earning family members, the usual measures of income can appear more unequal. In this argument, the fact that the official measures have shown *unchanged* inequality therefore means that the actual pattern of income distribution is becoming more equal. Only the population change — what social scientists call a *demographic* change — keeps us from seeing what is really a trend toward equality (Paglin, 1975).

Likewise, the conventional, intact husband-wife family (other things being equal) is likely to have a higher income than a family headed by a single parent, especially one headed by a single woman. So to the extent that the proportion of single-parent families has increased, according to this argument, the official income picture will also be misleading. By failing to account for a changing population, with a changing mix of expected incomes, the official statistics show greater inequality than actually exists, and fail to reflect an actual trend toward greater equality in the United States.

We will look more carefully at both of these trends later in this chapter and again in Chapters 6 and 7. Both trends *are* important — and both tell us much about the changing patterns of inequality and poverty. But do they mean that the official figures are seriously misleading and that there has actually been a strong trend toward equality in recent years?

The most careful studies show that these demographic trends *have* had an effect on the pattern of income inequality, but a relatively small one and not quite in the way the critics have argued. One study, for example, found that contrary to the official statistics, overall income inequality *increased* substantially between the mid-1960s and mid-1970s. Most of that increase, the study concluded, was accounted for by demographic changes in age structure and family composition. But when those were taken into account, though there was no longer a significant increase in inequality, there was no decrease either (Danziger and Plotnick, 1977).

Table 4-1

Income shares received by each fifth and top 5 percent of families and index of income concentration, 1947–1981

Year	Percent distribution of aggregate income					Top 5%	Index of income concentration
	Lowest fifth	Second fifth	Middle fifth	Fourth fifth	Highest fifth		
1981	5.0	11.3	17.4	24.4	41.9	15.4	0.370
1980	5.1	11.6	17.5	24.3	41.6	15.3	0.365
1979	5.2	11.6	17.5	24.1	41.7	15.8	0.365
1978	5.2	11.6	17.5	24.1	41.5	15.6	0.364
1977	5.2	11.6	17.5	24.2	41.5	15.7	0.364
1976	5.4	11.8	17.6	24.1	41.1	15.6	0.359
1975	5.4	11.8	17.6	24.1	41.1	15.5	0.358
1974	5.5	12.0	17.5	24.0	41.0	15.5	0.356
1973	5.5	11.9	17.5	24.0	41.1	15.5	0.356
1972	5.4	11.9	17.5	23.9	41.4	15.9	0.360
1971	5.5	12.0	17.6	23.8	41.1	15.7	0.356
1970	5.4	12.2	17.6	23.8	40.9	15.6	0.354
1969	5.6	12.4	17.7	23.7	40.6	15.6	0.349
1968	5.6	12.4	17.7	23.7	40.5	15.6	0.348
1967	5.5	12.4	17.9	23.9	40.4	15.2	0.348
1966	5.6	12.4	17.8	23.8	40.5	15.6	0.349
1965	5.2	12.2	17.8	23.9	40.9	15.5	0.356
1964	5.1	12.0	17.7	24.0	41.2	15.9	0.361
1963	5.0	12.1	17.7	24.0	41.2	15.8	0.362
1962	5.0	12.1	17.6	24.0	41.3	15.7	0.362
1961	4.7	11.9	17.5	23.8	42.2	16.6	0.374
1960	4.8	12.2	17.8	24.0	41.3	15.9	0.364

Another argument holds that the official picture is misleading because it fails to take into account a variety of benefits that people at the lower end of the income scale receive. These so-called in-kind benefits (including food stamps, Medicaid, and federal housing subsidies) are not counted as income in the official data but have become an increasingly important part of the overall income of the poor. We'll return to this argument later in discussing the impact of the welfare system on inequality. For now, we'll note that this argument raises a host of related issues, some of which lead to the opposite conclusion — that the official statistics probably *underestimate* the degree of inequality in American incomes. Once we begin looking at forms of income that are not officially counted, we also have to include many benefits that wealthy and middle-income people receive that low-income people rarely do, such as tax loopholes, government contracts, or income from capital gains. All of these add to the inequality of incomes. For example, if all capital gains income were counted, the richest 1 percent of American households, which now receives a substantial 5 percent of official income, would receive about 11 percent (Thurow, 1980, p. 168).

Year	Percent distribution of aggregate income					Top 5%	Index of income concentration
	Lowest fifth	Second fifth	Middle fifth	Fourth fifth	Highest fifth		
1959	4.9	12.3	17.9	23.8	41.1	15.9	0.361
1958	5.0	12.5	18.0	23.9	40.6	15.4	0.354
1957	5.1	12.7	18.1	23.8	40.4	15.6	0.351
1956	5.0	12.5	17.9	23.7	41.0	16.1	0.358
1955	4.8	12.3	17.8	23.7	41.3	16.4	0.363
1954	4.5	12.1	17.7	23.9	41.8	16.3	0.371
1953	4.7	12.5	18.0	23.9	40.9	15.7	0.359
1952	4.9	12.3	17.4	23.4	41.9	17.4	0.368
1951	5.0	12.4	17.6	23.4	41.6	16.8	0.363
1950	4.5	12.0	17.4	23.4	42.7	17.3	0.379
1949	4.5	11.9	17.3	23.5	42.7	16.9	0.378
1948	4.9	12.1	17.3	23.2	42.4	17.1	0.371
1947	5.0	11.9	17.0	23.1	43.0	17.5	0.376

	Upper limit of each fifth, 1981						
	Lowest	Second	Middle	Fourth	Top 5%		
	10 918	18 552	26 528	37 457	58 554		

Source: Adapted from U.S. Bureau of the Census, *Current Population Reports*, series P-60, no. 137, Washington, D.C., April 1983, p. 47.

Accounting for the persistence of this pattern of inequality (over and above the demographic changes) is more complicated than simply describing it, and we will be examining this problem in one way or another throughout the chapter. But some parts of the explanation seem fairly clear from recent research; we will note them briefly here, and they will reappear later in the chapter, particularly as we look at the patterns of poverty in the United States.

On the one hand, it is clear that cash transfer payments from government (including welfare payments and Social Security benefits) have acted to decrease inequality. How *much* they have done so is a matter of considerable controversy. A careful review of many recent studies estimates that the total impact of all cash transfer programs reduces the Gini index of inequality by 19 percent, or about a fifth, from what it would be in the absence of such programs (Danziger, Haveman, and Plotnick, 1981). Though government, as we shall see, "transfers" money to the upper as well as to the lower parts of the income scale, the main overall effect of the expansion of transfer programs has been to boost the income share of the bottom fifth. Without cash benefits of one kind or another, the bottom fifth's share of the country's total income would probably be only about 1 to 2 percent, rather than 5 percent (Danziger, Haveman, and Plotnick, 1981).

But if transfers tend to reduce inequality, other factors have simultaneously tended to increase it. One is unemployment. A recent study esti-

Extremes of wealth and . . .

Leonard Freed/Magnum Photos Inc.

poverty persist in the
United States.

mates that each one-percentage-point rise in the unemployment rate
increases the Gini index by about a third of a percent (Budd, 1982, p. 17).
This increase is caused by the declining income of people in the bottom two-
fifths of the income distribution, who are far more likely to be unemployed
than more affluent people. It's likely that a substantial part of the rise in
measured inequality in the past few years reflects the high and increasingly
stubborn unemployment rates we noted in Chapter 3. But recent studies
have also found a slow but persistent pattern of growing inequality even in
the earnings of workers who are *employed,* year round, full time (Henle and
Ryscavage, 1981). Part of this disturbing trend is the result of a greater proportion of younger workers (who tend to have lower and more variable earnings) in the labor force. But the trend toward growing earnings inequality
remains even when the factor of age (as well as work experience and education) is accounted for (Dooley and Gottschalk, 1982).

To an important extent, the relatively stable, though slightly increasing,
pattern of income inequality reflects an uneasy balance between two opposing tendencies. In the realm of jobs and earnings, we appear to be becoming
steadily less equal, but government assistance has, to some extent, offset
that trend — at least until very recently.

We will return to this issue in a moment, for it is crucial to an understanding of America's successes and failures in the battle against poverty. But let's
look first at another aspect of economic inequality in America.

The Concentration of Wealth

The gap in incomes, wide as it is, is only one aspect of economic inequality. In many ways, a more crucial one is the difference between those who own and those who do not own substantial wealth. Most people's income is tied to a job and/or to some form of government benefits. As we've seen, the differences in income are quite large between different groups; but even at the top, the upper fifth of income earners includes many people who would hardly be considered wealthy. But the ownership of wealth is another matter. At the highest levels it provides a different kind of income than most people ever receive, such as large amounts of "unearned" income from stock dividends and bond interest. And, unlike even most well-paid jobs, ownership of large amounts of wealth implies a degree of control over economic resources that few besides the wealthy ever possess. Wealth, much more than income alone, sharply divides the population between those people who have the capacity to shape and control economic life and those who do not. And wealth is much more narrowly concentrated than income.

Accurate estimates of the *precise* degree of wealth concentration, however, are almost impossible to come by. Even more than personal income, the wealth of a family or individual is usually a well-guarded secret, especially for tax reasons. (Much of the information on wealth holdings available to social scientists only appears when someone dies and estate taxes must be filed.) One careful student of wealth distribution states flatly that "the only truthful answer I, or anyone else, can give you at this time is that we do not know" the exact trends in wealth ownership in America in recent years (Smith, 1982, p. 197). But even the crude data available paint a striking picture.

Table 4-2 shows the share of all personal assets held by the richest 1 percent and 0.5 percent of the population in 1976 — about 2 million and 1 million people, respectively. Though the share these wealthy individuals hold is greater for some forms of wealth than others, it is disproportionate for all of them; ranging, among the top 1 percent, from 8 percent of the cash value of life insurance policies to an astonishing 44 percent of corporate stock. The concentration of wealth among the richest 0.5 percent is even more impressive. A little more than a million people own over a fourth of all bonds and well over a third of corporate stock. Overall, they hold almost one-sixth of the country's total personal assets.

Has there been a shift toward a more even distribution of wealth? Historical studies suggest that the most egalitarian period in American history, measured in terms of wealth concentration, was from the colonial era to the end of the period just following the American revolution. On the whole, the concentration of wealth increased during the nineteenth and early twentieth centuries, declined somewhat during the Depression and World War II, stabilized until the late 1960s, and *may* have declined somewhat since then

Asset	Share held by richest	
	0.5%	1.0%
Corporate stock	36.9	44.2
Bonds	26.4	30.6
Debt instruments	18.7	24.6
Miscellaneous and trusts	15.7	18.8
Real estate	8.9	13.1
Cash	6.7	11.1
Life insurance (CSV)	4.9	8.0
Total assets	14.0	18.6

Source: Adapted from James D. Smith, prepared statement, in Hearings, *1982 Economic Report of the President,* U.S. Congress, Joint Economic Committee, February 1982, part 2, p. 204.

Table 4-2
Share of personal wealth owned by the richest 0.5 percent and 1 percent of the American population, 1976

(Williamson and Lindert, 1980; Smith, 1982). Figure 4-2 illustrates these trends.

Does the downturn in the 1970s indicate a trend toward redistribution? Probably not. More likely, it represents a shift from the upper 0.5 and 1 percent to the upper 2 or 3 percent — as one scholar puts it, "redistribution from the superrich to the nearly superrich" (Smith, 1982, p. 200) — a genuine shift, but "hardly of social or economic significance."

Ownership of very large assets, then, remains highly concentrated within a very small proportion of the population. Traditionally, such concentrated wealth has been thought to give its owners disproportionate power to control the resources of the economy as a whole. It means not only an affluent standard of living but the ability to determine other people's standard of living as well.

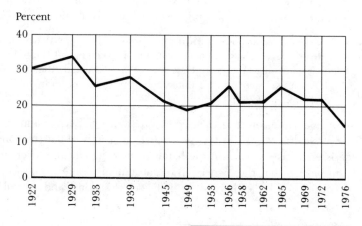

Figure 4-2
Share of net assets owned by 0.5 percent of American population 1922–1976 (data for 1976 are preliminary.)

Source: James D. Smith, prepared statement, in Hearings, *1982 Economic Report of the President,* U.S. Congress, Joint Economic Committee, February 1982, part 2, p. 209.

Stock Ownership and Inequality

Some social theorists have argued that this link between wealth and economic power has been exaggerated. One main argument has been that the spread of stock ownership to a wider segment of the population means that economic decision making is now diffused among many social groups. For a while, it was even common to refer to the American economy as a kind of "people's capitalism," in which average citizens could, and did, own a share — and therefore have a voice — in the big corporations.

But if we look carefully at the pattern of stock ownership, it turns out to mirror the larger economic inequalities in the United States, only more so. A considerable number of Americans, about 31 million in 1980, do own stock, up from about 25 million in 1975. But over a longer period, there has been a decline both in the number of stock owners and their percentage in the population as a whole. There were about a million fewer stockholders in 1980 than in 1970, and their proportion of the population fell from 15 percent to about 13 percent.

People with higher incomes, unsurprisingly, are much more likely to own stock. According to a survey by the New York Stock Exchange, the median income of stock-owning households in 1979 was nearly $28,000, while the median income for the country as a whole was $16,600. Someone in a professional or technical job was almost six times as likely to own stock as a blue-collar operative or laborer. A University of Michigan survey of asset ownership throws more light on the unequal distribution of stock:

- A fourth of all families owned stock in 1977, but half of families with incomes over $25,000 did, versus just 6 percent with incomes below $5,000 and 21 percent with incomes between $10,000 and $15,000.

- Twenty-eight percent of families with incomes above $25,000 owned more than $5,000 worth of stock, versus only 1 percent of those making less than $5,000 a year (Curtin and Neubig, 1979).

But it's at the top, as we've seen already, that the bulk of stock ownership is concentrated. One study has found that the 6 percent of the population with assets worth more than $60,000 in 1972 owned *two-thirds* of all corporate stock. As the study points out, this means that control of corporate assets rests, for all practical purposes, within this fraction of the population:

> The concentration of wealth in the hands of the superrich is arrestingly high for assets which connote economic power beyond the index of raw dollars. Looking at corporate stock, one must conclude that the superrich who own 66.7 percent of it potentially control all corporate assets. (Smith and Franklin, 1976, p. 178)

A final issue concerns the role of inheritance in perpetuating the inequality of wealth. We might feel somewhat differently about the concentration of assets in a few hands if the hands *changed* significantly over time. Those who believe that the ownership of substantial wealth necessarily indicates the fruits of a life of hard work, judicious risktaking, and careful saving, of course, tend to assume that the former is true. But the evidence suggests otherwise (Brittain, 1978). As one analyst observes, "Wealthy parents do indeed have wealthy children, though most of the children were not quite as wealthy as their parents were" (Menchik, 1979, p. 360). There are, of course, exceptions to this pattern of what Paul Menchik calls "wealth immobility" (1979, p. 360); in every generation some individuals do newly join the ranks of the very wealthy. But the *broader* pattern is one of very little movement from one wealth class to another across generations; the chances that the children of wealthy parents will remain wealthy are as high as 80 percent (Brittain, 1978, p. 88; Menchik, 1979, p. 360).

Executives' Earnings: Competence and Compensation at the Top

The statistics in this chapter show that the distribution of income in the United States is highly unequal. But even these statistics minimize the extreme differences between those at the *very* top of the income scale and almost everyone else. If we look more closely at the income of the highest-paid corporate executives, an even more skewed picture emerges.

In 1981, according to an article in *Fortune* dramatically titled "The Madness of Executive Compensation," the average compensation (including salaries, bonuses, and other cash benefits) of the chief executives of the country's 10 largest conglomerates was just over $1 million. The highest-paid executive, *Fortune* calculated, was J. Peter Grace, head of the W. R. Grace corporation, a conglomerate with interests in chemicals, food, and other industries. Grace's compensation in 1981 was about $1.8 million (Loomis, 1982, pp. 42–45).

The compensation of the 10 highest-paid conglomerate executives, if distributed directly to the poor, would have brought 3,415 families over the poverty line in that year. J. Peter Grace's compensation, by itself, could have lifted 601 American families out of poverty (calculated from U.S. Bureau of the Census, 1983, p. 26). The inequality between what these executives receive

for their work and what most other workers receive for theirs is startling: 100 skilled craft-workers could have been hired (at average 1981 wages) or 260 unskilled youth at the minimum wage with J. Peter Grace's earnings (calculated from *Statistical Abstract of the U.S., 1982–83*, pp. 400, 402).

These differences, of course, are usually justified by the argument that they reflect the "free market's" judgment that the skills and effectiveness of these executives are worth the price. Is this true? *Fortune* noted that the evidence suggests that executive compensation is actually unrelated to performance on the job. "In the upper reaches of corporate America," the magazine concluded, "the market frequently does not seem to work." In a more reasonable world, corporate managers would be paid "handsomely" for top performance and "would lose out when they flopped. But to an extraordinary extent, those who flop still get paid handsomely" (Loomis, 1982, p. 42). W. R. Grace and Company showed a "distinctly low grade" performance in 1981; the head of ITT, which performed poorly over the five years ending in 1981, earned almost twice as much as the head of Raytheon, which outperformed ITT on every measure of business performance (Loomis, 1982, pp. 42–43).

As an interesting footnote, J. Peter Grace was appointed to head the Reagan administration's Private Sector Advisory Council on Cost Control, a body charged with the task of finding ways of reducing costs in government operations.

The Persistence of Poverty

In 1964, the federal government formally declared a War on Poverty. For a while, we seemed to be winning that war. When it began there were 36 million Americans below the government-defined poverty line; by 1969, only 24 million. As a proportion of the population, the poor dropped from 19 percent in 1964 to about 12 percent by the end of the 1960s.

But the progress turned out to be short-lived. The number of poor people in the United States fluctuated along with the ups and downs of the economy during the 1970s. By 1979, there were over a million *more* poor Americans than there were in 1969, and the *rate* of poverty was essentially unchanged. And as the 1980s began, the poverty count took a sharp, dramatic leap upward. Between 1979 and 1982, more than 8 million people newly joined the ranks of the poor; the *rate* of poverty jumped by 28 percent (see Table 4-3 and Figure 4-3).

But these figures give only part of the picture. Things appear even worse when we begin to look beneath them at the long-term trends in poverty and what they may imply about the future. We will see in Chapters 5 and 6 that poverty has always been more severe for minorities and women, and is becoming even *more* so. But several other trends also make for a more ominous pattern than the statistics show at first glance.

1. Even in the 1960s, the successes against poverty were mainly confined to some areas, and to some kinds of people, and not others; and most of even those successes have undergone sharp reversals in the 1980s.

2. Even more disturbingly, conventional economic growth no longer seems to have much effect in reducing poverty.

3. The official poverty line does not adequately measure the much larger group of people whose incomes don't support an adequate standard of living — or who live precariously close to poverty.

Let's consider each issue in turn.

Rural Success, Urban Failure

Most of the successes against poverty, even in the 1960s, took place in rural areas, especially in the South. In the inner cities, especially in the economically depressed Northeast and Midwest, poverty has always been more stubborn. And it worsened considerably during the 1970s.

There were almost as many poor people in the northern and western states in 1981 as in 1959, well before the War on Poverty began. Put another way, of about 7 million people who moved above the poverty line since 1959, almost 6 million were southern. The South still has higher rates of poverty, but improvement there has been greater (U.S. Bureau of the Census, 1983a, p. 15). Why? Part of the answer is that the civil rights movement

Table 4-3
Trends in poverty,
1959–1981

Years	Number below poverty level (in thousands)			Percent below poverty level		
	All persons	65 years and over	Related children under 18 years	All persons	65 years and over	Related children under 18 years
1982	34 400	3 844	13 440	15.0	14.6	21.7
1981	31 822	3 853	12 068	14.0	15.3	19.5
1980	29 272	3 871	11 114	13.0	15.7	17.9
1979	26 072	3 682	9 993	11.7	15.2	16.0
1978	24 497	3 233	9 722	11.4	14.0	15.7
1977	24 720	3 177	10 028	11.6	14.1	16.0
1976	24 975	3 313	10 081	11.8	15.0	15.8
1975	25 877	3 317	10 882	12.3	15.3	16.8
1974	23 370	3 085	9 967	11.2	14.6	15.1
1973	22 973	3 354	9 453	11.1	16.3	14.2
1972	24 460	3 738	10 082	11.9	18.6	14.9
1971	25 559	4 273	10 344	12.5	21.6	15.1
1970	25 420	4 709	10 235	12.6	24.5	14.9
1969	24 147	4 787	9 501	12.1	25.3	13.8
1968	25 389	4 632	10 739	12.8	25.0	15.3
1967	27 769	5 388	11 427	14.2	29.5	16.3
1966	28 510	5 114	12 146	14.7	28.5	17.4
1965	33 185	(NA)	14 388	17.3	(NA)	20.7
1960	39 851	(NA)	17 288	22.2	(NA)	26.5
1959	39 490	5 481	17 208	22.4	35.2	26.9

Source: Adapted from U.S. Bureau of the Census, *Current Population Reports*, series P-60, no. 138, Washington, D.C., April 1983, p. 7.

Figure 4-3

Poverty rates, 1959–1982

Source: Data from U.S. Bureau of the Census, Current Population Reports, Series P-60, # 139, April 1983, and Press Release, August 1983.

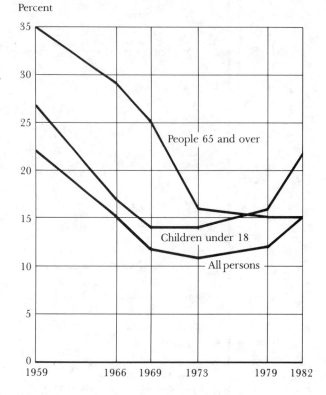

in the South led, directly or indirectly, to many improvements in both jobs and welfare benefits, especially for southern blacks. The relatively rapid economic development of the South also brought better jobs and higher incomes for southerners of both races, especially during the 1960s. And it also helped cause a massive movement to the North and West by many of the southern poor.

That exodus was primarily the result of the transformation of southern farming and, more generally, of American agriculture as a whole. And one of its effects is crucial for understanding the nature of poverty today. Machines and chemicals were used to do much of the work formerly done by the rural poor. Literally millions of jobs were eliminated, and millions of people left for the cities. This had two results. Many of the formerly rural poor simply changed location and became the urban poor. Also, the rural poor sometimes ceased being poverty statistics by a statistical slight-of-hand. Their standard of living may have actually improved little, or even deteriorated. But by moving to areas where earnings and welfare benefits were higher, they had higher incomes — enough to bring them above the official poverty level.

The change from southern to northern poverty is closely bound up with the wider change from rural to urban poverty. Almost all of the (slight) reduction in poverty during the decade of the 1970s can be accounted for by the continuing decline in poverty for people living on farms. As Table 4-4 shows, the poverty rate in central cities rose during the 1970s, while it fell in nonmetropolitan areas. But the even-deeper, nationwide recession of the early 1980s affected the rural poverty rate, too, reversing the hard-won gains of the 1970s.

Another limitation of the success of the War on Poverty involves age rather than residence or region. Most of the people who officially moved out of poverty, especially in the 1970s, were older. And even their relative gains began to be reversed in the early 1980s.

Between 1970 and 1978, the number of poor people over 65 dropped by almost a million and a half. Most of this decline resulted from improved Social Security benefits. But this didn't mean that the low-income aged achieved genuine comfort and security. Many still lived uncomfortably close to the poverty line, and the poverty rate for the elderly remains higher than that of most other groups. (And the Social Security system itself, of course, has become ever more precarious in the face of economic stagnation and political criticism.)

But the more drastic change is at the other end of the life cycle. Table 4-3 (page 113) shows that there were almost *200,000 more* poor children and youth (under 18) in 1979 than there were in 1969. At the close of the 1960s, the youth poverty rate was less than 14 percent. By the end of the 1970s, it was 16 percent; and it approached 22 percent by 1982. The harsh recession years from 1980 through 1982 added more than 3 million children to the poverty figures, bringing the number of poor children in America close to what it was when the War on Poverty began.

The antipoverty warriors of the 1960s shared with many of today's economists the idea that poverty could best be fought through increased economic growth. This belief underlies much social policy in the past few years. But the evidence suggests that though the situation may have been different in the past, overall economic growth now seems to have a diminishing impact on poverty.

One way of looking at this is through the technical distinction between what economists call *posttransfer* and *pretransfer* poverty. Posttransfer poverty, what official poverty statistics measure, includes income from cash transfer payments such as Social Security or welfare benefits. Pretransfer poverty counts only the income people receive from earnings. It therefore provides a rough estimate of how well the economy enables people to make a living by working. Obviously, there will be more pretransfer than posttransfer poor at any given time. We've seen that, by the official — posttransfer — measures, about one in eight Americans were poor during

Suffer the Children

The Declining Significance of Growth

Table 4-4
The changing geography of poverty: the poor by residence and region, selected years, 1959–1981

Residence and region	Number and percent of all races below poverty level, in thousands											
	1981		1980		1979		1975		1970		1959	
	No.	%	No.	%	No.	%	No.	%	No.	%	No.	%
Total	31,822	14.0	29,272	13.0	26,072	11.7	25,877	12.3	25,420	12.6	38,766	22.0
Nonfarm	30,562	13.8	28,282	12.9	26,072	11.7	24,562	12.3	23,483	12.2	NA	NA
Farm	1,260	23.0	990	17.5	793	13.3	1,316	16.4	1,937	21.1	NA	NA
Metropolitan areas	19,347	12.6	18,021	11.9	16,134	10.7	15,348	10.8	13,317	10.2	17,019	15.3
In central cities	11,231	18.0	10,644	17.2	9,720	15.7	9,090	15.0	8,118	14.2	10,437	18.3
In poverty areas	4,485	40.7	4,284	38.1	3,937	35.4	4,446	34.9	NA	NA	NA	NA
Outside central cities	8,116	8.9	7,377	8.2	6,415	7.2	6,259	7.6	5,199	7.1	6,582	12.2
In poverty areas	1,271	28.3	1,368	28.9	1,144	23.0	900	20.8	NA	NA	NA	NA
Nonmetropolitan areas	12,475	17.0	11,251	15.4	9,937	13.8	10,529	13.4	12,103	16.9	21,747	33.2
North and West	18,566	12.3	16,919	11.3	14,973	10.1	14,818	10.4	13,994	10.0	19,650	16.0
Northeast	5,815	11.9	5,369	11.1	5,058	10.4	4,904	10.2	4,204	8.7	NA	NA
Northcentral	7,142	12.3	6,592	11.4	5,639	9.7	5,459	9.7	5,842	10.3	NA	NA
West	5,609	12.7	4,958	11.4	4,276	10.1	4,454	11.7	3,947	11.3	NA	NA
South	13,256	17.4	12,353	16.5	11,098	15.0	11,059	16.2	11,462	18.6	19,116	35.4

Source: Adapted from U.S. Bureau of the Census, *Current Population Reports*, series P-60, no. 138, Washington, D.C., April 1983, p. 15.

Gays on Campus

Newsweek

April 5, 1982 / $1.50

REAGAN'S AMERICA

And The Poor Get Poorer

There were more poor children in America in the 1980s than at the close of the 1960s.

most of the 1970s, and that by 1981 the proportion was closer to one in seven. But about *one in five* people are poor before transfers are counted. One in five Americans, in other words, do not get enough income from working to subsist at the poverty level. Some of these people are aged, and would not be expected to have earnings under most circumstances. But even among the nonaged, about one in six has earnings that, by themselves, leave them below the poverty level.

The Persistence of Poverty   **117**

What is striking is that this proportion hasn't changed much since the mid-1960s. 21 percent of the population was poor before transfers in 1965, 20 percent in 1980 (Danziger, 1982, p. 60). Let's pause to consider what this seemingly obscure technical point means; despite the rapid growth of the economy in the late 1960s, the proportion of Americans able to earn a decent living did not increase. Put another way, the only thing that really helped bring down the poverty rate — *even when the economy was doing well* — was transfer payments. Table 4-5 shows how this can change our understanding of the recent trends in poverty. The second column is the official poverty rate as measured by the Census Bureau on the basis of a person's total money income. The first is the rate of poverty when transfer payments are subtracted. Without transfer payments, poverty would have decreased only 6 percent (rather than 17 percent by the official measure) during the entire decade and a half, and all of the decrease would have occurred before 1972.

Something about the way the economy has grown in recent years, then, has meant that growth by itself (even when we achieve it) seems no longer capable of altering the deeper inadequacies of work and earnings that keep people in poverty. "Trickle down," as one study of this phenomenon puts it, has "petered out" (Thornton, Agnello, and Lind, 1978). In later chapters, especially Chapters 5, 6, and 8, we'll consider how and why this has happened. For now, we'll simply note that the declining impact of growth obviously has important and ominous implications for the future of poverty in America.

Redrawing the Poverty Line

But there is still another reason why the official statistics may understate the dimensions of poverty. What we've said so far has assumed that the way the government now *defines* and *measures* poverty is satisfactory. But, in fact, the poverty line is one of the most criticized of official statistics. Some people believe it exaggerates the true amount of poverty in the United States. Others believe that it minimizes the severity of the problem of poverty.

How does the government decide who is poor and who isn't? The poverty level is based on an estimate of nutritional needs, a so-called *thrifty food plan*, developed in the 1950s by the U.S. Department of Agriculture. The cost of a basic subsistence diet was estimated and then multiplied by three, because surveys had shown that the poor spend about a third of their income on food. Three times the cost of a minimal diet therefore would give a plausible estimate of the cost of a minimal level of subsistence. The poverty line is adjusted for different family sizes (and for individuals). It is also adjusted each year for the cost of living. Beginning at $3,000 for a family of four in 1964, the poverty level reached $9,287 by 1981.

Critics have long noted several problems with this measure. One of the most crucial is that the thrifty food plan, by the Department of Agriculture's own admission, is not enough to provide a sound diet, even of the most

Year	Pretransfer poverty rate	Posttransfer poverty rate
1965	21.3	15.6
1968	18.2	12.8
1970	18.8	12.6
1972	19.2	11.9
1974	20.3	11.6
1976	21.0	11.8
1978	20.2	11.4
1980	20.0*	13.0
Percentage of change		
1965–72	−9.9	−23.7
1972–80	+4.2	+9.2
1965–80	−6.1	−16.6

*This is a preliminary figure.
Source: Adapted from Sheldon Danziger, prepared statement, *1982 Economic Report of the President*, U.S. Congress, Joint Economic Committee, February 1982, p. 60.

Table 4-5
Pretransfer and posttransfer poverty: the effect of transfer payments on poverty rates, 1965–1980

minimal kind. So a poverty line based on it is bound to understate what it really costs to live even at the bare subsistence level (Blaustein, 1982, pp. 48–49).

Many studies have confirmed this point. One, undertaken by the National Social Science and Law Project, surveyed the actual market costs of basic necessities (food, rental housing, clothing, and so on) in New Jersey. On the basis of that survey, the researchers calculated a "minimum adequacy budget," defined as what it cost to attain a minimally adequate standard of living. (This budget did not include any expenses for such "nonnecessities" as child care, reading materials, recreation, or education.) In 1980, when the poverty level for a four-person family was $7,450 in New Jersey, the cost of this minimum adequacy budget was $12,192. The official poverty level, in other words, was less than two-thirds of what was necessary to buy "those goods and services which the federal government defines as essential to the maintenance of adequate nutrition, housing, safety and health" (Blaustein, 1982, p. 49).

Another measure, sometimes offered as an alternative to the poverty level, is a *lower family budget* estimated each year by the Bureau of Labor Statistics of the U.S. Department of Labor. (The Bureau of Labor Statistics also estimates an *intermediate* and a *higher* budget.) As in the New Jersey study, this budget, while slightly less basic, leaves very little room for anything beyond the bare essentials. In 1981, for example, the lower budget amounted to $15,323 for a family of four. It allowed about $87 per week for food. This falls within the range of what the Department of Agriculture calls a moderate food cost for that size family, which assumes that no food is eaten away from home. The lower budget allowed about $235 a month for *all* housing expenses, including furnishings (it assumes that the family rents, rather than owns a home), and about $1,160 a year for all transportation, including the cost of a car and gas.

In the past few years, the official poverty level for a family of four has usually amounted to only about three-fifths of the Department of Labor's lower budget. Using the lower budget as a more reasonable measure of the upper limit of true poverty, as some have suggested, would more than double the proportion who are poor by the usual measure.

Equality and Progress

Traditionally, the United States has been considered to be the country in which the democratic vision of economic equality has come closest to realization. And, as we've seen, it has even been argued that the American commitment to equality has gone too far, with unfortunate consequences for economic growth and well-being. In this view, the wealthy need the lure of potential riches in order to maintain the incentive to invest in profitable enterprises. And, at the other end of the scale, coddling by the welfare state makes people too content with their lot in life, reduces their motivation for hard work, and ultimately weakens the economy as a whole (Kristol, 1979; Gilder, 1981; Scott, 1982).

But if we compare the United States with other industrial countries, these arguments seem unconvincing. Most of those countries have gone further than we have in reducing inequality of incomes — *and* are outperforming the United States economically. The shares of the wealthiest and poorest segments of the population in several countries are compared in Table 4-6. It's apparent that there is a wide variation among these countries, both in the share of income held by the relatively wealthy and, even more strikingly, in the share held by the relatively poorest people. The income share of the most affluent fifth of the population ranges from just over a third in Sweden to nearly half in France, with the United States toward the more unequal end of the scale. The share of the lowest income fifth shows a similar but sharper pattern. The most unequal countries are Spain and France, with the United

States, Canada, and Australia not far behind. The poorest fifth of the Dutch population gets, proportionately, twice the share of income as their Spanish and French counterparts, and nearly twice the share of the poorest fifth of Americans.

Dividing the share of the richest by the share of the poorest gives a ratio of rich to poor that can serve as a shorthand guide to the width of the income gap in these countries. In the relatively egalitarian Netherlands, the most affluent fifth receives only about four times the income of the poorest. Sweden, Norway, and Japan also rank high on income equality. Only Spain and France, among these countries, have a more unequal distribution of income than the United States.

Does the greater income equality in countries like Sweden, Holland, or Japan interfere with economic efficiency? Simply mentioning a country like Japan is enough to suggest the limits of this argument. The evidence in the table, in fact, supports the opposite conclusion: Greater equality and a stronger economy most often go hand in hand. Measured by gross national product per capita, *most* of the countries with a smaller income gap have moved ahead of the United States in economic performance. Those with similar or greater income inequality remain behind. There are exceptions; England has relatively high income equality and a smaller GNP per capita. Japan does, too, but in this case, the measure is misleading since Japan is simply moving up from further behind — and at a pace that has become the envy of other industrialized countries. (The French data are somewhat misleading, too; France has an unusually large agricultural population, which tends to make its income data less di-

Finally, it's important to understand that all of these measures consider only the number and proportion of people who are poor *at any one point in time*. But not all of those who are poor at some point stay poor all their lives. And not all nonpoor manage to stay out of poverty for very long. When we talk about "the poor," we are not describing an unchanging group of people who are poor year in and year out, but a fraction of a much larger population that is at risk of falling into poverty. For these people, one misfortune — the loss of a job, a serious illness, an accident — could make the difference between being in or out of official poverty.

rectly comparable with those of other advanced countries and masks a lower spread of inequality in its urban population.)

The reasons for this positive relationship between equality and economic progress are complex. One of the most important is the amount of unemployment a society is willing to tolerate. High unemployment is part of the explanation for the very low share of income earned by the lowest fifth in the United States. Full employment policies are one of the most important reasons why countries like Sweden or Japan have a more equal spread of income. At the same time, of course, full employment means that these countries are making better and more productive use of their human resources, leading to a stronger, more competitive economy.

Table 4-6

Income inequality and economic performance, selected countries

Country	Income share of lowest fifth, %	Income share of highest fifth, %	Ratio of highest fifth to lowest fifth	GNP per capita	Rank according to GNP per capita
Netherlands	9.1	36.3	4.0	$10,841	4
Sweden	7.3	35.0	4.8	12,337	2
Norway	6.6	36.9	5.6	10,860	3
Japan	7.1	41.9	5.9	8,891	8
United Kingdom	6.1	39.3	6.4	7,054	10
West Germany	6.5	46.3	7.1	12,387	1
Canada	5.2	40.5	7.8	9,257	7
Australia	4.8	40.9	8.5	8,259	9
United States	4.9	42.1	8.6	10,739	5
Spain	4.2	45.0	10.7	5,294	11
France	4.2	47.1	11.2	10,656	6

Income equality figures are for various periods in the late 1960s and early 1970s. GNP per capita is from 1979, standardized to value of American dollar. Shares of income are adjusted to account for differences in average size of households.

Source: Adapted from Malcolm Sawyer, *Income Distribution in OECD Countries* (Paris: Organization for Economic Cooperation and Development, 1976). Reprinted with permission.

How large is that fraction? A University of Michigan study, following the economic progress of 5,000 American families since the late 1960s, estimates that about 25 percent of Americans can expect to fall below the official poverty line in at least one year over a nine-year period. Again, this means that more than 55 million Americans are now poised precariously close to the poverty line.

Like the remarkable stability in the distribution of income and wealth, the persistence (and recent growth) of poverty presents a striking paradox. How can there have been so little progress despite the growth of the welfare state — a welfare state that has been criticized for pushing too hard for equality and for throwing money at the poor?

To understand this paradox, we need to look more carefully at that much-maligned abstraction, the welfare state, itself.

Welfare: Myths and Realities

The argument that American society has become overly egalitarian centers on the modern welfare system. We often hear that too many able-bodied people are on welfare and that welfare benefits are so high that it is possible to live all too comfortably without working. We also hear that the growth of the welfare state has sapped the strength of the economy and contributed to the problems of inflation and recession. These arguments are frequently used to justify sharp cutbacks in government spending — at least in spending for those government activities that mainly benefit people with low incomes. This perspective was strongly argued by the incoming president in 1981:

> Our society's commitment to an adequate social safety net contains powerful, inherently expansionary tendencies. If left unchecked, these forces threaten eventual fiscal ruin and serious challenges to basic social values of independence and self-support. The Federal government has created so many entitlements for unnecessary benefits that it is essential to begin paring them back. (Reagan, 1981)

But, if an overgenerous welfare state has channeled so much money from the affluent to the poor, why has there been so little change in the distribution of income? And why has poverty remained such a stubborn problem?

Part of the answer is that the popular image of a huge, out-of-control welfare state is misleading. In fact, the American welfare state turns out to be quite meager when compared with the welfare spending of other industrial countries. It has grown much less in recent years than is often supposed, especially in the programs that directly transfer money to the poor. It provides little beyond a minimum level of subsistence for most of the people who depend on it. And the great majority of those people are not lazy shirk-

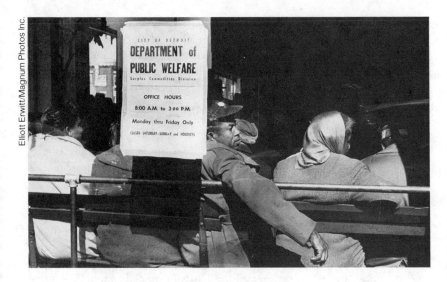

Elliott Erwitt/Magnum Photos Inc.

"The social safety net is pitched precariously close to the ground in the United States."

ers or cheaters, but people who, for one reason or another, are unable to work regularly enough, at high enough wages, to earn an adequate living in our present economy. Let's consider each of these points in turn.

The Myth of the Exploding Welfare State

The picture of an overgrown welfare state is usually based on the sheer amount of money the government spends on social welfare. And at first glance, this seems a very large amount, indeed. What the federal government calls *social welfare expenditures* grew from about $24 billion in 1950 to $428 billion in 1979. As a proportion of all government spending, social welfare expenditures were about 37 percent in 1950. By 1979 they had grown to 57 percent of all government outlays. (This figure includes local, state, and federal government spending.) As a proportion of gross national product, the growth of social welfare appears even more striking. From just under 9 percent of GNP in 1950, it rose to almost 19 percent by 1979.

On the surface, this would appear to be a dramatic surge of egalitarianism. But remember the trickiness of figures on the growth of government. We need to probe more deeply, to ask several questions about the apparent explosion in welfare spending.

To begin with, how much of this spending is actually targeted to the poor? Much less than it first appears. Most of these funds pay for what are called *social insurance programs,* such as Social Security, unemployment insurance, retirement systems for public employees and railroad workers, and workers compensation for people injured on the job. In 1979 these programs together accounted for about 45 percent of all social welfare spending.

These programs share two characteristics. First, they are paid for (at least in substantial part) out of special "trust funds" to which the recipients have contributed in one way or another. Second, they are for everyone, not just the poor. They do involve a great deal of money. But they are not what most people mean when they speak of "welfare." Nor, certainly, is government spending for schools, which accounted for another 25 percent of social welfare spending in 1979. If these are taken out of the picture, how much is left?

At the end of the 1970s, only 15 percent of all social welfare spending went for what the government calls *public aid,* chiefly the Aid to Families with Dependent Children (AFDC) program and the Supplemental Security Income (SSI) program for low-income people who are aged, blind, or disabled.

In both of these programs, the number of recipients has declined considerably, whether measured in absolute figures (as in Figure 4-4) or as a proportion of the total population. There were about 300,000 fewer people on SSI in 1981 than in 1975, and almost 900,000 fewer people receiving benefits under AFDC. Not surprisingly, the total amount the government spent on these programs, when corrected for inflation, dropped as well during the same period. Up to now, we've looked at social welfare spending without factoring in the decline in the value of the dollar. But this gives a very misleading picture of the "growth" of welfare expenses. The total cost of AFDC payments was about $9.2 billion in 1975 and rose to nearly $12.5 billion in 1980 — an increase of about 35 percent. But the consumer price index jumped 53 percent, so that, in constant dollars, welfare payments actually declined substantially.

Figure 4-4

The shrinking welfare system: recipients of AFDC and SSI, various years

Source: Adapted from *Statistical Abstract of the United States, 1982–83* (Washington, D.C.: Government Printing Office, 1983), p. 344.

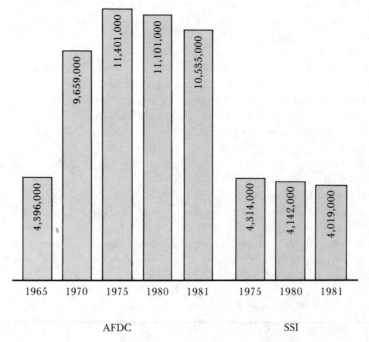

	Income-tested transfers	
Year	Cash	Cash and food stamps
1965	.71	.71
1966	.69	.69
1967	.75	.75
1968	.79	.79
1969	.89	.89
1970	1.11	1.18
1971	1.26	1.44
1972	1.16	1.36
1973	1.07	1.28
1974	1.24	1.49
1975	1.34	1.73
1976	1.29	1.71
1977	1.10	1.55
1978	1.08	1.38
1979	1.02	1.36
1980	1.05	—
1981	—	—

Income-tested benefits are those that, like AFDC, require that their recipients have incomes below a certain set level.
Source: Adapted from Peter T. Gottschalk, "Have We Already Lost the War On Poverty?" in Hearings, *The 1982 Economic Report of the President*, U.S. Congress, Joint Economic Committee, February 1982, part 2, p. 94.

Table 4-7
The shrinking welfare system: transfer payments as a proportion of national income

The same picture emerges if we consider the trends in cash transfers to the poor as a share of national income. Table 4-7 shows that the greatest growth in the system of benefits for the poor came during the late 1960s and early 1970s. Since the mid-1970s, cash transfers have declined significantly in proportion to the rest of the country's income. Even if we add in food stamps, one of the most important "in-kind" benefits for the poor and near-poor, the trend is the same. As the economist Peter Gottschalk puts it, "the 'welfare explosion' was contained well before the budget cuts of 1981. . . . By 1980 we were spending the same proportion of national income on welfare as we were spending a decade earlier" (1982, pp. 90–91). It's important to bear in mind, too, that this proportion was only *1.4* percent of the nation's total income, even before the sharp cutbacks in welfare spending that began in 1981.

The Myth of Lavish Welfare

Even though the total spending on welfare payments is declining, we often hear that individual's welfare *benefits* are too high. In this view, the welfare system has become so generous that the poor can now live better by going on welfare than by working. Newspapers occasionally print highly indignant stories of welfare mothers who have been discovered to own pleasant homes and luxury cars. And public officials sometimes juggle statistics and announce that welfare families can now receive $20,000 (or some other startling figure) by adroit manipulation of different benefits. No one seriously doubts that some people may manage to take advantage of the welfare system in this way; but is this a useful or accurate understanding of what *usually* happens in that system?

The available statistics show clearly that, on the contrary, the social safety net is pitched precariously close to the ground in the United States. Some illustrations:

- AFDC benefits vary widely across different states (see Table 4-8). But *in none of them* can welfare alone pull a family with no other earnings above the poverty line. In 22 states, the maximum payment is below $300 per month, less than *half* the poverty line for a family of three; in 11 southern states, it is below $200. In Mississippi, the maximum payment is less than $100 for a three-person family per month, or a shade over $3 a day. The average welfare payment in Texas was smaller in 1980 than it was 10 years earlier, despite a decade's worth of inflation in the cost of living.

Table 4-8
State monthly AFDC payments for a family of three, November 1981 (poverty level = $589)

State	Monthly welfare payment	State	Monthly welfare payment	State	Monthly welfare payment
Alaska	$571	Oregon	$339	Missouri	$248
New York	$507	North Dakota	$334	Nevada	$241
Vermont	$506	Pennsylvania	$332	New Mexico	$233
California	$506	New Hampshire	$326	West Virginia	$206
Connecticut	$498	South Dakota	$321	Arizona	$202
Wisconsin	$473	Wyoming	$315	Florida	$195
Hawaii	$468	Colorado	$313	North Carolina	$192
Michigan	$464	Virginia	$310	Kentucky	$188
Minnesota	$446	Idaho	$305	Georgia	$183
Washington (State)	$415	Illinois	$302	Louisiana	$173
Massachusetts	$379	Maine	$301	South Carolina	$129
Rhode Island	$367	Oklahoma	$282	Arkansas	$122
Iowa	$360	Montana	$278	Tennessee	$122
New Jersey	$360	Maryland	$270	Alabama	$118
Kansas	$353	Delaware	$266	Texas	$118
Nebraska	$350	Ohio	$263	Mississippi	$ 96
Utah	$348	Indiana	$255		

Source: Benefits from Walter Guzzardi, "Who Will Care for the Poor" *Fortune*, June 28, 1982, p. 39. Reprinted with permission. Poverty level for three-person family, 1981, calculated from *Statistical Abstract of the United States, 1982–83* (Washington, D.C.: Government Printing Office, 1983), p. 417.

- Inflation reduced the real value of average welfare benefits nationwide by almost 20 percent during the 1970s, according to an analysis by the U.S. Department of Health and Human Services (Joe, 1982, p. 3).

- Even though most welfare recipients *can* combine more than one kind of benefit, the resulting total still usually remains very low; it is very difficult to make a good living on welfare alone, even in those states that provide relatively high benefits. In only *one* state, Alaska, would the combined maximum benefits from AFDC and food stamps bring a family over the poverty line in 1981; in half of the states, the combination would produce an income of 75 percent of the poverty level (Joe, 1982, p. 4). The New Jersey study cited earlier found that even in that relatively high-benefit state, AFDC and food stamps combined only brought a family 59 percent of what it took to purchase a "minimally adequate" amount of food, shelter, transportation, and other necessities (Blaustein, 1982, p. 44).

- Families that combine work with welfare have a better chance of breaking the poverty barrier. But even combining earnings with several kinds of benefits usually only brings these families just over the poverty line. In 1981, according to calculations by the University of Chicago's Center for the Study of Social Policy, the monthly disposable income of working AFDC families ranged from 69 percent of the poverty level (in Texas and Alabama) to 130 percent (in Vermont), with an average for all the states of 101 percent of the poverty line. Disposable income, in this study, included earnings plus benefits from AFDC, food stamps, and low-income energy assistance. Moreover, changes in welfare rules in the early 1980s make eligibility for these benefits much more difficult for the working poor, considerably diminishing the potential income from combining work and welfare (Joe, 1982, p. 16).

Thus, the American welfare system is a fairly skimpy one overall. This is especially true if we compare it, as Figure 4-5 does, with welfare benefits in other industrial societies. And the low American benefits help explain why poverty has persisted here in spite of the growth of the welfare state, and why the overall picture of income inequality has changed so little.

Here we need to look at another view of welfare and poverty that has gained considerable currency in recent years. We have already seen that a large and growing share of the benefits the welfare state provides to the poor are in-kind benefits. In 1964, at the start of the War on Poverty, only about 19 percent of total benefits were in-kind, the rest were cash. By 1980, 61 percent were in-kind, 39 percent cash. In that year, in-kind benefits amounted to about $71 billion, of which $50 billion (70 percent) went for medical care, $9 billion for food stamps, $4 billion for child nutrition programs, and about $5 billion for housing subsidies (*Statistical Abstract of the U.S., 1982–83*, p. 318). Critics have pointed out that these in-kind benefits are not counted as income when the government counts the number of

Figure 4-5

Public spending on social welfare, selected countries, 1977. (The benefits covered in this chart include public assistance for children and the disabled, unemployment insurance, workers compensation, health care and old age insurance. Because these benefits are defined differently in the various countries, the comparisons should be understood as rough ones.)

Source: Data from Ira Magaziner and Robert Reich, *Minding America's Business* (New York: Harcourt Brace Jovanovich, 1982), p. 16.

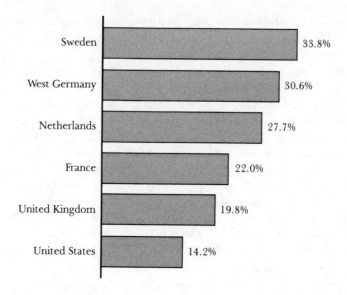

Sweden	33.8%
West Germany	30.6%
Netherlands	27.7%
France	22.0%
United Kingdom	19.8%
United States	14.2%

people below the poverty line or estimates the shares of income received by different groups in the population. As a result, these critics argue, the usual statistics greatly overstate the number of poor people in the United States. And they correspondingly underestimate the trend toward equality. Some even argue that the growth of in-kind benefits has, for all practical purposes, abolished poverty in the United States (Anderson, 1980).

The argument is technical, but important. It could profoundly change the way we look at poverty and inequality, and how we design the social policies to deal with them. How accurate is it?

The growth of in-kind benefits *is* significant — but not to the degree that this argument maintains. First, not all of the money the government spends on the poor actually reaches them. This has serious, and sometimes bizarre, consequences for the argument about in-kind benefits and poverty. Consider the case of medical benefits, which represent the largest proportion of in-kind benefits for the poor. When we say that the government spends this money "on the poor," what we really mean is that the government reimburses doctors and hospitals for *treating* the poor. The poor do not receive the money and cannot use it as if it were money. The problem with calling such benefits "income" can be illustrated by considering that, using this logic, a poor person who became seriously ill and incurred thousands of dollars worth of government-subsidized hospital expenses would suddenly and miraculously be counted as no longer poor — and might even have to be considered rich!

Taking out the presumed money value of medical benefits dramatically reduces the impact of in-kind benefits on the official poverty rates. Thus, according to the most recent attempt to calculate the effect of noncash benefits on poverty (a study done for the Census Bureau by the economist Timothy Smeeding), counting such benefits at the level of what they would actually cost in the "market" would have reduced the official poverty rate by almost half in 1979, from 11.1 to 6.4 percent. But without the inclusion of medical care costs as "income," all the other in-kind benefits together would have reduced the rate by just 1.7 percent (*Newsweek*, April 26, 1982, p. 35). Clearly, these noncash benefits are important, and they have certainly contributed to the well-being of low-income people. But they have not "abolished" poverty, nor even come close to doing so.

A second, more subtle problem is that these arguments, painstakingly applied to the income of poor people, aren't applied equally to the sources of income for middle-class people or the rich. But if we want to understand how various noncash benefits have affected the pattern of inequality, we must look at the noncash benefits of all groups, not just the poor. Some of these benefits come from private employers, such as employer-paid health plans and other fringe benefits that now are an important part of the compensation of middle-class workers. Also, about 16 million households above the poverty level received government benefits under the Medicare program for the aged in 1980. And, as we'll see in a moment, there are many other ways in which the government transfers forms of income to the affluent that do not appear in official statistics.

Most of the growth in the welfare state, then, has come about through the growth of social insurance programs. Only a fraction of government spending for social welfare has gone to the typical public assistance programs, which have declined in recent years. And benefits to needy individuals are typically both low and declining. It isn't just the *amount* of government welfare spending that is at issue in debates about welfare, however, but its appropriateness.

It's often argued that the welfare system supports people who don't really need it and who ought to be working instead. We have all heard about able-bodied welfare chiselers who live lavishly on the taxpayer's money. We've seen that few welfare recipients are lavishly supported in any case. Now let's look at the characteristics of those people who receive welfare payments and try to understand why social welfare spending increased so much during the 1960s and 1970s. Who receives welfare — and why? Did the growth of welfare really represent a sudden surge of excessive demands for equality? Did it represent a case of throwing money at problems — what some critics have called a "social pork barrel"?

The reasons for the growth of the modern welfare system are complex. They involve not only changing attitudes toward welfare, but changing social needs as well. Those changing needs, in turn, are related to broad demographic shifts in American society. Two such changes are especially important: the rising proportion of older people in the population and the growth in the proportion of families headed by women.

The Myth of the Welfare Chiselers

The largest part of social welfare spending goes for the needs of a growing population of older people.

The largest part of government social welfare spending goes to the aged, and the aged's share of that spending has grown rapidly. The reasons are clear. Between 1960 and 1981, the number of people 65 and over jumped from 16.7 to 26.3 million, from a little more than 9 percent to more than 11 percent of the population. By comparing the proportion of older people in the population to those in the conventional working-age range of 18 to 64, we get what is called a *dependency ratio*. In 1960 the dependency ratio stood at just over 16; that is, there were 16 over-65s for every 100 people between 18 and 64. By 1981, there were 19 (*Statistical Abstract of the U.S., 1982–83*, p. 324).

The rise in the number and proportion of older, and often economically dependent, people is compounded by another important change in modern American society. Many more people now live alone, apart from their families and from the material support that families can provide. This is especially true for the aged. The number of people living alone rose by almost 12 million between 1960 and 1981; 4.5 million were over 65, and almost 4 million were women over 65 (*Statistical Abstract of the U.S., 1982–83*, p. 44).

The aged, then, are both more numerous and less often supported by a larger family. This helps explain why their share of government spending has grown so rapidly, and it explains a large part of the overall rise in government spending on the welfare state.

A somewhat similar change helps explain the growth in welfare for the nonaged. We've seen that the welfare rolls expanded rapidly during the late 1960s and early 1970s: There were 4.4 million AFDC recipients in 1965, 9.7 million in 1970. What caused this rise? Many factors, including improved benefits, easier eligibility, and more aggressive assertion of legal rights by people eligible for benefits. But underlying all of these was another broad demographic change — the increase in families headed by women. In 1960 about 1 in every 10 American families was headed by a woman; by 1981, better than 1 in 7.

For reasons we'll examine further in Chapter 6 (including gender discrimination in the labor market and the lack of adequate child care), this trend has resulted in a growing number of families who are disproportionately dependent on public aid. (It is sometimes argued that the welfare system itself is responsible for the rising proportion of women heading families. We will look at this issue, too, in Chapter 6, but we'll anticipate the conclusion here: Most research suggests that, if welfare does have an effect on family stability, it is not a very large one.)

Both trends mean that the number of people on welfare who are of working age, able-bodied, and without severely limiting problems of child care, is quite small (Table 4-9). Seven out of ten AFDC recipients are children, and among them, seven out of ten in turn are eleven years old or younger. Only 1 in 25 AFDC families consists of a couple with an able-bodied father in the home. As Senator Daniel P. Moynihan (D–N.Y.) has written, AFDC "is not a program to subsidize leisure, it is a program to enable a hard-pressured woman to keep a roof over the heads, clothes on the backs, and food in the mouths of her children" (cited in Weinraub, 1981). (Note that Table 4-9 also undermines two other common stereotypes about welfare in America: Most welfare families are not large, and most are white.)

These demographic trends also affect the distribution of medical benefits under the Medicaid program. Of the roughly $23 billion in health-care payments under Medicaid in 1980, well over a third went to the aged, close to another third to the disabled and blind, and another seventh to children in the AFDC program. All told, more than four-fifths of Medicaid benefits went to people whose age, youth, or disability prevented them, for all practical purposes, from regular participation in the labor force (*Statistical Abstract of the U.S., 1982–83*, p. 334).

Does all of this mean that there are no welfare cheaters — able-bodied, working-age people collecting welfare when they could be working? Of course not. But it does show that *most* of the benefits and services of the modern welfare system go to people who genuinely need some form of public support.

The fact that the welfare system is mainly a response to the needs of the old, the ill and disabled, and women facing severe obstacles to steady (or well-paid) work should make us think twice about some of the popular beliefs about how welfare affects the economy. It isn't clear how cutting back on benefits to the disabled, or to unskilled single mothers with preschool

Table 4-9

Characteristics of
families and children on
AFDC, 1979

Families	Year		
	1975	1977	1979
Recipient families (1,000)	3,420	3,523	3,428
	Percent distribution		
Metropolitan areas	78.5	77.1	77.8
Nonmetropolitan areas	21.5	22.9	22.2
White	50.2	52.6	51.7
Black	44.3	43.0	43.9
Native American and other	5.5	4.4	4.4
Families with 1 child	37.9	40.3	42.5
Families with 2 children	26.0	27.3	28.0
Families with 3 children	16.1	16.1	15.5
Families with 4 or 5 children	15.0	12.7	11.4
Families with 6 or more children	5.0	3.6	2.5
Years as recipient:			
Under 1 year	27.7	30.8	28.5
1–3 years	27.3	29.1	28.2
4–5 years	18.8	15.4	15.4
6–10 years	19.3	18.5	19.9
Over 10 years	6.3	5.4	7.1

Children	Year		
	1975	1977	1979
Recipient children (1,000)	8,121	7,836	7,230
	Percent distribution		
Basis for eligibility:			
Father is—			
Deceased	3.7	2.6	2.2
Incapacitated	7.7	5.9	5.3
Unemployed	3.7	5.0	4.1
Absent from home:			
Divorced	19.4	21.4	20.3
Separated	28.6	25.5	24.4
Not married to mother	31.0	33.8	37.8
Other	4.3	4.1	4.4
Mother is absent, not father	1.6	1.6	1.5
Age:			
Under 6, including unborn	34.6	35.1	36.5
6–11	33.7	33.9	33.0
12–17	28.5	27.6	27.1
18–20	2.4	2.6	2.7
Unknown	.8	.9	.9

Source: Adapted from *Statistical Abstract of the United States, 1982–83* (Washington, D.C.: Government Printing Office, 1983), p. 343.

children, could boost the incentive to work — and hence boost the economy — in any meaningful way. This is *not,* by any means, to say that the present welfare system is necessarily the best or the most efficient way to meet the needs of these groups. But it does mean that those needs must be taken into account in considering realistic alternatives to the current system.

At the same time, the distribution of welfare helps us understand one of the reasons why the growth of the welfare state hasn't significantly changed the picture of income inequality. Most welfare spending doesn't shift money so much from rich to poor, as from people of working age to the old and the very young, and from the relatively healthy to the ill and disabled. To an important extent, then, the system transfers money sideways rather than up and down the income scale (Gough, 1979, chap. 6).

A final issue about the distribution of welfare deserves mention. It is commonly assumed that the welfare population consists of a vast "underclass" (Auletta, 1981) of people who are more or less permanently dependent on the welfare system. This perception, in turn, is partly responsible for the widespread belief that welfare itself fosters dependency in those who receive it (Kristol, 1979; Mead, 1982). Welfare is often said to demoralize the poor, to turn its recipients into incompetent wards of the government. But the University of Michigan's Panel Study of Income Dynamics (Duncan and Coe, 1981) has found that the vast majority of welfare recipients do *not* fit the stereotype of the underclass. Over the course of the 10-year period between 1969 and 1978, almost a fourth of the studied population received some kind of welfare benefits. But less than 1 in 100 people lived in families who were dependent on welfare for more than half of their income throughout those 10 years. Contrary to common assumptions, most people who received some welfare *also* worked; and relatively few remained persistently dependent on welfare for years at a time. For most of those who received it, welfare operated as a kind of "insurance" to cover temporary periods of lowered resources. Most recipients eventually found other sources of income, either enough to take them off welfare rolls altogether or, at least, to reduce greatly their reliance on welfare.

The Michigan study did find a group of recipients who appeared to fit the image of a permanent welfare underclass, but it was only a fraction of the total welfare population. About 8 percent of welfare recipients depended on welfare benefits to provide more than half of their income for at least eight of the ten years studied. For this smaller group, the more normal process of eventually moving out of dependency seems to have been blocked.

Now let's consider a final reason why government policy has had less impact on the distribution of American income and wealth than is often supposed. We have just seen one of the reasons: The scope and generosity of the system of government benefits to the poor has been greatly exaggerated. We now need to consider another reason: The government does not

A Permanent "Underclass"?

simply transfer money *downward* from the affluent to the poor. It also, in a bewildering variety of ways, transfers money upward, to the middle class and the wealthy.

The "Upside-Down" Welfare System

The government is often seen as a huge, bureaucratic Robin Hood, taking from the rich and giving to the poor, with what some regard as disastrous results. But the actual workings of the modern welfare state are far more complicated. The poor are by no means the only group that receives welfare — if by welfare we mean money and other forms of support that are not earned in the market and that are paid for by public funds. We have already encountered some of these benefits — government subsidies to business, for example. But there are many other examples as well. In modern American society, the government is less a Robin Hood than a giant machine that sifts and sorts the country's wealth in several directions at once. Virtually every decision made at any level of government, about how it will get money as well as how it will spend it, has consequences — sometimes very large ones — for the pattern of inequality in America. Taken together, these decisions add up to a largely hidden welfare system, alongside of, and often counterbalancing, the more visible one.

How much is transferred to the affluent, and to large corporations, through the hidden welfare system is unknown. (We know much more about the scope of welfare for the poor since every penny is doled out under the increasingly watchful eye of public officials. But no one looks as hard at the many forms of welfare for the affluent.) It's safe to say, though, that the overall amounts are enormous, and that they are growing. We'll now look at three main ways in which public resources are shifted upward by the government toward the more affluent: through loopholes in the tax system, through special subsidies and loans, and through the broader pattern of government spending in support of some activities rather than others.

The Hidden Welfare System I: Tax Expenditures

Most people think of the tax system as a *collector* of money. But the tax system also *spends* money in a number of ways. Most importantly, it can allow an individual, or a corporation, to pay lower taxes, or no taxes at all. In the United States, the government does this for many different groups, for many different reasons.

Popularly, these mechanisms are called tax loopholes. Officially, they are called *tax expenditures* because, by offering these tax breaks, the government is doing in effect what it does when it spends money directly. That is, the money cannot be used for other purposes. And, in both cases, someone wins and someone else loses. Most often, as one study puts it, tax expenditures "result in an upside-down welfare program — the richer the taxpayer, the greater the benefit he, she, or it receives" (*Common Cause*, 1978, p. iii).

Tax expenditures are a fast-growing form of hidden welfare. In 1975, they amounted to about $93 billion; by 1984, about $342 billion. And as a proportion of gross national product, they have grown much more rapidly than ordinary government spending (U.S. Office of Management and Budget, 1983, p. G-28).

What does this hidden spending pay for — and who gets the benefit? Table 4-10 shows the 12 largest categories of tax expenditures in 1981. Some of these go directly to businesses, like the investment tax credit — the largest single item — which allows businesses to deduct a substantial part of the costs of new plants or equipment. In 1981, of $206 billion worth of tax expenditures, $48 billion went directly to corporations. But some tax expen-

Tax expenditure	Amount ($ billions)
Investment tax credit (other than on employee stock ownership plans and rehabilitated structures)	19,975
Deductibility of nonbusiness state and local taxes (other than on owner-occupied homes or gasoline)	17,305
Capital gains (other than for farming, iron ore, timber, and coal)	15,695
Exclusion of employer contributions for medical insurance premiums and medical care	15,215
Deductibility of interests on owner-occupied homes	14,760
Net exclusion of pension contributions and earnings—employer plans	14,740
Deductibility of property tax on owner-occupied homes	8,975
Exclusion of OASI benefits for retired workers	8,695
Reduced rates on first $100,000 of corporate homes	7,510
Deductibility of charitable contributions other than education and health	7,095
Exclusion of interest on general-purpose state and local debt	6,525
Capital gains at death	5,085

Table 4-10
Major tax expenditures, fiscal year 1981

Source: U.S. Congressional Budget Office, *Tax Expenditures: Current Issues and Five-year Budget Projections for Fiscal Years 1981–1985* (Washington, D.C.: Government Printing Office, April 1980) p. 22.

ditures are available to a wide range of individuals on a relatively equal basis, like the deduction of OASI (Social Security) benefits. And a few (not listed because the amounts are smaller) are only for low-income people, such as the tax deductibility of public assistance payments. But even a quick look at the table suggests that *most* tax expenditures, even when they don't go to corporations, are still most likely to favor upper-income people. And a congressional study of how some of them are distributed among different income groups confirms this.

Table 4-11 shows that more than 90 percent of all income from the capital gains tax exclusion in 1979 went to people with incomes above $30,000 a year, and more than half went to people who made more than $200,000. Among the latter, the average amount of money saved through the capital gains exemption was almost $162,000 per taxpayer. At the bottom, for those few taxpayers with incomes under $5,000 who received the capital gains tax benefits, the average benefit was $58 (U.S. Congress, House, Committee on Ways and Means, 1980, p. 19).

Moreover, these statistics understate the tax benefits for the affluent because they do not reflect changes in the tax laws in the early 1980s that further reduced tax rates on capital gains (and on other forms of unearned income, such as dividends and interest). For example, the Economic Recovery Tax Act of 1981 reduced taxes on long-term capital gains from 28 to 21 percent — about the level paid by a married couple with an annual taxable income of $12,000 (U.S. Congress, Joint Economic Committee, 1982a, p. 106).

Matched against direct government spending for low-income people, these tax benefits are impressive indeed. In 1979, people making over $50,000 a year received *more than twice as much money from the capital gains*

Table 4-11
Tax distribution of capital gains tax exclusion, by income group, 1979

Income group	No. of tax returns (millions)	Amount of benefit ($ billions)
Below $5,000	$ 51	$ 3
$5,000–10,000	489	88
$10,000–15,000	636	182
$15,000–20,000	641	300
$20,000–30,000	1,075	773
$30,000–50,000	1,030	1,487
$50,000–100,000	548	2,441
$100,000–200,000	143	1,967
$200,000+	51	8,241
Total	4,664	15,482

Source: Adapted from U.S. Congress, House, Committee on Ways and Means, "Estimates of Federal Tax Expenditures, for Fiscal Years 1980–1985," Washington, D.C., March 1980.

exclusion alone than the federal government paid to all recipients of AFDC, and slightly more than the federal government spent on AFDC and food stamp benefits *combined (Statistical Abstract of the U.S., 1982–83*, p. 318). And little-known changes in the estate-tax laws in 1981, raising the income level at which estates may begin to be taxed at death, will lower yearly federal revenues by an amount at least as large as what the government spent on public service employment programs for low-income people in 1980 (Kinsley, 1981, p. 20; and *Statistical Abstract of the U.S., 1982–83*, p. 319).

Tax expenditures help explain why corporate taxes have fallen consistently in recent years. And they are the source of the spectacular tax inequities often reported in the media. In 1978, for example, 14 major corporations with combined earnings of $3.5 billion paid *no* federal income taxes, while the average rate paid by 145 corporations in a congressional survey was about the same as that paid by a family of four making $31,000 a year (cited in the *San Francisco Examiner*, June 29, 1980). In 1977, according to Internal Revenue Service data, tax loopholes enabled more than 500 people with incomes in excess of $100,000 to pay *no* federal taxes (*U.S. News and World Report*, April 28, 1980, p. 56).

Even more importantly, tax expenditures help explain why the American tax system, on balance, has had little overall impact on the distribution of income. Though, of course, the absolute amounts of money the government takes from rich individuals (or corporations) are larger than those taken from the less affluent, the best evidence suggests that the *proportions* taken from different income groups are roughly *equal*. In the language of tax economics, the tax system is thus a roughly *proportional* one when all its various parts and levels are put together, including state and local sales and property taxes as well as income taxes. (Taxes that take a greater share as they move up the income scale are called *progressive* taxes, while those that take a greater share at lower income levels, such as sales taxes, are called *regressive*.) According to a study by the economists Morgan Reynolds and Eugene Smolensky, the fact that the tax system shifted from slightly progressive in the 1950s to proportional or even slightly regressive by the 1970s (caused in part by the decline in the share of corporate income taxes) helps explain why American income distribution remained so persistently unequal, despite the substantial growth of government transfer during that period (Reynolds and Smolensky, 1977).

Besides tax expenditures, the government offers a number of special subsidies and loans that, by serving some social interests at the expense of others, also affect the distribution of income and wealth in the United States. The subsidies and loans take many forms, from outright bailouts of corporations in trouble and loan guarantees enabling businesses to compete more effectively against foreign corporations to federally backed loans, at favorable rates, for home mortgages or farm expansion.

The Hidden Welfare System II: Subsidies and Credit

In 1981 the federal government spent an estimated $142 billion on these credit arrangements. About two-fifths were direct loans, the rest loan guarantees (where the government promises to back up loans issued by other sources). A substantial part of this sum doesn't appear in the federal budget; and most of it escapes attention in the usual debates about government spending. But, as the Congressional Budget Office bluntly put it in a 1980 study, "some people — those who get more credit and income — are made better off; others, who get less, are made worse off" (U.S. Congress, Congressional Budget Office, 1980, p. 20).

The best-known examples of this kind of "public welfare" are the huge federal bailouts of major corporations that (like other welfare recipients) have failed to make it in the "free" market. All told, federally assisted credit to a few key, troubled industries, such as shipbuilding, aircraft, steel, and autos, came to about $4 billion in 1981, or about the same as the government paid for child nutrition programs. But other, less spectacular subsidies have been more important — and costly — over the long run. They include subsidies for farmers, housing, and businesses.

The federal government has been deeply involved in subsidizing agriculture since the 1930s. Most people still identify the farmer as a particularly bright example of rugged American individualism in action. But much of America's farming is now in the hands of corporate business. And these large farmers, as one critic puts it, are "protected against every contingency by a dizzying array of federal assistance programs that make the Chrysler bailout look like small change" (Chapman, 1980). The most important are price support programs that guarantee farmers a predetermined level of prices for many crops, whatever may happen in the market. The government also lends money on favored terms to farmers for new land and other investments, provides emergency loans in case of natural disasters or poor market conditions, and in many other ways provides protection against the ups and downs of the economy — again, much as public assistance does for poor people, only with less public fanfare and less hassle for the recipients.

This type of "welfare" aggravates inequality in two ways. First, like most items on the hidden welfare budget, it provides more money for the affluent than anyone else. The biggest beneficiaries of these subsidies are the largest farmers. In 1978, according to the U.S. Senate Committee on Agriculture, the largest 10 percent of farms receiving payments under the price support program got almost 50 percent of the total payments. The smallest 50 percent of farms got less than 10 percent (U.S. Congress, Senate, Committee on Agriculture, 1979, p. 34).

The second effect is indirect. By guaranteeing prices, the government keeps food prices from falling, even when the market demand for food crops is low. The government therefore fuels inflation in food prices, which transfers money upward from consumers (especially the poor, who spend a bigger proportion of their income on food) to food producers.

In 1981 federal subsidies for public low-income housing cost about $2 billion. But subsidies for homeowners are far more costly. In that same year, the federal Housing Administration and the Veterans Administration had outstanding loan guarantees of more than $150 billion for residential mortgages. Like tax expenditures for mortgage interest, these programs have allowed many people to afford homes of their own. But they have also been applied unequally, since the population of homeowners is considerably better off than the population as a whole.

There are many other kinds of federal subsidies. One of the most important is the Export-Import Bank, a federal agency that grants credit and offers direct loans at reduced rates to American businesses engaged in export. The goal is to give them an edge against foreign competition. In fiscal year 1984, the special low interest rates on direct loans amounted to a tax-supported subsidy of about $3.8 billion.

Like most of the hidden welfare system, these loans work in ways that are mysterious to most people. An example: In 1980, American taxpayers (though few of them were aware of it) loaned the national airline of *Belgium,* Sabena, $31 million (at 8 percent interest) and promised to guarantee another $62 million, so that Sabena would buy two American-made DC-10 jets instead of the European-built Airbus (U.S. Congress, Congressional Budget Office, 1980, p. 40). By loaning money to the Belgians, the public helped support the McDonnell-Douglas Corporation and its stockholders; again, a process that shifted money upward toward the higher end of the income scale.

There are many more of these credit and subsidy programs. What all of them have in common is:

1. They transfer money, often in very substantial amounts, from average- or lower-income people upward to large corporations and the individuals who hold stock in them.

2. They are prime examples of what is often called "socialism for the rich" — that is, they supply money and support to corporate businesses, not according to the much-applauded principles of the free market, but according to need as determined by the government.

3. They are complicated, often hidden from public view, and therefore difficult to monitor or control.

This isn't to say that the *purposes* of such spending are necessarily wrong or inequitable. Loaning money at low rates to a floundering industry may save the jobs of thousands of workers and may help keep entire communities intact in the face of what would otherwise be economic disaster. What is important is that we recognize that a similar principle underlies government spending for *individuals* who have floundered in the "free" market. There, the government seeks to maintain the individual as a productive member of society. Applauding the government's commitment to corporate welfare while condemning its support for individuals facing economic difficulties seems less than consistent.

The Hidden Welfare System III: The Direction of Government Spending

Before leaving this subject, let's make a final, more general, point about the hidden welfare system. Government spending on goods and services now amounts to about a fifth of GNP. Given the sheer size of the government's economic role, every major spending decision it makes affects the living standards of large numbers of people and alters the distribution of income and wealth.

We can only touch on this complex and many-faceted process here. The government's decision to shift money into defense production, for example, offers a long-term subsidy to those corporations, usually among the biggest, which win most large defense contracts. This means more money and a higher living standard for high-level technical and managerial workers in defense industries and for the stockholders in those corporations. But it also means less money, fewer jobs, and a declining standard of living for (among others) teachers, construction workers, or the unskilled unemployed in the inner cities. Likewise, the decision to build superhighways that serve suburban commuters, instead of mass transportation for central cities, transfers public funds from inner-city residents to suburban ones. Both of these processes, like many other decisions about government spending, tend to increase inequality. None of these processes is easy to describe in precise, quantitative terms. None shows up in official statistics on the distribution of income and wealth. But all are crucially important in understanding how different groups fare in the welfare state.

Inequality and the Future

Looking at all the ways that the government is involved in the distribution of income and wealth, then, helps explain why inequality has persisted with so little change. What does the future hold for the pattern of inequality?

At least for the near future, the prospects are troubling. Many of the forces that have kept inequality from becoming greater are likely to be less effective in the future, while some of the forces working in the opposite direction, toward greater inequality, seem likely to grow in importance. Some of these changes involve public policies, others deeper shifts in the economy as a whole.

We'll look at these forces in more detail later, especially in Chapter 8, on the changing nature of work, and in Chapters 5 and 6, on the problems of racial and sexual discrimination. Here, we'll just sketch out a few broad trends that make the future ominous for the ideal of equality.

- *Persistent recession:* Unemployment tends to increase economic inequality by reducing the income of working people. And with each recent recession, the country has been left with higher unemployment than before. To the extent that it continues, this trend promises to increase economic inequality. The same point applies to the deliberate use of recession as a tool of government policy. Those who wind up unemployed as a result of being "drafted" into the "war on inflation" are disproportionately lower-income workers. And the trend toward rapid deindustrialization threatens to add an entire stratum of new poor (blue-collar workers displaced from declining industries) to the already fast-growing ranks of the disadvantaged.

- *The problem of the "shrinking middle":* The same trend toward industrial decline raises the spector of another long-term threat to economic equality: the disappearance of many of the kinds of jobs that in the past provided a path into the middle-class levels of the income scale. The crisis of manufacturing industry in the United States may mean a shift from relatively good jobs to a greater proportion of poorer ones. This trend will be a main focus of Chapter 8, so we'll only touch on it here. But its implications for economic inequality are profound — especially for young people. It may well mean a widening gulf between those able to secure high-level jobs and those consigned to the bottom of what has sometimes been called an "hourglass" economy.

- *The dismantling of the welfare state:* As we've seen, the pattern of inequality results not only from impersonal economic changes but, to an important extent, from deliberate government policy as well. Thus, one of the most important developments for the future of inequality is the attack on the welfare state. Dramatic cutbacks in transfer programs for lower-income people have already sharply increased the level of poverty in America and have deepened our already harsh inequalities in the distribution of income and wealth.

We've heard that shifting government funds from the poor will ultimately stimulate the economy and bring about a better standard of living for everyone. How realistic is this scenario? We have already noted some reasons for doubting that sheer economic growth, without more direct measures to develop jobs and services, can any longer promise to reduce poverty or to narrow the gap between rich and poor. But these are complex questions, and to approach them properly we'll need to consider two other aspects of inequality in America that we've held, somewhat artificially, out of the discussion so far: the problems of race and gender.

Summary

This chapter has examined the trends in economic inequality in the United States in recent years. Though it is often argued that American society has become quite egalitarian — even excessively so — in the distribution of income and wealth, the evidence suggests otherwise.

The distribution of income is highly skewed toward the most affluent fifth of the population. Though this pattern improved slightly up till the early 1970s, it has probably worsened somewhat since then. Personal wealth is distributed even more unequally, and is typically handed down from generation to generation.

Poverty in America declined during the 1960s, remained roughly stable throughout most of the 1970s, and has risen sharply in the 1980s. The slowdown in the War on Poverty has had especially harsh consequences for children and for those living in the inner cities.

The spread of inequality in the United States is considerably wider than in most other advanced industrial countries — including many whose economies have performed better than ours in recent years.

The American welfare system is neither as large, as expensive, or as wasteful as many critics argue. Our welfare benefits are meager compared with those of many other advanced industrial societies; most states pay benefits that are well below the poverty level; and most welfare recipients are needy women and children who lack realistic opportunities for jobs and earnings under current economic conditions.

At the other end of the scale, the government provides many benefits — often hidden — to corporations and affluent individuals, which distribute income upward and thus help maintain the pattern of inequality.

For Further Reading

Blaustein, Arthur I., ed. *The American Promise: Equal Justice and Economic Opportunity*, New Brunswick, N.J.: Transaction Books, 1982.

Blumberg, Paul. *Inequality in an Age of Decline*. New York: Oxford University Press, 1981.

Gough, Ian. *The Political Economy of the Welfare State*. London: Macmillan, 1979.

Green, Philip. *The Pursuit of Inequality*. New York: Pantheon, 1980.

Piven, Frances Fox, and Richard A. Cloward. *Poor Peoples' Movements: How They Succeed, Why They Fail*. New York: Pantheon, 1977.

5

Social Inequality II: Race

The ideal of racial equality, like that of economic equality, has had an ambiguous history in America. We have officially enshrined the belief that people of all races are created equal and that all should have an equal chance at society's benefits. But American history is also the history of the conquest, enslavement, and exclusion of racial minorities. The vision of racial equality and the harsh reality of unequal treatment have coexisted uneasily from the beginning, with the reality typically dominating the vision.

That uneasy balance was upset in the 1950s and 1960s as first blacks and then other minorities challenged the social, legal, and economic bases of racial inequality. These challenges created a legislative and judicial revolution that established equal treatment as the law of the land — in the school desegregation decision of 1955, the Civil Rights Act 10 years later, and the creation of affirmative action programs in every major American institution by the 1970s.

And these weren't just paper victories. They quickly began to produce results in the even tougher realm of social and economic practices. Minorities began, in significant numbers, to move into jobs and income brackets from which they had traditionally been excluded.

By the 1970s, though, these gains produced a counterreaction. We began to hear that the movement for racial equality had gone "too far." If anything, it was argued, minorities now received too much preferential treatment. The balance had tipped to the point where whites had become the victims of "reverse discrimination," bringing inequity, resentment, and social conflict. And the cost of enforcing the new antidiscrimination policies was, in this view, beginning to smother efficiency and productivity.

For some, the time had come to shift priorities. Here is how *Fortune*, echoing many influential social scientists, saw the issue in 1981:

> In the 1970's, however, the egalitarian thrust went too far. Its meaning became too muddled, its costs too high, its supporters too militant . . . egalitarians have neglected the truth that equality must live in tension with other values just as cherished. Now, without overreacting and subordinating equality too much, we need to restore and balance our values . . . with the understanding that perfect balance — precisely the proper measure of equality for every American — can never be achieved. (Guzzardi, 1981, p. 99)

These sentiments have gained a substantial foothold among intellectuals, government officials, and the public. And they lie behind a political agenda that, during the past several years, has sought to put the further pursuit of racial equality on the back burner, and even to dismantle some of the programs, notably affirmative action, which have so far been the chief weapons in that pursuit.

One argument often used in support of this trend is that antidiscrimination programs have already "done their job" — and that, as a result, serious economic discrimination no longer exists. Let *Fortune* have the floor once again:

> Few groups have risen economically as rapidly as American blacks have in the past 15 years, although in our heap-ashes-on-our-head mood our society has not congratulated itself much for the gains. A lot of social discrimination persists. But economically, discrimination seems no longer of major significance. . . . The inescapable conclusion is that blacks as a community have now entered the mainstream of American economic life. (Guzzardi, 1981, p. 100)

Another variant of the same theme, one that has become increasingly voiced by some academic social scientists, holds that government programs designed to promote racial equality are *themselves* responsible for a good part of the problems that minorities experience today. Those who believe this usually argue that minority progress in recent years has been uneven, and that gains in jobs and income for some have been offset by stubborn, perhaps worsening problems of unemployment, dependency, and social pathology for others. And, in this view, these problems are now due less to overt racial discrimination than to cultural obstacles that hinder some minority groups from taking advantage of the opportunities now available to them (Glazer, 1977, 1981), or to government policies that have encouraged dependency and blocked minorities from pulling themselves up by their own bootstraps (Sowell, 1979; Williams, 1982).

These are difficult and complex issues that go well beyond what we can cover in a single chapter: They involve the vastly different historical experiences of racial and ethnic groups in America (Lieberson, 1981; Steinberg, 1981). We will touch on these historical and cultural issues from time to time in this chapter, but our main focus will be more modest. We'll look at the evidence on minority progress in recent years, focusing on basic trends in income, employment, wealth, and poverty, and we'll consider a variety of explanations for the continuing differences between whites and minorities. Again, we'll save most of the discussion of other aspects of racial inequality (such as differences in the quality of health care or in victimization by crime) for later chapters.

Gains and Losses:
Income and Poverty

We've seen that income distribution in the United States has remained highly unequal, more so than in most other advanced industrial societies, and that it has changed little, government intervention notwithstanding, in

A Note on
Racial Statistics

Like many other kinds of social statistics, those dealing with race must be handled cautiously. There is a wide disparity in the amount and quality of data available on different minority groups. The most extensive statistics are for blacks. Only since the early 1970s have reasonably comparable data on income, poverty, and employment been routinely gathered on Hispanic-Americans; and Asian-Americans and native Americans are still only sporadically included in most official statistics. Much of the year-to-year data regularly gathered on such characteristics as income, poverty, or unemployment are based on samples that are too small to cover groups with smaller populations. The 1980 census produced a wealth of new information on American racial and ethnic groups, but not all of it was available as this book was written and much of it is not strictly comparable with earlier data.

We will discuss more specific data problems as they arise. But first let's emphasize a few basic cautions.

It's important to understand that data on American blacks are often presented under the category *nonwhite* or *black or other*. This category includes Asian-Americans and native Americans and can be misleading because these groups are very different socially and economically. But because blacks are the overwhelming majority of this group (about 92 percent in 1980), most government surveys and academic studies use this category interchangeably with *black*.

Another problem is that *white*, in most official statistics, nearly always includes most Hispanics, over 90 percent of whom are classified as white in recent census data (National Commission on Employment Policy, 1982, p. 25). Comparisons of whites and nonwhites, then, most often lump Hispanics with non-Hispanic whites — a misleading procedure since Hispanics, on the average, are far less well off, measured by most social indicators, than non-Hispanic whites.

Some of the statistics we'll use in this chapter address this problem by using a separate category of *majority* or "*non-Hispanic*" *whites;* others do not, and it's important to keep this difference in mind.

recent years. Indeed, if anything, it has increased in the 1980s. The egalitarian "revolution" that has so disturbed some observers has yet to take place. But what about the relative position of minorities within that income spread? How have different groups fared under the impact of changes in the economy and in public policy?

A simple comparison of different minority groups and whites shows that sharp inequalities still persist. Measured in terms of median family incomes, most minority groups (with the partial exception of some Asian-American groups, see page 145) are far behind whites. The general pattern shown in Figure 5-1 is one we'll see repeated in many other areas of social and economic life: whites are still well ahead, with blacks and Puerto Ricans toward the bottom, and Mexican-Americans somewhere in between.

As usual, these figures must be qualified in several ways. For one thing, official statistics on income ignore a large part of the income that comes from owning property, especially capital gains. Minorities much less often own income-producing property (it's estimated that only about 1 percent of all capital gains income goes to blacks, for example, though they are almost 12 percent of the population), so that conventional income statistics underestimate the inequality between minority and white incomes. The usual statistics on income also underestimate racial inequality for another reason — they are not adjusted to reflect differences in family size. Because minority families tend to be larger than white families, the same level of family income equals a lower per capita income and, presumably, a lower level of family well-being (Bianchi, 1981, p. 115). But the limitations of the official figures work the other way, too. Minorities receive a higher proportion of in-kind welfare benefits, such as food stamps or subsidized housing, which are also not counted as income. To that extent, the figures understate minority groups' income.

More importantly, such raw figures don't convey either the complexity or the direction of the trends in minority living standards. Let's consider first the pattern of black versus white incomes over the past several years. Table 5-1 shows that the economic gap between black and white Americans is widening. In 1965, when Congress passed the Civil Rights Act, the median income of black families was about 55 percent of white income, a proportion that had hardly changed since 1950. By the early 1970s, stimulated by antidiscrimination efforts and a growing economy, that ratio reached a peak of about 61 percent. At its highest level, in other words, black family income has never been more than a fraction above three-fifths that of white family income.

As the national economy slid downward after the mid-1970s, blacks fell farther behind. By the early 1980s, black median family income had dropped back to 56 percent of white income — depressingly close to their position at the end of World War II and, for that matter, not far from their estimated level at the *turn of the century* (Reich, 1981, pp. 18–19).

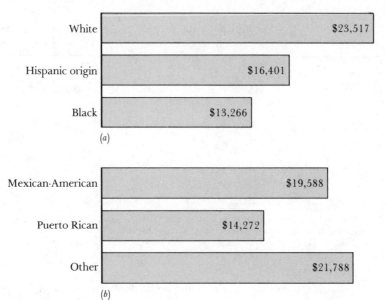

Figure 5-1

(*a*) Median family income by race and Hispanic origin, 1981. (*b*) Mean family income by type of Hispanic origin, 1981

Source: Data from U.S. Bureau of the Census, *Current Population Reports*, series P-60, nos. 137, 138, Washington, D.C., 1983. Data on percentages of Hispanic-origin groups from National Commission for Employment Policy, *Hispanics and Jobs: Barriers to Progress* (Washington, D.C.: Government Printing Office, 1982).

Note: Median income is the income at the midpoint of a particular population; thus, half of black families have incomes above $13,266, half below. *Mean* income is the arithmetic average of all incomes in a group; mean income levels are somewhat higher than median incomes.

"Other" refers to persons of Cuban, Central and South American, and mixed Hispanic origin. About 60 percent of persons of Hispanic origin in the United States are Mexican-American, 14 percent are Puerto Rican.

Trends in the family income of Americans of Hispanic origin (for which comparable data are only available from 1972 onward) show a somewhat different pattern. In the 1970s, Hispanic incomes fell slightly to about two-thirds of those of white families. They apparently recovered fractionally in the early 1980s. But by 1981 Hispanic families remained slightly worse off, in relation to whites, than they had been 10 years before.

As the 1980s began, to look at income from another angle, blacks, who accounted for more than 10 percent of American families, brought home less than 7 percent of total personal income. Had black families received a share of income equal to their proportion in the population, they would have had (in 1980) an extra $50 billion — about half again the total income they actually received, and a sum averaging nearly $8,000 for every black family in the United States (calculated from *Statistical Abstract of the U.S., 1982–83*, p. 435).

These trends in income reveal a consistent pattern. Real and important gains were made, especially during the late 1960s, toward racial equality. But those gains did not bring minorities to a position of equality with whites.

Table 5-1

Trends in minority and white income inequality. Ratio of minority median family income to white median family income, selected years, 1950–1981

Year	Black percentage of white income	Hispanic percentage of white income
1950	54	—
1955	55	—
1960	55	—
1965	55	—
1970	61	—
1972	59	71
1975	61	67
1980	58	67
1981	56	70

Source: Calculated from U.S. Bureau of the Census, "Money Income of Families and Households in the United States, 1981," *Current Population Reports,* series P-60, no. 137, Washington, D.C., 1983, pp. 39–40.

And, especially for blacks, the gains began to be reversed in the middle 1970s: By 1981, virtually the entire improvement in the ratio of black to white family income had been wiped out.

Southern Gains, Northern Losses

When we look at racial income patterns in different regions, the picture of racial progress looks even less bright. Most of the improvement in the ratio of nonwhite to white income took place in the South. The situation in the North has deteriorated — in some areas with startling speed. We've already seen, in looking at trends in poverty, some of the forces at work here. Overt racial discrimination in jobs and welfare was worse in the South than the North before the passage of civil rights legislation. And the South was less developed economically than the rest of the country. Changes on both fronts during the 1960s and early 1970s helped raise southern black income. At the same time, many poorer southern blacks migrated to the North and West, which had the (purely statistical) effect of raising the average level of black income in the South. Racial disparities in income were greater in the South to begin with, but they improved rapidly there while showing little change elsewhere.

Since the 1970s this regional difference has become even more important. In the northern and western states, the ratio of black to white family income dropped in the 1970s, especially after 1975. (Progress in the South, too, stagnated in the late 1970s, but without the sharp declines that characterized the North.) The ratio of black to white family income in the heavily urbanized Northeast dropped by more than 15 percent in the six years from 1975 to 1981. Were it to continue to fall at the same rate, black income would be less than half that of white by the late 1980s, and by the early 1990s would fall to levels not witnessed since the Jim Crow era in the South.

A similarly disturbing picture emerges for recent trends in minority poverty. We have seen that poverty rates for all races rose sharply in the early 1980s, and that overall progress against poverty had ground to a halt even before that. This trend has been especially devastating to the prospects for racial equality because it comes on top of already starkly disproportionate rates of minority poverty, as Table 5-2 illustrates. In 1981 the number of poor blacks was higher than it had been since 1965, and the black poverty rate was roughly triple the rate for whites. An astonishing 45 percent of black children lived in families below the poverty level, as did more than a third of all children in families of Hispanic origin. Rates of minority poverty reached

White	No. below poverty level		% below poverty level	
	Total persons (millions)	Children	Total persons	Children
White				
1981	21,553	7,429	11.1	14.7
1979	17,214	5,909	9.0	11.4
1973	15,142	5,462	8.4	9.7
1969	16,659	5,667	9.5	9.7
1965	22,696	8,595	13.3	14.4
Black				
1981	9,173	4,170	34.2	44.9
1979	8,050	3,745	31.0	40.8
1973	7,388	3,822	31.4	40.6
1969	7,095	3,677	32.2	39.6
1966	8,867	4,774	41.8	50.6
Hispanic Origin				
1981	3,713	1,874	26.5	35.4
1979	2,921	1,505	21.8	27.7
1973	2,366	1,364	21.9	27.8

Percent below poverty level by type of Hispanic origin, 1981

	Total persons	Children
Mexican-American	25.5	32.6
Puerto Rican	42.8	57.1
Other Hispanic origin	19.9	28.7

Children means related children in families under 18.
Source: U.S. Bureau of the Census, *Current Population Reports*, series P-60, no. 138, Washington, D.C., 1983, pp. 7, 152.

Table 5-2
Persons below poverty level by race and Hispanic origin, selected years, 1965–1981

Challenges to racial inequality: troops enforce the integration of Little Rock, Arkansas High School, 1957.

levels unknown since the mid-1960s, at the start of the War on Poverty and the antidiscrimination programs sparked by the Civil Rights Act.

Moreover, as is true of poverty for all races, a number of underlying trends, often hidden by the broad national statistics, make the picture even less encouraging:

- The successes in the War on Poverty took place mainly in the South, even in the 1960s. There was a substantial improvement in black poverty rates up until the early 1970s. But that was the result, in large part, of improvements in jobs (and welfare benefits) in the South, and also of the movement of many poor black southerners to states with higher incomes, benefits, *and* costs of living — a phenomenon that improved the poverty statistics while leaving many blacks in the same position. In 1981 there were slightly fewer poor blacks in the South than there had been in 1970. But there were over 2 million *more* in the North and West (U.S. Bureau of the Census, 1983a, p. 15). Poverty among Hispanic-Americans rose sharply in the North and Midwest during the 1970s, too, while it declined in the Southwest.

• We've seen that the successes against poverty have occurred mainly outside the central cities. Again, this is even more true of minority poverty. Indeed, all of the increase in the black poverty rate in America in the 1970s took place in the central cities. As Figure 5-2 shows, a fourth of central-city blacks were poor in 1970, a *third* by 1981 (U.S. Bureau of the Census, 1983a, p. 18).

• Even more disturbing is the fact that inner-city poverty among non-whites doesn't seem to respond well to economic growth. Poverty is always more likely when the economy declines into recession. But even when the economy has been booming, the minority poor of the cities have increasingly been left behind. Their rates of poverty during the economic recovery of the late 1970s were greater than they were at the height of the recession in 1975 (U.S. Bureau of the Census, 1983a, p. 16).

• The official measure of poverty understates the severity of minority poverty. For one thing, poor blacks and Hispanics are poorer on average than poor whites. In 1981 it took $1,000 more to bring an average

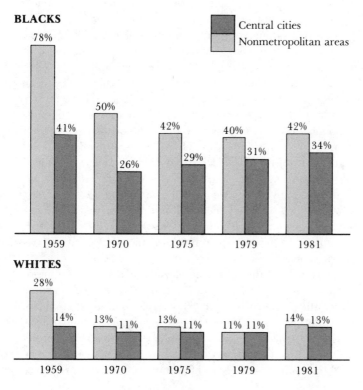

Figure 5-2
Trends in central-city and nonmetropolitan poverty rates, selected years, 1959–1981

Source: Data from U.S. Bureau of the Census, *Current Population Reports*, series P-60, no. 138, Washington, D.C., 1983b, pp. 15–16.

black family out of poverty than it did an average white family (U.S. Bureau of the Census, 1983a, p. 150).

- Minorities are overrepresented among the *persistently* poor — those who remain poor year after year. The likelihood of moving out of poverty is much greater for whites than blacks. More than three-fifths of the households characterized as "persistently poor" in the University of Michigan's Panel Study of Income Dynamics — those who remained poor in eight of the ten years studied — were black (Duncan and Coe, 1981, p. 98).

Progress and Paradox

By the 1980s, then, the condition of blacks, Puerto Ricans, and Mexican-Americans appeared to be deteriorating. Gains achieved in the 1960s had slowed in the 1970s, and the new decade of the 1980s was ushered in with sharp losses for minorities. What makes this trend especially disquieting is that, as the economist Michael Reich has noted (1981, pp. 61–62), it has occurred in spite of a number of social changes that should have *improved* the position of minorities.

Growing urbanization and migration of minorities out of the South and rural areas and out of agriculture into manufacturing and white-collar jobs is one such favorable change. The increasing similarity in educational attainment between whites and minorities, especially blacks, is another. By the beginning of the 1970s, the median years of school completed by blacks were almost equal to those of whites; and among younger blacks under 35, schooling levels had become completely equal (*Statistical Abstract of the U.S., 1982–83*, p. 145). Levels of schooling for Hispanics had not improved as much, but they had also increased dramatically. In 1970 less than a fourth of Mexican-Americans and Puerto Ricans in the United States had finished high school; by 1981, two-fifths had (*Statistical Abstract of the U.S., 1982–83*, pp. 142–143). That left them still distinctly behind both whites and blacks, but it was still a sharp improvement that could be expected to bring their incomes more into line with non-Hispanic whites and to have reduced their chances of poverty.

Furthermore, the resistance of white Americans to minority progress, at least on the level of attitudes and beliefs, seemed, according to virtually every survey taken by opinion pollsters and social scientists, to have subsided during this period. Whites were more likely to express a willingness to live next to blacks, to work alongside them, to send their children to school with them, and to support their claims for a better chance at the good life. And they were less likely to hold some of the most prejudiced beliefs about the incompetence or inferiority of minorities (*Public Opinion*, 1981, pp. 34–37; Governor's Task Force on Civil Rights, 1982, pp. 124–125). Substantial prejudice, both overt and subtle, did remain, as numerous studies discovered (Crosby et al., 1980; *Public Opinion*, 1981). But, on the whole, the climate of racial opinion improved during the period when, paradoxically, racial economic inequality began to increase.

A similar paradox appears when we look at residential segregation in the cities. A 1983 study by the sociologist Karl Taeuber shows that most major American cities with large black populations (with some notable exceptions) became somewhat less segregated during the 1970s, continuing a slow downward drift that began during the 1960s (Taeuber, 1983, p. 5). In several cities, including Gary and Oakland in the North and West, and Dallas, Jacksonville, and Houston in the South and Southwest, the 1970s brought relatively rapid declines in residential segregation. Again, though the successes were far from uniform, they showed an improving trend, probably resulting both from more effective (and better enforced) laws mandating fair housing practices and the general decline in overt racial prejudice.

A final aspect of the paradox is that minority economic losses seemed to coexist simultaneously with rises in black and Hispanic political representation. Between 1972 and 1982, for example, while urban black poverty rates were increasing, the number of black mayors in America rose from 86 to 223 and the number of black state legislators rose from 169 to 347, according to data from Howard University's Joint Center for Political Studies (*Newsweek*, April 11, 1983, p. 24). And the stagnation in Hispanic economic gains appeared just as Hispanics, especially in parts of the Southwest, were beginning to flex their political muscle.

How can we explain the stagnation in minority economic progress, especially in the face of these favorable trends?

Class versus Race?

One line of thought holds that the picture of racial progress that emerges from broad, undifferentiated data on income and poverty is misleading. Those who hold this view point to different data, especially those that distinguish racial gains and losses by age and family structure, to argue that the overall economic situation of nonwhites is much better than it seems at first glance. (At least by implication, this would be true of some other minority groups as well, though the argument has been usually about black progress.) In this view, it's not that *all* blacks are suffering from the effects of continuing discrimination and economic stagnation. Rather, the slowing — or reversal — of black gains in recent years reflects an increasing split between two parts of the black population.

On one side (according to this argument) is a growing, affluent, middle class, mainly composed of younger, better-educated families who have been able to take advantage of the improved racial climate and declining discrimination and prejudice in the schools and the job market. Such families, it's

Inner-city minority poverty has worsened in the past decade . . .

argued, now do as well as comparable white families. And because they are presumably the first generation of nonwhites to show the full effects of changing attitudes and forceful antidiscrimination policies, their situation is a more accurate indication of the future of racial equality.

On the other side, however, is a growing "underclass" of families disproportionately headed by women and often trapped in the inner cities in a self-defeating cycle of welfare dependency, crime, drug addiction, and other social pathologies.

The implications of this view are far-reaching. To some observers, it implies that discrimination itself — at least, discrimination in economic life — is no longer a serious problem. Blacks (or Puerto Ricans or Mexican-Americans) with the right characteristics (good education and a sound family) can now expect to do as well, or nearly as well, as whites in the competition for jobs and income. Moreover, they can expect to pass on these advantages to their children, in the traditional pattern of upward mobility followed by many other American ethnic groups (Kilson, 1981).

Those who hold this view don't argue that blacks and other minorities no longer face real problems. They argue that these problems are now due mainly to cultural deficiencies and the effects of *past*, rather than present,

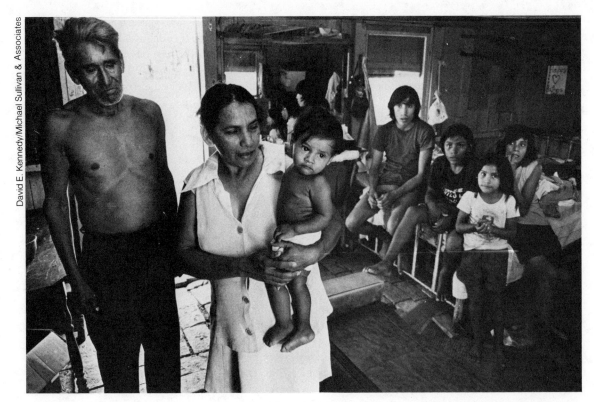

while rural poverty improved — until the 1980s.

racial discrimination (Glazer, 1977). Others believe that nonwhites still suffer from severe economic and social barriers, but see these barriers as being those of class rather than race (Wilson, 1978). In other words, the barriers mainly affect a minority lower class, and they reflect what one writer has called the "burden of background" — the obstacles of poor schooling and family disorganization — rather than the more traditional "burden of race" (Freeman, 1978a, p. 61).

For some (though by no means all) of these theorists, this growing separation between a healthy, thriving middle class and a pathological lower class also implies that many of the policies developed to combat racial inequality in recent years need to be reconsidered. Affirmative action and other anti-discrimination programs designed to overcome barriers caused by racial discrimination are, in this view, less and less important today. And government transfer programs, especially AFDC, are said to be largely responsible for the growth and persistence of the minority lower class.

How accurate is this view? The best evidence suggests that it contains some important insights, but also considerable exaggeration. The situation of some kinds of minority families did indeed improve substantially over the past two decades, and more so than the broad, average statistics indicate.

But this stratum is not as affluent, as secure, or as free from the impact of discrimination as some writers have argued. It remains a "minority within a minority" — a relatively small proportion of the nonwhite population. Its growth has slowed, and even suffered serious setbacks, in the less favorable economic and political climate of more recent years. And, at the other end of the spectrum, among the minority poor, the relationship among poverty, family disorganization, welfare, and economic discrimination is far more complex than this argument suggests.

A Growing Middle Class?

During the 1970s, as we've seen, the ratio of black to white family income declined. But a closer look reveals that this combines opposing trends. Table 5-3 shows that from 1970 to 1980, the ratio for *all* black families dropped from 61 to 58 percent. For families with a year-round, full-time worker, however, the ratio wound up about the same at the end of the decade. But the stable income picture for those families is the result of a *decline* for families with just one worker and a significant *rise* for those with at least two people working for pay. By 1980 a black family that could put two people to work — at least one of them full time and year round — could expect to bring home 85 percent of what a similar white family did. Meanwhile, a black family with *no one* working could expect to have less than half the income of a comparable white family — a ratio that declined sharply over the decade.

Such statistics lend some support to the idea of a fundamental split between a successful middle class steadily catching up with whites and a stagnating, even declining, workless underclass. Some other evidence also points in that direction. For example, the most notable gains during the 1970s were among highly educated, younger blacks, especially those from relatively higher-status family backgrounds. By the mid-1970s blacks with Ph.D.'s in some fields were earning as much as whites with comparable education; black men with some postgraduate training were earning roughly 94 percent of whites with similar postgraduate training (Freeman, 1978a, p. 59).

But several qualifications prevent us from making as much of this phenomenon as some other writers have. First, of course, there is the remaining unexplained racial disparity even for the most successful families. We may well ask why, after a decade of affirmative action, increasing educational achievement, *and* dual-career labors, black families with two earners still make 15 percent less than whites. And remember that higher family incomes may simply mean that more people in a family are working. It takes more people working to bring a minority family the same level of income as a comparable white family. Thus, in 1981, white families with a middle-class income of between $30,000 and $32,500 a year had, on average, two earners, while black families with the same total income had an average of two

Year and number of earners	Black-white median family income ratio	
	All families	Families with householder year-round full-time worker
All families, 1970	.61	.74
No earners	.64	NA
1 earner	.56	.66
2 earners	.74	.78
3 earners	.68	.75
4 earners or more	.64	.71
All families, 1975	.61	.77
No earners	.62	NA
1 earner	.58	.67
2 earners	.79	.84
3 earners	.75	.82
4 earners or more	.75	.75
All families, 1980	.58	.75
No earners	.48	NA
1 earner	.57	.61
2 earners	.81	.85
3 earners	.73	.75
4 earners or more	.77	.84

Table 5-3
Median family income in constant 1980 dollars, by number of earners and race, 1970–1980

Note: NA means not applicable.
Source: Adapted from *Statistical Abstract of the United States, 1982–83* (Washington, D.C.: Government Printing Office, 1983), p. 436.

and a half earners, and Hispanic families had only slightly fewer earners than blacks. It took about two and a half minority workers in a family, in other words, to make what two white workers did (U.S. Bureau of the Census, 1983c, pp. 94–95).

Much of the extra income in black families is the result of wives working longer, on the average, than wives in white dual-earner families. About two-thirds of black working wives, as compared to just over half of white wives, work year round, full time. And they contribute a considerably larger share of their families' total income (Shaw, 1981).

Moreover, the relative income gains for these families, though they didn't decline, came to a halt in the late 1970s and early 1980s. Whatever forces had operated to bring younger, better educated, longer-working families toward greater equality with whites were either slowing or being countered by other factors. Moreover, the threat of *downward* mobility for the minority middle class, as we'll see later in this chapter, is now especially great, for many of the gains in jobs and income that put more minority families into the middle class took place in just those parts of the American economy that have become more precarious in recent years.

Minority Poverty and Family Structure

Substantial economic gains, then, did take place in the 1970s for a growing segment of the minority population. But (1) these gains were largely confined to a relatively small proportion of families that are both intact and in which both husband and wife worked outside the home, (2) they were achieved in part only through extra work on the part of minority families, and (3) they have slowed since the late 1970s, and may well suffer reversals in the future. None of these qualifications erases the gains, but they do put the successes of recent years into perspective. And the other side of the picture of minority progress is far gloomier. At that end of the scale, it is widely agreed that things have gone from bad to worse. Why?

The growth of minority poverty in recent years, even in times of relative economic growth and lower unemployment, is often linked to the breakup of the conventional husband and wife family and the consequent rise in the proportion of minority families headed by women. Some observers have argued that *most* of the problems of nonwhite communities may be attributed to this shift — that minority poverty and the social problems that flow from it are the result of family instability *rather than of discrimination* (Gilder, 1981, chapter 6). According to this argument, since intact minority families have done well in recent years in achieving better income and jobs, the source of poverty and social pathology among minorities must be the growth of female-headed families. Thus, one writer argues that female-headed families, "regardless of race, display a seemingly endemic incapacity to foster social mobility comparable to husband-wife and male-headed families" (Kilson, 1981, p. 61). Such families tend to "pass on interpersonal pathologies, like hypertensive and violent behavior, which result in a low proclivity for coping and achievement."

Again, there is a kernel of truth here. The growth of families maintained by women *is* strongly related to the trends in minority poverty and income inequality. Such families are much more likely to be poor and to require public assistance. And among some minority groups, especially blacks and Puerto Ricans, the growth of female-headed families has been especially rapid (Figure 5-3). By the beginning of the 1980s more than two out of five black families were maintained by a woman, as compared to less than one in eight white families. That imbalance has grown larger over the years. Since 1960 the growth in nonwhite families headed by a woman has been twice as fast as that among whites (Bianchi, 1981, p. 36). Two-thirds of black children in these families, and more than four out of five mainland Puerto Rican children, were poor at the beginning of the 1980s (*Statistical Abstract of the U.S., 1982–83*, p. 441; U.S. Bureau of the Census, 1983c, p. 152).

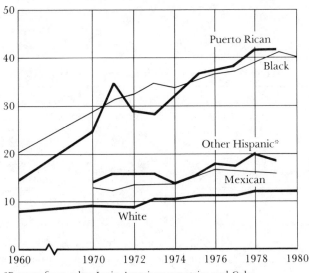

Figure 5-3
Percent of families headed by women, by race and type of Hispanic origin, 1960–1980

Source: National Commission for Employment Policy, *Hispanics and Jobs: Barriers to Progress* (Washington, D.C.: Government Printing Office, 1982), p. 31.

But this isn't the whole story, as a recent Census Bureau study (1982) makes clear. The Census researchers estimated what the poverty rate *would* have been in 1980, *if* the composition of families had remained the same as in 1970; if, that is, there had been no increase in the proportion of families headed by women. The role of family changes did indeed turn out to be important. In 1980 the official black family poverty rate was about 29 percent — only fractionally lower than in 1970. Adjusted for changes in family composition, the 1980 rate would have been about 20 percent. (Among white families, this exercise reduced the rate of poverty from the official 8 percent to about 6 percent.) Thus, without the growth in families headed by women, black poverty would have dropped by a third. A substantial difference — but even so, one in five black families would still have been poor in 1980.

This suggests that — like the "success" of the minority middle class — the negative impact of the rising rates of black families headed by women needs to be put in careful perspective. We must keep in mind that the break-up of the conventional family doesn't necessarily lead to poverty; nor is maintaining an intact family a guarantee against poverty, especially for minorities. On the one hand, *white* families headed by women have much higher average incomes than minority families in the same situation, as Table 5-4 illustrates. On the other, even among minority families that are *persistently* poor, a substantial proportion are headed by men. About 20 percent of all families that were poor in eight out of ten years in the University of Michigan survey were headed by black men of working age (*Employment and*

	Median family income					
	Two-parent families			One-parent families maintained by women		
	White	Black	Hispanic	White	Black	Hispanic
Total	$24,200	$20,200	$17,100	$ 8,800	$6,300	$5,300
Mother in labor force	26,900	23,200	21,400	11,900	8,900	8,900
Mother not in labor force	21,700	14,900	14,000	5,000	4,400	5,400

Source: Adapted from Allyson Sherman Grossman, "More than Half of All Children Have Working Mothers," *Monthly Labor Review,* February 1982, p. 43. Reprinted with permission.

Table 5-4
Median incomes of different types of families, by race and Hispanic origin and participation in the labor force, 1980

Training Reporter, 1982, p. 98). Clearly, something besides family disruption is at work to cause the higher rates of poverty among minority families.

This is confirmed in more systematic fashion in a careful study of the impact of family structure on racial inequality by the sociologist Suzanne Bianchi (1981). Like other researchers, Bianchi began from the observation that "the position of Black families relative to white families seems to have deteriorated in the 1970s" (Bianchi, 1981, p. 125). How much of that deterioration was due to the faster increase of female-headed families among blacks? Some of it was, but Bianchi found that a greater proportion was due to racial inequalities between families of *any* type. That is, low levels of income for black husband and wife households compared to white husband and wife households, or of black female-headed households compared to white female-headed ones, accounted for most of the overall inequality between black and white households in the 1960s and 1970s. If there had been no changes in the distribution of families across the different types of households over time (the same procedure used in the census study discussed earlier), the average per capita income of black families would have been only $145 higher in 1976 than in 1960 (Bianchi, 1981, pp. 125–127).

What caused the racial differences in income *within* family types? Among intact, husband and wife families, Bianchi argues, the problem was primarily the lower earnings of black, as compared to white, *husbands.* Within female-headed families, it was primarily lower welfare and other transfer benefits for black women (1981, p. 129).

As this suggests, to understand the stalemate in minority gains, we need to consider much more than the (admittedly significant) role of changing family structure. We also need to understand why family disruption so often does lead to poverty for women and their children (a crucial, complex issue we'll come back to in the following two chapters). And we need to know more about the factors that cause minorities to have lower incomes and higher risks of poverty *whatever* their family structure. To approach *that* question, we need to examine how minorities have fared in one particularly decisive arena — the labor market.

Minorities and the Job Market

Work, or the lack of work, crucially determines the way all of us live, so it isn't surprising that the distinctive pattern of significant gains for some groups in the minority population coupled with stagnation and even decline for others is intimately connected to the fortunes of minorities in the job market.

Untangling these issues is difficult because several different factors in the job market may contribute, simultaneously or in various combinations, to the inequality of minority and white income. One source of that inequality may be differences in the amount of work — or, put another way, the risks of not working — between the groups. Another may be differences in the earnings they receive when they do work. Both of these, in turn, are partly reflections of the kinds of jobs different groups typically hold, for this affects both the wages or salaries they receive when they work and the chances they face of being unemployed or intermittently employed. And all of these factors differ in their impact not only among the various minority groups but also among men and women within those groups.

In this section, we'll see that, as with income, the trends in the situation of minorities in the labor market are a mixture of positive and negative developments. Minorities have made real gains in breaking into jobs that were once almost exclusively the preserve of whites. Minority workers are now much more equally distributed throughout the range of occupations than before the growth of antidiscrimination programs. They still have a long way to go in many areas, and celebrations of the arrival of genuine equality are premature. But in the 1980s, the chances of a black or Hispanic getting a high-level job with good pay are considerably better than they have been in the past, and the chances of being confined in the lowest-paid, poorest-status jobs, though still harshly disproportionate, are less overwhelming.

But there is an underside to this progress. While the proportion of minority lawyers, bank managers, and engineers has risen, so has the proportion who are unemployed, sporadically employed, or who have dropped out of the labor force altogether. Even among those who do work regularly, substantial inequalities in wages and earnings remain — inequalities that are not wholly explained by age or regional differences, or differences in the skills, education, or other qualifications that different groups bring to the labor market.

Let's begin by looking at what is probably the most troubling part of the problem: minority unemployment and labor-force withdrawal.

Minority Joblessness: Bad and Getting Worse

Figure 5-4 illustrates official unemployment rates for blacks, Hispanics, and "majority" whites, by sex, from 1971 to 1980, based on a 1982 analysis by the U.S. Commission on Civil Rights. Two disturbing facts are clearly apparent. Unemployment rates are disproportionately high for Hispanics, and drastically so for blacks. And the size of the gap between black and white unemployment rates has tended to increase over time. Ominously, though the rates for all groups are clearly affected by broad fluctuations in the economy, many of the minority group rates have remained strikingly high even in years when the economy is in a state of recovery. Thus, all groups were adversely affected by the 1974 to 1976 recession, but, with the partial exception of Hispanic men, none of the jobless rates fell far enough in the late 1970s recovery to match the levels before the recession.

The unemployment picture for Hispanics is somewhat muddled by statistics that do not distinguish the experience of the *different* groups of people of Hispanic origin in the United States. Figure 5-5 shows that, though unemployment rates are high among most Hispanic groups, they are especially high for Puerto Ricans and somewhat lower, particularly for men, for Mexican-Americans. (For Mexican-Americans in the labor market, an even more serious problem than unemployment is low *earnings*.)

These differences are much more apparent if we also consider another aspect of joblessness, low rates of participation in the labor force. In Chapter

Figure 5-4
Minority and white unemployment rates, by sex, 1971–1980

Source: U.S. Commission on Civil Rights, *Unemployment and Underemployment among Blacks, Hispanics, and Women* (Washington, D.C.: Government Printing Office, 1982b), p. 15.

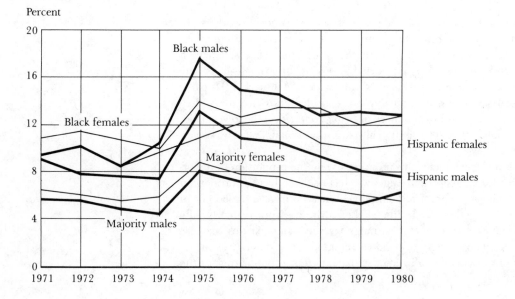

8, we'll examine in more detail the technical issues involved in the various measures of unemployment and labor-force participation. Here we will simply note that the measure of labor-force participation includes both those who are working and those who are looking for work. The labor-force participation rate thus helps tell us how many people have dropped out of the world of paid work altogether, or have never entered it in the first place. As

MALES

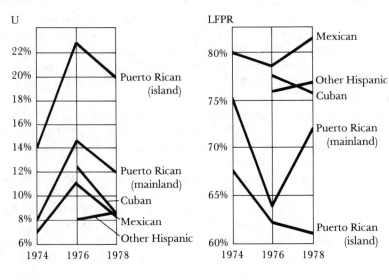

FEMALES

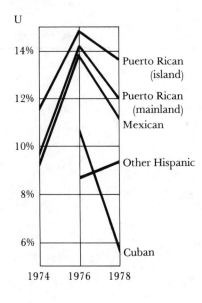 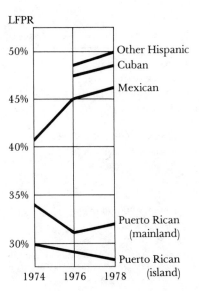

Figure 5-5
Unemployment (U) and labor-force participation rates (LFPR), by type of Hispanic origin, selected years, 1974–1978

Source: National Commission for Employment Policy, *Hispanics and Jobs: Barriers to Progress* (Washington, D.C.: Government Printing Office, 1982), pp. 33, 35.

Figure 5-5 shows, labor-force participation is strikingly low, and generally declining, among Puerto Ricans; it is high (especially for men), and generally rising, among Mexican-Americans. The latter trend explains why labor-force participation is considerably higher among Hispanic men generally than white men, as Table 5-5 shows.

The proportion of black men who are either working or looking for work, on the other hand, is lower (as Table 5-5 shows), and it has fallen substantially in the recent past. The proportion of men in the labor force is influenced by the age structure of the population; if the percentage of a group's population that is past the normal working age increases, *then*, other things being equal, the group's labor-force participation rate will fall. But the decline in labor-force participation for black men reflects much more than a changing age structure. Between 1960 and 1976, the percentage of black men of working age (under 65) who had worked at all in the previous year, according to census surveys, dropped from about 94 percent to about 86 percent. Among white men of working age, the proportion dropped as well, but by 1976 about 94 percent of them had worked in the previous year. In other words, by the late 1970s, about twice as many black men as white men had *no* work at all (Bianchi, 1981, p. 72).

These differences in unemployment and labor-force participation by race and sex provide part of the explanation for the different incomes, and the varying trends in income, that we've observed. Thus, the dramatically high rate of poverty among Puerto Ricans not only reflects their high rate of households headed by women but also the fact that the women heading those households suffer high rates of joblessness, and also that Puerto Rican

Table 5-5
Labor-force participation and unemployment rates by race, sex, and age, 1981

Race, sex, and age	Labor-force participation rate	Unemployment rate
Hispanic		
Males 20 and over	84.8	8.8
Females 20 and over	49.9	9.5
Both sexes, 16–19	46.3	24.1
Black		
Males 20 and over	74.1	13.3
Females 20 and over	56.0	13.4
Both sexes, 16–19	37.4	41.5
White		
Males 20 and over	79.6	5.6
Females 20 and over	51.7	5.9
Both sexes, 16–19	59.0	17.3

Source: Adapted from National Commission for Employment Policy, *Hispanics and Jobs: Barriers to Progress* (Washington, D.C.: Government Printing Office, 1982), p. 19.

In the 1970s, some minorities began to reach the higher rungs of the job ladder . . .

while others didn't get on the ladder at all.

Minorities and the Job Market   **165**

men suffer much more from the lack of work than men in most other groups, including other Hispanics. The income gap between blacks and whites reflects not only the growing proportion of black women heading families but also the high rates of unemployment among those women — and the declining rates of steady employment for black men. At the same time, black income has been affected in a positive direction by the growing labor-force participation of black women.

What accounts for these disparities in employment? We'll look at some explanations in Chapter 8. For now, let's look at another aspect of minorities' labor-market problems: the earnings they receive when they *do* work.

Minority Earnings: Differences and Explanations

The grave problems of joblessness for some minority groups, particularly blacks and Puerto Ricans, lend some credence to the view that the economic problems of these groups are largely concentrated among a predominantly workless urban underclass and that problems have receded for those with a foothold in the labor market. As the economist Richard Freeman put it in a review of black economic progress since the mid-1960s:

> The big problem in the labor market [for minorities] is not wage or occupational discrimination within businesses, but lack of employment altogether. . . . For those "in the system," particularly those with more education and better background, the improvement in the job market after 1964 has greatly reduced economic differences between black and whites. For those who have not yet entered the mainstream of the labor market, for whatever reasons, sizeable problems remain. (Freeman, 1978a, p. 68)

What this says about the plight of those outside the system is on target. But the assumption that discrimination in wages and jobs for the employed is no longer a problem is premature. In fact, substantial inequalities in earnings remain between minorities and whites even among full-time workers. And though it is difficult to pin down, with the methods of social science, how *much* of those inequalities are the result of discrimination, research does show that a significant amount of inequality remains even when a variety of other potentially influential factors are taken into account.

Table 5-6 shows average earnings among full-time white, black, and Hispanic workers, separated by sex, age, education, and occupation. Let's look first at the broad differences among the three groups. Not surprisingly, whites are well ahead and blacks and Hispanics are close together at the low end of the scale. When broken down by sex, these differences exhibit a more complex and startling pattern. White men's earnings are *far* ahead of those of any other group. Indeed, their earnings are farther away from those of the next highest group, black men, than black men's are from any other group's.

The table illustrates another point: The economic situation of Hispanics in America is less favorable than we would infer from their unemployment rates alone, for what they earn on the job is not only much less than white workers, but less than blacks as well.

Table 5-7 illustrates this disadvantage from another angle. Hispanic workers not only bring home lower earnings on average, compared with whites and even blacks, but they are also overrepresented among those at the very bottom of the earning scale. Hispanics were 5 percent of all full-time workers, but were 10 percent of all full-time workers earning $150 or less a week. Black workers were only slightly less disadvantaged. (This amount is only slightly more than the minimum wage, and considerably less than what was needed to bring a family of four over the poverty line in 1981.)

How do we explain these low wages? Several external factors, including differences in regional distribution, age structure of the population, and levels of education, skills, and training explain part of these disparities (Sowell, 1981). But, even in combination, they do not explain *all* of them. Part of the explanation, for example, is that blacks and Hispanics are concentrated in the South and Southwest, respectively, which are regions where wages for *all* workers are lower. More than half of all black men with jobs are employed in the South, compared to less than a third of white men. By itself, this would bias the national averages for black workers downward, giving a false picture of the severity of racial inequality. But it also turns out that the gap in workers' earnings between the South and other regions is even greater for blacks than for whites. And black earnings are lower than white earnings in *every* region, not just the South. This implies both that blacks remain, on the whole, less equal on the job in the South than elsewhere in the country and that they have not achieved economic equality in the North either (Bianchi, 1981, p. 99; Mellor and Stanas, 1982, p. 17).

Much the same is true of Hispanics. Their low average earnings relative to other groups partly reflect their concentration in the Southwest, which has lower wages and generally lower living costs. But this difference applies primarily to Mexican-Americans, and not to Puerto Ricans, who are concentrated in the high-wage, high-cost urbanized Northeast. And even considering Mexican-Americans alone, the regional difference accounts for only *part* of the inequality in wages (National Commission for Employment Policy, 1982; Reimers, 1982).

Another part of the explanation is the differing age structure of the various racial and ethnic groups. A group with a higher proportion of young people of working age will have a lower average earnings level, as well as higher rates of unemployment and lower rates of labor-force participation. Younger workers have had less time to gain the skills, education, and experience that lead to higher earnings, and they are more likely to work intermittently, moving in and out of jobs. Since most minority populations, particularly Hispanics, are younger on the average than the white population, age may account for what appear to be racially determined inequalities.

And indeed, age distribution *does* explain *some* of the differences in earn-

Table 5-6

The racial earnings gap: median weekly earnings of full-time wage and salary workers, by selected demographic characteristics, 1981

Age, major occupational group, and years of school completed	All races			White			Black			Hispanic		
	Both sexes	Males	Females	Both sexes	Males	Females	Both sexes	Males	Females	Both sexes	Males	Females
Age												
Total, 16 years and over	$289	$347	$224	$296	$356	$226	$238	$271	$210	$229	$252	$192
16 to 24 years	204	225	184	206	227	185	185	196	174	187	197	172
16 to 19 years	163	173	150	164	174	151	148	150	145	—	—	—
20 to 24 years	219	241	193	222	244	195	192	207	179	246	282	201
25 years and over	316	378	237	325	389	239	251	290	220	—	—	—
25 to 34 years	302	346	242	310	354	245	248	280	223	—	—	—
35 to 44 years	335	406	241	345	416	243	267	311	227	—	—	—
45 to 54 years	329	408	231	340	417	234	248	295	213	—	—	—
55 to 64 years	317	386	227	326	395	231	243	281	198	—	—	—
65 years and over	227	270	190	228	275	189	216	233	*	—	—	—
Occupation												
Total, 16 years and over	289	347	224	296	356	226	238	271	210	229	252	192
Professional and technical workers	377	439	316	381	443	315	324	352	308	336	386	285
Managers and administrators, except farm	407	466	283	410	471	282	347	391	303	347	381	271
Salesworkers	306	366	190	311	372	191	221	249	182	240	286	*
Clerical workers	233	328	220	233	335	219	230	286	220	226	280	214
Craft and kindred workers	352	360	239	356	364	239	309	314	239	296	304	*

Operatives, except transport	242	298	187	246	304	189	222	267	179	199	231	169
Transport equipment operatives	303	307	237	314	319	237	257	258	*	261	261	*
Nonfarm laborers	238	244	193	241	247	193	217	220	*	222	225	*
Service workers	192	238	165	195	245	165	182	214	166	173	190	147
Farmworkers	179	183	148	181	185	148	147	154	*	185	191	*
Years of school completed												
Total, 25 years and over	316	378	237	325	389	239	251	290	220	246	282	201
Less than 4 years of high school	242	290	180	249	301	182	211	241	172	210	232	167
8 years of school or less	227	259	169	232	268	171	203	225	160	199	221	158
1 to 3 years of high school	256	314	187	268	326	190	217	257	177	235	266	185
4 years of high school or more	333	402	249	341	409	251	273	317	237	293	349	234
4 years of high school	291	363	222	298	372	224	243	294	209	264	319	211
1 to 3 years of college	334	398	259	342	405	261	283	325	246	316	370	258
4 years of college or more	417	482	325	422	490	326	350	396	326	371	414	308
4 years of college	393	459	299	402	471	301	321	354	296	340	384	285
5 years of college or more	443	507	362	445	510	359	416	449	384	421	446	*

Note: Dashes indicate that data was not available. * indicate that base was less than 50,000, so median income is not shown.
Source: Earl F. Mellor and George D. Stanas, "Usual Weekly Earnings: Another Look at Intergroup Differences and Basic Trends," *Monthly Labor Review,* April 1982, p. 16. Reprinted with permission.

Table 5-7
Low-wage workers, 1981

Workers	Percent of full-time workers	Percent earning under $150
Workers 16 to 24 years	19	41
Women	39	66
Blacks	10	17
Hispanics	5	10

Source: Earl F. Mellor and George D. Stanas, "Usual Weekly Earnings: Another Look at Intergroup Differences and Basic Trends," *Monthly Labor Review*, April 1982, p. 19. Reprinted with permission.

ings (and in unemployment) among the different groups. But a number of studies show that the overall effect of age is small (U.S. Commission on Civil Rights, 1982b, pp. 50–53; National Commission for Employment Policy, 1982, p. 51). And when we look at racial and ethnic economic inequalities by age, we can also see another troubling pattern. The degree of inequality in earnings *increases* sharply after the teenage years and the early 20s, as a glance back at Table 5-6 (pages 168–169) shows. White men under 25 earn somewhat more than blacks or Hispanics of the same age; as men get older, moving toward their peak earning years, the racial and ethnic disparities become much greater.

What this suggests is that youth of all groups start out in the labor market by working intermittently, in poorly paying jobs. But white men move out of that condition much more often and much more quickly, acquiring work experience, skills, and job advancement in a much steadier fashion. The U.S. Commission on Civil Rights reports that, as teenagers, white youth are actually somewhat more likely than Hispanic or black youth to work in marginal jobs, jobs that don't require serious training and that pay badly. But after age 20 or so, whites tend to move out of those jobs quickly, while minorities tend to stay in them (U.S. Commission on Civil Rights, 1982b, p. 53).

Still another part of the explanation for racial inequalities in earnings involves education and skill levels. Workers with limited education and few marketable skills unsurprisingly, make less money. And though differences in school attainment are narrowing among the races, they still exist, particularly between Hispanics and whites. How much does this affect their different fortunes in the labor market?

Some, but not enough to account for all of the inequality in earnings. These inequalities *do* tend to decrease among the more highly educated. Table 5-6 (pages 168–169) shows, for example, that black workers with some graduate-school education earn about 90 percent of similarly educated whites.

And studies do show that limited school attainment has important consequences for Hispanics' levels of jobs and earnings. Their problems are further compounded by the language difficulties still faced even by many younger Hispanics. As many as 45 percent of Hispanic adults, according to

John Meyers/Picture Group

Minority youth often re-
main trapped in low-wage
jobs.

one estimate, have difficulties with English; as many as 40 percent of Mexican-Americans and 50 percent of mainland Puerto Ricans aged 20 to 24
have not graduated from high school (National Commission for Employment Policy, 1982, pp. 3–4). These differences translate into substantial
problems with both earnings and unemployment. But — as is true for the
educational levels of blacks — they do not explain all of the inequality these
groups suffer in the labor market. At *every* level of education, there are still
differences between whites and minority groups in earnings (and
unemployment).

Table 5-6 (pages 168–169) again shows this in raw figures. Black men
with four years of college earn less than white men with four years of high
school, and Hispanic men with four years of college earn only slightly more.
More elaborate social science research consistently finds that what researchers call the *returns to education* (the payoff in earnings for each further stage
of school completed) are greater for whites than for minorities. One recent

Minorities and the Job Market   **171**

study, for example, found that black high school graduates earned 65 percent of what white high school graduates earned. If they had had the same level of training and experience, their earnings would have risen, but only to 69 percent of whites'. If they had been *paid* at the same rate as whites, though, for their experience and education, they would have earned closer to 90 percent of white earnings (Hanushek, 1982). The Civil Rights Commission's study, similarly, concluded that increased education "helps everyone, but it helps majority males the most" (U.S. Commission on Civil Rights, 1982b, p. 53).

Some studies have estimated how much of the racial differences in earnings can be attributed to several of these factors (age, region, education), plus other individual and group characteristics (such as amounts of job training) put together. Again, the conclusion has been that though the combination of characteristics that different groups bring to the labor market does have a significant effect on what happens once they get there, it still leaves a substantial amount of inequality unexplained (Bianchi, 1981; Darity, 1982; Reimers, 1982; U.S. Commission on Civil Rights, 1982b).

Not all of that unexplained inequality can necessarily be attributed to current discrimination in the labor market. But the evidence for a continuing impact of such discrimination is strong.

Moreover, as many critics have noted, the argument that economic inequality is now due mainly to "background" characteristics, *rather* than current discrimination, sidesteps the fact that many of those characteristics may themselves be the product of systematic discrimination *outside* the labor market itself. Thus, despite the growing equality in levels of schooling completed among blacks and whites, few would argue that the *quality* of the schools they attend is the same — or that the differences in school quality are unrelated to racial discrimination. Health status also affects success in the labor market, and health, as we'll see in detail in Chapter 9, is in turn deeply affected by race and ethnicity, often in ways that clearly indicate the presence of discrimination in living conditions and the provision of health care. And the overall quality of local community life also has an important impact on individuals' chances of success in the job market. Growing up in neighborhoods with low income and high levels of segregation has been shown to have an independent, negative effect on young men's earnings later in life (Datcher, 1982).

The "Job Ladder": Progress and Marginality

Explaining racial differences in earnings and unemployment is obviously complicated. But it's also clear that an important part of these differences involves the way in which — for whatever reasons — minorities remain unequally represented in different *kinds* of jobs. Recognizing this, much of the government's civil rights effort since the 1960s has attacked the problems of discrimination and segregation that have traditionally kept minorities confined to the lower rungs of the occupational ladder in the United States. In this section, we'll examine this issue. What kinds of jobs do minorities hold? Has their job distribution changed much under the impact of antidiscrimination policies?

Table 5-8, based on surveys by the U.S. Equal Employment Opportunity Commission, shows how various minority groups are distributed in today's economy. The table reveals wide inequalities. At the beginning of the 1980s, blacks were roughly 12 percent of all workers, but only 4 percent of officials, managers, and professionals; more than 20 percent of service workers and almost 20 percent of laborers were black. About 1 in 20 workers were Hispanic, but only 1 in 50 Hispanics were professionals, officials, and managers, and 1 in 9 were laborers. Among all the groups surveyed, only Asian-Americans were overrepresented, in light of their proportion of total employees, in the highest-level jobs, and even then they were overrepresented only among professional and technical workers, not among managers or officials. Members of other minority groups are disproportionately service workers, laborers, and semiskilled operatives, and are much less often found in upper white-collar jobs. Blacks are also greatly underrepresented in the relatively high-paying skilled blue-collar craft jobs.

What about the trends in minority employment over time? Here the picture looks somewhat better. Since 1973, as Table 5-8 shows, blacks have significantly improved their representation in professional and managerial jobs, while their concentration at the bottom of the scale, among laborers and service workers, has decreased somewhat. The pattern is a bit more complicated for Hispanics. The gains they made in representation in higher-level jobs must be qualified by their substantial increase as a proportion of *all* workers. Hispanics did best over the 1970s in moving into managerial and skilled craft jobs, achieved slight gains in the professions, and slight declines in the lower-skilled service and blue-collar jobs.

These gains are real ones, but they do not leave us with anything remotely approaching occupational equality for most minorities. Overall, Hispanics, blacks, and native Americans were 17 percent of the workers surveyed in 1980, but they were less than 7 percent of professionals, and almost 33 percent of laborers. Clearly, at this pace, it would take many years before their representation in the job distribution equaled their proportion of the population.

Moreover, as is so often the case, these gains must be qualified in several ways. The qualifications show up most clearly in the case of blacks, the group for which we have the most detailed data. Though black job gains in the 1970s were significant, for example, they came at a much slower pace than they had in the 1960s: The number of blacks in professional and craft jobs grew only about *half as fast* in the 1970s as in the previous decade of economic expansion and the first flush of the federal civil rights effort (Westcott, 1982, p. 29). In addition, an important part of the black job gains reflects two historically limited changes — the continued shift of black workers out of farm work and domestic service (Table 5-9). The *single most* striking shift in black employment in recent years has been the movement

Table 5-8

Minority employment in firms with 100 or more employees, by sex and occupational group, 1973 and 1980

Year, minority group, and sex	Total employed	White-collar workers						Blue-collar workers				Service workers
		Total	Professional	Technical	Managers and officials	Sales-workers	Clerical workers	Total	Craft workers	Operatives	Laborers	
1973												
Both sexes												
Number (thousands)	31,838.9	15,060.5	2,702.5	1,439.5	3,065.6	2,745.2	5,107.7	14,287.4	4,172.8	7,220.5	2,894.1	2,490.9
Percent												
Black	10.8	5.6	3.2	7.5	2.7	5.1	8.5	13.9	6.5	15.4	20.7	24.7
Hispanic	4.1	2.3	1.4	2.6	1.4	2.5	3.1	5.7	3.6	5.4	9.5	6.2
Asian	.8	1.1	2.4	1.3	.4	.6	1.0	.4	.3	.4	.5	1.0
Native American	.4	.3	.2	.3	.3	.3	.3	.5	.4	.4	.6	.4
Male												
Number (thousands)	20,204.7	8,114.2	1,923.7	982.5	2,673.9	1,469.2	1,064.9	10,883.3	3,860.2	5,002.3	2,020.8	1,207.3
Percent												
Black	10.1	3.7	2.2	4.5	2.3	4.3	8.1	13.3	6.1	15.3	21.9	24.8
Hispanic	4.2	2.0	1.3	2.6	1.3	2.4	3.9	5.4	3.4	5.2	9.7	7.9
Asian	.7	1.1	2.2	1.3	.4	.6	1.2	.3	.3	.3	.4	1.2
Native American	.4	.2	.2	.3	.3	.3	.2	.4	.4	.4	.7	.4
Female												
Number (thousands)	11,634.1	6,946.4	778.9	457.0	391.7	1,276.0	4,042.8	3,404.1	312.6	2,218.2	873.3	1,283.6
Percent												
Black	12.1	7.9	5.7	14.0	5.2	6.0	8.6	15.9	11.9	15.6	17.9	24.6
Hispanic	4.0	2.6	1.5	2.8	1.7	2.6	2.9	6.6	5.5	5.7	9.2	4.6
Asian	.9	1.1	2.9	1.5	.6	.6	.9	.6	.8	.6	.6	.8
Native American	.4	.3	.2	.3	.3	.3	.3	.5	.5	.5	.6	.4

Year, minority group, and sex	Total employed	White-collar workers						Blue-collar workers				Service workers
		Total	Professional	Technical	Managers and officials	Sales workers	Clerical workers	Total	Craft workers	Operatives	Laborers	
1980												
Both sexes												
Number (thousands)	34,075.9	17,257.7	3,242.2	1,845.0	3,743.1	3,041.2	5,386.1	13,765.7	4,229.2	6,867.8	2,668.7	3,052.5
Percent												
Black	11.6	7.4	4.3	8.7	4.0	7.1	11.2	14.4	8.4	16.2	19.4	22.4
Hispanic	5.4	3.3	1.9	3.5	2.2	3.8	4.6	7.5	5.2	7.1	12.2	7.9
Asian	1.5	1.8	3.5	2.4	1.0	1.0	1.7	1.0	0.8	1.2	1.2	1.8
Native American	.4	.4	.3	.4	.4	.3	0.4	.5	.5	.5	.6	.5
Male												
Number (thousands)	20,115.4	8,557.0	2,037.3	1,103.9	3,049.9	1,437.3	928.6	10,186.5	3,824.1	4,605.4	1,757.0	1,371.9
Percent												
Black	6.1	2.5	1.9	3.7	2.7	2.7	2.0	9.8	7.1	10.3	12.9	10.1
Hispanic	3.3	1.4	1.2	2.2	1.7	1.8	1.0	5.3	4.5	4.6	8.4	4.7
Asian	.8	.9	2.2	1.5	.7	.5	.4	.6	.6	.5	.6	.9
Native American	.3	.2	.2	.2	.3	.2	.2	.4	.4	.3	.4	.2
Female												
Number (thousands)	13,960.5	8,700.7	1,205.0	741.0	693.2	1,603.9	4,457.6	3,579.2	405.1	2,262.4	911.7	1,680.6
Percent												
Black	5.4	4.9	2.4	5.0	1.2	4.4	9.2	4.6	1.3	5.9	6.5	12.4
Hispanic	2.1	1.9	.7	1.3	.5	2.1	3.6	2.2	.7	2.5	3.8	3.2
Asian	.7	.9	1.4	1.0	.2	.5	1.3	.5	.2	.5	.5	.9
Native American	.1	.2	.1	.1	.1	.1	.3	.1	.1	.2	.2	.2

These estimates are based on reports filed with the U.S. Equal Employment Opportunity Commission. Since the estimates cover only firms with 100 or more workers, they do not include smaller American businesses. They also provide only limited data on certain industries, such as agriculture and construction; and they are limited to *private* employers.

Source: Adapted from *Employment and Training Report of the President* (Washington, D.C.: Government Printing Office, 1983), pp. 337–338.

	Employment changes			
	Black employment changes, 1972–1980		White employment changes, 1972–1980	
Occupation	Number (thousands)	Percent	Number (thousands)	Percent
Total employment	1,344	17.3	13,306	18.2
White-collar workers	1,185	55.3	10,022	27.4
Professional and technical	354	55.4	3,592	33.8
Managers and administrators	168	69.1	2,639	34.2
Sales	88	51.9	698	13.5
Clerical	580	52.7	3,094	23.8
Blue-collar workers	215	6.8	1,760	7.0
Craft and kindred workers	217	32.3	1,427	14.2
Operatives, except transport	73	5.8	−209	−2.3
Transport equipment operatives	41	9.0	204	7.5
Nonfarm laborers	−116	−14.7	337	10.0
Service workers	21	1.0	1,826	21.2
Private household workers	−238	−41.8	−159	−18.6
Other service workers	259	15.9	1,985	25.6
Farmworkers	−74	−31.9	−302	−10.8
Farm managers	−23	−51.1	−187	−11.4
Farm laborers	−51	−27.3	−116	−9.9

Table 5-9

Occupational distribution of blacks: changes and continuities, 1972 and 1980

of black women from working as servants in private households to working in clerical jobs as typists, secretaries, and file clerks.

There is no doubt that these changes represent relative improvements, but both are self-limiting processes. By the beginning of the 1980s, the movement out of farm work was almost complete and the proportion of black women in household service was bottoming out.

But there is a more complex problem as well. The broad statistics on changes in wide occupational groups obscure the issue of just what *specific jobs* minorities have been able to attain in recent years. Thus, the category of professional and technical workers, so commonly used in social science, includes some very well paid occupations (such as doctors, engineers, and judges) but also some (such as recreational workers, vocational counselors, and health technicians) that are paid considerably less than most skilled, or even some semiskilled, blue-collar jobs. As Table 5-10 shows, when we look more closely at the job ladder, the minority gains appear in a much different light. Black men in professional and technical jobs were most concentrated,

Occupation	Distribution							
	Black males		White males		Black females		White females	
	1972	1980	1972	1980	1972	1980	1972	1980
Total employed (thousands)	4,347	4,704	45,769	5,033	3,406	4,394	27,305	36,043
Percent	100.0	100.0	100.0	100.0	100.0	100.0	100.0	100.0
Professional and technical	6.4	8.2	14.3	16.1	10.6	13.8	14.9	17.0
Managers and adminstrators	4.0	5.6	14.0	15.3	2.1	3.4	4.8	7.4
Sales	1.7	2.5	6.6	6.4	2.5	2.8	7.8	7.3
Clerical	7.6	8.4	6.8	6.2	22.7	29.3	36.2	36.0
Craft and kindred workers	14.8	17.6	21.2	21.5	.9	1.4	1.3	1.9
Operatives, except transport	17.4	15.5	12.1	10.7	14.8	13.8	12.5	9.4
Transport equipment operatives	10.3	9.9	5.7	5.4	.4	.7	.4	.7
Nonfarm laborers	17.4	13.0	6.8	6.5	.9	1.4	.9	1.2
Farm and farm managers	1.0	.4	3.4	2.6			.4	.4
Farm laborers and supervisors	3.5	2.4	1.7	1.5	1.1	.5	1.5	1.3
Private household workers	.3	.1			16.4	7.4	3.0	1.9
Other service workers	15.8	16.4	7.3	7.9	27.6	25.4	16.2	16.0

Source: Diane N. Westcott, "Blacks in the 1970s: Did They Scale the Job Ladder?" *Monthly Labor Review*, June 1982, p. 30. Reprinted with permission.

in 1980, in the kinds of jobs they had also held in 1972 — health technicians, counselors, social and recreational workers. Though their proportions increased in some higher-paying jobs, such as lawyers and engineers, they remained a very small fraction of men in those occupations; they made no progress at all in increasing their representation among doctors and dentists. In the broad managerial category, they showed a strong increase among bank and financial managers, but mainly remained concentrated in areas (such as restaurant and bar management) where they had been at the beginning of the decade. Blacks' share of skilled craft jobs improved slightly, but these traditionally good jobs remained the only realm of blue-collar work in which black men were underrepresented, relative to their numbers in the working population. Black women did somewhat better, measured in this way, than men, as their proportions in such fields as computer work, engi-

Table 5-10

Climbing the job ladder: employed blacks as a percent of all employed men and women in selected occupations, 1972 and 1980, annual averages

Occupation	Black males		Black females	
	1972	1980	1972	1980
Total	8.6	8.4	11.0	10.6
Professional and technical	4.0	4.4	8.0	8.8
Accountants	2.1	3.6	5.2	7.4
Computer specialists	3.5	4.1	6.5	9.3
Engineers	1.4	2.2	*	*
Personnel and labor relations	6.1	7.9	12.5	10.8
Physicians, dentists, and related practitioners	2.1	2.1	*	5.0
Nurses, dietitians, therapists	8.6	13.2	6.1	8.2
Health technologists and technicians	12.4	8.4	7.8	9.2
Lawyers and judges	1.3	3.1	*	7.1
Religious workers	10.0	5.7	*	*
Social and recreation workers	13.8	16.4	17.4	17.4
Teachers, college and university	3.6	3.3	5.4	5.3
Teachers, except college and university	7.0	5.5	9.0	10.2
Engineering and science technicians	3.5	5.6	*	6.7
Vocational and educational counselors	9.0	15.2	13.4	17.8
Writers, artists, and entertainers	4.2	4.1	2.8	3.6
Managers and administrators	2.6	3.2	5.0	5.2
Bank officials and financial managers	*	2.6	*	4.6
Restaurant, cafeteria, and bar managers	4.8	5.7	10.6	7.9
School administrators, elementary and secondary	6.7	6.0	6.9	12.2
Sales	2.4	3.5	3.8	4.4
Insurance agents, brokers, and underwriters	2.3	4.3	7.8	8.2
Sales clerks, retail trade	4.2	7.0	4.1	5.0
Clerical	9.5	10.9	7.2	8.9
Bank tellers	*	10.3	4.0	5.9
Bookkeepers	3.7	6.7	2.4	3.4
Cashiers	7.5	8.7	6.5	8.6
Counter clerks, except food	4.7	5.4	6.2	8.6
Estimators and investigators	2.5	6.0	7.3	11.7
File clerks	22.0	25.6	16.0	18.2
Library attendants and assistants	*	*	8.7	8.5
Mail carriers, post office	13.1	11.6	*	*
Mail handlers, except post office	25.0	22.1	12.5	17.9

Occupation	Black males		Black females	
	1972	1980	1972	1980
Messengers and office helpers	16.4	16.9	*	*
Office machine operators	9.8	14.0	11.9	15.1
Postal clerks	16.0	14.8	26.7	32.7
Receptionists	*	*	6.4	6.4
Secretaries	*	12.1	4.4	5.5
Shipping and receiving clerks	13.0	13.1	13.4	8.3
Statistical clerks	8.0	11.8	7.1	11.3
Stock clerks and storekeepers	12.2	10.5	10.3	11.0
Teachers aides	*	*	21.2	17.3
Telephone operators	*	*	*	14.8
Typists	*	*	10.9	13.2
Craft and kindred workers	6.2	7.0	8.0	8.1
Carpenters	5.1	4.4	*	*
Brickmasons and stonemasons	13.6	14.6	*	*
Bulldozer operators	13.6	11.7	*	*
Cement and concrete finishers	33.3	31.0	*	*
Electricians	2.8	4.1	*	*
Excavating, grading, and road machinery operators	6.6	8.2	*	*
Painters, construction and maintenance	9.3	10.5	*	*
Plumbers and pipe fitters	5.1	8.5	*	*
Machinists and jobsetters	5.6	6.3	*	*
Metal craftsmen, except mechanical, machinery, and jobsetters	4.9	6.2	*	*
Mechanics, automotive	7.4	7.7	*	*
Mechanics, except automotive	4.5	6.1	*	8.9
Printing craftsmen	4.5	7.3	8.5	8.6
Cranesmen, derrickmen, hoistmen	15.5	16.3	*	*
Operatives, except transport	11.9	11.7	12.7	14.6
Assemblers	13.3	11.2	11.8	11.9
Checkers, examiners, and inspectors (manufacturing)	7.6	9.6	9.3	10.8
Clothing ironers and pressers	28.9	*	38.4	40.4
Furnacemen, smeltermen, and pourers	23.9	25.4	*	*
Garage workers and gas station attendants	7.3	7.9	*	*
Laundry and drycleaning operators	24.0	21.9	28.7	23.3
Meatcutters and butchers	9.4	8.5	19.4	18.6
Packers and wrappers	12.6	20.4	13.4	15.4
Painters, manufacturing articles	14.5	10.7	*	*
Precision machine operators	6.9	6.7	10.3	18.2

Table 5-10
(*continued*)

Occupation	Black males		Black females	
	1972	1980	1972	1980
Operatives, except transport (*continued*)				
Punch and stamping press	10.5	11.0	11.6	9.1
Sawyers	19.1	17.4	*	*
Sewers and stitchers	*	14.3	11.3	13.8
Textile operatives	18.9	22.1	12.4	20.7
Welders and flamecutters	9.4	9.8	*	*
Transport equipment operatives	14.5	14.7	9.0	11.2
Busdrivers	21.7	24.0	7.0	13.1
Deliverypersons and routepersons	10.0	9.2	*	5.1
Forklift and tow motor operators	21.7	18.8	*	*
Taxicab drivers and chauffeurs	22.5	24.0	*	*
Truck drivers	13.9	13.5	*	7.3
Laborers, except farm	19.2	15.5	12.0	12.2
Construction laborers	24.7	15.4	*	*
Freight and material handlers	21.7	17.5	17.8	19.7
Garbage collectors	33.3	32.8	*	*
Gardeners and groundskeepers	16.5	14.1	*	*
Stockhandlers	8.8	10.4	10.7	10.0
Vehicle washers and equipment cleaners	21.9	18.4	*	*
Farm and farm managers	2.6	1.6	3.0	*
Farmers (owners and tenants)	2.6	1.6	3.0	*
Farm laborers and foremen	16.1	12.7	8.1	7.0
Farm laborers, wage workers	19.3	14.3	23.5	15.7
Service workers, except private household	16.8	15.7	17.3	15.9
Cleaning service workers	25.4	22.8	35.3	30.2
Food service workers	12.8	11.5	11.2	10.1
Health service workers	24.5	32.1	23.7	21.0
Personal service workers	13.9	15.0	11.2	12.6
Private household workers	*	*	39.8	31.9
Protective service workers	9.2	9.8	16.9	17.4
Private household workers	*	*	39.8	31.9
Child care	*	*	8.0	7.0
Maids and servants	*	*	71.1	52.5

*Data not shown where numerator is less than 4,000 or denominator is less than 35,000.

Source: Diane N. Westcott, "Blacks in the 1970s: Did They Scale the Job Ladder?" *Monthly Labor Review*, June 1982, p. 32. Reprinted with permission.

neering technicians, lawyers, and bank officials increased strongly. And, again, the movement out of domestic service has helped raise black women's overall job position considerably.

But despite those advances, the overall picture is one that shows a troubling continuity — a continuity that is apparent not only in the still-small numbers of blacks in many of the highest-level jobs but also in their long-standing concentration in some of the poorest-paying and lowest-status jobs in America. In 1972 the single job category with the highest percentage of black men was garbage collectors; it still was in 1980. The single job category with the highest percentage of black women — in both years — was maids and servants.

Racial Inequality and the Future

Recent trends in racial inequality, then, present a mixed picture. On the positive side, important gains have been made, especially in occupational status, helping to bridge the economic gap between minorities and whites. But those gains, though impressive, have been limited in crucial ways. With some exceptions, *most* of the progress against inequality took place in the late 1960s and early 1970s; it has slowed or even reversed since then. And even during the period of greatest progress, the gains were unevenly distributed among the minority population. The growth of an upwardly mobile, relatively affluent middle class, though often exaggerated, was a significant development. But it was accompanied by the stubborn persistence of wide — even growing — disparities in rates of poverty and unemployment, especially in the inner cities. While the chances of upward social mobility improved for some, the relative chances of being trapped in an urban underclass increased for others.

What is the outlook for the future? On balance, it isn't encouraging. To a large extent, the progress against racial inequality was the result of several *specific* favorable trends, some of which are not likely to repeat themselves, at least to the same extent, in the future. And new developments, both in the economy and in public policy, threaten to undermine the progress that has been made. We've looked at these developments already in discussing the outlook for poverty and income inequality in Chapter 4. Now let's look closer at what they could mean for minorities.

Economic Threats to Racial Equality

We've already noted one bad omen. Some of the most dramatic recent gains for minorities resulted from broad social and economic changes that are unlikely to reappear, at least not with the same magnitude or intensity. Improvements in minority poverty rates and in income inequality were partly a by-product of the social and economic transformation that brought the South closer into line with the rest of the country. Regional improvements on that scale aren't likely in the foreseeable future. Thus, the gloomier record of the North and West may be a more accurate indicator of what's to come.

Likewise, some of the most significant improvements in occupational status came about mainly through fundamental, one-time shifts in the structure of jobs itself: from domestic service to clerical work, from farm labor to manufacturing industries. It's conceivable that similar changes may come again — but it isn't clear what they would be or when they might come. And one of the most troubling portents for the future is that some of the jobs and industries in which minorities have made the most gains are precisely those that are being undermined by the massive, rapid changes now under way in the American economy. Since the start of World War II, for example, well-paying blue-collar jobs in manufacturing have been a main avenue of job security and mobility for blacks and Mexican-Americans. Movement into higher-level blue-collar jobs was one of the most important components of black occupational advancement in the 1970s. But these jobs are threatened as many basic industries have either undergone decline or are quickly restructuring themselves to meet the new, harsher demands of an age of "reindustrialization" (U.S. Commission on Civil Rights, 1982b, p. 38). In the late 1970s, black workers held about 9 percent of all jobs. But

Asian-Americans: Trials of a "Successful" Minority

The experience of Asian-Americans is often taken as proof that anyone who really works at it can succeed in America in spite of discrimination. The same kinds of discrimination and exclusion that are often held responsible for some groups' poverty, dependency, and social pathology, in this view, have actually strengthened the resolve of others to get ahead. One noted sociologist, for example, draws these lessons from the status of Asian-Americans:

> The gross discrimination, the collective frustrations, to which Chinese and Japanese have been subjected ordinarily result in a pattern of poor education, low income, high crime rate, and unstable family life, with each of these reinforcing all the other components of a self-sustaining slum. Efforts to assist members of such "prob-

> lem minorities" in achieving parity with the general population have seldom been altogether successful. However, these two minorities . . . themselves broke through the barriers of prejudice and, by such key indices as education and income, surpassed the average levels of native-born whites. This anomalous record, like the earlier one of Jews, challenges the premises from which the etiologies of poverty, crime, illegitimacy and other social ills are typically deduced. (Peterson, 1978, pp. 65–66)

In other words, from this perspective, discrimination creates real problems only for groups who are already, in some sense, "problem" minorities. This separation of different groups into problem minorities versus successful ones, however, has two unfortunate consequences. One, often noted by Asian-American writers, is that the image of success tends to mask the real problems the "successful" group faces. Asian-American communities have often wound up on the short end of government funds for social programs because of this bias; for that matter, they are often ignored

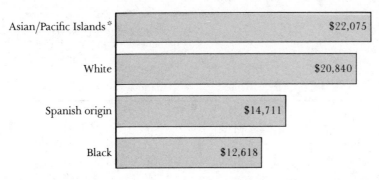

Figure 5-6
Median family income by race and Hispanic origin, 1979

Source: U.S. Bureau of the Census, *1980 Census of Population and Housing, Supplementary Report, Provisional Estimates of Social, Economic, and Housing Characteristics*, Washington, D.C., March 1982.

*Asian/Pacific Islander combines Japanese, Chinese, Filipino-Americans, and other Pacific and Asian-American groups. This masks important differences among the specific groups in family income; not all have higher income than whites.

they held more than 15 percent of the jobs in auto and steel, two of the industries most hurt by foreign competition and now rapidly shifting to greater automation and a smaller work force (Anderson, 1982, p. 8). More generally, blacks were about 18 percent of all unskilled manufacturing laborers and 17 percent of semiskilled manufacturing workers at the beginning of the 1980s, a time when the role of unskilled and semiskilled blue-collar labor

even in the collection of government statistics (U.S. Commission on Civil Rights, 1980a).

The second consequence of the success stereotype is that it implies that other groups' relative lack of success is their own fault. In this view, if blacks or Puerto Ricans haven't "made it" in American society to the same extent as Japanese- or Chinese-Americans, the problem must lie primarily in their attitudes or culture and not in continued discrimination by the larger society. After all, Asian-Americans have suffered their own harsh history of exclusion and persecution; as recently as the 1940s, Japanese-Americans were interned in camps and lost much of their property.

Some version of this reasoning has been used to argue against the extension of special consideration to other minorities. Instead, blacks, Puerto Ricans, Mexican-Americans, and others are urged to learn to pull themselves up by their own bootstraps, with the same perseverance that has presumably brought status and success to Asian-Americans (Sowell, 1979; Glazer, 1981).

What should we make of this argument? A careful analysis of the complex historical differences among the various Asian-American groups, and between those groups and other minorities, would take much more space than we have here. (For some useful leads, see Steinberg, 1980; Bonacich and Modell, 1981; Lieberson, 1981.) For now, let's look harder at the stereotype of Asian-American success itself, on which the broader arguments about ethnic culture and progress are based.

Have Asian-Americans really succeeded in America? Naturally, the answer depends on what we choose to define as "success." Without undervaluing the very real achievements of these groups, a closer look shows that their progress — while substantial (see Figure 5-6) — is also limited in revealing ways.

It's important, first of all, to distinguish the experience of different Asian-American groups. Japanese-Americans uniformly show the highest income and the lowest rates of poverty, while among Chinese-Americans and Filipino-Americans, median income is considerably lower, and rates of poverty are relatively high. Like blacks and Hispanics, the Chinese- and Filipino-Ameri-

Table 5-11
Poverty rate for states with highest Asian/Pacific Island population, by race, 1979

State	Persons below poverty level as a percent of total population			
	White	Asian/Pacific Island	Black	Hispanic
California	9	13	20	15
Hawaii	10	9	*	16
Illinois	7	16	34	19
New York	10	15	28	37
Texas	11	23	29	28
United States	9	14	30	24

Note: Poverty rates have been rounded to the nearest whole figure.
*Indicates that the base is too small to calculate.
Source: Calculated from U.S. Bureau of the Census, "Provisional Estimates of Social, Economic, and Housing Characteristics, States and Selected SMSA's," *1980 Census of Population and Housing,* Washington, D.C., March 1982, pp. 47–58.

can communities show a sharp division between those with better jobs and higher income and those suffering high rates of poverty and rising unemployment, especially for youth.

Success, then, hasn't been uniform among the different Asian-American groups. Data from the 1980 census indicate the dimensions of poverty among some Asian-Americans. These data are for the very broad, diverse category the census calls Asian/Pacific Islander, and that category mixes together the experiences of quite different groups, but the data are illustrative. In California, the state with by far the largest Asian/Pacific Island population, their rate of poverty was about 13 percent in 1979 — well below the Hispanic and black rates, but well above the white rate (see Table 5-11). In New York, a state with a high proportion of Chinese-Americans within the Asian population, the rate was about 15 percent, half again the white rate. And in Texas, at 23 percent, Asian/Pacific Island poverty was double the white rate and approached that of Hispanics and blacks.

But there are more subtle problems with the "success" stereotype. Most income comparisons fail to adjust for the fact that Asian-Americans are, on average, more highly educated than whites, and in other ways bring *higher* qualifications to the labor market. Studies adjusting for these differences show that, in terms of income and occupational status, Asian-Americans fare less well than whites *with comparable educations.* One recent study of minority gains in academic employment, for example, found that when the quality of their training and professional accomplishments were considered, Asian-American faculty members were consistently underpaid relative to both whites *and blacks.* "The presumption," the economist Richard Freeman notes, "is of some market discrimination" (1978b, p. 197).

In a 1978 study, the U.S. Commission on Civil Rights calculated the earnings of different minority groups as a percentage of white earnings, both before and after differences in age, state of residence, education, and weeks and hours of work were taken into account. When all these factors were considered, some groups' earnings relative to whites' improved over the picture given by the conventional statistics. But the opposite held for

seems likely to decline *permanently* in the American economy. Hispanics, less than 6 percent of workers in American private industry, are about 11 percent of manufacturing laborers (*Employment and Training Report of the President*, 1983, p. 340).

Just as this overconcentration of minorities in certain jobs and industries poses dangers for racial equality in the future, so, too, does the overconcentration of minorities in some of the areas and regions most disrupted by economic change. We've seen that minority income, relative to white, began to fall in the 1970s in the North and Midwest. This was partly the result of industrial decline in those regions, which meant disproportionately higher unemployment for minority workers, and a much slower growth of jobs in the economic recovery afterward. If present patterns of regional decline and uneven growth continue, they will perpetuate the shift of jobs and income away from traditional industrial areas with high concentrations of nonwhites. Should stronger economic growth continue in the South and Southwest, though, it might partially offset this trend by providing expanded job and income opportunities for blacks in the South and Hispanics in the Southwest.

both Chinese- and Japanese-Americans. Both have high median earnings, measured conventionally — higher than whites in the case of Japanese-Americans. And both improved through the early 1970s relative to the white average. But both groups tend to be older, to live in high-income areas, to be better educated, and to work longer and more regularly than whites. When these facts are considered, the adjusted earnings of both groups *dropped* relative to those of whites — and both turned out to have *lost* ground during the 1970s. In fact, measured this way, *the relative earnings of Chinese-Americans were the lowest of any minority group in America* (U.S. Commission on Civil Rights, 1978, p. 54).

Occupationally, Asian-Americans have done well — but again, not uniformly. Asian-Americans are highly concentrated in professional and technical fields. More than 30 percent of Asian-Americans, according to data from the Equal Employment Opportunity Commission, are in those two categories — double the proportion of whites and more than four times that of blacks and Hispanics. But they are also underrepresented in managerial and administrative positions. Though the proportion of Asian-Americans in those positions is nearly twice the comparable proportion of blacks, it is only about half that of whites. One interpretation of this distinctive pattern is that though Asian-Americans have high levels of education and achievement, they have only rarely been able to translate those qualities into economic power or official influence. Such a view is borne out by the position of Asian-Americans in business, which, according to a report from the U.S. Office of Minority Business Enterprise in the late 1970s, is marginal. Asian-Americans "are *not* in the mainstream of American business" and "are not competing well in securing a proportionate share of the market" (U.S. Commission on Civil Rights, 1980a, p. 10).

But this hope is clouded for several reasons. Some proportion of minority industrial workers might be able to pull up stakes to follow the shift of jobs out of the North and Midwest. But that option is less realistic for the inner-city minority poor, who are often women heading families with dependent children, lacking the skills, training, or adequate public services to help them make such a transition. And recent studies show that even in fast-growing regions, there are few jobs for the unskilled.

The accelerating flight of jobs and industries from central cities also has an unequal impact on minorities. The industries most likely to shut down or move away tend to be those with a higher proportion of minority workers; those that start up anew in the suburbs and outlying areas tend to hire fewer minority workers. Thus, between 1970 and 1976, the city of Chicago lost 92,000 jobs, about 7 percent of the city's total. But of those jobs, 50,000 were in predominantly black communities. Meanwhile, the counties surrounding the city, where the number of jobs *grew* by 72 percent, had very small minority populations. Illinois firms that relocated from central cities to

The State of Native America

American Indians — native Americans — are often neglected in discussions of the social problems of minorities in America. Part of the reason for this neglect may be that their numbers are relatively small (about 1.4 million, including Eskimos and Aleutian natives, according to the 1980 census); many are also isolated in rural areas and on reservations where their problems are less publicly visible. And urban native Americans, though a substantial population in several cities, are nevertheless a group that is dwarfed in size and political influence by others. During the 1970s, too, the energy boom in the American west brought some wealth to some of the native American tribes, which sometimes led to exaggerated portraits of newly affluent reservations growing rich off of mineral rights.

But data from the 1980 census show that native Americans are one of the most severely and persistently disadvantaged groups in America. In many places they are significantly worse off than other minorities, at least in those realms that are measurable by census statistics.

Nearly half of all native Americans live in the five states with the largest native American population: California, Oklahoma, Arizona, New Mexico, and North Carolina. As a *proportion* of the population, they are most highly concentrated in New Mexico — about 8 percent of the state's residents.

New Mexico can serve as a microcosm of the condition of native Americans in the United States as a whole. In 1979 the median annual family income among New Mexico's native Americans was $10,826; among blacks, $12,063; and among whites, $18,429. Measured in per capita terms, the income of native Americans was even lower relative to other groups: $2,972 compared to $4,731 for blacks and $6,886 for whites. Thirty-eight percent of native American families in the state were below the poverty line in 1979, compared to ten percent of white and twenty-six percent of black families. And among those below the poverty line, native Americans were typically poorer than either blacks or whites. Their average income deficit (the amount it would take to raise them to the poverty line) was $5,452, compared to $4,215 for poor black families and $3,387 for whites.

Similar disparities show up in the realms of employment and education. The native American unemployment rate in 1980 was about 15 percent in New Mexico, compared to 13 percent for

suburbs employed fewer workers after the move than before, and the workers most likely to lose their jobs in the process were blacks. And new firms, opening plants in the state for the first time, hired a smaller proportion of minority workers, on average, than the older firms that had shut down or left the state (U.S. Commission on Civil Rights, Illinois Advisory Committee, 1981, pp. 20–42).

So the problem is not just that recession and economic decline hurt minorities disproportionately. More ominously, the new patterns of economic *recovery* — the trends in economic "revitalization" or "renewal" — may not, by themselves, help minorities' economic situation very much. At worst, the changes now under way in the national economy threaten to block some of the most important past avenues to economic security and upward mobility while offering few real alternatives. Economic growth itself, in other words, once a key means of reducing racial inequality, now may even widen it — in the absence of programs specifically designed to ensure that its benefits are made equally accessible to all groups.

blacks and 6 percent for whites. Thirty-two percent of young native Americans aged 16 to 19 were neither working nor attending school. Less than half of native Americans older than 25, in fact, had completed high school, compared to more than three-fifths of New Mexico's blacks and almost three-fourths of whites. Native Americans, indeed, were the only racial/ethnic group in the state whose *median* level of education was below high school graduation.

For native Americans living on reservations, these problems are even worse than they are for the population as a whole. Many large reservations are among the most depressed pockets of poverty, joblessness, educational deprivation, and family breakup in the United States. On the largest reservation in the country, the Navajo reservation extending through parts of New Mexico, Arizona, and Utah, the poverty rate is 50 percent. Per capita income is less than $2,500. Only a third of residents older than 25 have completed high school; three out of ten youth aged 16 to 19 are high school dropouts. On the Pine Ridge reservation in South Dakota, 49 percent of all persons are below the poverty line, the unemployment rate is more than 21 percent, and less than 50 percent of all children under 18 live with both parents.

At least on the surface, as measured by census indicators, living standards are somewhat better for urban native Americans — but they remain severely disadvantaged. In Los Angeles (which, with about 19,000 native Americans, is the largest single urban concentration), native American family income, at $16,556, is well above that of blacks ($12,778) but far below that of whites ($23,300). In New York City, 28 percent of native Americans, 30 percent of blacks, and 13 percent of whites are below the poverty line. In Minneapolis, another major center of urban native Americans, the poverty rate — at 41 percent — approaches reservation levels. It is four times the white rate and a third higher than the rate for blacks.

Sources: Data from U.S. Bureau of the Census, *Current Population Reports*, series P-20, no. 374, "Population Profile of the United States; 1981," Washington, D.C., 1982, p. 22; U.S. Bureau of the Census, *1980 Census of Population, General Social and Economic Characteristics*, volumes for New Mexico (pp. 40–266) and South Dakota (pp. 268–269); U.S. Bureau of the Census, *1980 Census of Population and Housing, Advance Estimates of Social, Economic, and Housing Characteristics*, volumes for California (p. 131), New York (p. 112), and Minnesota (p. 67), Washington, D.C.: Government Printing Office, 1983.

Minorities, Public Policy, and the Welfare State

These disturbing trends all reflect adverse developments in the larger economy. But it would be a mistake to think that they are therefore inevitable. Instead, they are shaped and directed by deliberate public policies. Policies that encourage industries to pack up and move from one state to another, or out of the country, in search of lower labor costs, lighter taxes, and fewer regulations, are policies that, whatever their intention, ultimately promote racial inequality through their disproportionate impact on minority workers. Policies to tighten the supply of money or credit in order to slow down the economy, likewise, widen the racial economic gap by increasing unemployment unequally among white and minority workers.

Even more clearly, public policies designed to curb the growth of government generally — and of the welfare state in particular — promise to have a powerful effect on the course of racial inequality. We saw in Chapter 4 that much of the progress against economic inequality in the United States, especially in recent years, has been connected with the growth of government. This is particularly true for progress against minority poverty and racial inequality, for several reasons.

The growth of government employment has been a main factor in minority gains in jobs and income in recent years; growth in the private economy, on the other hand, has brought disappointingly small benefits for minorities. Only 5 percent of all new jobs in private industry went to blacks, for example, during the 1970s. But, at the same time, minority representation in government employment grew substantially. 12 percent of government employees in 1965 were minorities, but almost 16 percent were in 1979. A recent study estimates that fully 55 percent of the growth in nonagricultural employment for black workers between 1960 and 1976 was in the public sector, as compared to 26 percent of the growth in white employment. And much of the growth in professional and managerial jobs for blacks in this period has been in public sector social welfare occupations (Anderson, 1982, p. 7; Brown and Erie, 1982).

Another recent study finds that a major reason for the fairly impressive gains in earnings by black women, as compared with Hispanic women, has been the much greater rate of employment of black women in the public sector (Reimers, 1982). Moreover, these gains do not simply reflect a general growth in public sector jobs. In the federal government, as we saw in Chapter 2, the number of jobs actually *fell* during the 1970s. But the number and proportion of minorities — both black and Hispanic — in federal jobs increased significantly. And for both blacks and Hispanics, the growth in federal employment was fastest in the higher-paying jobs, though minorities were still clearly underrepresented by the end of the decade. So the drive to cut back government spending and employment, in the name of freeing the energies of the private sector, seems likely to further weaken what has been a main ladder of upward mobility and good earnings, especially for the minority "middle class."

An even more troubling development is the sharp reduction in the social programs that have provided jobs and transfer payments for the minority poor and near-poor. We have seen that nonwhite unemployment has remained at crisis levels, and that even in periods of economic recovery, a significant part of the black community remains in a state of "permanent recession." Without public employment and training programs, minority unemployment would have been even more disastrously high. It's been estimated, for instance, that about one-third of the total increase in black employment between 1976 and 1978 came through the much-criticized Comprehensive Employment and Training Act (CETA). In the late 1970s, before that program was severely cut back, CETA employed almost one in every four black teenagers who were employed at all. The argument that similar jobs will now be provided by a revitalized private economy requires us to assume that the private economy will prove capable of providing steady employment for groups it has never steadily employed in the past — and that is a very large assumption indeed.

The movement to reduce government spending on *income transfers* also affects the probable future of racial inequality. The minority poor are even more dependent on the welfare state for basic survival than are the white poor, especially because of the high proportion of women heading families with dependent children. Under present conditions — with few adequate provisions for child care and job training — these families are unlikely to be helped greatly by the growth of the private economy alone.

The reductions in these programs are often defended on the ground that the quest for equality has "gone too far." That belief, as we've already seen, also underlies recent criticism of the antidiscrimination and affirmative action programs that have been responsible for many of the tangible economic gains minorities have achieved in the past decade and a half. Some argue that these programs, once necessary, have now done their job and can safely be deemphasized, if not abandoned altogether. Others argue that they actually accomplished little that would not have been achieved anyway as the result of market forces in the normal economy — and that they may even have hurt minorities' chances for equality by making them dependent on the help of the state rather than their own efforts (Williams, 1982). As we've seen, it is difficult to estimate the precise share of minority disadvantages in jobs and income that is due to current discrimination; but virtually all of the recent social science research suggests that discrimination still plays a substantial role. And it's clear from other research that an important part of the progress minorities did make in the 1960s and 1970s would probably not have occurred without explicit government intervention through antidiscrimination programs (Freeman, 1978a; Anderson, 1982).

To probe these issues further, we will need to examine a range of questions that we have only touched on so far. One is the trend in inequality between the sexes. We've seen in this chapter that racial and gender inequalities are deeply interconnected. In the America of the 1980s, it is increasingly difficult to understand one without understanding the other, so we'll now turn to the patterns of inequality between men and women.

Summary

This chapter has examined trends in economic inequality between minorities and whites. After narrowing slightly during the 1960s and early 1970s, the racial economic gap has once again been widening. Minorities remain over-represented among the poor, and minority poverty increased sharply in the early 1980s.

Some writers have attributed these trends mainly to the high rates of family breakup among some minority groups. But though this is surely part of the explanation, it is not a sufficient one in itself. Whatever their family structure, minorities tend to have lower incomes than whites and greater risks of poverty.

Another part of the explanation for the racial gaps in income and poverty is the difficulties minorities face in the job market. Minority unemployment is disproportionately high, and among some groups — especially black and Puerto Rican men — labor-force participation is falling.

The problem of lack of jobs is compounded by low earnings for minority workers who are employed. Some of the disparity between minority and white earnings can be explained by such factors as educational differences, geographical concentration, and the younger age of the minority labor force. But these factors leave much of the earnings difference unexplained.

Still another part of the problem is the continued concentration of minorities in poor jobs. Though minorities have achieved important gains in breaking into more rewarding jobs in the past decade, they remain greatly overrepresented in low-paying, dead-end occupations, and are underrepresented in higher-level jobs with better pay and greater opportunities for mobility.

The decline of blue-collar industries and the reductions in government spending and social programs threaten to reverse some of the gains minorities have made toward greater equality.

For Further Reading

Bonacich, Edna, and John Modell. *The Economic Basis of Ethnic Solidarity: Small Business in the Japanese-American Community.* Berkeley, Calif.: University of California Press, 1981.

Lieberson, Stanley. *A Piece of the Pie*. Berkeley, Calif.: University of California Press, 1981.

Reich, Michael. *Racial Inequality*. New York: Cambridge University Press, 1981.

Sowell, Thomas. *Markets and Minorities*. New York: Basic Books, 1981.

Steinberg, Stephen. *The Ethnic Myth: Race, Ethnicity, and Class in America*. Boston: Atheneum, 1980.

U.S. Commission on Civil Rights. Illinois Advisory Committee. *Shutdown; Economic Dislocation and Equal Opportunity*. Washington, D.C.: Government Printing Office, 1981.

Wilson, William J. *The Declining Significance of Race*. Chicago: University of Chicago Press, 1978.

6

Social Inequality III: Gender

Like the drive for racial equality, the movement for women's equality came alive, and won many of its most significant gains, in the 1960s. A strong women's movement had been vibrant and active in the nineteenth and early twentieth centuries, but had declined during the Great Depression and during and after World War II. By the 1950s the position of women in American society was rarely raised as a public issue or considered a major subject for social scientific research. It had become what the feminist author Betty Friedan (1962) called a "problem that had no name."

Yet little more than a decade later, a revitalized women's movement began to transform public and private life in every corner of American society. This transformation was aided by some of the same laws and social policy that helped pave the way for progress for minorities, such as the Civil Rights Act, laws mandating equal pay for equal work, and affirmative action programs. And, like the reaction to minority progress, there was soon a chorus of disapproval. By the 1970s it was frequently argued that the egalitarian impulse had gone too far for women as well as for other groups that had traditionally suffered discrimination. The efforts to fight present discrimination, however justified in the beginning, had, in this view, overstepped proper bounds. Some argued that the attempts to ensure equality between the sexes in workplaces and schools were costly, unrealistic, and threatened to interfere with "rational business practice" and even with "the fundamental institutions of society" (Hoffman and Reed, 1981, p. 23). For others, the drive for equality was felt to be upsetting a "natural" balance between men and women, with what could only be dire results for social and personal stability and family integrity (Gilder, 1981).

192

Affirmative action programs have become the most frequent target of these criticisms. They have been accused of fostering discrimination in reverse by penalizing qualified men — barring them from jobs, education, and training in favor of less qualified but suddenly privileged women. As the 1980s began, one American Senator publicly described affirmative action as "an assault upon America, conceived in lies and fostered with an irresponsibility so extreme as to verge upon the malign" (Senator Orrin Hatch, Republican from Utah, cited in *Working Women*, 1981, p. 2).

The criticism of antidiscrimination laws and policies usually rests on the belief that women have either already made enough (or too much) progress toward social and economic equality or that, at least, they would achieve more *without* the dubious benefit of government intervention. Even some feminist writers (though from a much more supportive viewpoint) began to argue in the 1980s that many of the most important battles to ensure women's equality in job opportunities and income had been largely won. At least by implication, women could now, in this view, safely concentrate their energies more on improving personal and family life (Friedan, 1981).

In this chapter, we will look carefully at women's progress in jobs, earnings, income, and social services. We will consider the dimensions and sources of continuing economic inequality between men and women and of what some writers have called the growing "feminization" of poverty (Pearce, 1982). Finally, we will assess the prospects for women's equality in living standards and on the workplace in the future, in the light of recent economic developments and trends in public policy. Later chapters will take up, in greater detail, the position of women in the contemporary family, in health and medical care, and other areas.

Let's begin by considering one of the most important social changes of recent years — the rapid increase in the proportion of women in the American work force.

The "Revolution" in the Labor Force

At the turn of the century, less than one in five American women worked for pay outside their homes. By the 1980s, over half did. This dramatic change has appropriately been called a "revolution" (Smith, 1979), and it has had enormous effects on virtually every aspect of American life — from childrearing to the workplace, from patterns of unemployment to the relations between the sexes. Let's take a closer look at the nature and magnitude of this change.

Over the past decade, about 6 out of every 10 new additions to the American work force have been women (U.S. Department of Labor, Women's

The continuing struggle
for women's equality;
then . . .

Bureau, 1982). Between 1975 and 1982 alone, more than 10 million women entered the work force. By the 1980s, more than half of all women over the age of 16 were working outside the home (Table 6-1). (This proportion varies, though not greatly, by race and ethnicity; slightly higher proportions of black women, and slightly lower proportions of Hispanic women, are in the labor force than white women.)

Figure 6-1 shows that the rapid increase of women in paid labor has been accompanied by a less dramatic, but steady, decline in the labor-force participation of men. Since 1960, women's rate has risen by more than 36 percent; men's has decreased by more than 7 percent. As a result, the chances of a man or woman being in the work force have become increasingly similar. In 1950 a man was about two and a half times as likely to be in the paid work force as a woman; by 1981 this had dropped to one and a half times. But even these figures somewhat understate the changes in women's role in the labor force. Like most such statistics, they are a kind of snapshot that freezes the action at one point in time. But while about half of all women today are in the work force at any given point, more than *90 percent* of women alive today have been or will be working outside the home at *some* point in their lives. And the statistics understate the speed with which men's and women's participation in the work force is converging for another reason. The male and female populations in the United States are not strictly comparable: Because women tend to live longer, they are an older population, on average, and more of them have left the labor force because of age. Among *working-age* women and men, the proportions actually at work or looking for work are closer than the usual statistics indicate. And this is

194 Social Inequality III: Gender

EQUALITY OF RIGHTS UNDER THE LAW SHALL NOT BE DENIED OR ABRIDGED BY THE UNITED STATES OR BY ANY STATE ON ACCOUNT OF SEX

and now.

especially true for the young. While women's labor-force participation as a whole is about 66 percent that of men's, it is 80 percent of the comparable male rate for women aged 20 to 24, and 70 percent of the rate at ages 25 to 34.

To complete the picture of the "revolution" in women's work, we need to add two qualifications to the description of a recent rapid shift of women into paid labor. Though the average numbers of women in the work force historically were relatively low until recently, this has not been true for all groups of women. Black women have traditionally had a much higher rate of labor-force participation (the rate for white women has only recently largely caught up). Similarly, immigrant women have often been an important part of the labor force in many American industries. And, in general, work in the paid labor force has long been a common experience for lower-income women (Kessler-Harris, 1982).

Moreover, this is not the first time in American history that women have moved rapidly into the paid labor force. During World War II, millions of women entered what had formerly been considered men's jobs. When the war began, less than 30 percent of women older than 16 were in the paid labor force; at its end in 1945, more than 38 percent were, a rate that was not reached again until the early 1960s. In a story often told, many women who had worked throughout the war years in traditionally male jobs were ousted from them at the war's end to make room for men returning from military service. By 1947, only two years after the war, women's labor-force participation rate had fallen back to just over 30 percent (F. D. Blau, 1978; K. Anderson, 1981).

The "Revolution" in the Labor Force **195**

Table 6-1

Labor-force participation rates of males and females, by race and Hispanic origin, 1960–1981

	Percentages			
	1960	1970	1975	1981
Total				
Females	38	43	46	52
Males	83	80	78	77
By race				
White females	37	43	46	52
Black females	48	50	49	54
Hispanic females	NA	NA	42	48
Black males	83	77	72	71
Hispanic males	NA	NA	79	80
Ages 20–24				
Females	46	58	64	70
Males	88	83	85	86
Ages 25–34				
Females	36	45	55	67
Males	98	96	95	95

Note: NA means not available. Figures for black include blacks and others. Rates are rounded to nearest whole number.

Source: Adapted from *Statistical Abstract of the United States, 1982–1983* (Washington, D.C.: Government Printing Office, 1983), pp. 377, 380.

Still, even in wartime, the proportion of women in the work force never came close to its current level. And even more significant than these sheer numbers is the change in the marital status of women who work outside the home. Traditionally, the highest labor-force participation was among women who were never married or who had lost husbands through death, separation, or divorce — and who were often childless. In 1890, the first year for which we have reasonably reliable data, all but a million of the 3.7 million women in the American labor force were single. Less than 5 percent of all married women worked outside the home. As recently as 1940, nearly half of the female labor force was single; but only a quarter was by the beginning of the 1980s. It is estimated that by 1990 two-thirds of all married women under 55 will be in the paid labor force (R. E. Smith, 1979, pp. 3, 18).

The increasing tendency for women with *young children* to work outside the home is another major, dramatic change. Where once it was considered inappropriate for a woman to work while her children were young, today the difference in labor-force participation between women with and without young children is fast narrowing. Since the 1950s, the labor-force participa-

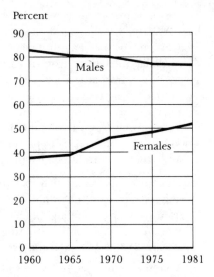

Percent

Figure 6-1
Trends in labor-force participation, by sex, 1960–1981

Source: Data from *Statistical Abstract of the United States, 1982–1983* (Washington, D.C.: Government Printing Office, 1983), p. 377.

tion of married women with no children under 18 has risen by a little more than half, that of women with children aged 6 to 17 has more than doubled, and that of women with children under 6 has nearly *quadrupled*. By 1982, 55 percent of children under 18 had mothers in the labor force; as did fully 46 percent of preschool-age children, up from 12 percent in 1950 (U.S. Department of Labor, Women's Bureau, 1982, pp. 1–2).

Increasingly, then, women from all types of family situations — single, married, divorced, with or without children — have come to occupy similar roles in the paid work force and to share similar needs with regard to jobs, earnings, and supportive services.

The Earnings Gap: How Much Progress?

Some have argued that women's growing role in the work force has put them well on the road toward economic equality with men, even if they haven't yet arrived at that goal. As one observer puts it, "The dramatically increasing participation rates for younger women and the emerging favorable employment trends demonstrate that mobility is working" to sharply reduce the inequalities between women and men (Livernash, 1980, p. 21). But this hopeful expectation is belied by the stubborn fact that women are still *far* from equal to men in the economic rewards that work ought to bring. The paradox of increasing labor-force participation coupled with persistent inequality in wages and earnings is one of the most enduring aspects of American women's experience in recent years.

Let's look first at the general pattern of men's and women's relative earnings. As Table 6-2 shows, the ratio of women's earnings to men's has fluctuated around 60 percent throughout the past two decades — that is, for every dollar men earn, women earn roughly 60 cents. (Historical studies suggest that this pattern extends back throughout the twentieth century.) These figures, moreover, refer to *full-time* work; they ignore the additional inequality resulting from women's more often having to work part time when they want to work full time. In 1981, about two-thirds of all part-time workers were women (U.S. Department of Labor, Women's Bureau, 1982, p. 2). And other important points emerge from the table:

1. Though the *percentage* gap between men's and women's earnings has remained about the same since 1960, the *absolute* dollar gap has risen — nearly doubling, in fact, between 1970 and 1981. By 1981 the average woman working full time in the paid labor force could expect to earn $8,000 less than the average man.

2. A close reading of the table shows that the sex/earnings ratio improves for women (becomes slightly less unequal) in times of economic recession and *declines* for women in periods of economic growth. Thus, the ratio was at its lowest in 1973, a "good" year for the economy, and rose somewhat through the 1974–1976 recession.

3. From what we have seen about the persistence of racial inequality, it should not surprise us that minority women fare less well than white women. For every dollar earned by a white man in 1981, Hispanic women earned 54 cents, black women 59 cents, and white women 63 cents.

Note, however, that these racial and ethnic differences among women are *far* smaller than the gap between women of any race and white men. Indeed, the relative income of black women has increased significantly. In fact, when we separate the women's earnings picture by race, it becomes clear that the overall pattern of women's relative earnings in recent years has been composed of two different trends. White women's earnings, compared with those of white men, have remained remarkably stable since the late 1960s, while black women's have *risen* (though they still remain lower than white women's) from 48 percent of the earnings of white men in 1967, to 59 percent in 1981 — just four cents on the dollar lower than the relative earnings of white women (Mellor and Stanas, 1982, p. 19). This phenomenon also turns up in long-term studies of the careers of women workers. In an Ohio State University study (Mott, 1981) of 5,000 young women from 1968 to 1978, white women's wages actually declined, on the average, during the period, despite substantial increases in their participation in the work force. Black women's wages and earnings improved, however, significantly narrowing the racial gap during the decade.

These differences in *average* earnings between men and women translate into even sharper, more specific differences in their chances of bringing

Year	Annual earnings		Female earnings as percent of males'*
	Females	Males	
1960	$ 3,293	$ 5,417	60.8
1961	3,351	5,644	59.4
1962	3,446	5,794	59.5
1963	3,561	5,978	59.6
1964	3,690	6,195	59.6
1965	3,823	6,375	60.0
1966	3,973	6,848	58.0
1967	4,150	7,182	57.8
1968	4,457	7,664	58.2
1969	4,977	8,227	60.5
1970	5,323	8,966	59.4
1971	5,593	9,399	59.5
1972	5,903	10,202	57.9
1973	6,335	11,186	56.6
1974	6,970	11,889	58.6
1975	7,504	12,758	58.8
1976	8,099	13,455	60.2
1977	8,618	14,626	58.9
1978	9,350	15,730	59.4
1979	10,151	17,014	59.7
1980	11,197	18,612	60.2
1981	12,001	20,260	59.2

Table 6-2
The male-female earnings gap: median annual earnings of year-round full-time workers 14 years and over by sex, 1960–1981

Note: Data for 1960–1966 are for wage and salary workers only and exclude self-employed workers. Data for 1979–1981 are for persons 15 years and older.

*Earnings of full-time female workers as a proportion of white male earnings, 1981: white females: .63; black females: .59; Hispanic females: .54.

Source: Janet L. Norwood, "The Female-Male Earnings Gap: A Review of Employment and Earnings Issues," U.S. Bureau of Labor Statistics (Washington, D.C.: Government Printing Office, November 1982), p. 9. Earnings by race and Hispanic origin from Earl F. Mellor and George D. Stanas, "Usual Weekly Earnings: Another Look at Intergroup Differences and Basic Trends," *Monthly Labor Review*, April 1982, p. 16. Reprinted with permission.

home relatively high or relatively low earnings. Women are greatly over-represented among low-wage workers. In 1981, women were 39 percent of all full-time workers, but 66 percent of all full-time workers earning less than $150 a week (See Table 5-7, page 170). At the other end of the income scale, among professional and technical workers who enjoy the benefits of year-round, full-time work, about 1 in 6 men — but only *1 in 75* women — earn more than $40,000 a year (U.S. Bureau of the Census, 1983c, pp. 178–180).

These earnings differences vary considerably across different occupations. As we'll see shortly, the most important reason for women's persistently lower earnings is that they typically work in different kinds of jobs — and the jobs they tend to work in the most are among the lowest-paid ones in the American economy. But men and women also earn different amounts of money within the *same* kinds of jobs, though the magnitude of that difference varies widely. Table 6-3 shows the 10 jobs with the most equal earnings between the sexes and the 10 with the least equal. At the top, women post-office clerks earn 94 percent of men doing the same work; at the bottom, women working as sales managers or department heads in retail stores earn less than 60 percent of what men earn in similar jobs.

Life-Cycle Differences

But there is an even more significant gender difference that is not revealed by the statistics on average earnings. At any given point, women's rewards for full-time work are considerably less than men's — and dramatically so in many kinds of jobs. But beyond this, there is also a sharp difference in the pattern of earnings *over time*, in what economists call *life-cycle earnings*. Figure 6-2 illustrates this graphically. Men's earnings tend to rise steadily once they leave school, and to continue rising until at least their middle 40s. After that, their earnings tend to fall, especially, of course, after retirement age. Men, in other words, can usually look forward to a steadily rising income as they move more deeply into careers. Women's earnings, on the other hand, typically rise very little from the start and peak much sooner, at about age

Figure 6-2

Earnings profile of full-time wage and salary workers, by sex and age, 1981

Source: Earl F. Mellor and George D. Stanas, "Usual Weekly Earnings: Another Look at Intergroup Differences and Basic Trends," *Monthly Labor Review*, April 1982, p. 17. Reprinted with permission.

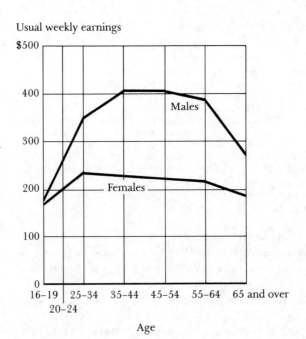

Usual weekly earnings

Occupations with highest ratios of female to male average weekly earnings	Percentage of female to male earnings
Postal clerks	93.9
Cashiers	92.0
Guards and watchmen	90.7
Food service workers, not elsewhere classified, excluding private household	90.0
Ticket, station, and express agents	88.3
Clinical laboratory technologists and technicians	88.1
Therapists	87.5
Packers and wrappers, except meat and produce	85.4
Editors and reporters	85.0
Bartenders	84.4
Occupations with lowest ratio of female to male average weekly earnings	
Insurance adjusters and investigators	64.7
Personnel and labor relations workers	64.3
Blue-collar supervisors	64.2
Clerical supervisors	63.4
Checkers, examiners, and inspectors, manufacturing	63.1
Buyers	62.3
Advertising agents and salesworkers	61.7
Bank and financial officers	60.2
Construction and services salesworkers	59.1
Sales managers and department heads, retail trade	57.0

Table 6-3
The earnings gap within occupations, 1981

Source: Adapted from Nancy F. Rytina, "Earnings of Men and Women: A Look At Specific Occupations," *Monthly Labor Review,* April 1982, p. 300. Reprinted with permission.

30. This flatter "earnings curve" means that women and men start out much closer to each other — at all levels of education and across all kinds of occupations — than they end up.

It is sometimes argued that these different life-cycle patterns result from women dropping out of the labor force to have children. Because their work experience is interrupted, in this view, they usually have to start all over again in entry-level jobs and thus never get the chance to develop a "normal" career pattern. It is true, of course, that women often interrupt their work lives to have children. But it also turns out that women who have *never* married and who do *not* have children tend to have earnings over their life cycle quite similar to those of married women with children — despite the fact that their job commitments resemble that of men's. In other words, even though single women's typical work patterns are like men's, their earnings are like other *women's* (Barrett, 1979a, p. 38).

Explaining the Earnings Gap: Education and Experience

Many other common explanations for the persistence of the earnings gap (like those purporting to explain racial earnings inequalities) are likewise based on the idea that women earn less than men because, in one way or another, they bring less to the job than men do in terms of skills, education, or experience: the endowments that some economists call *human capital.* How much do these characteristics matter? Research suggests that they *do* make a difference — but not nearly enough of one to explain all of the gender inequality in earnings.

Education, for example, is one path to higher earnings, and, other things being equal, more education does improve women's earnings — as it does men's. But, as is so often the case, other things are not equal, for the *effects* of education are very different for women than for men. This is strikingly clear from Table 6-4: Full-time working women who have graduated from high school *earn less than men with a grade school education or less*, and women with four years of college earn less than men who have not graduated from high school. Both working men and working women average about the same (12.7) years of schooling, but women tend to get less "payoffs" from their education.

Another way of illustrating this is by estimating how much money additional years of education are worth to men and to women. In the mid-1970s, according to one study, a man in his middle 40s earned about $9,000 more a year if he had finished college than if he had only graduated from high

Table 6-4
Schooling and earnings, full-time workers, 1981

Years of schooling completed	Median weekly earnings	
	Males	Females
Total, 25 years old and over	$378	$237
8 years of school or less	259	169
Less than 4 years of high school	290	180
4 years of high school	363	222
4 years of college	459	299
5 years of college or more	507	362

Source: Adapted from Earl F. Mellor and George D. Stanas, "Usual Weekly Earnings: Another Look at Intergroup Differences and Basic Trends," *Monthly Labor Review,* April 1982, p. 16. Reprinted with permission.

school. A woman also earned more if she had graduated from college, but only $4,000 more than if she had only finished high school. Astonishingly, these differences remained even among men and women who received the *same* types of degrees from the *same* types of colleges. So it is not just that women tend to go to poorer schools or to choose majors that are less likely to lead to better-paying jobs. Instead, a wide gap in the returns to college education remains even when these factors are taken into account (Barrett, 1979a, p. 42).

Another study, aptly titled "Does college pay?," found, similarly, that a college education does pay, for both sexes — but within every level of education, the women in this study, members of the high school class of 1972, earned less than their male classmates during the 1970s. The size of the male-female earnings gap was reduced at higher levels of schooling, but it didn't disappear. Women who went to work straight out of high school had starting wages about 95 cents an hour less than men who did the same; those with an undergraduate degree earned 72 cents an hour less than comparably educated men; and women who earned advanced degrees started work at 38 cents less an hour (National Center for Education Statistics, 1982).

These differences in the returns to schooling translate into widely divergent earnings over the life span. Figure 6-3 shows just how wide these disparities are. On average, a man 25 years old in 1979 who worked year round, full time, could expect to earn $954,000 over his working life if he was a high-school graduate, and $1,329,000 if he had completed four years of college. A woman the same age — again, working full time, year round — could expect to earn $567,000 if she had only graduated from high school, and $722,000 if she was a college graduate (U.S. Bureau of the Census, 1983b, p. 3).

These differences in the payoff to education might be explained by differences in *other* characteristics that women and men bring to their jobs. A large body of research has attempted to assess the effects of a variety of these factors (including training, work experience, age, and regional differences, separately and in combination). These studies have generally found that differences in these qualities do account for *some* of the persistent sex differences in earnings — but not all of them. For example, because a larger proportion of women workers are either young women new to the job market or older women returning after long absence, they are more often found in entry-level jobs, which, of course, have lower pay. And though women's patterns of work attachment and experience are coming more and more to resemble men's, they are still sufficiently different to have an important impact on average earnings. Men more often work overtime, tend to spend more hours at work, work more continuously through the year and through the life cycle, and invest more in skill training.

Having said this, however, it is still true that virtually all studies find a substantial part of the earnings gap that remains unexplained even when all such factors are taken into account. How wide is this unexplained part?

The Earnings Gap: How Much Progress?   **203**

What college is worth: lifetime earnings estimates in 1979 for Males (a) and Females (b) working year-round full time, by years of school completed and age, in constant 1981 dollars

Source: U.S. Bureau of the Census, *Current Population Reports*, series P-60, no. 139, Washington D.C., 1983, p. 5.

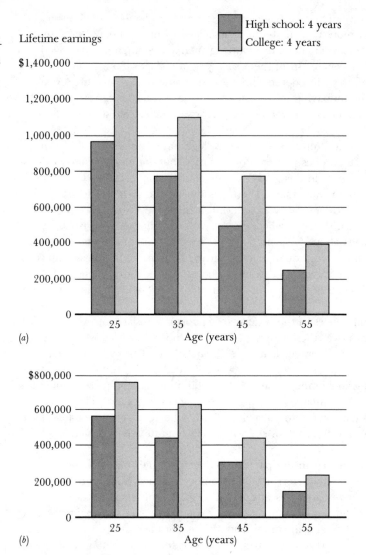

Different studies have arrived at different estimates, depending, in large part, on the kinds of jobs and of workers being investigated. One analysis, tracking the work experience of men and women over a period of several years, found that men earned an average of about 87 cents more per hour than women in similar jobs. When factors like work continuity, training levels, and education were accounted for, they explained only about 9 cents of that difference. The other 78 cents, according to the researchers, could be considered as "an upper-limit estimate of the impact of discrimination" (Shapiro and Carr, 1978, p. 28). A review by the National Research Council of many similar studies concludes that all these characteristics combined "usually account for less than a quarter and never more than half" of the earnings differences between men and women (National Research Council, 1981, p. 42).

Moreover, there is an important caution to be kept in mind in weighing the evidence in such studies. By their very nature, they tend to *understate* the role of discrimination in the male-female earnings gap. This is because so many of the factors that are being "controlled" or "held constant" in these studies are themselves often shaped by past or present patterns of discrimination, as we suggested in Chapter 5 in the case of racial inequalities. Thus, many studies have found that the single most damaging job-related characteristic women bring to the workplace is less experience: shorter experience in the work force in general, less in their present job, and less relevant on-the-job training. But, obviously, the fact that women have less job experience is likely to reflect both discrimination in hiring and training policies and the constraints of household work and child care. The same point applies to many other current "explanations" of women's position in the labor force, as we will see in the next section.

Women in the Labor Force: Some Myths and Realities

As women have moved into the work force in greater and greater numbers — but without gaining economic equality with men — a number of myths have emerged that serve to "explain" the continuing gap between men's and women's economic status and sometimes to justify the social policies in education and job training, child care, taxes, and other areas that help perpetuate it.

Most of these myths revolve around one of two basic assertions: first, that women are only temporary or marginal participants in the work force, with less commitment to work than men; second, that they don't really need to work and that any paid labor they do is, in some sense, "extra" work. Both ideas are deeply rooted in our culture and social institutions — both are increasingly distant from the reality of most women's lives.

Are women less committed to paid work than men? It's certainly true that, on average, women still work less — *outside the home* — than men and are likely to have a shorter work life in the paid labor force. (We will look more closely at the patterns of work *in* the home in Chapter 7.) But that difference is fast diminishing. In fact, one of the main reasons why women's overall labor-force participation rate has risen is that more women are not only

Less Committed Workers?

The Bettmann Archive

Women have always worked; an early twentieth-century "sweatshop."

entering the labor force, but, once in the labor force, are staying longer. At the same time, the average length of time *men* spend in the labor force has declined slightly. A woman born in 1970 can expect to work about 25 years in the paid labor force, on average, as compared to about 15 years for women born in 1950. Men's expected years of labor-force participation, on the other hand, were about 40 for those born in 1970 and 41 for those born 20 years earlier (U.S. Department of Labor, Women's Bureau, 1980, p. 11).

Pregnancy and childrearing once meant long-term interruptions in most women's work experience. This helped define women of childbearing age as unpromising candidates for jobs requiring extensive training or long-term commitment. But recent studies show that, increasingly, most working women stay on the job until only a few months before the birth of their first child, and they often move back into the work force very shortly afterward.

And dropping out of the labor force while their children are small turns out to have no substantial effect on women's longer-term attachment to the work force. In general, as one study following women workers over a several-year period concludes, "The lifetime work orientation of women is gradually approaching the more continuous pattern followed by men" (Mott and Shapiro, 1978, p. 49).

Besides their reputation for a less enduring commitment to the labor force, women are often typed as unreliable workers who quit jobs easily and often. Again, the conventional statistics appear to grant a superficial support to this view. On average, women have higher turnover rates than men do. But a harder look shows that this statistic mainly reflects women's greater concentration in low-level jobs — ones with low pay, little intrinsic interest, and few chances for advancement — which have traditionally high rates of turnover for *both* sexes. When job status is taken into account, men and women show similar levels of attachment to jobs. This is indicated, from another angle, by the fact that though women tend to quit jobs somewhat more frequently than men do, they generally get another one very quickly — showing, as some studies put it, that women often develop a stronger attachment to *work* generally than to the specific (often unsatisfying) *jobs* they hold at any given point (Barrett, 1979a, p. 45).

Another study, by the sociologist Paul Osterman (1982), sheds an interesting light on this issue. Osterman found that the enforcement of federal affirmative action guidelines reduced the amount of job quitting among women workers. Industries more closely watched by federal antidiscrimination agencies, and more dependent on federal contracts, had lower turnover among women. The study concluded that antidiscrimination enforcement probably created better job opportunities for women and, therefore, more incentive to stay on the job.

Work, Family, and Gender Expectations

These issues are further complicated by the fact that many of the statistical differences that lend superficial credence to traditional arguments about the "irresponsibility" of women workers are, themselves, partly reflections of pervasive gender differences in expectations about work and family life.

The shortest way of describing these different gender expectations is that, in American society, men's work, unlike women's, is rarely viewed through the lens of home and family responsibilities. In this sense, men's relationship to the labor force is a simpler one: their job opportunities and career tracks are rarely much influenced by such things as the number of children they have or the competing responsibilities of housework. But women's *are* — and this distinction affects every aspect of their working life.

We will examine how these different norms affect the division of labor within the American *family* in Chapter 7. For now, we want to focus on how they affect women's role in the paid labor force and, through that role, their income and earnings. For, though traditional attitudes about the sexual division of labor are changing (Cherlin and Walters, 1981), they are not changing fast enough to remove the obstacles most women face in moving into the paid labor force. Thus, in 1978, according to opinion polls, about 72 percent of Americans approved of married women earning money even if their husbands could support them — up from about 64 percent six years earlier. But *50 percent* of both men — and women — believed that women with children should not go to work until their children were grown, except out of "economic necessity" (American Council on Life Insurance, 1981).

These at best ambiguous attitudes about the importance or justification of women's outside work create a kind of double bind for many women. The result is that many women are placed in a kind of double bind. A growing number both want and need to work outside the home, but they are granted inadequate support to do so comfortably, either at home or by the larger society. The assumption that women will remain responsible for running the household, for example, means they must often drop out of the labor force periodically or work part time. The differences with men on this score are revealing. When men work part time, their most important reasons for doing so are that they can't find full-time work or that they are in school. For women, the most important reason for working part time is that they are taking care of the home. Similarly, only about 1 percent of men working part time, but about 50 percent of women, give home responsibilities as their primary reason for nonparticipation in the labor force. (For men, again, being in school is the most important reason, illness or disability second.) And these proportions have not changed significantly for a decade (Barrett, 1979b, p. 83).

All of these expressions of the traditional sexual division of labor in the home are compounded by others in the larger society, especially by the relative absence of effective social services to lighten home responsibilities for working women. The most important example is child care. Studies show that the lack of adequate child care is a powerful constraint on women's ability to take outside work, and an even stronger obstacle to their being able to follow the kinds of career paths typically followed by men. Close to one in five women with children who are not in the labor force, according to one recent survey, said they would look for work if satisfactory child care were available at reasonable cost. One in four women working part time said they would work more hours if such care were available (Presser and Baldwin, 1980).

Without either a measure of equality at home or adequate child care and other supports outside it, a vicious cycle is created. Many women are effectively locked into low-status, poorly paying jobs — often part-time or intermittent ones that allow frequent movement in and out of the labor force. Women's confinement in these jobs reinforces, in the family and the larger society, the view of women's work as "secondary," which in turn helps justify the expectations that women will continue to do most of the housework, stay home with the children when necessary, and relocate or leave school or training in order to build a husband's career (Barrett, 1979a and b).

This vicious cycle helps explain why women themselves sometimes fail to take opportunities for higher-level jobs or training when they have the chance. Some writers (especially those critical of affirmative action pro- grams for women) make much of this phenomenon in order to argue that the reason women aren't well represented in higher-level jobs is not that they face real discrimination in the labor market, but that they don't really *want* the better jobs. One recent analysis, for example, discovered that a main reason why women in a large Fortune 500 corporation were under- represented in higher-paying jobs was that many were insufficiently moti- vated to compete for promotions. Those women who *did* have the level of aspiration and motivation that most men had did considerably better in moving up in the company. On this basis, the study concluded that sex discrimination had nothing to do with the unequal position of women in the company (Hoffman and Reed, 1981).

The problem with this line of reasoning is its artificial separation of what happens to women's expectations outside of the workplace and what hap- pens *inside* it. Thus, a variety of studies *do* show that women's expectations about their own future work role often tend to be low and highly traditional. Teenaged women still most often aspire to typically "female" jobs, such as beauticians, nurses, or secretaries, and only rarely to nontraditional jobs. Surveys of high-school seniors show that well before they enter the labor force, young men and women are already "lined up" for very different kinds of work. Though most high-school women expect to be employed by the time they're 30, they mostly choose clerical work, almost never skilled craft jobs (Lueptow, 1981; Herzog, 1982). And young women often underes- timate the extent of their future attachment to the work force, expecting to achieve most of their economic status through marriage. As a result, they often don't prepare adequately for what will in reality be many years of labor in the paid work force, too quickly accepting dead-end jobs in place of long-term training and investment in career planning (Mott and Shapiro, 1978, p. 140). But to argue that this means that these women "choose" not to strive for better jobs is simplistic (National Research Council, 1981, pp. 53–54). For many women, opting for traditional jobs is less a matter of real choice than the expression of a deeply ingrained set of expectations, rooted in the realities of the constraints they face, in and out of the home.

An enormous body of social science research exists on the ways in which these gender-typed expectations about work roles are inculcated in both women and men from childhood onward, but we can only touch on it here. (For comprehensive summaries, see Maccoby and Jacklin, 1974; Laws, 1979; Richardson, 1981.) It's important to emphasize how *early* the process begins. A recent study of children aged from two and a half to eight years found that, even at the *youngest* ages, children of both sexes already clearly defined certain occupations as "women's" and others as "men's" (Gettys and Cann, 1981).

Absenteeism is another case in point. On average, women are more likely to be absent from a job, on any given day, than men are, a fact that is sometimes taken as yet another indication of women's flighty attitude toward paid work. Part of the problem, obviously, is that this fails to take into account differences in the kinds of jobs men and women hold. But, more importantly, it may simply reflect the degree to which women's paid work is defined as secondary to their other socially defined roles. When problems come up at home, for example, women are most often called on to take care of them, whether or not they work full time at an outside job. Data from the University of Michigan's Survey Research Center show that when both husband and wife work outside the home, if one must stay at home to cope with some household problem, four out of five times the one who stays is the wife (Wirtz, 1979, p. 214).

Such conflicts between home and work remain pervasive at all levels of American society. Even for women in high-level professional occupations, demands of home and family are often given priority over career development. In a recent study of men and women microbiologists, 93 percent of the women said they would accept a job in another part of the country *only* if a good job could also be found there for their husbands. Only 20 percent of *male* microbiologists, on the other hand, would have made a job for their wives a criterion for their own career relocation (Safilios-Rothschild, 1979, p. 424). This attitude helps explain the frequent finding that when working-couple families move, the husband's earnings generally *rise*; the wife's earnings generally *fall* (Barrett, 1979a, p. 44).

In general, then, the reasons why women drop out of the labor force, or move in and out of it without building up substantial experience on the job, are different from men's. The assumption that women should bear most of the responsibility for running a home means that their work *outside* the home is taken less seriously — by employers, by social service agencies, by their families, indeed, sometimes by women themselves — which, in turn, justifies denying them access to more stable jobs and longer-range training. All of which upholds the conception of women as intermittent workers whose "main job" is running the household.

Do Women Need to Work?

Another often-heard argument is that most women in the labor force don't really "need" to work. Again, the underlying premise is that most women are secondary earners who could be living comfortably enough on their husbands' paychecks. When they do work, it's mainly because of boredom or the desire to earn a little "extra" money. This argument serves to minimize the social and personal costs of both the low earnings women workers typically bring home and their high rates of unemployment. It is also often marshalled against vigorous antidiscrimination efforts for women. Since women do not really *need* the jobs, the argument runs, it is unfair for them to "take them away" from men who do — especially when the economy is faltering and jobs are scarce.

How does this argument stand up against the facts? Certainly, most working women see the issue differently. In 1979, 54 percent of working women in a national survey said they worked mainly for the basic support of themselves or their families (President's Advisory Council for Women, 1980). A frequently cited statistic backs up that response: As of 1982, two-thirds of women in the paid labor force were either single, widowed, divorced or separated, or married to men who earned less than $15,000 a year (U.S. Department of Labor, Women's Bureau, 1982, p. 2). (In 1981 the Bureau of Labor Statistics' lower budget for an urban family of four was $15,323.)

Especially in times of periodically high inflation and persistently high un-employment, women's earnings are often essential to basic economic secu-rity — in some cases, to economic survival. This is obvious when a woman maintains a family or lives alone. Of every eight women in the labor force, one maintains her own family (Norwood, 1982, p. 1). But it is also true in many married-couple families as well, for a wife's earnings are sometimes all that stands between some of these families and poverty. An Ohio State Uni-versity study of women workers' careers from the late 1960s to the late 1970s found that the rate of poverty among husband-wife families would have been 50 percent higher if the wives had not worked (Shaw, 1981). And even for families not so close to the poverty line, the wife's earnings often provide the critical edge that allows them to buy a house, send the children to school, or pay off debts. Those earnings also provide a cushion against catastrophes like a husband's illness, death, or job loss. On average, accord-ing to this study, white working women contributed about 28 percent of their family's income, black women 37 percent. Such dual-earner families (as we saw in Chapter 3) were the only ones who managed to stay ahead of the rate of inflation during the 1970s.

Because of the size of women's contribution to family income, women's *loss* of a job can be a devastating experience even in married-couple, dual-breadwinner families. A recent study of women laid off from production jobs in declining industries in New England, for example, found that the majority lived in two-earner families, and their earnings had amounted to between 35 and 45 percent of their families' total incomes (Rosen, 1982, pp. 96–97).

Occupational Segregation: How Much Change?

If these "explanations" fail to explain the earnings gap between men and women, its stubborn persistence presents something of a paradox. How can it be that women are still so far from economic equality, in the face of laws and programs that, since the 1960s, have mandated "equal pay for equal work"?

The data we've already examined offer a clue to one part of the answer. Much research suggests that some of the earnings gap reflects the persistence of overt or subtle discrimination in pay and promotion practices. Discrimination of this kind does, in fact, violate existing equal-pay laws and has been the subject of several important legal victories for women in recent years (National Research Council, 1981, chapter 1).

But there is another, and deeper, problem. An even larger part of the economic gap between the sexes reflects differences in the *kinds of jobs* men and women hold and in the *industries* that employ them. It's not just that women are often paid less for doing the *same* work as men (though that remains the reality in all too many workplaces). The more pervasive and more stubborn problem is that — despite some breakthroughs into less traditional occupations and industries — most women still do *different* work than men do. And this inequality is only marginally affected by laws requiring equal pay for equal work (National Research Council, 1981, chapter 1).

The vast majority of women in the paid labor force are still channeled into a small number of typically "women's" jobs, most of which are poorly paid, unstable, and offer few chances of advancement. The technical term for this sex-typed channeling is *occupational segregation*, and it has so far proven difficult to combat through antidiscrimination laws. It is increasingly recognized that today, as a recent Labor Department analysis puts it, "The single most important problem continuing to face all women in the labor force is job segregation and its resulting low earnings" (U.S. Department of Labor, Women's Bureau, 1980, p. 3).

The problem of job segregation is actually two somewhat different problems rolled into one. On the one hand, occupational segregation reflects the obstacles hindering women from taking jobs traditionally defined as "male" ones — jobs with predictably higher status and pay. On the other, occupational segregation reflects the *undervaluing* of the jobs that most women *do* perform. "Women's" jobs often bring less pay and other rewards than many "men's" jobs requiring considerably *less* skill — a disadvantage that has led to demands that jobs be rewarded according to some assessment of *comparable worth*. Let's now look at both of these problems in more detail.

Women's Jobs

Why hasn't the rush of women into the labor force had much effect on their level of income? A good part of the answer is that women have moved mainly into those jobs and industries that have *always* employed most working women, such as clerical work, retail sales, and the "service" occupations. (We'll describe this pattern of job growth in more detail in Chapter 8.) Women's gains in breaking into higher-paying jobs and industries have been counterbalanced by an even greater crowding of women into lower-level, traditionally "female" jobs.

Despite gains, most women still work in routine jobs.

What kinds of jobs do women hold today — and how has this changed in recent years? Let's look first at the broad, standard occupational categories. Of the approximately 43 million women in the paid work force in 1981, roughly 15 million (about 35 percent) were clerical workers. Another 8.3 million (almost 20 percent) were service workers; 7.3 million (17 percent) were professional and technical workers, and about 4.5 million (10 percent) were semiskilled operatives. Roughly four out of five women in the paid work force worked in those four broad categories (*Statistical Abstract of the U.S., 1982–83*, pp. 388–390).

It is instructive to compare these percentages with the distribution of men in the labor force. Only 6 percent of working men are clerical workers; about 9 percent are service workers. The other big differences between the sexes in the work force are the much greater proportions of men in managerial and especially in skilled craft jobs. Proportionately, more than twice as many men as women are managers or administrators, and 12 times as many men work in skilled crafts. Figure 6-4 shows that this distribution has changed in some ways in recent years — but it has remained remarkably stable in others. Since 1960 the most important changes have been that

1. Women have moved *out* of jobs as private household servants.
2. Women have moved *into* service jobs outside private households.
3. Women are *less* often blue-collar operatives.
4. Women are *more* often clerical and professional/technical workers.

With some exceptions, most of these shifts do not involve women moving, in large numbers, into formerly "male" jobs — nor even, necessarily, into jobs that are significantly *better* ones. Instead, these shifts most often reflect broad changes in the economy, notably the decline of household service and the growth of clerical and service jobs outside the home. [Ninety-five percent of "servants and cleaners" in private households are still women, however, and more than 50 percent of them are black (*Statistical Abstract of the U.S., 1982–83*, p. 390).]

The shifts in women's occupational distribution have not changed the basic fact about women's employment — women generally work in jobs where *other* women work. Put in another way, most of the movement of women into the labor force has been into jobs that were heavily female to begin with. A study by the U.S. Department of Labor defines jobs with less than 25 percent women workers as "traditionally male," and defines as "traditionally female" those with more than 55 percent women. By the end of the 1970s, only about 10 percent of working women held "traditionally male" jobs; more than 66 percent held "traditionally female" jobs; and about 22 percent held more "sex-integrated" jobs in between (U.S. Department of Labor, Women's Bureau, 1980, p. 9). [Some historical studies suggest, in fact, that the percentage of women in female-dominated jobs has *increased* since the turn of the century (Rosenthal, 1978, p. 242).]

A look at more specific jobs illustrates both the gains and the limitations of women's progress in the occupational hierarchy in recent years. The first and most striking fact that may be gleaned from Table 6-5 is how many jobs remain either disproportionately male or disproportionately female, despite more than a decade of efforts to promote job equality that some critics believe went "too far." By 1981 just 1 in 7 physicians, 1 in 25 engineers, and less than 1 in 50 carpenters and mechanics were women. And, at the other end, those jobs that were overwhelmingly female at the beginning of the 1970s still were in the early 1980s. In both years, virtually all private household workers, secretaries, and registered nurses were women. If anything, the concentration of women in some kinds of clerical jobs increased.

On the positive side, it's clear from Table 6-5 that more progress has been made in women *entering* formerly "men's" jobs than in getting *out* of "women's" jobs. The rate of change, especially in some professional and craft jobs, has sometimes been very rapid. But we need to keep in mind the

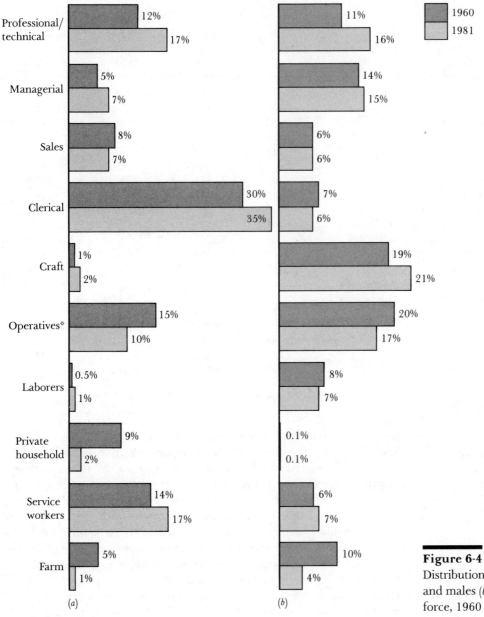

	1960
	1981

Professional/technical
12%
17%
11%
16%

Managerial
5%
7%
14%
15%

Sales
8%
7%
6%
6%

Clerical
30%
35%
7%
6%

Craft
1%
2%
19%
21%

Operatives*
15%
10%
20%
17%

Laborers
0.5%
1%
8%
7%

Private household
9%
2%
0.1%
0.1%

Service workers
14%
17%
6%
7%

Farm
5%
1%
10%
4%

(a)   (b)

Figure 6-4
Distribution of females (*a*) and males (*b*) in the labor force, 1960 and 1981

Source: Data from *Employment and Training Report of the President* (Washington, D.C.: Government Printing Office, 1980), p. 245; *Statistical Abstract of the United States, 1982–83* (Washington, D.C.: Government Printing Office, 1983), p. 386.

*Semiskilled blue-collar worker.
Note: Percentages do not add up to 100 due to rounding of figures.

Occupation	Number (in thousands)		Females as percentage of all workers in occupation	
	1970	1981	1970	1981
Professional-technical	4,576	7,173	40.0	44.7
Accountants	180	422	25.3	38.5
Computer specialists	52	170	19.6	27.1
Engineers	20	65	1.6	4.3
Lawyers-judges	13	80	4.7	14.0
Physicians-osteopaths	25	60	8.9	13.8
Registered nurses	814	1,271	97.4	96.8
Teachers, except college and university	1,937	2,219	70.4	70.8
Teachers, college and university	139	202	28.3	35.3
Managerial-administrative, except farm	1,061	3,098	16.6	27.4
Bank officials-financial managers	55	254	17.6	37.4
Buyers-purchasing agents	75	164	20.8	35.0
Food service workers	109	286	33.7	40.5
Sales managers-department heads; retail trade	51	136	24.1	40.4
Salesworkers	2,143	2,856	39.4	45.4
Salesclerks, retail	1,465	1,696	64.8	71.3
Clerical	10,150	14,645	73.6	80.5
Bank tellers	216	523	86.1	93.7
Bookkeepers	1,274	1,752	82.1	91.2
Cashiers	692	1,400	84.0	86.4
Office machine operators	414	696	73.5	73.7

Table 6-5

Women employed in selected occupations, 1970 and 1981

difference between the *rate* of change and the actual *proportions* of women in these jobs by the early 1980s. Consider engineering, traditionally one of the most male-dominated of all occupations in America. In 1970 less than 2 percent of engineers in the United States were women. In 1981 more than 4 percent were women, an increase of about 170 percent. But it is still true that only about 1 in every 23 engineers is a woman. If the same rate of change continues, less than one in five engineers will be women by the beginning of the twenty-first century. Or consider carpenters, one of the better-paying, traditionally male-dominated skilled crafts. In 1970 only about 1 out of every 75 carpenters was a woman. By 1981 the proportion had increased by more than half — but that still means that only 1 in 50 carpenters was a woman. At that rate of change, women would manage to hold about 4 percent of carpentry jobs by the year 2000.

Still, women *did* make substantial strides toward equality in some important fields in the 1970s. They made real gains in professions such as accounting and law, in some technical fields, including fast-growing, relatively high-paying computer-related jobs, and in a few other traditionally male-dominated craft and service jobs, such as police work and printing.

Occupation	Number (in thousands)		Females as percentage of all workers in occupation	
	1970	1981	1970	1981
Clerical (*continued*)				
Secretaries-typists	3,686	4,788	96.6	98.6
Shipping-receiving clerks	59	116	14.3	22.5
Craft	518	786	4.9	6.3
Carpenters	11	20	1.3	1.9
Mechanics, including automotive	49	62	2.0	1.9
Printing	58	99	14.8	25.0
Operatives, except transport	4,036	4,101	38.4	39.8
Assemblers	459	599	48.7	52.3
Laundry and dry cleaning operatives	105	125	62.9	66.1
Sewers and stitchers	816	749	93.8	96.0
Transport equipment operatives	134	304	4.5	8.9
Bus drivers	68	168	28.5	47.3
Truckdrivers	22	51	1.5	2.7
Service workers	5,944	8,184	60.5	62.2
Cooks	546	723	62.5	51.9
Food service	1,913	3,044	68.8	68.5
Health service	1,047	1,752	88.0	89.3
Personal service	778	1,314	66.5	76.1
Private household	1,132	988	96.9	96.5
Protective service	59	145	6.2	10.1

Source: Janet L. Norwood, *The Female-Male Earnings Gap: A Review of Employment and Earnings Issues* (Washington, D.C.: U.S. Bureau of Labor Statistics, 1982), p. 5.

But the distribution of occupations between the sexes remains highly unequal. And new openings at the top have not been accompanied by any significant lessening of the concentration at the bottom. If we add together all the women newly working as engineers, lawyers, judges, doctors, accountants, computer specialists, college teachers, and managers in banking and finance in 1981 as opposed to 1970, about three-quarters of a million women broke into these high-level, male-dominated jobs. But well over a million women joined the ranks of secretaries *alone* during the same years.

Moreover, what is remarkable about the separation between men's and women's work is the extent to which it reappears, over and over again, in a variety of different forms and settings, some subtle and some glaring. Thus, in every broad occupational category, women are still found clustered in the specific jobs at the lower-paying end, as Table 6-6 illustrates. In sales work, men are manufacturing or wholesale sales "representatives," or they sell stocks, bonds, insurance, or real estate; women are mainly clerks in retail

Table 6-6

Average weekly earnings
and percent of female
workers, selected
occupations, 1981

Occupations	Median weekly earnings	Percent female workers
Professional and technical workers		
Lawyers and judges	$550	20.7
Engineers	$540	4.7
Physicians	$501	21.7
Registered nurses	$332	95.8
Elementary school teachers	$322	82.2
Sales workers		
Stock and bond sales agents	$535	17.1
Manufacturing sales representatives	$434	16.0
Retail salesclerks	$178	60.3
Clerical workers		
Mail carriers	$406	11.7
Secretaries	$230	99.3
Service workers		
Police and detectives	$363	5.3
Firefighters	$362	1.4
Waiters	$150	85.1
Maids and servants	$126	91.8
Craft workers		
Tool and die makers	$433	3.0
Electricians	$419	1.7
Decorators and window dressers	$210	65.2

Source: Data from Nancy F. Rytina, "Earnings of Men and Women: A Look at Specific Occupations," *Monthly Labor Review*, April 1982, pp. 26–29. Reprinted with permission.

stores. In service jobs, women are waitresses, household workers, or nurses' aides; men are police officers and firefighters. In the professions, men are doctors, lawyers, and engineers; but more than half of the 7.3 million women professional and technical workers are schoolteachers or nurses. Even in the generally female-dominated realm of clerical work, certain jobs (like mail-carriers) remain largely male preserves, and they are invariably better paid than most clerical work.

Even in relatively sex-integrated jobs, women are often disproportionately found in specific workplaces or specific functions that are different from men's. Women accountants, for example, are often employed by a relatively few employers in a particular city, who tend to hire mainly women — and to pay them less (F. D. Blair, 1977; National Research Council, 1981, pp. 49–50). Women in academic teaching are much less likely to teach in large universities than men and much more likely to teach in two-year colleges (National Center for Education Statistics, 1980, p. 2).

And at the highest levels of the American economy — managerial positions in the largest corporations — sex segregation appears again in a very revealing way. We have seen that women gained some important footholds into management jobs in the 1970s. But a look at the *kinds* of jobs women attained shows the limits of those gains and the persistence of traditional conceptions of women's work. Thus, an analysis of women employed as officers of the top 1,000 industrial corporations and the top 50 banking, communications, insurance, and utilities corporations gives this picture, as of 1980 (Hedrich and Struggles, 1980):

- There was one woman corporate officer for every 3.3 industrial corporations and every 1.6 nonindustrial corporations.

- Of these women officers, 37 percent had the title of assistant secretary, and another 14 percent, secretary.

- Only 0.8 percent were chairmen [sic], vice-chairmen, or company presidents — *down* from 1.4 percent in 1979.

- 98.8 percent were non-Hispanic whites.

Authority and Women's Work

Women's work, even at the *highest* levels of conventional status and pay, often becomes defined as an extension of the type of work women have traditionally done at home: teaching, nurturing, feeding, cleaning. On the other hand, certain functions tend to be predictably male-dominated, even within groups of professional or managerial workers. This is especially true for the exercise of *authority*. Women in science and engineering, for example, are overrepresented in basic research and are very rarely found in managerial roles with authority to set policy or supervise other professionals (National Academy of Sciences, 1980). Women in education are typically teachers, more rarely administrators with authority over curricula or educational policy (Barrett, 1979a, pp. 4–6).

A number of studies have confirmed this tendency for women to be excluded from positions of authority, even in high-level jobs. The power to hire and fire or to determine others' pay or their working conditions is disproportionately lodged in men's hands. A University of Michigan survey found that about one-fourth of working men have some supervisory responsibilities that give them a say over other workers' pay or promotion; only one-tenth of working women do (Hill, 1980). Like other inequalities in jobs and earnings, this difference is partly explained by other differences men and women bring to the workplace — but only partly. Better education and training help a worker of either sex land a position of authority and responsibility over others — but they are far more likely to do so for men than for women. Women are more likely to remain in subordinate positions even *with* high levels of education.

Better for Younger Women?

These differences must be kept in mind when assessing women's progress in breaking the barriers of job segregation. But, as with minorities, it can be argued that the magnitude of the progress becomes more visible if we look specifically at the experience of younger women. Presumably, their situation more accurately reflects the beneficial impact of antidiscrimination laws and policies, as well as a more accepting attitude in society as a whole toward nontraditional work.

And, indeed, the statistics do show a trend toward improvement: younger women are more often found outside of traditional "women's" jobs. The proportion of women aged 20 to 34 in professional-managerial-technical jobs rose from 20 percent in 1968 to almost 25 percent 10 years later (Barrett, 1979a, pp. 52–53). This is significant progress, but it must be qualified by the fact that *most* young women now entering the labor force are still moving into lower-level, traditionally female jobs and industries. Indeed, most younger women now entering the labor force not only *expect* to enter traditionally female jobs, but *aspire* to them. A survey of 5,000 women aged 21 to 31 showed that among women without a college education, 81 percent of white and 87 percent of black women who expected to work outside the home by age 35 said they would prefer typically "female" jobs. Among college-educated women, the proportions favoring traditional jobs were somewhat smaller, but a majority of both white (75 percent) and black (78 percent) women said they would prefer a job typically defined as women's work (Barrett, 1979a, p. 53).

Moreover, a crucial question we are not yet able to answer is whether (or how much) better *initial* job opportunities for some women will be translated into greater chances for advancement and upward mobility *thereafter*. We have seen that women's earnings, unlike men's, tend to stay at much the same level throughout their life cycle. To a large extent this is because they tend to stay in relatively low-status jobs over the course of their lives, while men more often move upward through the job hierarchy over the years. One recent longitudinal study even shows that a substantial proportion of women workers experience *downward* mobility in the occupational hierarchy over their life cycle. Women reentering the labor force in their middle years most often enter in a job with *lower* prestige and pay than the one they first held (Rosenthal, 1978).

It isn't certain, then, that women's gains in landing a good job in the first place will necessarily be followed by the chances for advancement and mobility that many men enjoy. And, as we've seen, for many women the chances of *ever* landing a well-paying job remain elusive in the 1980s. This is one reason why poverty in America is increasingly a women's issue.

Non-traditional work: women's gains have been important, but limited.

Women, Work, and Poverty

We saw in the previous chapter that economic progress for American minorities has followed an uneven path. Some, with better access to good jobs and earnings, have gained a foothold in the middle class; others are trapped in a stubborn cycle of poverty and unemployment. The trends in women's economic progress show a similar division. Some women have made important gains in moving into nontraditional, better-paying jobs, reaching a more equal footing with men. But at the other end of the spectrum is what the sociologist Diana Pearce (1982) has called the "feminization of poverty" — a trend that haunts the progress of all women, but is especially severe among minority women. Two out of every three adults living in poverty are women. One in three Americans living in a family maintained by a woman is poor, as compared to just one in nine in families maintained by a single man and only one in *nineteen* in intact husband-wife families. And, as Figure 6-5 illustrates, this gap is generally widening. More and more, poverty in the United States is becoming a "women's issue" (U.S. Commission on Civil Rights, 1983).

The "Women's Economy"

The problem of job segregation by sex has two somewhat different, but overlapping, components. Women are segregated into particular *occupations* and in different kinds of *industries*. And in every case, a high proportion of women workers in a given industry goes hand in hand with relatively low wages — even for work that seems otherwise indistinguishable from work in other industries that are quite similar — except that they employ more *men.*

Within the American economy as a whole, we can discern the outlines of a fairly distinct "women's economy," an economy with its own special characteristics that profoundly shape the lives of the majority of working women in America. The outline of the women's economy coincides, to some extent, with what we've called the "secondary" sector of the economy. But it has some specific, and sometimes unpredictable, boundaries all its own.

The most obvious feature of the women's economy is that it is made up of industries that traditionally pay very poorly and are less likely to be unionized, as Table 6-7 indicates. The highest-paid workers in the table are those in the oil and coal industries. At the other end of the scale, the lowest-paid workers are those who worked in private households. Nine-tenths of workers in private households are women, but only one-fifth of workers in the petroleum and coal industries are. This difference turns up throughout the table.

But, even more tellingly, the women's economy also appears *within* industries. It can be de-

tected by the presence of sharp, sex-linked pay differences for virtually the same kind of work. Within the food and beverage industry, for example, the workers who earn far and away the most money are brewery workers. In 1981 they earned $497 a week, quite high up on the scale of American industrial workers. The lowest-paid food industry workers are found in poultry dressing plants. They earned an average of $169 a week in 1981, a wage which, for year-round, full-time work, amounted to almost exactly a poverty-level income for a worker with three dependents. 85 percent of brewery workers are men, while 53 percent of poultry dressers are women.

Much of American industry has, historically, been based on the organizing principle of the factory assembly line. But how much a worker *earns* on an assembly line depends greatly on just *what* is being assembled, which, in turn, is closely related to the *gender* of the typical worker. People who assemble motor vehicles made a little more than $500 a week in 1981, while people who assembled electronic components made only half as much. More than half of electronic component assemblers, but only one in nine auto assemblers, are women.

Sometimes the rationale for these distinctions between the men's and women's economies is extremely difficult to comprehend. Thus, more than 90 percent of the workers who make tires or inner tubes out of rubber are men, and earn about $450 a week in 1981. Two-thirds of the workers who make *footwear* out of rubber are women and earn $169 a week. Or consider the apparel (clothing) industry, which has traditionally been among the poorest-paying industries in America. Apparel workers averaged only

We have already seen that poverty in the United States increased sharply in the early 1980s after declining up to the early 1970s and remaining at a relatively stable level in between. A closer examination reveals, however, that most of the gains even in the period of greatest success against poverty took place for poor *men* and their families. Figure 6-5 illustrates this disturbing trend. Between 1959 and 1981, the number of poor Americans living in families headed by a woman grew by more than 5 million, while the number in all other families *fell* by 13 million. Most of this latter improvement took place between 1959 and 1970, and it can justly be regarded as one of

about $175 a week in 1981, again barely above the federal poverty level for a family of four. By now it shouldn't surprise us that more than four out of five clothing workers are women. Yet within this generally poor industry there is a category of workers who make automotive and apparel trimmings. In striking contrast to all *other* apparel workers, these workers make almost $400 a week — far above the average for American manufacturing. And *half* of these workers, also in striking contrast to other apparel categories, are men. At the other end of the scale in the clothing industry are the workers who produced women's and misses' blouses. At about $150 a week, these women — for *9 out of 10 are women* — cannot support three dependents at the federal poverty level through full-time, year-round work without an extra job or welfare.

It is sometimes argued that these inequalities in pay reflect basic differences in the type of work performed. In 1981 the highest-paid industrial workers in America were those in the basic steel industry, who averaged $550 a week. (Steelworkers, of course, have also suffered devastating unemployment in recent years.) Steel is one of the *durable goods* industries, which tend on the whole to have higher than average wages. There are some low-paying durable goods industries, however. The lowest paying is costume jewelry manufacturing, whose workers averaged only $175 a week in 1981. The fact that less than one in ten steelworkers, as compared to three out of five costume jewelry makers, are women might, in this viewpoint, be explained by the nature of the work. Steel mill work is heavy and dangerous, while costume jewelry manufacture requires dexterity, patience, and other characteristics long

considered typically feminine. But that sort of explanation doesn't help us understand why workers in copper or aluminum foundries, who make only a little over half of what steelworkers do — and *also* work at heavy, dangerous jobs — are almost *twice* as likely to be women as workers in steel mills.

The same logical difficulty appears if we look at people who work in stores of various kinds rather than in factories. Like the clothing industry, the retail sales industry is one of the poorest paid in the United States. Unsurprisingly, it is a very large employer of women: about 7.5 million of them in 1981, who comprise about half the industry's work force. But within the retail industry as a whole there are sharp, revealing differences. All retail sales workers sell something for a living — but *what* they sell depends heavily on their gender and is, in turn, fateful for their standard of living. Though women are half of all retail sales workers, they are only *15 percent* of auto dealers, the highest-paid people in the retail industry. The people who sell women's ready-to-wear clothing are nearly all (89 percent) women themselves, and in 1981 they made only $118 a week — oddly enough, $50 a week less than the people selling men's and boy's clothes, more than half of whom are men.

Source: Data from U.S. Bureau of Labor Statistics, *Employment and Earnings*, April 1981.

Table 6-7

Earnings and
unionization in
"women's" and "men's"
industries, 1981

Industries	Median weekly earnings	Percent represented by a union	Percent female
Total full-time workers	$289	29	39
Highest-paying industries			
Petroleum and coal products	433	36	20
Mining	423	36	15
Railroad transportation	422	82	7
Aircraft and parts manufacture	414	50	23
Ordnance	410	37	22
Motor vehicle and equipment manufacture	407	63	15
Lowest-paying industries			
Private households	114	1	90
Apparel manufacture	170	27	79
Eating and drinking places	174	8	55
Leather and leather products	185	24	61
Personal services	188	18	59
Agriculture	189	4	16

Source: Earl F. Mellor and George D. Stanas, "Usual Weekly Earnings: Another Look at Intergroup Differences and Basic Trends," *Monthly Labor Review*, April 1982, p. 19. Reprinted with permission.

the most positive legacies of the 1960s. But even then the sheer number of poor people (though not the *rate* of poverty) in families headed by women was still increasing. Whatever forces reduced overall poverty in those years clearly worked best for men and much less for women.

The result has been a striking, fundamental change in the composition of the poverty population. In 1959, more than three times as many poor children lived in male-headed families than in ones headed by a woman; since the mid-1970s, the majority of poor children are in female-headed families.

Even more disturbingly, this trend shows up most strongly among the young. While some young women have reaped the advantages of changing attitudes, laws, and social policies, winning better jobs and higher incomes, a rising number of others are being left behind in a trap of poverty and frequent dependency. The *overall* poverty rate for women heading families is about 35 percent, but about *two-thirds* of women under 24 who head their own families are poor. And their numbers have grown with astonishing speed; there were more than half a million such families in 1981, up from 150,000 in 1959 (U.S. Bureau of the Census, 1983a, p. 24).

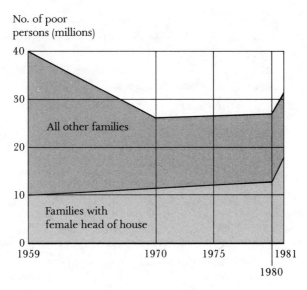

No. of poor persons (millions)

All other families

Families with female head of house

1959   1970   1975   1981
1980

Figure 6-5

Poverty in families with female householder and in all other families, 1959–1981

Source: Data from U.S. Bureau of the Census, *Current Population Reports*, series P-60, no. 138, Washington, D.C., 1983, pp. 8–9.

From what we've seen already about women's jobs and earnings, it shouldn't surprise us that *persistent poverty* (the rarer and more stubborn variety that entraps families year after year) is disproportionately a *women's* problem. Among those of the persistently poor who are not aged, two-thirds live in households headed by women, according to the University of Michigan's Panel Study of Income Dynamics (*Employment and Training Reporter*, August 1982, p. 99). Thus, women are not only more often poor, but, much more importantly, are far more likely to *stay* poor.

Why? How do we explain this dual character of women's experience today — substantial gains on the one hand, deepening poverty on the other? How can so many women be entering the ranks of the welfare poor while others are moving into executive suites? And why haven't years of antidiscrimination efforts stopped the widening inequality between the sexes in the risks of poverty?

The answers lie in several trends we've already noted: job segregation, the persistence of the women's economy, the sexual division of labor in childrearing and family responsibilities. All of them combine to force many women into poverty, especially, though not exclusively, when they are the heads of families. These gender inequalities generate poverty among women in several, often overlapping ways. One is high rates of joblessness — especially for minority women, the young, and those maintaining families. (Since we'll look at unemployment in greater detail in Chapter 8, we'll only mention one important aspect of it here.) By any measure, unemployment among women heading families has been at crisis proportions for years. But the problem of joblessness for these women is much greater than the unemployment statistics alone indicate, since official unemployment statistics minimize the extent of joblessness by ignoring people who have temporarily or permanently dropped out of the work force and those who work only part time when they need full-time jobs. Both of these problems of measurement and definition distort our understanding of women's unemployment more than men's. As we've seen, mainly because of their traditional responsibilities for childrearing, women drop out of the labor force much faster and more frequently than men do and also more often take part-time work in order to balance income needs with the demands of the home. Thus, only about 11 percent of the women heading poor families were officially unemployed in 1981. Yet only 29 percent were employed. The other 60 percent were counted as "not in the labor force" (U.S. Bureau of the Census, 1983a, p. 25).

Another important reason why so many women are increasingly found in the American underclass is low earnings. This confirms, once again, that the *sources* of poverty are typically different for men than for women. Men are most often poor because they don't, for one or another reason, have a job; when they *do* have one, they almost always earn enough to bring them over the poverty level. But one of the most telling effects of the segregation of men's and women's work is that a substantial proportion of women who work fairly regularly — even a significant minority of those who work year round and full time — remain poor. In 1981 about 7 percent of women heading families who worked full time, year round were poor as compared to about 3 percent of male family heads (U.S. Bureau of the Census, 1983a, p. 23). Moreover, the number of poor families headed by a male full-time, year-round worker dropped dramatically during the 1960s and has not risen even close to its pre–War on Poverty level. The number of poor *women* family heads who worked year round, full time dropped much more slowly in the 1960s and is now *higher* than it was in 1959.

The problem of low women's earnings helps explain the persistence of poverty among married-couple families as well, for though women's earnings help bring many such families over the poverty line, they are often insufficient for others. Overall, as the National Advisory Council on Economic Opportunity has noted (Blaustein, 1982, p. 10), "If wives and female heads of households were paid the same wages that similarly qualified men earn, almost half of the families now living in poverty would not be poor."

A final factor in women's high rates of poverty is inadequate levels of public and private support. We have seen that the American welfare system has been attacked for excessive generosity — and we've noted some of the misunderstandings that often underlie that view. How well *do* women fare in the welfare system today?

In 1981, the average income of all families maintained by women, where the family had no earnings and therefore received almost all of its income from public welfare, was more than $2,000 below the poverty level for a family of three, the average size for an AFDC family (U.S. Bureau of the Census, 1983a, p. 139).

Not only is the welfare state considerably less generous than is sometimes supposed, but its generosity divides sharply along gender lines — not unlike the economy as a whole (Pearce, 1982). In one "sector," the welfare state offers support — through unemployment insurance, trade adjustment assistance, and other programs — to those people, mainly (though not entirely) men, who lose high-paying, often unionized jobs in the "primary" economy. This part of the welfare state offers more substantial benefits (though not *as* substantial as some critics have argued) — and generally provides them with less hassle and degradation. But the other "sector" is for those people, disproportionately female, whose work outside the home is confined to the lower reaches of the women's economy and whose main source of support in case of job loss or other catastrophe is AFDC or local public assistance. The benefits of this "sector" of the welfare state are usually granted grudgingly and are rarely sufficient to lift these women out of what has aptly been called a "workhouse without walls" (Pearce, 1982, p. 31).

Prospects for the Future

On balance, then, women's progress against inequality has been decidedly mixed. Better jobs, with higher pay and better chances for advancement, have opened up for some women. And, to some extent, traditional attitudes in the home and in the larger society are shifting toward greater acknowledgement of the importance of women's work outside the home. But there is a dark side to this progress. Even in those areas where they have achieved the most success in breaking down traditional barriers, women have a very long way to go before they reach anything close to equality with men. The segregation of women's work still pervades the entire economy, even at its highest levels. And despite the velocity of change in some male-dominated fields, women are still underrepresented in most of them in absolute terms — and even at current rates of change, will remain so far into the future. Moreover, the persistence of the gender-based division of labor in the home, in spite of women's increased work outside it, helps feed a vicious cycle of poor jobs, lowered expectations, and interrupted careers.

But what is even more ominous is that the progress of some women has been offset by a decline for many others. It is not just that progress hasn't been rapid enough. The deeper problem is that many of the forces that have brought greater equality and improved life chances for some women have largely passed others by. The feminization of poverty continues, with its crippling features of low-wage work in segregated jobs, high levels of joblessness, and welfare dependency.

What can we say about the future direction of these trends? For women, as for minorities, the prospects for equality depend crucially on larger trends in the economy on the one hand, and in public policy on the other. Both currently show some troubling directions.

Women's Work and Economic Change

The position of women in American society will be greatly influenced by whether, and in what direction, their extraordinary rate of movement into the paid labor force continues. Most projections estimate that it *will* continue, bringing a still greater proportion of American women into the work force, though there is also some evidence that the trend may be slowing. But what is virtually certain is that *most* women entering the paid labor force will continue to move into "women's" jobs. With some exceptions, most of the fastest-growing sectors of the economy will probably continue to be those that have traditionally employed high proportions of women, such as service and clerical work. (We will explore these trends further in Chapter 8.) There will be more jobs for women, but they will still be in some of the poorest parts of the economy. As a result, the earnings gap between women and men is unlikely to be narrowed much in the near future.

Some women will also move into fast-growing, male-dominated jobs outside the largely segregated women's economy. But many of these jobs, especially in engineering, computer science, and other skilled technical fields, are among those where women are now least represented and where, even at present rates of change, they will still be underrepresented in the future. Short of an unprecedented shift in the sex composition of these occupations, their growth seems unlikely to have a very strong effect on the overall distribution of women in the job hierarchy.

Other changes in the American economy seem likely to have a powerful, if not easily predictable, impact on gender inequalities. The long-term process of deindustrialization has so far struck hardest at blue-collar jobs and industries that, on the whole, have traditionally been male-dominated. Many of the "new poor" displaced in this process have been men. Yet the same trend has also hit some women particularly hard, especially those who recently gained a foothold in well-paying blue-collar jobs, only to see them eliminated through economic decline and technological change. Moreover, as we'll see in Chapter 8, those parts of the economy that have been less devastatingly hit by the economic shifts of recent years (particularly clerical and service work) may themselves soon undergo fundamental technological changes as automation moves more and more into the office. And since these are the sectors of the economy that have traditionally employed most women, these changes may have profound repercussions on women's economic position and prospects.

Public Policy, Affirmative Action, and the Welfare State

On the level of public policy, the outlook for women is similarly precarious. Three related trends, in particular, have ominous implications for women: the waning commitment to affirmative action, the shrinking of the public sector, and the attack on the welfare state.

We've seen that women's recent gains in jobs and earnings, though sharply limited, have been real and significant. It's sometimes argued that they would have occurred *without* specific government antidiscrimination ef-

Automation in the office may deeply affect women's work in the future.

forts, simply as a by-product of economic growth and changing attitudes. But the evidence suggests that, on the contrary, much of the progress women have made in jobs and earnings has been, at least in part, the result of vigorous antidiscrimination policies. For example, the greatest improvement in women's job distribution in the banking industry came during the 1970s — a time of slow economic growth but relatively strong federal affirmative action efforts. Between 1950 and 1960, before affirmative action, the percentage of bank managers who were women rose barely at all — less than 5 percent. From 1970 to 1979, after affirmative action plans, the percentage rose by more than 80 percent (*Working Women*, 1981).

In the past several years, it's often been argued that these programs, while well intentioned, are too costly. But, some facts about the costs of antidiscrimination programs gathered by Working Women, a national organization of office workers, are enlightening. In 1977, for example, the nation's third largest bank, Citicorp, spent more to sponsor auto racing than it did on affirmative action programs. The chairman of Citibank was paid almost twice as much as the bank spent on affirmative action. And, as of 1980, the budget for the agency that oversees the *entire* federal effort to ensure compliance with antidiscrimination provisions in companies with federal contracts (the Office of Federal Contract Compliance) was only about $50 million (Working Women, 1981, pp. 5–10). A study of 48 large corporations by the Business Round Table, a major corporate lobbying organization, found that the costs of affirmative action programs amounted to about 0.01 percent of their revenues, or a little more than $12 per employee per year (Working Women, 1981, p. 9).

The weakening of commitment to the programs that have helped bring gains for women is compounded by the effects of the broader attack on government. Like racial minorities, women have generally fared much better in the public sector than the private, in terms of jobs and pay. Though total employment in the federal government did not grow in the 1970s, the fastest growth of employment *shares* for women took place there. The earn-

Women, Work, and Pay in Other Countries

Like many other social problems in contemporary America, the wide gap between men and women in jobs and earnings is often regarded as an inevitable fact of life. For some, it reflects biological necessity (Goldberg, 1974). For others, it's simply another aspect of "the way things are." Both attitudes, needless to say, imply that not much can be done through deliberate social policy to reduce these inequalities.

Few would deny that gender differences exist, on a variety of levels, and that they deeply influence virtually every facet of social and personal relations. But looking at the economic situation of women in some other advanced societies shows that the way in which gender affects employment, wages, and living standards is very much affected by explicit *social* policies.

If women were intrinsically less suited for some kinds of work rather than others, for example, we would expect their occupational distribution to be similar across different countries. But this isn't the case. Some of the basic features of women's job segregation in the United States are indeed recapitulated in other countries — women in other advanced industrial societies also remain, *on the whole,* concentrated in lower-paying, traditionally female occupations like clerical work and are underrepresented in skilled crafts

and many technical and professional jobs (United Nations, 1980). But there are very important exceptions, and the range of variation is wide. Thus, the proportion of women doctors in England, Sweden, France, Denmark, and Austria is about double that in the United States; in Finland and Germany, closer to three times. In Eastern Europe, the proportions of women doctors are typically even greater: more than 40 percent of doctors in Czechoslovakia are women, more than *70 percent* in the Soviet Union. These differences are even more pronounced for engineering, one of the areas in which women are most dramatically underrepresented in the United States. In 1970, 4 percent of engineers and architects in the United States were women. In most European countries women were still relatively unlikely to be in these fields, but much *more* likely than in the United States: There were, proportionately, between two and three times as many women engineers and architects in England, Switzerland, Belgium, and Denmark as in the United States. In most of the countries of Eastern Europe roughly 20 percent or more of architects and engineers were women; in the Soviet Union, 45 percent. And these differences aren't limited to the highest-level occupations. In the Soviet Union, for example, a number of blue-collar jobs that are male bastions in the United States are dominated by women, including electricians, metal workers, and painters (United Nations, 1980, pp. 40–51).

ings gap between men and women scientists and other professionals is *far* less wide in the federal government than in private industry. Similarly, women are much better represented in management jobs — and their pay is much more equal in them — in public administration than in the private sector. Regardless of occupation, in fact, women's earnings, relative to men's, are *consistently better* in public sector jobs, though gaps still exist. [Women public elementary school teachers, for example, earn 86 percent of what males earn; women social workers, 87 percent. (Rytina, 1981, p. 50).]

These differences strongly suggest that antidiscrimination policies for women have been much more firmly promoted in the public sector than in private industry (National Academy of Sciences, 1980). This makes the current shift toward reliance on the private sector to accomplish social goals an ominous one for women.

Both the continuities and the differences between the United States and some other industrial countries also appear in the case of differences in earnings. Women earn less than men, on the average, in every country in the world. But the range of this inequality is very wide. There are, of course, formidable problems in measuring the earnings gap across different countries. But careful studies indicate that the ratio of women's to men's pay varies from a low of about 60 to 65 percent in the United States and England to a high of 85 to 90 percent in Sweden. Most of this difference remains even when a number of potentially complicating factors (such as the age of the work force) are taken into account. Moreover, in many European countries, *unlike* the United States, pay differentials by sex have been *decreasing* in recent years as a result of the vigorous enforcement of clear-cut national antidiscrimination policies (United Nations, 1980, p. 118).

The specific kinds of policies used to reduce women's economic inequality vary widely among European countries (Ratner, 1980). The Swedish approach is one of the most interesting and, so far, most effective. Part of Sweden's success in reducing (though not eliminating) wage disparities between the sexes is the result of what Swedish planners call a *solidary wage policy* (Cook, 1980). Swedish unions have long adopted the policy of bargaining with employers to reduce the *overall* inequality of wages within industry and thus narrow the *spread* of earnings throughout the economy. "The goal," as one observer describes it, "is to abolish low incomes [by] narrowing the gap between high and low earnings. . . . Equality in Sweden means accepting a system under which all workers earn a reasonable but not a widely differentiated standard of living" (Cook, 1980, pp. 64–65). Since the biggest proportion of low-wage workers are women, such a policy has the effect of raising women's wages substantially relative to men's.

The solidary wage policy is complemented by a range of measures designed to lower the barriers *outside* the labor market that hinder women from equal access to good jobs. As we'll see in more detail in Chapter 7, this includes a strong commitment to the public provision of child-care and to national-level policies granting extensive leaves and more flexible and shorter working hours for both sexes. All of these policies are designed to lessen the conflicts between work and family life. They have not yet entirely succeeded; nor have they eliminated deeply entrenched gender differences in the traditional division of labor in the Swedish family (Liljestrom, 1980). But they do represent important — and partly successful — *steps* toward equalizing work and family roles in Sweden.

Sharp cutbacks in public programs — ranging from education and health care to food stamps and AFDC — also have harsh implications for women in America. This is true both for those who have been relatively successful in jobs and income and those who remain dependent on the welfare state. On the one hand, women in higher-level jobs are concentrated disproportionately in some of the parts of the public sector most vulnerable to budgetary austerity. Most women professionals are teachers, nurses, or social workers — all fields that grew rapidly through the expansion of state and local government spending in the 1960s and 1970s. That growth was responsible for much of the increase in the proportion of women in professional jobs. (We saw in Chapter 2 that though government spending is often identified with a vast, bloated, and distant bureaucracy, *most* of the growth in domestic public spending in the 1970s was state and local spending for education and health care, and most of the "bureaucrats" thus funded were teachers and nurses.)

At the other end of the spectrum, the prognosis is even worse. Because of their high rates of joblessness and their inadequate earnings when they *do* work, poor women are extraordinarily dependent on the income support provided by the welfare state. And, as we have seen, the welfare state's support for poor women — especially for young women maintaining families — is rarely, by itself, sufficient to raise most of them out of poverty. For those it has lifted over the official poverty line, the margin of safety usually remains narrow. Less than one child in five in a family maintained by a black woman enjoys a family income more than 1.5 times the federal poverty level (Blaustein, 1982, p. 52). Severe reductions in benefits and services bear part of the responsibility for the rapidly rising numbers of women and their children living in poverty in the early 1980s.

In defense of these policies, it is often argued that reducing the drain of welfare spending will stimulate economic growth, which, in turn, is the most effective way to reduce poverty. The vision is appealing; it professes to offer a way out of the present morass of welfare dependency and its accompanying pathology. But would this kind of growth really address, by itself, the roots of women's poverty? Probably not. Unfortunately, as one critic notes, women are already disproportionately "denied access to the additional employment opportunities which faster growth could create" (Sawhill, 1979, p. 545). We have seen why: many lack either the training, the mobility, or the freedom from home responsibilities to benefit from the higher-level jobs that conventional growth in a high-technology economy might create.

For these women, it seems clear that substantial change will require much more direct strategies of intervention on many levels — in the workplace, the division of labor in the home, and in the provision of social services. To explore these questions, we need to examine a range of further issues — the changing nature of work in America and trends in the structure of the family — in more detail than we've allowed so far. We will turn to these issues in Part Two of this book.

Summary

This chapter has looked at trends in social inequality between the sexes. Women have entered the labor force in unprecendented numbers. Their participation in the work force is coming increasingly to resemble that of men. But this shift has not brought women to a position of economic equality with men.

The earnings gap between women and men has remained relatively unchanged for decades. Women still earn about 60 cents for every dollar men earn. And women's earnings, unlike men's, tend to remain low over the life cycle.

These differences are only partly explained by differences in women's educational levels, work experience, or patterns of movement in and out of the work force.

A major source of these inequalities in income and earnings is that traditional sex role expectations and inadequate child care often limit women to intermittent and poorly paid jobs.

Thus, despite genuine gains in their representation in some high-level jobs, occupational segregation remains the norm for women in the American economy. Women still most often work where other women work, especially in clerical and service occupations.

Occupational segregation, along with the low level of public and private supports for single women with children, helps explain the increasing "feminization" of poverty in the United States.

Attacks on public services, affirmative action programs, and public sector employment are likely to widen gender inequalities and stall the progress that has been achieved in recent years.

For Further Reading

Kessler-Harris, Alice. *Out to Work: A History of Wage-Earning Women in the United States*. New York: Oxford University Press, 1982.

National Research Council. *Women, Work, and Wages: Equal Pay for Jobs of Equal Value*. Washington, D.C.: National Academy Press, 1981.

Pearce, Diana. "Women in Poverty," in Arthur I. Blaustein, ed., *The American Promise: Equal Justice and Economic Opportunity*. New Brunswick, N.J.: Transaction Books, 1982.

U.S. Commission on Civil Rights. *A Growing Crisis: Disadvantaged Women and Their Children*. Washington, D.C.: Government Printing Office, 1983.

Part II

Impacts and Institutions

7

The Family

Americans of every generation have worried about the state of the family. In the 1920s, rising divorce rates, changing attitudes toward birth control and premarital sex, and the stirrings of greater independence for women led to fears that the family was in deep trouble. A standard textbook on social problems written in 1925 devoted its first 11 chapters to the problem of "Family Disorganization and Personal Demoralization" and noted ominously that "probably no social fact is more commented on in popular discussion than the increase in the divorce rate" (Queen and Mann, 1925, pp. 57–58).

During the period immediately following World War II, these fears didn't disappear, but they were moderated by what seemed to be the considerable strength and durability of the family. This was particularly true of what many social scientists of that era regarded as the family's "ideal" form: the intact nuclear family of wedded parents who either had or planned to have children. For most of the late 1940s and the 1950s, divorce rates were relatively stable, and the strong commitment of this generation to raising a family was powerfully demonstrated in the rising birth rates of the postwar baby boom.

But, as was true for so many other aspects of American life, the sense of complacency about the family turned out to be short-lived. The relatively stable patterns of family life that seemed, at least on the surface, to characterize the 1950s soon began to crack in highly visible ways. Divorce rates shot upward in the 1960s and 1970s, as did illegitimate births. Conventional marriage and childrearing was rejected, at least temporarily, by a small but vocal minority of the young. And this rejection was sometimes accompanied by the exploration of a variety of alternative approaches to intimacy and sexuality. Birth rates fell, in strong contrast to the baby boom era immediately before.

To some observers, all this seemed to signal the approaching doom of the family. Assertions that the family was "dying" were common among both supporters and detractors of the conventional nuclear family, and the question of whether the family "had a future" was hotly debated (Cooper, 1970; Lasch, 1977).

This rather apocalyptic approach to the family's problems has abated in the past few years. It is widely acknowledged that the family, in the well-known phrase of the sociologist Mary Jo Bane, is "here to stay" (Bane, 1976). After all, as Figure 7·1 illustrates, recent surveys find that the vast majority of Americans still consider having a good family life as their *most* important goal — ranking it even higher than good health, self-respect, or general happiness. Among younger people, the central importance of family life is slightly — but only *slightly* — lower; in a recent Gallup poll, more than three-fourths of those 18 to 29 ranked a good family life at the top of the scale of personal values (Gallup Poll, 1982).

Even so, the family has become, if anything, a focus of even hotter public debate in the 1980s. The terms of the debate, however, have shifted. Those who describe themselves most vociferously as "pro-family" rarely argue that the family is on the verge of extinction. Instead, they worry that the family's vitality as an institution of socialization and social control is being eroded, with drastic and wide-ranging consequences for the quality of contemporary social and personal life. In this view, the family is still with us and is likely to be so for the indefinite future, but it needs defending against a host of threatening forces. The erosion of the family's strength is often held responsible for

> not only the juvenile crime rate, but the adult crime rate; the fact that only one-eighth of our youth have got enough sense of responsibility to register for the draft; the fact that we have so much drug addiction; the fact that we have so much loss of drive in terms of the work ethic (Denton, 1982, p. 5)

among other social ills.

The villain in this drama is often portrayed as the destructive "permissiveness" of the modern welfare state, which, in turn, is regarded as just one manifestation of a general decline in the values of personal responsibility, self-denial, and — often — the "proper" role of women as guardians of the home. Proponents of this view are particularly disturbed over several recent trends that have deeply affected American families: more "permissive" attitudes toward divorce, sexuality and childrearing; the spread of birth control, abortion, and family planning information; the rising participation of women in the labor force; the growth of public welfare and subsidized health care for poor families and of demands for day care for children of working parents. All of these developments are said to be undermining the

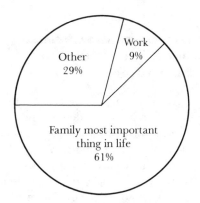

Figure 7-1
Percentage of responses to
question: What's the most
important thing in your
life?

Source: From *Public Opinion*, Au-
gust/September 1981, p. 26.
Reprinted with permission of
American Enterprise Institute
for Public Policy Research.

"self-sufficiency" that American families are thought to have enjoyed in the
past. As one U.S. senator argued in 1982,

> Many of the family's historical responsibilities have been taken over by the
> State . . . The strength of American society has come from families' aware-
> ness that they are working together and helping one another. Parents took
> care of their own children . . . What might be called the modern welfare
> state has removed much of that awareness of loving and being loved and
> working together and has removed much of the sense of responsibility . . .
> It is not surprising that as government expenditures on social welfare in-
> crease, our concerns over the family and who is taking care of the nation's
> children have also increased . . . We must restore the American family to
> self-sufficiency. (Denton, 1982, p. 5)

Restoring that presumed self-sufficiency, in this view, means reducing
many of the public programs designed to cushion economic problems for
families, such as AFDC and subsidized health care, as well as programs designed to enlarge families' choices about contraception and family planning.
It also usually means resisting the further provision of public child-care facilities for working parents, and it often at least implies that family life would
be vastly improved if most women remained in the home as full-time housewives and mothers.

We cannot address all of these issues in this chapter, but we will look
carefully at some of the kinds of data and research that should inform these
contemporary debates about the family. We will first examine some recent
trends in family structure, particularly the rates of marital disruption and
the growth of single-parent families. We will then consider some of the consequences of these trends for personal and economic well-being. In the following three sections, we will look at three of the most important problems
facing many American families today: the continuing gender inequality in
the home, the inadequacy of social services and public supports for families
and children, and the persisting tragedy of family violence — a set of problems that are often intimately connected. Finally, we will reflect on what
these problems tell us about recent trends in social policies toward families.

The Family   **239**

Some Trends in Family Structure

Both critics and defenders of the traditional family often agree that a number of cultural and demographic changes are eroding its historic roles as a central social institution and a source of deep personal values and satisfaction, care, and support.

On the surface, at least, there is much evidence that lends support to that view. In particular, the proportion of Americans who, through choice or necessity, no longer live in an intact nuclear family of husband, wife, and children all under the same roof has increased remarkably in recent years. The 1970s were, moreover, a time of very rapid shifts in the composition of families. The broadest expression of this trend is the declining number of households that consist of married couples (see Table 7-1). In 1970 about 71 percent of all households consisted of married couples; by 1982, only 59 percent did. By 1990, married-couple households will probably be closer to 55 percent of the total (Masnick and Bane, 1980, p. 57).

Several different components account for these trends. One is that more people are living outside of families altogether; another is that more people are living in families maintained by a single parent rather than a married couple. Thus, about 8.5 million more people lived alone in 1982 than in 1970. Some of them (about 2.5 million) were aged. Some were couples living together without being married. (Contrary to some rather sensational exaggerations of this trend, there were less than 2 million of these couples in 1982, and they represented less than 4 percent of all couples in the United States. Ninety-six percent of couples who live together, even in an age supposedly characterized by a rejection of enduring commitment, are formally married.)

A substantial number of people are *delaying* marriage, however, and this helps account for the rising proportion of people living outside of family households, especially among the young. And the young today are likely to set up their own households rather than remaining with their parents (Cherlin, 1981, pp. 72–73). Table 7-2 shows, for both men and women, that the *overall* proportion who are single (never married) changed little during the turbulent 1970s. But there are crucial differences among the different age groups. *Younger* people are increasingly likely to stay single longer. Those aged 25 to 34 were almost twice as likely to be single in 1982 as they were at the start of the 1970s. This trend toward a longer period of singlehood may or may not mean that a substantial proportion of those now single will never marry. As the sociologist Andrew Cherlin has pointed out, more than 90 percent of all Americans, from the mid-nineteenth century onward, have *eventually* married, despite variations in the age at which they did so (Cherlin, 1981, p. 10).

What will happen to these couples once they do marry, if they do, is another story. While the vast majority of Americans will still get married at some point, the chances of remaining in original marriages have dropped sharply. There are two ways of measuring the trends in the rate of divorce: we can describe the proportion of those who are divorced (as compared to

Table 7-1

The changing structure of the family, 1970, 1980, 1982

Type of household	Households		Persons in households		
			All persons		Persons per household
	No. in thousands	Percent	No. in thousands	Percent	
1982					
Total households	83,527	100.0	226,891	100.0	2.72
Family households	61,019	73.1	200,196	88.2	3.28
Married-couple family	49,630	59.4	165,191	72.8	3.33
Other family, male householder	1,986	2.4	5,688	2.5	2.86
Other family, female householder	9,403	11.3	29,317	12.9	3.12
Nonfamily households	22,508	26.9	26,694	11.8	1.19
Male householder	9,457	11.3	12,113	5.3	1.28
Female householder	13,051	15.6	14,581	6.4	1.12
Living alone	19,354	23.2	19,354	8.5	1.00
1980					
Total households	80,776	100.0	222,540	100.0	2.76
Family households	59,550	73.7	197,311	88.7	3.31
Married-couple family	49,112	60.8	164,677	74.0	3.35
Other family, male householder	1,733	2.1	5,064	2.3	2.92
Other family, female householder	8,705	10.8	27,570	12.4	3.17
Nonfamily households	21,226	26.3	25,228	11.3	1.19
Male householder	8,801	10.9	11,395	5.1	1.29
Female householder	12,419	15.4	13,833	6.2	1.11
Living alone	18,296	22.7	18,296	8.2	1.00
1970					
Total households	63,401	100.0	199,030	100.0	3.14
Family households	51,456	81.2	185,582	93.2	3.61
Married-couple family	44,728	70.5	163,888	82.3	3.66
Other family, male householder	1,228	1.9	3,677	1.8	2.99
Other family, female householder	5,500	8.7	18,027	9.1	3.28
Nonfamily households	11,945	18.8	13,438	6.8	1.12
Male householder	4,063	6.4	4,822	2.4	1.19
Female householder	7,882	12.4	8,616	4.3	1.09
Living alone	10,851	17.1	10,851	5.5	1.00

Source: U.S. Bureau of the Census, *Current Population Reports,* series P-20, no. 376, "Households, Families, Marital Status and Living Arrangements: March 1982 (Advance Report)," Washington, D.C., October 1982, p. 2.

Age and sex	1982		1980		1970*	
	Total persons in thousands	Percent never married	Total persons in thousands	Percent never married	Total persons in thousands	Percent never married
Males, 15 years and over	83,958	29.7	81,947	29.6	70,559	28.1
15 to 19 years	9,831	97.5	10,425	97.3	11,497	97.4
20 to 24 years	10,363	72.0	10,134	68.8	7,198	54.7
25 to 29 years	9,968	36.1	9,513	33.1	6,592	19.1
30 to 34 years	9,122	17.3	8,538	15.9	5,599	9.4
35 to 39 years	7,408	10.0	6,792	7.8	5,439	7.2
40 to 44 years	5,996	7.4	5,642	7.1	5,838	6.3
45 to 54 years	10,761	5.4	10,938	6.1	11,224	7.5
55 to 64 years	10,198	4.6	10,014	5.3	8,835	7.8
65 years and over	10,310	4.4	9,953	4.9	8,336	7.5
Females, 15 years and over	92,228	22.5	89,914	22.5	77,766	22.1
15 to 19 years	9,751	92.0	10,337	91.2	11,432	90.3
20 to 24 years	10,716	53.4	10,557	50.2	8,409	35.8
25 to 29 years	10,224	23.4	9,741	20.9	6,841	10.5
30 to 34 years	9,390	11.6	8,824	9.5	5,829	6.2
35 to 39 years	7,714	6.4	7,052	6.2	5,708	5.4
40 to 44 years	6,281	4.7	5,939	4.8	6,171	4.9
45 to 54 years	11,561	4.1	11,760	4.7	12,029	4.9
55 to 64 years	11,672	4.2	11,462	4.5	9,807	6.8
65 years and over	14,920	5.6	14,242	5.9	11,539	7.7

*Figures for 1970 include persons aged 14.
Source: U.S. Bureau of the Census, *Current Population Reports*, series P-20, no. 376, "Households, Families, Marital Status and Living Arrangements, March 1982 (Advance Report)," Washington, D.C., October 1982, p. 2.

Table 7-2

Persons 15 years old and over and percent never married, by age and sex, 1970, 1980, 1982

those still married) in any given year, and we can also estimate the proportion of married people who will divorce at *some* point in their married lives. Measured either way, the recent changes are dramatic.

Table 7-3 shows that in 1960 the *divorce rate* (that is, the number of divorced people as a proportion of current married people) was 35 per 1,000. By 1981 it had *tripled* to 109 per 1,000. The rise was even greater for black marriages, even though the black divorce rate was already almost twice the white rate in 1960. By 1981 the black rate was 233 per 1,000, meaning that almost 1 in 4 blacks who had ever married were now divorced (and had not remarried). The picture becomes even more disturbing when we look at divorce among younger married people. The rate for people under 30, for example, more than quadrupled from 1960 to 1981.

This suggests that the long-term chances of a married couple divorcing are increasing; and that, as Figure 7-2 shows, is clearly the case. This trend is a long and remarkably steady one, reaching back at least to the late nineteenth century. And it is a *dramatic* one — a marriage begun in the early 1970s has about five times the chance of ending in divorce as one begun in 1890. Roughly half of all 1970 marriages will end in divorce, if the trend prevails.

The rising divorce rate is the main reason, though not the only one, for a key social trend we've already encountered: the fast-growing proportion of families headed by a single parent. Between 1970 and 1981, the number of children living with only one parent rose by 54 percent. About one in five American children lived with a single parent in the early 1980s — about 90 percent of them with their mothers.

The broad figures on the rising proportion of single-mother families blur several different trends. Not only has the *number* of such families grown, for example, but their composition has changed as well. Women maintaining families today are typically younger than before, and they are more likely to be divorced, separated, or to have never married, and to have young, depen-

The Growth of Single-Parent Families

Table 7-3

Trends in the divorce rate: divorced persons per 1,000 married persons, by age, sex, race, and Hispanic origin; selected years

Year and sex	Total	Race			Age			
		White	Black	Hispanic origin	Under 30 years	30 to 44 years	45 to 64 years	65 years and over
Both sexes								
1981	109	100	233	110	103	138	101	65
1980*	100	92	203	98	96	125	91	64
1970	47	44	83	61	38	47	53	47
1960	35	33	62	(NA)	23	33	46	32
Males								
1981	88	82	178	73	85	118	82	44
1980*	79	74	149	64	78	104	70	48
1970	35	32	62	40	28	33	40	32
1960	28	27	45	(NA)	16	25	39	24
Females								
1981	129	118	289	146	116	158	121	95
1980*	120	110	258	132	108	147	112	89
1970	60	56	104	81	46	61	66	69
1960	42	38	78	(NA)	28	41	53	44

*Revised using population controls based on the 1980 census.
Note: NA means not available. Persons of Hispanic origin may be of any race.
Source: U.S. Bureau of the Census, *Current Population Reports*, series P-20, no. 372, "Marital Status and Living Arrangements, March 1981," Washington, D.C., June 1982, p. 3.

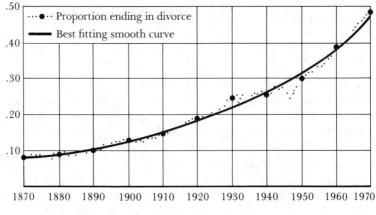

Proportion ending in divorce

···•·· Proportion ending in divorce
—— Best fitting smooth curve

Year marriage was begun

dent children. This is an important historical shift in the character, as well as the dimensions, of family disruption. There have always been many "broken" families (not as many as today, but a significant number nevertheless) in America. But in the past, death, rather than conflict or incompatibility, was the primary disrupter of marriage. As recently as 1970 more than 43 percent of women heading families were widows, about double the proportion who were divorced. By 1980 less than 30 percent of women heading families were widows, while 35 percent were divorced (*Statistical Abstract of the U.S., 1981*, p. 48).

The rising divorce rate, then, accounts for a sizable part of the increase in single-mother families. But there has been an even faster growth of families with children maintained by women who have *never* married (see Table 7-4). Like the number of unmarried couples who live together, this trend is often exaggerated: America is not about to be inundated by "illegitimate" babies. Yet the rapid pace of change in the number of families headed by a never-married mother is a real and significant phenomenon. Less than 3 percent of American children live in those families, but their number more than *tripled* during the 1970s.

It's important to keep all these factors in perspective. Some of the growth in single-mother households results simply from a greater tendency on the part of single women to establish their own separate households after a marital breakup or the birth of a child out of wedlock instead of moving in or remaining with other relatives, which was often the case in the past. And data from the University of Michigan's Panel Study of Income Dynamics show that a large proportion of women heading families move, fairly rap-

Living arrangements of children and marital status of parent	1981 Number	1981 Percent	1980* Number	1980* Percent	1970 Number	1970 Percent	Percent change, 1970–81
Total children under 18	62,918	100.0	63,427	100.0	69,162	100.0	−9.0
Living with							
Two parents	48,040	76.4	48,624	76.7	58,939	85.2	−18.5
One parent	12,619	20.1	12,466	19.7	8,199˙	11.9	53.9
Mother only	11,416	18.1	11,406	18.0	7,451	10.8	53.2
Divorced	4,912	7.8	4,766	7.5	2,296	3.3	113.9
Married	3,540	5.6	3,610	5.7	3,234	4.7	9.5
Separated	3,112	4.9	3,086	4.9	2,332	3.4	33.4
Widowed	1,158	1.8	1,286	2.0	1,395	2.0	−17.0
Single (never married)	1,807	2.9	1,745	2.8	527	0.8	242.9
Father only	1,203	1.9	1,060	1.7	748	1.1	60.8
Divorced	614	1.0	515	0.8	177	0.3	246.9
Married	296	0.5	288	0.5	287	0.4	3.1
Separated	261	0.4	241	0.4	152	0.2	71.7
Widowed	181	0.3	183	0.3	254	0.4	−28.7
Single (never married)	112	0.2	75	0.1	30	—	B
Other relatives only	1,911	3.0	1,949	3.1	1,547	2.2	23.5
Nonrelatives only	348	0.6	388	0.6	477	0.7	−27.0

Note: Table excludes persons under 18 who were maintaining households or family groups. Numbers are in thousands — represents less than 0.1. B means the base was less than 75,000.

*Revised using population controls based on the 1980 census.

Source: U.S. Bureau of the Census, *Current Population Reports*, series P-20, no. 372, "Marital Status and Living Arrangements, March 1981," Washington, D.C., June 1982, p. 3.

Table 7-4
Living arrangements of children under 18, 1970, 1980, 1981

idly, out of that status. About 16 percent of families in that survey were headed by a woman during at least one year of a five-year period, but only 9 percent were headed by a woman for *all* five years (Levitan and Belous, 1981, pp. 113–114).

Despite these qualifications, however, the growth in single-parent families remains one of the major social trends of the past two decades. And it has even greater significance if we look at its racial dimension. For the rise of single-parent families has been *much* more rapid among nonwhites (as we saw in Chapter 5), and the result has been a widening racial disparity in family structure. The proportion of white women aged 25 to 44 who are currently married has actually dropped only a little since 1950 (82 percent to 77 percent) — but the black proportion dropped from an already-low 66 percent to about 45 percent (Cherlin, 1981, p. 98).

Is the Family Still a "Vital Center"?

The fact that the traditional intact nuclear family has lost some ground is often taken as a sign of what one critic calls a "growing cultural rejection of individual moral responsibility, robbing the family of its natural and transcendent role as the vital center for human life, growth, and development" (MacGraw, 1982, p. 64). Assessing this kind of claim isn't easy; measuring the degree to which American culture has or hasn't rejected "individual moral responsibility" is no simple task. But there is some significant counterevidence suggesting that — for *most* people — the family is a long way from losing its role as a vital center. The evidence includes such trends as the frequency of remarriage, the continuing importance of kinship, and the high level of satisfaction with family life.

The frequency of remarriage. Increasingly, the breakup of a marriage doesn't necessarily lead to permanent disengagement from marital ties; instead, growing numbers of divorced people remarry. About 15 percent of Americans over 40 have been married twice (Miller, 1982, p. 29). At 1980s rates, about five out of every six divorced men and three out of four divorced women will remarry, most of them within a few years of their divorces. Moreover, the rate at which divorced people remarry is considerably *higher* today than it was 40 years ago (Cherlin, 1981, p. 10).

The continuing importance of kinship. Until recently, sociologists often argued that the nuclear family was the end product of a long historical shift away from the *extended* family (including uncles, aunts, cousins, grandparents). It was widely believed that the typical family of 75 or 100 years ago was a richer and more complex institution, often including three generations in the same household. The contemporary nuclear family was said to have become more and more isolated, lonely, and atomized as these traditional kinship systems eroded.

There is still probably some truth in this view — and many people can point to something similar in their own family histories. But both sides of the portrait have increasingly been challenged by historians and sociologists. On the one side, many historians now dispute the idea that the multigeneration extended family was ever as typical a form as we once thought. On the other, recent sociological research has almost uniformly turned up evidence that extended kinship ties are still extraordinarily important in most American communities today.

Theodore Caplow and his co-workers looked at family life in "Middletown" 50 years after the classic sociological study by Robert and Helen Lynd of life in a middle-sized midwestern town in the 1920s. They found that extended kinship ties were still surprisingly strong. Far from being "isolated urbanites," Middletown's residents were enmeshed in a varied and complex system of mutual supports and obligations with their relatives. Strong relationships were the norm between adults and their older parents, and there was a substantial and highly appreciated amount of regular social activity among relatives. The researchers concluded that kinship was, in the 1970s, still by far the most important "affiliative bond" in Middletown — a conclusion reached by numerous studies of other modern American communities (Caplow et al., 1982).

Similarly, a study of the coping patterns of working women by the sociologist Sheila Kamerman found that relatives and family were by *far* their most important source of support and help. Some of the families in her study felt these ties so strongly that they had actually moved in order to be closer to relatives. More generally, these women saw the "family in the larger sense" (that is, including extended kin) as "the focus of daily living" and as a "source of essential help and support, whether concrete and practical or reassuring and nurturing" (Kamerman, 1980, p. 115).

This finding of the importance of family ties puts the contemporary difficulties of the *nuclear* family in a broader perspective. Most of all, it suggests that the (very real) troubles faced by modern couples (Peltz, 1982), and reflected most clearly in the rising divorce rate, do not necessarily mean that family ties *in general* have been as badly eroded as some think. Even when marriages break down, the former spouses are usually still involved in complex and often strong family networks providing support, care, and a "vital center" for their lives.

As some researchers have shown, this is especially important in assessing the ramifications of the high rates of marital breakup and single-parent households among blacks. The difficulties faced by black single-parent families are certainly real (as they are for whites), but they do not mean — as some observers have argued since the 1960s — that these families are necessarily unstable and unsupportive. Often, women and children in these families can call on a diverse and rich network of relatives for aid (Stack, 1974).

The high level of satisfaction with family life. Despite the rising rates of divorce and the tendency to delay marriage, sociological research has found a high, and very likely *increasing*, level of satisfaction with the quality of family life in America. Whether it's measured in terms of parents' interactions with their children, the strength and quality of relations with aged relatives, or the quality of couples' sex lives, the evidence *often* suggests that things are getting better, not worse. Most opinion surveys find that people of every age still highly value family life (see Figure 7-1, page 239); they also are, at least on the surface, remarkably happy with it. The recent Middletown study suggests that, for blue-collar workers, family life has distinctly improved since the 1920s, when it was often dreary, bleak, devitalized, and burdened by the twin afflictions of too much work and too little income. By all accounts, it was also characterized by what we would now regard as an appallingly restricted level of communication between husbands and wives and a similarly unsatisfying and constricted sexuality (Caplow et al., 1982, pp. 117–135).

There is no longer any "typical" American family.

There is also evidence, from this and other studies, that parents now spend more time with their children than they did 50 (or 30) years ago. Again, the change is probably most significant for parents in working-class families, where the crushing burden of work once meant that some parents spent virtually *no* time with their children or that the time they did spend was typically harried and stressed (Caplow et al., 1982, p. 114).

The sources of the improvement in the quality of family life are no mystery. Advances in material well-being — in shorter working days and weeks, higher earnings, and better housing — have clearly helped make a more satisfying family life possible. So, equally clearly, have the spread of both technical knowledge and more flexible beliefs about sexuality, contraception, and family planning. These have not only enriched the relationships between men and women, but have also made possible smaller, better-timed, and therefore less harried and burdened families.

We will return to these issues later in the chapter. But now it will be helpful to examine some of the ways in which, despite its strengths and apparent durability, the family does remain an arena for a number of persistent social problems: the sometimes devastating personal and economic consequences of family disruption, the gender inequalities in the division of family roles, and the disturbingly widespread problem of domestic violence.

248 The Family

Michael Hayman/Stock, Boston

Susie Fitzhugh/Stock, Boston

The Consequences of Family Disruption

While the family seems remarkably resilient and often even thriving in the face of important social and demographic changes, this shouldn't blind us to the very real problems many families *do* face. In reaction to the sometimes overwrought fears that high divorce rates, fewer children, and the growth of one-parent families are signaling the "death" of the family, some commentators have too quickly leaped to the opposite view — arguing that the increase in marital disruption and the rapid changes in family composition represent only a healthy ferment, a benign diversity that will leave us all better off in the long run by expanding our "options" to choose among a wider, less restrictive range of life styles.

The reality is more complex than either extreme suggests. Changes in family composition *are* often painful and disruptive, but there is little evidence that — by themselves — they cause the level of social pathology often attributed to them. At the same time, the problems accompanying these changes, especially for single parents, are very real and create profound challenges for public policy. With the goal of separating real from imagined problems, let's look at what recent social research tells us about the consequences of family disruption.

The Impact of Divorce

What happens to spouses and children after divorce? Research on the effects of divorce has often led to conflicting findings, but some common themes have begun to emerge.

For the former spouses, there is — not surprisingly — every indication that divorce is a difficult and, at least initially, disorganizing experience. Studies that have closely followed the lives of divorced men and women after the breakup have found that, especially in the first year or so, they are likely to have difficulty organizing their home lives, sleep and eat poorly, and function badly at work. The divorced also often suffer, at least for a while, a restricted social life as mutual friends and associates drop away or align themselves on different "sides" (Goetting, 1983, pp. 367–372). They also typically experience at least an initial period of anxiety and depression (Cherlin, 1981, pp. 76–77), and a large body of research has consistently linked separation or divorce with higher rates of mental disorder. (Much of that research, however, is clouded by the difficulty of knowing whether the change in marital status *causes* mental ill-health, is caused *by* it, or is some combination of the two.) Suicide rates, too, are typically higher among the divorced than either the currently married or the never married, and there is evidence that death rates from cancer and other *physical* ills are also disproportionately high for the divorced or separated (Goetting, 1983, p. 371).

Marital disruption is obviously a powerful source of stress, which can underlie or at least aggravate a wide variety of physical and emotional problems, some very serious. But another frequent research finding complicates this picture somewhat. Studies that have looked at these effects through the lens of the *quality* of marriage, as opposed to the simple dichotomy of marriage versus divorce, have generally found that unhappy, conflict-ridden marriages are even *more* likely than divorce to cause emotional and social stress (Goetting, 1983, pp. 371–372). In some cases, divorce can be a way of escaping the conditions that breed the physical and psychological problems often loosely (and probably misleadingly) associated with divorce itself. And we must remember that divorce can lead to a more satisfactory remarriage. The picture of divorced people necessarily leading chaotic, isolated, and unhappy lives is certainly true for some, perhaps true for *most* in the beginning, but it must be qualified by the high proportion of the divorced who remarry, and do so happily.

In general, as Andrew Cherlin has pointed out, divorce may frequently have its "benefits" as well as its "costs" (Cherlin, 1981, pp. 88–92). The authors of the recent Middletown study argue that higher divorce rates may have helped make possible the *improvement* in the quality of intact marriages that, on balance, seems to have taken place both in Middletown and in the country as a whole. The growing social acceptability of divorce as a solution to a bad marriage may, in this view, mean that truly unhappy marriages are now likely to be terminated rather than dragging on out of inertia or convention. And intact marriages are, therefore, more likely to be reasonably satisfying or at least comfortable (Caplow et al., 1982, p. 135).

The same problem of marital instability versus marital conflict as a source of social and personal problems appears in studies attempting to assess the impact of parental divorce on children. As with adults, the initial period after divorce seems to be the hardest for children. Those of preschool age are especially likely to feel frightened, upset, and, often, to blame themselves for their parents' separation, while older children often become deeply angry at one or both parents (Hetherington et al., 1978; Wallerstein and Kelly, 1980). One study of affluent children of divorce in Marin County, California, found that a third of them were still unhappy and dissatisfied five years later (Wallerstein and Kelly, 1980).

A 1976 national survey found that about twice as many children in divorced as compared to intact households were described by their parents as "needing help" or as actually seeing a mental-health professional. But this was only about 14 percent of the children of divorced parents — meaning that about six out of seven of those children were *not* regarded, at any rate by their parents, as needing any special help with emotional problems (Cherlin, 1981, p. 79). And several studies suggest that the initial impact of divorce on children is most often eased over time. This is especially true where the marriage itself was conflict ridden; one study finds many divorced parents reporting that their relations with their children generally *improved* within two years after the end of a conflictual marriage (Hetherington et al., 1978).

A similar finding comes from studies of both children's conceptions of themselves and of their aggressiveness toward others. Both have turned out to be more closely related to marital *conflict* than to disruption itself (Goetting, 1983, pp. 375–376). And, most recently, a longitudinal study in New York, following children from infancy to early adulthood, found a strong correlation between parental conflict at age three and a variety of psychological problems in young adulthood. Children who had spent their early lives in families marked by strong disagreement and conflict between the parents over such issues as childrearing and discipline were considerably more likely, as young adults, to have problems with their families, school, or work, and to be troubled by substance abuse and a variety of psychological symptoms (Chess et al., 1983).

Single Parents and Social Pathology

These findings also throw light on some commonly held beliefs about the consequences of single parenthood. The female-headed family is often held heavily responsible for many of the social problems that bedevil contemporary American society, from juvenile delinquency through alcoholism and drug abuse, to the decline of the work ethic and the sapping of the entrepreneurial spirit. Being a member of a single-parent family, according to one sociological critic, is like "having a deformed physical body" (Burr, 1982, p. 232).

These beliefs are often based on the idea that children require a male presence in the home in order to grow into self-functioning adults. In this view, the growth in families without husbands present is, in itself, likely to cause a vast increase in the level of social pathology. What is the evidence for this belief?

There is a long tradition in social research attempting to link the prevalence of "broken homes" with such problems as adolescent mental illness, delinquency, and school failure. But both in early studies and in more recent ones, the answers have not been simple. There *is* frequently a simple association between growing up in a "broken" home and delinquency and other problems. But most studies that have also examined the effect of conflict, inadequate supervision, and violence in the family have concluded that it's these factors, rather than the family's "incompleteness," which are *most* strongly related to other social problems. On the whole, the *climate and quality* of home and family life, not just the presence or absence of two parents, are *most* important in influencing childhood and adolescent development (Bahr, 1979; Goetting, 1983, pp. 377–380). These qualities, in turn, are — unsurprisingly — strongly affected by the family's overall well-being, especially its level of income and the presence or absence of social and economic supports that can improve the single mother's capacity to "manage her life and her children adequately" (Cherlin, 1981, p. 80). In other words, there is nothing inherently pathological about women maintaining families alone; as Andrew Cherlin puts it, the problem such families face is "not the lack of a male presence but the lack of a male income" (1981, p. 80). Let's now look at how deeply these material problems afflict many families headed by women.

Women, Families, and Economic Supports

Recent research indicates that changes in family structure are the single *most* important determinant of changes in an individual's economic position over time (Duncan, 1981). The breakup of families causes dramatic changes in the economic condition of the former spouses, but typically strikes women very differently than men.

Data from the University of Michigan's Panel Study of Income Dynamics show that (for a period from the late 1960s through the early 1970s) couples who remained married enjoyed a rise in real income of about 21 percent. Men who divorced or separated saw their household income drop slightly in absolute terms. But when their household income was adjusted to account for the smaller size of their households, they enjoyed a rise in usable income of about 17 percent. For divorced or separated women, even adjusting for the shrinkage of their families didn't prevent their income from *dropping* by 7 percent (Cherlin, 1981, p. 82). Divorce, in short, typically *improves* men's economic condition — and makes women's *worse*.

Much of this difference results from men's more favorable position in the labor market. For women who may have been out of the paid labor force during their marriage, moving into it for the first time or reentering after long absence is a course loaded with obstacles, likely to end at best in a low-paying job. For *most* women who *had* worked steadily in the paid labor force (combining the roles of wife and employee), occupational segregation into "women's" jobs means that their own paychecks aren't usually enough to support themselves — much less themselves *and* their children — once their husband's income is gone.

As this suggests, the heart of the economic problems of these families is that, in most cases, women remain responsible for childrearing when their marriages break up or when they have children outside of formal marriage. As the sociologist Diana Pearce puts it, "the typical outcome of a marital breakup in a family with children is that the man becomes *single*, while the woman becomes a *single parent*" (Pearce, 1982, p. 12).

This burden is aggravated by several other economic problems single mothers often face. We've already seen one of them: The public welfare system offers very low benefits to most women who lack other sources of income. Another problem is that financial support from the fathers of their children is usually meager, at best. In 1978, according to the Census Bureau, of about 7 million women living with children of absent fathers, about 2.5 million (35 percent) received child-support payments and an additional million were entitled to payments but didn't receive them. The amount of child support averaged only about $1,800 a year for those women who *did* receive it (Grossman and Hayghe, 1982, p. 39).

The lack of both adequate earnings and adequate child support is compounded by the absence, in most families maintained by single women, of other workers who can bring in additional income. In 1981 almost four out of five families with children maintained by a working woman had no other earners. Only about one in ten had another family member working full time. This isn't surprising, since so many of the people in these families are young children. But in an age when achieving an adequate living standard almost *requires* two paychecks, having to make do on just one is often a crippling problem for single women maintaining families. Consider how they fare compared with both men and women in intact families: less than 10 percent of wives have no one else working in their families, and almost 50 percent of husbands have the benefit of another *full-time* worker in the family. It's this advantage, along with men's better jobs in the first place, that helps keep almost all married men out of poverty (U.S. Bureau of Labor Statistics, 1981, p. 82).

Another difficulty is that women are less likely to move back into relatives' (especially parents') households after a marriage breaks up than they were in the past (Levitan and Belous, 1981, p. 117). Among other things, this forces them into a housing market they are often unable to afford, at least without sacrificing other needs. Women who head families spend a much higher proportion of their income on housing after divorce or separation than before (and higher, too, than divorced men). They are still rarely able to afford homeownership, the most important means of accumulating significant assets for most nonwealthy families (Burgess, 1980; Levitan and Belous, 1981, p. 117).

All of these economic disabilities for single mothers are reflections of deeper gender inequalities running through several American institutions at once: including the labor market, the home, and the social services. We've already seen some of the dimensions of gender inequalities in the labor market in Chapter 6. Let's look now at two other, interrelated aspects of this complex problem: the continuing sexual division of labor within the family itself and the absence of effective *public* services for women and families in need.

Family Protection?

There have been many proposals in recent years for legislation to restore the family's strength. One of the most comprehensive has been a proposed piece of federal legislation called the Family Protection Act. The act, the creation of a coalition of self-described "pro-family" groups, was launched on the premise that many government policies have "undermined and diminished the viability of the American family." In response, the act was ostensibly designed to "promote the virtues of the family" by reversing many of what its sponsors saw as the most dangerous examples of governmental intrusions into family life.

First introduced in Congress in 1980 and revised in 1981, the Family Protection Act contains more than 30 proposals for specific legislation addressed to various aspects of governmental policy toward families and children, ranging from tax-law changes favoring married couples to provisions designed to prohibit the "intermingling" of the sexes in many school activities. Some of the proposals address more general social issues, such as prohibiting busing to achieve racial integration in the schools and reintroducing "voluntary" prayer in the public schools.

Though it is widely believed that the act is too wide-ranging to be passed in its entirety, parts of it have been passed — and others will surely remain live issues for some years. Perhaps more importantly, the act reflects a widespread attitude about the nature of the family's problems and what should be done about them. That attitude is laden with a number of curious contradictions — contradictions vividly revealed in the provisions of the act itself.

To begin with, the act seems less concerned with the "protection" of existing American families, in all their variety, than with enforcing a very specific conception of what families *should* be. It includes a provision prohibiting the use of federal funds for any educational materials or research that "do not reflect a balance between the status roles of men and women" and, even more generally, that "do not contribute to the American Way Of Life as it has been historically understood." It is particularly harsh on homosexuality. It would exclude homosexuals from provisions of the Civil Rights Act of 1964 and would prohibit any federal funds for groups or individuals who consider homosexuality an "acceptable life style." Presumably, such funds would include student loans, Social Security and disability payments, veterans' assistance, and/or federal unemployment benefits — to name only a few examples.

Other provisions are even less easily under-

Work and Inequality in the Family: The Persisting Division of Labor

Traditionalists have long feared that women's increased role in the labor force would undermine the long-standing division of labor in the home — with dreadful consequences for marital stability, child development, and the general moral tone of family life. A United States Senator, for example, recently declared that the trend toward husbands taking responsibility to "put on an apron and do the dishes [and] change the dirty diapers" was fraught with unacknowledged perils. "I guess that is progress," Senator Jere-

stood as "protecting" families — even if families are defined in an extremely traditional fashion. Thus, the act proposes scrapping all federal education and training programs for poor and handicapped children, replacing them, if at all, with reduced-funding block grants to be doled out at the discretion of state officials. It even proposes *prohibiting* private agencies from receiving federal funds for programs to prevent child abuse, unless a state legislature specifically approves the funding. And it proposes terminating all federally funded legal services for the poor in cases involving divorce, child custody, and child support.

Other contradictions abound as well. Thus, though the Family Protection Act, in theory, is designed to limit government influence on family life, it contains several proposals that would substantially *increase* it. One key provision, for example, requires family planning agencies receiving federal funds to notify the parents of any teenager asking for family planning or contraceptive advice. (As of this writing, a version of this so-called "squeal rule" has been made law and is being challenged in federal courts.) Whatever one may believe about the morality of teenage sexuality (or of the social and personal consequences of making it risky for young people to seek birth-control advice), what's noteworthy is that the act explicitly redefines teenage sexuality as *not* a pri-

vate matter between teenagers and their families, but one subject to control by the government. Agencies originally designed as purely *medical* ones would, in this approach, become redefined as enforcement arms for a particular *governmental* view of appropriate sexual morality.

A similar contradiction is apparent in a provision that would allow public schools to prohibit the "intermingling of the sexes in any sports or other school-related activities" — a measure that would clearly boost the power of the schools to enforce a state-determined conception of the "correct" sex roles for children.

The act proposes to levy harsh fines (up to $5,000 a day) on agencies or individuals who violate these and other provisions. Presumably, family planning nurses who do *not* "squeal" on teenage clients, or research agencies that produce literature suggesting that a more egalitarian approach to sex roles might be acceptable, could be in serious trouble. In this vision, the State would take on an unprecedented role as judge of the appropriateness — even the "Americanness" — of gender roles, as expressed in textbooks or on the playing field.

Sources: Wohl, 1981; Children's Defense Fund, 1982.

miah Denton (a Democrat from Alabama) noted in a 1982 congressional hearing, "but I definitely see a sort of neutered-like situation which has developed" (Denton, 1982, p. 43). Other observers, on the other hand, have *hoped* that increasing labor-force participation by women *would* undermine that conventional division of family labor.

So far, both the fears and the hopes have proven largely unfounded; the division of household labor between the sexes has remained astonishingly intact. Many American families remain distinctly, and sometimes harshly, unequal institutions that perpetuate the wider social and economic inequality of women in several ways. For some (though by no means all) women, work in the outside labor force has simply been added on to the long hours spent working in the home, creating what some writers have called a "double burden" and others, more sharply, a "treadmill" (Wirtz, 1979, p. 214; Duxbury and Shelendick, 1982). For some women, too, the dual role of traditional housewife and outside breadwinner helps keep them confined to the least desirable and least rewarding kinds of jobs.

Recent research shows strikingly how *little* the "revolution" in women's labor-force participation has affected the conventional role structure of family life. "A family with two wage earners," two rather optimistic observers recently suggested, "may be expected to have a far different pattern of sharing responsibilities than the traditional one-earner household . . . the slow evolution is toward family work roles based more on equality and less on sexual stereotypes" (Levitan and Belous, 1981, pp. 82, 101). The expectation seems reasonable enough, but the "evolution" is extraordinarily slow indeed. Two-thirds of the women in dual-earner families work 40 or more weeks a year, half work *full time* at least 40 weeks a year (Hayghe, 1981, p. 46). But studies suggest that a great many men (and at least some women) are still reluctant to abandon the traditional stereotypes of the husband as breadwinner and the wife as homemaker (Lein and Blehar, 1979). There is some evidence that this traditionalism is equally persistent among couples who live together outside of formal marriage — a generally younger group often thought to be less bound by conventional gender norms (Caplow et al., 1982, p. 67). Most couples divide the unpaid labor of child care and housework very unequally, and many cannot seriously envision doing things differently.

The Burdens of Housework

How much time and effort does household labor involve today? It's sometimes believed that advances in the technology of housework (such as labor-saving appliances) have dramatically reduced the time needed for home chores. Families, too, are smaller than in the past, which might also be expected to lighten the load of household work. But despite these changes, most research shows that the time spent on housework hasn't diminished nearly as much as expected over the last several decades. One recent study suggests that laundry is the only area of housework that has clearly been reduced by technological innovation. In other household chores, technological innovation mainly seems to *shift* the hours of work (from food production to child care, for example) or to raise the standards demanded from the work (cleaner homes, more "sparkling" dishes) (Hefferan, 1982, p. 13).

Recent estimates of the hours of work of full-time homemakers range anywhere from about 30 to about 70 hours a week, depending on what is defined as housework and on the age and number of children in the home (Hofferth and Moore, 1979, pp. 111–112). An analysis by researchers at the Department of Commerce calculates that American *adults* average 25 hours a week of housework, worth, all told, more than $750 billion in 1976 dollars — or an astonishing 44 percent of the country's gross national product at that time (see Table 7-5). This figure is arrived at by calculating what the same services would cost if they were purchased from specialists at prevailing wage rates. Another way of looking at the costs of housework is to estimate how much potential earnings are lost as a result of having to do housework rather than working in the paid labor force. According to the Department of Commerce studies, homemakers thus "lose" over half a *trillion*" dollars a year (Peskin, 1982, p. 19).

For our purposes, what is most striking about this is how thoroughly housework remains disproportionately *women's* work. As Table 7-5 shows, men average just 15 hours of household work to women's 34. Men and women also remain highly "specialized" in the tasks they perform in and around the home: Men do home repairs but rarely cook, do laundry, or clean up after meals. Moreover, these figures are *averages;* some men do considerably *more* housework than this, but (as other studies show) at least *a fourth* of American husbands do *no* housework other than some basic child care (Hofferth and Moore, 1979, p. 112). In a survey conducted as part of the recent Middletown study, wives reported doing *all* the housework in almost *half* the households sampled. Less than 10 percent reported that housework was equally shared, and just 2 out of 400 couples said that the husband did most or all of the housework while the wife brought in most of the income (Caplow et al., 1982, pp. 109–110).

How much does this division of labor change when women enter the paid labor force? Surprisingly little. What seems to happen most often is that (1) the total amount of time devoted to housework shortens somewhat when a married woman enters the paid work force, but (2) women continue to do most of the housework. Thus, the *overall* burden of labor within the family remains disproportionately on the wife.

In married couples where only the husbands are in the labor force, the husbands typically work long hours outside the home, while the wives average about the same number of hours *inside* it. Since the husbands also usually do *some* housework, they end up (on average) with a slightly longer total "work week" than their wives. But the opposite tends to happen when the

Housework as Women's Work

Table 7-5

How much is housework worth?, 1976

Type of housework	Totals				Average per adult		
	Annual hours		Annual value		Weekly hours	Annual hours	Annual value, dollars
	Billion dollars	Percent	Billion dollars	Percent			
Adults							
All housework	188.8	100.0	752.4	100.0	25.0	1,300	5,180
Women							
All housework	135.1	100.0	515.0	100.0	33.8	1,756	6,694
Cleaning and gardening	35.2	26.1	137.5	26.7	8.8	458	1,787
Shopping and other	32.7	24.2	150.9	29.3	8.1	425	1,961
Meal preparation	29.0	21.5	101.2	19.7	7.3	377	1,316
Child care and instruction	16.3	12.1	40.8	7.9	4.1	211	531
Laundry	9.7	7.2	35.6	6.9	2.4	127	463
Meal cleanup	9.4	7.0	31.5	6.1	2.4	122	409
Home repairs and hobbies	2.8	2.1	17.5	3.4	0.7	37	227
Men							
All housework	53.7	100.0	237.4	100.0	15.1	786	3,475
Shopping and other	19.5	36.3	90.2	38.0	5.5	285	1,322
Cleaning and gardening	13.1	24.4	50.9	21.4	3.7	191	745
Home repairs and hobbies	9.9	18.4	60.6	25.5	2.8	145	888
Meal preparation	5.6	10.4	19.7	8.3	1.6	83	289
Child care and instruction	3.9	7.3	10.0	4.2	1.1	58	146
Meal cleanup	1.3	2.4	4.3	1.8	0.4	19	63
Laundry	0.4	0.7	1.6	0.7	0.1	6	23

Source: Janice Peskin, "Measuring Household Production for the GNP," *Family Economics Review*, Summer 1982, p. 19.

wives enter the paid labor force. Even when they work full time, their husbands rarely step in to take on a significantly bigger share of the housework. The wives end up working an average of about 67 hours a week, while the husbands' week averages about 63 hours (Peskin, 1982, p. 10).

The time spent in unpaid housework does shrink when wives enter the paid labor force — especially for families able to afford child care, cleaning services, and meals away from home. But, particularly for women with lower incomes, these options can be prohibitively expensive. And some home tasks — time spent with children, for example — cannot reasonably (or happily) be replaced altogether by market alternatives. What generally happens, according to most studies, is that working women both use some of their extra income to buy paid housework and *also* lengthen their own working day and week to cope with both paid and unpaid tasks (Vickery, 1979, p. 190). And obviously, some time spent elsewhere has to give. Some studies find that working married women sacrifice an average of about 14 hours of their own time a week, taking it mainly from such activities as sleeping, eating, watching TV, visiting friends and relatives, or gardening, and often using their weekends to "catch up" with housework (Hofferth and Moore, 1979, p. 115). This helps explain why 50 percent of women working in clerical, service, retail, and blue-collar jobs reported, in a survey by the National Commission on Working Women in the late 1970s, that they had *no* leisure time (Wirtz, 1979, p. 215).

Changing Attitudes?

There is some evidence that the sexual division of labor in the home is beginning to change. Some recent surveys have found that husbands are now somewhat more amenable to sharing household tasks than they were in the past. Oddly, though, this seems to have virtually no relation to whether or not their wives are in the paid labor force. Instead, it apparently represents a more general shift in attitudes that leads *some* men to adopt a more egalitarian attitude toward household work, whatever the role of their wives in the outside work force (Hofferth and Moore, 1979, p. 114). There is also some evidence that, in working couples, black husbands are somewhat more likely than white ones to share housekeeping and child-care duties (Beckett and Smith, 1981). Suburban working women studied in the late 1970s by Sheila Kamerman believed that, though the division of household tasks was still highly unequal in their own lives, it was less so than in the families in which they grew up (Kamerman, 1980, p. 124).

Still, some recent research indicates that the sexual division of labor in the home is widely accepted by both sexes — at least on the surface. Middletown's husbands *and wives* still apparently agree that husbands should be the main providers and experts in home and auto repair, wives the primary housekeepers and specialists in the care and nurturing of children. Only a fifth of the men and women surveyed supported an egalitarian approach to housework (Caplow et al., 1982, pp. 67, 112).

Despite some evidence of changing attitudes, the traditional division of labor in the family persists.

How deeply these attitudes go — and how slowly they seem to be changing — is illustrated by a recent study of the sexual division of household chores (and outside jobs) among *children*. In this study of children aged 2 to 17, the sociologists Lynn White and David Brinkerhoff found that though the kind of work boys and girls perform is roughly similar at very early ages, it begins to diverge distinctly as they get older. Boys soon do less and less kitchen and general housework, girls less and less outdoor work. As they get older, girls also begin putting in more *total* hours on chores than boys. Children's work *outside* the home is even more sex-typed: girls' primary job is baby-sitting and, a distant second, restaurant work, while boys typically work on lawns and sidewalks. Somewhat ominously, the study discovered that one result of the mothers' outside work was often to increase the total amount of housework done by their children — but for girls much more than boys, with the result that women's work "sinks their daughters even deeper into the domestic role." The study found some indications that parents with higher levels of education and more flexible attitudes about sex roles were more likely to encourage both sons and daughters to adopt less stereotyped tasks, in the home and outside it. But they concluded that, even by 1979, "the major changes in women's adult roles within the last two decades have yet to reach childhood" (White and Brinkerhoff, 1981, pp. 177–181).

One result of the gender division of labor in the family is the perpetuation of the vicious cycle we observed in the last chapter: Women's domestic roles and their disadvantaged position in the paid labor force reinforce each other. Shouldering the major burden of household work doesn't prevent women from entering the labor force, but it *does* hurt their chances for achieving stable, successful, and rewarding jobs. It is likely to lead to frequent moves in and out of the labor force. This, in turn, means interrupted training, the depreciation of previously learned skills, and the loss of seniority and of career contacts and networks. The process comes full circle when these problems become defined as "proof" that women are flighty or uncommitted workers whose main interest — and most important role — lies in caring for home and family. This cycle is compounded by the relative absence, in American society, of adequate, accessible social services and workplace policies to ease the pressures and constraints on working women with children — a problem we'll now consider.

Housework and the "Vicious Cycle"

Maurice Rosen/Magnum Photos Inc.

Work, Family, and Social Supports

More than almost any other advanced industrial society, the United States has been slow in developing policies to respond to the changing character of family life — especially the rapid rise in women's participation in the paid labor force and the growing proportion of families maintained by women.

The relative absence of supports in the community and the workplace that could ease the strains of combined work and parenthood both reinforces women's unequal position on the job and at home and aggravates stresses that are felt throughout family life — especially for single-parent families and those with lower incomes. For a society that claims to place a central value on both work and family life, we do remarkably little to help make the two compatible. As Sheila Kamerman puts it, "Being a member of the labor force and a full-time parent means trying to manage against overwhelming odds in an unresponsive society" (Kamerman, 1980, p. 129).

Minding the Children

The biggest single problem faced by the 200 working women with young children in Kamerman's study was the lack of accessible and acceptable child care — a finding that reappears in many other studies as well. In 1980, 7.5 million children under the age of six had mothers in the paid labor force; by 1990 there will be an estimated 10.5 million (U.S. Bureau of the Census, 1982, p. 38). Data from the University of Michigan's Quality of Employment Survey in the late 1970s show that about one in four employed women find that their child-care arrangements often cause them to be late for work or to miss work altogether. Child-care problems make it especially hard for women to undertake training programs or advanced education, especially since evening child care is hard to find. Married women with very young children often find they can only take jobs during the hours their husbands do *not* work, so that the husband can take care of the children (U.S. Commission on Civil Rights, 1981, p. 12).

Lack of child care, or worries about its adequacy, keeps many women out of the labor force altogether, or confines them to part-time work. Some studies estimate that as many as one in five unemployed women are jobless simply because they cannot find satisfactory child care (U.S. Commission on Civil Rights, 1981, p. 12). Similarly, almost one out of five mothers with preschool children who are not in the labor force, according to a Census Bureau survey in the late 1970s, said they would enter it if adequate care for their children were available. Not surprisingly, the problem is most severe for single mothers; the same survey found that a third of divorced or widowed mothers with children under five said they would look for work (and half of those working part time said they would work full time) if good child care were available (Presser and Baldwin, 1980).

Inadequate child care, then, is very often another key part of the cycle that traps many women in low-paying, dead-end work or joblessness. Given the rhetorical importance we place on work and family in America, the paucity of adequate day care seems strange indeed. Yet, despite the rapid growth of dual-earner families with preschool children, the primary caretakers of children in the United States are still the nuclear family and the public school — other kinds of child care remain only supplementary. Table 7-6 shows that, compared with some other advanced industrial societies, we lag far behind both in the availability and, even more importantly, the affordability of child care.

In many European countries, most preschool children aged three to six are eligible for free, usually public, child-care programs that cover the entire school day. The United States *has* such programs, but they are mainly private, and often too expensive for low-income people. They also reach a smaller proportion of children, and typically enroll them for fewer hours of the day (Kamerman, 1980, pp. 139–140).

Child Care in Other Countries

Table 7-6

Family supports in three countries

Type of benefit	United States	Sweden	West Germany
Cash			
Income replacement	None	Paternity or maternity leave	Maternity leave
	None	Care for a sick child at home	Care for a sick child at home
Income substitution	Aid to families with dependent children	None	None
Income supplementation	None	Child and housing allowances	Child and housing allowances
	None	Child health services	Child health services
	Tax allowance for dependents	Tax allowance for dependents	None
	Child-care tax credit	None	Child-care tax credit
Employment			
Right to leave work and job security	None	Parental leave up to 9 months	Maternity leave up to 7½ months
	None	Unpaid leave up to 18 months	None
	None	6 hour workday up to child's 8th birthday	None

Source: Adapted from U.S. Bureau of the Census, *Current Population Reports*, series P-23, no. 117, "Trends in Child Care Arrangements of Working Mothers," Washington, D.C., June 1982, p. 36.

Some countries, such as Sweden and France, also have extensive day-care programs for younger children aged 3 months to three years old — in contrast to the United States where care for *very* young children is especially hard to find. France provides a broad range of public and private day-care arrangements, all of which are free for low-income parents. Sweden's program is entirely public and, though it enrolls fewer children than the French programs, is free for *all* parents. Swedish parents are also entitled — by law — to take off a few days from work with pay to help their children make the transition into a day-care program (Kamerman, 1980, pp. 141, 161).

Most countries in both Western and Eastern Europe provide a somewhat similar range of child care. The specific mix of programs and types of support vary, as does, of course, the quality and comprehensiveness of the care. But most of these countries share the belief that society as a whole bears some responsibility both to ease the stresses on working parents and to ensure a nurturing environment for all children.

In the United States, on the other hand, substantial public support for day care has only been provided during wars and depressions, and, more recently, for children of welfare mothers enrolled in mandatory work training (McConnell-Condry and Lazar, 1982). Comprehensive legislation to upgrade and extend federal support for child care and development was vetoed by the Nixon administration in the early 1970s on the ground that such legislation would commit "the vast moral authority of the government to the side of communal approaches to childrearing over the family-centered approach" (quoted in MacGraw, 1982, p. 66). No comprehensive approach has fared better since.

Part of the reason for this attitude may be the lingering belief that any form of care other than that provided by the child's mother may be harmful to the child's well-being and personality development. Especially during the 1950s, the notion of "maternal deprivation" as a crucial cause of childhood pathology helped give day care a bad name. But more recent research has failed to turn up evidence that outside care is, by itself, bad for children's health and growth. What's important is the quality and consistency of the care and of the transition between home and outside child care (Kagan, Kearsley and Zelazo, 1978; Rallings and Nye, 1979). (In any case, those who most fervently argue that the absence of a mother is bad for children often display a notable inconsistency by arguing — equally fervently — that women with dependent children should have to work outside the home as a condition of public support.)

Whose Responsibility? The relative lack of comprehensive support for child care in the United States seems to reflect the broader themes of private versus social responsibility that, as we've seen, have profoundly shaped American institutions in every realm of personal and social life. Thus, American public policy toward child care rests on the idea that caring for children is strictly an individual matter, barring obvious abuse, neglect, or some other social pathology. It is assumed that parents (and particularly mothers, since child care is also viewed as primarily a woman's problem) will find their own arrangements for care and will come up with the money to pay for them. (The fact that so many women with preschool children are working *despite* the lack of comprehensive or subsidized child-care programs, indeed, is sometimes taken as proof that such programs aren't really needed.) One result is that, according to a mid-1970s estimate by the Urban Institute, more than 30,000 children of *preschool* age may be caring entirely for themselves during much of the day. Others estimate that more than 2 million school-age children under 13 are routinely left alone without supervision (U.S. Commission on Civil Rights, 1981, p. 9).

The Working Day

But child-care problems are by no means the only obstacle working parents must overcome. Another is the problem of the relative inflexibility of work roles and policies in the United States. Working parents — especially single parents — are often caught in a double bind: it's not only financially necessary for them to work but increasingly *expected* that they will do so, yet the traditional organization of work simultaneously discourages their participation in many ways.

The most pervasive problem is the rigid organization of *time* in the American workplace. Most full-time jobs are tightly structured around a nine-to-five (or some other eight-hour block) working day; most offer little or no time off to cope with family problems, and little time off even for childbirth.

Again, the contrast with other industrial societies is revealing. Many European countries have widely implemented some form of flextime arrangement, where working hours are allowed to vary, within limits, usually around a central core of a few hours in the middle of the day. But flexible work time is rare in the United States; according to one estimate, only one in six American employers has experimented with some kind of rearrangement of the working week. [One result is that women with family responsibilities are often forced into typically lower-paid part-time work without fringe benefits or opportunities for advancement (Levitan and Belous, 1981, p. 165).]

Several European countries also have legislation requiring paid leave for parents to care for their sick children at home, another rarity in the United States. (In Sweden, *either* parent may take a paid leave of up to 60 days to care for a sick child.) In most Northern and Eastern European countries, families are entitled to a lengthy (by American standards) maternity leave at childbirth; the average is six months (9 months in Sweden, where the benefit is referred to as *parent insurance*). (By contrast, the women in Sheila Kamerman's study of working mothers took an average of six *weeks* off after childbirth.) Both Sweden and Norway provide for *fathers* as well as mothers to take parental leave at the time of childbirth. Sweden, in addition, has recently adopted legislation entitling either parent to a six-hour workday, with income supplements, until a child's eighth birthday (Kamerman, 1980, pp. 125, 131).

In the United States, at least a fourth of American workers who are married or have children under 18 report moderate to severe conflicts between work and family life (Pleck, Staines, and Lang, 1980, p. 36). Our failure to do much to resolve these conflicts may reflect continuing ambivalence about the roles considered truly appropriate for women. Our economy is increasingly one in which women's labor-force participation is a fact of life, but since it's often still felt that most women "really" belong at home, we also perpetuate an obstacle course for women who, through choice or necessity, try to combine outside work and family roles.

The Family as a Crucible of Violence

The contemporary American family, then, remains highly unequal in its division of work roles and expectations. An even more dramatic expression of inequality in the family is the problem of domestic violence.

How Violent Are American Families?

That question isn't easy to answer, partly because much (perhaps *most*) violence within families is never reported and partly because the answer depends crucially on how violence is defined. We know that violence between spouses, between parents and children, and between siblings is widespread. Just *how* widespread, however, is difficult to judge.

One of the most extensive recent studies of family violence, conducted by the sociologists Murray Straus, Richard Gelles, and Suzanne Steinmetz, concluded that "violence between family members is probably as common as love" (Straus, Gelles, and Steinmetz, 1980, p. 13). On the basis of a sample survey of more than 2,000 families, the researchers estimated that in the course of a year, about one-sixth of married people have engaged in at least one act of violence against their spouse, ranging from pushing, shoving, or "throwing something" to "beating up spouse" and "using a knife or gun." And that over the course of their marriages, more than one-fourth of the spouses would be involved in an act of violence. The researchers argued that those figures probably *underestimated* the amount of serious violence between husbands and wives, partly because many failed to report or admit family violence and partly because the study didn't include divorced couples, who might be expected to have experienced even higher levels of violence while married. The informal estimate was that *50 to 60 percent of couples* had engaged in violence at some point over the course of their marriages (Straus, Gelles, and Steinmetz, 1980, p. 13).

The same study found a considerably higher rate of violence by parents against *children* — with close to two-thirds of the couples sampled acknowledging at least one violent act against a child. And almost four-fifths of families reported violence between brothers and sisters. The survey also revealed a surprisingly high percentage of violence *against parents* by children; the authors recently estimated that almost 900,000 parents are victimized by "severe" violence at the hands of their children each year (Cornell and Gelles, 1982).

These researchers concluded that "the family is the most physically violent group or institution that a typical citizen is likely to encounter" (Straus, 1980, p. 13). This judgment, however, depends on accepting a fairly *wide* definition of *violence,* which included pushes and shoves, "grabbing," and throwing almost *anything* at a family member in anger — a very wide net indeed and one which may define as "violent" many families in which serious or physically harmful violence never happens. But, when these minor forms of family violence are excluded, levels of violence are still high. Thus, about 6 out of every 100 couples had slapped their spouse or worse, and 14 percent had done the same to a child during the previous year (Straus, 1980, p. 13).

These modified estimates, however, are still notably higher than most. A more recent survey by the U.S. National Center on Child Abuse and Neglect estimated conservatively that about 650,000 American children under 18 suffered *serious* abuse and/or neglect every year — a rate of about 10.5 per 1,000. These smaller, more cautious figures nevertheless reveal a human tragedy of enormous proportions (U.S. Department of Health and Human Services, 1982):

- More than 200,000 children a year are victims of *serious* physical assault.
- More than 100,000 children a year are victims of such severe neglect that they suffer injury, death, or impairment.
- Nearly 45,000 children a year suffer some form of *sexual* exploitation at the hands of a parent (or a parent's lover).
- About 1,000 children a year *die* as the result of a maltreatment-related injury or impairment; another 137,000 suffer *serious* injury.

These figures are regarded as a bare minimum by the researchers — and the actual extent of severe child abuse probably falls somewhere between them and those offered by Murray Straus and his co-workers.

Is family violence *increasing?* It's difficult to tell from the current studies because no really comparable or sufficiently sophisticated surveys were done in the past. Moreover, it's virtually certain that the *reporting* of both child abuse and spousal violence has improved greatly in the past few years.

Therefore, though the bare figures suggest a sharp increase in recent years, the opposite is probably likely. And historical evidence does suggest that wife and child abuse may have slightly declined over the past half-century (Straus, 1980, p. 28; Caplow et al., 1982, p. 336).

The Social Context   If we look more closely at the patterns of family violence in America we may better understand *why* it may have declined and perhaps also gain some insight into what it would take to decrease family violence even more. Despite the difficulties of reporting and definition, some of the social sources of serious family violence seem quite clear from the evidence we have. They include economic inequality and instability, the lack of social supports, and gender inequality.

Economic inequality and instability. Violence within families is sometimes described as being widespread *throughout* American society, afflicting families of all groups and classes. There is superficial truth to this — both wife-beaters and child-abusers *can* be found among the affluent as well as among the poor, among professionals with satisfying and rewarding jobs as well as among the unemployed and badly employed. But, like many other partial truths, the belief that serious violence is distributed evenly across American families — what the sociologist Leroy Pelton has called the "myth of classlessness" (Pelton, 1981) — is extremely misleading. *Serious* violence within families is disproportionately a problem of the poor and the economically insecure.

Consider child abuse and neglect. During the 1980s, several studies found that maltreatment of children was concentrated not only among low-income families, but among what one study describes as the "poorest of the poor." Among families poor enough to be receiving public welfare, those with high levels of child abuse and neglect were typically even *poorer* than the rest of the welfare population (Horowitz and Wolock, 1981, p. 138; Pelton, 1981, pp. 24–28). Figure 7-3, from the National Center on Child Abuse and Neglect's 1980 survey, graphically reaffirms the association of child maltreatment and poverty. The rate of serious reported abuse and/or neglect of children is *10 times* as high among families with income below $7,000 as among those over $25,000.

These differences *could,* as some critics have suggested, be due to differences in the *reporting* of child maltreatment. It is widely believed, for example, that lower-income people are much more likely to come under the scrutiny of public agencies (such as welfare agencies and the police) that deal with child abuse, and are much less likely to be able to keep incidents of abuse hidden with the help of discreet private physicians. (As we'll see in Chapter 11, this is a key research issue for other forms of crime as well.) But there is good evidence that these income disparities are *not* simply the result of different reporting practices. For one thing, though it is probably true

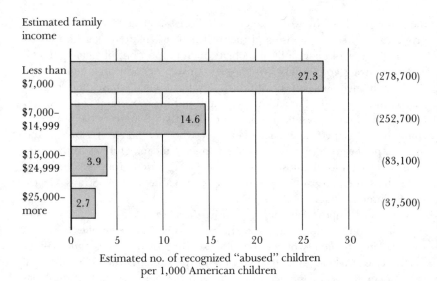

Estimated family income

Less than $7,000	27.3	(278,700)
$7,000–$14,999	14.6	(252,700)
$15,000–$24,999	3.9	(83,100)
$25,000–more	2.7	(37,500)

Estimated no. of recognized "abused" children per 1,000 American children

Figure 7-3

Poverty and child abuse (national incidence rates and incidence numbers, in parentheses, by estimated annual family income of maltreated children

Source: U.S. Department of Health and Human Services, *National Study of the Incidence and Severity of Child Abuse and Neglect* (Washington, D.C.: National Center on Child Abuse and Neglect, 1982), p. 10.

that public agencies may underreport the child abuse of the more affluent, there is counterbalancing evidence that relatives, friends, neighbors, and other *informal* sources of information on abuse may underreport its incidence in poor communities. For another, the belief that these differences result from different official attitudes to the poor doesn't explain why strong variations in child abuse by income show up even among *poor* welfare clients. Finally, the *death* of a child through physical abuse is not easily hidden, even among the affluent; and statistics on the distribution of child homicides at the hands of their caretakers are therefore fairly reliable ones. And the picture they give is unambiguous: A study of child deaths in New York City found that 70 percent of the families of murdered children lived in extreme poverty areas (Garbarino, 1981; Pelton, 1981, p. 41).

What is true of child abuse is also true of other forms of family violence. Straus and his co-researchers found several indicators of economic deprivation high on a list of characteristics that predicted much of the variation in spouse-beating: low family income; unemployment, part-time employment, or manual work for the husband; worries about economic security; and a wife "very dissatisfied with standard of living" (Straus, Gelles, and Steinmetz, 1980, pp. 203–204). (As we saw in Chapter 3, many other studies have linked family troubles with unemployment.)

Lack of social supports. Another factor associated with severe family violence is the absence of *social* supports, creating what the psychologist James Garbarino calls *social impoverishment* to distinguish it from sheer *economic* deprivation. Families who are isolated from kin, friends, and others who can provide support and assistance in times of crisis (or just help lighten the daily overload of work, household chores, and child care) are more prone to both spouse abuse and maltreatment of children. Neighborhoods with high rates of geographical mobility, high proportions of single parents, and few strong community ties through kinship or local organizations are predictably neighborhoods with high levels of child abuse and neglect (Garbarino, 1981). In the survey by Straus and his co-workers, fathers who have lived in their present neighborhood less than two years had a rate of child abuse 137 percent higher than those who were longer residents. And these fathers were also much less likely to have meaningful ties to the community through local clubs, unions, or other organized groups. Not surprisingly, the same pattern holds true for spouse-beating as well (Straus, Gelles, and Steinmetz, 1980, pp. 215–216).

The social impoverishment of abusive families is, of course, not really separable from economic impoverishment. More affluent families can cope with moving frequently or the lack of close, supportive friends and relatives much better by being able to buy some of the supports they need like day care, adequate health services, or help with the housework. The combination of severe poverty with social isolation, on the other hand, is a potentially explosive one. It helps produce what the family therapist Donald Bloch calls "a kind of impoverishment of familial social options" in which violence becomes virtually the only response to family problems or stresses that these families know how to use. Bloch's summation of the character of many abusive families fits the results of much other research:

> These are under-cared-for families. They are families that are impoverished economically, educationally, in their psychological resources, and in terms of their ability to function in the world. They could be characterized as coerced families. They are families most of whose lives are led in response to reasons they know not why. (Bloch, 1980, p. 35)

Gender inequality. Bloch also describes most violent families bluntly as "authoritarian and sexist," with a role structure that is typically "brittle and rigid" (Bloch, 1980, p. 34) — a conclusion shared by many others who have studied such families. Traditional gender inequalities, both in the family and outside it, nourish family violence in several different ways. The most direct is by providing a set of normative expectations about the "proper" roles of men and women that helps justify wife abuse and, perhaps less obviously, the abuse of female children.

Thus, Straus and his colleagues, along with several other researchers, find wife-beating *much more likely* in families where power over major decisions (such as those involving work, expenses, and children) was concentrated in the husband's hands — about *20 times* the rate found in families where decision making was democratically shared. This was especially true where male power, or the belief that the husband *should* be dominant in the home, was

Sepp Seitz/Woodfin Camp & Associates

American society lags behind many others in the provision of care for children.

not backed by the economic or educational resources to "legitimize" it. Men who *believe* that they should rule the home, in other words, but who also lack the economic and personal authority to do so, are the most likely to use violence against their wives (Straus, Gelles, and Steinmetz, 1980, p. 193).

The same social norms that foster the abuse of wives also tend to legitimize the abuse of female children. Figure 7-4 illustrates a stark gender difference in child maltreatment that becomes more and more apparent as children get older. Based on data from the National Center on Child Abuse and Neglect's 1980 survey, the graphs show that rates of *all* forms of abuse diverge sharply, especially after early childhood, with overall abuse rates for girls reaching about three times those for boys by mid-adolescence. (At the same time, as the other half of the figure shows, the rate of *neglect* shows the opposite trend.)

Because the norms that tend to legitimize male violence in the pursuit of control in the home also operate outside the home, there is a tendency for police, courts, and other agencies to take a "hands-off" attitude toward domestic violence, which probably helps perpetuate abuse. As we will see in Chapter 11, there have been some serious efforts to make the police and courts more responsive to domestic violence. But, on the whole, the criminal

Figure 7-4

Gender and child abuse: national incidence rates per 1,000 children for major forms of maltreatment by age and sex of maltreated children

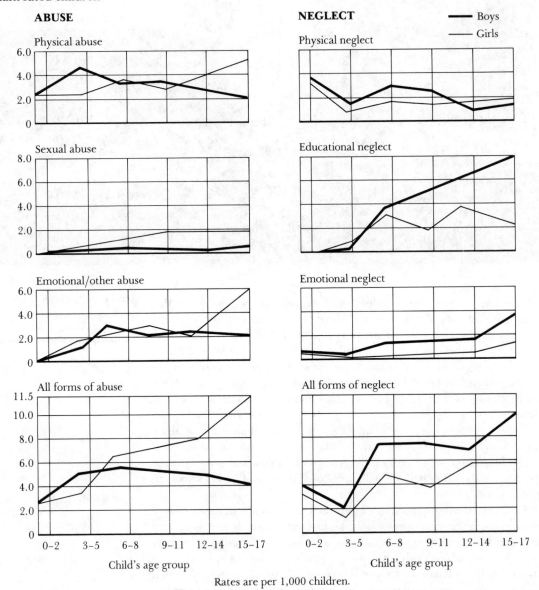

ABUSE

Physical abuse

Sexual abuse

Emotional/other abuse

All forms of abuse

NEGLECT

Physical neglect

Educational neglect

Emotional neglect

All forms of neglect

—— Boys

— Girls

Child's age group

Child's age group

Rates are per 1,000 children.

Source: U.S. Department of Health and Human Services, *National Study of the Incidence and Severity of Child Abuse and Neglect* (Washington, D.C.: National Center on Child Abuse and Neglect, 1982), p. 10.

justice system often still retains the traditional attitude that "a man's home is his castle" — that men's use of force in the home, as long as it isn't "excessive," is natural and emphatically a man's "own business" (Dobash and Dobash, 1981).

Sexual inequality also promotes both spousal and child abuse through limiting the economic and social options available to women. This problem is illustrated by the fact that full-time housewives are more likely than employed women both to be victims of wife-beating *and* to commit child abuse. In the first case, the woman's complete dependence on her husband often forces her into a choice between remaining with a violent husband or facing an uncertain and unrewarding job market. For women who lack salable job skills (especially if they also have small children) the alternative to continued abuse is, as they know, often deeper poverty and welfare dependency. In the second case, the overload of home and child-care responsibilities, coupled with the strains of a low family income, increase the possibilities of child abuse. Women who are "stuck" in the home with preschool children, either because of poor job chances and/or the husband's unwillingness to have them work outside the home, are at high risk for serious child abuse (Gelles and Hargreaves, 1981).

What all these factors show is that family violence cannot be adequately understood in isolation from the broader social forces that make *some* kinds of families more likely settings for violence than others. As we've already seen, those forces are much larger than the family itself. They involve the deep-seated problems of poverty and economic insecurity, a sex-typed division of labor and segregated job opportunities for women, and inadequate social supports for families and children. This point has broader implications for the way we think about the troubles of the contemporary family and about social policies to address them — issues to which we'll now turn.

Families, Social Policy, and the Future

One of the most important lessons that can be gleaned from this examination of some trends and problems affecting American families is that to speak of the problems of "*the* family" probably obscures more than it reveals. Not all families are alike, and different kinds of families, located at different points on the terrain of American social structure, face very different kinds of problems. Sorting out what those problems are, and thinking about specific ways of addressing them, is likely to be more fruitful than issuing declarations, one way or another, about the general state of "the" family as a whole. Thus, when we look at family problems this way, we discover some recurring themes.

Does Welfare Break Up Families?

The rising rate of family disruption is one of the most dramatic social trends in contemporary American life. As we've seen, it has a profound impact on many other social issues, including poverty, income distribution, and the persistent inequalities of race and gender. But *why* do families break up today at such a high rate —especially among the poor and some minority groups? That question is a large and highly controversial one, and there is no consensus among social scientists on the answers.

To get closer to some of the issues involved, let's look at what research tells us about one crucial part of the question: the impact of the welfare system on family stability. This is where the question of the causes of family instability becomes most relevant for social policy. And, especially in the past few years, the argument that welfare causes the breakup of poor families and encourages unmarried women to have children out of wedlock has become highly fashionable, especially among critics of the social programs of the welfare state. In this view, the welfare system encourages illegitimacy by paying for the support of children born out of wedlock: presumably, without that cushion, young people would be more careful. And by giving support (in most cases) only to women without husbands in the home, the system provides an incentive, as well as an opportunity, for families to break up.

The economist Thomas Sowell, for example, echoing many other critics, argues that "the current large and rising numbers of female-headed families among blacks is a modern phenomenon stemming from the era of the welfare state — when the government began to subsidize desertion and teenage pregnancy" (Sowell, 1979, p. 35). Is this an adequate explanation?

The evidence suggests that the sources of family disruption (among races) are much more complex, and that the role of welfare in particular has several — perhaps contradictory — aspects.

Part of the rise in both the proportions of families headed by women and illegitimate births, for example, reflects a simple demographic change — the increasing proportion of *young* people in the population during the 1960s and early 1970s. The young are generally more likely both to have children out of wedlock and to divorce or separate, so this shift in the age structure by itself causes rising rates of illegitimacy and family instability. And because this shift was especially pronounced in the black population, it helps explain the emerging differences in family structure between the races.

But this shift doesn't explain *all* of the trend toward one-parent families (or out-of-wedlock births), so the potential impact of welfare remains a question. Studies that have attempted to sort out welfare's impact have reached mixed and sometimes perplexing conclusions. There is little support for the belief that welfare benefits lead to increases in out-of-wedlock *births;* studies find no consistent effect of either the *amount* or the *availability* of AFDC benefits, for example, on teenage childbearing outside of marriage (Bianchi, 1981, p. 39). The evidence on AFDC's effects on *marriage* itself is less clear-cut.

A look at the percentage of female-headed families among different states, with widely different welfare benefits, illustrates the complexity of the problem (Table 7-7). Thus, in California, a state with one of the highest average welfare payments in the country, the proportion of female-headed black families with children is about the same as in Mississippi, with one of the *lowest* welfare benefits. The percentage of such families in California is also considerably lower than in the District of Columbia or such states as Missouri or Illinois, all of which also have welfare benefits that are lower than the national average and *much* lower than California's. The proportion of black families with a female head is, in fact, high in *all* the states listed, even those in which welfare benefits are minimal, suggesting that something else about the black experience in the United States bears an important part of the responsibility for generating this problem.

More elaborate research has sometimes found no connection between welfare benefits and family dissolution, and sometimes a small but noticeable one. This issue is complicated by the fact that the income provided by welfare benefits may well have two *opposing* effects on family stability.

State	Average monthly welfare payment	Percent of all families with children under 18 maintained by female householder	
		White	Black
California	$399	17	40
New York	371	14	48
Illinois	277	12	51
District of Columbia	252	15	51
Missouri	217	11	47
Georgia	133	11	38
Tennessee	122	11	44
Texas	109	12	35
Mississippi	88	10	38
U.S. average payment	280		

Table 7-7
Average welfare payments and percentages of female heads of families, by race, selected states, 1980

Source: Benefit levels from Walter Guzzardi, "Who Will Care for the Poor," *Fortune,* June 28, 1982, p. 39; family percentages from U.S. Bureau of the Census, *Provisional Estimates of Social, Economic, and Housing Characteristics, States and Selected SMSA's,* Washington, D.C., March 1982, various pages.

In the language of social science research, these have been called an *income effect* and an *independence effect* (Hannan and Tuma, 1978). Other things being equal, having more income is conducive to family stability. Poor income (along with unemployment, which often contributes to it) unsurprisingly tends to lead to conflict and discord in families, which often result in divorce or separation. But greater income *also* provides the means by which dissatisfied spouses, particularly wives, are able to afford to set up their own households (the independence effect of income support programs).

These opposing effects were illuminated in federally financed experiments during the 1970s that offered low-income families a "guaranteed income" in place of conventional welfare benefits (U.S. General Accounting Office, 1981). The experiments were not really designed to test the impact of the guaranteed income on family stability, and no consistent effects were found in *most* of the experiments across the country. One set of

experiments, however, in Denver and Seattle, did find that providing a guaranteed income apparently stimulated a substantial amount of family breakup among some kinds of families.

This finding caused considerable stir in the late 1970s, since it was often taken as evidence that income support was bad for the family. But its implications are actually much more complicated. The researchers discovered, for example, that the guaranteed income only seemed to cause family disruption if the benefits were very *low;* families given *higher* levels of income were unaffected. Why? One explanation has been that the income effect of the benefits canceled out the independence effect when the benefits were high enough. That is, giving participants in the program *low* benefits might have been just enough of an incentive to cause some unhappy marriages among poor families to break up. But *higher* benefits may have provided enough income to make the marriages more satisfactory and *less* likely to break up.

Families, Social Policy, and the Future   **275**

What this suggests is that there is no *simple* relation, as critics have argued, between the benefits of the welfare state and the rise of family instability. These findings, indeed, imply the rather startling conclusion that *higher levels of income support,* as well as the provision of stable jobs for poor families, might eliminate whatever adverse effects the welfare system may now have on families. And they also raise the important question (which some critics of welfare don't confront) of whether providing poor women a way out of bad marriages might not be a good thing.

Sources: Hannan and Tuma, 1978; Sowell, 1979; Bishop, 1980; Bianchi, 1981; Sandell, 1981; U.S. General Accounting Office, 1981; Blaustein, 1982, pp. 80–81.

One is the pervasive fact of *gender inequality.* Whether the issue is the division of labor in the home, the pattern of family violence, or the (inadequate) provision of child care, the unequal status of women is revealed at every turn as a major shaping influence on the problems faced by many families — and on the social response to them.

Another theme is the destructive impact of *economic inequality and insecurity.* For some families, poverty and/or unemployment are virtually unchanging facts of life, and they are less constant, but still painful, stresses for many others. Whether the issue is child abuse, the impact of divorce, or the quality of family life for single parents, economic deprivation is a brutally accurate predictor of both the extent and the seriousness of the problem.

Still another running theme is the often harsh impact on family life of a peculiarly American *ideology of social irresponsibility.* That ideology is revealed most clearly in the relative impoverishment of the kinds of social supports (including child-care programs and changes in the workplace) that many otherwise comparable societies have established to help manage the emerging shifts in the labor-force participation and family composition.

As this suggests, some of the criticisms often leveled at what are defined as destructive trends affecting contemporary families seem, on balance, to be curiously misdirected. Thus, as we've seen, critics of the welfare state blame it for undermining the American family. Yet in family-related programs, as in many other respects, the American welfare state is among the *least* developed of any advanced society, and that underdevelopment is itself a source of some of the most stubborn difficulties faced by many American families. Similarly, critics of the movement for equality for American women hold it partly responsible for the weakening of the family. Yet it is precisely the continuing *inequality* of women that, as we've observed, frequently lies at the root of many family problems, from violence and abuse to unemployment and low income. Others attack the growing openness about sexuality and the increased availability of family planning services as symptoms of an insidious "permissiveness" undercutting family life. Yet the evidence suggests that these trends may be partly responsible for what appears to be an increasing *satisfaction* with family life for a great many Americans.

Reducing economic supports for single parents, eliminating funds for child care, and slicing the budgets of family planning agencies — even the deliberate use of high unemployment to fight inflation — have all been justified on the grounds that the government will thereby "help families" by "boldly promoting a truly productive economy" (MacGraw, 1982, p. 69). From the evidence we've seen, such measures are more likely to reverse the recent, unsteady progress toward improving family life than to help families. But to understand these issues more clearly, we need to examine some trends in other American institutions, such as work and health care, which have profound effects on the character of family life.

Summary

This chapter has examined some problems of the contemporary American family, with special attention to four issues: the trend of family instability and its consequences; the gender division of labor within the family; the state of social services for families and children; and violence in the family.

Though some argue that the family is losing its central role in American life, the trends are actually far more complicated. Divorce rates have risen, along with illegitimate births. But remarriage is also common, family and kinship ties are still highly valued, and there is a high level of reported satisfaction with family life.

Still, the consequences of family instability can be severe. Divorce brings social and personal stress for both parents and children. The evidence suggests, however, that many of the problems faced by single-parent families are caused largely by a lack of resources.

Despite some evidence of changing attitudes, the division of labor in the home is still dictated by sex-role stereotypes.

The United States has been slow to develop adequate support services for children and families, such as child care and flexible working schedules.

Though its prevalence is difficult to measure precisely, family violence is widespread in America. Both child abuse and spouse abuse are aggravated by economic insecurity and the inequalities of income and gender.

For Further Reading

Caplow, Theodore, et al. *Middletown Families: Fifty Years of Change and Continuity*. Minneapolis: University of Minnesota Press, 1982.

Cherlin, Andrew. *Marriage, Divorce, Remarriage*. Cambridge, Mass.: Harvard University Press, 1981.

Kamerman, Sheila B. *Parenting in an Unresponsive Society.* New York: Free Press, 1980.

Straus, Murray A.; Richard J. Gelles; and Suzanne Steinmetz. *Behind Closed Doors: Violence in the American Family.* New York: Doubleday, 1980.

U.S. Commission on Civil Rights. *Child Care and Equal Opportunity for Women.* Washington, D.C.: Government Printing Office, 1981.

8

The Changing Workplace

As the 1980s began, Americans found themselves witnessing scenes reminiscent of the Great Depression: long lines outside unemployment offices; once-independent families lined up for free meals and shelter; young people hitting the road to look for work, sleeping in their cars or living in hastily built tent cities; college graduates scrambling for jobs waiting tables. But these tragedies were only the most recent and most dramatic expressions of a deeper crisis in the institution of work in America.

That institution, like many others in American life, is shot through with contradictions. Despite much talk about the decline of the work ethic, opinion polls consistently find that most Americans regard work as central to their lives and that they value working hard and doing a job well above most other pleasures and personal satisfactions (Figure 8-1). The vast majority also believe that work is so important that government should ensure that everyone who wants to work has a job. Yet despite this abiding belief in the value of work, Americans have tolerated levels of unemployment that, until very recently, were routinely the highest of any country in the developed world. We spend billions on education to prepare people for a more productive role in the work world and then allow many of them to languish on public assistance or in jobs that would not challenge a moderately intelligent 10-year old.

Throughout much of the postwar period, the contradictions of work in America were at least partly hidden by the phenomenon of affluence. Many Americans assumed that good jobs would come naturally, along with so much else, as a by-product of economic expansion. And so they did, for a while. Several severe recessions did throw millions out of work in the 1950s

279

Figure 8-1

Percentage of responses to the question: Do you agree or disagree with the statement: People should place more emphasis on working hard and doing a good job than on what gives them personal satisfaction and pleasure

Source: From *Public Opinion*, August/September 1981, p. 25. Reprinted with permission of American Enterprise Institute for Public Policy Research.

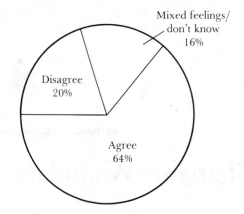

Mixed feelings/ don't know 16%

Disagree 20%

Agree 64%

and 1960s, but the economy bounced back, or so it seemed, after each. The economy of abundance seemed to produce so many jobs that the fear of massive or long-lasting unemployment, so strong in the generation that had endured the Great Depression, largely receded from view. Hard as it may seem to believe today, a college education provided an almost automatic ticket to a good job; good enough, at any rate, to pay for the basic prerequisites of the middle-class life-style. The same was increasingly true for high-school graduates who entered unionized jobs in the big "primary" industries like auto and steel. These were often tough and dangerous jobs, but they also paid the bills.

Two shadows emerged in the late 1950s and gathered momentum in the early 1960s, casting a pall over these expectations. First, it became increasingly clear that not everyone was able to participate fully in the work world and therefore in the general abundance of postwar American life. The excluded were concentrated in the inner cities and were disproportionately young and members of minority groups. By the early 1960s it was widely feared that this "social dynamite" would explode — and it did, to no one's great surprise, in the riots of the mid-1960s.

A second specter was "technological unemployment" — the fear that America's greatest postwar achievement, its growing technical prowess, might have the drastic, unintended consequence of creating machines so sophisticated that they would begin to eliminate human labor — and human livelihoods.

The postwar optimism did not survive the stagnation of the 1970s. Not only were more people thrown out of jobs in the recessions of the mid-1970s and early 1980s than at any time since the Great Depression but, worse, the economy no longer seemed to recover as well afterward, leaving millions still out of work even in "good" years. The problem of concentrated unemployment in the cities grew worse, not better. The number of urban minority youth out of work shot up more than 50 percent — despite more than a decade of government job training and education programs for the disadvantaged.

Meanwhile, even college graduates saw their futures shrinking as their degrees became less and less valuable in an economy that seemed to have simply run down like an old watch. And industrial workers who had struggled to achieve homes of their own and the good life in stable communities watched those expectations disintegrate as American industry collapsed around them. Not surprisingly, many Americans felt a real sense, not only of insecurity, but of betrayal, captured in Billy Joel's popular hit of 1982, "Allentown":

Massive unemployment is no stranger to American life.

> Well, we're waiting here in Allentown
> For the Pennsylvania we never found
> For the promises our teachers gave
> If we worked hard
> If we behaved
> So our graduations hang on the wall
> But they never really helped us at all
> No they never taught us what was real
> Iron and coal, chromium steel.
> [Copyright © 1981, 1982 by Billy Joel Songs (BMI)]

No one disagrees that the job crisis has been one of the most critical social issues of the 1980s, but there is no consensus on what to do about it. Much recent thinking among social scientists and policymakers about the job problem is based on the premise that the best way to create jobs is to

The Changing Workplace   **281**

Counting the Unemployed

The unemployment rate is one of the most common — and controversial — of social statistics. Since it's one of the most important measures of the success or failure of economic policies, its publication in the newspapers each month can cause fear and trembling at the highest levels of government. But what does the unemployment rate really measure — and how much does it really tell us about the state of the economy?

A national commission charged with evaluating the government's employment and unemployment statistics has pointed out that a good statistic "measures the right things — and it measures them well" (National Commission on Employment and Unemployment Statistics, 1979, p. 8). It is usually agreed that our present unemployment statistics *do* measure what they measure fairly well. But whether they measure the "right things" is another, more controversial, question.

Most regularly published data on unemployment are collected in a monthly survey of about 60,000 households carried out by the Census Bureau for the U.S. Department of Labor. On the whole, the survey is thought to have a high degree of accuracy, though the sample (while large enough to give reliable estimates of national conditions and of the working population as a whole) may be less reliable for smaller population subgroups and geographical areas. And like other census-based data, these surveys may be somewhat biased by the undercounting of some groups (like inner-city blacks) who tend to be especially hard-hit by unemployment.

But another, more serious question concerns the way the surveys *define* employment and unemployment. Deciding when someone is or isn't "working" might seem simple, but it is quite complicated in practice, and the choices government statisticians have traditionally made in response to these complications are by no means always obvious ones. Let's look at some of the issues now.

Unemployment versus Not Working

The official measure of unemployment includes only a fraction of those people who are not working for pay, and this has very important consequences for the way we understand unemployment as a social problem. Some of those left out are excluded for obvious reasons: Both the very young and the very old who do not work are not usually considered as unemployed, nor are those too seriously ill or disabled to work. Others, however, are excluded for less clear-cut reasons.

Most readers of unemployment statistics are unaware, for example, that several million people at any given time who are not working *want* a job and yet are not classified as "unemployed" but as "out of the labor force" (see Table 8-1). They are excluded from the government's measure because they have not *actively looked for work in the four weeks* before the Census Bureau interviews them. In mid-1982, there were nearly 7 million people "out of the labor force" who said they "wanted a job now" — roughly 4.5 million women and 2.5 million men (2 million of these were teenagers). The most common reasons cited for not having looked for work in the past month (and thereby failing to pass muster as truly "unemployed") were school attendance and home responsibilities, the latter being the biggest single reason for women (U.S. Department of Labor, 1982, pp. 39, 47).

Within this group defined as out of the labor force is a smaller subgroup which the Bureau of Labor Statistics calls "discouraged workers." They differ from the rest of those "out of the labor force" only because of the *reasons* why they haven't looked for work. They are classed as discouraged if they believed that no work was available, that they lacked the necessary skills or education, or that potential employers would think they were too young, too old, or otherwise unattractive as employees. In mid-1982 there were nearly 1.5 million discouraged workers — about two-thirds white and one-third black (three-fifths of them were women) (U.S. Department of Labor, 1982, p. 48).

Underlying this complicated scheme is a set of assumptions about people's availability for work. The discouraged are assumed to be less available

Reason and race	Total in thousands	Sex	
		Males in thousands	Females in thousands
White			
Total not in labor force	53,298	16,078	37,220
Do not want a job now	48,602	14,493	34,109
Current activity			
Going to school	5,072	2,574	2,498
Ill, disabled	3,275	1,789	1,486
Keeping house	25,608	253	25,355
Retired	11,131	8,018	3,113
Other	3,516	1,859	1,657
Wants a job now	4,697	1,584	3,113
Reason not looking			
School attendance	1,219	662	557
Ill health, disability	532	244	288
Home responsibilities	1,025	—	1,025
Think cannot get job	1,042	380	662
Other reasons*	879	298	581
Black and other			
Total not in labor force	8,769	2,996	5,773
Do not want a job now	6,909	2,369	4,540
Current activity			
Going to school	1,356	656	700
Ill, disabled	762	400	362
Keeping house	2,801	55	2,746
Retired	1,194	805	389
Other	796	453	343
Wants a job now	1,859	626	1,233
Reason not looking			
School attendance	513	261	252
Ill health, disability	235	80	155
Home responsibilities	366	—	366
Think cannot get job	526	207	319
Other reasons*	219	78	141

*Includes a small number of men not looking for work because of home responsibilities.

Source: Adapted from U.S. Department of Labor Statistics, *Employment and Earnings,* February 1983, p. 173.

Table 8-1

Persons not in labor force, by reason, race, and sex, in 1982

because they have opted, at least temporarily, out of the search for work; but they are considered sufficiently connected to the job market to be counted separately. The several million others who say they want a job but are not now looking for one are assumed to be unavailable for work and thus are more definitively out of the labor force. But, as the National Commission on Employment and Unemployment Statistics has argued, these definitions are "both arbitrary and subjective" (National Commission on Employment and Unemployment Statistics, 1979, p 10). The evidence suggests that many of the people defined as out of the labor force would, in fact, take a job if one were offered. Many are quickly pulled into the labor force during economic upswings. And many move in and out of the labor force quite regularly. In one study, almost half of the discouraged in a given year were back in the labor force a year later or had worked at some point in between. Among all people who were out of the labor force in mid-1982, 9 million had held a job in the previous year. And, about two-fifths of them had left the labor force because of school or home responsibilities; almost a fourth had left for economic reasons (slack work or the end of a temporary or seasonal job). About 4 million people who had worked in the past year but were now out of the labor force intended to seek work during the coming year (U.S. Department of Labor, 1982, p. 40).

It may be, of course, that many of those not in the labor force truly don't want a job and are not available for work even if they say they are; or they may want only the kinds of jobs they can't realistically get. On balance, though, the rather arbitrary exclusion of these hidden unemployed from the official count results in a considerable *underestimate* of the depth and seriousness of the problem of joblessness in America.

Underemployment and Hardship

Another major issue is that the official unemployment rate only counts people *without* jobs (or some of them). It doesn't tell us much about the *hardships* faced by those without work and it ignores the hardships suffered by many of those who *do* have jobs.

Historically, unemployment and economic hardship were very intimately linked. Most people in the labor force were adult men and single women who were usually the sole support of themselves and their families (the main exception was lower-income families in which wives and children often worked). Most families had one earner; fewer teenagers worked for pay; and there were few income-support programs for those out of work. So losing a job often meant a fall into desperate poverty and nearly always meant severe economic hardship.

Today, those conditions have changed. More families have multiple earners, many teenagers are in the labor force, and government transfer programs, particularly unemployment insurance, help cushion the financial impact of losing a job. As we'll see later, the extent to which these changes have eased the burden of joblessness is often exaggerated, but they *have* made the official unemployment rate, by itself, a less direct or precise measure of economic hardship. The unemployment rate lumps together a single mother with two children and no other source of income, a married blue-collar worker with three children and a mortgage, and a teenager from an affluent suburban family looking for a Saturday job. Given this diversity, the real-life experiences that the unemployment rate so coldly measures can range from minor inconveniences to a life-shattering disaster.

The other side of the same coin is that the mere fact of having a job — being counted as employed in the government's statistics — doesn't tell us whether the job provides the person with an adequate living standard. For one thing, an imposing fraction of people counted as employed are working in part-time jobs when they believe they need full-time work. Especially in bad economic times, these part-time workers often include people who are the sole support of families. In October 1982 almost 6.5 million Americans were working part time (at an average of about 22 hours a week) for economic reasons — nearly all because of slack work or because they couldn't find a full-time job.

Moreover, as we've seen, even those counted as being employed full time may not be able to

Calculations	No. in thousands
Total in labor force	108,276
Minus voluntary part-time workers	− 9,094
Minus those in labor force fewer than 40 weeks	−24,250
Plus discouraged workers	+ 700
Equals redefined labor force	75,632
Workers suffering hardship	
Workers earning less than poverty line	15,526
Workers earning less than poverty line	
with family income less than twice poverty line	7,563

Hardship index (workers earning less than poverty line with family income less than twice poverty line, as a percentage of redefined labor force)

$$\frac{7,563}{75,632} = 10.0\%$$

Hardship rates for specific groups	
Groups	Percent
All groups	10.0
Men	8.7
Women	12.1
Blacks	24.2
Hispanics	20.7
Other minorities	14.4
Whites	8.3
Ages	
16–19	26.4
20–24	12.9
25–64	8.7
65 and over	15.8
Family composition	
Husband-wife families	8.4
Families with female head	24.2
Unrelated individuals	10.7

Table 8-2
The hardship index, 1976

Source: Adapted from U.S. National Commission on Employment and Unemployment Statistics, *Counting the Labor Force* (Washington, D.C.: Government Printing Office, 1979), pp. 76–77.

make ends meet through earnings alone. In 1982 about 2 million Americans worked *full time all year round* but remained below the poverty level (U.S. Bureau of the Census, 1983e, p. 25). For these "underemployed" people, economic hardship is typically greater than that faced by those of the unemployed who, for one or another reason, have access to other sources of income.

Because of this, it's often suggested that a measure of economic hardship itself might be a better measure of the real problems of the American labor market than the conventional unemployment rate. One example, an "index of labor-market-related economic hardship," is illustrated in Table 8-2. It is calculated by first redefining the labor force to include discouraged workers and to exclude people who need only part-time work. The index then counts all those workers who for whatever reason (lack of work or poor wages) earn less than the official poverty level. Finally, it subtracts from this group those whose total *family* income is more than twice the poverty line. The result is a measure of those people who need full-time work but whose earnings aren't sufficient to provide more than a poverty-level income, and who lack *other* sources of income to bring their families to an adequate living standard.

Note that this measure shows, more sharply than the unemployment rate, the disproportionate problems faced by minorities, and especially by women, in the labor market. It also indicates, once again, the crucial role of family structure in economic well-being: Labor-market hardship is most frequent among families maintained by women. Other studies show that, compared to the unemployment rate, the hardship rate is both higher and more stable over time, fluctuating less sharply with the ups and downs of the general economy. What this indicates is that *underemployment* is both more widespread than official unemployment and in some ways is an even more stubborn, intractable social problem.

Working versus "Employment"

One final issue deserves mention. Historically, the government has defined employment as limited to work done for *pay* (a minor exception is the inclusion of people working in a family business). This means, most importantly, that most housework is excluded from the concept of employment. Under this definition, a "housewife" doesn't "work" — and someone who has done housework for years and then stops is not "unemployed." Somewhat curiously, a woman (or, in the much rarer case, a man) doing child care, cooking, and cleaning in her (his) own home is considered not in the labor force, unless she or he has an outside job, while the same person doing the *same* work in someone else's house for pay is considered "employed," and is "unemployed" if she or he *loses* that job. Thus, this definition of work offers a misleading picture of the extent of women's work and, by extension, of the severity of their employment problems. And it means that displaced housewives are not eligible for unemployment-related benefits.

unleash the private economy. According to this premise, if we eliminate wrongheaded policies that discourage investment (such as excessive regulations and taxes on businesses, and costly welfare and government job programs), business will invest more heavily and that investment will generate jobs. The Reagan administration's Program for Economic Recovery, for example, declared that public employment and training programs of the kind developed in the 1960s and 1970s would not be needed if the economy were allowed to grow without government interference: "In the context of a healthy expanding economy," it argued, "normal market forces will be relied upon to achieve present program goals" (Executive Office of the President, 1981, p. 21). *Fortune* agreed that though the plight of displaced blue-collar workers was severe, retraining them for new jobs was "no place for a government program" (Lubar, 1982, p. 118).

Another perspective emphasizes stimulating certain kinds of industries (especially the so-called sunrise industries such as microelectronics, robotics, or genetic engineering) in order to speed up and guide the transformation of the United States from a declining industrial power to an emerging post-industrial one (Democratic Caucus, U.S. House of Representatives, 1982).

Though different, both perspectives share the assumption that a booming private economy will indeed produce enough jobs to put Americans to work — just as it did in the 1940s and 1950s. This approach seemed, at least on the surface, to work reasonably well then — will it also work today?

This chapter will approach that question, and others, by considering several aspects of the current crisis of work in America. We'll look first at the problem of unemployment: how it is defined and measured; the groups it strikes the hardest; and some common, if often misleading, explanations for its rise and persistence. But unemployment is only *one* part of the problem of work in America — a problem that also involves fundamental changes in the structure of the American labor force: in the kinds of jobs that will be available to American workers, the kinds of skills the jobs will require, and the rewards they will offer. In the second part of the chapter, we'll examine some of these changes: the emergence of a "service" economy, the changing relationship between education and jobs, and the impact of new forms of automation based on microelectronics and robotics. All these trends have important implications for the way we think about resolving the job problem, and in the final part of the chapter we'll consider some recent social policies in the light of those trends.

The Deepening Shadow of Joblessness

The specter of massive unemployment, as we saw in Chapter 3, is no stranger to American life. Even if we ignore the Great Depression and consider only the years since World War II, unemployment has been a perennial problem that has receded only to return again in disturbingly recurrent cycles. Even during what we now regard with some nostalgia (and some truth) as an era of unparalleled economic growth and promise in the 1940s, 1950s, and 1960s, the jobless rate rose to the neighborhood of 6 percent (and even beyond) in 1949, 1958, and 1961. In the latter two years, joblessness was higher than it was in 1978 and 1979, years we regard as ones of economic decline.

Nevertheless, by the 1980s it was apparent that the job problem had been worsening over time. The jobless rate reached levels higher than any since the Great Depression; in early 1983 the number of unemployed in the United States was roughly equal to the entire Canadian labor force. Moreover, the peaks of unemployment had become progressively higher, while economic recovery hadn't brought the jobless rates down as significantly as in the past. Each successive recession of the 1970s and 1980s began with a higher level of unemployment than the one before; the level of joblessness just *before* the 1981–1982 recession began was much higher than any experienced in postwar America in any recession year before 1975.

The severity of the job problem is hidden, as we've seen, by the conventions of measurement and definition. An unemployment rate of around 10 percent means that roughly 11 million individuals are officially counted as out of work. But the true number of the jobless also includes the more than 1.5 million "discouraged" workers and the several million others who are "out of the labor force" but want work. And even the lower figure of 11 million individuals out of work means that *25 to 30 million people in families* are touched by the unemployment of one or more members. Moreover, the official unemployment rate is a kind of "snapshot" measure that freezes the action at one point in time. But 11 million people out of work *at any given point* during the year means that close to 25 million people will suffer unemployment *at some time* during that year — or more than one in every five people in the American labor force (U.S. Bureau of Labor Statistics, 1982).

These broad statistics also mask important differences in the way unemployment strikes different groups in American society — differences that are crucial not only for understanding the dimensions of the job problem, but for developing strategies to respond to it. Recent research suggests that three groups bear a disproportionate share of the burden of unemployment and underemployment: youth, disadvantaged adults, and displaced industrial workers.

Youth Unemployment: Pinpointing the Hard Core

A glance at Figure 8-2 reveals that younger people, especially teenagers, face much higher rates of unemployment than older adults, and have throughout the last several decades. By the end of 1982, on an average day, one in four youths aged 16 to 19 were officially unemployed, as compared to about one in six of those aged 20 to 24, and only about one in twelve of those over 25. Similarly, "discouraged worker" rates among teenagers were roughly double those for "prime age" adults and 1.5 times those of youth 20 to 24.

How serious is youth unemployment? It is often argued that despite what these numbers imply, youth joblessness isn't as serious a social problem as it seems on the surface since most young people are still in school and supported by their families and don't really need to work. Much teenage unemployment is often regarded as a normal part of growing up, a harmless movement between school, leisure, and occasional jobs. And it is widely felt that this kind of unemployment has few, if any, adverse consequences for young people's jobs or income later in life (U.S. General Accounting Office, 1982d).

The evidence generally supports the view that an important *part* of teenage unemployment is of this fairly mild variety. But it would be a mistake to conclude that youth unemployment is therefore a minor social problem. For one thing, some studies suggest that the overall level of youth unemployment may actually be *higher* than the already high official figures indicate. Longitudinal studies tracking youths' work experience over time have found

Figure 8-2
Unemployment rates, selected groups, 1960–1982

Source: U.S. Congressional Budget Office, *The Outlook for Economic Recovery,* Part 1 (Washington, D.C.: Government Printing Office, March 1983), p. 91.

Percent

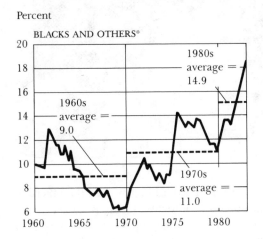

Percent

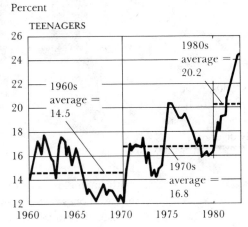

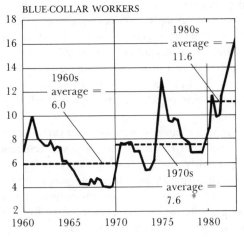

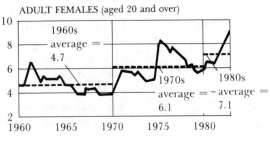

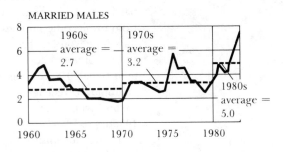

*"Others" include native Americans, Alaskan natives, Asians, and Pacific islanders.

The Deepening Shadow of Joblessness   **289**

Since the 1960s, unemployment rates for black and white youth have increasingly diverged.

youth unemployment rates more than a third higher than the official, census-based ones (U.S. Commission on Civil Rights, 1980b, pp. 13–14).

Also, the notion that work is more or less optional for young people, while doubtless true for some, is widely off the mark for others. A substantial fraction of unemployed youth badly need jobs, especially if they are from low-income families or — a surprisingly frequent condition, especially for young women — are the sole or main support of their own children. The *majority* of unemployed black and Hispanic youth live in families making less than $10,000 a year, as do a fourth of unemployed white youth. Among unemployed teenage women, a third of blacks, a fifth of Hispanics, and a sixth of whites have already had children (U.S. Commission on Civil Rights, 1980b, pp. 14–15).

Though it's misleading to say that teenage unemployment isn't a particularly painful experience, it *is* true that the most serious youth unemployment is concentrated among a fairly small proportion of young people. These youth tend to have many recurring spells of unemployment and to be unemployed for exceptionally long periods. About three-fourths of the total weeks of unemployment among youth, for example, is accounted for by the roughly 8 percent of jobless youth unemployed for 15 weeks or more (National Commission for Employment Policy, 1981, p. 48). These youth are not only likely to be out of work in any given year, but also to be unemployed in subsequent years as well (Bowers, 1982, p. 13).

The racial factor. Who are these especially hard-hit youth? What makes them different from the larger population of young people for whom the lack of a job is usually a short-term problem?

The most striking difference is race. The racial disparities in youth job-lessness are so large, in fact, that one scholar has argued that the problem of explaining the rise in youth unemployment is "largely one of explaining the reduced employment of minority youth" (Freeman, 1980, p. 7). Figure 8-3 shows that these *extreme* racial differences in youth unemployment are a relatively new phenomenon. White and nonwhite teenage unemployment rates were close in the mid-1950s. By the mid-1960s (during a period of relatively low *overall* unemployment) the rates had become quite divergent and were even more so in the 1980s. This pattern also occurred, though it began somewhat later, for young men past their teens but under 25. During the mid-1960s, unemployment rates rose considerably for young black adults, while those for whites scarcely rose at all.

But even these sharply diverging unemployment rates describe only the most *visible* part of the racial difference in joblessness. Another part is the "hidden" unemployment of those youth who have dropped out of the labor force. One way of looking at the depth of this problem is through what the Bureau of Labor Statistics calls the *employment–population ratio* (*EPR*): the proportion of people in a specific population group who are *working*. Since this measure excludes both the officially unemployed *and* those not in the

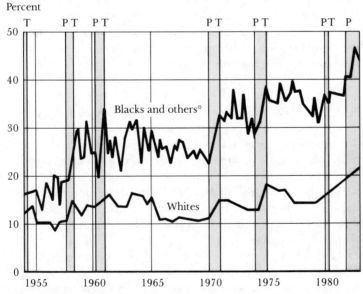

Percent

Figure 8-3
Teenage unemployment rates by race (ages 16 to 19)

Source: U.S. Congressional Budget Office, *The Outlook for Economic Recovery*, Part 1 (Washington, D.C.: Government Printing Office, March 1983), p. 93.

*"Others" include native Americans, Alaskan natives, and Pacific islanders.

Note: P and T lines represent business cycle peak and trough dates.

labor force, it can be a revealing indicator of the amount of joblessness hidden by the official unemployment rate itself. White teenagers have a somewhat higher EPR today than they did in the mid-1950s to mid-1960s, but the EPR for black youth has dropped greatly. Somewhat *more* black than white teenagers were working in the 1950s. But by the end of the 1970s, the proportion of all teenaged black males at work was only about *half* that of young whites. Blacks aged 18 to 19 are now less likely to be working than teenage whites aged 16 and 17, though more of the latter are in school full time and fewer have family responsibilities of their own (Bowers, 1979).

Part of the decline in black youth employment, especially for younger teens, reflects their increasing enrollment in school — but only a part, and less for youths over 18. By the end of the 1970s, an estimated 3 out of 10 black youths over 18 were neither working nor in school (Wrigley, 1982, p. 232).

Severe and recurrent unemployment is not, of course, confined to black youth. Mexican-American youth have unemployment and labor-force dropout rates that generally fall in between those for blacks and whites, while among Puerto Rican young people jobless rates have generally been equal to, or even higher than, those of blacks (National Commission for Employment Policy, 1981). And a significant group of lower-income white youth experience the same problems of high and prolonged joblessness; only the proportions are different. [In urban poverty areas in 1982, more than half of black teenagers were officially unemployed, but so were more than a third of white youth (National Commission for Employment Policy, 1981, p. 58).] Nevertheless, when we add together the growing gap in official unemployment rates and the equally striking decline in employment ratios among young blacks (and to a somewhat lesser extent young Hispanics), it's apparent that the most stubborn forms of youth joblessness are increasingly linked to race and minority status.

Disadvantaged Adults: The Persistence of Underemployment

Since the 1960s, American public policy has focused more on youth unemployment than on that of adults; and given the disparity between youth and adult unemployment rates, that emphasis isn't surprising. Nevertheless, some adults face equally severe problems in the labor market. And, as with youth, the *most* serious problems are concentrated in a relatively small stratum of the population. Many adult Americans endure some unemployment during their lives, but severe economic hardship — the result of long-term joblessness, low earnings, or both — is found most often among certain fairly specific groups.

According to a recent study of the dynamics of unemployment by Kim Clark and Lawrence Summers, two Harvard economists, almost three-fourths of the total weeks of adult unemployment are accounted for by people out of work at least 15 weeks; a surprising 40 percent of adult unemployment was experienced by the *2.5 percent* of the work force who suffered more than six months of unemployment (Clark and Summers, 1980). This concentrated, long-term unemployment also tends to persist from year to year. The University of Michigan's Panel Study of Income Dynamics, tracking the jobs and income of family heads over a several-year period, for example, found that less than 9 percent of the adult men were unemployed in 1972, but half of those were also unemployed a year later (Corcoran and Hill, 1980).

Similar findings appear when we consider the broader problem of under-employment. Many people find themselves in jobs that pay poorly at some point in their lives, but *persistently* poor earnings are concentrated among a small proportion of the work force. The Michigan researchers tried to determine the size of this persistently underemployed group by counting the proportion of people who fell, from year to year, into the lowest tenth of the earnings scale in America. During the 1970s, about 70 percent of men heading families *never* fell into that bottom tenth of American earners. At the other end of the spectrum, 5 percent were found in the bottom tenth at least seven out of the ten years, and another 3 percent for four to six of those years. These represent a persistent core of workers who are apparently permanently disadvantaged in the labor market (National Commission for Employment Policy, 1981b, p. 50). On the average, these men worked almost as many hours as the average for all working men — but they earned only about a third as much. Even if they had been employed as regularly as other men, they would still have brought home only poverty-level earnings (Freeman, 1981, pp. 120–121).

Race, sex, and underemployment. Who are the persistently under-employed? Some of their distinguishing characteristics are demographic, others reflect the kinds of jobs they hold, and still others involve the education and training (what economists often call "human capital") they bring to the labor market. Like hard-core unemployed youth, they are more likely to be members of minority groups and to be poorly educated; a disproportionate number never finish high school. [Low education, as we saw in Chapter 5, is an especially severe part of the job problem for Hispanic workers (National Commission for Employment Policy, 1981).] The persistently disadvantaged are also more likely to work in unskilled jobs in agriculture or personal-service industries, retail trade, and some low-paying manufacturing industries like textiles and apparel.

But it is *gender* that most sharply differentiates the persistently disadvantaged — suggesting, again, that the unemployment rate by itself is a misleading indicator of the labor-market problems of women. In the University of Michigan study, while 5 percent of men fell into the lowest earnings tenth seven out of ten years, almost 20 percent — one in five — of women family heads had earnings that put them at the bottom of the scale in *every one* of the ten years studied. And the difficulties these women face in earning an adequate living, like those of the smaller proportion of men in the same situation, seem little affected by economic growth. They remain disadvantaged through both the ups and the downs of the economy (Freeman, 1981, pp. 122–124).

Recognizing the stubbornness and concentration of underemployment has important implications for the way we think about strategies to combat the job problem — a point we'll discuss in more detail in the conclusion to this chapter. In particular it suggests that policies designed to create *any* kind of jobs won't do much to address the problems faced by the most disadvantaged men and women in American society. Behind the (bad enough) problem of a shortage of work, is an even deeper problem of a shortage of *good* jobs. We'll soon return to these issues when we examine trends in the structure of the American labor market itself. In the meantime, we turn to consider a third group suffering severely from unemployment in the 1980s: displaced industrial workers.

Displaced Workers: Casualties of Deindustrialization

The decline of many traditional American industries during the 1970s and 1980s has been one of the most profound social developments in our recent history. We saw some of the dimensions of this deindustrialization in Chapter 3. Here we'll focus on its most troubling result, the displacement of hundreds of thousands of workers from what had been relatively stable jobs that once enabled them to enjoy many of the rewards of American abundance. These "new" unemployed are different, in many ways, from the hard-core unemployed and underemployed groups we've looked at so far. But as the American economy continues its shift away from basic manufacturing industries, their numbers are increasing — and their chances of regaining jobs comparable to the ones they lost are shrinking.

According to the Congressional Budget Office, nearly 900,000 workers lost jobs in declining industries by 1983, almost half of them from just four basic industries: auto, primary and fabricated metals, and apparel. These are most often (though by no means always) former semiskilled workers in traditional manufacturing. These workers are concentrated most heavily in the industrial heartland of the northeastern and central states, but are also found in the industrial south and west (U.S. Congressional Budget Office, 1982b, pp. xii–xiv).

Dislocated workers are likely to be better educated and more highly skilled than the rest of the long-term unemployed; they are also more likely to be white and non-Hispanic and to have some access to other sources of income after they lose their jobs — either unemployment insurance (sometimes supplemented by other benefits from employers or unions) or the earnings of other family members (Bendick and Devine, 1981). Because of these resources, it is sometimes assumed that these workers will have few long-term problems in adjusting to the economic shifts that have cost them their jobs.

But the evidence suggests otherwise. A substantial fraction of displaced workers spend many months, or even years, out of work or drop out of the

A disproportionate number of disadvantaged workers are women.

labor force completely. A recent study found that, among workers laid off as a result of foreign competition, even those who were ultimately able to find new jobs had been unemployed for an *average* of nine months — and were now receiving wages a third lower than what they had earned before (U.S. Congressional Budget Office, 1982b, pp. xii–xiv). In a study of more than 1,000 New York City typesetters displaced by automation in the late 1970s, more than 400 went directly into early retirement when their jobs were lost (U.S. General Accounting Office, 1982a, p. 20). And among workers displaced by a steel-plant shutdown in Youngstown, Ohio, 35 percent retired early, 15 percent were still looking for work months after the shutdown, and 10 percent were forced to move from the area in search of work. Ten percent of a group of displaced blue-collar workers studied in New York State

The Deepening Shadow of Joblessness **295**

were still jobless two years after their layoff. And the average unemployment of displaced workers from a chemical company shutdown in Massachusetts was 60 weeks (Bluestone and Harrison, 1982, pp. 49–53).

The problems of long-term joblessness and lower earnings strike some displaced workers — especially older workers and women — even harder. Many of these workers withdraw from the labor force after losing a blue-collar job, often after exhausting unemployment benefits without finding a new job. And if they do find new jobs, women and older workers typically suffer even greater declines in earnings than other displaced workers. A study of workers laid off from New England's aircraft industry found that about one in eight of the displaced women, as compared to one in fifty of the men, had fallen into a "secondary" job five years later; 40 percent of the women, but just 14 percent of the men, had suffered a significant long-term loss of earnings as a result of losing their original jobs (Bluestone and Harrison, 1982, p. 61).

Though they are usually less obviously disadvantaged than the typical hard-core unemployed, then, the situation of displaced industrial workers is both bleak and ironic. They are generally people who have worked hard and steadily for years and who have never lacked the capacity or the motivation to hold down a job. But — as we'll see in a moment in examining changes in the structure of jobs in America — none of these qualities can guarantee them a secure future. Many may *never* attain the same kinds of jobs or the same level of earnings they enjoyed in the past.

Understanding Unemployment: Some False Leads

The high levels of unemployment in the 1970s and 1980s — especially the stubborn, hard-core joblessness of urban youth — have spawned an almost bewildering variety of explanations from social scientists, economists, editorial-page writers, and politicians. Though they differ widely in specifics, many of these explanations share some common themes. One persistent theme is that the problem of unemployment is, in one way or another, largely the result of faults or deficiencies in the unemployed themselves, sometimes compounded by unwise government policy. Few regard the labor market itself as a social problem; many, indeed, seem to accept our present mix of economic policies as if they were inevitable facts of life.

Bad Attitudes? The belief that unemployed people "really don't want to work" is deeply embedded in American folk wisdom. The accusation is most often leveled at the young and, at least by implication, at minority youth, since they are among the most visible casualties of unemployment. A more sophisticated, but fundamentally similar, version is offered by some economists who argue that much unemployment, especially among young people, is "voluntary," a deliberate choice of leisure over work — or at least over the kinds of jobs realistically available. People remain unemployed, in this view, because they have inflated expectations, leading them to reject jobs they could easily get if they weren't so choosy.

All of us know people who don't like to work, and it would be silly to suppose that there are not *some* youth (and adults) who fit this description. But acknowledging that this may apply in *individual* cases (as we argued in Chapter 1) is not the same as explaining unemployment as a *social* problem — and here the "explanation" fails.

To begin with, studies of unemployed youth have found that (as one puts it) "virtually no unemployed young jobseeker" actually rejects a job offer; nearly all take the first job they are offered. The image of picky young people disdainfully spurning an array of job offers is false. For the kinds of youth hardest hit by unemployment, there are few offers of *any* kind even in the best of times, and virtually none in times of recession. Whatever jobs are offered are almost invariably taken (Freeman, 1981, p. 23; Wrigley, 1982, p. 146).

Surveys of the job preferences of youth give a similar picture. A recent study by the economist Michael Borus (1982) found that many youths were willing to take any of several jobs listed (including dishwashing and working in a hamburger place) even at $2.50 an hour; the great majority would have accepted *any* job at $5 an hour. More than a million 18 to 19 year olds were willing to accept a job at a checkout counter or a hamburger place at well *below* the minimum wage. Even more revealingly, black youth showed considerably greater willingness to accept even very poor jobs at any wage.

This is especially damaging to the argument that unemployed youth don't want to work, since it's the disproportionate increase in unemployment among black youth that most requires explanation. Poor youth of all races, too, were much more willing to take jobs at $2.50 an hour than the more affluent. We can understand that for more affluent young people, having a job is less crucial and the willingness to take one is more likely to be balanced by other options, including schooling and leisure. But lower-income and minority youth, who bear much of the burden of serious joblessness, rarely have these choices. "To find the causes of high minority unemployment," Borus concludes, "we need to look for other explanations, such as discrimination, geographical distance from jobs, and lack of adequate knowledge of the labor market" (Borus, 1982, p. 592).

A review of the impact of job training programs on the work attitudes of disadvantaged youth affirms this conclusion from another angle. Few of these programs actually changed young peoples' attitudes toward work, though many of them tried to. Even when they *did* have some impact on youths' attitudes, the changes didn't help youths get jobs. Why not? Partly, the study concludes, because the youths' work attitudes weren't particularly negative to begin with. Even if their attitudes changed for the better, the real problem these youths faced was the sheer lack of enough jobs in the labor market and of the concrete skills to compete for the few jobs available. These youth often did display what the researchers called an "intermittent and casual" connection with the labor market. But, the study argues, this was largely because the labor market offered only minimal job opportunities for them to "connect" with (Forcier and Hahn, 1982).

A common variation of the "unemployed don't want to work" argument is that the pages of help-wanted ads in the newspapers "prove" that there are plenty of jobs for anyone who wants one. But that argument (popularized by Ronald Reagan during his first year in office) has often been exposed as fallacious, even by business-magazine writers. The most thorough refutation, in fact, was achieved by *Fortune* in an article exploring the realities behind the help-wanted ads in a small city in New York State in 1978. *Fortune*'s investigation showed that there was much less to the pages of want ads than met the eye. Of 228 want ads in the Sunday paper, only 142 were actual job offerings within reasonable commuting distance of the city (many others, for example, were ads for "business opportunities," not jobs). Of those 142, just 42 didn't require special skills, like those of nurses, mechanics, or X-ray technicians. What was the response to those 42 ads that offered work for the typical jobless worker?

According to *Fortune*, the employers offering those ads were "fairly swamped by a tidal wave of applicants." A $3-an-hour night-clerk job in a motel drew 70 applicants in 24 hours. The city's jobless, *Fortune* concluded, "are not people who are out of work because they are overly fussy about

A Stampede for 250 Jobs

More than 3,000 people, many of them vaulting counters and climbing over desks, converged on a state employment office yesterday to get applications for 250 jobs at a hotel.

"I almost had a riot down here," said Marvin Noll, supervisor in charge of the employment service.

Police were called, but employment service workers had the situation under control by the time officers arrived.

"These people just want to work," said police Sergeant John Paul.

Noll said more than 3,000 people picked up applications during the first hour his office was open.

"It was just wall-to-wall people. I've never seen anything like this," Noll said. He said a sizable turnout is expected today.

The applicants hope to be picked for the 250 jobs — 200 of them permanent — at the Radisson Muehlebach Hotel in downtown Kansas City.

Ron Juneman, the hotel's personnel director, said the hotel expects to fill all the jobs in March.

The initial plan, Noll said, was to hand out applications and interview the applicants on the spot. "We had to tell most of them to come back later in the week for interviews," he said.

Unemployment in the Kansas City area was 8.7 percent in December and an estimated 9.4 percent in January.

Source: San Francisco Chronicle, February 15, 1983. Used by permission of Associated Press.

how to make a living; they are people who are eager, even desperate, for jobs that pay $3 an hour." (For a dramatic illustration of this desperation, see the box below.) Even if all the full-time jobs listed had in fact gone to unemployed people (and none to people moving from one job to another, as is usually the case), the local unemployment rate would have dropped only insignificantly, from 7.4 to 7.2 percent (Meyer, 1978). A more recent study of Boston-area want ads found that even for the poorest, least-desirable jobs, there were an average of 15 to 20 responses to each ad within 2 days of its appearance (Clark and Summers, 1980, p. 14).

Closely related to the idea that the unemployed don't want to work is the belief that unemployment insurance and other social benefits keep people from working by making *not* working too attractive. The Harvard economist Martin Feldstein, later head of the Reagan administration's Council of Economic Advisors, argued in the late 1970s that the "private costs" of being unemployed, for many workers, had become "quite small" because of generous unemployment insurance and other benefits. "The relatively low cost of unemployment," according to Feldstein, "is a substantial cause of our high permanent rate of unemployment" (Feldstein, 1978, pp. 155–158). This belief led, in 1982, to a quickly dropped administration proposal to tax benefits to the unemployed and thereby increase the costs of joblessness. What is the evidence for this view?

Social Benefits: Too Much Welfare?

Not much. We've already seen that there is simply *no* good evidence that a significant number of realistic job opportunities are *ever* refused by members of those groups with the most serious labor-market problems. The idea that unemployment insurance or other transfer payments *keep* unemployment high requires us to believe that actual work opportunities are rejected by the hard-core unemployed in favor of living off "handouts" — and we simply have no evidence that this happens to any *considerable* extent (though again, of course, it doubtless happens occasionally).

This argument also exaggerates both the extent and the generosity of benefits for the unemployed. Consider unemployment insurance, the usual villain in this piece and the most important source of income support for the unemployed. The argument that it causes unemployment ignores, first of all, that only a fraction, and a dwindling fraction at that, of the unemployed actually receive unemployment benefits. Only about 40 percent of the officially unemployed were getting unemployment insurance during the 1982 recession, as compared to about 60 percent in the recession of 1974–1975. In large part this is because the eligibility requirements for unemployment insurance exclude many of the unemployed, including people entering the labor force for the first time or reentering after a long absence, and most of those who *leave* their jobs. Moreover, especially during lean economic times, many who are eligible exhaust their benefits before they find another job. In a recent study, only 65 percent of those who had exhausted their unemployment benefits had found a job even a year afterward (Freeman, 1981, p. 151).

Since youth are less likely to be eligible for unemployment insurance, we would expect them to have lower unemployment rates if this argument were a strong one; but the opposite, of course, is true. [Some European countries, in fact, do not exclude youth first entering the labor market from unemployment benefits and still have *lower* youth unemployment rates than we do (Reubens, 1980, pp. 125–126).]

The degree to which unemployment benefits compensate for lost earnings from work (what economists call the *wage replacement ratio*) is also relatively low in the United States compared with other industrial societies, including many with lower unemployment rates (Havemann, 1978).

Studies attempting to estimate more precisely whether, and how much, unemployment insurance may raise unemployment, suggest that though there may indeed be *some* impact, it's certainly a small one — and incapable of explaining more than a minor fraction of the unemployment problem. Thus, no relationship has been found between the level of unemployment benefits and the rate at which workers *quit* their jobs. Some studies do suggest that unemployment benefits may increase the *duration* of unemployment for those already out of work, but the effect is minimal. Thus, one study estimates that increasing the wage replacement ratio by about 25 percent might increase the length of an average spell of unemployment by about four days; another, that extending unemployment benefits by ten weeks might decrease average employment during a year by one week. Neither effect quite clearly would make much of a dent in the multiple-month spells of joblessness faced by the hard-core unemployed (Danziger, Havemann, and Plotnick, 1981).

Similar findings apply to other public benefits for the unemployed. Some have argued that the generosity of the welfare state as a whole has provided so much potential affluence for those who "choose" not to work that rising unemployment is a predictable response. Certainly the welfare state has provided important cushions for those unable to work. But the major flaw in this argument is that there has *not* been a substantial shift of income toward the disadvantaged in recent years. Instead (as we saw in Chapter 4), there has been a striking continuity in both the income shares of low-income families and in the size and distribution of public assistance benefits for over a decade, with an apparent slight *increase* in income inequality and a *decrease* in the value of welfare benefits since the late 1970s. It's difficult, therefore, to explain the sharp *rises* in unemployment as resulting from a supposed increasing level of comfort enjoyed by the nonworking poor (Freeman, 1980, p. 28). Again, too, the size and spread of many public benefits is far greater, and their rate of growth faster, in most European industrial countries, many of which, like Austria or Sweden, have far *lower* levels of joblessness (Havemann, 1978).

Studies experimenting with guaranteed income plans in the 1960s and

1970s, moreover, found that even when low-income people were guaranteed an income whether or not they engaged in paid work, the effect on their work habits (what in economists' jargon is called *labor supply*) was small. On average, the income guarantees reduced the work hours of family heads by less than 1 percent; somewhat more — not too surprisingly — for other earners in a family. Even with a minimum income assured, then, the desire for work is a very powerful one at all levels of American society (Danziger, Havemann, and Plotnick, 1981, p. 1018).

Finally, it's important to remember that some of the time the unemployed spend not working is actually quite productive in both social and economic terms. One of the original purposes of the unemployment insurance system, indeed, was precisely to allow workers sufficient time to search for jobs that best fit their skills and interests and therefore enhance their productivity. Similarly, benefits that support unemployed parents of very young children may help keep them out of paid work, but the benefits also help support such *unpaid* work as running a household and caring for children. Those who are critical of the potential of public welfare to create what are sometimes called *work disincentives* have rarely offered convincing alternative ways of supporting those important tasks.

Is the Minimum Wage Too High?

This argument holds that federally enforced minimum wages cause unemployment by requiring employers to pay more for some workers, especially youth, than they're "worth." As minimum wage levels have risen, in this view, they have outstripped the market value of less productive workers. An employer willing to hire a youth at $2 an hour may not find it worthwhile at $3.50 or more. As *Fortune* claimed in a 1982 article, "by now, of course, many economists have come to agree that the minimum wage has been a cause of unemployment" (Lubar, 1982, p. 121).

Have they? Actually, the evidence shows that the connection between minimum wages and unemployment is by no means that simple. One problem is that (as in the case of social benefits for the jobless) our minimum wages have risen less rapidly than those of some European countries with lower unemployment rates (Havemann, 1978). Moreover, minimum wages in the United States have *not* risen, except on paper, in recent years; relative to the average wage American workers receive, the minimum wage is lower today than in the 1950s and 1960s. In 1961, for example, the minimum wage was an even 50 percent of the average earnings of production workers in American manufacturing industries; 20 years later, it had fallen to 43 percent. Inflation, too, has meant that, in real terms, federal minimum wages have declined slightly from the late 1960s. Even more damaging to this argument, though, is the fact that unemployment has *never* been as high in the United States as it was during the Great Depression, which began years before the passage of the first federal minimum wage law in 1938 (Currie and Rosenstiel, 1979).

It's often forgotten, too, that many youth — including about half a million students working in small service and retail enterprises — are already *exempt* from minimum wage legislation; increases in the minimum wage obviously have little to do with their unemployment problems.

Despite these basic contradictions, this argument has inspired an extraordinary amount of research attempting to calculate just what fraction of the unemployment rate, especially for young people, may possibly be attributable to the inhibiting effects of minimum wages. None of this research, though, has convincingly demonstrated large negative effects of the minimum wage on employment. A recent review of dozens of such studies finds that most of them estimate that a 10 percent increase in the real minimum wage (that is, the minimum wage adjusted for inflation) might reduce teenage employment by anywhere from 0 to 3 percent, most likely in the "lower half of that range" (Brown, Gilroy and Cohen, 1982). (At the level of unemployment faced by black teenagers in 1982–1983, this "explanation" might account for somewhere between one-sixteenth and one-twenty-fifth of the problem.)

Another difficulty is the failure of this explanation, like some others, to plausibly account for the *racial differences* in youth unemployment — which account for much of the overall increases in youth joblessness. The minimum wage, where it does apply to youth, applies to all races equally, of course; but black teenage unemployment has typically been in the neighborhood of 2.5 times that of white youth in recent years. It is hard to see how the minimum wage could be responsible for this key difference.

If excessive minimum wage requirements were what kept employers from hiring young people, we would expect them to jump at the chance to hire youth if someone else were footing the bill. But this isn't the case. Experiments in giving government subsidies to businesses to encourage them to hire low-income youth have generally failed to motivate employers. Recent Labor Department studies in Baltimore and Detroit found that only 5 percent of employers eligible for a *50 percent* wage subsidy (the government would pay half the youth's wage) hired even *one* new young employee. Only *18 percent* of eligible employers hired a low-income youth even when they were guaranteed a subsidy covering *100 percent* of the youth's wage. Clearly, something besides wage costs keeps employers from hiring young people, if they won't even hire them at *no* cost (*Employment and Training Report of the President, 1983*, p. 115).

If the impact of the minimum wage on teenagers is difficult to pin down, it's even more difficult for adults. Researchers completely disagree on whether there is *any* impact of the minimum wage on adult jobs at all and, if so, in which direction that effect operates. That is, while some adult workers with very low skills might be kept from being hired by the minimum wage, others are probably kept *on* the job because the minimum wage helps protect them from teenage competition (Brown, Gilroy and Cohen, 1982). In this sense, the often-heard proposals to lower the minimum wage for teenagers run the risk of substituting cheaper teenage labor for that of disadvantaged adults (especially women, who tend disproportionately to fill lower-paid adult jobs).

But there is an even deeper problem with the argument about the negative effects of the minimum wage on jobs. As we've seen, the job problem in America is not simply a matter of a *shortage* of jobs. It is also the inability of many of those who *do* have jobs to earn a standard of living adequate to meet fundamental human needs. In the early 1980s, full-time, year-round work at the federal minimum wage supplied an income more than $1,500 *below* the poverty line for a family head with three dependents, and just barely squeaked over the poverty line for a female head of household with two children (*Statistical Abstract of the U.S., 1981*, pp. 408, 445). In this sense, to argue that the minimum wage causes unemployment misses the point, since work at wages *below* the minimum is, itself, part of the job problem — not part of the solution.

A less judgmental, and more plausible, explanation of high unemployment (again, one with special relevance for the young) focuses on the effects of demographic changes in the composition of the American labor force — in the kinds of people working and looking for work today. Two of these changes have been particularly important in recent years: the growth in the teenage labor force and in the labor-force participation of women. According to some observers, both have helped boost unemployment rates, even when the economy is generally performing well.

Demographic Changes: Is the Labor Market Too Crowded?

Thus, the growth in the youth labor force means that the work force now contains a bigger proportion of those people who tend to have higher rates of unemployment, which pushes up the unemployment figures as a whole. Relatedly, it's argued that the great influx of young and female workers means there are now simply too many people competing for jobs. In this view, though the economy has performed well in generating millions of new jobs in recent years, the pace of job creation still hasn't kept up with the even more rapid growth in the demand for work. (Interestingly, this argument bases itself on a premise diametrically opposed to some of those we've just examined — here, the problem isn't that people *don't* want to work, but that they *do*.)

Certainly, there is important truth in this perspective. To some extent, a rapidly increasing number of people wanting jobs is bound to cause some strains on an economy's capacity to put them to work. How *much* of an explanation it provides, however, is another matter.

Again, one important source of insight is the experience of other countries. Some other industrial societies saw a less rapid growth in their youth labor force in recent years than the United States did, but others, such as Japan, saw a faster rate of increase — without the high youth unemployment that accompanied that increase here (Sorrentino, 1981, p. 9). In the

United States itself, the rate of growth in the teenage labor force, while quite rapid for many years, began to taper off in the mid-1970s and actually declined beginning in 1979. [Youth aged 16 to 19 were almost 10 percent of the American labor force in 1975, but were less than 8 percent in 1982 (Sorrentino, 1981, p. 9; *Monthly Labor Review*, December 1982, p. 60).] Meanwhile, youth unemployment, after a slight dip in the late 1970s, rose again sharply, as we've seen, in the early 1980s. And minority youth were suffering severe labor-market problems back in the 1960s, at a time when youths' proportion of the labor force wasn't high by current standards. Though it may have aggravated the rise in youth unemployment, then, the growth in the share of youth in the labor force can't really explain either the continuing rise of youth joblessness in the early 1980s or its persistence for minorities in earlier periods.

Nor is there much evidence that the influx of women into the labor force has been a major cause of unemployment — that women have "crowded out" other groups from the labor market. For the most part, as we've seen, women have moved into traditionally "female" jobs rather than into those traditionally held by men or younger people. And again, the experience of other countries casts doubt on this explanation. Sweden, with an unemployment rate of only 2.9 percent in 1982, has a significantly *higher* proportion of women in the labor force than the United States.

The best evidence is that the changing composition of the labor force resulting from the baby boom of the 1950s and 1960s and the rising participation of women has had *some* effect on the jobless rates, but not a large one. According to an analysis by the National Commission for Employment Policy, if the American work force had had the same proportion of women and youth in 1980 as it did in 1957, the unemployment rate in 1980 would have been *one percentage point* lower than it actually was (National Commission for Employment Policy, 1981, p. 49).

Are Undocumented Workers Taking Too Many Jobs?

A recent federal commission estimates that between 3.5 and 5 million illegal aliens were in the United States in the late 1970s, and that as many as half a million more entered the country during 1980 alone (mostly from Mexico and Latin America, and increasingly from the Caribbean and Southeast Asia (Martin, 1982, p. 37). Since most of these immigrants, whether or not they remain in the country, come here in search of work and income, it's widely believed that they increase unemployment by crowding American workers out of jobs. What do we really know about the impact of illegal immigration on jobless rates?

Surprisingly little. Though on the surface it seems logical that the employment of alien workers should displace native workers from jobs, hard evidence that it actually happens is difficult to come by. As the Commission on Immigration and Refugee Policy concluded, there is no consensus among researchers on whether illegal aliens displace American workers at all, much

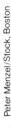

Fewer workers now make
their living from the land.

less on how much. Estimates run the range from *no* American workers displaced to one displaced for every illegal worker hired. The most plausible
recent estimates are that illegal immigration probably does displace some
American workers and thus has some impact on the jobless rate, but most
likely a small one (U.S. Select Commission on Immigration and Refugee Policy, 1981; Martin, 1982).

Why such a small and uncertain effect? One of the most important factors is that most immigrant workers, including many legal as well as illegal
aliens, apparently work in different labor markets than do American workers. They are typically found in the poorest-paying service jobs (like dish-

washing), in agriculture, or in those manufacturing jobs with the lowest pay and worst working conditions. For two reasons, this concentration may mean that alien labor has minimal impact on American workers. For one thing, these jobs won't support an American worker — at least one with any dependents, but they may offer much higher wages than are available in most of the immigrants' countries of origin. Thus, the jobs usually filled by immigrants are rarely sought by American workers. One recent study found only a small proportion of adult unemployed American workers willing to work as sewing-machine operators in the local garment industry at the minimum wage or less — a typical job for alien workers from poor countries (*Employment and Training Report of the President, 1983*, p. 91). At the same time, employers in these low-wage, often marginal industries may not want native workers, preferring, instead, an immigrant work force that is likely to be more docile and less inclined to complain about substandard (even illegal) working conditions and subminimum wages (Currie and Rosentstiel, 1979, p. 53–57; Cornelius, 1982).

What's most clear is that most of the kinds of jobs illegal aliens apparently fill — even if "opened" to native workers — wouldn't do much to address the larger problem of underemployment in the United States; they would most likely simply increase the number of Americans who, despite even full-time work, are unable to earn enough to assure an adequate living standard.

The shortcomings of these explanations, taken singly or together, suggest that understanding the unemployment problem demands that we focus our attention on the American labor market itself — on the way our economy produces, or fails to produce, enough jobs of sufficient quality to put Americans to work at living wages. In the following section, we will turn to some of the key changes that have been taking place in the patterns of employment in the United States and consider what these changes may mean for American jobs in the future.

A "Service" Society?

It is widely agreed that there has been a profound shift in the way Americans earn their livings in the twentieth century, especially during the last quarter. The shift is frequently described as one from a society primarily engaged in the production of *goods* to one primarily engaged in the provision of *services*. Since World War II, this shift toward a service economy has proceeded with extraordinary speed. In 1948 the goods-producing industries (agriculture, mining, manufacturing, and construction) produced 46 percent of our gross national product; service industries (including trade, communications, banking and insurance, entertainment, social services, and all others not directly producing goods) accounted for the other 54 percent. Thirty years later, the production of goods accounted for just 34 percent of GNP, services 66 percent (Ginzberg and Vojta, 1981).

The same development can also be described as a series of changes in the proportions of people working in agricultural, blue-collar, or white-collar jobs. As Figure 8-4 shows, the most striking trend throughout this century is the sharp decline of agriculture as a source of jobs and livelihoods. At the turn of the century, agriculture engaged about a third of American workers. By the end of the 1930s, spurred by the economic calamity of the Depres-

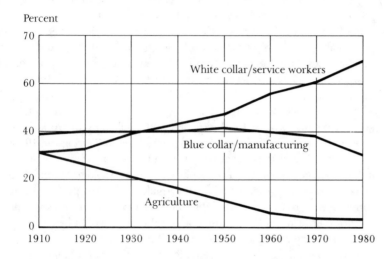

Figure 8-4

The changing structure of work in America

Source: From *Public Opinion*, August/September 1981, p. 22. Reprinted with permission of American Enterprise for Public Policy Research.

	Agriculture	Blue collar/ manufacturing	White collar/ service workers
1910	31%	38%	31%
1920	27	40	33
1930	21	40	39
1940	17	40	43
1950	12	41	47
1960	6	40	54
1970	3	37	60
1980	3	30	67

Note: For 1910–70, agriculture = farmers; farm laborers/supervisors. Blue collar = crafts people/supervisors; operatives, laborers except farm and mine. White collar/service workers = professional/technical; managers/officials/proprietors: clerical; sales; household: service workers. 1980 figures based on employed persons.

sion and the growing substitution of machines for human labor on the farm, the proportion had been halved, to about one in six. By 1970 just 3 percent of American workers made their living from the land.

Meanwhile, the kinds of jobs we loosely call white-collar or service work (professionals and managers, technical workers, clerical, sales, and service workers) grew rapidly. In 1910 these occupations accounted for roughly the same proportion of Americans as did agriculture. But by 1970, as farm work dwindled, the proportion of white-collar jobs doubled. Between 1970 and the present, white-collar employment continued to increase; but with the bottoming out of the decline in farm work, the growth of white-collar work has been mainly at the expense of blue-collar jobs.

With the mounting troubles of American manufacturing industries in the 1970s and 1980s, there has been much talk about the coming end of blue-collar work. This "death" has been exaggerated: Blue-collar jobs still employed about 3 out of every 10 working Americans in 1980. But, as a recent review notes, "the long-term trend in manufacturing remains unmistakably downward," and it accelerated in the late 1970s and early 1980s (Freedman, 1982, p. 75).

The existence of this trend toward a service economy is not in doubt. What it means in terms of the quality and availability of work, however, is another question — and the answers are not yet in. During the 1960s, some social theorists argued that these trends would culminate in a "post-industrial" society (in the famous phrase of the sociologist Daniel Bell, 1969) in which, among other benefits, the quality of work performed by most Americans would be greatly "upgraded." Dirty, dangerous, low-skilled jobs requiring little more than muscle and endurance would be increasingly replaced by more sophisticated ones calling for brains, not brawn. More recent versions of the same idea envision the coming of a "high-tech" society based on new developments in microelectronics and robotics, in which increasingly sophisticated machines will do most of society's dull and dirty work. Meanwhile, the blooming new industries themselves will involve work that is increasingly challenging and intellectually demanding, requiring, as *Fortune* recently prophesied, "a new order of worker — well-educated, highly skilled, strongly motivated, and capable of taking the initiative" (Lubar, 1982, p. 115).

How likely is this hopeful scenario? From the evidence we have, the coming shape of work in America seems much more problematic — and less easy to discern. While the rapid shift away from traditional blue-collar labor does have the potential of ushering in an era of more rewarding and fulfilling jobs, it also poses the opposite danger — the threat of eliminating some of the better jobs in the economy without creating nearly enough new ones to take their place. The changes we are now witnessing in the technology and organization of work could bring us a richer, healthier, and more challenging work life. They could also create even greater and more stubborn mass unemployment while eroding the quality of many jobs that now exist.

To assess these different possibilities, we need to look more closely at what the developing service economy and the accompanying technological changes in the workplace have meant, so far, for the kinds of jobs Americans hold. On close inspection, it's clear that, on balance, these changes have *not* brought the general upgrading of work that many observers anticipated. There are two main reasons why. One involves the *kinds of jobs* the service economy has typically generated and the other involves the way in which advancing technology has affected the character of particular occupations. Both are related; both raise some disturbing questions about the future trends in work in America.

The first problem is that, though the growth of the service economy has generated millions of new jobs (and at a fairly rapid pace — faster, indeed, than in many other industrial countries), too many of these jobs have been poor ones, with low pay, poor working conditions, and little security or chance for advancement. Between 1950 and 1976, according to the economist Eli Ginzberg, the American economy produced about 2.5 times as many jobs in industries with below-average wages as it did in industries paying above the average (Ginzberg, 1977, p. 47). About three out of every five jobs created in this period were in two industries, retail trade and services, alone. These two industries also accounted for more than 70 percent of new jobs in private industry from 1973 to 1980. Most of these new jobs have been in just three specific categories: eating and drinking places, health services, and what the Labor Department calls business services (a broad category that includes everything from photocopying to data processing to janitorial work). In these three areas, as Emma Rothschild notes, employment in the 1970s grew *16 times* as fast as in the goods-producing sectors of the economy. The increase in the number of people working in eating and drinking places from 1973 to 1980 was greater than the *total* number working in the auto and steel industries combined at the end of the 1970s (Rothschild, 1981, pp. 12–13).

The problem is that these are often some of the worst jobs in the service economy. Eating and drinking places pay the lowest wages of any American industry; the work, like that in retail trade, is often part time and offers few chances for promotion. And this trend toward the creation of more poor jobs than good ones is expected to continue at least through the near future. According to the Labor Department, by 1990 there will be more than 4 million new jobs in private medical care (mainly in poorly paid occupations like hospital aides and nursing-home workers) and another 5 million in retail trade (especially in fast-food restaurants, food stores, and department stores) (Currie, Dunn and Fogarty, 1982, p. 98).

Not all jobs in the emerging service economy are poor ones, of course. The service economy includes not only dishwashers and fast-food cashiers, but also doctors, social workers, and systems analysts. Nevertheless, the *typical* workplace of the modern service society is not the computer analyst's or doctor's office, but the fast-food franchise, the hospital kitchen, and the "convenience" store. Many of these jobs are in small enterprises that operate with low profit margins in a fiercely competitive environment. Only rarely do they offer the protections and amenities that workers traditionally achieved in the more stable, more unionized, and more profitable primary sector of the economy. According to one estimate, almost 69 percent of small firms with fewer than 20 employees went out of business over a recent seven-year period (Gordon, 1979, pp. 54–55). Another study suggests that between 7 and 8 percent of jobs in very small businesses are lost each year (Greene, 1982, p. 109).

The much-celebrated postindustrial economy, in short, turns out to be heavily (though by no means entirely) made up of jobs that, far from offering unprecedented challenges and rewards, more often provide only low-paid dead-end work that can neither support a family, provide for the future, nor engage the mind. And there is troubling evidence that the growth of automation may aggravate this trend.

The Uncertain Impact of Automation

The rapid emergence of sophisticated microelectronic technology, it's widely agreed, will help speed the transformation of American society toward a service-based economy. But how much, and in exactly what ways, this will affect the kind of work we do is an open question. Some argue that this "second industrial revolution" will improve both the quality and, at least in the long run, the quantity of work. Like the earlier technological transformation of agriculture, it's argued, automation in industry will increasingly enable workers to move from dull and perhaps dangerous jobs into more sophisticated and interesting ones — improving workers' lives and the productivity of the economy at the same time. Those who take this view also usually argue that fear of massive loss of jobs through the new automation is groundless; "there is ample historical evidence," one enthusiast writes, "that automation in the past has led to greater employment" (Vedder, 1982, p. 25).

Automation and Job Skills

A closer look, however, again suggests that things aren't that simple. To begin with, like the growth of the "service" economy, it's by no means clear that the overall effect of new technological development has upgraded the quality of work in America. In fact, there is much evidence that the opposite has occurred. The introduction of new technology in the American workplace has often led to what the economic historian Harry Braverman has called the "degradation" of work: eliminating or modifying many jobs with traditionally high skills and replacing them (if at all) with less skilled, more routine and alienating ones (Braverman, 1974; Zimbalist, 1979). Though

Robots have begun to re-place workers in many industries.

these new jobs are sometimes called white-collar work, there's little evidence that many of them involve greater skills than the jobs they've replaced in the factory and on the farm. As one critic describes the "growing routinization of clerical and sales work":

> In modern fast-food outlets, for instance, the cash register keys that clerks punch are marked only by pictures of hamburgers, french fries, milk shakes, and the like. Clerks punch the order in pictures, not prices, and the register does all the numerical computing. (Lucy, 1980, p. 83)

This process has also occurred within many formerly high-skill jobs such as printing, machining, and other crafts. Job satisfaction has generally been high in these jobs, and workers have traditionally enjoyed substantial control over their working conditions. The introduction of electronic technology has often lowered the skills needed in these jobs, simultaneously reducing work-ers' job satisfaction and control of the work process (Wallace and Kalleberg,

1982). A description in *Newsweek* of a highly automated jet-engine components plant operated by General Electric illustrates what this process has done to the jobs of skilled machinists:

> Computer-aided design terminals send exacting engineering specifications from distant parts of the country while digital information orders inventories, controls automatic warehouses, keeps records and precisely regulates 137 numerically controlled lathes, milling machines, and drills. . . . It used to take someone three to ten years to become fully qualified as a machinist. GE now can train its Wilmington workers in six months. (*Newsweek*, October 19, 1982b, p. 81)

As automated production methods reach more and more industries, more and more skilled jobs may undergo the same transformation.

At the same time, it's also true that new high-tech industries have created many jobs that *do* require high-level skills — jobs for computer specialists, technicians, engineers, and others. It's difficult to sort out the net impact of these contradictory developments on skill levels in the economy as a whole. One recent analysis concludes that, overall, the distribution of skills in American industry has narrowed — that there has been a decline in both extremely high-skilled jobs and in the lowest-skilled ones, and a corresponding growth of jobs requiring middle-level skills (Rumberger, 1981).

Automation and Unemployment

If the new technology's potential impact on the *quality* of work is still uncertain, its impact on the *quantity* of work is even more so. There is no question that, in the short run, some kinds of jobs in certain key industries have already been hard hit by automation. The American Society of Manufacturing Engineers estimates that half of all auto assembly will be done by automated machines by 1995. Another study estimates that by the 1990s it will be technically possible to replace almost *all* semiskilled manufacturing workers in the auto, electrical equipment, machinery, and fabricated-metal industries — all bastions of relatively well-paid blue-collar employment — through automation and robotics (Levitan and Johnson, 1982, p. 12). A recent analysis by the National Science Foundation warns that rapid automation in the textile industry in response to foreign competition could cost the jobs of 400,000 workers by 1990 (*San Francisco Chronicle*, May 3, 1983). Many factors (including the depressed state of the economy as a whole and a sluggish rate of investment in these basic industries) might slow this trend, but they are unlikely to stop it.

Beyond the immediate impact on blue-collar jobs looms the threat that automation could soon eliminate millions of jobs in those areas of the economy — especially clerical office work — that have been the main sources of new livelihoods in recent years, the heart of the emerging service economy itself. According to one estimate, the new computer-based technologies that make up what the electronics companies like to call the "office of the future" may affect at least 20 to 30 million white-collar jobs by 1990 (Levitan and Johnson, 1982, p. 12).

But it is much more difficult to predict what effect these trends will have in the longer run. According to rough projections by the Bureau of Labor Statistics, automation may cause job *growth* in almost as many occupations as job *loss*. Table 8-3 lists 33 occupations, employing roughly 8 million people at the end of the 1970s, which will be adversely affected by automation. Note that these are by no means all low-skilled "rote" jobs; some are, but others have traditionally offered opportunities for skilled work, both blue and white collar. On the other hand, the table also lists 26 occupations,

Table 8-3

Occupations expected to be adversely or positively affected by automation

Adversely affected occupations	Positively affected occupations
Boiler tenders	Accountants
Bookkeeping workers	Bank clerks
Broadcast technicians	Bank officers and managers
Buyers	Business machine repairers
Cashiers	Ceramic engineers
Central office telephone crafts	Chemical engineers
Credit managers	City managers
Drafters	Computer operators
Electroplaters	Computer programmers
Electrotypers and stereotypers	Computer service technicians
File clerks	Economists
Hotel front office clerks	Electrical engineers
Insurance agents and brokers	Engineering and science technicians
Insurance claim representatives	Industrial engineers
Machine setup workers	Instrument makers (mechanical)
Machine tool operators	Librarians
Molders	Maintenance electricians
Motion picture projectionists	Mathematicians
Office machine operators	Medical record administrators
Photoengravers	Metallurgical engineers
Photographic laboratory occupations	Physicists
Postal clerks	Political scientists
Printing compositors	Sociologists
Production painters	State police
Radio and television announcers	Systems analysts
Railroad brake operators	Technical writers
Railroad conductors	
Railroad locomotive engineers	
Railroad telegraphers, telephoners, and tower operators	
Shipping and receiving clerks	
Stock clerks	
Telephone operators	
Tool-and-die makers	

Source: Adapted from U.S. General Accounting Office, *Advances in Automation Prompt Concern Over Increased U.S. Unemployment* (Washington, D.C.: Government Printing Office, May 1982), pp. 34–35.

almost all computer-related, which should *grow* as a direct or indirect result of automation.

Whether automation will ultimately produce more jobs than it destroys will depend on many factors — including public policy. At present, there are simultaneous pressures in both directions. On the one hand, the modernization of the work process in many industries may make American industry more productive and more competitive in the world market, stimulating enough general economic growth at home to boost the number of jobs. But on the other hand, several forces — including some inherent in the new technology itself — make this outcome less likely.

One of these elements is what is sometimes called the "reproductive potential" of microelectronic technology — the potential for automation *within* the electronics and robotics industries themselves. The possibility of computers being increasingly able to program themselves and of "robots building robots" is a qualitatively new development in modern industry. It may sharply curtail job growth even in the heart of the high-tech industries, even assuming strong growth in the economy as a whole (Levitan and Johnson, 1982, p. 12). Another problem is that the new high-tech industries are just as drawn to the lures of cheaper labor costs in foreign countries as other American industries before them. Even the computer-game industry has not been immune, as dramatically illustrated by the Atari corporation's shift of several hundred jobs from California to the Far East in 1983.

It's even less certain that — even granting the most optimistic scenario of economic growth — the emerging high-tech economy will provide livelihoods for the *same* people whose jobs it has eliminated, and will continue to eliminate, in the coming years. The evidence we have so far isn't encouraging. One study of high-tech reindustrialization in New England, for example, by the economists Barry Bluestone and Bennett Harrison (1982, p. 97), shows that most of the workers who lost manufacturing jobs in the region's textile industry did *not* move into high-tech jobs, even though a substantial number of such jobs have been created in New England. Instead, most of the displaced industrial workers moved into lower-paying, often unstable jobs in services or retail trade — or moved out of the labor force altogether. Similarly, studies of typesetters in New York's printing industry who had been displaced by automation found that many remained unemployed for months, retired, or were forced to take poorer jobs much below their former levels of skill and pay (U.S. General Accounting Office, 1982a, pp. 23–24).

What these experiences suggest is that nothing *guarantees* an automatic "adjustment" of the American work force to the emerging technological trends in the workplace. How these trends will affect jobs, skills, and the quality of working life will depend crucially on the policies we develop to guide them. What is the outlook for the intelligent development of policies to shape the impact of the new technology? To approach that question, let's turn now to consider some recent trends in American policies toward work and unemployment.

The Future: Where Will the Jobs Come From?

The problem of jobs is clearly one of the most urgent issues in the American agenda in the 1980s. But despite that urgency, the response to the job crisis has seemed haphazard at best, self-defeating at worst. For the past several years, the main approach of public policy to the problem of unemployment has been to "unleash" the private sector of the economy in the hope that doing so will stimulate business investment, thus creating economic growth and more jobs. Yet, in spite of many efforts to provide incentives to business and the sharp reduction of the government's own role in creating jobs and training and retraining unemployed workers, the problems of unemployment and underemployment remain with us with a vengeance.

The evidence we've presented in this chapter offers several insights into why this impasse has occurred — and why this approach is unlikely to "put America back to work."

One problem is that, as we've seen, even substantial prosperity has not, by itself, been an effective remedy for the most severe problems of unemployment and underemployment in the past. Even if we regain strong economic growth in the future, there is little reason to believe that the benefits will "trickle down" sufficiently to reverse this pattern. Overall economic growth *does* benefit many disadvantaged workers. One study estimates that with every drop of one percentage point in the national unemployment rate, the unemployment rate for white men heading poverty families falls 1.3 percent, for black men 1.6 percent. But we've seen that hard-core youth and adult unemployment, as well as the underemployment of the extremely disadvantaged, tend to persist even during the upswings of the economic cycle — and so do the disparities in joblessness between minority and white (Bendick, 1982, p. 252).

This problem is made much more acute by the impact of deindustrialization on some of the traditional paths to decent jobs for the less skilled. The automobile, steel, and other basic industries once provided a crucial source of jobs for low-skilled workers; when the economy expanded, these industries pulled in many otherwise hard to employ people and put them to work at good wages. The increasing automation of these basic industries threatens to close off these traditional avenues for jobs and income even if these industries enjoy a strong recovery. As the Nobel Prize winning economist Wassily Leontieff has pointed out, even large investments in reindustrialization are unlikely to generate the numbers of jobs that similar investments once did. A new copper smelter costing $450 million, Leontieff points out, employs just 50 workers per shift (Leontieff, 1982, pp. 190–191).

The Limits of Conventional "Growth"

Even an extraordinary spurt of economic growth under these circumstances will not, by itself, create new, good jobs and the necessary retraining for workers displaced from blue-collar industrial jobs; nor is it likely to offer much hope for an unemployed teenager in the inner city or a subemployed woman heading a family with preschool children.

The impact of automation on industry's capacity to create jobs is just one part of an even larger problem — the decreasing connection between investment and job creation in the American economy. As we've seen, many large corporations have used the capital they already possess *not* to build job-producing plants or to refurbish old ones, but often to buy other, typically unrelated businesses — a process that rarely creates jobs and sometimes destroys them. When corporations *have* invested in labor-intensive production, it has often been in foreign countries where labor costs are much cheaper. In the absence of some means of controlling where and how these corporations may invest the fruits of tax reductions and other business incentives, it is not clear that even substantial economic growth will generate many new American jobs (Gordon, 1979).

On the other hand, it's equally unclear that small businesses will be able to supply what the large corporations won't. There is some evidence that small businesses may be better at generating jobs than larger ones, but the jobs they do create are most often both poorly paid and insecure. So the stubborn problems of underemployment and the trend toward a prolifera-

---

Education and Jobs: The Declining Returns of Schooling

The idea that a good education will lead to a good job is solidly engrained in our national culture, and is partly borne out by statistics. As Table 8-4 shows, there is a clear relationship between levels of schooling and the risks of unemployment. For all races, increases in formal schooling are almost invariably accompanied by reduced unemployment rates. Other data bear out the same point. People with only one to three years of high school were about 15 percent of the labor force in 1980 but were 30 percent of the unemployed. People with four or more years of college, meanwhile, were about 18 percent of the labor force but less than 6 percent of the unemployed (*Statistical Abstract of the U.S., 1981*, p. 385).

A recent analysis by the General Accounting Office argues that inadequate education is the *most* significant contributor to hard-core youth unemployment and underemployment. The General Accounting Office estimated that of roughly 1 million disadvantaged youth aged 16 to 19 who required serious help in the labor market, at least 44 percent had severe educational deficiencies — and a substantial proportion were illiterate (U.S. General Accounting Office, 1982a).

These facts lend support to the often-expressed view that much of the job problem results from a mismatch between poorly educated jobseekers and increasingly sophisticated jobs. In turn, this implies that the best way to attack the job problem is through better education and training.

But — even though these links between schooling and jobs are real ones — there is another side to the story, one that suggests grave limits to a strategy of attacking unemployment and underemployment *mainly* through education and training. It is increasingly apparent that edution of inadequate jobs in the lower reaches of the service economy are unlikely to be much affected even by a rapid growth in the small-business sector of the economy (Gordon, 1979; Birch, 1982).

Given these dilemmas, it seems logical for the government to take on a larger role through expanded job-creation and training programs. Some studies estimate that, per dollar spent, a public jobs program specifically targeted to the long-term unemployed would create *twice* as many jobs as would "trickle down" from a general cut in taxes designed to stimulate business (Bendick, 1982, p. 258). But the main thrust of recent social policy has been in the opposite direction. The government's role in employment and training was dramatically reduced in the early 1980s. Two main arguments helped justify that reduction: First, that private employers would do better at hiring the kinds of people who were served by public employment and training programs than the government itself; second, that the programs themselves were little more than costly and ineffective make-work. But the evidence does not bear out either argument.

The record of private employers in taking up the slack left by the demise of government employment and training programs for the jobless and disadvantaged has not been impressive.

The Reduction of Employment and Training Programs

cation is no guarantee of a good job — or even of a job at all — and that Americans, especially young Americans, may be increasingly *over*educated in relation to the jobs they will hold.

One disturbing sign is that the educational level of the American labor force has *risen* steadily throughout the past decade, simultaneously with the rise of unemployment. Between 1970 and 1982, the proportion of American workers with less than four years of high school was cut almost in half, while the jobless rate nearly doubled. This trend is expected to continue, with the 1990s seeing sharp declines in the proportion of the work force who have less than a high school education and a continuing rise in the proportion having four or more years of college (Table 8-5).

Increasingly, even a college education is no certain protection against unemployment, as most college students are well aware. This is most apparent for black college students; a closer look at Table 8-4 shows that blacks with some college,

in 1982, had an unemployment rate roughly equal to whites with an *elementary school* education or less. But college is no longer a guarantee of a decent job for graduates of any race. During the 1950s and 1960s, college attendance expanded dramatically and, in general, so did the demand for college-educated labor. But in the 1970s, "the labor market for the educated underwent a major, unprecedented downturn" (Freeman, 1976, p. 2), especially for *new* college graduates. This decline is reflected, in part, in growing numbers of graduates forced to take jobs outside the professional and managerial areas their training led them to expect. In 1958 just 10 percent of new college graduates were employed in nonprofessional, nonmanagerial jobs; by 1972 more than 30 percent of male and 25 percent of female graduates were (Freeman, 1976, p. 5). In 1966, 81 percent of women college graduates were working in professional and technical jobs; in 1978 just 65 percent were. Meanwhile the proportion of women college graduates working in *clerical* jobs

© Paul Conklin

Employment and training programs brought benefits for the economy as a whole as well as for participants.

rose from about 10 to 15 percent (Rumberger, 1981, p. 14).

By the 1970s new college graduates also began to face *higher*-than-average unemployment rates, reversing a long tradition. In 1972, when the national unemployment rate was about 5.5 percent, the rate for graduates of the class of 1972 was more than 9 percent — and it was far higher for graduates in some fields. Those who had majored in humanities and social sciences had unemployment rates of more than 15 percent (Freeman, 1976, p. 7). And these Depression-level rates of joblessness continued for some new graduates into the 1980s.

What happened to the once-glowing job prospects for college graduates? Part of the explanation lies in the generally poor performance of the economy during the 1970s and early 1980s. But another part reflects a growing disparity between the still-increasing numbers of college-trained workers and a labor market no longer providing the same mix of jobs as in the recent past. During

the 1950s and 1960s, the demand for college graduates was fueled by the expansion of jobs in government, education, and certain key industries (such as aerospace and electronic computing) that called for large numbers of highly trained professionals, and by the growth of spending on research and development. During the 1970s, however, the rapid growth rates in what the economist Richard Freeman calls the "college-intensive" parts of the economy slowed markedly relative to the growth in those sectors traditionally employing fewer graduates. Sharp cuts in the growth of federal employment and in education are especially crucial parts of this shift (Freeman, 1976, pp. 17–18).

The declining value of the college degree in the labor market, however, is only the most dramatic expression of a more widespread problem of "overeducation" — or, more accurately, of underutilization of educational skills — throughout the economy. In 1977 more than a third of working adults described themselves as having skills

As we noted earlier in the chapter, efforts to lure private business to hire the disadvantaged — through subsidies, tax credits, and other incentives — have not been successful in the past. Studies show that business involvement in such efforts has usually been minimal. In many cases, employers have used the subsidies to pay workers they had hired already or would have hired even without the subsidy, thus defeating the aim of creating new jobs. Such programs can only be effective, it's widely agreed, if employers are genuinely willing to add new and sometimes difficult workers to their present work force; but there is considerable evidence that most regard the costs of hiring, training, and keeping these workers as simply too high (Ripley and Franklin, 1981).

The fate of disadvantaged workers who lost their jobs as a result of the cutbacks in federal job programs in the early 1980s affirms this point. According to government studies of about 300,000 workers who lost public jobs in the spring and summer of 1981, only about 45 percent were reemployed by October. And of those officially working, only a little more than half held regular full-time jobs; the rest did part-time or temporary work. Moreover, only half of those who *were* employed had been hired by private business, the rest by public agencies or nonprofit organizations. Several months after the elimination of these programs, then, the private economy had *not* succeeded in putting more than a fraction of these people into pro-

that they were unable to use in their jobs (Rumberger, 1981, p. 17). The relatively unchanging skill requirements of most American jobs coupled with rising educational attainment means that overeducation has strongly increased during the past two decades. Though the problem has been worst for the more highly educated, it reaches high school graduates as well: Today, "even workers with a high school education hold jobs incommensurate with their level of training" (Rumberger, 1981, p. 17).

Indeed, even the least-skilled workers may be overtrained for many jobs, especially the kinds of jobs usually available to youth. One study of what young workers actually *did* at work found that many "were almost never required to read, write, or use arithmetic skills on the job":

Most spent their time cleaning or carrying objects; interaction with others was limited. . . . It has been suggested that for many young jobseekers, filling out a job application may actually re-

quire more literary skills than doing the job. (Wrigley, 1982, p. 247)

The underutilization of abilities leads to widespread job dissatisfaction, especially among the most overeducated but also among those with little education who are nevertheless confined in jobs that require virtually no use of their minds (Rumberger, 1981, p. 105). And it wastes precious skills in jobs of low productivity and little economic value. But — barring either significant declines in the proportion of American youth who choose to engage in extended schooling, or substantial increases in the number of jobs calling for high skills — the indications are that the mismatch between education and jobs can only worsen in the future.

ductive work; for many, the result was the replacement of work by welfare dependency (Bendick, 1982, p. 256; U.S. General Accounting Office, 1982c).

But aren't government job programs useless "make-work"? No one argues that all of these programs have been efficient, well-run, or carefully designed. But there is a large body of evidence that some achieved impor-

Labor force status and years of schooling	Race		
	Whites	Blacks	Hispanics
Population, total	95,479	11,429	6,058
Elementary: 8 years or less	9,067	1,959	2,274
High school: 1–3 years	11,113	2,456	855
4 years only	39,606	4,154	1,728
College: 1–3 years	16,104	1,752	707
4 years or more	19,590	1,109	494
Labor force, total	71,632	8,318	4,272
Elementary: 8 years or less	5,119	1,056	1,357
High school: 1–3 years	7,244	1,580	562
4 years only	29,433	3,181	1,343
College: 1–3 years	12,768	1,486	592
4 years or more	17,067	1,016	417
Labor-force participation rate	75.0	72.8	70.5
Elementary: 8 years or less	56.5	53.9	59.7
High school: 1–3 years	65.2	64.3	65.7
4 years only	74.3	76.6	77.7
College: 1–3 years	79.3	84.8	83.7
4 years or more	87.1	91.6	84.4
Unemployed, total	4,904	1,159	460
Elementary: 8 years or less	653	158	203
High school: 1–3 years	851	221	90
4 years only	2,238	522	107
College: 1–3 years	691	187	41
4 years or more	472	72	20
Unemployment rate	6.8	13.9	10.8
Elementary: 8 years or less	12.8	15.0	15.0
High school: 1–3 years	11.7	14.0	16.0
4 years only	7.6	16.4	8.0
College: 1–3 years	5.4	12.6	6.9
4 years or more	2.8	7.1	4.8

Source: U.S. Bureau of Labor Statistics, *Education Level of the Labor Force Continues to Rise* (Washington, D.C.: Government Printing Office, 1982), table 2.

Years of schooling completed	Percent completing		
	1972	1978	1990 (projected)
11 or less	34.1	26.5	19.9
12–15	52.3	56.6	58.5
16 or more	13.6	16.9	21.7

Source: Marcia Freedman, "The Structure of the Labor Market and Associated Training Patterns," in National Society for the Study of Education, *Education and Work* (Chicago: University of Chicago Press, 1982), p. 84. Reprinted with permission.

Table 8-5
More education for fewer jobs? Educational attainment of the civilian labor force 16 years and over, 1972, 1978, and 1990 (projected)

tant successes in jobs and improved earnings, especially for the *most* seriously disadvantaged, for women, and for those with very poor job histories (U.S. General Accounting Office, 1982b). Often, such programs have provided strong benefits to the economy as a whole as well as to the individuals participating in them. The Job Corps program (an intensive skill training program for the most severely disadvantaged youth), for example, brought benefits per participant that exceeded its costs by 45 percent (Bendick, 1982, pp. 260–261).

In the short run, such programs are expensive. In the long run, they offer substantial savings in reduced welfare costs, higher productivity, and lower social pathology. But whether the long-term vision will prevail is an open question. The same tension between short- and long-term goals runs through many other areas of American social policy, including health and medical care, energy use, and environmental quality — areas we will now explore.

Summary

This chapter has examined work in America as a social problem. Both the critical problem of unemployment and the question of the future of work in America have become more urgent issues with the recurrent economic stagnation of recent years.

The problem of unemployment is deepening in many ways. Jobless rates in the early 1980s reached levels not seen since the Great Depression; ominously, unemployment rates haven't fallen as low during periods of economic recovery.

Though unemployment and underemployment touch all corners of American society, three groups have been especially hard hit; jobless youth (especially minority youth); disadvantaged, underemployed adults; and workers displaced from declining industries.

Many common explanations for the unemployment problem — that the unemployed don't want to work, that the minimum wage or social benefits keep them out of jobs, and that teenagers, women, or illegal aliens take away many jobs — are not supported by the evidence.

Despite glowing predictions, the transition from the production of goods to the production of services in the "post-industrial" economy has not necessarily upgraded the quality of work in America.

The advance of automation in the workplace has eliminated millions of jobs. Whether continued advances in workplace technology will create or destroy jobs, on balance, is uncertain.

Simply stimulating the growth of the private economy, the strategy most often proposed for dealing with the job problem, will not suffice by itself. Private investment no longer leads necessarily to good jobs; partly because of automation, and partly because the jobs it does create are often either in foreign countries or, if in the United States, poorly-paid and unstable ones.

For Further Reading

American Assembly. *Youth Unemployment and Public Policy*. Englewood Cliffs, N.J.: Prentice-Hall, 1980.

Braverman, Harry. *Labor and Monopoly Capital: The Degradation of Work in the Twentieth Century*. New York: Monthly Review Press, 1974.

Gordon, David. *The Working Poor: Towards a State Agenda*. Washington, D.C.: Council of State Planning Agencies, 1979.

Levitan, Sar A., and Clifford M. Johnson. *Second Thoughts on Work*. Kalamazoo, Mich.: W. E. Upjohn Institute, 1982.

Maurer, Harry. *Not Working*. New York: Penguin, 1980.

Scientific American. Special Issue on "Mechanization of Work." September 1982.

9

Health: Gains and Losses

Health care in America has long been the focus of intense controversy. Few things tell more about a society than the level of preventable suffering and disease it is willing to tolerate. During the 1960s we discovered that in this regard, as in so many others, American society contained some disturbing paradoxes. As citizens of the most affluent society in the world, Americans had access to some of the best health care money could buy. And as a result of our generally rising living standards and the onrush of formidable new medical technologies, we seemed to be on the verge of conquering forever many of the most feared diseases of the past.

But there was an underside to this progress. It was perhaps most vividly demonstrated when a group of physicians toured some impoverished areas of the rural South in 1967 and found children who showed startling levels of malnutrition, preventable disease — and even the effects of starvation. The doctors concluded that the children were "living under such primitive conditions that we found it hard to believe we were examining American children of the twentieth century" (quoted in Amidei, 1981, p. 458). Meanwhile, similar conditions were found in the inner-city ghettos of the North.

The discovery of the tragic paradox of starvation in the midst of affluence and of traditional, avoidable diseases side by side with the most advanced medical technology helped spur a commitment to government action to reduce some of the harshest inequalities in health care. And that commitment brought substantial results. The poor, minorities, many of the aged, and others who had been largely excluded from the benefits of modern medicine and nutrition were brought within their reach. The gap between their health status and that of the more affluent began to narrow —

so much so that, by the end of the 1970s, a prominent health scholar could write that "with respect to the most precious good of all, life itself, the United States is approaching an egalitarian distribution" (Fuchs, 1979, p. 6).

But there were other disturbing discoveries as well. By the late 1960s, it was becoming frighteningly clear that many health problems were linked to technological changes that affected the environment, the workplace, and the consumer products that represented the fruits of the affluent society. Whether it was the discovery of miners crippled by black lung disease, or the threat of cancer in food dyes and preservatives, or of leukemia and neurological damage from poisonous industrial wastes, we were fast learning that the economic growth we had taken for granted had its fearful costs as well as its obvious benefits. Most Americans, to be sure, were getting a bigger share of the economic pie. But the pie, as some put it, was increasingly toxic.

Once again, the response was a new commitment on the part of government — in this case, a commitment to exert some control over the dangers lurking in the air, the water, the shop floor, and the supermarket shelves. And like the commitment to narrowing inequalities in health care, it bore fruit in more stringent control of the hazards of work and consumption.

But, by the end of the 1970s, we began to hear that we had gone overboard in an overzealous concern for occupational and consumer health. Government regulations were seen as stifling productivity and crippling economic growth. In an ironic twist, it was even argued that regulation of industrial and environmental health hazards would make people sicker in the long run by undermining economic growth and thus slowing the rise in living standards, which was ultimately the most significant source of improvements in health (Wildavsky, 1980). As one critic put it, "With today's consumer advocates heading the way, we are heading toward not only zero risk, but zero food, zero jobs, zero energy, and zero growth. It may be that the prophets of doom, not the profits of industry, are the real hazards to our health" (Whelan, 1981, p. 5).

If the government's regulation of workplace and environmental health hazards was often seen as utopian and counterproductive, its spending on health care for the disadvantaged was often regarded as a source of inflation and a general burden on an already strained economy. The proposed remedies that have followed from these views mainly involve reducing the government's role in health care. One thrust is toward dismantling the system of public care for the poor and aged through cuts in public spending. Another is toward relaxing occupational health and safety and consumer-product standards, in the name of restoring both economic efficiency and personal freedom. Still another thrust would place strong constraints on the use of family planning services, in the name of restoring traditional morality.

Beyond these specific targets, the very idea that health ought to be a matter for *social* concern at all — so basic to the health-care policies of the recent past — is now being challenged in fundamental ways. In its place is a tendency to regard health as being mainly an *individual* matter. We are urged to eat better, to jog farther, to abandon our attachment to coffee and cigarettes, to freely express our feelings, and to avoid stress. All of these are surely important aims, and the evidence increasingly shows their strong influence on the chances of good health. But if the mood of the 1960s was to confront the social and economic aspects of health and illness, the mood of the 1980s is often to look narrowly inward and to seek both the sources of ill-health and the prospects for well-being in our own personal life-styles.

This chapter will address these complex issues. We'll begin by examining how far we've come — and how far we still need to go — in achieving a more healthy society. We will look at changes in death rates, life expectancy, and infant mortality, and in the incidence of serious diseases. And we will compare our progress with the progress achieved in other industralized societies. We will then look more closely at the health status of several specific groups: the poor, minorities, women, and industrial workers. Along the way, we'll touch on the problem of rising health-care costs and on the arguments for and against a national system of health care. In the final part of the chapter, we'll consider some recent trends in our health-care policy in the light of these developments.

The Picture of Health

It is widely agreed that (with some exceptions) the overall health of Americans has improved substantially in the recent past. But the precise extent of that improvement turns out, like so many other social questions, to be surprisingly hard to measure.

Some of what we know about the health status of the population as a whole is derived from interview studies, mainly from a periodic National Health Survey carried out by the National Center for Health Statistics of the U.S. Department of Health and Human Services. Like other data based on interview surveys, these are subject to a variety of biases and misperceptions; but they do provide a useful broad picture of the way most people view their own health. And, on the whole, that view is remarkably positive. Only about 12 percent say that their health is only fair or poor, and about half describe it as excellent. These proportions have even improved slightly since the mid-1970s. Only about 7 percent of the population describe themselves as limited in some major activity because of health problems, and that percentage has changed little in recent years.

Another way of measuring health status is to look at the incidence of specific diseases. Here some of the most important data are gathered from doctors' and hospitals' reports by the Center for Disease Control of the U.S.

In general, Americans are enjoying healthier lives.

Public Health Service. These measures are also subject to problems of interpretation. Increases in the reported rates of a given illness, for example, may mean that more people are getting the disease, or that doctors have come up with a better way of diagnosing it, or that more people who get the disease are willing or able to seek treatment for it. For that matter, they may mean that, because of medical advances, people who get the disease live longer than they did before.

Despite these limitations, the general picture is, again, encouraging, with some exceptions. As Table 9-1 indicates, there has been a spectacular decline in some infectious diseases that were still common even fairly recently. Some, like poliomyelitis and whooping cough, have been virtually eliminated. Others, including measles and tuberculosis, have been dramatically reduced.

Mortality rates (overall rates of death and death rates from specific causes) are probably the most reliable indicators of broad patterns of health and illness. Even these are not infallible; diagnoses of causes of death can be highly subjective and variable. These problems are aggravated, too, when we compare mortality rates across different countries. Nevertheless, these rates do provide a reasonably reliable portrait of trends in health in this country — and how we stack up relative to others.

Table 9-2 shows recent changes in mortality rates for the most important causes of death. These rates are *age-adjusted* to take into account changes in the age composition of the population. Other things equal, an older population will have higher death rates; and since our population is aging, a simple comparison between years would understate the decline in mortality.

Fewer Americans are now dying from most major causes of death than they were 30 years ago. The declines are especially apparent for some of the most deadly diseases of the past. Heart disease mortality has fallen by a third, and deaths from cerebrovascular disease (mainly stroke) by nearly half. Tuberculosis was the eighth largest killer of Americans as late as 1950, but had declined to virtual insignificance by the 1970s. (But the incidence is rising in at least one city; see page 357.) Some parts of the picture are less encouraging, though. Cancer — especially lung cancer — has risen, and so have cirrhosis of the liver (a disease usually associated with alcoholism), homicide (as we will observe in more detail in Chapter 11), and suicide.

The patterns of disease mortality are even more striking if we consider specific age groups rather than the population as a whole. Proportionately, for example, heart disease kills only about half as many men in the age

Table 9-1

Trends in the incidence of selected diseases, 1950–1980 (number of cases per 100,000)

Disease	1950	1960	1965	1970	1975	1980
Diphtheria	3.83	0.51	0.08	0.21	0.14	0.00
Hepatitis A	*	23.15	17.49	27.87	16.82	12.84
Hepatitis B				4.08	6.30	8.39
Measles (rubeola)	211.01	245.42	135.33	23.23	11.44	5.96
Mumps	*	*	*	55.55	27.99	3.86
Pertussis (whooping cough)	79.82	8.23	3.51	2.08	0.82	0.76
Poliomyelitis, total	22.02	1.77	0.04	0.02	0.00	0.00
Paralytic		1.40	0.03	0.02	0.00	0.00
Rubella (German measles)	*	*	*	27.75	7.81	1.72
Tuberculosis†	80.50	30.83	25.33	18.22	15.95	12.25

*Data are not reported nationally.

†Data subsequent to 1974 are not comparable to prior years because of changes in reporting criteria that became effective in 1975.

Source: Adapted from U.S. Department of Health and Human Services, *Health—United States, 1982* (Washington, D.C.: Government Printing Office, 1982), p. 79.

Causes	1950	1960	1970	1975	1979	1980
All causes	841.5	760.9	714.3	638.3	588.8	594.1
Diseases of heart	307.6	286.2	253.6	220.5	203.5	205.3
Cerebrovascular diseases	88.8	79.7	66.3	54.5	42.5	41.5
Malignant neoplasms	125.4	125.8	129.9	130.9	133.2	134.2
Respiratory system	12.8	19.2	28.4	32.5	35.8	36.7
Digestive system	47.7	41.1	35.2	33.6	33.8	33.4
Breast	22.2	22.3	23.1	22.8	22.8	—
Pneumonia and influenza	26.2	28.0	22.1	16.6	11.4	12.6
Chronic liver disease and cirrhosis	8.5	10.5	14.7	13.8	12.2	12.6
Diabetes mellitus	14.3	13.6	14.1	11.6	10.0	10.1
Accidents and adverse effects	57.5	49.9	53.7	44.8	43.7	43.4
Motor vehicle accidents	23.3	22.5	27.4	21.3	23.7	23.7
Suicide	11.0	10.6	11.8	12.6	11.9	12.2
Homicide and legal intervention	5.4	5.2	9.1	10.5	10.4	11.4

Note: Rates are age-adjusted to reflect changes in the age structure of the population.
Source: U.S. Department of Health and Human Services, *Health—United States, 1982* (Washington, D.C.: Government Printing Office, 1982), p. 59.

Table 9-2

Trends in mortality rates, 1950–1980 (deaths per 100,000)

range from 30 to 45 as it did in 1950. Lung cancer, however, killed twice as many — suggesting that *part* of the changed American health picture has been a shift in the *kinds* of diseases most likely to take American lives (U.S. Department of Health and Human Services, 1982a, pp. 107–110).

Another dramatic decline has been in infant mortality, as Figure 9-1 shows. By 1980 considerably less than half as many infants could be expected to die as 30 years before. The sharp decline in the late 1960s and early 1970s — when the infant mortality rate dropped by a third — is especially striking. One recent study puts the magnitude of this change in concrete terms: "More than 21,000 babies survived in 1978 who would have died if the 1970 rate had prevailed, and *52,000* survived who would have died at the 1950 infant mortality rate" (Kovar, 1982, p. 5).

Older children, too, are far less likely to die than they were even in the quite recent past. Death rates for children under 15 dropped at a rate of 3 percent a year during the 1970s. If we go only a little farther back in American history, this change is enormous. Of every 100,000 children aged 1 to 4, 564 died in 1930; 139 in 1950; and just 69 in 1978 (Kovar and Meny, 1981, p. 41).

The Limits of Progress

These are genuinely important strides forward. But a distinctly different side of the picture appears when we compare some key indicators of health in America with those in other industrialized countries. Table 9-3 shows that,

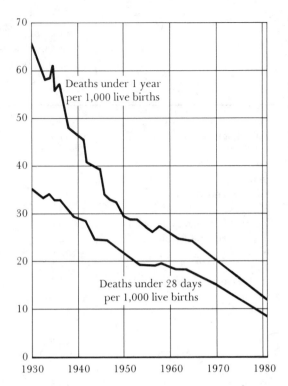

Figure 9-1
Trends in infant mortality,
1930–1981

Source: U.S. National Center for
Health Statistics, *Monthly Vital
Statistics Report, Annual Summary
of Births, Deaths, Marriages and
Divorces, United States, 1981*
(Washington, D.C.: Govern-
ment Printing Office, Decem-
ber 1982), p. 9.

despite the rapid declines in infant mortality, we still lag well behind many industrialized societies. Sweden's infant death rate is only a little more than half of ours. The Japanese, Swiss, Danish, and Dutch rates are also far below ours. In concrete terms, this means that if we had the same infant mortality rate as Sweden, about 20,000 fewer babies would die in America every year.

As we'll see, infant death rates in this country are crucially affected by race. But it is important to realize that America's problem of infant mortal-ity goes beyond race as well — even the *white* rate of infant death in the United States is higher than the rates in much of Western Europe and Japan.

Our high rates of infant mortality are a major reason why (as Table 9-4 shows) Americans' life expectancy, especially for men, is somewhat lower than that of people in many other industrial societies. Life expectancy at birth is a tricky statistic; it represents an average of the chances of dying at any point in the life cycle. Thus, the fact that an American male at birth, at the end of the 1970s, could expect to live almost four years less than a Japanese and three years less than a Swede largely reflects the much higher chance that the American male might die during his first year. But these differences also persist through childhood and adolescence into young adult-hood. In the mid-1970s, an American girl aged 1 to 4 had nearly twice the chance of dying as a Swedish girl those ages; a young American woman

Table 9-3

Infant mortality rates, selected countries, 1973–1978

Country*	Infant mortality rate (infant deaths per 1,000 live births)		Average annual percent change 1973–78
	1973	1978†	
Canada	15.5	12.4	–5.4
United States	17.7	13.8	–4.9
Austria	23.8	15.0	–8.8
Denmark	11.5	8.9	–5.0
England and Wales	16.9	13.1	–5.0
France	15.5	10.6	–7.3
German Democratic Republic	15.6	13.2	–3.3
German Federal Republic	22.7	14.7	–8.3
Ireland	18.0	15.6	–3.5
Italy	25.7	17.7	–8.9
Netherlands	11.5	9.6	–3.5
Sweden	9.9	7.8	–4.7
Switzerland	13.2	8.6	–8.2
Israel	22.8	17.2	–5.5
Japan	11.3	8.4	–5.8
Australia	16.5	12.5	–6.7
New Zealand	16.2	14.2	–3.2

*Countries are grouped by continent.

†Data for Canada, Ireland, Italy, Australia, and New Zealand refer to 1977; data for Denmark and France are provisional.

Source: Adapted from U.S. Department of Health and Human Services, *Health—United States, 1982* (Washington, D.C.: Government Printing Office, 1982), p. 57.

aged 15 to 24 had almost twice the chance of death faced by a young British woman (Sidel and Sidel, 1977, p. 12).

Comparing death rates for specific causes among different countries is somewhat risky, too, since there are often slight differences among them in defining and reporting disease. But some broad patterns are unmistakable. On balance, our standing relative to other industralized societies is mixed, at best. Our death rates from cancer and stroke are in the average range, even better, perhaps, for stroke. But our death rates from heart disease and accidents are exceptionally high. Again, too, these *overall* rates mask the tragic fact that Americans are much more likely to be felled by serious disease (particularly heart disease) at relatively *younger* ages. American men in their late 30s and early 40s, for example, were almost three times as likely to die of cardiovascular disease as Swedish men the same age during the 1970s (Sidel and Sidel, 1977, p. 19).

Country*	Life expectancy in years					
	Males			Females		
	1973†	1978‡	Average annual change in years	1973†	1978‡	Average annual change in years
Canada	69.5	70.5	0.3	77.0	78.2	0.3
United States	67.6	69.5	0.4	75.3	77.2	0.4
Austria	67.4	68.4	0.2	74.7	75.7	0.2
Denmark	71.1	71.7	0.1	76.6	77.7	0.2
England and Wales	69.2	70.2	0.3	75.5	76.3	0.2
France	69.5	69.9	0.1	77.3	77.9	0.2
German Democratic Republic	68.9	68.9	—	74.2	74.5	0.1
German Federal Republic	67.8	69.2	0.3	74.4	76.0	0.3
Ireland	68.5	69.0	0.2	73.4	74.3	0.3
Italy	68.9	69.8	0.3	75.2	76.1	0.3
Netherlands	71.2	72.0	0.2	77.2	78.7	0.3
Sweden	72.1	72.5	0.1	77.7	79.0	0.3
Switzerland	71.1	72.0	0.2	77.2	78.9	0.3
Israel§	70.2	71.6	0.3	73.2	75.1	0.4
Japan	70.9	73.2	0.5	76.3	78.6	0.5
Australia	68.3	70.0	0.4	75.3	77.0	0.4
New Zealand	69.2	69.4	0.1	74.8	75.6	0.2

*Countries are grouped by continent.
†Data for the German Democratic Republic refer to the average for the period 1969–70; data for Ireland and Italy refer to 1972.
‡Data for Ireland and Italy refer to 1975; data for France, German Democratic Republic, and New Zealand refer to 1976; data for Canada, England and Wales, and Australia refer to 1977.
§Jewish population only for 1973.
Source: U.S. Department of Health and Human Services, *Health—United States, 1982* (Washington, D.C.: Government Printing Office, 1982), p. 58.

Table 9-4
Life expectancy at birth and average annual change in years, by sex; selected countries, 1973 and 1978

All things considered, then, there has been substantial progress — but there are still formidable problems. And the diseases and disabilities that are increasing tend to be ones that have been linked to the stresses of modern social and economic life (like cirrhosis and accidents) or (like cancer) to some of the massive environmental changes that have accompanied our techno-logical and economic development. These problems take on clearer shape when we begin to look at how health and health care in America vary among different groups.

As we'll see, these differences are pervasive and often striking. And they show, more clearly than any other evidence, how deeply the problems of health and disease are *social* as well as medical problems. Our chances of suffering disease, accident, or early death, despite important improvements in recent years, still depend very much on whether we are born into affluent families or poor ones, whether we are minority or white, male or female, blue-collar industrial workers or professionals. And though some of these differences, particularly *some* of those between men and women, result from factors over which society has little or no control, others reflect choices about the organization of our social life: the inequalities of income, race, and gender we tolerate (or encourage); the attitude we take toward the regulation of workplace hazards; and the social priority we place, or fail to place, on the prevention of disease.

Health Care and the Poor: How Much Progress?

The 1960s brought a new commitment to improving the health of the poor. The Medicaid program, which amounted to only half a billion dollars in 1960, rose to about 23 billion dollars by 1979. It's generally agreed that this expansion in care for the disadvantaged has narrowed the gap in health status between the poor and the more affluent. But how much remains?

At the end of the 1970s, a noted medical economist declared that "other things being equal, there is no longer any systematic effect of income on health" (Fuchs, 1979, p. 5). Two years later, another group of researchers stated flatly that "despite some improvements in health status, the poor are significantly sicker than the nonpoor" (K. Davis, Gold, and Makuc, 1981, p. 60).

Which assessment is correct? Evaluating just how equal the health of Americans has become is complicated by the lack of reliable measures (mortality rates, for example, are not usually broken down by income level) and also by some stubborn problems of interpretation. It is difficult, for example, to separate the effects of low income on health from the often simultaneous effects of low education or poor personal care. And since health status doubtless affects an individual's (or family's) level of income, just as income affects the chances of health or illness, it is often difficult to pinpoint the direction in which the relationship runs. Someone who is chronically ill may be unable to work or at least unable to keep a demanding, and hence well-paying, job; at the same time, the illness may be related to a number of typical accompaniments of low income: inadequate nutrition, inferior medical care, and poor sanitation. Teasing out these relationships from the broad-brush data usually available isn't easy. But several points do seem clear.

Poor people, for example, report that their health is only fair or poor, or that they are limited in activity by some chronic illness or disability, about *three times* as often as people with incomes more than double the official poverty level (K. Davis, Gold, and Makuc, 1981, p. 162). Between one-fourth and one-fifth of people in low-income families suffer limited activity because of illness or disability, as compared to less than one-tenth in high-income families (Fingerhut, Wilson, and Feldman, 1981, p. 26). (This is an age-adjusted figure, moreover, which cancels out the possibility that this link is due to the large proportion of older people living in poverty.)

These differences *could* reflect the impact of illness on the ability to earn a good living, rather than the other way around. But the same relationship between income and health holds, though somewhat less strongly, for children — for whom the effects of poor health on income are, obviously, less significant. Though even most poor children are rated by the parents as in good to excellent health, they are twice as likely as the national average to be judged as having some health problems (Kovar, 1982, p. 9).

A recent study by the sociologist Robert Mare (1982) of childhood deaths (see Table 9-5) provides further evidence of the independent effect of low income on poor health. Mare found that the differences in the risks of death for children according to their families' income level are at least as great as those for adults, mainly because of a much higher risk of death by accidents faced by lower-income children.

Better health care for low-income people has substantially reduced the risk of those illnesses and disabilities considered most susceptible to improvement through increased medical attention: infant and maternal mortality, influenza and pneumonia, some kinds of cancer (such as breast and cervical cancer) that are often curable with early detection, diabetes, and cerebrovascular disease (K. Davis and Schoen, 1978, p. 18). But many of these diseases still remain disproportionately afflictions of the poor. Diabetes is a clear example: It is the ninth leading cause of death in the United States, and its incidence is sharply divided along lines of income and education. Figure 9-2 shows that the diabetes rate of the very poor is double that for people of moderate means or better.

The disparities in health status also show up as sharp regional differences in health. People who live in wealthier states are healthier than those in traditionally poorer ones, despite considerable improvement in the quality of health care, especially in the South and other predominantly rural states. Infant mortality is a strong example. Even considering only white infants (to cancel out, for the moment, the strong effects of race on infant death), the poorer states remain badly behind. A white baby in West Virginia, for instance, has almost half again the chance of dying before its first birthday as one born in some New England states (U.S. Department of Health and Human Services, 1982, p. 55).

How do we explain these continuing inequalities? One line of thought puts the emphasis on differences in *education* (and, by implication, on differ-

	Mother's schooling	Annual family income		
		Less than $10,000 (percent)	$10,000 or more (percent)	Total (percent)
Males				
0–9 years	Less than 12 years	2.16	2.14	2.15
	More than 12 years	2.09	1.62	1.74
	Total	2.45	1.70	1.96
10–19 years	Less than 12 years	4.64	2.87	3.68
	More than 12 years	2.75	1.99	2.13
	Total	3.74	2.18	2.59
Females				
0–9 years	Less than 12 years	1.54	1.69	1.60
	More than 12 years	1.77	1.04	1.23
	Total	1.67	1.13	1.32
10–19 years	Less than 12 years	1.98	2.16	2.08
	More than 12 years	2.10	1.48	1.59
	Total	2.04	1.63	1.74

Source: Adapted from Robert Mare, "Socioeconomic Effects on Child Mortality," *American Journal of Public Health*, June 1982, p. 543. Reprinted with permission of American Public Health Association.

Table 9-5

Income inequality and childhood death: percentages of white children dead, by total family income, mother's schooling, years since birth, and sex

ences in personal care and life-style). Evidence that these factors are important comes from studies showing that the level of education achieved by an individual (or, in the case of children, by their parents) has a strong relationship to health status — stronger than income itself. The relationship holds even when income is "controlled"; that is, even relatively well-off children, for example, may have health problems (such as dental problems, obesity, or anemia) if their mothers have had few years of schooling (M. Grossman, 1982, p. 192).

Some writers take this to mean that it is no longer income inequality itself that is responsible for the remaining differences in health between affluent and poor, but the absence of adequate health habits among poor people. At the extreme, this implies that the ill-health of the poor is now, in some sense, "their" problem — that we've done all we can as a society to equalize access to health care, but some people are simply unable to take advantage of that care or to practice elementary methods of prevention (Fuchs, 1979).

Though no one would deny that people do differ in the quality of their attention to their own and their children's health needs, or their understanding of the importance of good nutrition, exercise, and other staples of personal health care, the tendency to regard the health problems of the poor as mainly a result of their own personal failings stretches the evidence consid-

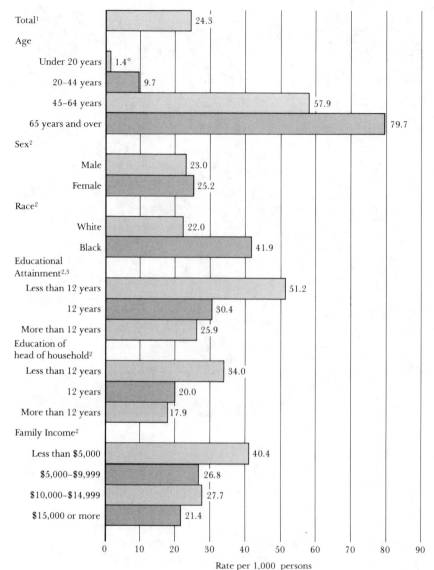

Total[1] — 24.3

Age
Under 20 years — 1.4*
20–44 years — 9.7
45–64 years — 57.9
65 years and over — 79.7

Sex[2]
Male — 23.0
Female — 25.2

Race[2]
White — 22.0
Black — 41.9

Educational Attainment[2,3]
Less than 12 years — 51.2
12 years — 30.4
More than 12 years — 25.9

Education of head of household[2]
Less than 12 years — 34.0
12 years — 20.0
More than 12 years — 17.9

Family Income[2]
Less than $5,000 — 40.4
$5,000–$9,999 — 26.8
$10,000–$14,999 — 27.7
$15,000 or more — 21.4

Rate per 1,000 persons

Figure 9-2

The risk of diabetes in selected groups, 1979

Source: Thomas F. Drury et al., "Prevalence and Management of Diabetes," in U.S. Department of Health and Human Services, *Health — United States, 1981* (Washington, D.C.: Government Printing Office, 1981), p. 26.

[1]Includes all other races not shown separately and those for whom education and family income were unknown.

[2]Age adjusted by the direct method to the 1979 civilian noninstitutionalized population, using four age intervals.

[3]Data for persons 20 years of age and over.

Not everyone is adequately protected by the American health-care system.

erably. The best evidence suggests that *both* income and education have independent impacts on health. Robert Mare's study of childhood deaths, for example, found that both the family's income *and* the mother's years of schooling shaped a child's risks of death (Mare, 1982, pp. 541–543; see also Table 9·5); the same independent effect of low income has been found in the case of high rates of infant mortality among the poor (Gortmaker, 1979).

A great deal of research in the past several years has shown that the incidence and severity of illness are profoundly affected by social and personal stress. And, as a recent review of this evidence makes clear, poverty "constitutes one of the major sources of chronic stress, thereby increasing susceptibility to illness" (Starfield, 1982, p. 533).

Unequal Access to Care

There are other problems with the argument that the health problems of the poor are no longer the result of persistent social inequalities. Most importantly, the central premise of this argument — that people of all income levels now enjoy *equal access* to health care — is, unfortunately, decidedly premature. Despite important changes, "Equity," as a recent study concludes, "— equal access according to need — has not been achieved" (Kovar, 1982, p. 13). Some of the problems:

- Low-income people are about 25 percent of the American population, but are 55 percent of those without medical insurance. The problem is especially severe for the so-called near-poor — those not poor enough to be eligible for subsidized programs like Medicaid but too poor to be able to afford private insurance (Aday, Anderson, and Fleming, 1980).

- Low-income people are less likely to have a regular source of health care or a regular personal physician, and are much more likely to get most or all of their care from hospital emergency rooms or outpatient clinics (K. Davis, Gold, and Makuc, 1981, p. 168).

- Low-income women are far less likely to see a physician in the early stages of pregnancy, and they are also generally less likely to receive other kinds of preventive care. Though periodic exams can greatly reduce the risks of breast and cervical cancer, for example, poor women have far fewer of these exams.

- Low-income children are considerably less likely to have had a skin test for tuberculosis or to have received complete vaccinations against common diseases like measles and polio.

- Low-income people now visit doctors slightly more often than the nonpoor, but this must be seen in light of the fact that they are also *sicker*. When their higher levels of sickness are taken into account, the poor, especially poor children, are underserved relative to the more well off. In one survey, for example, children from families earning less than $5,000 a year and those in families earning more than $15,000 both saw a doctor an average of about four times a year. But measured in terms of the number of days of school lost due to illness, the poor children saw a doctor 46 times for every 100 school days lost, the moderate-income children 77 times (Kovar, 1982, p. 12).

Part of the reason for these continuing disparities lies in the limits of government health programs for the poor. Though Medicaid and other public programs have reduced health-care inequalities considerably, they still failed to reach many of the medically needy, even at their peak in the 1970s. Medicaid actually covers only about a third of America's poor — partly because eligibility is limited mainly to the disabled, the aged, or people in single-parent families, and partly because different states are allowed to set their own (sometimes very low) income eligibility standards. [In Texas, in the late 1970s, a family that earned more than *one-tenth* of the federal poverty level was disqualified for Medicaid benefits (K. Davis, Gold, and Makuc, 1981, p. 175).] Individual states, too, vary widely in the services they actually provide under Medicaid. Many do not cover dental care, eyeglasses, or inpatient psychiatric care for children and youth; several do not even provide hospital emergency care (Budetti, Butler, and McManus, 1981, p. 517).

More than a third of the poor, moreover, live in areas so lacking in accessible health-care facilities that they have great difficulty getting adequate care even if they *are* covered by Medicaid. Among the most significant innovations in health care for the poor have been publicly funded Community Health Centers, most of which were targeted to low-income rural or inner-city people. But by the late 1970s, such centers still reached only an estimated 8 percent of the poor. Similarly, less than half of the women and children eligible for the federally funded Women, Infants, and Children (WIC) Program, which provides nutritional supplements for low-income mothers and young children, received benefits from it — and the proportion was much lower in many states (K. Davis, Gold, and Makuc, 1981, pp. 177–178; Kovar and Meny, 1981, p. 37). Health care for the poor has improved greatly, but it has never come close to reaching all of them.

Why Health Care Costs So Much

As the 1980s began, about 10 cents out of every dollar of gross national product in America was spent on health care, and the total bill was approaching $300 billion a year. Between 1960 and 1980 health-care expenditures rose at an average rate of almost 12 percent a year; a hospital room cost 2.5 times as much at the end of the 1970s as it did at the beginning.

Why do we spend so much on health care — and why has the bill gone up so much, and so rapidly, in recent years? The answer has several parts: more people are using health care, they are using it more intensively, and the prices they pay for health services are much higher.

Increasing Use

The most important reason for increased use of health care — and, therefore, one of the most important reasons for rising health expenditures — is the changing age structure of the American population. As a greater proportion of the population becomes concentrated at the higher ages (over 65 and, especially, over 75), the use of medical services increases. This is especially true for some of the most expensive kinds of health care, like nursing homes and other long-term institutional care. In 1950, people over 65 were 8 percent of the population; they were 11 percent 30 years later, and the proportion over 75 has increased even faster.

That 11 percent of the population now consumes about 29 percent of all health-care expenditures. They are more likely to go to doctors, to be hospitalized (and for longer periods), and they are most of the population in nursing homes.

In turn, the rapid growth of nursing homes and other forms of extended care reflects not only the rise in the numbers of aged but also an important shift in the family relations of older people. Until recently, many of the routine care needs of the elderly were met at home by their families. Today, far fewer older people live with other family members. In 1950, for example, only 25 percent of widows 65 years old and over lived alone; by the mid-1970s, two-thirds did. In this sense, the growth in institutional care for the aged — which represents a large fraction of rising health spending — may be less a real increase in the level of care they receive than a shift in the *source* of care, away from the more traditional and unpaid provision by the family to more formal organizations.

Minorities and Health: The Persistence of Inequality

Another important goal of health-care reform in recent years has been to reduce the disparity in the health status of minorities and whites. How close have we come to that goal?

We have some answers about the specific health differences between blacks and whites. But much of the most relevant data on health and health care is not broken down for other minority groups. Moreover, because race and income are so closely linked in American society, it is often difficult to disentangle the health effects of one from the other. We do know that the trends in racial differences resemble those in the disparities between affluent and poor. And, though traditional racial gaps in health have generally narrowed, wide differences still remain, and in a few areas, the gaps have increased.

Wider Access

In part, too, the sheer growth of expenditures on health reflects the thrust toward equality in health care. Extending health care to the poor and other underserved groups did not come for free. Some cautions, however, must be kept in mind in placing those costs in context.

1. In looking at the billions spent on health care for those formerly denied it, we often forget to factor in the benefits — even in sheer economic terms — of that spending. The benefits are often difficult to measure, but it's clear that our assessment of the costs would be different if we subtracted the gains of reduced disability, fewer lost working days, expenses for treating preventable illnesses, and unnecessary institutionalization.

2. Though few are aware of it, the government actually spends more on health care for the affluent and people of average income than for the poor. That reality is easily overlooked because most government health-care spending on the more affluent is in the form of tax expenditures (see pages 134 to 137). One of the biggest of these is the tax deduction for employer-paid health insurance premiums, a tax break that cost the government an estimated $21 billion in 1981 — a sum approaching that of the *entire* Medicaid program. Though the government spends more money *per capita* on lower-income people, it spends nearly the same *total* amount on the affluent as on the poor. Thus, it spent $9.7 billion on those making more than $32,000 a year in 1977, and $10 billion on those making less than $10,000.

3. It is important to understand the *components* of the costs of government health spending on the needy. There is much concern over fraud and abuse in health programs for the poor, but though these problems exist, they've never amounted to more than a tiny fraction of total program costs. Some critics describe Medicaid as if it were a massive trough at which the able-bodied poor feed at the taxpayer's expense. But two-fifths of Medicaid costs are for long-term institutional care for the elderly; three-fifths of Medicaid recipients are aged or disabled adults, and most of the rest are children living below the poverty line.

Rising Prices

Two important reasons for the growth of health-care spending, then, are an aging population and a commitment to providing care for the disadvantaged. But studies show that the *most* important cause is simply that the prices for any

These differences appear very early in life. Figure 9-3 shows that though rates of infant mortality have declined for both races, the racial *gap* remains equally wide. In 1979, 11 out of every 1,000 white babies died before their first birthday, but 22 out of 1,000 black babies did. In Washington, D.C., almost *30* black infants die out of every 1,000 born. The black rate of infant death in 1979, in fact, was almost exactly the same as the white rate *15 years earlier* (U.S. Department of Health and Human Services, 1982, p. 54). That historical lag can be expressed in plain numbers. If blacks had been blessed with the white infant mortality rate in 1978, over 6,000 of the roughly 13,000 black infants who died that year would have lived (Kovar, 1982, p. 5).

The roots of the racial disparity in infant mortality are planted well before birth. Black infants are born weighing an average of about 8 ounces less than white infants. They are more than twice as likely to be of low weight at birth as white babies, and low birth weight, in turn, is one of the most reliable predictors of early infant death (U.S. National Center for Health Statistics, 1981b, pp. 5–9).

Nevertheless, the black infant death rate has dropped substantially (especially from the mid-1960s to the mid-1970s) with the spread of health care

given medical service have risen greatly, even faster than most other prices. Since 1950 the consumer price index has risen at an average of about 4.2 percent a year, its medical-care component about 5.5 percent. And as most people who have had the misfortune to fall ill are aware, physicians' and hospital services have risen even faster than most other medical costs. Why? There are several key factors, among them:

- *Technology:* Medical technology has expanded rapidly in the past 25 years. Some of that development has been both cost-effective and clearly beneficial in reducing illness (for example, the development of new vaccines). But other aspects, especially the more capital-intensive innovations, such as CAT scanners and other complex diagnostic devices, are both very expensive and generally of more limited effectiveness in improving the health status of the general population. These new technologies raise the costs of health care not only for their immediate users but across the board, since their costs are spread out in higher medical bills for everyone.

- *Financing:* Probably the biggest single source

of rising medical prices is a payment system that, in effect, allows doctors and hospitals to charge almost whatever they want and offers virtually no incentives to hold prices down. Most health care in this country is provided on what's called a fee-for-service basis — meaning that health-care providers have a stake in performing more services, and more elaborate services, than might be needed. In turn, the fees they charge are usually paid for by "third parties": in private health care, by insurance companies such as Blue Cross; in public health care, by the taxpayers. In neither case is there any mechanism for scrutinizing the fees charged, or for exerting some restraint if the fees seem excessive. Instead, doctors and hospitals are simply reimbursed for whatever they declare to be their costs. In that sense, the health-care sector of the economy is a lot like the defense sector (as we'll see in Chapter 12). It tends to reward inefficiency and cost padding and to discourage the search for less costly alternatives.

Sources: Fuchs, 1979; Weichert, 1981; Case, 1981; U.S. Department of Health and Human Services, 1982a, pp. 130–147; Wilensky, 1982.

Deaths per 1,000 live births

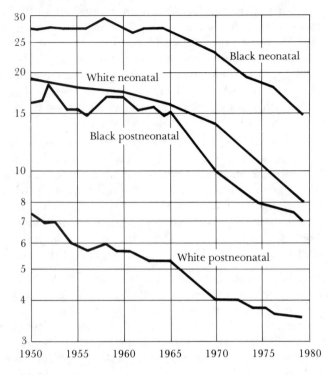

Figure 9-3

Racial differences in infant mortality, 1950–1980

Source: U.S. Department of Health and Human Services, *Health — United States, 1982* (Washington, D.C.: Government Printing Office, 1982), . p. 9.

Note: Neonatal deaths are those occurring within the first month of life; postneonatal deaths are those occurring during the second through twelfth months of life.

and nutrition programs into rural poverty areas and inner-city ghettos. That decline also accounts for much of the narrowing of the racial gap in life expectancy. In the 1970s, about 3.5 years were added to the average life expectancy for blacks, about 2 for whites (Fingerhut, Wilson, and Feldman, 1981, pp. 8–9). But despite the positive trend, a white male, at birth, can still expect to live some five years longer than a nonwhite; a white female, about four years. At later ages, these differences almost disappear. By the end of the 1970s, life expectancy at age 65 was about the same for both races (for both sexes). But at the *middle* of life, as at the beginning, the risks of death from many causes are strikingly greater for black Americans. For example:

- *Heart disease:* Black men in their late 30s have more than double the white rate of death from heart disease; black women in their late 30s have 3.5 times the risk of death from heart disease as white women. And though heart disease generally kills men at a far higher rate than it kills women, the death rate for black *women* in their early 30s is higher than that for white *men*.

- *Cancer:*   The age-adjusted death rate for cancer is over a third higher for black men than for white men, more than a fifth higher for black women than for white women. Cancer rates among black men rose sharply during the 1960s and 1970s; white men's rates also rose, but the black rate rose three times as fast (Fingerhut, Wilson, and Feldman, 1981, p. 11). These differences are typically greatest in middle age. In general, the chances of dying of cancer increase with age. But the cancer death rates of middle-aged black men tend to resemble those of white men who are about *five years older.*

- *Stroke:*   Racial differences in death from cerebrovascular disease are dramatic. Black men die from strokes at a rate almost twice that of whites. And though, like heart disease, stroke is typically more common for men than for women, it is much more likely to strike a black *woman* than a white *man.* What is especially disturbing is how early in life the risk of stroke becomes a serious one for blacks; the death rate for black men aged 35 to 44 is more than *four times* the white rate (U.S. Department of Health and Human Services, 1982, pp. 59–69).

Similar, though often less dramatic, differences show up as routinely poorer health and higher levels of disability among blacks. Black parents rate their children's health as just fair or poor about 75 percent more often than white parents do (Kovar, 1982, p. 9). Forty-two out of every thousand blacks suffer from known diabetes, as compared to twenty-two out of every thousand whites. Washington, D.C., with a population about 70 percent black, has the highest rate of tuberculosis of any city of comparable size, about four times the national average (Rice and Payne, 1981, p. 129).

How do we explain these differences? The reasons are complex, but it seems clear that part of the disparity reflects some general features of the social, economic, and cultural context of black life in America today, while part reflects the specific effects of racially unequal health care.

Part of the problem, for example, is the long-standing one of inadequate nutrition. There has been much improvement since the doctors uncovered starvation among southern children in the 1960s, but much remains to be done. As the Children's Defense Fund has pointed out, for all important nutrients except iron, undernutrition is *twice* as common among black as among white children (Children's Defense Fund, 1981, p. 164).

It is increasingly understood, too, that minority health (like that of the poor of all races) is adversely affected by the physical and psychological impact of socioeconomic stress. This is vividly illustrated in the racial disparities in the risks of certain diseases generally understood to be stress related. Hypertension (high blood pressure) is a striking example. High blood pressure is much more common among blacks, which helps explain the higher black rates of death from stroke and heart disease. But why are blacks more likely to suffer from high blood pressure?

At one time, it was often argued that the difference was largely genetic.

The quality of health care remains unequal for minorities and the poor.

But it was soon discovered that blacks in Africa don't suffer disproportionately from hypertension. Instead, as several recent studies have shown, hypertension is closely linked to high levels of stress in black communities, particularly ones with low-income. Some of those stresses are economic, such as the greater threat of unemployment or the chances of being trapped in a poorly paying and unpleasant job. Others are closely-related emotional stresses, including the need among many poorer blacks to suppress feelings of hostility and anger over racial discrimination and economic injustice (Harburg, 1973).

The effects of social and economic disadvantages like poor nutrition and high stress are aggravated by enduring inequities in access to adequate health care. These inequities, too, begin early. Thus, though it is now well understood that early screening to detect high-risk pregnancies can significantly reduce infant mortality, and that early prenatal care strongly reduces the chances of both infant and maternal death, black women are far less likely to receive adequate prenatal attention. And they are more likely to receive it, if at all, later in their pregnancy (Kovar and Meny, 1981, pp. 14–15, 32).

Assuming that they survive the risks of birth and the first year of life, black children are much less likely than white children to be completely immunized against common preventable diseases such as polio or diphtheria. They are also less likely to have a regular doctor (only half of black, as compared to four-fifths of white, children did in the mid-1970s) or even a regular source of medical care of any kind — a problem also found among low-income Hispanics (Aday, Anderson, and Fleming, 1980, p. 57; Kovar and Meny, 1981, p. 32).

Even in government-funded health programs for the poor, minorities often wind up with the short end of the stick. They tend to receive lower Medicaid benefits, especially in the rural South and West. Black (and Hispanic) Medicaid patients in some areas still faced segregated waiting rooms and long, discriminatory waits for routine care in the late 1970s (Davis and Schoen, 1978, p. 73). And even before a changed social and political climate led to severe reductions in funding for health programs for the poor, they never reached more than a fraction of the medically needy minority population. Most of the nutritional deficiencies of black children, for example, could have been largely remedied through the subsidized school lunch and breakfast programs of the 1970s. But even *before* those programs suffered losses in funding, only about half of black welfare families benefited from them.

A National Health System?

It is often argued that some form of national health insurance for everyone would help alleviate the inequalities in American health care. The appeal of such a system is not hard to understand. Not only do many people receive less-than-equal care, but others are not covered, or only partly covered, by public or private health insurance. By the end of the 1970s, an estimated 18 to 20 million Americans had no health insurance; another 37 million had some coverage, but not enough to pay for high medical bills resulting from long hospital stays or complicated surgery. An even larger number of Americans lacked coverage for long-term care in nursing homes or extended-care facilities.

The uninsured and inadequately insured are disproportionately drawn from the poor and the near-poor (those not poor enough to be eligible for Medicaid or other public programs, and neither affluent enough to afford private insurance nor employed in a job that provides health benefits). Health-care protection in the United States,

it's often said, is "broad but not deep," leaving at least a fifth of the population completely unprepared for major medical bills, and many more vulnerable if they lose a job or suffer a drop in income.

Though we usually take this medical insecurity for granted, the United States is actually the *only* Western industrial society that lacks some form of comprehensive, universal national health program. What makes this situation especially surprising is that most of the American public — about 75 percent, according to recent opinion polls — supports the idea of national health insurance, and that majority sentiment has been with us since the Great Depression.

Why haven't we heeded that sentiment and followed the road every other industrial society has taken? The reasons include successful resistance by the organized medical profession and private insurance companies and the widespread belief that a comprehensive medical program for all represents "socialized" medicine that would necessarily be cumbersome, inefficient, and, perhaps most important, costly. (The polls show that though most Americans support national health

Women's Health: Gender and Medical Care

Women are the principal consumers of health care in the United States, and are also the *least* satisfied with the care they receive. The problems women face in health care are often obscured by the fact that, according to most (though, as we'll see, not all) measures, women tend to be healthier than men. In some important ways, too, that comparative advantage is increasing.

The most striking gender differences in health status are in life expectancy and the risks of mortality from most major killer diseases and major nondisease killers (such as accidents, suicide, and homicide). Of the top ten causes of death, women's mortality rates exceed men's in just two: diabetes and cerebrovascular disease. But even these apparent disadvantages occur because women tend to live longer than men and therefore represent an older and more vulnerable population. Adjusted for age, men die from *every* one of the ten major causes at a higher rate than women (though black women die of diabetes at a higher rate than black men) (U.S. Department of Health and Human Services, 1982, pp. 59–60).

insurance in the abstract, they balk somewhat at being willing to pay for it.)

What can we learn about the validity of these fears from the experience of other countries? The exact form that national health programs have taken in different countries varies widely, from elaborate insurance systems (as in Sweden) to public control of most aspects of health care (as in Great Britain). But for an approach that may be most applicable to the United States we might look closer to home: to Canada, which has had a comprehensive national health insurance system since 1947.

Under Canada's tax-supported system, every Canadian is covered for the costs of all medically necessary expenses. Measured against the goal of achieving security against devastating health expenses, the system has been an unqualified success. As a recent study of the Canadian system sponsored by the U.S. Public Health Services puts it,

> For all Canadians, the fear of not being able to meet the cost of the hospital or doctor's bills is a thing of the past — and no Canadian citizen has to go begging to the welfare department to pay a hospital or doctor's bill. Canadians have obtained equal access to medical care and medical care with dignity. (Hatcher, 1981, p. 1)

Has the provision of quality health care to all caused Canadian health costs to skyrocket? That was the main objection raised in Canada when the system was introduced in the 1940s, and that fear remains a major obstacle in the minds of many people in the United States. If everyone is entitled to "free" care, it was argued, doctors' offices and hospitals would be swamped with patients demanding excessive care and creating a massive increase in costs. But these fears didn't materialize. Health care in Canada now takes a considerably *smaller* fraction of GNP than it does in the United States. In 1960 that fraction was between 5 and 5.5 percent in both countries. By 1978 it had risen to more than 9 percent in the United States, but to only a little more than 7 percent in Canada. Our costs of *hospital* care *doubled* in that period as a percent of GNP, while Canada's increased by about a third.

What about efficiency? The Canadian health-

These differences begin very early, in higher mortality rates for male infants and much higher male mortality rates among adolescents (especially from accidents and suicide, the leading adolescent killers), and continue into adulthood. Men under 45 have about three times the risk of death from heart disease, the number one cause of death in the United States, as women the same age.

Much of the overall decline in mortality rates in recent years, in fact, is accounted for by the especially rapid declines for women. One result is the well-known gulf in life expectancy between women and men. Women's life expectancy at birth in the United States now exceeds men's by about eight years. Interestingly, American women's longevity comes much closer than American men's to equaling that in other, generally healthier industrial countries.

But focusing solely on mortality exaggerates the comparative healthiness of women compared to men in the United States. There are some disturbing exceptions to the rule that women's chances of death have declined faster than men's. The most striking is the rapid rise in women's deaths from lung cancer [generally attributed largely to the rise in smoking (Fingerhut, Wilson, and Feldman, 1981, p. 11)]. And it's *only* women, of course, who face

care dollar is put to more efficient use, by most measures, than its counterpart in the United States. One way of seeing this is to compare administrative costs — how much is spent simply to manage the health-care bureaucracy rather than deliver services to patients? Administrative costs in Canadian health care are, proportionately, about a fourth of those in the United States; 95 cents of the Canadian health-care dollar goes directly to doctors and hospitals for services. In private health insurance programs in the United States, administrative expenses account for about *20 percent* of the total costs. Our administrative costs rose about 2.5 times between 1960 and 1978 as a proportion of GNP; Canada's were the *same* proportion in both years.

How is this possible? One key to the relative success of the Canadian system is its simplicity, made possible by the standardization of health benefits in a single comprehensive plan, administered uniformly within each province. A crucial part of the plan is that decisions about most issues affecting costs and the quality of services are the responsibility of health-planning authorities and are not left simply to the "market." Standard fee schedules for doctors, for example, are nego-

tiated periodically, and doctors are required to stick to them. Doctors who encourage the overuse of services can be disciplined by health authorities. The introduction of costly new facilities or equipment is carefully regulated according to the need for them, not simply left to the decisions of hospital administrators.

The simplicity of having only a single package of benefits helps reduce costs considerably. We often think of government planning as being inevitably cumbersome and bureaucratic. But the opposite seems to be true of health care. In the United States, the effort to devise many different and competing structures of benefits for different kinds of people (in the hope that no one will get more than they "ought to") generates innumerable complex exclusions and rules about eligibility, which in turn require an enormous — and expensive — set of bureaucracies just to implement and enforce them. Paradoxically, our concerted attempt to ensure that no ones gets "something for nothing" costs us dearly — and keeps us from reaping the potential benefits of a more efficient health-care system.

Sources: Hatcher, 1981; Schroeder, 1981.

death in pregnancy and birth. Though maternal mortality rates have declined greatly in the United States in the past several decades, they remain considerably higher, especially among black women, than in many comparable societies (Moore, 1980, p. 10).

Moreover, though women's health appears better than men's when measured by the risks of mortality from serious diseases, other measures draw a different picture. Although women are less likely to be carried off at relatively young ages by catastrophic diseases, accidents or violence, they are *more* likely, especially at older ages, to suffer some chronic, limiting impairment or disability (Lebowitz, 1980; Moore, 1980). Partly for that reason, women seek doctors' services more often than men do, and are considerably more apt to use many medications. Two-thirds of all prescriptions for tranquilizing drugs are written for women, and the overpromotion of drugs as a typical response to women's medical needs has become a problem of increasing proportions. In a generally overmedicated society, women are the chief targets of legal drug advertising and marketing, and are also three-fifths of the people admitted to hospital emergency rooms for drug-related problems (Moore, 1980, p. 37). But this overmedication of women is a response, however inappropriate, to a set of real problems, emotional as well as physical. Women, particularly low-income and minority women, report higher levels of tension and anxiety than men, as well as a lower general sense of psychological well-being and more severe feelings of stress (Moore, 1980, p. 12).

What accounts for these differences? There is considerable debate about the sources of women's health advantages, and the answers are not yet all in. One common argument is that they reflect the influence of traditional sex roles. Men tend to be locked into a way of life, particularly at work, which emphasizes competition and striving and generates health-destroying stresses from which, it's sometimes argued, women have been traditionally sheltered. As women move into formerly male-dominated jobs and generally adopt more traditionally "male" social roles, it's argued, their health patterns will come to resemble men's. This argument is sometimes used as ammunition against removing occupational and cultural barriers to women's equality at home and in the workplace. But is it true?

The evidence suggests that it isn't. Generally, women's rising participation in the paid labor force *hasn't* reduced the male/female disparities in mortality from those illnesses (like heart disease) typically linked to the stresses of competition and achievement. On the contrary, the male disadvantage has usually *grown* (Moore, 1980, p. 10). A recent study of women listed in *Who's Who* shows that women who have achieved considerable social and economic status haven't lost their life-expectancy advantage over men. And a major long-term study of the risks of heart disease has demonstrated that, on the whole, women who work in the paid labor force have no greater risk than those who do not (Moore, 1980, p. 35).

In general, as recent research shows, women who work outside the home are typically *healthier* than those confined to housework. One study found that housewives reported almost *twice* as many days of restricted activity due to illness as either employed men or employed women. Women who worked outside the home went to the doctor less often and reported their health as excellent much more often than women who worked only in the home. And housewives had higher death rates at all ages up until age 60 than women who worked in the paid labor force (Nathanson and Passannante, 1983).

But the issue is more complicated than this. The impact of paid labor on women's health varies greatly, depending on the nature of the work itself and on the other obligations they must shoulder at the same time. "Women's" work is sometimes thought to be inherently less stressful, dangerous, or demanding than "men's." But women workers actually predominate in several highly dangerous industries. Fifty-six percent of textile workers, who face high risks of brown lung disease (bysinnosis) and lung cancer, are women. Two-thirds of the workers in laundry and dry-cleaning plants, who suffer high rates of some cancers induced by chemical solvents, are women. Similar risks abound in many other industries that mainly employ women, such as electronics assembly, plastics manufacturing, and hospital work. These industries are often scattered in a multitude of small work sites that are often only superficially scrutinized by occupational health and safety authorities (Stellman, 1979; Lebowitz, 1980).

The health hazards for working women, moreover, aren't confined to blue-collar industrial or service work. Evidence is accumulating that health-threatening levels of stress are associated with many kinds of clerical work, the biggest source of jobs for American women (Stellman, 1979). The same study that found no significant differences in heart disease between women

Abortion, Family Planning, and Mortality

The liberalization in the early 1970s of laws and regulations governing such emotionally charged issues as abortion, contraception, and family planning was a significant development in health policy in America. Supreme Court rulings made abortion a matter of choice to be settled between a woman and her doctor. Federal health policy extended the use of legal abortions and improved family planning services to the poor through Medicaid and other public programs. Teenaged women (and men) were informed about family planning techniques and contraception, with or without their parents' knowledge. These developments gave women (especially poorer and younger women) much greater control in decisions affecting reproduction.

More recently, these policies — and the deeper philosophy behind them — have been increasingly and sometimes successfully attacked. Some court decisions have restricted the scope of legal abortion generally and particularly the use of federal funds to provide abortions for lower-income women. Family planning services have been cut back severely, and a variety of restrictions have been proposed on the use of those services by younger women.

Often lost in the debates over these policies are the facts about what women's increased reproductive rights have accomplished, strictly in *health* terms. Whatever one's personal views on contraception or abortion, these outcomes must be an important part of any intelligent discussion of public policy toward them. And the evidence is mounting that the widening of reproductive choice for women was a major factor in reducing deaths related to childbirth and pregnancy —

in and out of the paid labor force also discovered that it was almost *twice* as prevalent among women who were working in clerical jobs and had children as among women in blue-collar or professional work or women who worked only in the home (Moore, 1980, p. 11).

The researchers found that three features common to much clerical work were particularly correlated with heart disease among women: lack of job mobility, suppressed hostility, and an unsupportive boss. Among women clerical workers with children, these negative job characteristics combined with the "double duty" of household work to produce a much higher susceptibility to stress-related disease. As this suggests, what counts in determining women's health (as it does, of course, for men as well) is not simply the fact of working itself, but the quality and quantity of the work and the way it fits with the rest of one's life. In a nutshell, though there is no evidence that achieving rewarding jobs will hurt women's health, there is every evidence that overwork in poor jobs coupled with an unequal division of housework *will*.

Health and the Changing Workplace

It is now widely understood that medical care itself is only one of many influences on health, and that what we broadly term "environmental" factors are also crucially important. Indeed, some writers have argued that nei-

both maternal mortality and, even more strikingly, infant mortality.

The reduction of the number of high-risk pregnancies has been one of the most important health advances in America in recent decades. We've seen one of its effects in the dramatic decline in infant deaths; another has been the reduction of maternal mortality to a fraction of its level of even 30 years ago. Dying in childbirth was once an ever-present risk for American women. Even as late as the end of World War II, more than 200 women died in childbirth for every 100,000 live births. Better birth techniques and prenatal care, and improvements in their delivery, brought that rate down to about 50 per 100,000 by the late 1950s. By the close of the 1970s, the rate had fallen to less than 10 per 100,000 births — a striking and welcome decline in one of the most significant risks of death for younger women (Figure 9-4). This decline re-

flected several developments: an increase in good prenatal care, especially for low-income women; the spread of contraception and family planning knowledge, allowing women better control over the timing and planning of pregnancy; and the increased availability of legal abortion. During the 1970s, the number of women receiving publicly funded family planning services increased almost 10 times (from 400,000 in 1970 to about 4 million in 1978).

The liberalization of abortion laws also resulted, even more directly, in reducing deaths related to abortion itself. The difficulty of obtaining abortions legally before the 1970s reduced the overall number of abortions performed, but it also meant that a far greater proportion of those that *were* performed were done illegally, often under dangerous and unsanitary conditions. (Prior to the Supreme Court decision in the early 1970s, there were an estimated 1 million illegal abor-

Figure 9-4

The decline in maternal
mortality, 1950–1981

Source: U.S. National Center for
Health Statistics, *Monthly Vital
Statistics Report, Annual Summary
of Births, Deaths, Marriages, and
Divorces, 1981* (Washington,
D.C.: Government Printing Of-
fice, December 1982), p. 7.

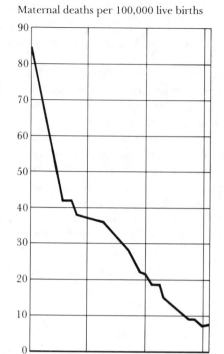

Maternal deaths per 100,000 live births

tions a year.) Liberalization reduced abortion-
related deaths dramatically, cutting them by two-
thirds between 1972 and 1975 alone (according to
U.S. Public Health Service data). (These figures
are necessarily somewhat limited since illegal
abortion is by definition clandestine and hard to
measure, but they are carefully estimated.)

The most precise accounting of the health impact of liberalized abortion, however, comes from
studies of its impact on infant mortality. We've
seen that infant mortality declined greatly for
both blacks and whites in the 1960s and, even
more rapidly, in the early 1970s. A study by the
economist Michael Grossman has shown that the
increase in the rate of legal abortions was the
"single most important factor" in that decline —
more important than improved income and levels
of schooling, or better health care generally.
Grossman calculates that the growth in legal
abortions reduced infant death among whites by

about 1.6 per every 1,000 live births between
1964 and 1977, and by 2.5 per 1,000 for nonwhites, with the most rapid reductions coming in
the 1970s, after the changes in abortion laws. According to Grossman, this has crucial implications
for the way we think about abortion and public
policy. A policy banning legal abortions which reduced them to the pre-1970s level would cause a
rise of 1.8 deaths for every 1,000 white births,
and 2.8 for every 1,000 nonwhite births. At 1978
birth rates, that translates into the death of more
than 1,800 nonwhite and more than 4,800 white
infants a year.

Sources: Moore, 1980; U.S. National Center for Health Statistics, 1981; M. Grossman, 1982; Tietze, 1982.

ther the quantity nor the quality of medical care has had *any* significant positive impact on health in the modern age; or, worse, that our highly technological medical system causes more harm to health than it does good (Illich, 1978). It's clear, however, that some medical advances have made an important difference — including improvements in immunization against major diseases and improved screening and detection techniques for many others, which make possible early and effective treatment (Fuchs, 1979).

Still, few now doubt that the environment has a profound effect on health and illness. In a widely cited figure, the World Health Organization estimated in the 1960s that up to 80 percent of human cancers were environmentally related (Environmental Defense Fund, 1979, p. 5) — reflecting both the impact of carcinogenic substances in the technological and natural environments and the role of such more personal factors as smoking and dietary habits. Another, more recent estimate is that between 15 and 25 percent of all deaths in the United States each year (between 270,000 and 480,000 people as of 1979) are "related to technology" — including a considerably higher proportion of two major causes of death: accidents and cancer (Derr et al., 1981, p. 8).

The implications of this, however, are hotly debated, especially as they affect the way we think about society's responsibility to regulate health dangers in the environment and the workplace. We will look more closely at the relation between health and the broader environment in Chapter 10; now, we'll focus on the heated issue of the problems of health and safety in the workplace.

We know that many workers are injured or made ill on the job — but how many? As usual, the answer is not easy to find. For one thing, the time lag between exposure to a disease-causing condition at work and the appearance of the disease itself is often very long for many typical occupational illnesses, notably cancer and some other long-term chronic diseases — as long as 20 years and more for many work-related cancers. It's difficult, too, to separate out the effects of occupational exposures from other factors (such as smoking or poor diet) that may have helped bring on or aggravated a disease. And some of the potentially most useful sources of information, like employers' health records, are likely to be biased for financial and public relations reasons (U.S. Department of Labor, 1980, p. 1). But we have a ballpark idea of the magnitude of work-related health problems, and they are staggering:

- An estimated 1 in 4 American workers (more than 25 million people) are potentially exposed to a major health hazard at work.
- An estimated 75,000 deaths a year are "job-induced," and about 10 million injuries and 30 million separate bouts of illness are related to working conditions (Derr et al., 1981, p. 9).

Occupational Illness and Injury: Dimensions

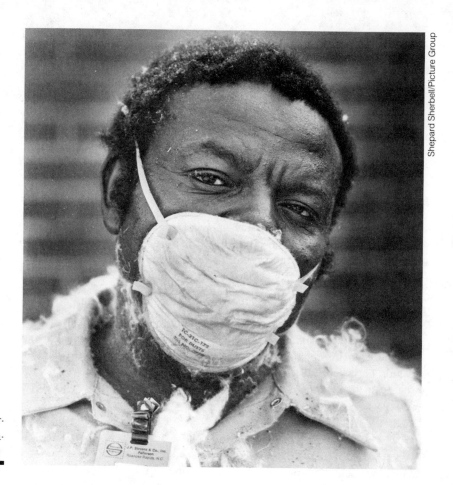

An estimated 1 in 4 Americans are exposed to a major health hazard at work.

- Almost 2 million workers report that they suffer some degree of disability from a work-related disease; 700,000 of them report long-term, total disability (U.S. Department of Labor, 1980, p. 2).

- Estimates of the percentage of occupationally related cancer vary widely, from less than 5 percent up to 20 percent and more. But even if the *lowest* estimates are correct, occupational exposure accounts for close to 20,000 cancer deaths a year (D. L. Davis, 1981, p. 36).

All of these estimates, moreover, almost certainly understate the magnitude of the problem of industrial health. We may only now be beginning to see the long-term health impact of some of the new technologies that expanded so rapidly after World War II, especially the enormous proliferation of industrial chemicals. The federal government now lists about 26,000 different chemicals on its roster of known toxic substances, 2,000 of which are suspected of causing cancer. About 1,000 *new* chemicals are put on the mar-

Michael O'Brien/Archive Pictures

We allow levels of exposure to toxic chemicals in the workplace that would be illegal if inflicted on the public.

ket every year. We know a great deal about the effects of *some* toxic chemicals, but almost nothing about the vast majority of new substances that are constantly being introduced into the workplace. And because of the long lead time for the appearance of cancer and other industrially related diseases, the rates we see now may be only the tip of the iceberg. Some evidence for this frightening prospect is provided by estimates that the specific forms of cancer most often associated with industrial exposure rose at about 4 percent a year during the 1970s, while other kinds rose at about 1 percent (D. L. Davis, 1981, p. 36).

Given the enormity of these threats, it isn't surprising that the debate over the proper role of the government in regulating occupational health and safety has intensified. On one side are those who believe that the risks of

Health and Safety Regulation: Limits

Health and the Changing Workplace   **353**

occupational disease are so great that they call for a larger commitment of social resources to control them — and that we may be heading for catastrophe if that commitment isn't forthcoming (Epstein, 1980). On the other side are those who believe that government regulation of the workplace has already gone too far, putting such an intolerable burden on businesses that it threatens to strangle the economy (Whelan, 1981). Economic growth and workers' health have been increasingly pitted against each other as mutually exclusive goals. Is that perception accurate? Does an effective attack on occupational illness and accidents necessarily hinder economic efficiency?

An adequate answer must begin by noting the *limits* of existing health and safety regulation in the United States. Since the early 1970s, much of the regulatory task has been shouldered by the federal Occupational Health and Safety Administration (OSHA) and its state-level counterparts. OSHA is frequently described as an all-powerful bureaucracy capable of harassing and intimidating private employers. But the reality is considerably less imposing. Of the roughly 25 million American workers routinely exposed to hazardous substances, only about half a million are in workplaces inspected by OSHA each year (U.S. Department of Labor, 1980, p. 114). There were enough OSHA inspectors, in the late 1970s, to visit every American work site about once every 80 years (Witt and Early, 1981, p. 21). From its establishment in 1970 until the late 1970s, OSHA set only 11 new standards governing toxic substances (keep in mind that there are about 26,000 of those substances on the list, and that 1,000 *new* chemicals are introduced each year) and adopted about 400 others from preexisting agencies (U.S. Department of Labor, 1980, p. 114). The main reason for the slow development of new standards has been the strong resistance of private business, which has repeatedly forced newly proposed standards into costly and lengthy court litigation. Of all the new standards OSHA attempted to issue in the 1970s, only *two* did not face a court challenge by employers (U.S. Department of Labor, 1980, p. 113).

Once standards for workplace health *are* established, moreover, the government's ability to inflict serious penalties on employers who violate them is minimal. In the late 1970s, the *maximum* fine for a single serious violation of an OSHA standard was $1,000. In the chemical industry, according to a study by the Council on Economic Priorities (1981), the average fine per violation in 1979 was less than $75. [The giant Du Pont chemical company, which the study labeled the "worst violator" in the entire industry, endured an average fine per violation of about $415 in 1979. In 1981 Du Pont — the twelfth largest American industrial corporation — had about $24 billion in assets and earned about $1.4 billion in profits (*Fortune*, May 3, 1982a, p. 260).]

Health standards for American workers, too, are usually far more lax than for the public as a whole. We typically permit levels of chemical exposure in the workplace that would be grossly illegal if they were inflicted on the general population. OSHA and the Environmental Protection Agency

(EPA), which regulates air and water quality for the general public, are often charged with setting standards governing the same substances — but the EPA standards are generally far more stringent. The EPA's standards limit the allowable level of carbon monoxide in the air to about 9 parts per million over an eight-hour period; OSHA's workplace standard is 50 parts per million. The OSHA standard for exposure to sulfur dioxide (a major culprit in respiratory disease) is about 12 times the level the EPA allows for the public, and the disparity for many highly toxic chemicals (including such cancer-causing agents as lead and beryllium) is much greater still (Derr et al., 1981, pp. 13–14).

As in many other health measures, the United States also lags behind many other industrialized societies in the stringency of its regulation of occupational safety and health, as Table 9-6 shows. American standards for exposure to a number of toxic chemicals are considerably more permissive than in many Western European countries (especially Finland and Sweden) and far more so than in the Soviet Union. These differences show up in other ways as well. Finland, for instance, has about 500 specialists in occupational health research serving a work force of about 2 million, while the United States has about 700 for a work force of more than 100 million (A. Anderson, 1982).

Health and Safety Regulation: Costs and Benefits

Beyond these sheer quantitative differences are broader differences in underlying philosophies. In countries like Finland or the Soviet Union, standards for exposure to hazardous conditions are based almost wholly on *medical* considerations alone. Conditions that are believed to be harmful for workers are treated as a first priority, and industries must often, if necessary, redesign their work processes or technology to eliminate them. In the United States, medical considerations are allowed to *compete* with other concerns — in particular, with the "economic feasibility" of a proposed health

Table 9-6
Occupational exposure standards for various chemicals, selected countries (in milligrams per cubic meter)

Country	Nickel	Benzene	Cadmium Oxides	Carbon Monoxide	Lead	Mercury
Finland	NA	32	0.01	55	0.15	0.005
Italy	1	20	0.01	55	0.15	NA
Sweden	0.01	30	0.02	40	0.1	0.05
USSR	0.5	5	0.1	20	0.01	0.01
United States	1	30	0.1	55	0.2	0.05

Note: NA means not available.
Source: Adapted from Patrick Derr et al., "Worker/Public Protection: The Double Standard," *Environment*, September 1981, p. 15. Reprinted with permission.

standard or the *prior* existence of "available control technology" (Derr et al., 1981, p. 31). More than many other countries, in short, we *already* balance the value of workers' lives and well-being against the presumed economic costs of reducing workplace hazards.

What, exactly, *are* those costs? Most studies find them to be less formidable than is often supposed, particularly when balanced against their benefits. One example comes from the Council on Economic Priorities' study of the chemical industry. With one of the worst violation records of any American industry (second only to mining), the chemical industry was a main target of OSHA regulation during the 1970s. What were the results? Recorded rates of work related illness and injury dropped by about 23 percent after the adoption of OSHA standards — translating into the prevention of as many as 90,000 illnesses and injuries. The cost to the industry was estimated at about $140 per worker per year, or only 1.8 percent of total capital invested.

Did that investment in health hurt the chemical industry's productivity? On the contrary, output per hour rose faster *after* the introduction of OSHA standards (Council on Economic Priorities, 1981, pp. 1–4). Similarly, the Swedish government regulates many workplace chemicals more stringently than we do, and also spends *more* annually on workplace health and safety training, though its work force is only about one-twentieth the size of ours. One estimate is that Sweden's rate of industrial accidents is about half ours (Witt and Early, 1981). But the tougher regulations haven't visibly hurt the Swedish economy, which outperformed ours on virtually every measure of efficiency in the 1970s.

Despite the lack of evidence that health and safety regulation has damaged the economy, that belief has already led to basic changes in workplace health policy in the United States. Increasingly, measures to lower workers' risks of illness or injury are required to be justified in narrow cost-benefit terms — balanced on a scale against employers' beliefs about the hardships of complying with them. That shift is only one part of a broader thrust in American health-care policy. Where it will take us is not entirely clear, but it does involve far-reaching changes — changes we'll now consider.

Health and Social Policy: The Prospects

We've seen that, in many respects, Americans' health has improved significantly in recent years. Can we expect those improvements to continue? Some recent trends in health policy give us considerable cause for worry.

Consider first the crucial exception to the overall picture of recent progress in health — the frightening rise in some forms of environmentally related cancer. The magnitude of that increase is understated when we look simply at overall statistics on the rate of increases in cancers among the general population. Because of the long lead time before the effects of an increasingly carcinogenic environment become apparent, it may be more appropriate to focus on the rate of cancer increase among older people. Ominously, cancer deaths have increased dramatically for people over 65, especially for men. Black men were more than twice as likely to die of cancer by the end of the 1970s as they were in 1950 — a shockingly short span of time to witness that amount of change (U.S. Department of Health and Human Services, 1982, pp. 128–130). It seems likely that some of the increase reflects increased smoking, but some of it may reflect the effect of industrial carcinogens. "It is absolutely certain," one group of researchers writes, "that if voluntary and involuntary exposure to environmental carcinogens continues, cancer rates will soar even higher." And they conclude that "If we remain on our present course, we are not simply inviting disaster, we are rushing to embrace it" (Environmental Defense Fund, 1979, p. ix).

But this threat is being met, increasingly, by health policies whose underlying philosophy is to deemphasize society's collective responsibility for the health of its members. In part, this involves a retreat from government regu-

The Resurgence of Tuberculosis in New York City

Tuberculosis was once a major killer disease in the United States. As recently as 1950, it killed about 22 out of every 100,000 Americans, and about four times as many were known sufferers from the disease. Like many other infectious diseases, however, TB was largely controlled by advances in antibiotics and improved screening techniques. By 1979 the incidence had dropped to about 13 per 100,000, and less than 1 in 100,000 Americans died from TB.

What remains of tuberculosis represents a lingering disease of social neglect. The death rate from TB is five times higher for black men than for whites, for example; and the TB rate in 1980 in New York City's disadvantaged Lower East Side resembled that of the country as a whole in 1950.

Between 1979 and 1980, for the first time in decades, the incidence of TB in New York City increased. The increase was especially apparent among children and among people who had already had the disease, whose illnesses were reactivated. According to the director of New York's tuberculosis control program, both types of cases are "direct indicators of the success or failure of a tuberculosis control program." The rise in reactivated cases, for example, reflects the failure to adequately monitor people formerly ill with the disease, a major task of modern TB control programs. Similarly, the rise in child cases represents a failure to follow up known adult cases, since most children acquire the disease from being around infected adults.

Why is New York City's control program failing to control the disease? In the words of the program's director, "New York City's tuberculosis problem stems from reporting and financial difficulties combined with the loss of personnel that has taken place over the last few years due to loss of funds for the control program" (Vennema, 1982, p. 132).

Sources: U.S. National Center for Health Statistics, 1981b, p. 147; Vennema, 1982.

lation in the name of presumed requirements of economic growth. In part, too, it involves a more general rethinking of the balance between individual and social aspects of health and health-care policy. We now hear that most of Americans' remaining health problems, to the extent that they are susceptible to improvement at all, can mainly be corrected through individual effort. There is a new tendency to regard many health problems as essentially the result of voluntary actions (or inactions) — and to argue that similar voluntary changes in life-style hold the key to better health.

That emphasis certainly reflects real problems, as we've seen, and in the case of some major health issues, such as diet and smoking, it is critically important. But an overemphasis on the "voluntary" and personal sources of health and illness can be misleading. Even in the case of smoking, to take an obvious example, habits that appear to be personal turn out to be influenced by larger social and economic factors. How voluntary or "private" an act is smoking, for example, in a society in which millions of dollars a year are spent to advertise cigarettes — and in which the full power of government is used to divert tax monies to subsidize the tobacco industry?

If smoking is a less "personal" phenomenon than it might first appear, the same is clearly even more true of the kinds of jobs we hold, the air we breathe, or the water we drink. Yet some contemporary health-care writers have gone so far as to argue that, for example, the decision to accept a hazardous job is also a "voluntary" act (Wildavsky, 1980), with which government has no right to interfere. But — especially in an economy in which unemployment among blue-collar workers has been endemic for several years — can we really consider that taking a dangerous job is a matter solely of individual choice?

This tug-of-war between public and private responsibility also affects the provision of health care to the poor, the aged, and the disabled. Few disagree that better care for the disadvantaged has been a crucial factor in improving their health status (and thus in improving the American health picture as a whole). Some studies of the impact of specific programs illustrate this even further. Primary and prenatal care furnished to mothers and infants through the publicly funded Community Health Centers, according to one study, may have reduced infant mortality in their client populations by up to 50 percent. Preventive care for children in those centers may have reduced the rate of some preventable diseases (like rheumatic fever) by as much as 60 percent. (K. Davis, Gold, and Makuc, 1981, p. 177). A North Carolina study found that clients of a publicly funded family planning clinic had a 50 percent lower rate of mortality among infants past the first few weeks of life than a control group not receiving the clinic's services (Kovar and Meny, 1981, p. 23). A study in rural Louisiana found that the WIC program of supplemental nutrition for infants and children brought what the researchers called "significant enhancement" of "most intellectual and behavioral measures" (including IQ, attention span, and school grade-point average) for enrolled children (Hicks et al., 1982). And a New York study showed that a systematic screening program for breast cancer eliminated the long-standing differences in survival rates from the disease between black and white women, while simultaneously increasing the overall rate of survival for women of *both* races (Shapiro et al., 1982).

Yet all of these programs, as well as many others providing preventive care for lower-income people, have come under severe attack. Cutbacks in support for public programs in Maternal and Child Health, Family Planning, Community Health Centers — even in the Childhood Immunization program — have been justified in the name of reducing the costs of government. But that argument fails to consider the cost advantages of *preventive* care — the type of care that has been most fostered by the programs for the poor (U.S. House Committee on Energy and Commerce, 1982). Studies indicate, for example, that community primary-care centers reduced the rate of hospitalization among their clients by as much as 25 percent by offering a wide range of screening, prenatal care, and other preventive services (K. Davis, Gold, and Makuc, 1981, p. 177). Since hospitalization is the most expensive way to deal with illness, and prevention the cheapest, we may expect an actual *rise* in the costs of health care (in addition to a decline in health status) as a result of the cutbacks in preventive care services. Similarly, a Harvard University study, finding that the incidence of low birth weight was three times as great for infants of high-risk mothers who did *not* receive benefits from the WIC program, estimated that every dollar spent on delivering nutritious foods to these mothers would save *three* dollars in later health-care costs for their children (Amidei, 1981, p. 459).

This issue goes beyond the specific question of the impact of reductions in care for the disadvantaged. Most of the innovations in health-care policy in the 1960s and 1970s can be seen as experiments in improving our capacity to prevent disease by confronting its social, economic, and environmental sources. To the extent that we sidestep that confrontation in the future, we will shift the direction of American health-care policy back to an earlier, more passive role — a role that mainly involves attempting, *after* the fact, to undo the health damage wrought by unchecked technological and economic forces. Something very similar is also at issue in our environmental policy, and we'll turn to that problem now.

Summary

This chapter has considered recent trends in health conditions and the health-care system in the United States. Most of these trends are positive, but there are troubling exceptions.

According to most measures, Americans' health has improved in recent decades. Death rates from most diseases have fallen, sometimes dramatically, and infant mortality has declined considerably.

But the United States lags well behind many other advanced industrial societies in many measures of health, including life expectancy, infant mortality, and childhood death rates. And contrary to the general trend, some health problems — especially some forms of cancer — are increasing.

Progress in achieving a healthier society has also been markedly uneven. Many groups (especially minorities, people with low incomes, and workers in some industries) still suffer unequal access to health care and far higher risks of health problems.

The introduction of thousands of new, potentially harmful chemicals into America's workplaces has made occupational health an issue of growing concern. But we now devote few resources to the task of protecting workers' health, especially as compared to other industrial countries.

Changing health policies that reduce public responsibility for health care (especially cutbacks in preventive health services) may slow or even reverse some of the recent positive gains in health.

For Further Reading

Epstein, Samuel. *The Politics of Cancer*. New York: Doubleday, 1980.

Sidel, Victor W., and Ruth Sidel. *A Healthy State*. New York: Pantheon, 1983.

Starr, Paul. *The Social Transformation of American Medicine*. New York: Basic Books, 1982.

Stellman, Jeanne M. *Women's Work, Women's Health*. New York: Pantheon, 1979.

10

Energy and
Environmental Quality

Americans have historically taken abundant natural resources for granted, and the past few decades were no exception. The prosperity of the 1950s and 1960s was fueled by what we now recognize as a prodigal use of energy and a cavalier disregard for the impact of growth on the natural environment. Energy use *doubled* between 1950 and 1972, increasing as much in that brief period as it had in the entire 175 previous years of American history (Union of Concerned Scientists, 1981, p. 3). In the 1950s, few Americans worried about world oil supplies as they sped down highways in ever bigger, more powerful cars; few reflected on the human and environmental dangers generated by the production of the attractive consumer goods that contributed to an emerging affluent life-style.

One of the most profound social and cultural changes of our time has been the demise of that state of environmental unconsciousness. Growing concern over environmental integrity prompted an extraordinary growth of protective government legislation, especially during the 1970s: including the Clean Air Act in 1970, the Clean Water Act in 1972, the Safe Drinking Water Act in 1974, and the Toxic Substances Control Act in 1976.

Full recognition of the so-called energy crisis came a little later and, if anything, caused even greater repercussions in American life. The country that came of age with the private automobile found itself seemingly running out of gas. Suddenly our capacity to maintain an elevated standard of living, to sustain a growing and vibrant economy, and to preserve national security were all thrown into doubt with the awareness of our heavy dependence on imported oil.

Sepp Seitz/Woodfin Camp & Associates

The gasoline shortages of the 1970s helped change American attitudes about energy use.

Two broad, sharply contrasting tendencies have emerged in response to the twin crises of energy and the environment. One believes that the lesson of these crises is that we must learn to become a more conserving society, reducing dependence on scarce, nonrenewable fuels and exerting greater control over the environmental consequences of growth. Almost by definition, this approach implies a stronger role for public decision making, for the government to create policies, standards, and incentives to ensure that environmental goals are granted equal status with the more traditional one of economic growth.

The other tendency calls for a decreased role for government in regulating the quality of the environment and in shaping national energy policy. In this view, the government has itself been a large part of the problem and should be reduced in favor of "unleashing" the forces of the private market (Kneese, 1980). Behind this attitude is the assumption that the growth of environmental regulations has "hobbled the economy" [as *Fortune* put it in 1981 (Alexander, 1981, p. 239)], slowing economic growth and putting an intolerable and self-defeating burden on business. One recent critic goes even further, attacking the entire spirit of environmentalism as an "elitist" approach that opposes progress, industry, and prosperity — a doctrine "fearful of the future, despairing of human effort, worried about change, and wed to the status quo" (Tucker, 1982, as quoted in Stegner, 1982, p. 35).

Few issues more sharply illustrate the contrasts between competing social philosophies in America today — and few involve such high stakes. For the direction we now take on the problems of energy and the environment will shape not only our social and economic life but also the condition of the natural ecology on which both ultimately depend — for decades to come. The debate involves questions of enormous significance: the risks of nuclear catastrophe, of potentially irreversible contamination of water supplies, even of basic atmospheric and climatic changes affecting all life on earth.

In this chapter, we cannot, of course, do justice to all aspects of these broad, complex, and often highly technical issues. Instead, we will focus on the social and political questions they raise and on some of the evidence available to illuminate them. For it has become clear in recent years that the problems of energy use and environmental policy are profoundly *social* issues and not just scientific or economic ones. Whether the issue is balancing the costs and benefits of environmental regulation or the choice between alternative or conventional energy sources, the questions that are ultimately raised involve our deepest social priorities: our assessments of the relative importance of economic growth, the quality of urban and rural life, the benefits of intensive production in the present versus reducing the risks of illness and environmental degradation for future generations.

This chapter has two parts. In the first, focused on energy use and policy, we consider some of the potentials and limits of both conventional energy sources (oil, gas, and coal) and nuclear power, and of alternative energy sources (conservation and solar power). In the second we examine the closely related problems of the environment, with particular attention to recent debates about the costs, benefits, and consequences of environmental regulation.

Energy: The Hidden Revolution

With 6 percent of the world's population, the United States consumes almost 30 percent of its energy (Table 10-1). As we entered the 1980s, American energy consumption reached the equivalent of about 14 tons of coal or 2,600 barrels of oil a year for every man, woman, and child in the country

Region and energy source	Consumption, in million metric tons*					Percent distribution		
	1960	1965	1970	1975	1980	1960	1970	1980
World total	3,970	4,971	6,430	7,462	8,548	100.0	100.0	100.0
United States	1,477	1,783	2,227	2,284	2,370	37.2	34.6	27.7
Western Europe	783	1,003	1,295	1,407	1,559	19.7	20.1	18.2
Japan	109	178	317	354	431	2.7	4.9	5.0
Centrally planned economies†	1,201	1,444	1,783	2,292	2,745	30.3	27.7	32.1
Rest of world	400	563	808	1,125	1,443	10.1	12.6	16.9
Energy source:								
Solid fuels	1,981	2,070	2,184	2,309	2,669	49.9	34.0	31.2
Liquid fuels	1,311	1,902	2,798	3,374	3,709	33.0	43.5	43.4
Natural gas	593	882	1,293	1,556	1,871	14.9	20.1	21.9
Electricity	85	116	155	223	300	2.1	2.4	3.5

*In tons of coal equivalent. Metric ton = 1.1023 short tons.

†Includes China, North Korea, Mongolia, Vietnam, Albania, Bulgaria, Czechoslovakia, Hungary, Poland, Romania, the U.S.S.R., and West Germany.

Source: Adapted from *Statistical Abstract of the United States, 1982–83* (Washington, D.C.: Government Printing Office, 1983), p. 577.

Table 10-1
World energy consumption, by region and energy source, 1960–1980

(Union of Concerned Scientists, 1981, p. 4). The total bill for all this now amounts to about $400 billion a year (Friends of the Earth et al., 1982, p. 30).

Unlike some other industrial countries, the United States is also a major *producer* as well as *consumer* of energy — the largest energy producer in the world, in fact. But we are nevertheless heavily dependent on outside sources for energy, especially for oil. As one observer notes, "We *import* more oil than any other industrial nation *consumes*" (Yergin, 1982, p. 16). Because of that dependence, the sudden shortages of imported oil in the 1970s quickly rocked the country out of its complacency about energy use. In its place came the sense that assuring an adequate supply of energy was one of the most pressing of social and economic problems.

This much is generally agreed on. But *how* we should respond to the threatened security of energy is not. Since the oil shortages of the 1970s, one response has been a flurry of proposals designed to help the country "produce its way out of the energy crisis." The proposals include removing all controls on the prices of oil and gas, in the hope that this will encourage oil companies to undertake more domestic exploration and production, and continuing the massive subsidies to nuclear power and development begun in the 1950s. Several interlocking assumptions underlie these proposals:

1. It is assumed that the main energy problem the United States faces is *not enough* energy — that in order to sustain our standard of living, let

alone promote economic growth, we will need ever-expanding energy supplies.

2. It is assumed that *conventional* sources of energy, including some combination of oil, natural gas, coal, and nuclear power, can provide for those expanding needs, if given enough political and economic encouragement.

3. It is assumed that "alternative" energy sources, including the various forms of solar power and energy-conservation measures, can make only a minimal contribution to the country's energy needs in the foreseeable future.

How do these assumptions stand up against the evidence? Though the issues are certainly complex, much recent research casts considerable doubt on all three. There is a remarkable degree of convergence, in fact, around these different points:

1. A greatly expanded overall supply of energy may *not* be necessary for continued economic growth and material well-being; indeed, we are already using less energy per unit of economic output than we did during the 1970s.

2. The long-term potential for much greater exploitation of oil and other nonrenewable fuels (and for nuclear power) is probably much less than often supposed; while

3. The potential of alternative energy sources is probably much greater — not only in the distant future, but in the short term as well.

Let's consider each of these points.

The sharp increases in oil prices imposed in the 1970s by the oil-producing countries sent shock waves throughout the world, throwing the economies of both the industrial and developing countries out of gear. But there is wide agreement that these shocks were only the leading edge of a much deeper problem: Most of the energy sources we have historically relied on to do the work of society are finite — they are nonrenewable. This is especially true for two of our most heavily used fossil fuels, oil and natural gas. Both will probably be largely depleted — or so difficult to extract and produce that they will become prohibitively expensive — within an uncomfortably short time. Increasingly, debates over appropriate energy strategies begin from the understanding that we cannot, even if we wished, continue for too much longer our current level of dependence on these fuels (Stobaugh and Yergin, 1982, Chapter 1).

Nonrenewable energy sources (the basic fossil fuels such as coal, oil, and natural gas, as well as nuclear fuels) now account for roughly 95 percent of America's energy use. Currently, by far the largest single source is oil; about half our energy is derived from it, about three-fourths from oil and natural

The Limits of Fossil Fuels

gas combined. [This marks a dramatic historical change: In 1920 only about one-sixth of energy in the United States came from oil and gas (Union of Concerned Scientists, 1981, p. 2).] About half of the oil we use is imported. Oil is not, however, uniformly used to supply energy throughout the economy. About half of all oil used domestically is used for transportation.

How much oil do we have left? That question is not easy to answer and has been the subject of intense debate. But several recent estimates suggest that proven and unproven *domestic* oil reserves are in the range of 20 to 35 years' worth, at current use levels, or 40 to 70 years if we assume that about half our oil will continue to be imported from abroad (Stobaugh and Yergin, 1979, chap. 1).

There is much more oil, of course, *outside* the United States. But how much of it we will be able to count on for domestic use is impossible to predict. This is partly because of political uncertainties, dramatized by the behavior of the major oil-exporting countries in the past decade. But it also reflects the increasing intensity of competition for world oil resources, both from other industrialized countries and from developing countries with rapidly increasing energy needs. Table 10-1 shows that countries besides Western Europe, Japan, and the centrally planned economies increased their share of world energy consumption by about 70 percent over the past two decades.

Even if the United States were guaranteed a substantial share of world oil reserves — which it is not — the long-term problem of finite oil supplies would not be changed, only postponed. At some point in the not very distant future, we will have to shift to other sources of energy.

Much the same problem applies to natural gas, though, unlike oil, a large proportion of natural gas is domestically produced. About a quarter of domestic energy now comes from natural gas, especially to power industry and to heat and cook in homes and businesses. Natural gas has the additional advantage of being a relatively "clean" fuel and therefore relatively benign in environmental terms, compared to other nonrenewable fuels. But it, too, is finite. One study estimates that we have another 35 to 60 years of domestic natural gas supplies left, at current rates of consumption (Union of Concerned Scientists, 1981, chap. 2).

Is decontrol the answer? One argument often raised in response to these shortages is that they are mainly artificial ones, resulting less from natural scarcity than from unwise social policy. Specifically, the relatively low prices for oil and gas on the American market are held partly responsible for a supply problem that, it's held, is more apparent than real. Historically, oil and gas prices have been held below their potential market levels through government regulation. Some writers argue that these controls have discouraged efforts by oil companies to locate and develop more domestic supplies. Especially as those supplies become more difficult to discover and extract, the economic incentive to do so begins to disappear. The result, in this view, is that we really don't know how much oil and gas may be beneath the surface — and we will only find out when we allow prices to rise high enough to make more intensive exploration worthwhile.

While it is certainly true that government policy has historically kept fuel prices under control, there is little evidence that *decontrol* (allowing the prices to rise to whatever level the market will bear) will have much long-term effect on the problem of dwindling domestic oil reserves. One important indication: The oil companies' level of new exploration and drilling actually went up substantially during the 1970s, while proven oil reserves continued to decline. In 1970 the American oil industry drilled 13,000 crude oil wells, and proven oil reserves were about 39 billion barrels. In 1979 it drilled 19,000 wells, but proven oil reserves had nevertheless shrunk to about 27 billion barrels. Clearly, despite already stepped-up efforts by the industry to discover new oil, it had not turned up enough new reserves to slow the clock significantly. As a Harvard Business School study sums up this experience, "There is no domestic oil solution to the problem of increasing U.S. oil imports . . . any hopes rest, to varying degrees, on the other energy sources" (Stobaugh and Yergin, 1979, p. 46).

The social consequences of rising energy costs. Another side of the strategy of decontrol deserves mention — its *social* impact. As critics have pointed out, a strategy of attempting to increase energy production by raising prices can have harsh consequences, and its worst victims are people with low incomes (Olsen, 1981, p. 67).

While the poor use less total energy than the more affluent, they spend a large proportion of their budget for energy — and often pay *higher prices* for it as well. According to a Department of Energy study, the average poor household in the 1970s spent about 22 percent of its budget on energy, as compared to just 5 percent for middle-income households (Thompson, 1980). This difference is partly because middle-income people enjoy a much larger total budget, while the poor's budget is almost entirely consumed by necessities — and energy is a major necessity (Hatch and Whitehead, 1981). But the poor also pay more *per unit* of energy used — about 5 percent more than the national average, according to one study (Grier, 1979), mainly because current utility company rates, somewhat perversely, favor large consumers of energy over small ones. (Big industries that use enormous amounts of electricity, for example, pay lower unit rates for it than households do.) In the western states, according to one study, poor black households paid half again as much for electric power, per unit consumed, as the average, so that many black households actually paid more for energy than white households while using *less* of it (Thompson, 1980).

Under these conditions, energy price increases in the name of freeing market forces may aggravate an already harshly unequal situation. Since,

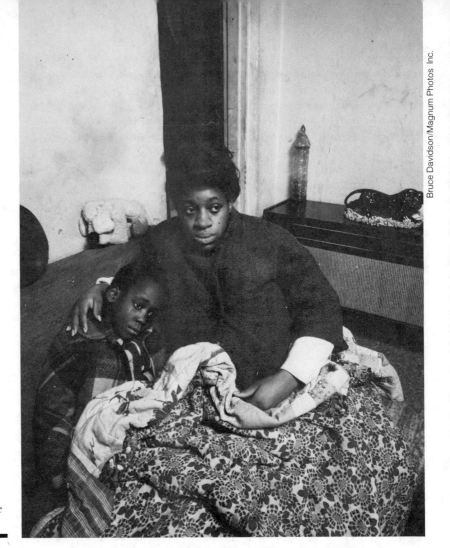

Rising energy prices are not an abstraction for the poor.

unlike the more affluent, the poor use most of their energy for necessary uses like heating and cooking, they have no slack to cut back on in the face of cost increases and (as studies have shown) tend to respond to higher energy costs by cutting back other necessities, especially food. For some of the poor, rising energy prices may mean a choice between "heating or eating" (Hatch and Whitehead, 1981; Blaustein, 1982, chap. 4). In theory, this choice might be avoided by special government programs to target energy assistance to the poor; in practice, it hasn't. A 1982 study for the Joint Economic Committee of Congress found that between 1979 and 1981, the decontrol of oil prices cost low-income people more than $9 billion, of which only between one-fourth and one-third was offset by federal energy assistance programs. In addition to its disappointing impact on oil supplies, then, oil decontrol, according to the Joint Economic Committee, "has been a social policy failure" (U.S. Congress, Joint Economic Committee, 1982b, pp. 4–5).

Before the ascendence of the automobile, coal was the most important energy source in the United States; it is still a major one, supplying more than a fifth of our total energy in the early 1980s (*Statistical Abstract of the U.S., 1982–83*, p. 571). Americans consumed more than 700 million tons of coal in 1980, largely for electric power generation; but, unlike oil and gas, we are a long way from running out of coal. The United States has been called the "Persian Gulf of coal" (Stobaugh and Yergin, 1979, p. 80); we have almost a third of the world's known reserves, enough to last at least 400 years at current rates of consumption.

The problem with coal is not its availability, but the severe environmental problems that accompany its heavy use. These hazards appear at all stages in the process of coal use, from mining to burning. Underground coal mining has traditionally been one of the most dangerous of occupations; aboveground, strip mining (increasingly common, especially in the West) produces fewer occupational hazards but even greater environmental ones.

But the hazards of *burning* coal are even more troubling. Coal burning produces great amounts of hazardous pollutants, especially sulfur dioxide, ash, and carbon dioxide. Historically, these have been responsible for a major part of the air pollution problem in most industrial countries; more recently, they have presented the specter of even more severe problems. Sulfur dioxide emissions from coal-fired power plants are one of the chief sources of the acid rain (see pages 388 to 389) that has threatened waters and forests, especially in the northeast. The large amounts of carbon dioxide may create what scientists call a *greenhouse effect* (where a "blanket" of carbon dioxide absorbs heat radiated by the earth's surface and significantly raises the average temperature, with potentially catastrophic effects on climate, crops, and even the level of the oceans).

Some of these hazards may be mitigated by more advanced coal-burning technologies that allow coal to be burned in cleaner ways. But though coal will undoubtedly remain an important source of fuel for decades to come, enough hazards remain to create wide agreement that coal can only be one part of a long-term energy mix. The hazards of heavy dependence on coal, in fact, are one of the main arguments to justify an even more controversial nonrenewable energy strategy: nuclear power.

Not long ago, nuclear power seemed to promise an end to worries about America's future energy supplies. In the early stages of the country's budding nuclear program, it was sometimes argued that electricity produced by nuclear power plants would be "too cheap to meter" (Council on Economic

Coal

Nuclear Power: High Promises, Grave Dangers

Priorities, 1979, p. 2). The United States accordingly plunged into a huge investment in nuclear energy, fueled by massive government subsidies.

Since World War II, the overwhelming bulk of federal funds for energy research and development have gone to nuclear energy (Union of Concerned Scientists, 1981, p. xvi), and the government also subsidized nuclear power indirectly through legislation (the Price-Anderson Act) limiting the insurance liability that nuclear power companies face in case of even a massive reactor accident. One study estimates that by the beginning of the 1980s, the public had subsidized nuclear energy to the tune of $37 billion (Friends of the Earth et al., 1982, p. 29). But despite an amount of government support that dwarfs anything allotted to any other energy form in recent American history, it had become increasingly apparent by the late 1970s that, as the Harvard Business School's study put it, "the nuclear promise has turned into nuclear disappointment" (Stobaugh and Yergin, 1979, p. 108). Other critics, going even farther, have called the decline of nuclear power "the greatest collapse of any enterprise in industrial history" (Lovins and Lovins, 1980, p. 54). Is this an accurate prognosis?

Certainly the momentum that characterized the nuclear industry in the 1960s and 1970s has subsided. By the 1980s orders for new nuclear facilities had come to a virtual halt in the United States (as they had in many other

Breeding Catastrophe?

In 1970 a hitherto obscure river in Tennessee, the Clinch, entered history. In that year it was chosen as the site for a proposed experimental nuclear reactor, cumbersomely termed the Liquid Metal Fast Breeder Reactor (LMFBR). The breeder was announced with much fanfare as the newest answer to America's long-term energy problems. Virtually shelved during the late 1970s, because of rising costs and doubts about its safety and usefulness, it was revived again in the early 1980s, in the face of strong protest from scientific and environmental groups. What is the breeder's potential role — and why is there such intense opposition?

In principle, the breeder reactor, besides simply consuming nuclear fuel (as other nuclear reactors do) also creates new fuel by causing nuclear reactions within otherwise nonusable but "fertile" uranium. Thus, the breeder reactor can potentially provide very long-range supplies of energy. One estimate holds that a "breeder economy" could provide the United States with between 500 and 1,300 years of energy at current levels of consumption. That potential has made investment in breeder technology seem tempting. (Though, it should be stressed, breeders are not a *currently* available technology; they would not provide a significant contribution to America's energy needs until well into the next century.)

But the problems are equally formidable. Many of them are the same ones encountered in conventional nuclear technology, only intensified. The first is cost. The $500 million cost estimate for the Clinch River project in 1970 had, by the early 1980s, multiplied to $3.5 billion. Breeder reactors, if actually constructed, are expected to cost 25 to 75 percent more than conventional nuclear reactors, which are now priced beyond other electric power plants in cost per unit of output. With such high costs, the breeder could only survive through massive infusions of public funds since it would be unable to compete economically, at least for the forseeable future. These extreme relative costs are a main reason why five of six breeders scheduled for development by the French government have been scrapped.

countries as well). Between March 1979 (when the Three Mile Island reactor accident occurred) and the close of 1982, only 6 new reactors were licensed for operation, while 37 new plants under construction or in the planning stage were canceled by utility companies. The U.S. Nuclear Regulatory Commission estimated in 1982 that another 19 proposed plants would soon be canceled or postponed indefinitely (*New York Times*, November 1, 1982). In the 10 years prior to 1980, more proposed reactors were canceled than were actually in operation at the end of the period.

Why this sudden reversal in the fortunes and potential of the nuclear power industry? There have been several reasons, including high costs, declining demand, and questions of safety.

Cost. Nuclear power advocates seriously underestimated the costs of nuclear power plant construction. Cost overruns have generally been double or triple the initial cost estimates. One recent projection holds that in the mid-to-late 1980s, nuclear plants may cost, per unit of electrical output, *twice* as much as coal-fired power plants. As a result, nuclear electricity will be less and less able to compete with coal-fired electricity in the marketplace. Many proposed nuclear plants have run so far over projected costs that they may simply never be completed. In Washington State, for example, $4 billion

In 1983, Congress halted federal funds for the Clinch River project on the ground that no acceptable plan for *private* financing of the reactor had been developed; apparently, private investors were too wary to be interested. This lack of enthusiasm, in turn, has resulted from the uncertainty that an economic need exists for the project in the first place. A 1982 study by the U.S. Congressional Research Service estimated that the southeastern region in which the Clinch River project is located will have a comfortable margin of electrical generating capacity until at least 1995; the Tennessee Valley Authority, the major potential customer for the plant's electricity, declared that it wouldn't need new generating capacity until well after the year 2000. In this glutted market, the breeder's only plausible role would be in the distant — and uncertain — future.

But the even more serious problem with the breeder reactor involves *safety;* in particular, the enhanced potential for breeder material to be diverted into the production of nuclear weapons by unstable governments or terrorist groups. The breeder reactor creates large amounts of pluto-

nium, one of the most toxic materials on earth (thus presenting grave dangers in case of reactor accident) and also a main ingredient in nuclear weaponry. The magnitude of this threat is ominous. Every year, according to a recent estimate, just *one* breeder reactor could produce sufficient plutonium to make about 10,000 nuclear bombs, or about as many as are now in America's *total* current arsenal of strategic nuclear weapons.

Might it be possible to defend a "plutonium economy" in the future against the dangers of terrorism, sabotage, or devastating accidents? Possibly. But, as many critics point out, that would probably require an elaborate and costly security apparatus that would gravely threaten civil liberties. As the Union of Concerned Scientists sums up the problem, "The vigilant administration of a large-scale plutonium economy may in all likelihood prove to be incompatible with the exercise of civil liberties and democratic control" (Union of Concerned Scientists, 1980, p. 259).

Sources: Stobaugh and Yergin, 1979, chapter 5; Union of Concerned Scientists, 1980, p. 259; Marshall, 1983; Norman, 1983.

was invested in the early 1970s to build five new nuclear plants. By 1981 the cost had mushroomed to $24 billion; by 1983 construction on two of the plants had been abandoned. Only one of the original five was considered likely to ever produce electricity, and the project's more than $8 billion in outstanding debt would probably never be repaid (*Business Week*, July 11, 1983).

Declining demand. The nuclear planners also badly misjudged the demand for nuclear power. Current nuclear technology is feasible only for electric power generation, but the demand for electric power has not matched early expectations. Increasing energy efficiency and slower population growth, among other causes, have reduced the rate of increase in demand for electricity. By the late 1970s, the United States had an *excess* capacity to produce electric power, an excess more than twice as large as the entire share of electricity generated by nuclear plants (Lovins and Lovins, 1980, p. 61).

Safety. The problem of safety has been perhaps the greatest obstacle to the continued viability of nuclear power and the one most keenly felt by the public. Fears over nuclear safety center on two equally serious issues: the possibility of major nuclear reactor accidents and the more insidious problem of the disposal of radioactive wastes.

Two years before the terrifying accident at Three Mile Island, one highly placed nuclear advocate wrote:

Estimating the Risks of Nuclear Disaster

For many years, proponents of nuclear energy believed that reactor safety was not a major problem. The chance of a serious nuclear power plant accident releasing substantial amounts of radioactive material were, they argued, almost infinitesimal. These views were supported by a 1975 study commissioned by the U.S. Nuclear Regulatory Commission (the Rasmussen Report) that estimated the chances of a "worst-case" reactor accident at less than one in a million. The report also calculated that the worst accident would possibly cause about 3,300 "early" deaths (that is, not counting those resulting from the long-term effects of radiation) and that the economic costs would be a maximum of $14 billion in damages.

But in 1982, a massive, detailed study carried out by the U.S. Department of Energy's Sandia National Laboratories drew much different — and far grimmer — conclusions. On the basis of elaborate computer models of the risks at each of the 80 sites in the United States where nuclear power plants were in operation or under construction, the Sandia researchers came up with the astounding figure that the worst-case reactor accident could cause more than 100,000 deaths in the first year and more than $300 billion in damages.

These estimates were based on a hypothetical, very severe accident involving extensive damage to the reactor's core, partial melting of its nuclear fuel, the collapse of its safety system, and a breach in its containment structure sufficient to allow a substantial release of radioactivity into the atmosphere close to a densely populated

---

The safety of this present generation of nuclear reactors is not a major policy issue. These reactors have operated on ships and on land for over two decades and have never led to a reactor-related fatality. . . . Disposal of low-level wastes . . . is being handled safely, and indefinite term disposal technologies appear to be nearly at hand." (Laird, 1977, pp. 9-10)

The Three Mile Island accident, which caused over a billion dollars of direct damages and several more billions in indirect economic losses (*New York Times*, November 1, 1982) plus immeasurable psychological damage to residents, made this argument seem less than compelling. So did government studies in the early 1980s demonstrating that the likelihood — and the costs — of catastrophic nuclear accidents were much greater than had been confidently supposed (see below).

According to an analysis by the energy-advocacy group Critical Mass, there were 140 reactor mishaps of "major significance" in 1981 alone; a 1982 study by the U.S. Nuclear Regulatory Commission, the body that oversees the country's nuclear power program, counted 169 accidents between 1969 and 1979 that could have led to a meltdown of a nuclear reactor core (cited in *Environment*, September 1982, pp. 21-22).

Meanwhile, effective waste-disposal technologies have *not* yet materialized as hoped. By the 1980s some communities were voting on measures to prohibit the disposal of radioactive wastes within their borders. Nuclear waste had become an admittedly intractable problem that nobody wanted in their backyard. In 1980, for example, the residents of Washington State successfully passed an initiative forbidding the shipment of nuclear wastes

area. Though such an accident would be considerably worse than the most serious one in the United States so far (the 1979 incident at the Three Mile Island reactor in Pennsylvania), the chances of its occurrence, in Sandia's calculations, are much greater than earlier projections had envisioned. The probability of this worst-case accident, according to Sandia, was 1 chance in every 100,000 reactor/hours; a seemingly small figure, but one that translates into about *1 chance in 50 of such an accident happening in the United States before the year 2000.*

The toll in death, injury, and property damage from this kind of accident would vary greatly, depending particularly on the population density near the plant, the quality of emergency responses (especially the speed of evacuating the local population), and the specific weather conditions at the time of the accident. The worst site,

according to the Sandia study (ranked in terms of potential deaths) would be the Salem nuclear plant in Salem, New Jersey, where a worst-case accident could kill 100,000 and injure another 75,000 in the first year and cause an additional 40,000 deaths from radiation-induced cancer over the following 30 years. An accident at the Waterford plant in St. Charles, Louisiana, could kill 96,000 during the first year and injure 279,000. On the other hand, an accident at the LaCrosse reactor near LaCrosse, Wisconsin, would, according to the Sandia study, kill just 70 people in the first year and 200 over the following generation.

Source: U.S. Department of Energy data as cited in *San Francisco Chronicle*, November 1 and 2, 1982.

Roger Sandler/Picture Group

Public awareness of the limits and dangers of nuclear power has grown.

into the state (*Business Week*, July 11, 1983). And one critic noted, "With the nuclear enterprise now in its fourth decade, it is an acute embarrassment that the waste problem has not been solved" (Carter, 1983, p. 33). In late 1982, Congress approved a bill mandating the government to begin building nuclear waste-disposal repositories (probably in deep underground storage areas) by 1989. Most of the proposed possible sites for these facilities, however, turn out to have built-in uncertainties (like the possibility of contaminating groundwater or of earthquakes) in addition to the political ones of resistance by those who will have to live and work near the sites (Carter, 1983). In 1983, too, the U.S. Supreme Court, in what was widely described as a potential death blow to plans for further nuclear power plant construction, upheld a California law forbidding the building of new nuclear reactors until a "demonstrated technology" for radioactive waste disposal was available (in mid-1983, eight other states had similar laws) (*Environment*, June 1983, p. 21; *Science*, May 6, 1983, p. 587).

These problems mean that nuclear power is unlikely to supply anywhere near the share of America's energy that its proponents projected in the 1960s and 1970s. As the Harvard Business School's study noted in 1979, even if every nuclear plant then ordered or under construction was added to our current array of nuclear facilities, we would have less than half the nuclear capacity by the 1990s that was predicted in the 1970s (Stobaugh and Yergin, 1979, p. 111). Since that time, the process of "denuclearization" has proceeded even faster. Table 10-2 shows that we were generating less nu-

Table 10-2

Nuclear power plants—number, capacity, and generation, 1965–1981

	1965	1970	1973	1974	1975	1976	1977	1978	1979	1980	1981 preliminary
Operating reactors*	10	19	41	54	57	64	67	71	71	75	74
Capacity (million kW)	.9	6.5	24.7	36.9	35.6	44.6	47.1	50.8	50.9	54.7	55.8
Percent of total electric utility capacity	.4	1.9	5.6	7.7	7.0	8.4	8.4	8.8	8.5	8.9	8.8
Electricity generated (billion kWh)	.4	22	84	114	173	191	251	276	255	251	273
Percent of total electric utility generation	.4	1.4	4.5	6.1	9.0	9.4	11.8	12.5	11.4	11.0	11.9

*As of year-end. Includes plants shut down permanently or for extended periods.
Source: Statistical Abstract of the United States, 1982–83 (Washington, D.C.: Government Printing Office, 1983), p. 589.

clear electricity in 1981 than several years earlier. The public's support for nuclear power, too, has been rapidly eroding. An NBC poll in late 1981, for example, found that 56 percent of respondents believed that no more nuclear plants should be built (Friends of the Earth et al., 1982, p. 42).

But over and above the growing public rejection, sheer economics has most deeply undercut the promise of nuclear power. It has apparently ceased to be competitive with conventional fuels as a means of generating electrical power. "The free market," one study comments, "is killing nuclear power" (Friends of the Earth et al., 1982, p. 29). Without continuing federal subsidies to prop it up, according to some observers, the nuclear industry might well have collapsed already. This judgment is apparently shared even within parts of the nuclear industry itself: The chairman of General Electric, a major nuclear plant contractor, declared in 1982 that "If we were starting again, we would not enter this business" (quoted in *Environment*, April 1982, p. 21). Despite attempts to salvage the nuclear program (like the renewed commitment to the so-called breeder reactor, see below), there seems "no reasonable possibility," as the Harvard study puts it, that nuclear power will make substantially greater contributions to our energy needs during this century (Stobaugh and Yergin, 1979, p. 135).

Alternative Energy Strategies: Conservation and Solar

If the conventional fuels are inherently limited and nuclear energy is burdened with grave and possibly insurmountable problems, what will we do for energy in the coming decades? Strategies to increase conventional and nuclear energy production, even in the face of environmental and social dangers, are often justified on the ground that there is simply no other feasible alternative. But there is considerable evidence that the picture may not be that bleak — and the choices not that limited. Reducing our commitment to fossil fuels and nuclear energy need not mean a declining economy, a lower standard of living, or a new "dark age." Two alternatives seem especially promising according to current research, even *without* major new technological advances: energy conservation and solar power.

Conservation: The Hidden "Energy Source"

The average American home, according to one recent investigation, has a square yard of holes in it (Lovins and Lovins, 1980, p. 96). This homely fact illustrates that much of our traditional thinking about energy problems may have ignored a crucial side of America's energy problems. The scarcity of energy *supplies* is just one part of the problem; the other is the inefficient way in which we consume the energy we have.

Because that inefficiency is so widespread in American life, the potential for energy savings through conservation is enormous. One study estimates that a strong commitment to energy conservation would allow the United States to use 30 to 40 percent less energy than we now do and enjoy the same (or perhaps better) living standards (Stobaugh and Yergin, 1979, p. 136); another estimates that a shift to conservation, using only those technological tools that already exist, could cut American energy needs by roughly one-half. If the United States had fully invested in energy-efficiency improvements in the late 1960s and early 1970s, another analysis argues, we could have cut oil purchases (as of 1978) by about 28 percent, coal purchases by 34 percent, and electricity by 43 percent — thus allowing us to cut oil imports in half, reduce the environmental damages from coal use, and completely eliminate the need for nuclear power (Lovins and Lovins, 1980, p. 51). The National Academy of Sciences calculated in the 1970s that by the year 2000, depending on which energy strategy we pursued, and especially on the level of investment in conservation, we could expect to use as much as twice the amount of energy we now produce — or 20 percent *less* — assuming the same level of material living conditions (Stobaugh and Yergin, 1979, p. 176).

This astonishing flexibility is one consequence of the heedless use of energy long tolerated — and even encouraged — in the United States. Some of the most important examples are:

- Building construction in the United States has typically been enormously energy-inefficient, especially during the 1950s and 1960s. The modern office building is an energy-planner's nightmare. It is often a sealed system that cannot use outside temperature conditions for its heating and cooling, so it may have to be artificially heated even on warm days and cooled even when outside temperatures drop. It usually has centralized lighting systems instead of lights that can be turned on and off individually, so the entire lighting system must be either on or off — a sure prescription for the overuse of electric power. Large pre-1950 buildings used only *half* as much energy per square foot as those constructed in the early 1960s (Stobaugh and Yergin, 1979, p. 166).

- A similar loss of efficiency took place during the postwar era in some industrial products and consumer goods. Small electric motors, for example, of the kind used in many consumer appliances, were less energy-efficient in 1975 than they had been 20 years *earlier,* according to a study by the U.S. Department of Energy (Council on Economic Priorities, 1979, p. 39).

- American homes are also enormously energy-inefficient. Plugging the square yard of holes in the typical American home would save up to 50 percent of the oil and gas now used for space heating in the United States, according to some estimates. As many as 30 percent of American homes, moreover, may be completely lacking in insulation. During the 1970s, experimental energy-efficient houses built under federal programs achieved energy savings of 25 to 50 percent compared to conventional homes (Stobaugh and Yergin, 1979, p. 170).

• Transportation has been one of the most inefficient areas of energy use in America, though improvements in the past few years have been considerable. Our heavy reliance on the private automobile is part of the problem. But it is not just that we depend so much on the private car (and so little on more energy-efficient mass transit) but also that the cars themselves have been relatively inefficient users of energy. And, like construction and consumer appliances, they became even less efficient during the postwar era. In the case of the automobile, the main cause of declining efficiency was increasing weight: The average Chevrolet sedan gained a quarter of a ton between 1968 and 1973 (Stobaugh and Yergin, 1979, p. 148). Improvements in the energy efficiency of the American automobile (and the increased sales of more energy-efficient foreign cars) help explain why (as we'll see in a moment) energy use hasn't risen as much as was predicted a decade ago.

Evidence for the great potential of conservation comes from several sources. One is the experience of foreign countries, most of which (see pages 380 to 382) use *far* less energy per capita than the United States while maintaining equal — or better — rates of economic growth and per capita income. And Figure 10-1 demonstrates that *within* the United States, the new concern for energy conservation has already had a striking impact on energy use. Between 1973 and 1978, American industrial output went *up* by 12 percent, while total energy use went *down* by 6 percent. Between 1977 and 1981, conservation improvements (including better gas mileage in most cars) led to a one-third reduction in oil imports (Friends of the Earth et al., 1982, p. 70). Overall, by 1982 the United States was "more than 15 percent more energy-efficient than it was in 1973" (Yergin, 1982, p. 16).

Figure 10-1

Energy consumption per dollar of GNP, 1950–1981

Source: Conservation Foundation, *The State of the Environment—1982* (Washington, D.C.: Conservation Foundation, 1982), p. 190. Reprinted with permission.

Thousand Btu per dollar

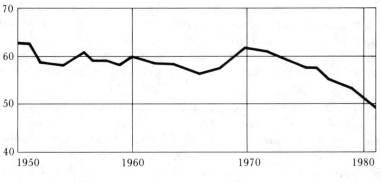

1972 constant dollars

These changes indicate that what was once considered an unbreakable link between the amount of energy consumed and the level of economic well-being is actually quite flexible. They mark a kind of quiet revolution in energy use; one that, if encouraged, will surely have an increasing impact in the future. And this emerging shift in energy use has taken place *without* wholesale austerity measures on the part of the public. As the Union of Concerned Scientists puts it, "No radical transformation of society or reversion to the life-styles of our grandparents is required to hold down growth in energy use" (1981, p. 16).

Solar Power: An Emerging Role

Opinion polls show that solar power is the most widely favored of all sources of energy and the one the majority of Americans most wish to see encouraged. But it is also widely believed that solar energy is at best a technology for the distant future, not an important source of energy for the near term nor a significant part of the answer to shrinking supplies of conventional energy. This belief has guided government policy: Only a fraction of federal energy subsidies have been devoted to solar research and development. Solar energy in all its forms (including wind power and wood, an indirect solar source) now account for only about 5 percent of America's energy. The idea that much of an advanced society's energy needs could be met from the sun still strikes many people as utopian and farfetched.

But there is growing evidence that solar technology may — if it is adequately encouraged — play a far more important role in meeting American energy needs in the *near* future, and play a much greater role within a few more decades. As with energy conservation, there is a striking amount of agreement in much recent research on the magnitude of that potential contribution. The Harvard Business School's study estimated that, with proper government incentives, solar energy could supply from 20 to 25 percent of America's energy by the year 2000 (Stobaugh and Yergin, 1979, p. 183). Reviewing many studies of the potential of solar energy, the Union of Concerned Scientists estimated the proportion at between 15 to 33 percent and felt that a wholly solar-powered economy could be largely completed by the year 2050 (Union of Concerned Scientists, 1981, p. 21). A report by the federally funded Solar Energy Research Institute (SERI) estimated that 20 to 30 percent of American energy demands in the year 2000 could be met by renewable sources, given a substantial commitment to increasing energy efficiency (Friends of the Earth et al., 1982, p. 66). It's important to note, however, that solar energy's potential is, so far, an uneven one. Solar power is capable of doing some things now, others only in the future.

There is no problem of availability in the case of solar energy; the energy contained in the sunlight that falls on the land mass of the United States over a given year is more than 500 times the total energy the country consumes (Union of Concerned Scientists, 1981, p. 110). The problem is transforming that energy into useful applications. Currently, we have the technology to make *some* of those applications now, while others will require more development. What solar energy does best at present levels of technology is provide space and water heating at relatively low levels of temperature, making it especially suitable for residential uses. Most studies now agree that residential solar heating systems are already economically competitive with conventional fuels, offering a "here-and-now alternative to imported oil" (Stobaugh and Yergin, 1979, p. 188). Higher-temperature industrial uses of solar energy are less well developed, as is the direct generation of electric power from sunlight.

The technology for solar electric power generation through photovoltaic cells (which transform sunlight into electrical current) is understood in principle. The obstacles to its large-scale development are now mainly economic; the cells are costly to produce. Yet many studies argue that this cost disadvantage could be eliminated through sufficient government support, especially through large-scale government purchases of solar cells that would enable the use of more efficient mass-production techniques. In the mid-1970s, a federal task force estimated that an investment of this kind of less than $500 million could make photovoltaic cells economically competitive by the mid-1980s. Indeed, the cost of these cells, even without massive government incentives, dropped drastically (about tenfold) during the late 1970s because of technological advances (Union of Concerned Scientists, 1981, p. 140).

These developments suggest that even the large-scale generation of electric power, which would make solar energy directly competitive not only

How Other Countries Use Energy

When we think about how much energy we need to sustain economic growth and material comfort, we typically extrapolate from our *present* levels of energy consumption. We tend to assume, in other words, that the way we now use energy is a more or less inevitable fact of life. If we want continued growth and a rising standard of living, we will need ever-increasing inputs of energy; and we will have to come up with new ways to produce it. In this view, the only alternative to vastly greater energy production is economic stagnation and a kind of modern version of the dark ages.

But this attitude ignores an important source of lessons about the uses and possibilities of energy: the experience of other countries. Many studies have concluded that we use energy less efficiently than otherwise comparable countries, including some that, by most measures, have a

higher standard of living. This suggests that we could achieve the same — or better — living standards as we now enjoy without massive increases in energy consumption, and perhaps while using *less* energy than we now do.

One recent study estimates that Americans use "twice as much energy per capita as do the West Germans, the Swedes, and the Swiss" (Nordlund and Robson, 1980, p. 4). Meanwhile, all three countries have performed better economically than we have in recent years and have higher per capita incomes as well. The United States, according to another analysis, was using about 490 more tons of oil (or its equivalent in other fuels) than Western European countries to produce each million dollars worth of gross national product (Darmstadter, 1981, p. 39).

What accounts for these striking differences? Studies show that the relative energy efficiency of many European countries applies across the board to every realm of energy use: in homes, transportation, and industrial processes. One

with conventional fuels but with nuclear power, may be fairly close at hand. Unlike both conventional and nuclear technologies, moreover, most solar technologies are environmentally benign. They cause little or no pollution and involve relatively insignificant safety hazards — and they are capable of creating large numbers of jobs.

Despite these advantages, though, recent social policy has not been generous to research and development in solar energy. Funding for solar research activities by the U.S. Department of Energy (never a high priority) dropped from $570 million in 1979 to $22 million in 1983 (*Environment*, November 1982, p. 23). Why — if the scientific knowledge already for the most part exists — have we done so little to promote the development of solar energy? We will leave the answer to the conclusion of this chapter, but it seems clear that, as the Harvard study puts it, "it's the political climate, not the weather, that will govern the future of solar energy" (Stobaugh and Yergin, 1979, p. 212).

Jobs and Energy

Debates about energy issues often become centered on economic questions, particularly the impact of different energy policies on jobs. The stakes can be high — and can generate strong emotions. Especially when unemploy-

study sums up Sweden's ability to use 40 percent less energy per capita than the United States by noting that the Swedes have "fewer large cars, flimsy products, leaky houses, and empty buses" (Schipper and Lichtenberg, 1978, p. 26). Swedish homes, for example, use only about half the energy American homes do, when the proportions are adjusted for differences in size and typical weather conditions. (This difference mainly results from stricter construction standards, better insulation, and more multiple-family housing units in Sweden.) In industry, West German companies use one-third less energy to produce a ton of steel than their American counterparts (Union of Concerned Scientists, 1981, pp. 38–42).

The largest single difference in energy efficiency between the United States and many other industrial countries lies in transportation. The Swedes use less than one-third the energy per capita in transportation than we do, mainly because of lighter private cars and a much greater use of public transit within cities. Similar —some-

times even lower — proportions exist in other European countries. American cars (mainly because of their weight) are 50 percent more energy-intensive, on average, than European cars (Darmstadter, 1981, p. 37).

Not all of these differences imply lax standards or simple inefficiency on the part of Americans. Some are "structural" differences; that is, they reflect largely unavoidable physical or demographic characteristics of the different countries. One reason why European countries use less energy for transportation per capita, for example, is that many of their cities are denser (less spread out) than American cities and therefore require less extensive commuting. Overall, one recent study estimates, about half of the differences in relative energy use between the United States and several Western European countries may be accounted for by these structural and largely unchangeable factors. But the other half is due to differences in the *intensity* of energy use (the amount of energy it takes to produce a given

ment is high, communities, workers, and businesspeople may support energy development programs — even those that may bring troubling social or environmental consequences — on the assumption that they will, at least, create jobs. The risks involved in building, say, a nuclear power plant near a community may come to be seen as a relatively small price to pay for its potential benefits in new jobs. The concern for the human and environmental consequences of nuclear development thus becomes pitted against the equally pressing one of jobs and material well-being — either the power plant or no jobs.

But a growing body of research suggests that this dilemma may be partly illusory because it ignores a third option: the job-creating potential of investment in alternative energy sources. In particular, solar energy and conservation, singly or in combination, generate considerably more employment than conventional energy technologies — and far more than nuclear power.

Studies comparing the job-creating potential of solar development with conventional energy technologies indicate that, for example, investment in solar heating can produce three to four times as many jobs as "hard" technologies producing the same amount of energy. One study estimates that California alone could create at least 375,000 new jobs a year during the 1980s through investment in already existing solar technologies (that is, solar space and water heating) alone (Nordlund and Robson, 1980, pp. 67–68). The U.S. Office of Technology Assessment, similarly, estimated that a con-

unit of output) and that in turn reflects differences in efficiency (Darmstadter, 1981, p. 39).

In part, the relatively efficient use of energy in Europe is the result of traditionally greater concern for energy conservation. Historical studies of the different patterns of industrial development between the United States and several foreign countries illustrate this tendency sharply. One study of industrial innovation in the United States, Japan, and Western Europe shows, for example, that the typical American approach to innovation has been to devise ways of eliminating *labor* — at the expense of capital and energy resources. Looking at almost 2,000 major industrial innovations in several countries, this study (from the Harvard Business School) found that 40 percent of American innovations were primarily "labor-saving" as compared to just 13 percent of Western European and 6 percent of Japanese innovations. Meanwhile, only 21 percent of innovations in American industries were classified as "material saving" as compared to 47 percent of

the Western European and 34 percent of the Japanese innovations. Traditionally, then, we have tended to squander energy resources in industrial growth, while many other countries have, for years, sought ways of conserving them (Vernon, 1980, pp. 151–152). Similarly, the United States has lagged well behind many other countries in the level of government support for energy conservation measures. We've seen that the government has heavily subsidized selected forms of energy production in America, especially oil and nuclear. The other side of the coin is the lack of support for energy conservation. Proportionately, the amount spent by the Canadian government to subsidize housing insulation alone would translate into $14 billion in the United States (as of the late 1970s), an amount much greater than what we actually spent to make homes more energy-conserving (Stobaugh and Yergin, 1979, p. 178).

Sources: Schipper and Lichtenberg, 1978; Stobaugh and Yergin, 1982; Nordlund and Robson, 1980; Vernon, 1980; Darmstadter, 1981; Union of Concerned Scientists, 1981.

ventional, coal-fired electric power plant would require about 2,300 person-hours of work per megawatt-year (a measure of electric power generation), while a solar hot-water system would require from 3,500 to 5,200, and a solar photovoltaic generating system between 11,000 and 15,000 person-hours (Nordlund and Robson, 1980, pp. 67–68). A study by the California Energy Commission found that *most* energy production typically provides fewer jobs, per dollar invested, than the average for the economy as a whole. But within the range of energy options, solar turns out to be a relatively effective job producer, nuclear an especially poor one. Solar water heating provides at least three times as many jobs per kilowatt-hour as any type of electric power plant; and among power plants, nuclear ones provide fewer jobs than those powered by coal or oil (Lerney and Posey, 1979).

Why so few jobs from conventional energy production? Like some other industries (the chemical industry, for one), most energy-producing industries are extremely capital-intensive — they require very large investment in materials and plant but relatively few workers.

Some alternative technologies, however, including most solar and conservation approaches, are labor-intensive — they require relatively little capital investment and relatively large amounts of labor, both in manufacturing (of solar panels or energy-conserving devices, for instance) and in installation. (For the same reason, they offer strong potential for small business development.)

This effect is especially strong when these "soft" energy technologies are combined with conservation efforts. Thus, one study calculated that a "conservation/solar package" could produce about 30 person-years of work for each million dollars invested, compared to less than 10 person-years in a nuclear power program (cited in Nordlund and Robson, 1980, p. 69). The Council on Economic Priorities (1979), similarly, estimated the job-producing effects of investing $4 billion in conservation and solar power for Long Island homes compared to a scenario based on existing use of conventional fuels (fuel oil, conventional electricity, and natural gas). The council found that the conservation scenario would stimulate up to more than four times as much local employment as the conventional one, and could, by itself, reduce the area's jobless rate from 6.3 to 5.5 percent. The conservation scenario was also compared to a proposed alternative, the construction of a new nuclear power plant. The study estimated that the conservation approach would create more than twice as many jobs in the local economy as the nuclear one, while costing less and saving considerable amounts of electricity.

Different energy strategies also create different kinds of jobs. Conventional energy production is top-heavy with highly skilled professional, managerial, technical, and craft jobs — even more so for nuclear power than other forms. According to the Council on Economic Priorities, 42 percent of employees in nuclear energy are scientists, engineers, managers, and other professionals; another 34 percent are highly skilled technicians and craft

workers. But most forms of solar energy and conservation are not only typically labor-intensive but also produce many less-skilled, easily learned jobs:
in weatherization, insulation, light manufacturing, and construction, among
others. Job growth in "soft" energy technologies can, therefore, reach a
much wider range of potential workers, including the blue-collar unemployed and unskilled minorities (Council on Economic Priorities, 1979, p. 5).
[Traditional energy industries are heavily white — and male. The extreme
case is coal mining, where 94 percent of the work force in the late 1970s
were white men. White men were also 74 percent of workers in oil refining
and 79 percent in electric power production (Humphrey, 1979, p. 69).]

Both in the sheer number of potential jobs and the possibility of targeting
them to those most in need of employment, therefore, an energy strategy
that gives special weight to conservation and renewable energy sources
could be an important part of the solution to America's job problems.

The Environment: Progress and Perils

Until the 1970s, the United States had no antipollution program at the national level, and the environment was deteriorating at a rapid pace. This
changed during the 1970s, as the government began to take on the job of
regulating some of the unwanted environmental effects of economic
growth. And though not all of the most serious environmental problems
have been rolled back (some, in fact, have been barely addressed), many
show encouraging changes.

Trends in Environmental Quality: Air and Water

The most visible improvement has been in the quality of the air we breathe.
Between 1974 and 1980, the number of days in which air pollution reached
what the U.S. Environmental Protection Agency defines as unhealthful levels
dropped by about a third, from almost 90 to less than 60 per year (Figure
10-2). (This is an average of pollution levels in 23 cities.) In Chicago, to take
just one example, air pollution controls cut the number of days in which it
was unhealthful to breathe from 240 in 1974 to just 48 in 1980 (National
Wildlife Federation, 1983, p. 35).

But the trend toward healthier air slowed toward the end of the decade,
and the number of days pollution reached officially hazardous levels showed
an increasing trend. In addition, though most cities have healthier air than
they did several years ago, some remain badly, even dangerously, polluted.
In the years 1978 through 1980, Los Angeles averaged 231 days of unhealthful air a year, including 113 days classed as very unhealthful or even hazardous (Table 10-3). Several other cities across the country averaged more than

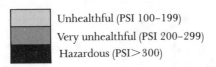
Unhealthful (PSI 100–199)
Very unhealthful (PSI 200–299)
Hazardous (PSI > 300)

Figure 10-2
National urban air quality: average number of days of polluted air [based on the Pollution Standards Index (PSI), which combines the concentrations of sulfur dioxide, nitrogen dioxide, ozone, carbon monoxide, and suspended particulates], averaged for 23 cities, 1974–1980

Source: Council on Environmental Quality, *Environmental Quality, 1981* (Washington, D.C.: Council on Environmental Quality, 1981), p. 33.

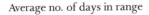
Average no. of days in range

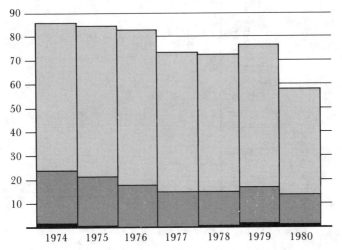

100 days of unhealthful air annually. And others became *more* polluted during the decade; in Houston, that paragon of "Sun Belt" economic growth, the number of days in which the air was officially defined as unhealthful or hazardous tripled between 1974 and 1980 (Conservation Foundation, 1982b, p. 48).

Trends in the quality of water are somewhat similar, though the improvements are less notable. The pace of deterioration of water quality was slowed and in some places halted in the 1970s, but rarely reversed. A 1978 Environmental Protection Agency (EPA) study found 20 percent of American drinking water systems to be contaminated; in 1982, the agency declared that more than 13,000 community water systems were not up to federal standards (National Wildlife Federation, 1983, p. 36). And though the condition of lakes and streams had improved in many areas, others still had far to go. The various states were supposed to meet federal guidelines making their surface waters "fishable and swimmable" by 1983; but 37 states in 1983 said they couldn't meet the guidelines (National Wildlife Federation, 1983, p. 36). Only 10 percent of Nebraska's waters "could safely support full body contact recreation" in 1980. In the states of Massachusetts and Washington, less than half of the surface waters were fishable or swimmable, mainly because of contamination by industrial wastes and municipal sewage (Council on Environmental Quality, 1980, p. 116). And beyond the

Table 10-3
Ranking of 40 Standard Metropolitan Statistical Areas (SMSAs) by the Pollutant Standards Index (PSI), 1978–1980.

Severity level (days with PSI greater than 100)	SMSA	3-year average of no. of days	
		"Unhealthful," "very unhealthful," and "hazardous" (PSI>100)	"Very unhealthful," and "hazardous" (PSI>200)
More than 150 days	Los Angeles	231	113
	San Bernardino—Riverside—Ontario	174	89
100–150 days	New York	139	6
	Denver	130	36
	Pittsburgh	119	18
	Houston	104	23
50–99 days	Chicago	93	14
	St. Louis	89	19
	Philadelphia	74	6
	San Diego	72†	8†
	Louisville	70	4
	Phoenix	70†	6†
	Gary	68	33
	Portland	62	11
	Washington	62	3
	Jersey City	58*	0*
	Salt Lake City	58	18
	Seattle	52	3
	Birmingham	50*	8*

	City		
25–49 days	Cleveland	46	11
	Detroit	39	4
	Memphis	37*	3*
	Baltimore	36	2
	Indianapolis	34	2
	Cincinnati	28	1
	Milwaukee	28	2
	Kansas City	28*	1*
0–24 days	Sacramento	22	1
	Dallas	21	1
	Allentown	21	2
	Buffalo	20†	4†
	San Francisco	18	0
	Toledo	15	2
	Dayton	15	1
	Tampa	8	1
	Syracuse	7	1
	Norfolk	6†	0†
	Grand Rapids	6*	0*
	Rochester	5	0
	Akron	4	0

*Based on 1 year of data.

†Based on 2 years of data.

Note: The Pollution Standards Index (PSI) combines the concentrations of five major pollutants (sulfur dioxide, nitrogen dioxide, ozone, carbon monoxide, and suspended particulates) into a single value.

Source: Council on Environmental Quality, *Environmental Quality 1981* (Washington, D.C.: Council on Environmental Quality, 1981), p. 33.

continuing pollution of surface waters loomed an even graver and more intractable problem, the increasing contamination of groundwater by toxic wastes (see pages 393 to 395).

Moreover, if substantial progress had been made against some kinds of pollution problems, others were only beginning to be seriously addressed. Three of them, in particular, are among the most urgent social problems in America in the 1980s: acid rain, toxic wastes, and contaminated groundwater. All three promise to be even more stubborn than most of the other problems of air and water pollution that were the main targets of legislation and regulation during the 1970s.

Acid Rain: "Airmailing Pollution"   Acid rain is used to describe the airborne acidic particles that, ultimately, are deposited (sometimes in rain, sometimes as dry particles) in distant waters, lands, and forests. Much of it is believed to result from the emission of two kinds of pollutants, sulfur dioxide and nitrogen oxides. Most of the former, in turn, are believed to come from coal-burning power plants (Conservation Foundation, 1982b, pp. 65–67). Once deposited in lakes or streams, acid rain can kill fish and other aquatic life; in forests, it can destroy vegetation. The economic impact varies in different regions, but was estimated at $5 billion a year in the early 1980s (*Newsweek*, April 25, 1983, p. 36). The impact has, so far, been greatest in the northeastern and upper midwestern states and in Canada (Figure 10-3), all of which are downwind from the heaviest concentrations of acid rain sources, the coal-burning industries, especially power plants, in the heavily industrialized midwest. In a 27-state area studied by the U.S. Office of Technology Assessment in 1982 (cited in *Environment*, May 1982, p. 23):

- Of 17,000 lakes, 3,000 were already damaged by acid rain and 9,000 were endangered
- Of 117,000 miles of streams and rivers, 25,000 miles were already damaged, 49,000 were at risk

More recently, EPA analyses show that acid rain may be threatening other parts of the country as well, including part of the South, the mountain states, and the Pacific Northwest (*Environment*, November 1982, p. 21). And in southern California, recent studies have discovered that local fog is even more heavily acidic than rainwater (Waldman et al., 1982).

Though there is now considerable agreement about the major sources of acid rain, there's much less agreement about the strategies to control it, for — like other environmental problems — the control of acid rain raises a number of difficult social and economic issues, as well as technical ones. One of the most important of those issues involves the social and economic effects of attempts to reduce the emission of acid rain's components at their source. As we've noted, a major source of the pollutants is coal-burning power plants. A number of technologies are available to reduce emissions from these plants, but many involve costs of their own. For example, emissions could be reduced by switching the kind of coal used from the high-sulfur-content variety now mainly mined in the East to lower-sulfur coal produced in the West. But this strategy could have a destructive impact on the coal-mining economy (and on coal miners' jobs) in the East, while raising the specter of environmental damage from accelerated strip-mining of coal in the West (Rhodes and Middleton, 1983, p. 32). Other technologies, including techniques to clean or "wash" coal before it's burned and to chemically "scrub" the gases produced afterward, also hold promise, but both are also expensive.

We can't, of course, resolve these technical issues in this book. We raise them to reaffirm a more general point: Problems that seem, on the surface, to be purely technical or scientific ones usually carry broader *social* implications — implications that are sometimes hidden but nevertheless have important human consequences.

Several highly publicized tragedies — like the toll of severe illness and social disruption caused by the dumping of toxic chemicals at Love Canal in New York State or the closing of the entire town of Times Beach, Missouri, in 1983 — brought the problem of hazardous wastes strongly into public con-

Toxic Wastes: Legacy of Neglect

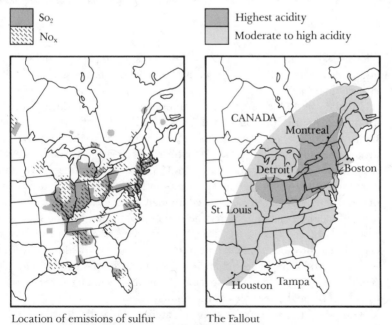

SO₂

NOₓ

Highest acidity

Moderate to high acidity

CANADA

Montreal

Detroit   Boston

St. Louis

Houston   Tampa

Location of emissions of sulfur dioxide (SO₂) and nitrous oxides (NOₓ)

The Fallout

Figure 10-3

Acid rain: sources and destinations

Source: For emissions, Conservation Foundation, *State of the Environment, 1982* (Washington, D.C.: Conservation Foundation, 1982), p. 68; for fallout, *Newsweek*, April 25, 1983, p. 37. Reprinted with permission. All rights reserved.

Social consequences of environmental neglect: dioxin contamination, Times Beach, Missouri.

sciousness in America. But these catastrophic examples are only the most visible elements of a *much* larger problem whose dimensions are still not entirely understood.

In 1980 the EPA estimated that American industry produced from 30 to 40 million metric tons of hazardous wastes a year and predicted that the figure would rise at a rate of about 3 percent a year (U.S. Environmental Protection Agency, 1980, p. ix). Yet later research suggests that this estimate may have been overly optimistic. In 1983 the U.S. Office of Technology Assessment (OTA) released a report estimating that 250 million metric tons of hazardous wastes were produced annually in the United States, of which just 40 million tons came under the regulatory auspices of the EPA (cited in *Science*, April 1, 1983, p. 34). Much of that unregulated waste is not especially hazardous, but a significant fraction of it is. (The federal government exempts producers of less than a ton of hazardous waste a month from regulation, and a number of specific chemicals, including some of the *most* toxic, fell through loopholes in the regulations.)

Thus, despite government steps initiated in the early 1980s, the problem continues to grow. Part of the difficulty is the huge gap between the size of the toxic waste problem and the resources allocated to coping with it. In

1980 Congress authorized a "Superfund" to clean up existing toxic waste dumps. But that fund (raised mainly by a tax on producers of chemicals and petrochemicals) would total only an estimated $1.6 billion by 1985. That sum seems large at first. But the OTA's study estimated that it would cost anywhere from $10 to $40 billion to clean up even a substantial *fraction* of the roughly 15,000 toxic waste sites already pinpointed as needing immediate action (cited in *Science*, April 1, 1983, p. 34). In 1983 the EPA identified 418 of what it considered the *worst* hazardous dumpsites — but in the previous two years, the agency had actually cleaned up only 5 of over 100 sites it had already identified (*Newsweek*, January 3, 1983). (Figure 10-4 maps the worst of the dumps as of 1981.) And at the rate of toxic waste cleanup achieved from 1981 to 1983, the worst 1,000 of these dumps might be rendered safe in just 400 years. Meanwhile, new toxic wastes are being poured into the ground at the rate of hundreds of millions of tons annually. Is this situation necessary?

Although the issues involved are highly complex, the evidence suggests that it isn't. The OTA report argues that the process of dumping toxic wastes in the earth or the oceans is not *technically* necessary. About four-fifths of federally regulated hazardous wastes are now dumped on land. Yet (as a recent report from the National Academy of Sciences affirms), "there currently exists some technology or combination of technologies capable of dealing with every hazardous waste in a manner that eliminates the need for perpetual storage" (quoted in *Christian Science Monitor*, April 7, 1983). Many industrial wastes can be safely burned away at extremely high temperatures; others can be detoxified through the use of other chemicals or even certain bacteria. In West Germany, roughly 85 percent of hazardous industrial wastes are detoxified through one or another method (Council on Environmental Quality, 1980, pp. 218–219; *Newsweek*, March 7, 1983, p. 24). And some wastes may be reusable by other industries, "on the principle that one company's wastes may be another's raw materials" (Council on Environmental Quality, 1980, p. 218). Also, according to the EPA, about 60 percent of all hazardous wastes in the United States could be safely incinerated; in the Netherlands, half of all hazardous waste is now burned (Conservation Foundation, 1982b, p. 171).

Why don't we make more use of these alternative technologies? One reason, surely, is that they are more expensive — in the short run. Because of that, they have been unattractive to most American industries and have received little encouragement from our government. (Table 10-4 shows that the generation of hazardous wastes is overwhelmingly concentrated in just a few industries, most notably the chemical industry.) But the short run, as usual, is not the whole story. It's estimated, for example, that proper disposal of the chemical wastes at Love Canal would have cost $2 million or less. But by mid-1980, the costs of dealing with the problem after the fact, including the cleanup and the relocation of residents, already added up to more than $36 million (Council on Environmental Quality, 1980, pp. 220–221).

Figure 10-4

The worst toxic waste dumps: hazardous waste sites with highest priority for remedial action under Superfund program, 1981

Source: Conservation Foundation, *State of the Environment, 1982* (Washington, D.C.: Conservation Foundation, 1982), p. 154. Reprinted with permission.

ALABAMA
Triana

ARIZONA
Phoenix

ARKANSAS
Ft. Smith
Jacksonville
Mena
Walnut Ridge

CALIFORNIA
Glen Avon
Keswick
Rancho Cordova

COLORADO
Denver

CONNECTICUT
Naugatuck

DELAWARE
Delaware City
New Castle
Red Lion

FLORIDA
Between Alford
  and Cottondale
Clermont
Davie
Ft. Lauderdale
Galloway
Hialeah
Jacksonville
Miami
Pensacola
Tampa
Warrington
Whitehouse
Zellwood

GEORGIA
Athens

ILLINOIS
Waukegan

INDIANA
Bloomington
Seymour

IOWA
Council Bluffs

KANSAS
Arkansas City

KENTUCKY
Brooks

MAINE
Winthrop

MARYLAND
Baltimore

MASSACHUSETTS
Ashland
North Dartmouth
Tyngsborough
Woburn

MICHIGAN
St. Louis

MINNESOTA
Andover
Oakdale
St. Louis Park
St. Paul

MISSISSIPPI
Greenville

MISSOURI
Ellisville
Springfield

NEW HAMPSHIRE
Epping
Kingston
Nashua

NEW JERSEY
Bridgeport
Edison
Elizabeth
Freehold
Hamilton
Marlboro
Monmouth County
Pitman
Pleasantville
Plumsted

NEW MEXICO
Church Rock
Clovis
Milan

NEW YORK
Batavia
Elmira
Niagra Falls
Olean
Oswego
Oyster Bay
Philipstown
Wheatfield

NORTH CAROLINA
Highway dumping
  in fourteen
  counties

NORTH DAKOTA
Rural south-
  eastern corner

OHIO
Ashtabula
Cleveland
Deerfield
Hamilton

OKLAHOMA
Criner
Ottawa County

PENNSYLVANIA
Bruin
Buffalo
Chester
Girard
McAdoo
Natrona Heights
Old Forge
Pittston

RHODE ISLAND
Burrillville
Coventry
Smithfield

SOUTH CAROLINA
South of Columbia

SOUTH DAKOTA
Deadwood

TENNESSEE
Memphis

TEXAS
Crosby
Grand Prairie
La Marque

UTAH
Salt Lake City

VERMONT
Burlington

VIRGINIA
West of Salem
York County

WASHINGTON
Tacoma

WASHINGTON, D.C.

WEST VIRGINIA
Point Pleasant

Table 10-4
Hazardous waste
generation by industry,
1980

Industry	Quantity, in thousand metric tons	Percent of total
Chemicals and allied products	25,509	61.9
Primary metal industries	4,061	9.8
Petroleum and coal products	2,119	5.1
Fabricated metal products	1,997	4.8
Nonmanufacturing industries	1,971	4.8
Paper and allied products	1,295	3.1
Transportation equipment	1,240	3.0
Electrical and electronic equipment	1,093	2.7
Leather and leather tanning	474	1.1
Machinery, except electrical	322	0.8
Miscellaneous manufacturing industries	318	0.8
Rubber and miscellaneous plastic products	249	0.6
Textile mill products	203	0.5
Printing and publishing	154	0.4
Instruments and related products	90	0.2
Lumber and food products	87	0.2
Furniture and fixtures	36	0.09
Stone, clay, and glass products	17	0.04
	41,235	100.0

Source: Conservation Foundation, *State of the Environment, 1982* (Washington, D.C.: Conservation Foundation, 1982), p. 149. Reprinted with permission.

Troubled Waters: Groundwater Contamination

We've seen that the antipollution efforts of the past decade at least held the line against further deterioration of the lakes, rivers, and streams of the United States. But by the early 1980s it had become clear that this was only part of the problem with America's water — what was happening *below* the surface was much more disturbing. Indeed, the threat of chemical contamination of groundwater threatens (as one EPA official has put it) to become the "environmental horror story of the 1980s" (*Newsweek*, November 1, 1982).

Groundwater is the water trapped underground in permeable rock strata (called *aquifers*) that supplies, through wells, about half of the drinking water (and a quarter of the fresh water used for *all* purposes) in the United States. At one time it was generally believed that groundwater was safe from the kinds of contamination that affected surface waters. The soil usually acts as a giant filter removing most normal contaminants before they reach the water, and the groundwater itself sheds pollutants as it "percolates" through underground rocks.

But the introduction of new kinds of industrial chemicals has created a very different situation. Many of these chemicals are not broken down by

Handling toxic waste.

the usual processes of cleansing in the soil and rock. And once it has been contaminated by these chemicals, the groundwater may remain contaminated "for hundreds or thousands of years, if not for geologic time" (Burmaster, 1982, p. 9). Groundwater contamination, as the Conservation Foundation notes, "may be essentially irreversible"; unlike some other forms of pollution, it continues *long* after the initial source of the pollution has been stopped (1982b, p. 107). Because of this, groundwater contamination promises to be one of the most dramatic legacies of the heedless attitude toward the introduction of toxic chemicals in the course of America's economic development.

What makes groundwater pollution so threatening is that it strikes at the basic drinking water supplies of many communities. In the late 1970s and early 1980s, contaminated wells were discovered — many by accident — in a number of areas across the country. Some of the chemicals involved are among the most toxic produced by industry, including several known or suspected to cause cancer and/or genetic damage (Table 10-5). But, more disturbing is the fact that little is known about the precise health effects of these chemicals. Some of them, for example, may have worse health impacts when combined together (as they often are in contaminated

Chemical	Evidence for carcinogenicity
Benzene	H
alpha-BHC	CA
beta-BHC	NTA
gamma-BHC (Lindane)	CA
Bis (2-ethylhexyl) phthalate	NTA
Bromoform	NTA
Butyl benzyl phthalate	NTA
Carbon tetrachloride	CA
Chloroform	CA
Chloromethane	NTA
Cyclohexane	NTA
Dibromochloropropane (DBCP)	CA
Dibromochloromethane	NTA
1,1-Dichloroethane	SA
1,2-Dichloroethane	CA
1,1-Dichloroethylene	NTA
1,2-Dichloroethylene	NTA
Di-n-butyl phthalate	NTA
Dioxane	CA
Ethylene dibromide (EDB)	CA
Isopropyl benzene	NTA
Methylene chloride	NTA
Parathion	SA
Tetrachloroethylene	CA
Toluene	NTA
1,1,1-Trichloroethane	NA
1,1,2-Trichloroethane	CA
Trichloroethylene (TCE)	CA
Trifluorotrichloroethane	NTA
Vinyl chloride	H, CA
Xylene	NTA

Table 10-5
Toxic chemicals detected in drinking water wells.

H = Confirmed human carcinogen
CA = Confirmed animal carcinogen
SA = Suggested animal carcinogen
NA = Negative evidence of carcinogenicity from animal bioassay
NTA = Not tested in animal bioassay

Source: David Burmaster, "The New Pollution: Groundwater Contamination," *Environment*, March 1982, p. 33. Reprinted with permission.

groundwater) than they do separately. Based on admittedly limited research evidence, one study estimates that if a population of a million people were to consume water from one of the most heavily polluted wells so far discovered (near Princeton, New Jersey), it would cause an extra 2,500 cancer deaths over the life cycle (Burmaster, 1982, p. 33).

The Costs and Benefits of Environmental Control

Thus, it is clear that while the environmental protection measures of the past decade accomplished much, much still remains to be done, and some of the remaining jobs are *very* formidable. One response has been to press for stricter, more extensive regulations, both to more effectively control long-standing air and water pollution problems and to begin to confront the newer, more stubborn ones.

Increasingly, however, another approach has become more common — to attack much of the current arsenal of environmental regulations as unwise and unworkable. This view usually acknowledges that the growth of environmental concern and regulation has helped create a better, healthier environment, but it also insists that environmental regulations have turned out to be, as a *Fortune* article argued, "staggeringly expensive for the amount of cleanup achieved" (Alexander, 1981, p. 235). An overzealous approach to environmental regulation, in this view, however well intentioned, has hobbled the economy and thereby unwittingly made life poorer for everyone: "Through onerous regulations, the total economic pie is reduced to such an extent that all of us — Easterners, Westerners, industrialists, environmentalists — are losers" (Navarro, 1980, p. 44).

The idea that environmental protection has gotten out of hand and hurt the economy touches a nerve in a time of high unemployment and sluggish growth. Although a majority of the public (see Figure 10-5) believes that

Figure 10-5

Responses to the question, Which of these statements comes closer to your own feelings? We need to relax our environmental laws in order to achieve economic growth. Or, we need to maintain present environmental laws in order to preserve the environment for future generations?

Source: Survey by CBS News/ New York Times, September 22–27, 1981. From *Public Opinion*, February–March 1982, p. 35. Copyright © 1981 by The New York Times Company. Reprinted with permission.

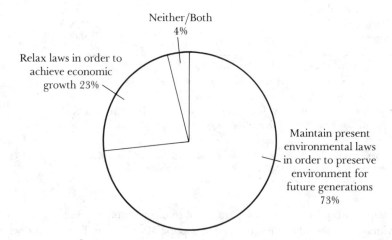

Note: Sixty-seven percent of Republicans, 80 percent of Democrats, 70 percent of Independents chose the "maintain present laws" category.

controling environmental pollution remains a high priority, these economic concerns have led to strong political demands that we carefully "balance" the claims of environmental quality with the imperative of economics. But is this an accurate assessment of the role of environmental regulation?

Let's consider, first of all, how much environmental protection actually "costs." On close examination, the dollar costs turn out to be less than is often supposed.

How Much Does Pollution Control Cost?

According to U.S. Department of Commerce estimates, total spending on pollution abatement and control amounted to just under $27 billion in 1980. But this figure is misleading because it includes *all* spending on such basic necessities as sewage systems and garbage treatment, not just spending to comply with environmental regulations. American *business* spent about $13 billion for *all* forms of pollution abatement control in 1980 (compared with corporate *profits* of about $246 billion). Moreover, the rate of increase in pollution spending began to slow in the late 1970s. The biggest single category of business expense for pollution control, capital spending for air and water pollution control equipment, actually *declined* between 1975 and 1980 at an annual average rate of 3 percent (Rutledge and Trevathian, 1982). Finally, a study by the Business Roundtable, an organization of executives of some of the largest American corporations, estimated that 48 of the largest firms spent, among them, a total of about $2 billion to comply with EPA regulations in 1977. But, at the same time, the same firms enjoyed net, aftertax profits of almost $17 billion (Congressional Quarterly, 1981, p. 126).

The sheer dollar cost of pollution control, however, is of less concern to critics than the wider effects of environmental regulation on economic performance. A number of studies have attempted to estimate the impact of these regulations on inflation, jobs, productivity, and economic growth. Do environmental regulations really hurt the economy, by these measures? The issues are complex, and the problems of measurement difficult, but the overall answer is generally negative. If anything, though it may sometimes involve fairly substantial short-range expenses, environmental protection appears to have a *positive* long-run impact on economic health, and could have an even greater one in the future.

Several studies suggest that environmental regulation may have a slight aggravating effect on inflation; but all find the effect to be small, and most find that regulation simultaneously increases employment. Thus, an EPA study calculates that environmental regulations may decrease unemployment by 0.2 or 0.3 percent a year (by creating jobs in antipollution equipment industries and services), while probably causing a 0.1 to 0.2 percent rise in inflation (Congressional Quarterly, 1981, p. 128). A 1981 study by the Data Resources Institute calculates that all spending on pollution and toxic waste control might add 0.6 percent annually to the rate of inflation during the 1980s, slow the growth of the gross national product by 0.1 percent, and

---

The Costs and Benefits of Environmental Control **397**

reduce unemployment by 0.4 percent (Portney, 1981, pp. 47–52). Another study reviewed many similar analyses and found that most estimates of the inflationary impact of environmental control range from 0.2 to 0.6 percent. The study concludes that, given the levels of inflation that have been common in recent years, even very drastic cuts in regulation would not make "an immediate and substantial contribution to lower prices" (Portney, 1981, pp. 47–52).

Another argument raised by critics is that pollution regulations require such costly, cumbersome changes in industrial processes or products that they lower industrial productivity. Again, the specter of declining productivity hits home when American industry's productivity gains have slowed, on average, especially in comparison with some other countries. As we saw in Chapter 3, however, productivity is a tricky concept, difficult to measure and even more difficult to interpret. And most studies indicate that to the extent that productivity has declined in the United States, it has been due to a host of factors other than regulatory activity. As one study argues, "the evidence for an adverse impact of environmental regulations on the capital stock and its productivity is very weak" (Havemann and Christianson, 1981, p. 74).

Several studies reviewed by the Council on Environmental Quality found that environmental controls might lower industrial productivity by no more than 0.05 to 0.3 percent — only a very small fraction of America's productivity slowdown. Moreover, the magnitude of this effect had *declined* by the late 1970s, suggesting that part of it reflected one-time expenses of complying with pollution regulations (installing equipment to control emissions from smokestacks, for example) (Council on Environmental Quality, 1980, pp. 388–389).

The Benefits of a Cleaner Environment

The small size of these effects is all the more remarkable because very few of these studies consider any of the *benefits* of pollution control in their calculations. To be sure, some (though not all) of these benefits are more difficult to measure than their dollar costs. But they are hardly less important: they include better health, reduced mortality, improved environmental quality, and longer-range gains in the productivity of the economy.

Air pollution controls, for example, improve agricultural production, reduce damages to industrial plants and equipment, and lower the costs of cleaning and painting. Water pollution controls increase commercial fishing yields and lower the costs of public waste and drinking water treatment. Estimates of the economic losses water pollution inflicts on recreational activity alone run to several billions of dollars a year (Portney, 1981, p. 50).

Beyond these economic benefits are those associated with human health. Evidence on the adverse effects of pollution on health is growing. Table 10-6 describes the health impacts of some toxic pollutants. Probably the two biggest pollution-related health problems are respiratory diseases and cancer.

Industrial pollutants, especially sulfur oxides and particulate matter, have long been linked to respiratory illnesses, particularly in vulnerable groups: children, the elderly, and people already suffering from lung or heart diseases. Children living in highly polluted areas have higher rates of acute respiratory disease and of poor lung functioning and are more likely to develop chronic respiratory diseases as adults. High levels of air pollutants are also linked with more lost workdays due to illness — another reason to look skeptically at the one-sided way in which the productivity costs of pollution controls are typically calculated (Freeman, 1979; Ostro and Anderson, 1981). The corrosive effect of one major class of industrial pollutants, acid sulfates, on the respiratory system may account for almost 190,000 deaths a year in the United States, according to a recent study (Congressional Quarterly, 1981, p. 21). Much of this health impact is hidden because it is usually long-term and subtle, not sudden and dramatic, and because it is often difficult to disentangle from other problems, such as age or excessive smoking, with which it is often combined.

We've already seen that rising rates of some kinds of cancer are the most troubling exception to the overall improvements in Americans' health. We saw, too, that a significant part of that increase has been linked to environmental factors, especially toxic chemicals in the workplace. More recent research makes it clear that toxic chemicals *outside* the workplace — in the air and drinking water — are also implicated in rising cancer rates. We've mentioned the potential carcinogenic effects of groundwater contamination. But cancer and *air* pollution are increasingly associated as well. One study calculates that between 11 and 21 percent of lung cancers in the United States are associated with air pollution, and that the threat of pollution-induced cancer is greater in urban areas (Karch and Schneiderman, 1981).

Another example of the health impacts of air pollution — and the potential benefits from environmental controls — is the effect of lead. Lead is an extremely toxic substance known to cause a number of severe health problems, particularly in children. Long-term exposures to high concentrations of lead can lead to progressive loss of kidney functioning, loss of fertility and risks of fetal damage in pregnant women, and anemia (Hattis, Goble, and Ashford, 1982). But probably the most telling effects of lead in the human body is its tendency to "wreak havoc in the nervous system, to destroy normal behavior and to result in crippling mental damage" (*Environment*, March 1982, p. 22).

We saw in Chapter 9 that the incidence of many health problems in the United States is profoundly shaped by the circumstances of race and income. Figure 10-6 shows that this is also true of lead exposure. A recent survey from the National Center for Health Statistics found that almost one-fifth of inner-city black children have seriously high levels of lead in their blood, as compared to less than 5 percent of inner-city white children, and just 2 percent of white children living outside the inner cities (cited in *Environment*, March 1982, p. 22). There are several sources for the lead that

---

The Costs and Benefits of Environmental Control   **399**

Table 10-6

Selected human health and environmental effects of 25 toxic chemicals

Chemical	Human health effects			Environmental effects
	Potential carcinogen	Potential teratogen	Other effects	
Aldrin/dieldrin	•		Tremors, convulsions, kidney damage	Toxic to aquatic organisms, reproductive failure in birds and fish, bioaccumulates in aquatic organisms
Arsenic	•	•	Vomiting, poisoning, liver and kidney damage	Toxic to legume crops
Benzene	•		Anemia, bone marrow damage	Toxic to some fish and aquatic invertebrates
Bis (2-ethylhexyl) phthalate	•	•	Central nervous system damage	Eggshell thinning in birds, toxic to fish
Cadmium	•	•	Suspected causal factor in many human pathologies: tumors, renal dysfunction, hypertension, arteriosclerosis; Itai-itai disease (weakened bones)	Toxic to fish, bioaccumulates in aquatic organisms
Carbon tetrachloride	•		Kidney and liver damage, heart failure	
Chloroform	•		Kidney and liver damage	
Chromium	•		Kidney and gastrointestinal damage, respiratory complications	Toxic to some aquatic invertebrates
Copper			Gastrointestinal irritant, liver damage	Toxic to juvenile fish
Cyanide			Acutely toxic	Kills fish, reduces growth and development of fish

Substance	Carcinogen	Teratogen	Human health effects	Environmental effects
DDT	•		Tremors, convulsions, kidney damage	Reproductive failure of birds and fish, bioaccumulates in aquatic organisms, biomagnifies in food chain
Di-n-butyl phthalate			Central nervous system damage	Eggshell thinning in birds, toxic to fish
Dioxin	•		Acute skin rashes	Bioaccumulates
Lead	•	•	Convulsions, anemia, kidney and brain damage	Toxic to domestic plants and animals, biomagnifies in food chain
Mercury	•		Irritability, depression, kidney and liver damage, Minamata disease	Reproductive failure in fish species, inhibits growth and kills fish, methylmercury biomagnifies
Methylene chloride (dichloromethane)	•			
Nickel	•		Gastrointestinal and central nervous system effects	Impairs reproduction of aquatic species
PCBs	•		Vomiting, abdominal pain, temporary blindness	Liver damage in mammals, kidney damage and eggshell thinning in birds, suspected reproductive failure in fish
Phenol				Reproductive effects in aquatic organisms, toxic to fish
Silver				Toxic to aquatic organisms
Tetrachloroethylene	•	•	Central nervous system effects	Toxic to aquatic organisms at high concentrations
Toluene	•			
Toxaphene	•			Decreased productivity of phytoplankton communities, birth defects in fish and birds

Notes: In many cases human health effects are based on the results of animal tests. For instance, the identification of a substance as a potential carcinogen indicates that there is at least one animal test that demonstrates carcinogenic effects. However, whether a substance actually produces the effects indicated depends on the duration and intensity of exposure, the form of the exposure (whether it is inhaled, ingested, and so on), the susceptibility of the person exposed, and other factors. If a substance is identified as a *carcinogen*, there is evidence that it has the potential for causing cancer in humans. If it is identified as a *teratogen*, it has the potential for causing birth defects in humans.

Source: Adapted from Conservation Foundation, *State of the Environment, 1982* (Washington, D.C.: Conservation Foundation, 1982), pp. 120–121. Reprinted with permission.

401

winds up in a child's blood system: some of it comes from food; some from peeling lead-based paint in older, often dilapidated urban housing; and some from the air, especially from automobile exhausts. Since the mid-1970s, these blood-lead levels have declined substantially. Why? Lacking systematic studies, the cause is difficult to prove. But the environmental regulation of lead in gasoline is the most likely factor: The decline in blood-lead levels parallels the decline in the use of leaded gas.

Overall, according to a 1979 study, cleaner air standards could result in a 7 percent reduction of mortality in the United States (Congressional Quarterly, 1981, p. 128). Again, these matters of life and death are not easily translated into quantitative cost-benefit terms and are, therefore, typically left out of the conventional calculations of regulation costs. But it is noteworthy that the Organization for Economic Cooperation and Development (OECD) has estimated that the health damage caused by air pollution *alone* may amount to between 3 and 5 percent of the gross national product of industrial countries — which translates (roughly) into a sum between $90 and $150 billion in the United States in 1981 (cited in *Environment*, September 1980, p. 22).

Environmental Control, Jobs, and Investment	Most critics of environmentalism would probably acknowledge that cleaner air and water do bring important benefits. But many would nevertheless argue that both the cost and the complexity of complying with pollution regulations have become so great that they discourage investment, hinder the construction of new plants, and generally block economic growth. Horror stories are told of plants closed or unbuilt, and jobs lost, because of "nitpicking" regulations.

But though the cost, in money and time, of meeting environmental standards *can* be significant, the evidence does *not* show substantial adverse effects on investment. And, at the same time, environmental protection turns out to have somewhat surprising potentials for encouraging, rather than hindering, economic growth.

It is often argued, for example, that tough environmental laws discourage businesses from locating in certain states or encourage them to leave the country. But a 1982 study by the Conservation Foundation (funded by several business-related organizations) argues that this view is a myth. The study found no evidence that environmental regulations had caused industries to avoid certain states. California, for example, which has very stringent environmental regulations, also had the *largest* gain in manufacturing jobs of any state during the 1970s (Conservation Foundation, 1982a).

Similar findings apply to the specter of plants closing because of the burdens of pollution regulations. Using data provided by industry (which we wouldn't expect to understate the problem) the EPA calculated that between 1971 and 1981, a maximum of 33,000 American workers may have

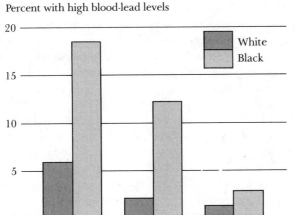

Percent with high blood-lead levels

Annual family income

White

Black

Less than $6,000 | $6,000 to $14,999 | $15,000 or more

Figure 10-6
High blood-lead levels in children 6 months to 5 years of age, by family income and race; averaged from 1976 to 1980

Source: U.S. Department of Health and Human Services, *Health — United States, 1982* (Washington, D.C.: Government Printing Office, 1982), p. 89.

been displaced by plant closures in which environmental regulations played *any* part at all (Kazis and Grossman, 1982, p. 13). (This was during a period when the average number of unemployed workers never dropped below 4 million.) And many of the plants turned out on closer inspection to have been marginal ones in any case — the inability to meet pollution regulations was often the *least* of their problems. Meanwhile, an EPA-sponsored analysis estimates that between 1970 and 1987, we can expect a net *gain* of over half a million jobs as a result of pollution controls. Some of those jobs are in government pollution-control agencies, but many others are in the private sector. By 1981, according to one estimate, about 600 new companies were in the business of pollution-control equipment manufacturing and installation (Kazis and Grossman, 1982, p. 18).

Of course, the loss of even a *few* jobs as a result of environmental controls is a painful, threatening experience for those affected. But the job losses seem small enough to be offset by serious retraining programs for the displaced workers.

More generally, pollution prevention, as an analysis in the *Harvard Business Review* notes, has been responsible for stimulating a substantial amount of new economic development, both in the United States and, even more, in some foreign countries. "Environmental business" had become a $50 billion-a-year industry by the beginning of the 1980s, and was growing at a rate of 20 percent a year — in a time generally characterized by a sluggish economy. "Environmentally induced economic activity" of all kinds, according to this analysis, was now an estimated 2 percent of America's GNP, employing more than 2 million people (Royston, 1980, pp. 12–13).

The importance of environmentally related industry is even greater in some other countries, where it has been deliberately developed as a high priority in order to spur economic growth. Both the Swedes and the Japanese used massive investments in pollution control (stimulated by very strict antipollution legislation) to boost their economies out of the recession of the mid-1970s. According to an OECD estimate, fully 20 percent of Japan's economic growth in the late 1970s was attributable to new, tough environmental regulations and the resulting large antipollution spending. Because of that investment, too, both Japan and Sweden benefited economically by emerging as leading world suppliers of the most advanced pollution-control equipment and technology (Royston, 1980).

Certainly, some forms of pollution control cost money — and controlling some of the more recently discovered problems, like carcinogenic wastes or acid rain, will cost even more. The evidence doesn't suggest that these costs are unimportant (or that *all* environmental regulations are equally sound and wisely conceived: there is certainly room for improvement and careful assessment of the value of particular regulations). What it most clearly suggests is that we need to distinguish between *short-term* costs and *long-term* ones. Like most other socially useful investments (and like many personal ones) the initial costs to an industry to "clean up its act" may be significant. But the economic benefits *alone* are usually even greater, when viewed in a longer time frame. Many European and Japanese companies have saved substantial sums, and increased their profits, by redesigning industrial processes to reduce pollution and to reuse industrial wastes at the same time. And in the United States, some corporations have discovered that, as the economist Ruth Ruttenberg has put it, "regulation is the mother of invention" (1981). Corporations that are forced to change their products and industrial processes to meet environmental requirements often design something more productive, more technologically advanced, and frequently more profitable. Unfortunately, though, as in the case of energy use, American industry has more often emphasized the short-term gains at the expense of potential long-term advantages.

The Outlook: Energy and Environmental Policy

That tension between short-term gains and the longer-range health of the economy and society underlies much of the debate over energy and environmental policy in the United States today. And, in the 1980s, it appears that, after a decade and more of greater attention to the long-term issues of energy supply and environmental quality, we began to shift back toward the kind of short-range approaches that have been an unfortunate, persistent part of the American tradition.

Much of American energy policy in the 1980s has stressed incentives for increased fossil fuel production (and nuclear energy), while downplaying the already minimal support for conservation and renewable energy — the strategies that now appear *most* likely to offer long-lasting, environmentally attractive solutions to the energy crisis. Tax incentives for energy production outweighed those for conservation by eight to one in the early 1980s. In the 1983 federal budget, almost 90 percent of the Department of Energy's funds for research in energy technology was slated for nuclear power (Friends of the Earth et al., 1982, p. 60). And this is in spite of the public's often expressed preference for a shift to renewable energy and conservation, and its growing wariness over the costs and perils of nuclear power.

These policies, somewhat curiously, are often justified in the name of allowing the unfettered operation of the free market. But most of these energy policies have little to do with the market — and are most certainly not free. The nuclear power industry has been saved from the market's verdict in recent years by nearly $40 billion worth of government subsidies. America's energy choices, in fact, have *never* been left to the forces of the free market: they have always been shaped by the government's funneling of taxpayers' monies to *some* energy strategies at the expense of others. According to a Department of Energy–sponsored study, from the end of World War I through the 1970s, direct federal subsidies for energy amounted to more than $250 billion: about half for the oil industry, a fourth for electric power, 8 percent for the nuclear industry — and just 0.15 percent for all forms of solar energy (Lovins and Lovins, 1980, p. 112).

Thus, our current dependence on energy sources that are either the least plentiful, the most polluting, or the most dangerous is not simply a result of consumers' free choices, or of fate, or even of technological obstacles to alternative energy strategies. Instead, it is to a substantial degree the result of deliberate government policies. And those policies are now pointing us toward an uncertain and perhaps perilous future in energy.

And the long-term care of the natural environment is also increasingly being counterposed to the short-term imperatives of economic growth. In 1982, the Conservation Foundation (a research organization not generally known for its social criticism) warned that "the bipartisan consensus that supported federal protection of the environment has been broken" (1982b, p. 1). In the name of a more "realistic" concern for economics, there has been a decided shift toward weakening pollution regulations — often, again, in favor of so-called market approaches. Funding for federal environmental programs was sharply reduced in the early 1980s, and the staffs of pollution control agencies were also reduced. Most of these changes were heralded as the beginning of a more cost-effective approach to environmental problems. But, as we've seen, assessing "cost" is a much more complicated matter than simply adding up the dollar figures on tomorrow's budget, or even next year's. And the possible longer-term costs are staggering. The Conservation Foundation's summation of these issues is hard to improve on:

> Environmental programs are not an expendable indulgence of an affluent society. The basic purpose of environmental programs is to protect us from ourselves by assuring that our activities do not destroy the natural functions on which we depend. . . . Delays in pursuing environmental programs may have serious consequences. At stake are human health, the condition of our farms and forests and rivers, and irreplaceable natural areas and animal species. Not only are the stakes high: many decisions are irreversible. (Conservation Foundation, 1982b, p. 8)

Summary

This chapter has examined two closely related issues: energy use and environmental quality. After decades of heedless attitudes toward these problems, the United States now faces tough choices in both realms.

Among potential energy sources for the future, the traditional fossil fuels (oil, natural gas, and coal) are crucially limited. Oil and natural gas are in relatively short supply. Coal, though more abundant, carries troubling environmental costs.

The potential of nuclear power (once thought to be the answer to America's energy problems) has been derailed by skyrocketing costs and unresolved safety problems.

Alternative energy sources (conservation and solar power) may have a much greater potential role in America's future energy policy than we once thought.

Some aspects of environmental quality have improved significantly in recent years. But other massive problems — including toxic wastes, acid rain, and groundwater contamination — have barely been touched by public policies.

Though environmental protection is often attacked as too costly, the evidence indicates that pollution regulations have little negative impact on the economy — and can have important economic benefits, in addition to the more obvious benefits in health and environmental quality.

Weakening the commitment to environmental protection in the name of short-term economic gains may have devastating long-term results.

For Further Reading

Conservation Foundation. *State of the Environment, 1982.* Washington, D.C.: Conservation Foundation, 1982b.

Peskin, Henry, Paul Portney, and Allen Kneese. *Environmental Regulation and the U.S. Economy.* Baltimore: Johns Hopkins University Press, 1981.

Schnaiberg, Alan. *The Environment: From Surplus to Scarcity.* New York: Oxford University Press, 1980.

Stobaugh, Robert, and Daniel Yergin. *Energy Future*, rev. ed. New York: Vintage, 1982.

Union of Concerned Scientists. *Energy Strategies: Toward a Solar Future.* Cambridge, Mass.: Ballinger, 1981.

Ward, Barbara. *Progress for a Small Planet.* New York: Norton, 1979.

11

Crime and Justice

When Americans are asked what worries them most about their society, crime is always high on the list — usually just below the cost of living and the threat of unemployment. Most of us feel intuitively that our streets and communities are more dangerous than they used to be, and many of us have the sense that violent crime is simply out of control. Opinion polls show that these fears are growing. In 1967, according to the Gallup poll, 31 percent of Americans surveyed answered affirmatively when asked if there were any areas in their immediate neighborhoods where they were afraid to walk alone at night. By 1982, the proportion had reached 48 percent, and in most urban areas the fear of crime is higher still (*San Francisco Chronicle*, March 11, 1982).

The most common response to this fear of crime has been the demand to "get tough" with criminals. Most Americans, again according to the polls, believe that the courts are too lenient with criminals. Legislators have responded to that feeling with stiffer sentences for serious crimes, a call for an end to special treatment for violent youth in the juvenile courts, and the appropriation of scarce public funds for new jails and prisons.

Though these sentiments have been with us for some time, the strength of the get-tough position in recent years marks an important shift in public attitudes — and those of some social scientists as well. In the 1950s and 1960s, American criminology emphasized the need to deal with what were assumed to be the social and economic root causes of crime. To a great extent, crime was regarded as one of the bitter fruits of disadvantage and discrimination. In turn, it was widely believed that crime could be largely overcome through reform of the larger social conditions that seemed to

408

breed it, such as poverty, racial discrimination, unemployment, and poor housing, coupled with innovative programs to rehabilitate delinquents and criminals. A former U.S. attorney general put it this way at the close of the 1960s: "Warring on poverty, inadequate housing, and unemployment is warring on crime. A civil rights law is a law against crime. Money for schools is money against crime. . . . Every effort to improve life in America's inner cities is an effort against crime" (President's Commission on Law Enforcement, 1967, p. 6).

Yet, by the 1970s, the view of crime as mainly the product of remediable social conditions was already under attack. It was weakened by what some writers described as a revealing paradox: The social programs of the 1960s, and the general improvements in educational opportunities and income levels, seemed to have had no discernible impact on crime (Wilson, 1975). If anything, crime had increased considerably — leading some critics to argue that efforts at social reform were at best irrelevant and at worst detrimental to community safety. Simultaneously, a series of widely publicized academic studies of programs for offenders and ex-offenders seemed to show that "nothing worked" (Lipton, Martinson, and Wilks, 1975), that the record of efforts to rehabilitate criminals was a dismal failure.

A sense of futility and desperation about crime began to grow. By 1981, *Newsweek* described the American attitude toward violent crime as a "dispiriting malaise" and acknowledged that there was now "none of the old optimism proclaiming that we know what the problems are and that we have the solutions at hand" (March 23, 1981, p. 43).

In contrast to the more active thrust of the 1960s, it is now often argued that we know little about the causes of crime and that even if we did know, we lack the means to intervene effectively to alter them. In 1981, for example, a presidential task force on violent crime cited at least three factors it believed were probably important sources of America's rising levels of violence: the weakening of the bonds of family and community, the persistence of social disadvantages among some groups, and the spread of "attitudes that favor immediate over deferred gratification." But the task force went on to reject any responsibility to examine — let alone confront — those issues, on the ground that "we are not convinced that a government, by the invention of new programs or the management of existing institutions, can by itself recreate those familial and neighborhood conditions, those social opportunities, and those personal values that in all likelihood are the prerequisites of tranquil communities" (U.S. Department of Justice, 1981, pp. 2–3).

By the 1980s, in short, the dominant attitudes about crime and its remedies were shaped by the themes of pessimism and rejection of social action that we charted in Chapter 1. In this chapter, we will consider these issues through the lens of the most recent research on crime and its control. As in other chapters, the vast amount of research available forces us to be very selective. We will focus on some of the key questions raised by current debates about crime and justice: Is crime increasing? If so, how much? Who are the typical victims? How much can we rely on courts, prisons, and police

Uncovering the
Crime Rate

At first glance, it might seem simple to determine how much crime we have and whether — and by how much — it has increased. In fact, despite improvements in the techniques of measuring crime, we are still a long way from being able to pinpoint its true dimensions with precision. Because of this, crime statistics are among the most commonly abused of all official data, and they require even more caution than most.

The fundamental problem is that there are several steps between the commission of a crime and its being recorded by officials. The first step is the initial reporting of the crime to the police. Most often, this is the responsibility of the victim; but for a variety of reasons, victims may fail to report crimes. Sometimes this is because the crime is a small one; many small thefts are never reported because the victims feel that going to the police is more trouble than it is worth. Sometimes, crimes are not reported because victims are afraid, ashamed, or alienated from the police and courts. Some groups, especially minorities, may distrust the police and prefer to avoid them even if that means not reporting a serious crime. Some victims are afraid of retaliation by their attackers, a problem that is especially severe in such crimes as child abuse or wife-beating. Many rape victims are afraid that the police response will be unsympathetic or degrading.

These problems are much more consequential for some crimes than for others. Some crimes are so severe, or so obvious, that they are nearly always reported. Murder is the best example of the first, auto theft of the second. This makes these crimes easier to compare over different time periods or across different cities, regions, or countries, than crimes like theft, which vary enormously in reporting rates.

But the difficulties, and potential biases, do not end when crimes are reported to police. Studies show that how the police classify and record the crimes that do come to their attention depends partly on a host of factors other than the crime itself. For example, a study of robberies in Chicago found that only about a fourth were ultimately recorded by the police as official robberies. Of the rest, some were not reported by the victims, and some that were reported were classified as "unfounded" by the police. Both for the victims and the police, the decision to classify an incident as a robbery or not depended primarily on their assessment of the larger situation in which the robbery took place. Robberies that were successfully resisted, for example, were less often recorded by police; robberies involving guns were more often recorded. Though these decisions make sense intuitively, they also cause considerable bias in our understanding both of the extent of robbery and of the nature of its victims and perpetrators (Block and Block, 1980).

The collection and recording of official crime statistics in this country begins with the many thousands of separate local law enforcement agencies. About 15,000 such agencies provide the information that goes into the FBI's *Uniform Crime Reports*, the annual compilation that is the basic source of official crime statistics in the United States (Federal Bureau of Investigation, 1982, p. 1). Though there has been a considerable effort to standardize the way these agencies record and report crimes, much variation remains. Especially in the not-too-distant past, some police agencies tended to record the local crime rate according to their own administrative needs rather than the call of accuracy and impartiality. A stunning example of this took place in New York City in the mid-1960s, and is illustrated in Table 11-1. As the table shows, the city's official rates of certain crimes shot up enormously, coincidentally just at the time when the police administration changed hands.

Despite the potential biases, the FBI's *Uniform Crime Reports* (UCR) remain the standard source for most of the crime rates and trends that are reported in the media and bemoaned by public officials. The UCR describes the number of crimes of various kinds reported to the police, with special attention to eight serious crimes that are often combined to form a *crime index*: murder, forcible rape, robbery, aggravated assault (assault intended to seriously injure, often with a weapon), auto theft, larceny (theft), burglary, and (since 1980) arson. These index crimes are, in turn, broken down into *crimes of violence* (murder, rape, ag-

Crime	Recorded crimes			Percent change between 1965-1966
	1964	1965	1966	
Murder and non-negligent manslaughter	636	631	653	3
Forcible rape	1,054	1,154	1,761	53
Robbery	7,988	8,904	23,539	164
Aggravated assault	14,831	16,325	23,205	42
Auto theft	32,856	34,726	44,914	29
Burglary	45,693	51,072	120,903	137
Larceny over $50	70,348	74,983	108,132	44

Table 11-1
Reported crimes before and after a 1965 change in police administration, New York City

Source: Adapted from Alfred Blumstein, Jacqueline Cohen, and Daniel Nagin, eds., *Deterrence and Incapacitation* (Washington, D.C.: National Academy of Sciences, 1978), p. 115. Reprinted with permission of the National Academy Press.

gravated assault, robbery) and *crimes against property* (burglary, larceny, auto theft). The UCR also records how many of these crimes *known* to the police are "cleared" by an arrest, and, for some crimes, describes the characteristics, insofar as they are known, of the people arrested and (for homicide) of the victims.

Like the process of reporting crime in the first place, but even more so, the official figures on *arrests* reflect many things other than the "true" crime rate itself, and must be treated even more cautiously. Police may arrest someone for a wide variety of reasons: a past criminal record, a "suspicious" appearance, or, in some places, unfavorable racial, ethnic, or class stereotypes. Again, these biases are likely to be more severe for certain kinds of crime than others.

Some crimes frequently lead to arrests; others are very rarely cleared in this way. Figure 11-1 shows the proportion of index crimes cleared by arrest in 1981; these range from almost three-fourths of murders to one-quarter of robberies and about one-seventh of burglaries and auto thefts. As we will see later in this chapter, this low rate of cleared crimes has important implications

for our understanding of strategies to prevent crime. For now, it is important to note that it limits the usefulness of arrest data in telling us much about either the underlying crime rate or the nature of the criminal population.

Because of the limitations of these official data, two other techniques have been used by researchers to get at the "true" rate of crime. One relies on the testimony of crime's victims, the other on its perpetrators.

Victim surveys ask a sample of the population (of a city or the country as a whole) about its experience with crime, usually in the past year. The most comprehensive of these surveys is the annual National Crime Survey of 60,000 households done for the Justice Department by the Census Bureau (begun in 1972). Because these surveys tap crimes that are not necessarily reported to police, they produce a very different picture than the FBI data. In particular, they show much *more* crime, even serious crime, than official figures reveal. Thus, according to the UCR, the 1978 robbery rate in the United States was about 191 per 100,000 population. According to the National Crime Survey it was 590 per 100,000. The rate of

Figure 11-1

Crimes cleared by arrest, 1981

Source: Federal Bureau of Investigation, *Uniform Crime Reports, 1981* (Washington, D.C.: Government Printing Office, 1982), p. 152.

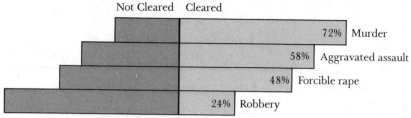

CRIMES OF VIOLENCE

Not Cleared   Cleared

72% Murder
58% Aggravated assault
48% Forcible rape
24% Robbery

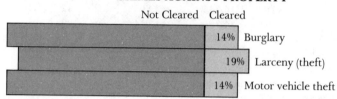

CRIMES AGAINST PROPERTY

Not Cleared   Cleared

14% Burglary
19% Larceny (theft)
14% Motor vehicle theft

forcible rape was about 31 per 100,000 as reported to the police, about 100 per 100,000 as reported directly by the victims.

Since the victim surveys show that a very large proportion of some crimes are not reported to the police, they imply that changes in people's ability or willingness to report crimes can make an enormous difference in the official crime rate without necessarily involving any change in the "true" incidence of crime. Because of this, it is often thought that victim surveys can give a more accurate picture of the trends (or lack of them) in crime over time.

But the victim surveys are not without limitations of their own. First, they only deal with "street" crime and not with "white-collar" offenses (see pages 442 to 445) — an important, though often neglected, aspect of crime in America. They also underreport crimes within families. Evaluations of these surveys, too, have found that though they catch more crimes than the official reports do, they still undercount the number of offenses. Most importantly, the surveys depend on victims' ability to remember incidents of crime accurately and to have perceived them correctly in the first place. But memory and perception are fallible, and reliance on them opens the victim surveys to some inaccuracies, especially when it comes to uncovering the characteristics

of the perpetrators of the crimes (Hindelang, 1981). Finally, some critics argue that the surveys exaggerate the real seriousness of crime by including many relatively unserious incidents in the category of serious crimes. Victims may define small thefts as robberies, for example, or consider a minor altercation a serious assault.

Another common approach to uncovering the crime rate is through "self-report" surveys, in which samples of some population, or of known offenders, are asked in confidence about the kinds of offenses they have committed. Like the victim surveys, self-report studies generally turn up much more crime than is recorded in official data — and show that the number of people who are willing to admit to having committed *some* sort of crime is very large indeed. But even more than the victim surveys, they are subject to strong biases reflecting the respondents' ability or willingness to report their own criminal acts accurately. And, again like the victim surveys, these surveys turn up a vast amount of minor crimes that may give a misleading picture of the distribution of serious crime (Hindelang, Hirschi, and Weis, 1979).

Sources: Hindelang, Hirschi, and Weis, 1979; Block and Block, 1980; Hindelang, 1981; Federal Bureau of Investigation, 1982.

to prevent crime? Are we as much in the dark about crime's causes as some writers suggest — and as powerless to develop strategies to combat them? Finally, what is the outlook for the future? Can we expect continuing rises in crime and violence, or is there reason to expect that we may begin to reverse the sense of fear and disintegration in American communities?

Is Crime Increasing?

In 1981 a major news magazine ran a cover story on what it called the "epidemic" of violent crime, and a presidential task force spoke of a "wave of violence" sweeping the country (*Newsweek*, March 23, 1981; U.S. Department of Justice, 1981). Many of us feel that violent crime has gotten worse and that life is more dangerous than it used to be, and, as we have seen, this feeling is increasingly expressed in public opinion polls. But some writers have argued that the true crime rate is exaggerated by public officials and the media, that the increase in crime has been much less than it seems. What do we know about the real dimensions of the American crime problem? Is crime really rising?

As we've seen in "Uncovering the Crime Rate" (pages 410 to 412), the answers are not simple.

The FBI's *Uniform Crime Reports* suggest that, aside from a slowdown in the mid-1970s, and a similar drop in the early 1980s, serious crime has generally risen since the early 1960s. Figure 11-2 shows the growth in the FBI's index crime rates since 1971. And Table 11-2 adds detail. Note that:

1. Most recorded crime is *property* crime, not violent crime. The combined rate for the three property crimes is roughly ten times that of the four violent crimes combined. Well over half of all officially reported crimes are crimes of theft alone.

2. Both kinds of crime rose rapidly until the early 1970s, leveled off slightly during the middle of the decade, and rose sharply again thereafter, easing off slightly in 1981.

The figures give the impression that crime in America has increased considerably, if unevenly, in recent years. But it is often argued that they overestimate both the seriousness and the growth of crime. One reason is that many recorded violent crimes are not as serious as the term implies; a robbery, for example, may mean anything from a youth demanding lunch money from another to a shoot-out at a liquor store that leaves someone badly injured. More importantly, the official data may exaggerate the increase in crime by mistaking changes in *rates of reporting* or *recording* crime for changes in the underlying crime rate.

Table 11-2
Index of serious crime, United States, 1972–1981

Population*	Crime† index total	Violent‡ crime	Property‡ crime	Murder and non-negligent man-slaughter	Forcible rape	Robbery	Aggra-vated assault	Burglary	Larceny theft	Motor vehicle theft
Number of offenses:										
1972: 208,230,000	8,248,800	834,900	7,413,900	18,670	46,850	376,290	393,090	2,375,500	4,151,200	887,200
1973: 209,851,000	8,718,100	875,910	7,842,200	19,640	51,400	384,220	420,650	2,565,500	4,347,900	928,800
1974: 211,392,000	10,253,400	974,720	9,278,700	20,710	55,400	442,400	456,210	3,039,200	5,262,500	977,100
1975: 213,124,000	11,256,600	1,026,280	10,230,300	20,510	56,090	464,970	484,710	3,252,100	5,977,700	1,000,500
1976: 214,659,000	11,304,800	986,580	10,318,200	18,780	56,730	420,210	490,850	3,089,800	6,270,800	957,600
1977: 216,332,000	10,935,800	1,009,500	9,926,300	19,120	63,020	404,850	522,510	3,052,200	5,905,700	968,400
1978: 218,059,000	11,141,300	1,061,830	10,079,500	19,560	67,130	417,040	558,100	3,104,500	5,983,400	991,600
1979: 220,099,000	12,152,700	1,178,540	10,974,200	21,460	75,990	466,880	614,210	3,299,500	6,577,500	1,097,200
1980: 225,349,264	13,295,400	1,308,900	11,986,500	23,040	82,090	548,810	654,960	3,759,200	7,112,700	1,114,700
1981: 229,146,000	13,290,300	1,321,900	11,968,400	22,520	81,540	574,130	643,720	3,739,800	7,154,500	1,074,000
Rate per 100,000 inhabitants§										
1972	3,961.4	401.0	3,560.4	9.0	22.5	180.7	188.8	1,140.8	1,993.6	426.1
1973	4,154.4	417.4	3,737.0	9.4	24.5	183.1	200.5	1,222.5	2,071.9	442.6
1974	4,850.4	461.1	4,389.3	9.8	26.2	209.3	215.8	1,437.7	2,489.5	462.2
1975	5,281.7	481.5	4,800.2	9.6	26.3	218.2	227.4	1,525.9	2,804.8	469.4
1976	5,266.4	459.6	4,806.8	8.8	26.4	195.8	228.7	1,439.4	2,921.3	446.1
1977	5,055.1	466.6	4,588.4	8.8	29.1	187.1	241.5	1,410.9	2,729.9	447.6
1978	5,109.3	486.9	4,622.4	9.0	30.8	191.3	255.9	1,423.7	2,743.9	454.7
1979	5,521.5	535.5	4,986.0	9.7	34.5	212.1	279.1	1,499.1	2,988.4	498.5
1980	5,899.9	580.8	5,319.1	10.2	36.4	243.5	290.6	1,668.2	3,156.3	494.6
1981	5,799.9	576.9	5,223.0	9.8	35.6	250.6	280.9	1,632.1	3,122.3	468.7

*Populations are Bureau of the Census provisional estimates as of July 1, except April 1, 1980, preliminary census counts, and are subject to change.
†Due to rounding, the offenses may not add to totals.
‡Violent crimes are offenses of murder, forcible rape, robbery, and aggravated assault. Property crimes are offenses of burglary, larceny (theft), and motor vehicle theft. Data are not included for the property crime of arson.
§Crime rates calculated prior to rounding number of offenses.
Source: Federal Bureau of Investigation, *Uniform Crime Reports 1981* (Washington, D.C.: Government Printing Office, August 1982), p. 39.

Rate per 100,000 inhabitants

Rate per 100,000 inhabitants

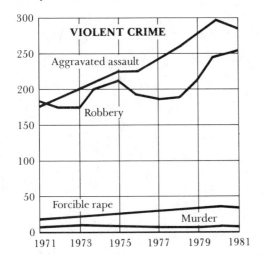

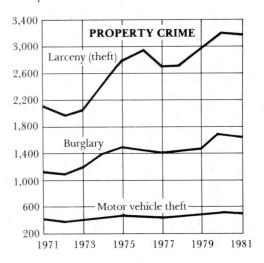

Figure 11-2
Selected crime rates,
1971–1981

*Source: Statistical Abstract of the
United States, 1982–83* (Wash-
ington, D.C.: Government
Printing Office, 1983), p. 173.

Surveys of the victims of crime throw some light on this question — and provide a somewhat different picture. Table 11-3 shows rates of crime over an eight-year period of the National Crime Survey. Compared with the official FBI rates for the same years, two points stand out sharply.

1. The victim survey shows far *more* crime than the police data; almost three times the rate of rape and robbery, for example. Seen in this light, the crime problem appears more, not less, serious and pervasive than the official data indicate.

2. The victim survey also suggests that the *increase* in crime may be significantly less than the official FBI data show. During these eight years, violent crimes (excluding murder, which for fairly obvious reasons is not included in victim surveys) rose less than 2 percent; the overall trend is one of virtually no change. Robberies, in fact, declined though assaults and rapes increased. (The FBI figures show violent crime increasing significantly over the same years.) For "household" crimes, burglary had declined in the victim surveys, while larceny increased.

Homicide rates provide another perspective on the increase in crime. As we have noted, they are much less likely to reflect serious reporting or recording biases than most other crime rates. Table 11-4 shows that official homicide rates have followed the same general trend as other violent crimes, though not as sharply: rising in the late 1960s, flattening out in the mid-1970s, and rising again in the late 1970s. Well over *twice* as many Amer-

Is Crime Increasing? **415**

Sector and type of crime	1973	1974	1975	1976	1977	1978	1979	1980	1981
Personal sector									
Crimes of violence	32.6	33.0	32.8	32.6	33.9	33.7	34.5	33.3	35.3
Rape	1.0	1.0	0.9	0.8	0.9	1.0	1.1	0.9	1.0
Robbery	6.7	7.2	6.8	6.5	6.2	5.9	6.3	6.6	7.4
Assault	24.9	24.8	25.2	25.3	26.8	26.9	27.2	25.8	27.0
Aggravated assault	10.1	10.4	9.6	9.9	10.0	9.7	9.9	9.3	9.6
Simple assault	14.8	14.4	15.6	15.4	16.8	17.2	17.3	16.5	17.3
Crimes of theft	91.1	95.1	96.0	96.1	97.3	96.8	91.9	83.0	85.1
Personal larceny with contact	3.1	3.1	3.1	2.9	2.7	3.1	2.9	3.0	3.3
Personal larceny without contact	88.0	92.0	92.9	93.2	94.6	93.6	89.0	80.0	81.9
Household sector									
Household burglary	91.7	93.1	91.7	88.9	88.5	86.0	84.1	84.3	87.9
Household larceny	107.0	123.8	125.4	124.1	123.3	119.9	133.7	126.5	121.0
Motor vehicle theft	19.1	18.8	19.5	16.5	17.0	17.5	17.5	16.7	17.1

Source: U.S. Bureau of Justice Statistics, *Criminal Victimization in the United States; 1980–1981 Changes Based on New Estimates* (Washington, D.C.: Government Printing Office, March 1983), p. 3.

Table 11-3

Victimization rates for personal and household crimes, 1973–1981 per 1,000 population

icans, proportionally, were the victims of homicide in the beginning of the 1980s than 20 years earlier.

On balance, then, the pattern of crime in recent years probably lies somewhere between the extremes often heard in public debate. Official data probably overstate the rate of increase in serious crime, but some significant increase is apparent (at least through 1980), and reflects a striking change in the quality of American life since the 1960s. Two things make this conclusion even more compelling. First, serious crime has increased in spite of the personal precautions many people have taken to avoid it. Second, it has increased despite the vast sums we have put into more and more sophisticated police and a greatly expanded prison system. We will return to this point shortly.

Who Are the Victims?

We have often seen in this book that broad, national figures can be misleading, masking sharp variations in the way social problems affect particular kinds of people in particular kinds of places. In turn, these variations are often crucial in shaping the way we think about the problem and its possible

Year	Total†	White		Black	
		Male	Female	Male	Female
1950	5.3	3.9	1.4	NA	NA
1955	4.5	3.4	1.2	NA	NA
1960	4.7	3.6	1.4	36.7	10.4
1965	6.5	4.4	1.6	43.4	10.5
1968	7.4	6.0	1.9	60.0	12.3
1969	7.7	6.1	2.0	63.8	12.5
1970	8.3	6.8	2.1	67.6	13.3
1971	9.1	7.3	2.3	74.2	14.9
1972‡	9.4	7.7	2.3	76.8	14.4
1973	9.8	8.3	2.8	72.5	15.8
1974	10.2	8.9	2.8	73.8	15.7
1975	10.0	9.1	2.9	69.6	15.1
1976	9.1	8.3	2.7	62.2	13.6
1977	9.2	8.7	2.9	59.7	13.2
1978	9.4	9.2	2.9	58.7	13.0
1979	10.2	10.1	3.0	64.6	13.8

Note: NA means not available.

*Rate is based on population figures as of April 1 for 1950, 1960, and 1970; July 1 estimates for other years.

†Includes races not shown separately.

‡Based on a 50 percent sample of deaths.

Source: Adapted form *Statistical Abstract of the United States, 1982–83* (Washington, D.C.: Government Printing Office, 1983), p. 178.

Table 11-4
Homicide victims, by race and sex, 1950–1979 (per 100,000 population)

solutions. Crime is no exception. National crime trends obscure the fact that different groups face dramatically different risks of being victimized by crime. In most respects, these risks reflect the broader inequalities characteristic of American society in the 1980s. In general, the victims of serious crime — and especially violent crime — are disproportionately the poor, minorities, and the young. The danger of crime, in this sense, is just one aspect of the larger pattern of unequal risks and rewards that fall along lines of class, race, age, and — in complex ways — sex.

Data from the victim surveys (for crimes other than homicide) and the UCR (for homicide) show that though crime can strike anyone, violent crime is disproportionately an affliction of the poor. With the exception of some property crimes, the chance of victimization for nearly all serious crimes rises, sometimes dramatically, as income levels fall. For violent crimes other than homicide, the rate of victimization for people whose family income is below $3,000 is nearly double the rate for families earning more than $15,000 a year. And this figure understates the difference for several reasons. First, many of these extremely low-income households are elderly (as

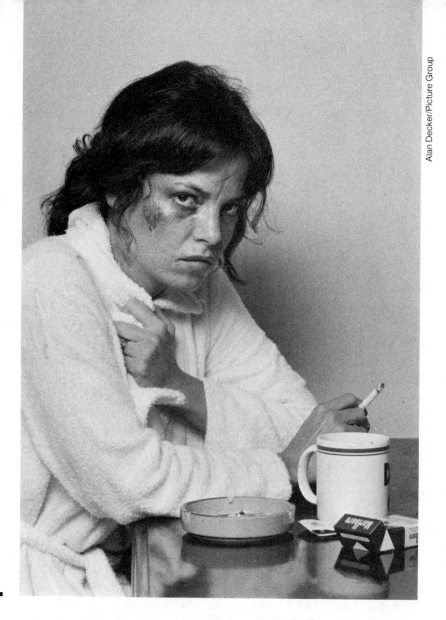

Alan Decker/Picture Group

Many crimes against women go unreported, though less so than in the past.

we've seen in Chapter 4), and the elderly, as we will see in a moment, are victimized at a lower rate than younger people. As a result, the data mask a considerably higher rate of victimization for the nonelderly poor. Second, the overall difference in the risk of violent crimes between poor and nonpoor obscures the fact that for all but one, relatively nonserious, violent crime (simple assault), the ratio of the risks of poor to nonpoor is much worse. The poorest stratum in the United States has more than four times the risk of rape or robbery with injury than Americans earning more than $15,000 a year (U.S. Bureau of Justice Statistics, 1982).

418 Crime and Justice

	Probability
U.S. total	1 out of 153
Male	1 out of 100
Female	1 out of 323
White total	1 out of 240
Male	1 out of 164
Female	1 out of 450
Nonwhite total	1 out of 47
Male	1 out of 28
Female	1 out of 117

Table 11-5
Probability of lifetime risk of murder, by race and sex

Source: Federal Bureau of Investigation, *Uniform Crime Reports, 1981* (Washington, D.C.: Government Printing Office, August 1982), p. 339.

Crimes against property are a somewhat different story. Poor homes, perhaps surprisingly, are somewhat *more* likely to be burglarized than middle-class homes; but the poor are slightly *less* likely to be the victims of simple theft or auto theft. (Some of this, however, may reflect their having fewer cars and reporting smaller thefts less frequently.)

And, though crime victimizes people of all races and ethnic groups, it strikes especially hard at minorities, particularly blacks. Again, this pattern is clearest for the more serious crimes of violence. Black women have more than twice the chance of being raped as white women; whites have about half the chance of being robbed as Hispanics and less than half that of blacks.

Data on the risks of homicide present a similar picture. Forty-four out of every hundred murder victims in 1981 were black, though blacks were only twelve out of every hundred persons in the general population (Federal Bureau of Investigation, 1982, p. 10). This translates into a striking racial difference in the *lifetime* risks of death by homicide, illustrated by Table 11-5: 1 in every 164 white men face that risk, 1 in 28 black men do. Homicide is the *leading* cause of death among black men aged 15 to 44 (U.S. Department of Health and Human Services, 1982, p. 20).

Violent crime is so often associated with the cities that the terms *crime* and *urban crime* are sometimes used interchangeably. And the connection is a real one: the cities — especially the central cities — are much more dangerous than the suburbs or, especially, nonmetropolitan areas. The latter have rates of rape, for example, around one-fourth the rates for cities of more than 500,000 population, and the robbery rate in nonmetropolitan areas is only about *one-eighth* what it is in central cities of more than a million people.

Almost half of Americans are afraid to walk at night in their own neighbor-hoods.

With one very important exception, rape, official violent crime strikes men more often than women. Overall, the male victimization rate is more than double women's for violent crimes other than murder; men's rate of aggravated assault is more than triple women's. (The latter figure should be treated cautiously, though, since assault against women within families is probably consistently underreported in victim surveys.) Homicide rates, fairly reliable indicators of the male risk of violent death, show a similar picture; in 1981, 77 out of every 100 murder victims were male. (The factor of race, as in so many aspects of American life, cuts across this distinction, however. Black women are somewhat *more* likely than white men to be homicide victims.)

We will see in a moment that the young commit much more than their share of violent crime. It is less often recognized that they are also disproportionately crime's *victims*. For most violent crimes, the worst risks are among youth aged 16 to 24; the risk drops sharply after age 35, so that the chances of being a victim of personal violence for people over 65 are less than one-eighth those of young adults.

Of course, none of these differences implies that any group is free from the risks of violence, or that some people's fears about crime are more justified than others. What these differences do illustrate is the truly disastrous level of violence faced by some kinds of people in some kinds of communities. Not too surprisingly, the communities most plagued by crime are those that accumulate a number of other disadvantages — especially if they combine inner-city residence with minority status and low income. And within these especially violence-ridden communities, some people, notably the young, face particularly high chances of death or injury from personal violence.

Crime, Courts, and Prisons

What can be done about crime? In the beginning of this chapter, we noted that the idea that crime is best attacked through social programs dealing with its causes has lost favor in recent years, while the older notion that the most effective way to reduce crime is to deal more swiftly and harshly with criminals has returned into fashion, fueled by the generally rising crime rates of the late 1970s and early 1980s.

The belief that criminals are treated too leniently is shared by a broad majority of Americans, according to opinion polls. About three-fourths of blacks and more than four-fifths of whites, according to data from the National Opinion Research Center, believe that the courts do not "deal harshly enough with certain criminals" (*Public Opinion*, April-May 1981, p. 40). But getting tough with criminals can mean several different things: arresting them more often, convicting them more predictably once arrested, and/or sentencing them to more severe punishment once convicted. In the past several years, it has become especially common to hear demands for more prisons and stiffer sentences in response to rising crime rates. Behind these demands is the argument that the reason we have such a serious crime problem is that we have allowed crime's "costs" to fall, relative to its "benefits" (Wilson, 1975; Ehrlich, 1979). In this view, crime is rising because punishment is declining. The remedy follows simply: If we increase our capacity to punish criminals more certainly and/or more severely, we can bring down the crime rate.

The argument has a compelling simplicity that appeals to our fears of being victimized by crime, as well as to our understandable moral sense that criminals should not go unpunished. But how well does it explain the nature of America's crime problem?

On closer examination, things are not nearly so simple. There are two main difficulties with the declining costs argument. First, it overlooks the crucial fact that the United States *already* has one of the harshest systems of punishment in the world and that we have been locking criminals up for several years now at an ever-accelerating rate — without a discernible effect on public safety. Second, careful studies have repeatedly found that it is much more difficult to increase the real "costs" of crime, in practice, than this argument supposes. Let's look at each point in turn.

Are We "Soft" on Criminals?

Compared to most other advanced industrial societies, the United States has traditionally imprisoned a very high proportion of its population. Table 11-6 shows what criminologists call *incarceration rates* (the number of people in prison as a proportion of the total population) for several Western European countries, Japan, and the United States. Our incarceration rate is from two to about eight times higher than that of the other countries. Yet, as the table also indicates, the rate of the most serious of violent crimes, murder, is strikingly *less* in all of the other countries.

Why the Prisons Are Crowded

The American prison system is almost literally bursting at the seams. At the beginning of 1983, about 412,000 Americans were locked in state and federal prisons — a rate of about 180 per 100,000 population. Between 1941 and 1970, that rate never rose above 120 per 100,000. But after 1972, the situation began to change rapidly. The prison population increased by 110 percent between 1970 and 1982.

The result has been massive overcrowding, despite considerable sums poured into new prison construction over the same years. By the late 1970s, many state prison inmates were being locked up in local jails, and many state prison systems were being sued because their facilities could no longer meet minimum legal guidelines for safe or humane treatment of prisoners. At the end of the decade, according to a federal study of prison conditions, "the living space available to the majority of the nation's prisoners failed to meet minimum standards of adequacy" (Mullen et al., 1980). About half of all state prison inmates, (90 percent of Texas inmates), were living in overcrowded cells.

Prison overcrowding has been linked to illness, suicide, psychiatric complaints, and inmate violence — and has been implicated in prison riots in several states (Lieber, 1981; Thornberry, 1982). It is often argued that these conditions result from an "epidemic" of violent crime in recent years. The implication is that we need more prisons — not only to protect the public from a mushrooming population of violent criminals, but to provide humane treatment for those inside the walls. Is this an accurate perspective?

Not entirely. We have seen, first of all, that violent crime — though it *has* increased overall in recent years — actually slowed in the mid-1970s, just when the prison population was rapidly grow-

Country	Incarceration rate	Homicide rate
United States	217	9.4
Canada	97	2.5
France	67	1.0
Denmark	63	1.3
West Germany	60	1.2
Sweden	55	1.2
Norway	45	1.0
Japan	44	1.0
Netherlands	21	0.9

Table 11-6

Incarceration rates and homicide, various countries, 1977–1980 (per 100,000 population)

Note: Incarceration rates include prisoners in detention centers and jails.
Sources: Incarceration rates from Eugene Doleschal and Anne Newton, *International Rates of Imprisonment* (Hackensack, N.J.: National Council on Crime and Delinquency, 1981); homicide rates from World Health Organization data, in *Statistical Abstract of the United States, 1982–83* (Washington, D.C.: Government Printing Office, 1983), p. 179.

Obviously, there are many differences in social, economic, and cultural patterns among these countries, making comparisons difficult. But, equally obviously, these differences do show that the relationship between rates of punishment and rates of violent crime are far more complicated than the declining costs argument suggests.

ing. More tellingly, what is often ignored is that much of the growth in the prison population has not come from a surge of *violent* criminals, but of people imprisoned for crimes against *property*. Between 1972 and 1978, the total number of violent offenders in state prisons rose by only 13 percent. (Higher, to be sure, in some individual states.) The *proportion* of violent offenders, relative to others, dropped substantially. In 1973, 52 percent of state prison inmates were imprisoned for crimes of violence, 32 percent for property crimes, and 16 percent for crimes against "public order" (mainly drug-related offenses). By 1978 the proportion of violent offenders had dropped to 47 percent, that of property criminals had risen to 37 percent, and the proportion of public order offenders had remained the same. In the northeastern states, there were actually *fewer* violent criminals behind bars in 1978 than there had been five years earlier (Mullen et al., 1980).

This does not mean that ensuring public safety by imprisoning dangerous offenders, or providing decent conditions of confinement once they are behind bars, are not important goals. It does suggest, however, that there may be other ways, besides more prisons, to reduce overcrowding without diminishing public safety, particularly through programs designed to deal with nonviolent property offenders outside prison walls. In the short term, the experience of some states suggests that *reducing sentences* for less-dangerous offenders may be an effective way to ease the immediate problem of overcrowding. Michigan, for example, has an "emergency release" program whereby certain prisoners may have their sentences reduced by 90 days when the inmate population exceeds the prison's capacity for 30 days or more (Tropin, 1983, p. 6).

Sources: Mullen et al., 1980; Lieber, 1981; Thornberry, 1982; Tropin, 1983.

Crime, Courts, and Prisons **423**

The same point emerges if we compare incarceration rates for different groups in the United States itself. Thus, by most measures, black Americans commit a disproportionate amount of street crime. Using the simple logic of the costs argument, we would expect blacks to be treated more leniently by the criminal justice system. In fact, the opposite is true. The black incarceration rate in state prisons is about seven times that of whites in the United States as a whole. Almost *20 percent* of black men can expect to spend some time in a jail or prison in their lifetime, as compared to less than 3 percent of whites (Blumstein, 1982, p. 1260). That difference partly reflects the higher crime rate among blacks, but it also seems to result from a tendency for some jurisdictions to deal more severely with blacks than with whites for the same types of crimes. The social-scientific evidence for this kind of racial bias in the courts is mixed (Blumstein, 1982), but several recent studies conclude that blacks are somewhat more likely to receive a prison sentence than whites once convicted of a serious crime — and that the sentence is likely to be longer (Thornberry, 1979; Thompson and Zingraff, 1981). By the simple logic of the declining costs argument, the disproportionate incarceration of blacks ought to bring their crime rate *down*. Since it has not done so, it seems clear that something other than judicial leniency must lie behind black Americans' higher crime rate.

The same problem appears when we examine differences in crime in different *regions* of the country. The South imprisons people at a considerably higher rate than other sections of the United States; with less than a third of the country's population, it holds almost half of all state prison inmates. Moreover, it imprisons people disproportionately, relative to its share of the country's total serious crime (Mullen et al., 1980). In other words, the "costs" of crime are typically *greater* in the South than elsewhere in the country. But, at the same time, many southern states and cities have among the country's *highest* rates of violent crime.

In comparative terms, then, the country with the *highest* rate of imprisonment has the worst rate of violent crime; within that country, the group with the highest rate of imprisonment accounts for a disproportionate share of violent crime; and the region that uses its prisons most heavily has among the highest rates of violence. These facts pose obvious problems for theories that, in effect, blame the leniency of our criminal justice system for our high crime rate.

So, too, does another piece of evidence — the fact that our rates of incarceration have been rising sharply for many years. This fact has, surprisingly, been left out of much of the public debate over crime. But it suggests that the declining costs argument may also be out of date. To the extent that there was a period of leniency in the American criminal justice system, it ended in the mid-1970s.

Figure 11-3 shows that, after a low point in the late 1960s and early 1970s, the American prison population began to increase rapidly, with the incarceration rate leaping by almost a third between 1975 and 1981 alone.

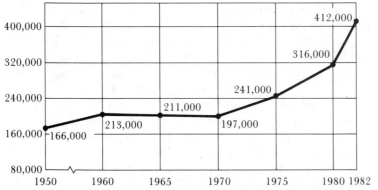

Figure 11-3

Inmates in state and federal prisons, 1950–1982

Source: Data from U.S. Bureau of Justice Statistics, *Prisoners in State and Federal Institutions on December 31* (Washington, D.C.: Government Printing Office, annual).

As the box on crowded prisons (pages 422 to 423) shows, the get-tough policies we have *already* adopted for many years have resulted in a prison system that is now almost literally bursting at the seams, with grim and sometimes terrifying results.

The problem, then, is not how to understand the growing "leniency" of American justice — but, rather, to understand why the increasing *harshness* of American justice has not reduced crime, and has, in fact, been accompanied by generally rising levels of violence. To approach that question, we need to look more closely at what recent research tells us about the complex relationship between crime and punishment in America.

Deterrence and Incapacitation

Criminologists have traditionally described two distinct, but related, ways in which the criminal justice system may act to prevent crime: *deterrence* and *incapacitation*. Deterrence refers to the inhibiting effect on potential criminals of the risks of being caught and punished. Incapacitation is the crime-reducing effect of taking particular criminals out of circulation and thus preventing the crimes they would otherwise have committed. Thus, imposing a stiff prison sentence on a convicted robber might reduce the crime rate in either or both of two ways: by deterring others who might be tempted to robbery (or deters the robber in question from *further* crimes), and/or by taking one active robber off the street. When we talk about reducing crime by building more prisons, giving convicted criminals harsher sentences, or improving the efficiency with which they are caught and brought to justice, we are making assumptions about the impact of some combination of these two effects. What do we know about how they actually influence the crime rate?

That question has generated an enormous amount of research, but the results are much less clear-cut than we would guess from politicians' speeches. On the whole, the evidence suggests that our capacity to reduce crime through either deterrence or incapacitation is crucially limited.

Deterrence: inconclusive evidence. The commonsense idea that punishment deters crime is based on the assumption that people choose their behavior according to some more or less rational weighing of the risks and benefits of different courses of action. Thus, the potential gains of, say, robbery are balanced by would-be criminals against the risks of being caught and punished. If those risks are high, the potential gains will not appear worth it, and the rate of robbery should go down. If, on the other hand, the chances of capture and punishment are low, robbery may seem a rational option, especially if the benefits of law-abiding behavior are also low. The result should be a higher rate of robberies.

Though this argument seems quite simple at first glance, it is less so in practice, for at least three reasons:

1. Research suggests that the model of rationally chosen behavior — the notion that criminals think through the relative costs and benefits of their actions in advance — fits poorly with the admittedly limited evidence we have on criminals' motivation. At best, it works better for some kinds of crime than others. Many crimes of violence, those we generally fear the most, are typically less planned and calculated than the model implies. One recent estimate is that between one-half and two-thirds of murders are unpremeditated, spontaneous results of arguments and moments of anger, often between people who know each other, and frequently among family members. A substantial proportion of violent crimes, too — including an estimated 40 to 65 percent of homicides — take place under the influence of alcohol or drugs (Green and Wakefield, 1979; U.S. Bureau of Justice Statistics, 1983a, 1983b). This does not mean that such crimes *cannot* be deterred by the threat of punishment, but it does limit the usefulness of an approach based *mainly* on appealing to criminals' rational avoidance of risks.

   A recent study sheds light on this problem by asking known, convicted criminals to evaluate how much planning had been involved in their crimes. Criminals were asked to recall the circumstances surrounding their first offense and their last one, presumably the ones they would remember most reliably. According to these offenders, only 17 percent of first offenses and 21 percent of "last" offenses had involved any advance planning at all, even as little as an hour before the crime. Only 6 percent and 14 percent, respectively, had been planned as much as a day in advance. The vast majority of violent crimes, in this study, were defined by their perpetrators as essentially impulsive ones (Erez, 1980).

2. Another fundamental limitation on the deterrent effect of punishment stems from the fact that this effect is actually a blend of two separate factors: the chances of being caught and punished, and the harshness or leniency of the punishment if it is inflicted. Criminologists have traditionally called the first the *certainty* and the second the *severity* of

punishment. Most studies show that of the two, it is the *certainty* of punishment that has the more important deterrent effect on crime (Blumstein, Cohen, and Nagin, 1978). Common sense suggests why this should be so: If the chances of punishment are low, the fear of even very harsh penalties is, realistically, likely to be slight. The problem is that the chances of being punished with certainty for a crime are not so much a matter of what happens to criminals once they are in the courts, but of whether they are caught in the first place. As we will see when discussing the effects of incapacitation, those chances are often quite small for many crimes, and they depend on factors that lie mainly outside the influence of the courts or prisons.

3. The third important limitation concerns the kinds of punishments that may be inflicted on criminals through the formal processes of the criminal justice system. Most studies of the role of deterrence have found that such "formal" sanctions have much less impact on crime than "informal" ones (the approval or disapproval of one's family, friends, and larger community). Sociologists have long argued that these informal, close connections of family and community exert a far more powerful influence on human behavior of all kinds than is usually recognized, and criminal behavior is no exception (Tittle, 1980). Thus, formal punishment may be inherently less effective than other means of social control.

Does all of this mean that tough sentences and the threat of prison have *no* deterrent impact on crime? No; most research suggests that the common-sense notion that punishment can have *some* effect on crime rates is probably correct. But how *much* of an effect — and for what kinds of crimes and on what kinds of criminals — is still a largely unknown quantity. A thorough review of dozens of studies of deterrence by the prestigious National Academy of Sciences recently concluded that

> The empirical evidence is still not sufficient for providing a rigorous confirmation of a deterrent effect. Perhaps more important, the evidence is woefully inadequate for providing a good estimate of the magnitude of whatever effect may exist. (Blumstein, Cohen, and Nagin, 1978, p. 135)

Incapacitation: yes, but. . . . The existence of what criminologists call an *incapacitation effect* is more easily documented. But, once again, the *magnitude* of that effect is difficult to determine. As with deterrence, common sense suggests that, other things being equal, putting known criminals behind bars will reduce crime. But the more important questions of how *much* crime — and at what cost — turn out to be far more difficult, and the results of research fairly discouraging. Why?

The amount of crime that can be prevented through incapacitating a given number of criminals depends partly on how much of the total crime in a community those criminals commit. Two extreme examples help illustrate this. Suppose, first, that *all* of the serious crime in a community is commit-

Longer sentences for offenders have resulted in overcrowded and turbulent prisons.

ted by a handful of extremely active criminals. In this case, imprisoning even one of this "hard core" for a long period could have a noticeable impact on the overall crime rate; locking up *all* of them would virtually end crime. But suppose, instead, that crime is much more evenly spread among a much larger number of criminals. In this case, locking up any one criminal will have little impact on the crime rate; or, to put it the other way around, making a large impact on crime would require locking up a much larger number of people, with a much greater investment of social resources.

Which example is closest to the truth? The reality clearly lies somewhere in between these extremes. No one knows exactly how much crime is accounted for by particular criminals since so much crime is hidden and since criminals have an important stake in keeping it that way. Most studies based on official crime records suggest that a disproportionate amount of crime is committed by repeat offenders; one study, by the criminologist Marvin Wolfgang and his co-workers, found that less than one-fourth of all delinquent youth in Philadelphia were responsible for about two-thirds of the city's serious youth crime (Wolfgang, 1981). But most research indicates that the often-heard idea that we could stop crime by getting tougher with a handful of hard-core criminals is greatly exaggerated.

A study of violent criminals in Columbus, Ohio, illustrates this problem. The researchers followed all serious violent offenders who were arrested through the courts over a period of a year and calculated, as closely as possible, how much crime would have been avoided by giving every one of them a minimum five-year prison sentence. Their estimate was that just *four percent* of serious violent crime in that city would have been prevented by that kind of sentence — one considerably more severe than most offenders actually receive, and one that, if adopted, would multiply the prison population many times over (Conrad, Van Dine, and Dinitz, 1979).

Other studies have put the amount of street crime that could be prevented through tougher prison sentences higher; but few argue that, even with extremely severe changes in sentencing, the rate of serious crime could be slashed by much more than 20 percent (Boland, 1978). And most agree that this level of prevention would be possible only through truly dramatic increases in our reliance on prisons. The National Academy of Sciences study concluded that in order to cut serious index crime by 10 percent, California would have to increase its prison population by 157 percent, New York by 263 percent, amd Massachusetts by 310 percent (Blumstein, Cohen and Nagin, 1978, p. 176).

Why would tougher sentences have so little payoff? In part, research suggests, because so much crime is *not* committed by repeat offenders — at least, not by repeat offenders who get caught. Among the Columbus study's sample, for instance, only 11 percent had a record of a previous conviction for a violent felony; less than a third had *any* previous felony conviction. (Roughly similar proportions have been found in studies of other urban criminal courts.) Thus, this study tends to affirm the first of our hypothetical examples — serious crime seems to be fairly widely spread among a large population of criminals, many of whom are first offenders, and many of whom apparently never reach the courts (Conrad, Van Dine, and Dinitz, 1979).

We noted this problem in looking at the effects of deterrence: for either deterrence or incapacitation to work, criminals must first be apprehended. We saw in the beginning of the chapter that the clearance rate for many kinds of crime is quite low; in the Columbus study, only 40 to 50 percent of the city's serious violent crime was ever cleared by an arrest. No one knows precisely how much of these unsolved crimes were committed by criminals who are ultimately arrested and tried. But we do know that the chances of being arrested for any given crime are small — for most types of crime — while the chances of being dealt with severely once arrested and convicted are much greater than critics often suggest, particularly for repeat offenders.

A Rand Corporation study of imprisoned felony offenders, for example, asked them to report how often they were arrested in comparison with the number of crimes they had committed. The results are revealing. According to their own testimony, these criminals had about 1 chance in 10 of being arrested for any robbery, slightly less for a burglary, and only 1 chance in 25 for an auto theft. Once arrested, on the other hand, these "repeat" offenders were quite likely to be dealt with strictly by the courts. Almost 9 out of 10 of those arrested for robbery were convicted; of those convicted, almost 9 of 10 were imprisoned. Other studies have found roughly similar proportions for the treatment of repeat or "habitual" offenders (Petersilia, Greenwood, and Lavin, 1978).

In the past few years, there has been an increasing interest in what some criminologists call *selective incapacitation* (Greenwood and Abrahamse, 1982), the attempt to predict which criminals are most likely to become repeat offenders and to sentence them to appropriately longer confinement. This approach has been criticized on several grounds. For one thing, though there is considerable controversy over the degree to which it's possible to predict future criminality, there is virtually no disagreement that the state of the art is very crude indeed. As a result, any formula for picking out just which criminals will be repeaters in need of special handling will cast its net too wide, snagging many offenders who would not have gone on to further crimes. Moreover, there are disturbing legal and ethical issues involved in sentencing people to greatly different punishments when they've committed the same crimes. Finally, and perhaps most importantly, courts *already* use a less formal version of the idea of selective incapacitation: judges already use background information and the criminal's past record in deciding how to sentence offenders. It's unlikely that efforts to make this process more exact would have *much* impact on crime, especially given the lack of precision in our capacity to predict future criminal behavior.

In general, attempts to prevent crime by changing the way we deal with offenders in the courts are probably focusing on the wrong end of the criminal justice process. Some criminals, certainly, do slip through the net of the criminal justice system, receiving a light sentence, or even no sentence at all, for even very serious crimes. But the weight of the evidence suggests that this is not the *main* way in which the criminal justice system "fails." Critics of the "leniency" of American criminal justice often point to figures showing that only a relatively small proportion of crimes ever end in a prison sentence. That is true, as many studies of the criminal courts have shown. But the *primary* reason is the varying, but usually small, proportion of crimes that result in arrest — not the failure to punish known, convicted repeaters.

That distinction is important because it helps us understand what the strategy of getting tough in the courts or building more prisons can and cannot do. Ultimately, our ability to increase the costs of crime depends more on increasing the chances of *apprehending* criminals than on dealing more severely with them once they are caught. And that is primarily a function of the police rather than the courts or prisons. We need to ask, then, what we know about the ability of the *police* to prevent crime.

Police and Crime

Here, too, the evidence isn't encouraging. It is not that the police do not want to prevent crime. It is rather that they are limited in their capacity to do so.

This is not to suggest that the police have no impact on crime. Historical studies of the rare occasions when cities have been without police are instructive. In England, a Liverpool police strike in 1919 resulted in mass looting of shops and attacks on the few remaining police officers. In 1944, in occupied Denmark, the Germans arrested the entire Danish police force. Although the Germans greatly increased the *severity* of punishment, the crime rate doubled during the seven-month absence of police. But the *total* absence of police is unusual and transient. Usually when we discuss the effectiveness of the police, we are talking about the ways in which marginal changes in the numbers of police officers assigned to different units of police departments influence police effectiveness or about how police effectiveness varies with different strategies of policing.

Consider for a moment how police officers work. They are obviously very dependent on information that they do not themselves generate. And, as we have already seen, victim surveys show that a very large proportion of some crimes do not come to the attention of the police. Obviously, if the police do not know a crime has occurred, they cannot move to apprehend the offender. Also, in one major area of crime, the police rarely, if ever, are offered information about criminal activities. These are sometimes called "vice" crimes, sometimes "crimes without victims," to suggest the consensual nature of the crime, but most accurately, from a law enforcement perspective, these are crimes without citizen complaints. The prevalence of these crimes (such as drug sales and use, prostitution, and illegal gambling) is captured neither by the *Uniform Crime Reports* nor by victim surveys. The narcotics sellers and purchasers, the prostitute's "John," and the bookmaker's bettor do not usually feel victimized. Therefore, they don't report such crimes to the police. They may also not report them to crime surveyors because they fear that they themselves have committed a crime.

How effective are the police in fighting *street* crime? Once again, the answer is: not very. Nor have police strategies for *increasing* effectiveness been very successful. As the criminologists George Kelling and Mark Moore argue, research suggests that "there is a limit to the deployment of police resources (squad cars, rapid-response police teams, investigators) beyond which the rate of violent crime is very insensitive" (1983, p. 56). Historically, the most important strategy was that of "preventive patrol," backed by the theories of the influential and innovative police manager, O. W. Wilson. Wilson's ideas on preventive patrol were aided by the availability of the automobile, which was first used to widen the range of foot-beat officers by enabling them to move more quickly from one beat to another.

As the idea of preventive patrol came to dominate thinking in police circles, the police came to see themselves as being "in-service" when they were cruising in their cars, and "out-of-service" when they were in contact with citizens. The goal of police action was to "bust criminals," while positive contact with citizens diminished in importance (Kelling and Moore, 1983).

In the early 1970s, the Police Foundation (a national research organization) carried out a study in Kansas City to test the impact of preventive patrol. The researchers created three types of experimental areas: in one, the police presence was increased by two or three times the customary amount; in another, it was held at the usual level; and, in a third, the police presence was withdrawn except to respond to calls for assistance. The results showed that police patrols had virtually no impact either on the incidence of crime or on citizens' perception of crime (Kelling et al., 1974).

Later studies found somewhat different effects of preventive patrols, but they were not so carefully constructed. A 40 percent increase in police presence was found to reduce the crime rate substantially in New York City's twentieth precinct, but the experimental precinct was not chosen randomly, nor was a control precinct selected until after the experiment had been completed. The study, moreover, depended on police crime reports as the sole measure of crime and did not evaluate other changes in police practices in the twentieth precinct. Crime rates did not appear to rise in adjoining precincts, but there was no attempt to evaluate more diffuse and distant "displacement" of criminal activities. Altogether, the results of this study, conducted by James Press for the Rand Corporation, must be regarded as mixed. Indianapolis, where Donald Fisk studied the Fleet Car Plan, was the site for another major study of preventive patrol strategies. The Indianapolis strategy was an effort to simulate police presence by having police officers use their cars while off duty, but few positive effects were found (Wilson, 1975, chap. 5).

Critics of preventive patrols suggest that the tactic contributes to an image of police officers as a remote and alien force — occupying the community rather than participating in it. This alienation is both ironic and costly when measured against the fact that police officers actually spend little time on crime-related matters. Considerable research has shown that most police time is spent breaking up fights in bars, clubs, and athletic stadiums; settling

Some communities regard the police as a remote and alien force.

family fights; responding to complaints about teenage misconduct; directing the flow of traffic; and maintaining public order in various other ways. Police officers talk the suicidal out of killing themselves, break into houses and apartments for those who have locked themselves out, administer first aid to heart attack victims, get cats down from trees, shoot loose and threatening animals, and rush accident victims to hospitals. These are important services, and some critics argue that the police might be able to increase their ability to provide such "order maintenance" to communities by, for example, getting out of their cars and back into the community on foot (Kelling and Moore, 1983). But while this approach may help bring police officers closer to the communities and help make residents feel more secure, there is no evidence as yet that it will do much to reduce serious crime (Police Foundation, 1981).

Police and Crime **433**

Understanding Crime:
Some Recent Evidence

In emphasizing the limits of the criminal justice system's capacity to reduce crime, we do not mean to imply that we could do without courts, police, or prisons — or that we should not continue to search for ways to improve their efficiency and fairness. What those limits *do* suggest, though, is that the criminal justice system is best seen as only one of a set of institutions that have a significant effect on crime. And this, in turn, directs our attention to the larger social context of American crime.

We have noted that the search for the causes of crime lost ground in recent years in favor of an emphasis on enhancing the means of punishment. In part, that shift reflected at least these key assumptions:

1. That the most frequently cited explanations of crime — especially the role of poverty and unequal opportunity — were largely irrelevant since the plight of America's disadvantaged had improved just when crime rates were sharply rising

2. That crime rose not only in the United States but in every other society throughout the world as well — so that attempts to explain crime by reference to the institutions of American society were misguided

3. That social programs (both within and outside of the criminal justice system) designed to attack the root causes of crime had turned out to be incapable of either rehabilitating offenders or reducing the crime rate

Are these assumptions supported by the evidence? In this section, we will look at what some recent research tells us about the role of several key factors — inequality, poverty, unemployment, family disorganization — on crime. The literature on these issues is enormous, and we cannot, of course, hope to cover all of it in this chapter. But even a beginning look at the best current research suggests that we know more about the social sources of crime (at least some of them) than is often supposed — and, by extension, that we may be considerably less helpless to deal with it in constructive ways.

Crime, Inequality, and Poverty

The social science of the 1950s and 1960s stressed the close connection between crime and racial and economic inequality. It was widely believed that poverty and discrimination caused crime and that ending those disadvantages would reduce (if not eliminate) it (Cloward and Ohlin, 1959; President's Commission on Law Enforcement, 1967).

This view was roundly attacked in the 1970s. Critics argued that, since crime and violence increased during a time of rising incomes, improved educational opportunities, and declining rates of poverty, it could not be explained by worsening social conditions.

But more recent research suggests that this conclusion was premature. For one thing, the critics' argument failed to acknowledge the uneven, spotty character of the rise in American living standards in the 1960s (a point we considered in detail in Chapters 4 and 5). As we saw, rising living standards, in the aggregate, masked a far more complex pattern. Some groups achieved real affluence, while others faced new forms of disadvantage and blocked opportunities. This was especially true of those — particularly minorities — who were uprooted from rural livelihoods and displaced into urban areas where a changing economy left many of them farther and farther behind as other groups advanced. The decline in poverty, too, as we have seen, was considerably less than often supposed, and — even more importantly — was concentrated among some groups

A Violent Society?

It is often said that America is a violent country. How does our level of criminal violence compare with that of other countries?

Those who believe that there is little we can do to reduce crime often argue that crime is increasing everywhere in the world — that rising crime results from inherent forces in modern society, over which we have little control (Wilson, 1975). There is *some* truth to that description, but it masks great differences in the experience of violent crime in different societies. First, some countries, unlike the United States, did *not* experience rapid rises in serious violent crime during the 1960s and 1970s. (Japan and Switzerland are two examples in the industrial world, Cuba one in the Third World.) And even among those societies that *have* suffered substantial increases in crime in recent years, some crimes of violence are so rare by American standards that focusing on the increases alone is highly misleading.

Crime rates, as we have noted, are difficult to compare even across different cities in the United States, much less across different countries (many of which use quite different ways of classifying and reporting crime). But homicide rates are less troublesome in this way, and they provide a fairly reliable, if inexact, indicator of the extent of violence in America vis-à-vis some other countries. The United States is not quite the murder capital of the world; but it *is* the murder capital among advanced industrial societies — and by a shocking margin. Table 11-7 shows homicide death rates for several countries, as compiled by the World Health Organization. Men in the United States have from 10 to 20 times the chance of being murdered as do men in several other Western industrial societies. And, though death by violence is almost everywhere less likely for women than men, the chances of being murdered are greater for an American woman than for *men* in almost every European country. Only Puerto Rico in this table (and a number of other Third World countries not included in it) exceed the American murder rate. [According to a recent United Nations survey, violent crime rates are generally highest in the Caribbean and parts of Latin America (Shelley, 1981).] If the United States had the same murder rate as Denmark, we would have about 1,600 homicides a year instead of the more than 20,000 we now typically have.

A detailed study of crime in Switzerland, where serious crime generally declined in the 1960s and early 1970s, found that murder rates in the biggest Swiss cities were considerably lower than those in American cities of less than 10,000 people. Switzerland's largest city, Zurich, is about the same size as Denver, Colorado; but in 1972, Denver had six times as many robberies as Zurich did over the preceding *10 years* (Clinard, 1978).

Sources: Wilson, 1975; Clinard, 1978; Shelley, 1981.

Table 11-7

Homicide in America and selected other countries, by sex (per 100,000 population)

Country	Male	Female
United States	14.6	4.2
Austria	1.6	1.2
Canada	3.5	1.7
Denmark	0.7	0.4
England	1.0	0.8
France	1.2	0.6
Japan	1.3	0.9
Netherlands	1.0	0.6
Norway	1.0	0.5
Puerto Rico	29.3	3.5
Sweden	1.4	0.6
Switzerland	0.8	0.7
West Germany	1.4	1.1

Note: Data are for various years in the late 1970s.
Source: Adapted from *Statistical Abstract of the United States, 1980* (Washington, D.C.: Government Printing Office, 1981), p. 187.

and regions (the elderly, the South) much more than others. Poverty — accompanied by rising youth unemployment and a growing, not narrowing, disparity between minority and white jobless rates — persisted stubbornly in the inner cities. Moreover, national trends in the overall inequality of income and wealth changed little if at all during those years, despite the growth of Great Society programs and the expansion of the welfare state.

So the supposed paradox of rising crime amidst rising prosperity turns out, on closer examination, to be far less paradoxical than it seemed at first glance. And the continuing connection between crime and inequality is also affirmed by a variety of different avenues of recent research.

We can approach this connection from several angles. If racial and class inequality lie behind America's high rates of crime, we would expect minorities and the poor to figure disproportionately in crime statistics. We have seen that crime disproportionately *victimizes* the poor and minorities. But is it also disproportionately *committed* by them?

Official data on arrests, which are broken down for most crimes according to race, provide one kind of picture — but one that, for the reasons we have already noted, needs to be examined cautiously. Arrest data may be biased by the police applying different practices to different groups, and data on convictions and imprisonment may be even more biased (we will return to these issues in a moment). Homicide rates, however, give a somewhat more reliable indication of group differences in crime rates (Blumstein, 1982, p. 1274) — and they show startling divisions by race. In 1981, for example, blacks were about 12 percent of the American population — but about 49 percent of those arrested for homicide. Hispanic Americans were overrepresented too, though less so than blacks. About 16 percent of homicide arrests were of Hispanics, while they amounted to about 6 percent of the total population. *Uniform Crime Reports* figures for arrests for forcible rape are very similar: Of those arrested for rape in 1981, 48 percent were black and 10 percent were Hispanic. Robbery arrests are even more sharply tilted toward minorities: 60 percent of robbery arrests were of blacks, 12 percent were of Hispanics (Federal Bureau of Investigation, 1982, pp. 8–18).

A similar picture can be drawn from prison statistics. In 1979 almost half (48 percent) the inmates in state prisons were black, 9 percent were Hispanic (U.S. Bureau of Justice Statistics, 1982, p. 2). The latter figure is almost certainly an underestimate. State prison data on Hispanics are not generally reliable since they are often not reported in many states. But it is clear that in those states with a high concentration of Hispanic Americans, they are strikingly overrepresented in the prison population: A fourth of prison inmates in Arizona and Colorado and more than half in New Mexico are of Hispanic origin.

Surveys of state prison populations also reveal a striking concentration of people whose "street" incomes were at poverty level or below. As the U.S. Bureau of Justice Statistics sums it up on the basis of its most recent survey, "Inmates of state prisons are predominantly poor young adult males with less than a high school education" (1982, p. 2). Table 11-8 shows this quite graphically.

Moreover, these broad indicators of the role of race and income are supported by more elaborate studies that also use official data. Thus, a classic analysis that followed the criminal careers of every youth born during 1945 in Philadelphia found that both lower socioeconomic status and being nonwhite — especially the latter — were associated with higher rates of youth crime. Nonwhite boys averaged three times as many offenses as white boys, and were much more likely to commit more serious offenses and to be repeat or "chronic" offenders (Wolfgang, Figlio, and Sellin, 1972). A more recent study of Philadelphia youth born in a later year, 1958, similarly found that nonwhite boys were three times as likely as white boys to commit a violent crime (Wolfgang, 1981, p. 141).

These proportions (and others based on official criminal statistics) have long been criticized on the ground that they reflect class and racial bias in the criminal justice system more than any real differences in groups' propensity to commit serious crimes. Critics have noted several potential sources of bias. First, these data deal only with the more serious street crimes — not with other kinds of crime, especially white-collar crime (see pages 442 to 445). If we include those crimes, ones more accessible to the relatively affluent, a different portrait appears. Whites, for example, are almost 70 percent of those arrested for crimes of fraud, 75 percent of those arrested for embezzlement, and about 90 percent of those arrested for drunken driving or violation of liquor laws (Federal Bureau of Investigation,

Table 11-8
Who goes to prison?
Selected characteristics
of state prison inmates,
1979

Characteristic	Number	Percent	Characteristic	Number	Percent
Total	274,364	100.0	Maximum sentence length		
			Less than 5 years	56,517	20.6
Age at survey			5 to 9 years	63,775	23.2
Under 30	173,093	63.0	10 to 14 years	39,062	14.2
30 and over	101,471	37.0	15 to 19 years	24,211	8.8
Median	27.3	NA	20 to 97 years	46,015	16.8
			98 years or more	2,143	0.8
Sex			median	103.6	NA
Male	263,484	96.0	Life	27,740	10.1
Female	11,080	4.0	Death	1,270	0.5
			Not available	13,832	5.0
Race					
White	136,296	49.6	Time served on current offense		
Black	131,329	47.8	Less than 1 year	95,634	34.8
Other	6,939	2.5	1 to 1.9 years	63,595	23.2
			2 to 2.9 years	40,133	14.6
Ethnicity			3 to 3.9 years	24,273	8.8
Hispanic	25,816	9.4	4 to 4.9 years	16,338	6.0
Non-Hispanic	248,748	90.6	5 to 9.9 years	27,344	10.0
			10 years or more	6,057	2.2
Prior incarceration record			median (in months)	18.0	NA
With prior incarceration	175,473	63.9	Not available	1,191	0.4
Juvenile only	21,666	7.9			
Adult only	79,652	29.0	Education		
Both	62,476	22.8	Less than 12 years	159,340	58.0
Not available	11,680	4.3	12 years or more	115,224	42.0
Without prior incarceration	97,866	35.6	median	11.2	NA
Not available	1,225	0.4			

Current offense		
Violent	157,742	57.5
Murder and attempted murder	37,352	13.6
Manslaughter	10,941	4.0
Sexual assault	17,053	6.2
Robbery	68,324	24.9
Assault	17,554	6.4
Other	6,517	2.4
Property	85,562	31.1
Burglary	49,687	18.1
Larceny	13,018	4.7
Auto Theft	5,138	1.9
Forgery, fraud, embezzlement	11,894	4.3
Other	5,825	2.1
Drug	19,420	7.1
Public order	10,982	4.0
Unspecified	859	0.3

Prearrest employment status		
Employed	192,800	70.2
Full time	165,577	60.3
Part time	27,223	9.9
Not employed	81,005	29.5
Looking for work	38,230	13.9
Not looking for work	42,433	15.5
Not available	342	0.1
Not available	759	0.3
Prearrest annual income		
Total*	25,940	100.0
With income	20,172	77.8
Less than $3,000	4,982	19.2
$3,000–$9,999	7,834	30.2
$10,000 or more	6,457	24.9
Don't know	899	3.5
median	$6,660	NA
Without income	5,768	22.2

Notes: Detail may not add to totals shown because of rounding.
NA means not applicable.
*Includes only persons admitted after November 1977.
Source: U.S. Bureau of Justice Statistics, *Prisons and Prisoners* (Washington, D.C.: Government Printing Office, 1982), p. 2.

1982, p. 179). In looking at the way crime is distributed by race and income, then, we need to keep in mind that it is not simply that whites (or the affluent) commit *fewer* crimes, but that they commit *different* ones.

Studies of the distribution of crime using self-report methods (asking respondents about their own involvement in crime) also support a somewhat different interpretation than the one provided by official statistics. For the most part, these studies have turned up a great deal of "hidden," unreported crime that, contrary to arrest figures, shows a much more equal distribution of offenses among different races and income strata. Some self-report studies have found *no* significant differences in offense rates by class or race; others have found some, usually relatively small, ones. Such findings have generally been taken to imply that the criminal justice system itself, by "labeling" members of some groups as criminals more often than others, is the main source of the differences in official crime rates. Obviously, this has crucial implications for our understanding of the causes of crime — if all groups are equally involved in crime, explanations that stress the role of inequality in causing high rates of crime are false. Is this a reasonable interpretation?

According to the "labeling" perspective, the criminal justice system, from the initial encounter with the police to the final slam of the prison door, acts as a kind of giant sifting mechanism that creates high crime rates among minorities and the poor by systematically channeling them into police stations, courts, and prisons. On the whole, however, studies of bias in the courts and by police give a mixed and inconclusive answer to the question of how much the differences in arrests and sentencing are determined by the characteristics of race or income level and how much by the differences in the amount and kind of crime different groups commit. It is easily shown, for example, that blacks are generally more likely to receive tougher sentences than whites for *generally* similar crimes. But when such factors as the seriousness of the specific crime and the offender's past record are also taken into account, the racial differences are less clear. On balance, the evidence does indicate some bias in the treatment of minorities in the criminal justice system, though the bias probably varies considerably depending on the kinds of crime involved and on the region of the country. But these biases do not, according to most research, loom large enough to explain the dramatic group differences in official rates of violent crime — especially for crimes like homicide and aggravated assault (Blumstein, 1982, p. 1274).

More recent research based on victim studies comes to a similar conclusion, suggesting that the official arrest and prison data may be a closer reflection of group differences in serious crime than some critics have thought. Based on victim reports in the National Crime Survey, for example, one study calculates that offense rates for personal crimes (robbery, rape, assault, and larceny from people) are about five times higher, in proportion to population, for black men than white men, and that the disparity is even sharper among young men aged 18 to 20 — an especially crime-prone age (Hindelang, 1981).

Why so wide a divergence with the findings of the self-report studies? In part because those studies rarely survey the most crime-prone groups, particularly poor, urban minority youth, and in part because they turn up a great deal of relatively unserious offenses (like vandalism or petty thefts) that a wide range of people readily admit to having committed. When the focus is on more serious or violent crimes, a different picture emerges (Hindelang, Hirschi, and Weis, 1979).

The effect of class and racial inequality on crime rates can be approached in other ways. For example, recent studies comparing crime rates among various American cities have found a strong association between high levels of crime and a high degree of inequality in a city's income distribution. Others have found that, *within* cities, the areas with the highest levels of violent crime are likely to be those split by the sharpest income inequalities — where poverty and affluence coexist uneasily side by side. These studies generally find that *poverty*, itself, is less clearly significant as a factor in high crime rates than is *sharp inequality* between the races and between the affluent and poor (Blau and Blau, 1982). The same association appears when crime rates are compared across different countries (Braithwaite and Braithwaite, 1980). Measured by their rates of homicide, many very poor countries have relatively low rates of personal violence. But harsh inequalities in living standards, especially but not exclusively in some "developing" countries, are closely associated with high levels of violence. And a high degree of inequality of income in the United States, relative to most other advanced industrial societies (see pages 120 to 121), goes hand in hand with our devastatingly high homicide count.

Poverty itself, however — in the stark sense of simply having too little money to survive through legitimate means — *can* be an important factor in crime rates, as the results of recent experimental programs for ex-offenders have demonstrated. Traditionally, ex-inmates coming out of prison have faced not only a difficult job market and the stigma of being an "ex-con" but also an immediate lack of income for basic necessities. The pressure to return to crime for survival needs alone has often been compelling under those conditions. During the 1970s, the U.S. Department of Labor initiated a series of programs designed to give a small stipend (at about the level of unemployment insurance benefits) to ex-offenders while they looked for jobs and tried to reestablish themselves in the community. Careful evaluation of these programs shows that even very *small* amounts of cash, offered for a period of a few months, had a substantial impact on rates of return to street crime (what criminologists call *recidivism* rates). Compared with a control group of ex-offenders receiving no payments, the experimental program groups had rates of rearrest up to 30 percent lower (Rossi, Berk, and Lenihan, 1980).

Unemployment, Subemployment, and Crime

The connection between inequality and crime is closely related to another relationship often affirmed by recent research: the association between unemployment and crime. Even many of those critics who argue that we know little about the causes of crime agree on this one — especially on the effect of the disastrously high jobless rates among urban minority youth.

But the precise relationship between unemployment and crime is more complex than it seems at first glance (Thompson et al., 1981). Surveys of convicted offenders give a startling picture of the poor job situation most of them faced while "on the street." American prison inmates are disproportionately drawn from the ranks of the unemployed and intermittently employed. In a recent study of imprisoned felony offenders in California, for example, only about half had gotten their usual income from work, and even among those, "most had earnings that were not much above a poverty level." Among these generally poorly employed offenders, those who were described as the "better employed" (meaning that they had worked during at least 75 percent of their "street" time and had earned at least $100 a week) had dramatically lower rates of crime than the rest. Adults in the better-employed group committed, per month of street life, less than a *fifth*

White-Collar Crime: Dealing with the Corporate Offender

Most of our discussion in this chapter has been about what is often called street crime: crimes against persons and property that strike with stunning immediacy in the streets and homes. But there is another variety of crime, usually less immediately tangible, which since the classic work of the sociologist Edwin Sutherland (1949) in the 1940s has been called "white-collar crime."

White-collar crime is often divided by criminologists into two somewhat distinct varieties. One is *occupational crime:* crimes usually committed by individuals in connection with their occupation (such as embezzlement or employee theft) as well as violations by public officials (such as taking bribes). *Corporate crime,* on the other hand, refers to business violations of laws and regulations that typically involve groups acting together as part of a larger organization (Clinard and Yeager, 1980, pp. 17–18).

We have encountered some aspects of the problem of corporate crime already in this book, such as violations of environmental and work-

place health and safety regulations. But corporate crime is a much broader phenomenon, including offenses ranging from price fixing to consumer fraud, from bribery of public officials to the illegal dumping of hazardous chemicals. Its precise extent is unknown, but it is widely agreed that, far from being a rare occurrence in American business, it is both widespread and deeply embedded in American corporate practice.

In 1979, more than 100 price-fixing conspiracies were under investigation by grand juries (M. Green, 1982b, p. 228). A study of almost 600 major American corporations, by Marshall Clinard and Peter Yeager, found that in just two years (1975 and 1976), more than 1,500 federal cases were begun against these companies, for an average of 2.7 cases apiece. Overall, *60 percent* of the corporations studied had at least one federal action brought against them (Clinard and Yeager, 1980, p. 113). Some of these corporations were "repeat offenders": 5 percent of the companies accounted for over *half* of all the violations in the two years studied, with an average of an astonishing *24* violations per firm.

The worst violators, in this survey, were the large corporations, and especially those in the oil, pharmaceutical, and motor vehicle industries.

of the crimes that the less well-employed committed. And the crimes they did commit tended to be not only less frequent but less serious as well (Petersilia, Greenwood, and Lavin, 1978, p. 89).

But this relationship between poor jobs and crime could mean that crime leads to unsteady employment, not, necessarily, the other way around. More elaborate studies, however, throw more light on the independent effect of unemployment on crime. Some have charted the relation between changes in the economy over time and changes in the rate of reported crime or of admission to prisons. One of the most comprehensive is the work of M. Harvey Brenner. Brenner's research calculates the effects of economic recession on crime with chilling precision. A one-percentage-point increase in the national unemployment rate, according to this study, would increase the rate of admissions to state prison by about 4 percent, and, by itself, would account for about 6 percent of robberies, 9 percent of narcotics offenses, and 4 percent of homicides in a given year (Brenner, 1976).

Not all studies have found such a strong and precisely calculable connection between unemployment and crime rates (Orsagh and Witte, 1981). There are several reasons why. First, these studies deal with the effects of

The oil industry alone was responsible for more than half of the violations of environmental laws in this survey and accounted for a fifth of *all* the legal actions taken against this sample of firms (Clinard and Yeager, 1980, pp. 116–120).

By many measures, the costs to society of corporate crime may be greater than those of conventional street crime. Violations of federal antitrust laws alone may cost consumers more than $60 billion a year: one admittedly rough estimate puts the total annual cost of illegal business activity at more than $200 billion (M. Green, 1982b, p. 229). By contrast, the average street robbery in the United States, in 1981, netted $441; even the average bank robbery brought its perpetrators just $3,564 (Federal Bureau of Investigation, 1982, p. 16). The total "take" from every street robbery in the country in 1981 was a little more than $130 million, while the cost of cleaning up one of the worst-known violations of environmental laws in recent years — the illegal dumping of the toxic chemical kepone into the James River in Virginia by the Allied Chemical Company — has been estimated at $8 billion. The hazardous waste cleanup at Love Canal in New York State had already cost more than $35 million by 1981; the total "haul" from every bank robbery in the United

States in that year was about $29 million (Federal Bureau of Investigation, 1982, p. 16).

Despite these costs — and the more tragic losses of human lives and health — research consistently finds that corporate crimes rarely incur severe penalties. Sutherland's study in the 1940s found that most white-collar criminals were let off with minor fines at worst, and often received no punishment at all. Most research since then has turned up a similar, though somewhat less extreme, pattern.

There *have* some been changes in the social response to corporate crime in America, both in public attitudes and in the seriousness with which courts and government agencies approach the problem. Recent surveys show that many kinds of corporate crime are regarded by the public as at least as serious as many "conventional" crimes (Clinard and Yeager, 1980, p. 5). And one study found a "significant shift" during the 1960s and 1970s toward increased prosecution of some white-collar cases (Hagan and Nagel, 1982). During the 1970s, too, there was an increase in the attention and resources devoted by the federal government to the problem of corporate crime, a movement described by two recent observers as "a modest redeployment of prosecutorial re-

changes in the unemployment rate on patterns of crime. But those economic fluctuations may have less importance in terms of crime rates than in the *persistence* of an urban underclass that, tragically, is relatively unaffected by the ups and downs of the economy. Thus, as we have seen, men who have rarely if ever held a decent or stable job now disproportionately fill America's prisons, and their situation changes little as a result of large-scale changes in the economy as a whole. (We will return to the future implications of this in a moment.)

Another reason why changes in unemployment rates sometimes show only a slight connection with crime rates is that unemployment affects different kinds of crime in different, even opposite, ways. A study by the Vera Institute shows that certain crimes, such as employee theft, predictably *decline* when unemployment rises, canceling some of the increases in other kinds of crime (Orsagh and Witte, 1981).

Finally, most research shows that it is not so much the fact of being without *any* job that increases the likelihood of crime, but the lack of reasonably *good* jobs with adequate pay and some chance of security and advancement — what one study calls "economic viability" (Orsagh and Witte, 1981,

sources from crime in the streets to crime in the suites" (Braithwaite and Geis, 1982, p. 293).

But the impact of this shift was never large, and it ebbed in the early 1980s. Though sanctions against corporate crime have been stiffened in the past decade, they remain relatively puny. As of the beginning of the 1980s, the maximum penalty for a violation of the antitrust laws was $1 million; violations of consumer product safety laws can add up to $500,000. And these are among the *largest* penalties; others are much smaller. Violations of Food and Drug Administration laws brought a maximum fine of $1,000 for the first offense and $10,000 for each succeeding one at the end of the 1970s (Clinard and Yeager, 1980, p. 91). (These penalties must be seen in the context of the multibillion dollar operations of most large corporations.)

In certain cases, criminal penalties may be invoked against corporate officials. In theory, these penalties can put them behind bars. In practice, criminal prosecutions are rare, and actual imprisonment even rarer. Clinard and Yeager's study found just 16 corporate executives who received prison sentences for the more than 1,500 prosecuted violations; 11 of these executives averaged just *nine days* of actual time in jail (1980, p. 291).

There are several reasons for this leniency. It is often difficult to penetrate the labyrinth of corporate decision making to pinpoint the individuals responsible for the violation. The complex, technical character of some kinds of corporate violations also makes it difficult to establish criminal intentions. As the criminologists John Braithwaite and Gilbert Geis note, "Pollution, product safety, and occupational safety and health prosecutions typically turn on scientific evidence that the corporation caused certain consequences. [But] In cases that involve scientific dispute, proof beyond reasonable doubt is rarely, if ever, possible" (1982, p. 299). And, finally, there is a deeply engrained attitude in America that the kinds of people who offer bribes to officials or conspire to fix prices or evade workplace safety regulations are not "really" criminals — at least, not like the people who commit street robberies or household burglaries. For the former, "respectable" people, the mere fact of being caught and made to suffer public shame is thought, by judges, prosecutors, and fellow corporate executives, to be punishment enough.

These limitations have inspired a number of proposals for more effective sanctions against corporate offenders. They include, among others:

p. 1071). Jobs that confine people to the disadvantages of the "secondary" labor market seem unable to provide a sufficient stake in law-abiding behavior or to promote the values and norms that keep people from crime (Currie, 1982).

As with the impact of inequality on crime, important evidence on the relation between jobs and crime can be gleaned from the results of social programs: in this case, ones designed to provide jobs for offenders and ex-offenders. A substantial body of research now suggests that we can reduce crime through increasing the "benefits" of work at least as well as by increasing the "costs" of crime. Both job programs for parolees and work-release programs for inmates still serving time in prison have been shown to have positive effects in reducing rates of recidivism (Manpower Demonstration Research Corporation, 1980). A recent, elaborate experiment in providing supported work for ex-addicts and other high-risk populations also shows important success. This program provides a sheltered work environment for people who have trouble functioning in the regular labor market. Participants start with low responsibilities (and low pay), and with intensive counseling and peer support, are gradually brought to greater and greater

- *Much higher economic penalties:* Corporations convicted of violations might, for example, be required to pay a fine up to double the amount they gained through the violation. This would ensure that the economic sanction isn't simply dwarfed, as it nearly always is now, by the potential illegal gains a corporation may envision when it bribes a foreign government official to buy a certain product or fails to correct a dangerous, illegal health and safety problem.

- *Barring convicted executives from performing similar work in the future:* Lawyers, doctors, or other professionals may be barred from practicing their professions if they commit a sufficiently grave violation of law or ethics. On the same principle, corporate executives could be disqualified from holding the same type of job, at least for a specified period of time. At present, corporate officials rarely lose their jobs, even when convicted of very serious offenses.

- *Holding corporate officials criminally liable for the actions of their subordinates:* Much corporate crime now goes unpunished because managers simply look the other way while those working under them actually carry out the illegal actions. This pattern could, it's argued, be re-

versed by making higher-level managers accountable even if they were unaware of the violations going on below them. (This principle would apply only to cases in which a manager's lack of awareness reflected a truly reckless disregard of the duty to oversee the actions of subordinates.)

- *Nationalizing the worst offenders:* As a last, most drastic resort, some critics propose that corporations that are serious, "habitual offenders" might be brought under public ownership and control. Short of that, but on a similar principle, a corporation might be forced to sell the part of its business that had repeatedly violated the law to a different company with a less-criminal track record (Clinard and Yeager, 1980, chap. 13; Braithwaite and Geis, 1982, pp. 307–308; M. Green, 1982b, pp. 231–234).

Sources: Sutherland, 1949; Clinard and Yeager, 1980; Braithwaite and Geis, 1982; Federal Bureau of Investigation, 1982; M. Green, 1982; Hagan and Nagel, 1982.

responsibility and higher rewards until they are ready to take on regular work. Extensive tests of this program found that it worked most effectively for ex-drug addicts — a group that has been especially difficult to reach through other programs — reducing their rearrests for serious crimes substantially. So far, supported work has proven less successful with some other groups of ex-offenders (Manpower Demonstration Research Corporation, 1980). But it shows real promise, and suggests, once again, that we may be less helpless in dealing with the roots of street crime than is often thought.

Family Patterns and Crime

A third set of factors, also widely accepted as being deeply implicated in crime in America, are those involving the family and early childhood development. As with youth unemployment, social scientists of nearly every persuasion agree that the family, as the primary agency through which children are socialized, is important in forming behavior that is law abiding or criminal, violent or cooperative.

Yet there is considerable disagreement over just *how* the family affects crime patterns. As we saw in Chapter 7, it is commonly argued that a "breakdown" of the family lies behind the rise in violent crime, especially youth crime. But the precise meaning of this is much less clear. One line of argument blames crime, as well as a host of other social pathologies, on the growing number of families with only one parent (especially those maintained by women). As the traditional two-parent family has lost center stage, especially in urban minority communities, the family has, in this view, lost the capacity to discipline and socialize its children. How accurate is this view?

A growing body of research does affirm that children in "broken" families face greater risks of delinquency (Rankin, 1983). But most research suggests that the reasons do not lie mainly in the fact of having a single parent, or in having that single parent be a woman. Instead, research most often pinpoints two other factors as the crucial ones: the effects of the tensions and problems that led to the family's breakup in the first place and, even more importantly, the absence of adequate supports for the one-parent family in the larger society -— including jobs, income, child care, and networks of personal support. Children from more "traditional" two-parent families where there is much hostility between the parents, capricious discipline, or systematic abuse and neglect fare at least as badly in terms of later delinquency. As Chapter 7 suggested, these facts should direct our attention to the broader social and economic structures that help shape early childhood development in the family rather than to the particular *form* the family takes.

As with the effects of inequality and unemployment, we can gain some insight into the relation between crime and family problems by looking at the results of programs designed to reduce delinquency by intervening in family life. For example, there is some evidence that programs offering a wide range of social services to low-income families (such as health care, nutrition, educational enrichment, and community advocacy) may have a substantial payoff in reduced rates of delinquency (as well as in better school performance and better health) (Currie, 1982). Again, what this suggests is that it is the social context surrounding the family that can be decisive in affecting the quality of life within it — and in affecting its ability to produce compassionate and nonviolent children. Where basic social services are absent or inadequate, where parental unemployment and poverty-level income is a way of life, that capacity may be seriously crippled.

Crime, Social Policy, and the Future

Even a brief excursion into research on the roots of crime, then, suggests that the question is not as murky as some would argue. And it also suggests that the recently popular view that government can do little or nothing about the causes of crime is off the mark. Government policy, in fact, is deeply implicated in crime — and our high crime rates become less mysterious when we view them in the context of policies that distinguish the United States from most other advanced industrial societies. We tolerate consistently higher levels of unemployment; perpetuate a much larger underclass of the permanently or semipermanently poor; support a far wider spread of income inequality; and are generally far stingier in our public commitment to providing supportive services to families and individuals. Whatever arguments may be marshalled to attempt to justify these policies, it seems clear that they have had a dismal effect on the safety of American communities.

Given what we know about the effects of these several factors on crime, what can we say about the potential effects of current social and economic trends and policies on our chances of building a less violent society in the future?

Economic Change and the Future of Crime

The implications of recent economic trends and policies are not encouraging. Continued high levels of unemployment bode ill for the stability and security of American communities. As we have seen, unemployment is often regarded as a necessary, if hopefully temporary, means of restoring economic health by fighting inflation. But from what we know about unemployment and crime, the deliberate use of unemployment as a social policy will very likely increase crime rates — not necessarily in the short run, but over time, as joblessness becomes virtually a way of life for even larger numbers of young Americans.

Even more ominously, the kind of economic growth we are now typically encouraging is unlikely, as we have argued, to trickle down to the groups in

America that are now most prone to street crime. Even if we achieve strong-er economic growth, in other words, the conditions for those at the bottom of the economy are likely to remain relatively unaffected — barring more deliberate programs to integrate the poor and unskilled into the growth pro-cess. Without such programs, conventional economic growth may well mean increasing inequality between those best able to benefit from the ex-pansion of the private economy and those for whom such expansion will largely leave behind: women heading families, inner-city youth without skills, and workers displaced (perhaps permanently) by industrial relocation and technological change. And that kind of inequality, as we have seen, is one of the factors most clearly and consistently associated with crime and urban violence.

Social Services, Social Support, and Crime

It seems likely, too, that these economic stresses will be aggravated by sharp reductions in key social services — many of which have traditionally pro-vided the opportunities and supports that, on the basis of recent research, appear to be crucial sources of crime prevention. We cannot calculate pre-cisely how much the potentially crime-generating impact of recession and long-term structural unemployment has been cushioned by public employ-ment and training programs, for example, but we *do* know that those pro-grams can play a role in preventing crime. As we abandon them, in the name of reduced public spending and a diminished role for government generally, we are clearly increasing the possibility of rising levels of crime and violence in the cities.

The same specter is raised by the reduction or elimination of programs that have provided educational and health assistance, counseling and mental health services to families and communities most at risk of involvement in crime. These programs can be especially crucial for low-income families, buffering some of the harshest effects of social and economic stress on the quality of life within the family. Again, the results — in terms of future lev-els of delinquency and crime — cannot be precisely calculated. And many of these effects may not make themselves felt for many years. Like our policies toward health care or environmental quality, these economic poli-cies raise longer-term questions about the kinds of legacies we will leave to future generations.

Summary

This chapter has explored some aspects of the problems of crime and crimi-nal justice in America. The complexity of criminal statistics makes it hard to pinpoint the dimensions of crime with precision, but it seems clear that (1) overall, serious crime has increased since the 1960s and (2) though crime can strike anyone, its victims are disproportionately the young, minorities, and the poor.

Much recent social policy toward crime has emphasized "getting tough" with criminals; we have been locking up offenders at an unprecedented rate. But this strategy has done little to reduce crime.

The evidence suggests that it is much more difficult to "deter" criminals through tough sentences than is often believed. One reason for that difficulty is that so few crimes ever result in an arrest. And we do not yet know how to increase the ability of the police to apprehend criminals.

Though public concern usually focuses on "street" crimes, white-collar crime also takes an enormous toll, and only rarely results in severe treatment by the courts.

It's sometimes argued that we know very little about the causes of street crime. But there is considerable evidence that economic and racial inequality, inadequate employment, and the lack of family supports are all important factors.

For Further Reading

Blumstein, Alfred, Jacqueline Cohen, and Daniel Nagin, eds. *Deterrence and Incapacitation.* Washington, D.C.: National Academy of Sciences, 1978.

Clinard, Marshall A. *Cities with Little Crime.* New York: Cambridge University Press, 1978.

————, and Peter Yeager. *Corporate Crime.* New York: Free Press, 1980.

Greenwood, Peter, and Allan Abrahamse. *Selective Incapacitation.* Santa Monica, Calif.: Rand Corporation, 1982.

Thompson, James W., et al. *Employment and Crime: A Review of Theories and Research.* Washington, D.C.: Government Printing Office, 1981.

12

National Security

The United States emerged from the trauma of World War II with a widespread desire for a return to international peace and domestic security. But by the early 1950s we were already embroiled in another war, in Korea, and by the close of that decade, the president of the United States warned us that what he called the "military-industrial complex" had grown to become a powerful and dangerous part of American life.

The military presence in America grew without much reflection or careful scrutiny until the close of the Vietnam War in the early 1970s. Until that war, the buildup of American military strength and its deployment around the world was widely accepted as one of the necessary costs of maintaining and extending America's economic growth and that of its allies, and of containing the spread of the power and influence of the Soviet Union and its allies.

The Vietnam era brought some important changes of direction. Though this wasn't the first time that many Americans had challenged their government's military priorities, it was the deepest and most serious challenge in decades. As the war in Southeast Asia wore on, taking American lives and resources without much discernible result, more and more Americans began to question the values and aims that lay behind the entire postwar military expansion — especially the fundamental belief that American military might should be a primary instrument of our foreign policy.

By the mid-1970s, these sentiments had helped put an end to the Vietnam War itself. They had also deeply influenced the way many people in the United States viewed the more basic, underlying issues the war had raised: the role of American military power in the international arena, the seriousness of the presumed threats to the United States and its way of life from countries that organized their economies and societies along different models, and the impact of a vast defense establishment on political, economic, and social life at home.

These new doubts didn't diminish the military's role, at home or overseas, to the degree that many critics have since argued. But the changes they brought in American policy were significant enough to generate a chorus of criticism, intensifying in the latter part of the decade, that the United States was neglecting its military. This neglect, they claimed, would have fearful results. America's world influence was being weakened as a result of a posture of "withdrawal, retrenchment, disengagement" (Podhoretz, 1980, p. 2). Meanwhile, according to these critics, the Soviet Union, less "weak-willed" and vacillating, was steadily building up its military strength to the point where it not only exceeded ours in technical terms, but gave the rest of the world a signal that it was willing and ready to use force to pursue *its* goals while the United States was not.

This threatened shift in the world's balance of military power, it was often argued, was caused not just by wrong-headed attitudes, but by what a later president of the United States called "a dramatic shift in how we spend the taxpayer's dollar." As Ronald Reagan continued, in a 1983 speech,

> Back in 1955, payments to individuals took up only about 20 percent of the federal budget. For nearly three decades, these payments steadily increased, and this year will account for 49 percent of the budget. By contrast, in 1955 defense took up more than half of the federal budget. By 1980, this spending had fallen to a low of 23 percent . . . The calls for cutting back the defense budget come in nice, simple arithmetic. They're the same kind of talk that led the democracies to neglect their defenses in the 1930s and invited the tragedy of World War Two. We must not let that grim chapter of history repeat itself through apathy or neglect. (Reagan, 1983, p. 13)

By the 1980s many Americans agreed that we needed more defense spending in order to bolster our sagging military capacities. Thus, what one critic called the "decade of somnolence" (Stein, 1982b) about defense was succeeded by the most rapid and massive diversion of American resources to the military since the early 1950s. But the new thrust toward more funds and bigger weapons for defense quickly ran into strong and vocal opposition. By the mid-1980s other critics were not only warning about the terrible destructive powers that were being created through the modernization of our military weapons systems but also casting doubts about the capacity of those weapons to further the goal of world peace or even to reliably protect the United States in the event of war.

In the 1980s, then, the role of the military in American society has once again become one of the most urgent, and fateful, areas of debate about social policy in the United States. In this chapter, we can only consider *some*

Protest against the Vietnam War helped make America's military priorities a focus of public concern.

of the many aspects of this debate. Space doesn't allow us more than a passing glance at most of the broad issues of international policy that have shaped it. Instead, we will concentrate on the effect of defense and military priorities on American social and economic life. Given that we need a system of national defense, we address some of the issues raised over how we go about providing it — and what different strategies for providing it really cost.

In the first section, we examine the growth of American military spending in recent years, giving special attention to the problems of measurement and definition that often make the defense budget difficult to unravel. We then consider what recent research tells us about the impact of defense spending on the economy, and some of the reasons for the skyrocketing costs of military weapons. Finally, we'll take a closer look at the weapons themselves — at what defense spending buys — and how they fit (or fail to fit) the realistic needs of America's national defense in the 1980s.

Understanding the
Military Budget

According to recent projections, the United States will spend more than $1.5 *trillion* on the military between 1983 and 1988. In sheer dollar terms, this is the largest military buildup since the Korean War in the early 1950s (U.S. Congressional Budget Office, 1983b, Table 1). Figure 12-1 shows that this sharp rise has been a major trend in American social policy in recent years. The rise is frequently justified on the ground that our defense spending dropped to perilously low levels during the 1970s, especially when compared to other kinds of public spending. As the secretary of defense put it in 1983, these enormous expenditures are required to offset a "decade of our neglect" of the fiscal requirements of the military (Weinberger, 1983). In this view, we've tended to ignore the most fundamental requirements of defense in favor of a shortsighted emphasis on government spending for social programs. In the meantime, the military readiness of the United States has crumbled, making the country ever more vulnerable to threats from abroad.

We'll look in a moment at some of the dimensions of those threats, as shown by data on comparative military strength. First, let's consider the course of military spending in the United States in recent years. Have we shifted the balance too far away from the military, too much toward domestic spending?

Obviously, the answer to that question depends very much on subjective assessments of what we wish to use social resources *for*. But it should also

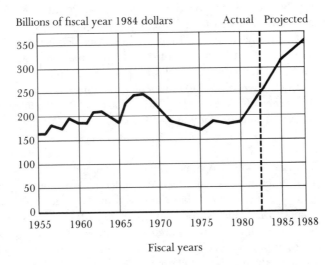

Figure 12-1
Budget authority for national defense (in constant 1984 dollars)

Source: U.S. Congressional Budget Office, *An Analysis of the President's Budgetary Proposals for Fiscal Year 1984* (Washington, D.C.: Government Printing Office, 1983a, p. 56.

rest on a careful analysis of the realities of the federal budget. Unfortunately, such an analysis is not as easy as it might seem. Like most official statistics, the figures on military spending (as well as those on nondefense expenditures) are very complicated, and they can be given many different interpretations depending on what kind of argument one wants to make. Read carefully, however, the figures show that the argument that defense has recently suffered a "decade of neglect" is very much overstated. And they also show that the supposed "tilt" toward nondefense social spending is a far more complex matter than its critics assume.

As we've seen in earlier chapters, government spending has grown substantially in recent years (though not as much as critics often imply). Thus, in constant dollars, actual federal spending (*outlays*) grew by about 46 percent between 1972 and 1982. Outlays for national defense, on the other hand, went up by just 8 percent in those years. At the start of the 1980s, national defense took about a quarter of all federal government spending and amounted to between 5 and 6 percent of the country's gross national product (GNP). In 1972, defense was a third of federal outlays and almost 7 percent of GNP. Going back another decade, to the early 1960s, defense accounted for 46 percent of federal outlays and almost *9 percent* of GNP (*Statistical Abstract of the U.S., 1982–83*, p. 350).

Meanwhile, that part of the federal budget devoted to what the government calls payments to individuals rose considerably, from about 23 percent of outlays in 1960, to 39 percent in 1972, and to almost 50 percent in 1982 (*Statistical Abstract of the U.S., 1982–83*, p. 247). (These general trends are sometimes described in slightly different terms, as increases in the proportion of government spending for income security and health, for example, or for "human resources.")

Figures like these are often presented to demonstrate the supposed decline in our military spending in recent years in favor of a vast array of social programs. But do they tell the whole story?

Not really. To gain a more accurate perspective, we need to look much more closely at both sides of this comparison. Two issues are especially important. One we've touched on already, in Chapter 4: it involves the nature and definition of the government's spending on domestic social programs. The other involves a more critical look at both the measurement and the history of military spending.

Types of Government Spending

The first problem is that this view of federal domestic spending blurs two very different ways in which the federal government receives and spends money. Thus, *most* of what the government spends on the category of payments to individuals does not come from the public's general tax money (what in budgetary jargon are called *general funds*) but from another source, called *trust funds*. These are funds based *primarily* on special contributions made by the groups for whose needs the funds will be spent. Because of this, trust funds are not available for other governmental purposes and are usually considered as relatively "uncontrollable" (not subject to the government's discretion as to how they should be spent). All told, trust funds accounted for close to two-fifths of the 1982 budget; of those funds, 70 percent were accounted for by two very large programs: Social Security and Medicare (DeGrasse and Murphy, 1981, p. 2). That is, the most important single part of the nondefense side of federal spending is money for health care and income support for the aged. As we've seen, the increase in this kind of government spending primarily reflects the overall aging of the population (and partly, too, the increasing costs of health-care services). Neither can fairly be said to reflect a decreasing commitment to defense in the name of *shifting* social resources to the needy.

Another important part of the trust fund component of federal spending is unemployment compensation. Unemployment insurance accounted for about $25 billion of federal outlays in 1982, up from less than $4 billion in 1970 (*Statistical Abstract of the U.S., 1982–83*, p. 253). This growth does represent an increase in the share of the budget devoted to income security versus defense. But it hardly represents a deliberate policy shift from national defense to pay for expanded social programs. Instead, it is a necessary response to the rising rates of unemployment that have accompanied the general stagnation of the economy in recent years. (Moreover, as we'll see in a moment, those rising unemployment rates are not unrelated to the size of our defense spending itself.)

A more accurate way of depicting the share of the military budget in overall federal spending is to subtract these trust fund outlays from the rest of federal expenditures. This will give us a better picture of the way the government spends the tax dollars over which it has more discretion, which do not so closely reflect fundamental demographic or economic changes, and which are paid for out of general tax funds. Figure 12-2 illustrates this "general funds" measure of the burden of military spending.

The figure also includes two further operations necessary to arrive at a clear picture of the size of the military budget. First, it also subtracts, along with trust funds, another uncontrollable part of the budget: the interest on the federal debt (what the government owes on its past borrowing of money). In 1982, interest on the debt was about 12 percent of the total federal budget, up from about 7 percent in 1960. It is another reason for the apparent increase in the share of the budget going for nondefense spending. But much of it — *about half* in 1982 — was interest on debts incurred to pay for *past* wars and military purchases (DeGrasse and Murphy, 1981, p. 2). Second, Figure 12-2 also includes in its calculation of the defense burden an important sum that, in more conventional portraits of federal spending, is placed, curiously, on the "nondefense" side of the ledger: veterans benefits (which amounted to nearly $25 billion in 1982).

Seen in this light, the military burden looms much larger — even before the recent buildup — than is usually acknowledged. Instead of a fourth, it

Figure 12-2

Two measures of the military burden, 1950–1980 and projected 1981–1986

Source: Robert DeGrasse and Paul Murphy, "Impact of Reagan's Rearmament," *Council on Economic Priorities Newsletter*, May 1981, p. 1. Reprinted with permission.

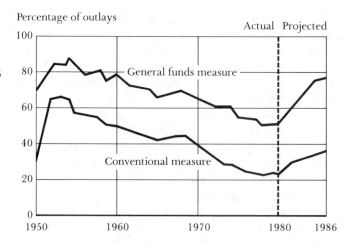

Percentage of outlays

Note: General funds measure: Conventional measure adding veterans benefits to the defense function and subtracting trust funds and interest on the debt from total federal outlays. Conventional measure: Defense function as a percentage of total federal outlays.

amounted to over *half* of the more controllable federal spending by the early 1980s, and it is projected to rise to more than three-fourths by 1986.

How this translates into the average American family's budget can be illustrated by the example of a family earning about $26,000 a year in 1983–84. Under the terms of the federal budget proposed for fiscal year 1984, this family would pay roughly $1,300 in taxes to support the military, $490 for interest on the national debt, and about $1,100 for *all* other federal expenditures (Women's International League For Peace and Freedom, 1983).

The Military Budget in War and "Peace"

Even with these qualifications, however, it remains true that the share of the national treasury spent on defense declined during the 1970s. It has only begun to move back up to its late-1960s level since the 1980s began. And it still has a long way to go before it reaches the share it held during the early 1950s. Does this mean, as critics argue, that American society has grievously neglected its defense needs?

On the contrary, what these trends more clearly suggest is that, measured in dollar terms alone, the military has become an ever-greater presence in American social life. This is apparent when we realize that the earlier periods in which defense spending as a share of the economy was higher than in the past few years were periods of *war*. One way of looking at the trends in military spending since the 1940s, therefore, is that we have never returned to the low levels of military presence we enjoyed just after

World War II. The "peacetime" military system has become institutionalized in America — so much so that, by the mid-1980s, the military budget in years of peace has approached the share of the American economy that it held during the height of the Vietnam War in the late 1960s.

Table 12-1 and Figure 12-3 illustrate this pattern. Thus (in constant dollars), military outlays nearly tripled from 1950 to 1953, during the Korean War, and though they fell somewhat throughout the early 1960s, they remained much more than *double* their level before that war began. They rose again in the middle and late 1960s, peaking in 1968 as the American involvement in Vietnam intensified. As the war in Southeast Asia wound down in the early 1970s, defense spending once again declined. But, again, it remained more than double what it had been before the Korean War. And by the mid-1980s, the peacetime military budget was estimated to be greater than at any time since World War II — much larger than at the height of the Vietnam conflict. The pattern shown in Figure 12-3 is similar. From less than 4 percent of GNP in the late 1940s, defense spending shot up to 14 percent in the Korean War period. And though it fell thereafter, it fell slowly, and the same pattern took place during and after the Vietnam War.

As our economy grows, and as the country disengages from its overseas military engagements, we would *expect* the military's share of economic activity to fall. And, indeed, that is what happened in the 1970s — up to a point. But what is striking is that this share remained so much higher than it was after World War II. Far from being a neglected stepchild of the American economy, the military had become an established, enormous, and perhaps inextricable part of it even before the massive buildup of the 1980s.

The Impact of Military Spending

But what is at issue in the debates over military spending is not just the trends in the numbers of dollars we spend on defense but the ways in which those trends affect both national security in a volatile world and the fabric of economic and social life at home. We will return to the first issue — how well our current approach to military spending addresses the real problems of national security — later in this chapter. First, let's look at what we know about the effect of defense spending on the domestic economy and society. As we might expect, there is considerable disagreement over this issue.

Some observers argue that defense production is inherently bad for the economy and that sharp increases in military spending will "wreck" it (Thurow, 1981b). On the other hand, the secretary of defense argued in 1983, in the midst of the largest defense buildup in 30 years, that "fears that

Table 12-1
Outlays for defense in constant dollars (billions), 1950–1980

Year	Total	
	Amount	Percent change
1950	69.1	
1951	107.3	55.3
1952	193.9	80.7
1953	207.3	6.9
1954	194.9	−6.0
1955	168.4	−13.6
1956	162.5	−3.5
1957	166.5	2.5
1958	162.7	−2.3
1959	165.4	1.7
1960	164.3	−0.7
1961	166.9	1.6
1962	179.6	7.7
1963	182.6	1.6
1964	181.6	−0.6
1965	165.6	−8.8
1966	183.2	10.7
1967	216.1	18.0
1968	236.0	9.2
1969	229.6	−2.7
1970	211.6	−7.8
1971	191.9	−9.3
1972	179.4	−6.5
1973	164.0	−8.6
1974	160.5	−2.1
1975	160.6	0.1
1976	155.1	−3.4
1977	157.9	1.8
1978	158.7	0.5
1979	165.0	3.9
1980	170.0	3.0
1981	177.8	4.6
1982	191.1	7.5
1983*	208.9	9.3
1984†	230.2	10.2
1985†	252.1	9.5
1986†	271.8	7.8
1987†	284.8	4.8
1988†	295.8	3.9

*Estimated.
†Projected.
Source: U.S. Congressional Budget Office, *Defense Spending and the Economy* (Washington, D.C.: Government Printing Office, 1983b), Table 1.

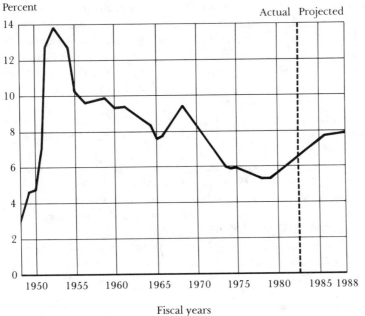

Percent

Actual   Projected

Figure 12-3
National defense outlays
as a percentage of GNP,
1948–1988

Source: Congressional Budget
Office, *An Analysis of the President's Budgetary Proposals for Fiscal Year 1984* (Washington,
D.C.: Government Printing Office, 1983a), p. 57.

Fiscal years

the defense budget of this administration will strain the economy are unfounded" (Weinberger, 1983, p. 2). Who is right?

Like so many other questions of social policy, the answer depends very
much on judgments about what kind of social priorities we want our economy to serve. With this in mind, let's consider several areas in which the
impact of defense spending has been of major concern: jobs, urban and
regional decline, and investment and productivity.

**Military Spending
and Jobs**

No one disagrees that military spending creates a great many jobs in the
United States. According to Bureau of Labor Statistics estimates, more than
2 million industrial jobs in America now depend on the military budget
(McFadden and Wake, 1983, p. 6). Moreover, as we saw in Chapter 2, the
Department of Defense is itself one of the largest employers in America,
providing more than 900,000 civilian jobs in the early 1980s.

But evaluating the employment impact of military spending involves
more specific problems: first, whether defense spending is an *effective* creator
of jobs as compared with alternative ways of using government monies; second, whether the *kinds* of jobs it creates are those most needed in American
society today — and most helpful in developing a vital economy; and, third,
whether the *location* of the jobs created by defense spending represents an
efficient or equitable use of the government's resources.

How many jobs from defense spending? Although it's easy to show that the investment of a given amount of money in military production will produce a substantial number of jobs, most research indicates that it will produce *fewer* of them than other uses of government spending. Recent estimates by the Council on Economic Priorities, on the basis of data from the Bureau of Labor Statistics, show that roughly 28,000 jobs are created for every *billion* dollars spent on military procurement. (*Procurement*, in the language of military budgets, means the purchasing of weapons and other supplies — as opposed, for example, to military spending for personnel salaries or maintenance of equipment.) The same amount of spending, however, would create 32,000 jobs if it were spent on public transit, and *71,000* if it were spent on education (DeGrasse, 1983a, p. 2).

Why does military spending produce such a relatively small number of goals? We've encountered part of the reason already, when we discussed the transformation of the modern American workplace through high-technology, automated forms of production. Most military production is extremely capital-intensive, using very large amounts of money and sophisticated machinery to produce *other* very sophisticated, complex products. (As we'll see later in this chapter, the growing complexity of military weapons systems has disturbing consequences in military terms as well.) This is especially true of some of the most advanced strategic weapons systems, which have been the fastest-growing part of the total military budget in recent years. Table 12-2 illustrates this. The military production of guided missiles produces fewer jobs, directly and indirectly, than other industrial production. (Indirect employment refers to jobs created among suppliers, subcontractors, and

Table 12-2
Jobs and military spending

Alternatives	Numbers of jobs per $1 billion*		
	Direct plus indirect employment	Direct employment	Indirect employment
Guided missile	53,248	25,055	28,193
Mass transit equipment	77,356	32,889	44,467
Public utility construction	65,859	32,173	33,686
Railroad equipment	54,220	20,260	33,960
Housing	68,657	31,016	37,641
Solar energy/energy conservation	65,079	NA	NA
Solar energy	57,235	NA	NA

*1972 dollars
Note: NA = not available.
Source: David Gold and Geoff Quinn, "Misguided Expenditure: An Analysis of the Proposed MX System," *Council on Economic Priorities Newsletter,* June 1981, p. 6. Reprinted with permission.

firms providing a variety of services to those working directly in the industry.)

Because the capital-intensive character of military production is increasing, the same amount of money invested in it no longer generates as many jobs for American workers as it once did. As we saw in Chapter 8, this is a growing problem in many American industries; but it is especially apparent in some of the defense-related ones, particularly the aerospace industry — one of those most dependent on military contracts.

Table 12-3 indicates the scope of this problem. In 1982, in a time of rising defense spending, total employment in the aerospace industry had not reached the level of 20 years before. This is apparent even for guided-missile production, which has been a major part of the overall buildup of weapons systems in the 1980s. While the military procurement budget, adjusted for inflation, rose by a *very* substantial 82 percent between 1965 and 1981 (*Statistical Abstract of the U.S., 1982–83*, pp. 353, 461), employment in the aerospace industry rose barely at all, while guided-missile employment declined. Put another way, it took almost twice as many defense dollars to put an aerospace worker to work in the early 1980s as it did 15 years before. Other figures pinpoint this shift more specifically. Between 1968 and 1979, one major aerospace firm in California saw its work force cut almost in half (from 31,000 to 16,000 employees) while its defense-contract funds doubled (McFadden, 1979).

The extreme dependency of some industries on defense contracting also means that their employees are quite vulnerable to unemployment as a result of shifting decisions about defense priorities or a changing international scene. Again, Table 12-3 bears this out. The drop in employment after the height of the Vietnam War in the late 1960s is dramatic and represents substantial hardship for the several hundred thousand workers who lost their jobs.

Jobs for whom? A second issue has to do with the *kinds* of jobs that military spending creates — and fails to create. Defense spending, like any other kind of spending, creates what economists call a *multiplier effect* — one that ripples out through the economy as a whole, providing jobs for many people only remotely connected with the defense industry itself. But it's still true that dollars spent on defense are dollars *not* spent on other things, and, like other spending decisions by the government, this has important effects on the distribution of jobs and income throughout the society. And by benefiting some occupations more than others, military spending affects the pattern of social inequality as well as the prospects for employment and unemployment.

An analysis by Employment Research Associates (1982) calculates that the 1981 spending by the Department of Defense resulted in the net *loss* of more than 1.5 million jobs in the rest of the American economy. According to this study, each $1 billion shifted to defense from ordinary purchases by

Table 12-3
Total employment in the
aerospace industry,
1961–1982, (in thousands
of employees)

Year	Total aerospace	Aircraft	Guided missiles, space vehicles, and parts	Communications and other equipment
1961	1,178	606	152	160
1962	1,270	634	165	193
1963	1,267	635	173	183
1964	1,209	601	166	171
1965	1,175	620	155	145
1966	1,375	748	159	166
1967	1,484	828	157	179
1968	1,502	846	150	184
1969	1,402	799	124	179
1970	1,166	664	98	152
1971	951	525	87	129
1972	912	495	93	132
1973	956	525	93	116
1974	982	539	94	121
1975	941	514	93	116
1976	896	487	86	115
1977	893	482	83	121
1978	977	527	93	129
1979	1,109	611	102	139
1980	1,185	652	111	147
1981	1,203	649	122	153
1982†	1,165	614	127	154

*Data not available before 1973.
†Estimated.
Source: U.S. Congressional Budget Office, *Defense Spending and the Economy* (Washington, D.C.: Government Printing Office, 1983b), p. 57.

taxpayers caused the loss of about 18,000 jobs. The heaviest losses, in this estimate, took place in a few key areas of the nondefense economy, especially retail trade, the textile and clothing industries, automobiles, banking, insurance, real estate, and residential construction. Earlier estimates support the same point. A 1970s analysis of the employment impact of the proposed B-1 bomber program by Chase Econometric Associates calculated that the same amounts then slated for the bomber would produce far more jobs if spent in either of two different ways: on a public housing construction program or as a simple cut in taxes stimulating more personal spending. Over a 10-year period, the tax cut would produce 30,000 more jobs than the bomber, and the housing program 70,000 more — with obvious benefits for the hard-pressed construction industry, which suffered very high unemploy-

In dollar terms alone, the military has become an ever-greater presence in American life.

ment throughout the economic troubles of the past decade (Edelstein, 1977, pp. 8–9).

These differences in the sectors of the economy boosted by military versus domestic spending also translate into differences in the types of workers who benefit from each. The Council on Economic Priorities' recent research shows that relatively few defense-related jobs go to blue-collar production workers. The bulk of jobs created by defense spending go to high-level workers, especially engineers and other workers with high-technology skills. Most of the major defense-related industries employ considerably higher proportions of professional workers and of managers than American manufacturing industry as a whole (DeGrasse, 1983b, p. 2). Again, the guided-missile industry offers a striking extreme. Almost two-thirds of its employees are professionals or managers, and it employs only a fourth the proportion of semiskilled operatives and less than one-twelfth the proportion of laborers than American manufacturing industry as a whole.

Obviously, this is a complicated issue to evaluate in social terms. On the one hand, the evidence suggests that high-tech defense-related jobs are relatively *good* ones — for those who get them. But, as we've seen, relatively few people *do* get them. Defense spending tends to distribute employment benefits toward workers who are relatively affluent, highly educated, and already blessed with relatively low risks of unemployment (DeGrasse, 1983b, p. 2). To a disturbing extent, these workers are also white and male. Although a few of the industries in which jobs tend to be displaced by military spending (notably construction) are also disproportionately filled by white men, most of the others are large employers of minorities and women. Some are the industries, in fact, which provide many of the *good* jobs traditionally available to those groups: including teaching, health care, nondefense government employment, and semiskilled blue-collar work in civilian manufacturing industries, such as autos and steel. This disparity is even greater if we compare defense procurement spending to other possible uses of public spending, such as job programs targeted toward the unemployed, which (as we saw in Chapter 8) are much more effective in providing jobs for minorities, women, and the disadvantaged. To the extent that military production "crowds out" such more targeted social spending, it tends to heighten, rather than diminish, the inequalities of race and gender.

The Urban and Regional Effect of Military Spending

Defense production is also distributed unevenly across the country. Thus, some areas benefit more than others. To some extent, this is true of any form of government spending. What makes this pattern especially troubling, however, is that shifts of government spending to military uses, on the whole, distribute those resources primarily to areas that are *least* in need of such public support, and away from those that have suffered the most from joblessness and economic decline in recent years.

Military contracting is heavily concentrated, though with important exceptions, in the Sun Belt states, and especially in California, whose industries have held, on average, about a fifth of all prime defense contracts in the United States since the early 1960s. Estimates of the number of California's direct defense-related jobs run from 450,000 to 600,000 (McFadden and Wake, 1983, p. 21). As more and more defense funds are poured into the economy, they obviously push up investment and employment in those areas of high defense-industry concentration.

Most of these regions, however, are precisely those that have been least hurt by the problems of industrial decline we saw in Chapter 3. The resulting imbalance between regional need and government funding is sharply revealed in a University of Michigan study of the impact of recent increases in the military budget in the different states of the union (Anton, Oppenheim, and Morrow, 1982). The researchers began by calculating what they graphically called a "pain index," the combined rates of unemployment and welfare dependency for each state and region of the country. They then calculated the per capita amounts of federal spending each region received. Table 12-4 shows the results. The pain index is worse in the Mid-Atlantic and East North Central states of the old industrial heartland. But the federal budget, in per capita terms, serves those areas *least* — mainly because they receive so little from the defense part of the budget (see the fourth column of the table). The hard-pressed states of Illinois, Indiana, Michigan, Ohio, and Wisconsin received about a fourth as many defense dollars per capita as the New England or Pacific states. And they gained much less, too, from the increases in federal spending in the early 1980s, since by far the greatest part of that increase went for defense.

Noting the rather perverse consequence that the hardest-pressed areas of the country received the least aid for their tax dollars, the researchers concluded that "it seems clear that little or no attention was paid to the regional consequences of policy decisions to reduce entitlement and social service programs while increasing defense spending" (Anton, Oppenheim, and Morrow, 1982, p. 43). Similarly, a study by the Urban Institute concluded that the defense buildup of the early 1980s would bring a net gain of less than 100,000 jobs across the United States in 1982; the bulk of them would be in about a dozen metropolitan areas, most with already low unemployment. In most states, the study argued, these minimal job gains wouldn't balance the jobs *lost* through cuts in domestic social programs (Muller, 1982, p. 455).

What is true for the declining industrial areas is generally even more true for many of America's most distressed cities. The shift of employment away from teaching, health care, and housing construction helps ensure that the inner cities remain disadvantaged in all these areas. Since few of the (limited) job opportunities created by defense expansion are accessible to most inner-city residents, particularly the low-skilled and unemployed, the shift of government spending to military procurement cannot deliver in new jobs what it takes from the cities in employment, training, and other supportive programs. Moreover, the evidence suggests that, for many older, "needy" cities, high levels of defense spending act as an enormous funnel that channels tax funds in the wrong direction, taking more public monies than it gives back in necessary urban services.

One result is that the hard-pressed cities have been blamed for fiscal problems that usually lie far beyond their control. Since the 1970s, it has been fashionable to argue that the cities brought many of their financial problems on themselves by "throwing money" at misguided social programs (Auletta, 1979). That argument, in turn, has been used to justify cutbacks in urban services, from public-service job programs to housing and even police and fire protection. But what's less often acknowledged is that these reductions in urban programs, undertaken in the name of a healthy trimming of the fat of social spending, took place while the citizens of many of these reeling cities were "throwing" considerably more money at the Pentagon than at local social programs. In the late 1970s, according to one esti-

Table 12-4
Distributing the spending: Federal budget resources by region, fiscal year 1983

Census divisions*	Pain index	Per capita dollars				
		Total budget (minus interest)	Change in total budget fiscal year 81 to 83	National defense	Change in national defense fiscal year 81 to 83	National defense change as percent of total change
New England	102	4,241	677	1,919	657	97
Mid-Atlantic	117	3,223	327	805	264	81
East North Central	124	2,516	236	515	160	68
West North Central	80	3,681	439	1,118	354	81
South Atlantic	85	3,822	485	1,361	354	73
East South Central	106	3,257	288	877	238	83
West South Central	72	3,585	425	1,295	371	87
Mountain	73	4,362	586	1,359	360	61
Pacific	105	4,558	785	1,991	592	75

*Census divisions include the following states:

1 New England: Connecticut, Maine, Massachusetts, New Hampshire, Rhode Island, Vermont.
2 Mid-Atlantic: New Jersey, New York, Pennsylvania.
3 East North Central: Illinois, Indiana, Michigan, Ohio, Wisconsin.
4 West North Central: Iowa, Kansas, Minnesota, Missouri, Nebraska, North Dakota, South Dakota.
5 South Atlantic: Delaware, Florida, Georgia, Maryland, North Carolina, South Carolina, Virginia, West Virginia.
6 East South Central: Alabama, Kentucky, Mississippi, Tennessee.
7 West South Central: Arkansas, Louisiana, Oklahoma, Texas.
8 Mountain: Arizona, Colorado, Idaho, Montana, Nevada, New Mexico, Utah, Wyoming.
9 Pacific: Alaska, California, Hawaii, Oregon, Washington.

Source: Thomas Anton, John Oppenheim, and Lance Morrow, "Where the Shoe Pinches: the 1983 Reagan Budget," University of Michigan, Survey Research Center, *Economic Outlook USA*, Spring 1982, p. 41. Reprinted with permission.

mate, the average New York City taxpayer paid 37 cents of every tax dollar for military spending, just 6 cents for the city's own government, 25 cents for all programs and services of the state of New York, and 32 cents for *all other* federal spending (Parenti, 1980, p. 28).

Booming defense, crumbling infrastructure. One long-range result of these priorities has been the steady deterioration of the infrastructure of American cities: highways, bridges, and other public facilities. Most of us can observe this first hand, in potholed streets, unkempt parks, insufficient and dilapidated public transportation. No one knows the precise extent of this problem, but some rough estimates of its dimensions ha *re* been provided in a study by Pat Choate and Susan Walter for the Council of State Planning Agencies. "America's public facilities," they wrote in 1981, "are wearing out faster than they are being replaced" (1981, p. 1). Among the most pressing problems they reported:

- One out of every five bridges in America needed "major" rehabilitation or reconstruction, at an estimated cost of as much as $33 billion.

- At least several thousand dams in the United States were plagued by "hazardous deficiencies," but not enough public funds were available even to *inspect* most of them, let alone repair them.

- New York City alone would require more than $40 billion of public investment over the 1980s to service, reconstruct, or repair bridges, reservoirs, streets, sewers, subways, public hospitals, firehouses, and other public facilities. The city was expected to be able to invest just $1.4 billion a year to do the job.

Choate and Walter argued that these were only a few examples of a more general "decline in both the quantity and quality of virtually every type of public works facility in the nation" (1981, p. 4). But, meanwhile, the government's investment in public works spending had actually declined considerably. As a proportion of GNP, for example, public works investments dropped from more than 4 percent in 1965 to 2.3 percent by 1977 (Choate and Walter, 1981, p. 7).

Not all of this decline reflects the impact of defense spending, to be sure. Some of it, for example, represents the declining share of spending on educational facilities as the school-age population has become a smaller proportion of the total (Choate and Walter, 1981, p. 7). But it seems clear that the kinds of sums thought to be required to rebuild America's infrastructure will be hard to find in the coming years, given the growing share of limited public resources now taken by defense.

We will return to this issue again in Chapter 13. Now, let's look at some of the ways in which high levels of military spending affect *private* investment — and, therefore, may aggravate the nagging problems of low productivity growth and declining competitiveness in the world economy.

**Defense,
Investment, and
Productivity**

As we have seen, many of America's basic industries have fared badly in recent years, especially when compared with those of a number of foreign countries. We examined some of the possible reasons for this comparative decline in Chapter 3. But there is growing evidence of the importance of another factor, one we haven't discussed yet: the negative impact of high military spending.

Some basic evidence is illustrated in Figure 12-4, based on recent research by the Council on Economic Priorities. The figure shows that countries with a high level of investment — the basic source of economic growth — tend to be those with relatively *low* military spending. Thus, Japan stands out from all the countries in the chart in the amount of its gross domestic product (GDP) devoted to investment — and it also has the *lowest* proportion devoted to military spending. At the other end of the scale, the United States stands out as the country with the *highest* proportion of its economy devoted to the military, and it is next to the bottom in its level of productive investment. It is second only to the United Kingdom, which, not coincidentally, spends the second highest percentage of its domestic product on defense.

Certainly, disproportionate spending for defense is not the *only* source of poor investment and declining economic performance in the United States. (We've looked at some others in earlier chapters, including, among other things, the inefficient use of human resources and the substitution of short-term gains for long-term planning and investment.) But the destructive role

Figure 12-4

Investment versus military spending in selected nations 1960–1980

Source: Robert DeGrasse, "Military Buildup Exacts Toll on Economy," *Council on Economic Priorities Newsletter*, May 1983, p. 3. Reprinted with permission.

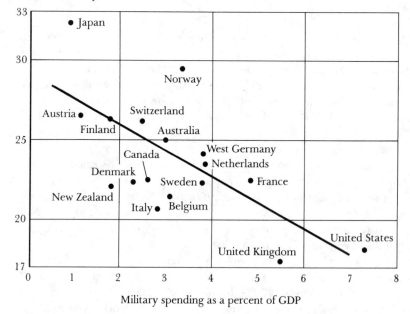

Investment as a percent of GDP

Military spending as a percent of GDP

of the extreme diversion of resources to defense is an important *part* of the explanation. Table 12-5 adds support to this from a somewhat different angle, by comparing *productivity* across different countries in relation to levels of military spending. Once again, as with investment, productivity growth is fastest by far in Japan, the country with the lowest defense share of domestic product. It is slowest in the United States, with the United Kingdom also near the bottom in productivity growth and near the top in spending on defense.

What causes these effects? In part, extremely high levels of defense spending apparently drain necessary capital away from civilian industry. This is a complicated issue because, as we saw in Chapter 3, a number of industries that have performed poorly in recent years have *not* suffered from a shortage of capital so much as from a misuse of the capital they have. But, nevertheless, across the economy as a whole, it's clear that an extraordinary amount of America's capital is siphoned off to the defense economy, a phenomenon one critic, Seymour Melman, describes as "looting the means of production" (Melman, 1982). As Melman notes (1982, p. 4), $46 out of every $100 of new capital formed in the United States is spent in the military economy, versus $14 in West Germany and less than $4 in Japan.

Country	Decade	
	1960–1970	1970–1979
United States		
Productivity growth	2.1	1.1
Defense share of GDP	8.7	6.1
Japan		
Productivity growth	9.7	4.5
Defense share of GDP	0.9	0.9
West Germany		
Productivity growth	4.6	3.4
Defense share of GDP	4.2	3.9
France		
Productivity growth	4.8	3.4
Defense share of GDP	5.4	3.9
United Kingdom		
Productivity growth	2.8	2.0
Defense share of GDP	5.8	4.9
Canada		
Productivity growth	2.4	1.3
Defense share of GDP	3.3	2.0

Table 12-5
Defense spending and productivity growth — comparisons over time and across selected countries, 1960–1979

Source: Adapted from U.S. Congressional Budget Office, *Defense Spending and the Economy* (Washington, D.C.: Government Printing Office, 1983), p. 40.

Military production drains not only capital, but skills and knowledge as well, from the civilian economy. The Council on Economic Priorities' study discovered that even in the late 1970s, when defense spending was at a (relatively) low point in the United States, it still "cornered the market" on many kinds of scientists and engineers: 60 percent of the country's aeronautical engineers, to take the most extreme example, worked in defense-related projects (DeGrasse, 1983b, p. 3). The military absorbs about two-thirds of *all* federal spending for research and development in the United States, as compared to about 10 to 15 percent in West Germany, and below 5 percent in Japan (McFadden and Wake, 1983, p. 10). The strong emphasis on high-technology weapons development in recent years has accelerated this trend. Thus, the nation's budget for research and development increased by $6.9 billion between fiscal years 1983 and 1984. Of that increase, $6.7 billion (97 percent) went to the Department of Defense, primarily for what it termed "advanced strategic systems," particularly nuclear-missile development (Office of Management and Budget, 1983, p. K-3).

It has often been argued that this concentration of scientific talent and research funding on defense shouldn't hurt the civilian economy because scientific and technological developments in the military will "spin off" into civilian uses. But the evidence provides only minimal support for this. Many of the industries that have a large part of their operations supported by defense contracts, for example, have *not* done well in their *commercial* enterprises, especially in comparison with their foreign counterparts (DeGrasse, 1983b, p. 3). One reason is that the products American industry creates for the military are increasingly unlike anything encountered in civilian life. As a result, much of modern military technology has only a peripheral application to civilian needs. Moreover, technological innovations originally heavily supported by military spending have rarely been developed by *American* industry into effective civilian applications. Here the classic example is the development of integrated circuit technology in electronics — a development that owed much initially to military research grants in the United States, but was translated into cost-decreasing, commercially successful uses in products like TV sets and radios not by American industry but by the Japanese (DeGrasse and Murphy, 1981, p. 4).

The overall result is that the absorption of innovations by the military may be partly responsible for reducing the international competitiveness of American goods. The economist Lawrence Klein estimated in the early 1980s that a 10 percent increase in American military budgets would generate, by 1986, an extra *$12 billion worth of losses* in the balance of trade between the United States and its economic competitors (cited in DeGrasse and Murphy, 1981, p. 4).

But the most crucial reason why military spending seems associated with the stagnation and poor performance of the economy is probably a more general one. It is not only that militarism "drains" the rest of the economy of capital and talent (though this is surely part of the problem). An even deeper problem may be that military production simply exhibits, in exaggerated form, many of the worst attributes of the modern corporate economy in America. From this perspective, both the problems of the defense economy and those of the civilian economy reflect the same, underlying problems of organization and goals. Both parts of the economy are dominated by the same priorities and suffer the same distortions. And the evidence is growing, as we'll see in the following section, that the results are not only bad for the civilian economy and society, but bad in terms of national security — in terms of defense itself.

The Costs and Aims of Defense Spending

All of this suggests that America's growing commitment to a massive system of defense carries some extraordinary social and economic costs — costs of lost civilian production, stifled innovation, inadequate and unevenly distributed job opportunities, and urban and regional decline. But we have not yet paid much attention to the more *immediate*, dollars-and-cents costs associated with the military buildup in recent years. In the 1980s the dramatically escalating cost of defense — particularly in the production of new, complex weaponry — has become the focus of concern and criticism from a surprisingly wide and diverse range of critics, from every point on the political spectrum. Whether from left, right, or center, the critics converge in their assessment that defense costs much more than it needs to. Moreover, there is also a surprising amount of consensus that the weapons Americans pay for, with a bigger and bigger share of their taxes, are problematic even in military terms. Viewed strictly from the perspective of enhancing the country's military security, what we buy is probably not what we need. Meanwhile, some things we *might* do to make the country's defense system more efficient and more reliable are usually the *last* items on the current military agenda.

Why Defense Costs So Much

It's widely agreed that military spending tends to be inflationary, pushing up prices throughout the economy as a whole. There are at least two major reasons why. One is that much military spending produces goods that cannot be purchased by consumers under ordinary circumstances: Most of us aren't allowed to buy rocket launchers or armored personnel carriers for home and neighborhood use. The result is that military production pumps dollars into the economy without increasing the supply of goods the dollars can buy. This creates the classic conditions for what many economists call *demand-pull inflation*: an excess of the demand for goods over their supply. This problem is especially acute because the use of so much industrial capacity to produce military goods means that it's less likely that the civilian economy can gear up rapidly to meet the demand for more nonmilitary goods and services. In times of high civilian unemployment and low use of the capacity of civilian industry, however, this problem is considerably less acute (U.S. Congressional Budget Office, 1983b, chap. 2). Since this situation prevailed in the late 1970s and early 1980s, it helps explain why the rising military budgets of the early 1980s went hand in hand with declining inflation in the overall economy. Rapid, intensive buildups in defense can, however, cause inflation by creating bottlenecks in the demand for certain products and skills — specific shortages in goods or occupations that tend to drive up their prices (U.S. Congressional Budget Office, 1983, chap. 3).

But the more pressing problem is the escalation of costs within the defense sector of the economy itself. During 1982, when the national rate of inflation had fallen to 5 percent, the rate of inflation *within* the defense industry amounted to 18 percent (Center for Defense Information, 1983, p. 6). As James Fallows points out, the cost of American combat fighter planes rose by a factor of 100, in *constant* dollars, in the 25 years following World War II (1982, p. 37). The vice president of Martin Marietta Aerospace, a major defense contractor, has noted in a well-known remark that, at these rates, the *entire* American defense budget would buy a single tactical aircraft by the year 2054 — and the air force, navy, and marines would have to share the plane, a few days a week each (quoted in Fallows, 1982, p. 38). Aircraft carriers cost 20 times what they did in World War II, tanks 15 times. A modern Trident nuclear submarine costs more than 270 times as much, per ton, as a World War II variety of submarine (Kaldor, 1981, p. 25).

Such figures have led even some of the staunchest supporters of increased American military power to accuse the government, as the conservative Heritage Foundation did in 1982, of "throwing money at the Pentagon" (quoted in J. Anderson, 1983). Why have the costs of defense risen so fast, and why can't they be held down?

The "Military-Industrial Complex" and the Costs of Defense

It seems clear that some of the reasons are *organizational* ones involving the nature of the institutions of defense production in the United States: the large private corporations that account for the lion's share of military production and the military agencies that plan, fund, and ultimately use the weapons. Other reasons for the rising costs of weapons involve the nature of the weapons themselves. Both, as we shall see, are related.

In a famous declaration at the end of the 1950s, former President Dwight Eisenhower warned that what he called the military-industrial complex was achieving a dangerous amount of influence in American life. In the 1980s that influence is considerably greater since the military-industrial complex is considerably bigger — and no less difficult to control. The Department of Defense itself is, by any measure, one of the largest economic entities in the world; with assets totaling more than $372 billion in 1981, it controls more property than most countries of the world (*Statistical Abstract of the U.S.,*

1982–83, p. 352). On the other side, the private corporations that provide most of the military's weapons systems are among the country's largest. Eight of those corporations (Boeing, General Dynamics, Grumman, Lockheed, McDonnell Douglas, Northrop, Rockwell International, and United Technologies) received about 25 percent of all Defense Department contracts during the 1970s, including 36 percent of all contracts for research and development (Adams and Quinn, 1981, p. 1). Five of these corporations were among the top 50 manufacturing corporations in the United States in 1982. The combined sales of all eight amounted to $54 billion in 1982, about the size of Norway's gross domestic product in 1980 (*Fortune*, May 2, 1983, pp. 228–252).

It isn't just the size of these corporations that gives them great influence over the defense production process, however, but, more importantly, the nature of their connection with the government. In an economy that is generally less and less "competitive" in the classical sense (of a large number of firms competing for the customer's dollar), the sector devoted to defense is an extreme example. Most defense contracts are not subject to competitive bidding among potential suppliers — they are negotiated with a few corporations that have longstanding ties to the Department of Defense and the various military services.

By itself this lack of competition is extraordinarily costly, as even many corporate managers (and Defense Department officials) have frequently pointed out. In 1983, the president's Private Sector Survey on Cost Control, undertaken by a staid assortment of corporate executives, concluded that opening up the military weapons procurement system to more contract competition might save the navy and air force each about $2 billion annually, the army $3 billion (*New York Times*, July 1, 1983). In the early 1980s, the Small Business Administration insisted on opening up the procurement of certain aircraft spare parts to competitive bidding, allowing more smaller companies to have a crack at supplying them. Over an 18-month period, this practice saved the air force almost $7 million on spare parts alone (Harvey, 1982).

Probably even more important than the absence of competition, however, is the tendency for the defense corporations and their government customers to develop intimate relations and common perceptions that often allow the defense firms to exert great influence over defense policy and especially over the acquisition of new weapons. According to a study by Gordon Adams of the Council on Economic Priorities, the ties between the top eight defense contractors and the Pentagon are very close indeed. Table 12-6 shows that an astonishing number of high-level executives move back and forth between the defense corporations and the Department of Defense or the National Aeronautics and Space Administration (NASA). As Adams points out,

> To the insider, this intimacy seems to foster technical and political knowledge that smooths the contracting process, ensuring a more efficient de-

Table 12-6

The military-industrial connection: personnel transfers to and from the Department of Defense (1971–1979) and NASA (1974–1979)

Company	Military	Civilian	Total personnel transfers
Boeing	316	82	398
Northrop	284	76	360
Lockheed	240	81	321
General Dynamics	189	50	239
Rockwell	150	84	234
McDonnell Douglas	159	52	211
Grumman	67	29	96
United Technologies	50	33	83
Totals	1,455	487	1,942

Note: Of the personnel in this table, 1,642 moved to the listed corporations from DOD and NASA; 270 moved in the other direction, from the corporations *to* DOD and NASA.
Source: Adapted from Gordon Adams and Geoff Quinn, "The Iron Triangle: The Politics of Defense Contracting," *Council on Economic Priorities Newsletter*, June 1981, p. 3. Reprinted with permission.

fense of national security and the public good. To the outsider, however, it suggests a closed community in which the private and government interests converge. (Adams and Quinn, 1981, p. 4)

In addition, the major defense corporations maintain influential lobbying offices in Washington. These spend large sums to develop friendly ties with members of the Congress and the executive branch of the government — much of which are ultimately charged to the taxpayers as normal expenses of government contracts. [Some of these expenses stretch the imagination: The Raytheon corporation charged taxpayers for lodging, meals, and guide service for goose hunts it organized for its executives and guests; General Dynamics charged to the government the cost of tie-pins it had made in the shape of its F-16 fighter plane, to be distributed as gifts (*Common Cause*, 1983.)] The large defense contractors also spend substantial sums, through political action committees and campaign contributions, to support friendly congressional candidates (Adams and Quinn, 1981, p. 2).

The most important consequences of these intimate relations are the ability of the defense corporations to shape the aims of national weapons policy and the absence of mechanisms for holding them accountable for the quality or the costs of what they produce. Most defense contracting is done on what's called a "cost-plus" basis: The firm bills the government for what it claims to be its costs to complete a project, plus an adequate margin of profit. Since the costs are virtually automatically reimbursed by the government, there is no incentive for the corporation to hold them down. (As we saw in Chapter 9, this is remarkably similar to what happens in the case of health-care spending.) The mentality this process creates was summed up by an expert, Admiral Hyman Rickover (the creator of the navy's nuclear submarine program) as he left the service in 1982: "They don't care how the work goes," the Admiral told a congressional committee. "The government pays for it. There's no incentive. There's no real responsibility" (Rickover, 1982, p. 13).

Sometimes this practice leads to outright fraud, as when corporations pad their bills in order to recover the costs of poor contract performance and inept management (Rickover, 1982, p. 13). More often, the lack of incentives for cost control and efficiency simply allows the costs of virtually anything the military contractors produce to rise inexorably upward — especially in comparison with the costs of similar products sold on the civilian market. The critic James Fallows (1982, p. 38) and other observers have pointed out that the cost of many civilian electronics products, from calculators to large computers, dropped dramatically during the 1970s as simpler, cheaper technology became available and was passed on to consumers as lower prices. But the opposite has happened with military electronics. Over the past decade the electronic systems that represent much of the new technology in advanced aircraft, guided missiles, and other sophisticated weaponry have become vastly more expensive.

This cost escalation affects even the most mundane military equipment, not just the super-sophisticated weapons systems. Thus, as a former high-level Defense Department executive, Jaques Gansler, has noted, standard, conventional equipment made for the military frequently costs *many* times more than the *same* equipment produced commercially: A military version of a videotape recorder cost three times as much as a commercial one and a naval shipboard tape recorder cost *47 times* as much as a commercial model (Gansler, 1980, p. 280).

The most often-noted result is what are called, in the language of government contracting, *cost overruns*: The costs of particular weapons systems almost invariably escalate far beyond their original estimates. In recent years cost overruns on major military weapons systems in the United States have *averaged* about 100 percent (Kaldor, 1981, p. 71). By the beginning of 1983, according to the Defense Department's own (probably understated) estimates, the costs of 62 major weapons systems under production in the United States had grown from about $257 billion to $540 billion. For most of those systems, the end wasn't yet in sight, since many were still *far* from completion. On some weapons, as Table 12-7 shows, the cost overruns have been much higher, more than 250 percent in the case of the F-15 fighter plane and the AH-64 helicopter (*Common Cause*, May-June 1983, p. 52).

Another factor feeding the ever-increasing costs of weaponry is the rivalry among the various armed services — a rivalry built deeply into American military traditions. It causes what a former head of the Joint Chiefs of Staff calls "an intramural scramble for resources" (quoted in *Newsweek*, December 20, 1982, p. 32). That scramble for resources — and for prestige — results in massive duplication of weapons systems, as each service comes to

Table 12-7

Cost escalations of selected weapons systems*

Weapon system	Original est. program cost	Dec. 31, 1982 est. program cost	Original est. unit cost	Dec. 31, 1982 est. unit cost	Percent increase in unit cost
F-16 fighter plane	$17.04 bil.	$43.49 bil.	$ 9.20 mil.	$ 20.01 mil.	118%
F-15 fighter plane	13.60 bil.	41.50 bil.	8.06 mil.	28.19 mil.	250%
F-18 fighter plane	14.06 bil.	39.83 bil.	15.88 mil.	28.93 mil.	82%
Trident II missile	24.26 bil.	37.65 bil.	30.59 mil.	50.88 mil.	66%
F-14A fighter plane	13.00 bil.	33.79 bil.	13.15 mil.	39.99 mil.	204%
SSN 688 nuclear attack submarine	10.90 bil.	29.38 bil.	165.80 mil.	473.88 mil.	186%
B-1 bomber	20.44 bil.	28.33 bil.	204.40 mil.	283.30 mil.	39%
CG-47 AEGIS cruiser	14.46 bil.	28.03 bil.	716.74 mil.	1.17 bil.	63%
M-1 tank	6.28 bil.	20.38 bil.	0.90 mil.	2.88 mil.	220%
AH-64 attack helicopter	2.70 bil.	7.37 bil.	3.74 mil.	14.06 mil.	276%

*Estimates based on figures compiled by the Defense Department. Members of Congress, private watchdog groups and others have questioned Pentagon figures in some cases. For example, the Congressional Budget Office has estimated that the eventual program cost for the B-1 bomber could be more than $40 billion, rather than the $28.33 billion projected by the Pentagon. Furthermore, the B-1's prime contractor, Rockwell International Corp., told a congressional committee two years ago that the B-1 program could be completed for $11.9 billion — far below the $20.44 billion the Pentagon now lists as the original estimate for the program. If Rockwell's figure were used, the current unit cost increase for the B-1 would be around 140 percent instead of 39 percent.

Source: *Common Cause*, May-June 1983, p. 52. Reprinted with permission.

476

believe it needs to outpace the others. Both the navy and the air force, for example, invest in tactical airplanes that are virtually alike, except that they are produced by different corporations. They thus have parts and systems that can't be interchanged and that cost more per unit and require more money and personnel to maintain. In the early 1980s, the overall cost of this duplication was estimated to be as high as $20 billion a year (*Business Week*, November 29, 1982, p. 76).

At the heart of the cost problem is the nature of much modern military weaponry itself. In the past several years a growing number of critics have begun to argue that, despite their admittedly awesome destructive power, many modern weapons systems have become so complex that they are not only incredibly expensive, but often of very limited use in achieving their stated purpose — the defense of the country in the event of war. They are examples of what the British social theorist Mary Kaldor (1981) has called "baroque" technology: marginal improvements tacked on, at ever-increasing expense, to conventional, and very likely outmoded, designs. Because of the drift toward this kind of expensive but marginally effective technology, as Kaldor (echoing many other critics, in and out of the military itself) notes, there are serious questions about "the ability of modern armed forces to fight wars" (1981, p. 175).

What the Dollars Buy

Sometimes the growing complexity of modern military technology results in the production of expensive weapons that simply don't work. A news magazine article recently described the ignominious failure of a weapon that has been termed the "most expensive gun in the world": the DIVAD (a military acronym for Division Air Defense) antiaircraft gun. As of 1983, the DIVAD was expected to absorb nearly $3 billion in defense monies by 1987. The DIVAD is elaborately controlled by sophisticated computers and guided by the most advanced radar systems available. This is what happened during its demonstration in 1982: ". . . the DIVAD trained its sights on a drone Huey helicopter hovering nearby — and failed to fire. After repairs to a disconnected cable, the DIVAD fired — this time, directly into the ground 300 yards away" (*Newsweek*, December 20, 1982, p. 31).

Other expensive weapons may ultimately perform better. But many of them turn out to be so cumbersome and complex that they seem astonishingly ill-suited to any imaginable conditions of actual combat. Thus, the program to develop the XM-1 tank, developed by the Chrysler Corporation to replace earlier (and much cheaper) models, was expected (in 1983) to cost Americans almost $20 billion during the 1980s. (Of course, like most weapons-cost projections, this sum is almost certain to rise.) In 1983 the XM-1 created a considerable stir when it became publicly known, as a result of field tests, that the tank's engine and transmission had to be removed in order to change the oil (Coates, 1983). The tank is also so voracious in its consumption of fuel that it must be accompanied into battle by military gasoline trucks (Children's Defense Fund, 1982, p. 16).

The Costs and Aims of Defense Spending   **477**

We may be building more complex and expensive weapons than we really need.

Such complexity often means that the newest weapons are not only more costly but also require more frequent maintenance, more spare parts, and more personnel to keep them going. Not surprisingly, the percentage of time during which many such weapons — from combat aircraft to armored vehicles — are out of service has increased very substantially over their less expensive predecessors. Mary Kaldor notes that at any given time (as of the early 1980s), two-thirds of the military's F-111 D Attack aircraft are out of service; the plane requires 98 hours of maintenance work for every flight. And only 23 of 66 F-15 fighter planes passed a test in 1980 of their readiness for mobilization in the event of a real war in the Middle East (Kaldor, 1981, pp. 175–76).

As James Fallows notes, "As an airplane or missile becomes more complicated, the probability that *all* its parts will be working at the same time goes down." Fallows uses the example of a mid-1950s jet aircraft engine versus a mid-1970s variety used in more recent fighter planes. The earlier engine contained a fuel-control system with about 1,000 separate parts, an astonishing number in itself. The later engine's fuel system has 4,500. The result is that the more recent engine breaks down almost eight times as often as the 1950s model, and "takes six times as long to fix when it does" (Fallows, 1982, pp. 38–39).

Such examples can be multiplied many times over. But the main message of much recent analysis of modern weapons systems is clear: the increasing costs they incur don't bring anything remotely comparable in terms of benefits, even in the most quantitative, military terms. And because the more elaborate, high-technology weapons require such vast sums to produce, even in an age of greatly expanded military budgets, it's impossible to produce very many of them. The long-term results of this should be disturbing to those interested in achieving a sound national defense. They mean that we are tending to produce a few, highly destructive, but remarkably unreliable weapons, rather than — *at the same cost* — producing a larger number of simpler, more reliable weapons that might serve much better should they ever be needed.

If so many weapons are so poorly designed and developed in relation to their enormous costs, why do they continue to be sponsored and paid for? The answer, it's increasingly argued, lies in the character of the military-industrial linkage we've already observed, what James Fallows calls the "culture of procurement" (1982, p. 38). Increasingly, the weapons are built less to suit any conceivable needs of military defense, and more to sustain the financial and organizational needs of the defense corporations themselves. This implies that it may be very difficult to break out of the cycle of ever more costly, ever less effective weapons production. But it also suggests, very clearly, that doing so would not hurt the possibilities for an efficient defense.

Alternatives to Military Spending

We've seen that the defense budget in the United States is swollen by cost overruns and the production of weapons that are sometimes unnecessary and often unreliable. The bright side to this otherwise grim picture is that these inefficiencies create room for considerable savings of money and human resources through reforming the way we spend our defense dollars. And it is becoming increasingly clear that, with careful planning, those savings could be turned to alternative uses — uses that could go a long way toward revitalizing the American economy and restoring equity in domestic social programs.

No one proposes that we scrap the entire defense budget. But research suggests that there are several ways in which it might be reduced without damaging national defense. Critics of our current patterns of defense spending have pointed to three such strategies, in particular: putting a cap on the level of *increases* we permit in the defense budget from year to year, reducing cost overruns, and halting or scaling down the further production and testing of nuclear weapons.

Putting a Cap on Defense Increases

The Center for Defense Information, a Washington-based advocacy group, has argued that one way to achieve savings in military spending is to establish on a "level" defense budget — that is, a budget that gives the Pentagon the same amounts from year to year, with an added adjustment to account for inflation. If inflation reached 4 percent, for example, the defense budget would be increased by no more than 4 percent each year. (The budgets requested in the early 1980s were closer to 12 percent above their predecessors.) Between 1984 and 1988, according to these calculations, capping the defense budget in this way would save about $422 billion over the actual projected spending for those years. And it would do so without requiring *cuts* in military spending, only a ceiling on increases.

Putting such a ceiling on defense spending, in this argument, would ultimately strengthen the national defense because it would force a greater degree of efficiency on the military and its suppliers — an efficiency that is now routinely demanded of all government programs *except* defense. "A level military budget," the center argues, "would encourage military officials to give more attention to *how* money is being spent and for what purposes." It would also "stimulate more careful planning of military programs and improve procurement practices," help to "limit spending on new weapons that may quickly become obsolete or will be too complex to function on the battlefield," and, over the long run, will also help to "focus attention on better long-range planning and valid military strategies" (Center for Defense Information, 1983, pp. 2–3).

Reducing Cost Overruns

One of the most obvious places where substantial savings could be achieved without a discernible negative impact on national defense is in holding down cost overruns in the procurement of military weapons. As we've seen, the amount of waste involved in the added costs of weapons systems alone is staggering, amounting to nearly $300 billion in just 62 major weapons systems by early 1983. As many critics have pointed out, these sums often dwarf the levels of spending on some supposedly "out of control" domestic programs. Thus, according to the Children's Defense Fund, the cost *increases* in the F-15 fighter plane up to fiscal year 1983 could have paid for the entire AFDC program in that year (Children's Defense Fund, 1982, p. 16). Some other examples:

1. The cost overrun on the MX missile during 1982 alone equaled the proposed reductions in federal student loans for the five years from 1984 through 1988.

2. If cost increases during 1982 for five major weapons systems (the MX, Trident submarine, Tomahawk missile, C-5 transport aircraft, and SH-60B helicopter) had been avoided, the resulting savings could have restored five years worth of reductions in Child Nutrition programs (calculated from U.S. Congressional Budget Office, 1983b, pp. 77–145).

3. The accumulated cost increases by 1982 in any *one* of the three most costly fighter plane programs, if distributed as cash grants, could have brought every poor family in the United States in 1981 above the poverty line (calculated from *Common Cause*, May-June 1983 and U.S. Bureau of the Census, 1983a, p. 150).

Accomplishing such reductions is no easy task, however, given the deeply entrenched practices of defense contracting in the United States. But there is obvious room for reform. By the mid-1980s, critics representing many different political and social views were calling for legislation to control cost escalation. The suggestions included (Coates, 1983):

• Forcing the Pentagon to increase the amount of procurement done under competitive bidding to about 50 percent from its 6 percent level in 1983;

• Insisting that the Pentagon require producers of military equipment to provide warranties, like those given with new car sales;

• Creating an independent government testing office to ensure that high-technology weapons actually work *before* they're purchased by the military;

• Requiring that major cost overruns incurred by defense contractors be made public knowledge.

Halting or Scaling Down Production of Nuclear Weapons

Controlling the growth of nuclear weapons (weapons that, as pages 484 to 485 show, we possess in amounts many times greater than would be required to meet any imaginable military need) could free tens of billions of dollars, at a minimum, during the 1980s, for other uses. According to one estimate, a "freeze" on nuclear weapons production in the United

States would save at least $84 billion over five years, with a potential for much more (McFadden and Wake, 1983, p. 13). Table 12-8 shows where those savings could be achieved. A considerable part would, initially, come from reductions in two of the most costly and widely criticized nuclear weapons programs, the MX missile and the B-1 long-range bomber. Other substantial savings would come from curtailing the production and testing of nuclear warheads and other materials. According to analyses by the Congressional Research Service, the savings from the first year of a nuclear weapons freeze would have been close to $7 billion in fiscal year 1983, a sum that could have restored most of that year's reductions in federal programs for community development, mass transit, child nutrition, student loans, income support, legal services, and subsidized health care (McFadden and Wake, 1983, p. 14).

The Importance of Planning

Achieving this kind of savings in defense spending, however, could not be accomplished without some significant impacts on those workers and communities now heavily dependent on defense contracts. This problem is especially serious for a strategy of limiting or reducing the production of costly, complex and destructive weapons systems.

The defense industries, as we've seen, are a major employer of American workers, especially in some parts of the country. The eight companies identified by the Council on Economic Priorities as the top defense contractors during the 1970s employed, among them, nearly 700,000 workers in 1982 (*Fortune*, May 2, 1983, p. 228). Because much defense-related work is a rela-

Table 12-8
Budget savings from a nuclear freeze

System or program that would be halted by a freeze in 1987	Budget savings, fiscal years 1983–1987 (in billions)
MX missile	$23.9
B-1B bomber	$27.2
Trident I submarine-launched ballistic missile (SLBM)	$2.5
Air-launched Cruise missile (ALCM)	$5.2
Sea-launched Cruise missile (SLCM)	$0.8
Pershing II missile	$1.1
Ground launched Cruise missile (GLCM)	
Nuclear warhead production	$11.5
Nuclear warhead development & testing	$3.6
Nuclear materials production	$6.0
Total	$84.2

Source: Adapted from Dave McFadden and Jim Wake, eds., *The Freeze Economy* (Mountain View, Calif.: Mid-Peninsula Conversion Project, 1983), p. 14.

Despite growing protest, nuclear-weapons production continues to escalate.

tively poor generator of jobs, careful, targeted reductions in defense production would boost employment and community well-being over the long run — especially given the notorious insecurity of military-related employment. In the short run, however, reductions could mean serious hardship and economic dislocation. A nuclear weapons freeze, for example, would ultimately produce many more jobs than nuclear weapons development now creates, since nuclear weapons production generates even fewer jobs per dollar of investment than other forms of military spending. A billion dollars taken from guided-missile production and invested in the iron and steel industry could create roughly 19,000 jobs to replace the 9,000 lost in the missile industry. But a freeze, according to one estimate, could cost more than 120,000 jobs in the short run.

Because of these problems, proponents of reduced weapons spending have directed their attention to ways of cushioning the impact of reductions through retraining defense workers and developing alternative uses of military production facilities. There is certainly no lack of needed goods that converted defense plants might produce, especially products that require some of the same skills (and even some of the same machinery), such as

Alternatives to Military Spending   **483**

mass transit vehicles, energy conservation devices, and agricultural machinery. In England, one of the most ambitious plans for military conversion, developed by the workers at one of Britain's major defense contractors, Lucas Aerospace, identified 120 alternative products their 17 plants might produce (Yudken and Goldenkranz, 1983, p. 5). In Massachusetts, workers at a General Dynamics shipyard, floundering because of reduced military and civilian orders, have proposed using the facility to build floating plants to convert ocean thermal energy into electricity (such "plantships" are already being produced in Japan) (Meacham, 1983, p. 3). In southern California, workers at a McDonnell-Douglas aerospace plant have identified a variety of alternative products that promise to be both marketable and feasible to produce within the plant, given some retooling and retraining. The products include commuter aircraft, mass transit vehicles, wheelchairs and other medical supplies, and energy-conservation equipment (Yudken and Goldenkranz, 1983, p. 5).

The Nuclear Balance

Debates over military spending and the kind of defense it should buy often focus on immediate questions like the technical characteristics of the weaponry or the economic impact that relatively more or less defense spending would create. But looming behind all of these issues, and giving shape and urgency to the debates, are the broader international realities the United States faces in the 1980s.

Shortly after World War II, a United States Senator advised the then-president of the United States that public support for spending billions on massive increases in military strength wouldn't be possible without "scaring hell out of the country" (cited in Barnet, 1983, p. 448). In the 1980s, as in the 1950s, what "scares the hell out of the country" is what has come to be called the "Soviet threat." It is widely argued that a rapid and single-minded military buildup by the Soviet Union has created an unprecedented threat to world peace and security — a threat that can be countered only if the United States rushes to "catch up." This belief has led much of the public to accept the massive increases in defense expenditures in the early 1980s. As Richard Barnet comments, "The 'Soviet threat' is an indispensable component of the weapons acquisition process" (1983, p. 448).

Addressing the complex history of Soviet/

American relations is a task far beyond the scope of this book. And comparing the strength and sophistication of American and Soviet military forces as a whole is itself a complicated and forbidding science that has generated an enormous, highly technical literature. We won't, therefore, try to sort out all of these issues here, but we will attempt the much more modest task of examining recent claims about the comparative buildup of nuclear weapons in the two countries — the most critical aspect of the presumed imbalance between Soviet and American military strength. (For some useful starting points on the wider issues of policy and military strategy, see the works by Holloway and by Barnet in the suggested readings at the end of this chapter.)

The dramatic increases in our own commitment to nuclear weapons development have been justified on the ground that the "stabilizing balance of forces" tentatively achieved after World War II has been "upset by the Soviet military buildup, which contrasts sharply with our own military restraint," as a U.S. State Department official put it in 1983 (Dam, 1983, p. 57). Is this an accurate assessment?

The evidence suggests that it isn't. It's certainly true that Soviet nuclear capacity increased significantly, and alarmingly, in recent years; but so did that of the United States. Table 12-9 illustrates these trends.

The most dramatic aspect of this buildup, on both sides, is the rising numbers of nuclear war-

Weapon	United States		Soviet Union		**Table 12-9**
	1972	1982	1972	1982	A decade of buildup
ICBMs					
Missiles	1,054	1,052	1,510	1,398	
Warheads	1,254	2,152	1,510	5,800	
SLBMs					
Missiles	656	576	440	950	
Warheads	1,232	5,072	440	1,500	
Long-range bombers	450	316	140	150	

Note: ICBMs are intercontinental ballistic missiles (land-based). SLBMs are submarine-launched ballistic missiles.

Source: Data from International Institute for Strategic Studies, in Leon V. Sigal, "Warming to the Freeze," *Foreign Policy*, Fall 1982, p. 65.

heads. Both the United States and the Soviet Union had several times as many by 1982 as they had a decade before. The proportionate growth of the Soviet nuclear weapons arsenal is slightly faster, but the increase for both countries has been dramatic. The situation by the 1980s is one of rough equality, at least in bare numbers, not drastic imbalance.

On balance, the United States is "ahead" in long-range bombers and in submarine-launched nuclear missiles, two of the "legs" of what in defense jargon has been called the "triad" of strategic nuclear weapons: those based on land, in aircraft, and at sea. The Soviet Union is "ahead" in the third "leg," land-based missiles. One of the most important arguments for the rapid buildup of American nuclear forces in the 1980s has, therefore, been the need to upgrade the land-based leg of the triad, through heavy investment in missile development.

But whatever technical issues may arise about the virtues or drawbacks of particular missile systems, the enormous number of nuclear weapons already capable of being delivered by the United States makes this argument seem less than credible. A single Trident nuclear submarine now carries enough nuclear warheads to destroy 192 Soviet cities or other comparable targets. The same capacity to destroy American cities is not *quite* so far advanced in the Soviet nuclear navy: It would take three of their most modern submarines to demolish an equivalent number of American cit-

ies (Sigal, 1982, p. 57). To date, no effective technology exists, on either side, to locate and disable these missile-launching submarines. The result is that an unimaginably devastating retaliation against even a completely successful attack on land-based nuclear weapons is impossible for either side to deflect. Since, at any given point, some of these submarines are in port or otherwise out of commission, not all of these sea-based warheads are actually deliverable at any one time. But, by most estimates, this still leaves us with an estimated 3,000 nuclear warheads that are now virtually incapable of being destroyed. Do we need more?

As three critics (one of them the former head of the Defense Department's Weapons System Evaluation group) have written:

The arsenals of the United States and the Soviet Union have long passed the point where the terms *parity* or *superiority* have any meaning. Making generous allowances for human and mechanical error and Murphy's law (if something can go wrong, it will) it may take as many as two or three hundred nuclear warheads to impoverish a continent for hundreds of years. Any weapons above and beyond that number, a number that exists on our fleet of submarines, are not "*superior*": they are superfluous. (Zacharias, Rathjens, and Gordon, 1983, p. 4)

Thus, it's generally understood that conversion isn't a simple or automatic process, but one that, to be successful, requires careful planning, local initiative, and national-level coordination and support. There have been several recent attempts to develop legislation to put the conversion of defense production on the political agenda. Though they vary in specifics, they focus on at least these priorities:

1. Providing assistance to workers and communities, through retraining programs, income support, and help in developing plans for alternatives production

2. Establishing local committees, representing workers, management, and the community, to develop specific approaches for plant conversion

3. Providing for early notification of workers when the government plans to reduce or eliminate defense-related projects

So far, no such comprehensive conversion legislation has made it through Congress. But with the growing awareness of the excesses and uncertainties of our current pattern of defense spending, the search for alternatives is likely to remain a key public issue throughout the 1980s.

International Insecurity and the Prospects for Change

For many years there has been a tacit assumption in American social policy that, when it comes to national defense, "more is better" — that a more effective defense necessarily means more money for armaments and, necessarily, less for other social purposes. We've seen how this attitude has affected the civilian economy and society. But one of the most important shifts in thinking about defense in recent years has been the growing awareness that this assumption has undermined the integrity and reliability of defense itself.

Thus, the choice is often posed to the American public — between pouring ever more money into a strong defense or supporting the rest of society's public needs — seems more and more to be a false one. "Throwing money" at defense *will* divert resources from other social goals, like providing stable jobs, or affordable housing, or rebuilding America's declining infrastructure. But it will *not* necessarily provide more security — even when security is defined in the narrow sense of military readiness (see Barnet, 1983).

There is a parallel here with the problem of revitalization of American

Arming the World

So far in this chapter, we have been considering the impact of military priorities on American society itself. But the military role of the United States does not, of course, stop at our own borders. We are also the largest supplier of arms and other forms of military assistance to the rest of the world. During the late 1970s, America's role as chief armorer to the world began, like many other aspects of our defense policy, to be questioned. But by the early 1980s the arming of foreign countries was once again viewed as "an indispensable instrument of American policy that both complements and supplements the use of our own military forces" — in the words of the State Department official in charge of military assistance programs (cited in Hartung, 1982, p. 2).

The United States supplies the military needs of other countries in three basic ways: cash sales of military equipment, grants and loans, and training programs for military personnel. American arms corporations can sell directly to foreign governments or foreign firms, particularly such smaller, "nuts and bolts" military products as small arms, ammunition, and spare parts. Most larger sales, especially of costly, sophisticated equipment like aircraft or missiles, are handled through the government's Foreign Military Sales program (FMS). Between 1950 and 1982, as Table 12-10 shows, FMS sales totaled *more than $116 billion* worldwide. Direct commercial arms sales by private firms added another $14 billion (U.S. Department of Defense, 1983, p. 32).

Until the late 1970s, the United States, in the military assistance program, also poured considerable sums into outright military grants to foreign countries, about $55 billion between 1950 and 1982. But economic realities, among other factors, have caused a shift in policy. Outright military assistance has been increasingly replaced, partly by cash sales of weapons and partly by loans, usually offered at very favorable rates, enabling foreign governments to buy American military equipment. Finally, the United States has trained more than half a million foreign military personnel since 1950 under the International Military Education and Training Program (IMET), an enterprise that has cost more than $2 billion.

Who gets this military assistance — and what are the consequences? The American arms industry's foreign customers are an extraordinarily diverse group — and very numerous, indeed. In 1982 the United States sold arms through the FMS program to 96 nations. The two biggest cash customers in the past three decades have been Middle Eastern countries: Saudi Arabia and (until recently, of course) Iran. Since the early 1970s, in fact, about two-thirds of FMS sales have gone to the countries of the Middle East, as well as about half of other military assistance.

What is most troubling is that American arms sales and military assistance have helped support some of the world's most repressive governments — and also probably increased the risks of destructive war, especially in the Third World. According to the Center for Defense Information, the United States has been a key supplier of arms to 28 out of 41 military-dominated governments around the world with records of severe violations of their citizens' human rights, including torture and arbitrary arrest (Center for Defense Information, 1982, p. 7). During the 1960s and 1970s, the United States trained more than 300,000 military personnel and transferred close to $30 billion in weapons to these countries, which include South Korea, the Philippines, Argentina, Brazil, and El Salvador. In the late 1970s, some halting steps were taken by the American government to restrict arms sales to some of the worst human-rights offenders. But these restrictions began to be lifted in the 1980s.

It has been argued that removing such restrictions and boosting the level of foreign arms sales generally will both help the American economy and promote world peace and stability by providing America's military allies with sufficient means to defend themselves in a hostile world. But the evidence suggests that this argument is wrong on both counts. Economically, massive arms sales aggravate the distortion of the domestic economy already set in motion by a disproportionate emphasis on military production. And though foreign sales do bring some revenues into the domestic economy, the low-cost loans and remaining military grants offered those countries to pay for the American arms represent a significant "hidden" expenditure (of the kind we described in Chapter 4) that diminishes the revenues available for other public uses.

And the impacts of arms sales on the foreign client nations themselves are far more troubling.

Intensive spending for weapons drains their economies, especially those of some of the poorer countries of the Third World, making more stable, long-term economic development difficult or impossible. In some of these countries, many of the weapons and military skills purchased with American help are used in part to repress internal dissent. And the scale and sophistication of the weapons we sell virtually ensures that any military conflict that does arise in tense regions of the world will be far more destructive than it would otherwise have been — especially since the

Table 12-10
Foreign military sales agreements, fiscal years 1950–1982

Sales, dollars in thousands	Countries	Sales, dollars in thousands	Countries
116,261,272	Worldwide	737,427	Morocco
		73	Nepal
19,000,950	East Asia and Pacific	98,660	Oman
6,160,637	Australia	2,070,817	Pakistan
305	Brunei	547	Qatar
6,913	Burma	23,297,174	Saudi Arabia
1,533	Fiji	4	Sri Lanka
8,542	Indochina	1	Syria
319,505	Indonesia	473,001	Tunisia
2,833,652	Japan	24,038	United Arab Emirates
3,877,351	Korea (Seoul)	340,489	Yemen (Sanaa)
171,225	Malaysia		
210,337	New Zealand	34,820,381	Europe and Canada
224,846	Philippines	201,326	Austria
377,998	Singapore	2,086,076	Belgium
3,391,703	Taiwan	1,969,306	Canada
1,415,238	Thailand	1,187,090	Denmark
1,167	Vietnam	182	Finland
		511,327	France
57,764,169	Near East and South Asia	8,157,751	Germany (Bonn)
12,587	Bahrain	2,216,042	Greece
5,369,542	Egypt	543	Iceland
80,523	India	784	Ireland
12,556,897	Iran	1,095,182	Italy
13,152	Iraq	4,566	Luxembourg
9,772,267	Israel	3,463,772	Netherlands
1,772,664	Jordan	1,836,379	Norway
950,060	Kuwait	104,193	Portugal
165,999	Lebanon	1,765,158	Spain
28,249	Libya	147,010	Sweden

United States sometimes arms *both* sides of potential conflicts (consider Saudi Arabia and Israel, Turkey and Greece).

The usual justification for increasing arms sales and military assistance to foreign countries is that doing so will boost America's influence around the world, thereby decreasing international tensions. But a glance back at the history of two decades and more of military aid should help put this claim in perspective. In the 1970s, the second-largest customer of American arms sales was Iran; the second largest consumer of American military assistance was South Vietnam. Obviously, arming these two countries did *not* produce the hoped-for results. It's important to note that the record of the Soviet Union in cementing its world influence through arms transfers is almost equally dismal: one of its biggest arms clients since World War II was the People's Republic of China.

Sales, dollars in thousands	Countries	Sales, dollars in thousands	Countries
1,159,826	Switzerland	14	Barbados
1,816,704	Turkey	2,100	Bolivia
7,008,609	United Kingdom	303,712	Brazil
88,555	Yugoslavia	184,385	Chile
		70,201	Colombia
753,906	Africa	1,480	Costa Rica
*	Benin	4,510	Cuba
21,445	Cameroon	6,358	Dominican Republic
99,904	Ethiopia	114,559	Ecuador
2,239	Gabon	36,021	El Salvador
662	Ghana	32,090	Guatemala
148,695	Kenya	1,300	Haiti
17,753	Liberia	28,419	Honduras
*	Madagascar	207	Jamaica
154	Mali	134,553	Mexico
8	Niger	5,229	Nicaragua
66,205	Nigeria	6,281	Panama
1,969	Rwanda	983	Paraguay
6	Senegal	186,788	Peru
75,503	Somalia	1	Suriname
3,149	South Africa	99	Trinidad-Tobago
230,520	Sudan	22,538	Uruguay
85,695	Zaire	935,716	Venezuela
2,273,777	American Republics		
196,234	Argentina	1,648,088	International organizations

*Less than $500.

Source: U.S. Department of Defense, *Foreign Military Sales, Foreign Military Construction Sales, and Military Assistance: Facts as of September 1982* (Washington, D.C.: Government Printing Office, 1983).

industry, which we discussed in Chapter 3. Simply boosting the amount of money that flows to American business won't rebuild economic vitality if it's used to speculate in real estate or buy other corporations. Similarly, the massive shift of government spending to the large defense corporations won't ensure national defense if the funds are spent to buy elaborate planes that rarely fly or weapons that don't fire.

But the gap between spending and performance in defense, though deeply troubling, has its positive side, too. It opens up an exciting possibility — the possibility that some of the resources we now devote to a mistermed "defense" effort could be shifted to alternative uses *without* jeopardizing the legitimate demands of a military that works (Kaldor, 1981, p. 229).

Still, the prospects for doing this aren't bright without larger changes in the way the United States approaches its role in the wider world. We've kept that issue out of our discussion in this chapter, somewhat artificially (it would take at least another book to do justice to the intricacies of foreign policy issues in the 1980s; some useful leads may be found in the suggested further readings). Still, some general comments are appropriate — and hard to avoid. As we argued in Chapter 1, the international situation has changed considerably in the past few decades. From the rather narrow viewpoint of the United States, the world has become in many ways a more volatile, less controllable place. Old balances of economic and military power have shifted, formerly dependent parts of the world have begun to flex their political muscles, and the longstanding technological superiority of the United States has been eroded. Ultimately there are two broad possible responses to these changes — and it's these responses rather than technical judgments or domestic social priorities that have largely shaped our choices about defense policies. We can adapt to the changed realities, maintain sufficient defensive capacity to cope with the genuine potential threats an unstable world produces, and also relinquish the idea that we can remold the rest of the world to our liking. Or we can take on the unpromising job of trying to turn back the clock, to reassert American power over the destiny of other countries through the threat of military force.

Given what we know about the irrationality and excess of current patterns of defense spending, the first response would very likely allow us to achieve, over time, both a more efficient, truly *defensive* defense *and* a more equitable, more productive use of social resources in civilian society. The second response commits us to building an elaborate, expensive — and terribly perilous — military presence whose purpose is more to project a symbolic image of America's "will" or "strength" than it is to defend us against realistic threats from other countries in the real world.

Ultimately, deciding on a rational approach to defense strategy means that we need to place our concerns about the military in the broader framework of the kind of society we want to build. As Mary Kaldor argues, "Prac-

tical aims, like getting rid of certain weapons or initiating experiments of industrial conversion, need to be located in a wider vision of the future to which we aspire" (1981, p. 23). In Chapter 13, we'll examine some of the different approaches to that future that have emerged on the political stage in the 1980s.

Given the vastly increased destructive power of nuclear weapons, there may be few — if any — survivors of the next nuclear war.

Summary

This chapter has examined national defense as a social problem, focusing on the social and economic impacts of defense spending and military priorities in the United States.

Though it is often argued that the military has been neglected in recent years, especially as compared to social programs, the actual trends in defense spending are more complex. Military spending takes a far larger share of available budget resources than is often assumed. Its decline as a share of the budget in the 1970s reflected the fact that the country was no longer at war, rather than a deliberate shift of funds to social programs.

Compared to most other industrial societies, the United States devotes a much greater portion of its resources to national defense. Research suggests that this has several negative effects:

1. Though military spending does create employment, it creates fewer jobs than most other kinds of spending and often bypasses areas with the greatest need for jobs and income.

2. Channeling public resources into defense has diminished funds available for other purposes, such as rebuilding the country's infrastructure.

3. Military spending hinders economic performance by shifting skills, research, and capital away from nonmilitary industries.

The high cost of defense results, in part, from wasteful and inefficient practices built into the "military-industrial complex" itself, such as lack of competition, "cost-plus" contracting, and duplication of effort among the military services.

In addition, the equipment that the defense dollar buys is not only expensive but often also cumbersome and ineffective.

The evidence suggests that it's possible to reduce military spending without damaging national defense. Some approaches include putting a cap on increases in the defense budget, reducing cost overruns, and stopping (or greatly reducing) the production of nuclear weapons.

For Further Reading

Barnet, Richard. *Real Security.* New York: Simon and Schuster, 1981.

DeGrasse, Robert. *Military Expansion, Economic Decline.* New York: Council on Economic Priorities, 1983.

Fallows, James. *National Defense.* New York: Random House, 1982.

Holloway, David. *The Soviet Union and the Arms Race.* New Haven, Conn.: Yale University Press, 1983.

Kaldor, Mary. *Baroque Arsenal.* New York: Hill and Wang, 1981.

McFadden, Dave, and Jim Wake, eds. *The Freeze Economy.* Mountain View, Calif.: Mid-Peninsula Conversion Project, 1983.

13

Social Issues and Public Policy

During the 1980s, there has been an unusual amount of agreement among people of almost all political persuasions that the dominant social policies of the past 30 to 40 years will no longer suffice to deal with America's problems in the future. It's probably true that every historical period has been regarded, by those who live in it, as a turning point or watershed for social policy. To some extent, the perception has probably been accurate. But there are reasons to believe that the perception applies especially well to *our* period — and this book has presented a number of those reasons. Though it's easy to exaggerate the depth and significance of the changes we've recently witnessed, it's also clear that we have come near to the end of an era.

The model of social and economic organization based on the economic expansion that characterized much of the postwar period was often regarded as an inevitable fact of life. But we can understand now, with the advantage of hindsight, that it was a temporary condition made possible by a fleeting combination of several factors: America's dominance of the international economy; the ready availability of cheap petroleum-based energy; and the still relatively uncluttered natural environment which, up to a point, absorbed the ecological by-products of unreflective affluence like a giant sponge.

As we've seen, severe and troubling problems revealed themselves even when that postwar development was working "well." There was nagging unemployment, high rates of crime and violence, sharp inequalities of race, class, and gender, and the less quantifiable but equally disturbing coexistence of what the economist John Kenneth Galbraith (1958) described as "private affluence and public squalor." But America's commanding position

493

Many of America's roads and bridges are rapidly decaying.

in the world's economy, coupled with abundant and seemingly inexhaustible natural resources, did act as a kind of buffer that allowed us to put off reckoning with the larger implications of those problems.

There's now little disagreement that the terms and conditions of American life are changing. We are increasingly aware that the only social policies that are likely to be effective will be those that appropriately come to terms with these changing realities: including the growing economic role of other countries, the limits of nonrenewable resources, and the limit of the capacity of the human and natural environments to absorb unchecked growth. It's increasingly understood that these changes force choices on us that we had been able to dodge up to now with some success — choices about economic growth versus ecological balance and about the distribution of social and economic resources among different groups and (more broadly) between private and public purposes. And, within the category of public purposes, there is the further choice between the domestic social programs of the welfare state and the claims of military spending. In turn, these choices force us to rethink some crucial concepts whose meaning may have been taken too much for granted in the recent past: concepts like "growth" itself, or "efficiency," or "security," or "costs," or "welfare." How such key terms are defined, and how those definitions are put into practice, is a good part of what social policy in the 1980s is about. And here, of course, the agreement ends.

Strategies for Social Policy

Obviously, it would take another book even to begin to describe the range of proposals for social change stimulated by America's recent problems. We've seen already that for virtually every significant question of contemporary social policy there have been a bewildering variety of proposed responses. Yet within the welter of policies proposed for dealing with particular problems, we can discern some larger organizing themes — themes that lead to fairly distinct *strategies* of approaching social problems. In this chapter, we will sketch the outlines of three such strategies that are shaping much of the debate over specific social policies in the 1980s. In earlier chapters we briefly touched on how these strategies apply to more specific issues, and we won't attempt to draw out all of their implications for particular social problems here. We want, instead, to outline their most important principles and underlying assumptions — and to suggest what we think, on the basis of the research we've examined so far, may be some of their probable social consequences.

Generalizing about these strategies is inevitably a little risky. In the real world of social action and social policy, such broad themes are only rarely clear-cut or mutually exclusive. The three broad strategies should therefore be considered examples of what one of the founders of modern sociology, Max Weber, called "ideal types": abstractions that help us illuminate the essential features of more complex and subtle realities (Gerth and Mills, 1954). We've encountered all three strategies before at various points in this book. If we now draw out their premises more explicitly, they may provide a framework that can help us understand a variety of more specific policy issues in the 1980s.

The Strategy of Reprivatization

The first strategy calls for what we may term a *reprivatization* of social and economic life. It often takes the form, at least rhetorically, of demands to reduce the role of government in the economy and in society as a whole in favor of greater reliance on "market forces" or "free enterprise." But, as we've argued before, this is a somewhat misleading description of the real thrust of this strategy, both now and in the American past. More accurately, it has meant making government less the servant of a broad range of social interests and more the powerful, if sometimes hidden, partner of those private economic interests considered most able to produce the benefits of economic growth (Lindblom, 1977).

As we've seen in earlier chapters, few segments of the American business community are genuinely opposed to using the resources and power of government, or even to very large-scale government spending. The important differences in contemporary debates about social policy are mainly over what government and its fiscal resources are *for* — and, not far behind, over who should be allowed to decide the answers. (For one portrait of how the *public* regards the proper role of government, see Figure 13-1.) As two political theorists have recently written, "The central phenomenon in advanced Western nations is public intervention in economic markets and property relations; the central issue is the form and goal of that intervention" (Furniss and Tilton, 1977, p. x). Whether the specific issue at hand is energy policy or national security or the supply of medical care, the driving vision of the strategy of reprivatization is *not* a return to a presumed golden age of small-scale, genuinely competitive capitalism with government a distinctly minor character in the drama of social and economic life. Instead, this strategy is rooted in the conscious belief that the vast resources of the modern state should be channeled toward *some* social ends and diverted from others. What are those ends?

Figure 13-1

Public attitudes toward the role of government

Source: Public Opinion, February-March 1982, p. 39. Reprinted with permission of American Enterprise Institute for Public Policy Research.

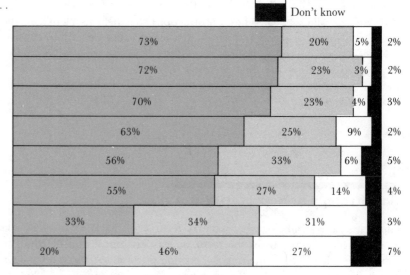

Role government should play in. . .

	Major role	Minor role	No role	Don't know
Seeing to it that all Americans get good health care	73%	20%	5%	2%
Protecting the environment	72%	23%	3%	2%
Encouraging economic development	70%	23%	4%	3%
Seeing to it that there are enough good jobs	63%	25%	9%	2%
Fostering basic research	56%	33%	6%	5%
Helping American business compete with foreign business	55%	27%	14%	4%
Increasing the number of blacks and minorities in good jobs	33%	34%	31%	3%
Fostering the arts	20%	46%	27%	7%

Social critics in the 1960s often warned against the growth of what they called the "welfare-warfare state" — a phrase that described the uneasy combination of the expansion of domestic social programs on the one hand and of massive military spending on the other. In the 1980s, the strategy of reprivatization aims at what, for want of a better phrase, we could call the "military-market state."

This would be a state strongly committed to ever-increasing military spending. But unlike the architects of the welfare-warfare state, the supporters of the military-market state are deeply hostile to the extension of the institutions of social welfare. Government — despite rhetoric to the contrary — remains of crucial importance to this strategy. But the ends of government are defended as mainly those of strengthening the country's capacity for warfare and of reasserting American economic and political influence in the international arena. These ends are to be pursued through a massive shift of public spending away from many domestic social programs to the government's military planners and, through them, to selected private corporations whose prosperity is now inseparable from government defense spending.

On the domestic front, reprivatization means a great deal more than just the frugal trimming of overblown social program budgets or the search for ways of reducing "waste" and "abuse" in these programs. If this was *all* it meant, not many would strongly disagree with it. Most public bureaucracies (like most private ones) can certainly stand some trimming, tightening, and an occasional shaking-up. But this strategy involves something much more fundamental; for its long-term goal is to greatly reduce the scope of the institutions developed in the past half-century to cushion the impact of economic forces on individuals and communities.

It is important to realize that the social changes in the welfare state that this strategy proposes are profound ones. Much of the growth of domestic social programs over the past several decades has been based on the principle that modern societies bear some degree of collective responsibility for the well-being of their members, over and above what happens to them and their families in the economic market. Slowly, often grudgingly, and by no means consistently, American society has made important strides in that direction, as this book has often shown.

The length of those strides shouldn't be overstated, as we've *also* shown. We remain the *least* developed of modern welfare states. [So much so that some scholars are unwilling to describe the United States as a true welfare state at all. (Furniss and Tilton, 1977, chap. 1).] We lag behind most other industrial societies in workplace health and safety, in child-care provisions, in cushions against unemployment and loss of income, in accessible and affordable health care. We are more unequal in the spread of personal income than almost every other developed country — mainly, as we saw in Chapter 4, because we allow more severe poverty at the bottom. We have few of the kinds of mechanisms for worker participation in decisions affecting the workplace that have become conventional in many European countries and Japan (see pages 93 to 95) (Carnoy and Shearer, 1980). We are already, in short, a far more "privatized" society than most and have been much slower to recognize both the obligations and the benefits of a more conserving approach to our human resources.

Yet American accomplishments along this line in the past several decades cannot be taken lightly. For all its (very real) limits, failures, and imperfections, the rudimentary American welfare state has brought many notable changes in American life. Traces of those changes have appeared again and again in the statistics we've presented — numbers that, however coldly, represent some of the life and death realities of our society. These include the dramatic decreases in infant death and other life-threatening health problems, attributable in part to publicly supported preventive health care; a better life for many of the aged, partly the result of better social benefits and improvements in the quality and delivery of medical care; the achievement of safer, more healthful workplaces through more effective social regulation, and many others.

But behind the strategy of reprivatization is the belief that these social benefits should come — if at all — as a by-product of the growth of the private economy. Proponents of the strategy of reprivatization argue that the sheer *expense* of these programs is a drain on private economic growth. But they also frequently make a more fundamental criticism of the idea that society as a whole ought to shoulder some responsibility to intervene in what they regard as the beneficial risks of interpersonal competition for economic rewards. It's this belief, for example, that leads one (rather extreme) partisan of this approach to argue for scrapping most social welfare and job programs on the ground that "what the poor need is the spur of their poverty" (Gilder, 1981, p. 118).

On another level, it's argued that since it's only through risk that we achieve economic growth, and only through growth that we create wealth and opportunities, any attempts to regulate or influence the direction of private economic growth will predictably make everyone poorer. At the extreme, this often sounds like a late twentieth century echo of the "social Darwinism" of a hundred years before — a sometimes chilling vision of a social world organized single-mindedly around interpersonal competition in which only the "fittest" will (or should) survive. "How could adaptation take place," writes one social scientist partial to this view, "if some behaviors and organisms do not die? Is it being suggested that everything live forever? . . . *neither everything nor everyone can survive*" (Wildavsky, 1980, p. 36).

There is more than a little illogic in this position, especially when it moves out of the lecture halls and into the less abstract world of social policy. Many of those who argue that the poor should be "spurred" by their poverty and insecurity, or that industrial workers ought willingly to accept greater risks to their health in the workplace in the name of economic growth, are *also* among those who clamor the loudest for a variety of cushions and protections — subsidies for investment, cost-plus contracts for defense production, emergency funding to stave off business failure — designed to shield *private corporations*, at *public* expense, from the consequences of their actions. Again, the true issue here is not whether protection against economic risks is itself a bad thing — but whose risks are to be considered, and who gets to choose. As the political theorist Michael Walzer (1982, p. 12) puts it, "There is no such thing as a risk-free society, but there are choices to be made about kinds and degrees of risk. When these choices are not made politically, they will be made privately."

The Consequences of Reprivatization: The Economy

Leaving such contradictions aside, what are the likely consequences for American social problems should this strategy come to dominate most of our social policy? We've now had enough of a chance to see this approach in operation to add some experiential evidence to what we've gleaned from social science research and analysis. The results are not encouraging.

As we've seen (especially in Chapter 3), even on economic terms alone, the strategy of simply stimulating the private economy — of "throwing money" at those who already have it — does *not* necessarily bring useful growth. Instead, it may mean the diversion of human resources, capital, and energy into nonproductive investments — into what Robert Reich of the Harvard Business School calls "paper entrepreneurship" (1983), and what other critics call a "short-term profit orientation" rather than a "long-term productivity orientation" (Bluestone, Thurow, and Shaiken, 1980, p. 52).

A fundamental tenet of the strategy of reprivatization is that productive investment follows directly from policies designed to promote the greatest short-term profit. But recent experience both in the United States and abroad belies this view. We've already described some examples in Chapter 3; one more here will help underscore the point. One of the provisions of the boldly titled Economic Recovery Act of 1981, which sought to strengthen the flagging economy by reducing taxes for the wealthy, was a tax exemption designed to stimulate speculative buying of racehorses by wealthy investors. As the Children's Defense Fund pointed out (1982, p. 13), this provision allowed someone who bought 600 racehorses to avoid about $1.25 million in federal taxes each year for three years, the equivalent of funding for a comprehensive services program for 538 American children. It is not clear how such a provision would help revive America's sagging productive industries — though it *is* true that the purchase of a $12,500 horse appears in our national economic statistics as an addition to gross national product and as an indication of economic growth.

But the fact that such transactions are counted as part of our GNP doesn't mean that they help solve either the economic problems of industrial decline or the *social* damage that follows in their wake. Nor does this strategy address some of the deep and troubling questions about the *quality* of such economic growth as America has witnessed in recent years — including its capacity to support either an acceptable standard of living or a sustainable environment. The strategy of reprivatization cannot distinguish between the social and economic virtues of an economy based on fast-food franchises and T-shirt shops and one providing stable, rewarding work and useful services. Its proponents have not, so far, been able to come up with clear answers to questions about how our finite natural resources and fragile environment will be preserved in the face of uncontrolled economic growth. At best, they typically offer a rather pious hope that human "ingenuity" will find some (as yet unknown) way of resolving the tensions between unregulated growth and the natural ecology. At worst, they often avoid the questions by attacking those who pose them as "elitist" and backward-looking (Tucker, 1982).

Economic Arguments, Social Consequences

Beyond these issues of economics and ecology are perhaps even more pressing questions about other potential *social* impacts of the strategy of reprivatization.

In the introduction to this book, we noted that one of the most important contributions of social science to public policy and the analysis of social problems is precisely its emphasis on the *social* dimension — on the complex and diverse interconnections of groups, communities, and institutions that make up the fabric of a society. What's striking about what we've called the strategy of reprivatization is its *lack* of this sense of the complexity of the social world — its unfortunate tendency to reduce nearly all social problems to questions of "economics," narrowly understood, and, as a result, to ignore or dismiss the social consequences of economic policies.

One very likely consequence of this strategy, for example, is increased social inequality. Such a strategy is *based,* in part, on the argument that inequality is a "good thing," a necessary precondition for economic growth and for ensuring incentives to work. And the other side of that belief is the assertion that the greater economic growth that inequality brings will, in turn, bring sufficient jobs and income to provide the basis for a healthy social order. "A rising tide," as the hoary economic platitude goes, "lifts all boats." The trouble is that it clearly *doesn't,* under modern social and technological conditions — a fact recently emphasized by the noted conservative economist Herbert Stein. "It is not sufficient to say that a rising tide lifts all boats," Stein writes (1982a, p. 50), "it is not true." In particular, "it is necessary to recognize that some sacrifice of economic efficiency and growth may be desirable for the sake of helping the poor."

Actually, it's far less clear than Stein assumes that "helping the poor" necessarily means sacrificing economic efficiency. As we saw in Chapter 4, the connection between equality and efficiency seems to run in the other direction. Greater equality, particularly as a result of adequate employment and the better use of productive skills throughout the society, is one of the main reasons for the relatively superior economic performance of several other industrial countries. But the rest of Stein's point is well-taken.

The benefits of the private economy do not "trickle down" to all Americans.

Undirected economic growth cannot, by itself, draw all of the poor, the jobless, or the displaced into productive work or ensure them an adequate living standard, for reasons we've touched on in Chapters 4, 5, 6, and 8. Many of the poor are members of groups (welfare mothers, older people, teenagers without salable skills, for example) that have not been effectively pulled into the economy in the past, even in periods of "prosperity." Others (like some displaced industrial workers) are among the "new poor" who, though once sought after for their skills, will not fit easily into a "revitalized" economy without substantial aid and retraining of a type this strategy usually explictly rejects. And, as we saw in Chapter 8, this problem will most certainly be aggravated by the continuing impact of automation in industry and the office. We do not yet know exactly how that impact will make itself felt. But it seems clear that without careful attention to the issues of job training and retraining and the pace of introduction of new technology, the impact will certainly sharpen the inequalities between those who, through luck, pluck, or skill, have a foothold in the emerging economy of the coming decades and those who do not.

The Strategy of Reprivatization **501**

As in the past, a disproportionate number of the latter are destined to come from the ranks of minorities and women if the strategy of reprivatization prevails. Though it has become fashionable to argue that the worst enemy of minority progress has been "government" and that the best hope for minorities is the removal of such government-created barriers as affirmative action programs (Williams, 1982), the evidence shows that the opposite is the case. We might all wish for a society in which the rights of minorities to equal employment, earnings, and educational opportunities come naturally as a result of the market's even-handed rewarding of individual abilities and motivation. American society, however, is not — and never was — that society of happy abstraction.

A good part of the progress made by minorities in the 1960s and early 1970s (as we saw in Chapter 5) was the result of the expansion of the public sector in general and of government antidiscrimination programs in particular. Thus, even for many of the relatively affluent among the minority middle class, a strategy of reprivatization could bring substantial suffering and the prospect of downward mobility. But for many of the minority poor and near-poor, it promises something like disaster. Forced to the margins of economic and social life even when the economy has performed reasonably well, the inner-city minority poor are unlikely to be lifted from that condition simply by more of the same. And if this gloomy prospect holds for the poor generally, it holds doubly for poor women maintaining families, for whom the lack of adequate child care and the still-segregated labor market combine to add extra obstacles to their chances of success.

This tendency to increase social inequality suggests that the strategy of reprivatization has a troubling potential for generating severe social conflict between those groups with a realistic chance at the "good life" and those without (U.S. Commission on Civil Rights, 1982a). A society that offers harsh and bleak futures to a wide stratum of its people — especially its young — while holding out the lure of ever-increasing consumption for others, is not a society that can ensure public order for long. We learned this painfully in the 1960s. The lesson may be equally agonizing in the 1980s and 1990s, if this strategy prevails.

One response to these issues has been the argument that the plight of many of the poor is the result of a decline in moral values brought on in large part by the welfare state itself (Gilder, 1981). "Permissiveness," in this view, has been mainly responsible for the growth of families headed by women and other social problems among minorities and the poor. From the perspective of reprivatization, what's needed is not more income supports or public services that merely reinforce the breakup of families, but a new enforcement of traditional morality among the poor. Indeed, it is characteristic of this strategy that if often seeks to resolve a host of social problems by increasing the role of the state in the enforcement of private morality. The fact that this conflicts philosophically with the idea of reducing the role of government hasn't stopped it from being a major theme for partisans of the strategy of reprivatization.

The Strategy of Managed Revitalization

A second broad strategy toward American social problems in the 1980s is distinguished from the first primarily by its emphasis on the need for a certain amount of government economic planning. Because of this emphasis, we can think of it as a strategy of *managed revitalization* of the economy. In the past several years it has usually taken the form of a call for some kind of "industrial policy" for America, but its implications run considerably deeper than the revitalization of industry alone.

Unlike the reprivatization strategy, proponents of this approach realize that modern societies are increasingly interdependent systems that require a substantial degree of planning and coordination. Moreover, they recognize that planning done wholly under *private* auspices is unlikely to add up to a coherent or socially effective policy. They also understand the crucial importance of the careful cultivation of human resources for a society's health and are critical of the more simplistic versions of "market ideology" for failing to adequately understand "the importance of human capital for America's future" (R. Reich, 1983, p. 108).

From this perspective, one of the main reasons America has "lost" in the competitive economic arena to countries like West Germany and especially Japan is that the latter have been much better at training and motivating workers as well as making more efficient use of their physical resources. Most often, this is seen as a failure of American management more than of American workers. Thus, the economist Lester Thurow notes that "in a number of American plants, Japanese managers have proved that they can get American workers to work more efficiently than American managers can" (1982, p. 25). And Japan and other countries have also, in this view, been much better at directing economic investment into areas promising long-run productive gains as opposed to the short-run search for profit that has dominated American management.

Because of this, it is argued that what's most needed to recreate American prosperity are new mechanisms of planning and coordination of the economy. In this model, business and government would enter into a partnership to promote American industry's ability to "win" in international competition. Without some explicit direction and planning, in this view, we will not have a truly productive economy — nor, by implication, a healthy society. This strategy understands that sheer growth, as measured by gross national product, is a misleading indicator of economic and social health: it masks too much waste, too much unproductive activity (such as corporations buying other corporations), and too much mere shifting of assets from one firm to another. Holders of this viewpoint are thus critical of the belief that simply offering ever-greater incentives for private investment will truly revitalize the American economy. As Robert Reich (1983, p. 107) notes, "It is no secret that the rich are likely to spend large chunks of any new income on Persian carpets, rare paintings, antiques, yachts, luxury cars and vacations" — none of which contribute to sound economic growth.

Instead, this strategy places most of its bets on targeting private investment into more productive uses, particularly through supporting the development of what are sometimes called "sunrise" industries — those that, like microelectronics, genetic engineering, or robotics, appear (at this point) to be the most promising future winners in the international arena. In this view, a policy of channeling investment to these industries, changing the tax system to reward productive investment rather than paper profit-making, and investing more heavily in education and training to develop a more sophisticated labor force, would lead to a revitalized economy and the return of some level of prosperity — though not, perhaps, the level America enjoyed before the 1970s (Democratic Caucus, 1982).

In the 1980s, this vision has a strong appeal — so strong that today nearly everyone now pays at least lip service to the need for a more conscious industrial policy. And, as we've seen, particularly in Chapter 3, much of the critique of the anarchy and irrationality of American economic policy and its destructive effects on the fabric of society as a whole strikes home. It seems likely that *some* kind of approach to public/private planning for economic revitalization will be a major item on the social policy agenda in America for years to come. But there are a number of troubling social questions about this strategy, at least in many of the versions we've seen up to now.

Revitalization for Whom?

Perhaps the greatest problem is that this strategy generally accepts, without much reflection, the premise that boosting the private economy will bring about a whole range of beneficial *social* impacts. Many approaches to the reindustrialization of America, in other words, share with more traditional ideologies the idea that jobs, income, and an enhanced community life will necessarily "trickle down" from the growth of the private economy. They differ, as we've noted, in believing that some government planning and coordination with business and labor are necessary to achieve that growth, but the assumption that growth will lead naturally to other social benefits remains central. Like the strategy of reprivatization, this approach often seems too enamored of purely economic solutions to social problems, and insufficiently concerned with the changing social and technological context of economic life.

One crucial problem can be illustrated by an example. During the early 1980s, some politicians who supported high-tech reindustrialization as a response to America's problems became known as "Atari Democrats" (from the computer corporation best known for its elaborate video games). As one of the most phenomenal examples of the rapid growth of the microelectronics industry in the 1970s, Atari seemed an appropriate symbol for a strategy of social and industrial revitalization. But in early 1983, Atari shut down

High-speed railways, like those in France and Japan, could become an important new industry in the United States.

some of its operations in California's Silicon Valley, shipping the production of many components — and thus several hundred California jobs — to the Far East.

The lesson would seem to be that there is no good reason to believe that the new sunrise industries won't follow the route of other American firms in search of lower labor costs and the other profit-maximizing advantages of moving abroad. Nor, as we saw in Chapter 8, can we be sure that investment in these industries will generate substantial numbers of good jobs even if they *do* remain within American borders. The technology of many of the sunrise industries is impressive, but much of it is designed precisely to *eliminate* jobs, not create them; so even a booming industry is no longer a guarantee of adequate livelihoods for many Americans.

A strategy based so thoroughly on boosting America's ability to compete in the international economy raises other questions as well. Beating other countries at the competitive game often means sacrificing a great deal — particularly since some of our new competitors are low-wage Third World countries with the economic "advantages" of minimal environmental or workplace regulations. Such competition often implies deliberate reduction of the standard of living of *some* groups in order to raise capital for private industry. As Lester Thurow puts it, "less consumption is the necessary converse of more investment" (Bluestone, Thurow, and Shaiken, 1980, p. 48).

The Strategy of Managed Revitalization   **505**

From this perspective, revitalizing the American economy — especially in the inner cities — may require rolling back many of the hard-won gains of working people, such as minimum wages and workplace regulations) (*Business Week*, June 14, 1980d).

If the past is any guide, the burdens of such a strategy would fall hardest on those groups in American society that are now most dependent on public services and most desperate for employment, such as urban minorities and women.

But it is not clear that, even on its own terms, this strategy can work — if working means successfully competing in the world market with countries that can probably be counted on to provide even *lower* wages, even *fewer* public services, and even *less* stringent social regulations than we could reasonably achieve. And it is even less clear why the kind of society we would create by trying to beat Third World nations at their own game would be one much worth striving for. Advocates of this strategy often tend to agree with those of reprivatization that "if we maximize justice we destroy the conditions of economic growth" (Tsongas, 1981, cited in Harrington, 1982a, p. 413). The lack of evidence for that view hasn't greatly weakened its appeal among political leaders searching for ways of justifying the imposition of a new austerity on some social groups, but not others. An editorial in *Business Week* at the beginning of the 1980s, for example, explicitly declared that the creation of what it called a new "social contract" to boost American industry's productivity "must take precedence over the aspirations of the poor, the minorities, and the environmentalists" (1980d, p. 146). And a noted sociologist similarly argued that reversing America's "industrial obsolescence" in the future would require us to diminish our concern for the "quality of life" — including such social goals as national health insurance, better air and water quality, public support for education, and child care (Etzioni, 1980).

What we've called the strategy of managed revitalization, in short, often rests on what turns out to be a rather harsh vision of social life, in which many other social goals are deliberately sacrificed in the name of improving productivity and international competitiveness. "The world is becoming a race course," one enthusiast writes, "in which the first producer to gain a dominant share of a new market is able to maintain a lead in future markets, because it enjoys higher profits than its rivals . . . " (R. Reich, 1983, p. 104). But one problem with regarding the world as an economic race course is that very little attention is paid to the effects of that "race" on social and personal well-being.

Again, the vision often seems a narrowly economic one that views the economy as an abstract system of exchanges, detached from its roots in living human communities. Many advocates of industrial revitalization argue that declining industries, cities, and even regions should be allowed to "die" so that investment may be channeled to new, more dynamic regions and more promising industries. Presumably, people who are displaced or made jobless through this process will simply move to where new opportunities are. But even if we granted the ability of this strategy to produce those new opportunities, the result would often be the disruption and fragmentation of entire communities. The potential human and financial costs of these impacts, ranging from increased welfare dependency to crime, family violence, and health problems, are rarely accounted for on the balance sheet of managed revitalization (Bluestone and Harrison, 1982).

Despite its tough-mindedness about some of the recent failings of the American economy, then, this approach is sometimes remarkably myopic about the *social* consequences of economic change and about the limited ability of economic growth to ensure, by itself, other fundamental social values. The view of social life as a race course implies that some will win and some will lose. But this perspective is often uncomfortably silent both about what will happen to the losers — and about what lies at the end of the race.

The Strategy of Social Reconstruction

A third strategy toward America's problems is distinguished by its central emphasis on just those social values and concerns that tend to be ignored or downplayed by the other two strategies. Because of this emphasis, we can call it a strategy of *social reconstruction* — one that includes, but also moves beyond, the pursuit of economic revitalization.

Like the others, this strategy recognizes that a productive economy is a necessary foundation for any successful attempt to cope with most social problems. And it also recognizes, like the others, that there has been considerable waste and irrationality in some of the programs of the welfare state. Like the strategy of managed revitalization, it emphasizes the need for more, rather than less, conscious planning of economic life. As the economist Jeff Faux puts it, "National economic policy remains the only significant organized human activity in America where planning ahead is considered irrational" (1982, p. 12). But the strategy also goes further. Less convinced that the social goals of equality, democratic participation, individual well-being, environmental health, and community stability will necessarily be accomplished through economic growth alone, it puts these ends *first*. It thus seeks to tailor economic policies and programs explicitly to social goals, rather than the other way around.

Since these goals may or may not coincide with the logic of the search for private profit, such a strategy leads to a much more explicit role for *public* investment and for *public* participation in economic decisions. The means to achieve this extension of democratic norms to the economy vary widely in this strategy. They necessarily include a stronger role for national-level government economic planning (a goal shared with the strategy of managed revitalization). But they may also include other mechanisms for public influence over economic policy, such as worker or worker/community ownership of some industries, or representation of workers or labor representatives on boards of directors, workplace health and safety committees, and other important functions now usually under private control (Zwerdling, 1980).

We saw in Chapter 2 that the United States is unique among other advanced industrial societies in the relatively small role played by the public sector in the economy — and the extent to which fundamental decisions about investment and economic priorities are concentrated in private hands. We've encountered this difference, in many ways, throughout this book: in national differences in policies governing employment and training, energy conservation, the regulation of occupational hazards, and much more. Bringing the United States closer to the practice of most other industrial societies is a central thrust of the strategy of social reconstruction. For example, such

Controlling the New Technology: Some Experiments from Europe

Some of the most profound issues for social policy in the next decade will be those surrounding the development of new technologies in the workplace. Computer-based, microelectronic technology has already had a powerful impact on the nature of work and the problem of unemployment in America, and that impact is certain to be even greater in the future. Yet there has been little effort to develop policies to govern the introduction of these new technologies or to control their social consequences. Like many other social concerns, the impact of revolutionary new technologies has usually not been considered a proper object of deliberate policy in the United States. Our approach has been to leave decisions about technology almost entirely up to the discretion of private employers, while allowing the social costs of those decisions — such as unemployment and its destructive impact on families and individuals — to be borne by society as a whole.

But America may be able to learn a great deal from the experience of European countries. Many of these countries have developed innovative policies that help prevent some of the ad-

verse effects of technological change by giving workers considerably more control over its direction and impact.

Much of the impetus for these policies has come from European unions. While the unions accept the need for new technologies, they have also insisted that changes be introduced in ways that enhance rather than diminish workers' skills and working conditions, and that maintain jobs and wages. European unions have been successful in sparking legislation and agreements with employers that improve workers' access to information about proposed new technical developments in the workplace, as well as giving them a voice in determining how these will be implemented.

In Sweden and Norway, workers have won legislation giving them the right to full information about any new technology planned for their workplace. The Norwegian "data agreement" gives workers access to company data banks and all other information available to a company's board of directors, and the right to attend company board meetings. Unions may veto proposed technological changes that could be harmful to workers' safety and health. Workers in several countries (including England, West Germany, Sweden, and Norway) can participate in government- or union-sponsored training programs on

a strategy often calls for a significant expansion of public-sector enterprises, common in many other industrial countries, to ensure enough investment in areas (such as mass transit or alternative energy development) typically neglected by private industry (Carnoy and Shearer, 1980, chap. 2). It also calls for legislation at both federal and state levels to reduce the arbitrariness of private investment decisions: legislation, for example, calling for closer regulation of industrial wastes or advance notification of plant closings (Bluestone and Harrison, 1982, chap. 8).

These proposals all address the issue of how decisions about social problems are made in the United States. The substantive goals of such a strategy are similarly varied, but they usually include, at a minimum, at least the following: assuring public investment for full employment, maintaining and strengthening measures to overcome the remediable inequalities of race and gender, enhancing public services, and recasting the balance of military and domestic spending. Let's consider each of these goals in turn.

new technology, subsidized by special government funds or by employer contributions. (In the United States, any such training must be paid for by workers themselves, through their unions.) Scandinavian, German, and British workers also have access to government funding to develop consulting programs with outside technical experts, such as computer specialists and engineers, of their own choosing.

This access to information on new technologies gives European workers the tools to engage successfully in "technology bargaining," — negotiating with employers over the nature and purposes of new techniques before they are put in place. Thus, German metal workers have won a contract provision guaranteeing that they will not lose income through technological changes in their jobs; Norwegian telephone workers won the right to block new computerized technology that would eliminate jobs or worsen working conditions; a German union of bank workers won a provision forbidding the layoff of workers as a result of technological change.

The principle behind these policies is not simply resistance to change for its own sake; the goal is to minimize the social and personal *costs* of such change and to broaden the control over the nature and pace of technological innovation beyond

the hands of employers. The contrast between this and the American practice is illustrated in an example of the computerization of machine operators' jobs in Norway and the United States. According to the labor writers Steve Early and Matt Witt, workers in an aircraft parts plant in Norway were given full information in advance about a proposed installation of computer-based machine tools. This enabled them to successfully demand, not that the new tools be rejected, but that the existing machine operators be trained to program and repair them. In a similar situation in a plant in Massachusetts, workers were neither consulted nor given a voice in the introduction of automated machine tools. As a result, the programming and repairing are done by specialized programmers or supervisors, and the machinists have had to settle for lower pay, less challenging work as mere "button pushers," and the prospect of losing their jobs altogether (Early and Witt, 1982).

What is most compelling about the European experience is that it has begun to bring technological change out of the realm of the inevitable and uncontrollable, and rendered it, for the first time, an issue that (in the words of the journalist Robert Howard) is "open to social action and control" (1980).

Public Investment for Full Employment

The crucial role of employment and unemployment in shaping many of America's problems (from racial inequality to family violence and ill-health) has appeared again and again in the preceding chapters. And, on the surface, there's not much disagreement in America today that dealing with the devastating joblessness that has wracked American society in recent years must be a main priority for social policy.

The idea of full employment is an example of what's sometimes called a "motherhood" issue: almost everyone is for it, at least rhetorically. But the superficial agreement conceals dramatic disagreements about what full employment *means,* not to mention how it should be achieved, or where it stands on the list of social priorities. Proponents of rebuilding American society through unleashing the "forces of the market" have, as we've seen, often opted for deliberately *increasing* unemployment on the ground that, however painful, it will help create the conditions for economic growth. Those who argue for a strategy of managed reindustrialization tend to believe that full employment will come as a natural by-product of government-stimulated growth of competitive industries. The limits of the first strategy in producing full employment are obvious. And from all the evidence we've examined, the second strategy's ability to provide adequate work for all is problematic, at best.

Recognizing these limitations, the strategy of social reconstruction emphasizes that genuine full employment will require a commitment to *public* as well as private job creation (Harrington, 1982a, pp. 417–418). Where the private sector fails to generate adequate jobs, public ones will need to be created if we want to avoid the systematic waste of human resources, the disruption of personal and community life, and the aggravation of social inequality that massive unemployment and underemployment generate.

In the United States, public job creation has often been dismissed as somehow inferior to private employment. As we saw in Chapter 8, government-supported jobs are often regarded as useless make-work. But it is not clear why, say, a public school teacher's job is less serious than that of a private go-go dancer or used car salesperson. It's also sometimes difficult even to *distinguish* public from private employment. What is the difference, for example, between working as a meter-reader for a public utility company or for a private company, between working as a nurse in a public health clinic or in a private hospital?

As we've seen, countries like Sweden or Austria, which have very low unemployment rates and have weathered the economic crisis of the last decade well, have done so partly through extensive public intervention in the labor market, including public job creation and extensive job training and retraining programs. And, as Figure 13-2 shows, the majority of Americans support the idea that the government should provide jobs for all those who want one. Moreover, though it's not much talked about, mandatory public job creation under conditions of high unemployment is already the law of the land in the United States. Under the provisions of the Full Em-

Percent

Figure 13-2
Attitudes toward government job creation: Responses to the statement, government should see that everyone who wants to work has a job

Source: From *Public Opinion*, August-September 1981, p. 34. Reprinted with permission of American Enterprise Institute for Public Policy Research.

ployment and Balanced Growth Act of 1978 (popularly called the Humphrey-Hawkins Bill), the federal government is *required* to create publicly supported jobs in areas of social need when the national jobless rate rises above 4 percent. Strictly speaking, the federal government's failure to do so in the 1980s has been a clear-cut violation of the law.

A basic premise of the strategy of social reconstruction is that high unemployment represents a failure to make the most rational use of our human resources, not a lack of necessary work to be done. (Some concrete suggestions on where such useful work could be found are offered in the proposals from the Joint Economic Committee of Congress, pages 514 to 517.) But many kinds of necessary work do *not* usually get done under private auspices because they are not regarded as sufficiently profitable, at least in the short-range calculus of American private industry. Because of this, the strategy of social reconstruction emphasizes the crucial importance of supplementing the decisions of the private labor market with public investment to create permanent jobs.

A strategy for full employment, from this perspective, is perhaps the single most important step toward reducing America's systematic inequalities of class, race, and gender. As the economist Robert Lekachman points out, "Full employment is the most efficient agent of equitable income redistribution" that is possible "within the parameters of market capitalism." Full employment is a strong catalyst for social equality in several simultaneous ways, as Lekachman notes:

Mechanisms to Overcome Social Inequality

> Full employment sucks into the labor force individuals who now strive desperately to survive on welfare, food stamps, Social Security and unemployment compensation. Full employment improves wages for low-paid workers whose financial situation is only slightly less precarious than that of the unemployed. It is a particular boon to blacks, Hispanics, teenagers, and women, last hired in good times and first hired in recessions . . . full

Renewable energy technologies may have a major role in the reconstruction of America's economy.

employment would substantially narrow the existing indefensibly wide differentials between the earnings of those groups and those of white males. (Lekachman, 1982, p. 201)

The other side of this coin is that protracted high unemployment makes a mockery of most of the instruments we now possess for reducing racial and gender inequalities. Laws against discrimination in employment, for example, are obviously limited when a sixth of a city's work force is unemployed. But the strategy of social reconstruction argues that the opposite is also true. Even sustained full employment will not, by itself, guarantee the equal treatment of women and minorities in the labor market, in education, or in other American institutions. In the case of minorities, this became clear in the 1960s, when a period of something approaching full employment on the national level coexisted with high rates of unemployment and continuing income inequality for the minority population. And, as we've seen in Chapters 6 and 7, the barriers of inadequate child care, sex-segregated labor markets, and traditional sex roles in the family will conspire to perpetuate gender inequality even in an almost full-employment economy.

Nor can we reasonably expect the inequalities of gender and race to be wiped out magically by the uncontrolled operation of the market system. After all, these inequalities were even more entrenched in the United States *before* government intervention in the market was so much as a gleam in the bureaucratic eye. Thus, the strategy of social reconstruction recognizes that the position of minorities and women reflects deeply rooted traditions in America that will not simply wither away without deliberate social action. A commitment to reducing these inequalities therefore means that explicit antidiscrimination measures, as well as extensive child care and other public supports that acknowledge the changing roles of American women, must have a central place in the social policy agenda for the 1980s.

What we've called the strategy of social reconstruction also emphasizes that the welfare state is here to stay. No social order can do without some systematic provision for the ill, the disabled, the very young, and the very old — a principle increasingly acknowledged even by serious conservatives (Will, 1983). And, as we've seen in this book, a number of social changes have made the extension of *public* provision for these needs even more crucial.

Coming to Terms with the Welfare State

One, for example, is the aging of the population. As we have learned to lengthen the life span, we will also have to learn to accept the responsibility to provide well for an increasing proportion of people who are past the age when they can reasonably be expected to support themselves in the labor force. Similarly, the changing pattern of labor-force participation among American women (especially coupled with the growing number of women heading families) creates greater responsibilities for the provision of child care, supplemental income supports, and more flexible approaches to work time.

It has sometimes been argued that these needs should, ideally, be taken care of within the family rather than by government. Or, in the case of women in the labor force and the needs of children in families headed by women, that these needs wouldn't exist if the traditional family had not been eroded by unwise policy and an attitude of permissiveness. As we've seen, this is one reason why the strategy of reprivatization also frequently involves efforts to enforce traditional family norms as a response to these social and demographic changes. A strategy of social reconstruction, on the other hand, seeks to support the family not by dictating its "correct" composition or "proper" gender roles but by protecting *all* families from the preventable stresses of economic insecurity, inadequate income, and absent or inaccessible public services.

Again, such a strategy is undeniably costly (though, as we've seen in Chapter 4, not nearly as costly as it's sometimes said to be). But there are several reasons why we need to look more carefully at the deeper, more complex issues surrounding the way we define the notion of costs. We have touched on these issues before. For one thing, just as in the business world or in the family budget, some of the "costs" of the welfare state are more properly seen as *investments*. Preventive health care, early childhood education, and nutrition, and community mental health programs, to name just a few examples, are not simply consumers of scarce funds, but investments in the quality of our human resources. And even in the barest dollars-and-cents

Reconstructing the Economy — A Congressional View

A multitude of proposals for rebuilding the American economy have been advanced in the past few years. Among the most comprehensive and detailed is a set of recommendations offered by the Joint Economic Committee of Congress in 1982. In a discussion ranging over many aspects of the contemporary troubles of the economy, the committee called for much more active public intervention in economic life. Its specific recommendations included, among others, ones dealing with credit policies, tax expenditures, special assistance to "catalyst" industries, rebuilding America's physical infrastructure, and rethinking energy policies.

Recommendation No. 6: Practice Credit Conservation

The administration and the Federal Reserve should encourage the banking system to develop an effective means to deter destabilizing bursts of bank-financed lending for unproductive purposes such as large corporate takeovers and speculation in commodities, collectibles, and land. Such measures will have the effect of conserving scarce credit resources in times of need for the use of small business, farmers, housing, automobile financing, and productive capital investments.

The year 1981 was a banner one for predacious corporate takeovers financed by the savings of ordinary American citizens. Spectacular examples included the takeover of Conoco by Du Pont, after a public battle involving Texaco, Mobil, and Seagrams; the takeover of Marathon Oil by U.S. Steel, after a public battle with Mobil; and the attempted takeover of Grumman by LTV. One can only imagine how millions of ordinary Americans who could not get credit in 1981 viewed the spectacle of such massive misuse of their savings by the corporate world and the banking system . . .

We recommend specifically that a policy in this area take the form of credit conservation. . . . We should effectively discourage bank lending for those few uses which conspicuously absorb large amounts of scarce credit to the detriment of more productive uses. This will not put an end to corporate takeovers. But it will make them more expensive to the acquiring firm, and therefore encourage a reallocation of that firm's efforts to more productive activity, which is the point. . . .

Recommendation No. 12: Review Tax Expenditures

For decades, Congress has made use of tax preferences and other forms of tax relief to channel resources into beneficial economic activities, such as business investment, homeownership, energy conservation, and support of charitable organizations. These should be continued. There are many other preferences in the tax code, however, which have channeled the nation's resources into activities whose economic benefit is not justified by their cost, and which have disproportionately favored the well-to-do at the expense of the average taxpayer. . . .

The "tax-expenditure budget" which is published each year with the budget of the United States government lists the special tax preferences which result in a loss of federal tax revenues. This budget, as drawn up for fiscal year 1983, consists of 96 items with a revenue loss of about $244 billion. By comparison, the tax expenditure budget for fiscal year 1977 consisted of 82 items with a total revenue loss of $106 billion.

For fiscal year 1983, the total revenue loss from tax preference items will amount to more than 32 percent of projected budget outlays. Despite the magnitude of the revenue loss, these tax preferences rarely come under close scrutiny or review. Many tax expenditures have outlived their usefulness, others are ineffectual in fulfilling their intended purposes or actually favor the well-to-do. All such provisions withhold revenue year in and year out from the U.S. treasury. These are revenues which other taxpayers who are not so favored must make up . . .

Recommendation No. 19: Promote Catalysts

There is a role for government policy in the pursuit of sensible industrial development goals. We have not come up with a single grand criterion which encompasses all of the right things to do and rejects all of the wrong ones. But we have agreed on a general approach which is consonant with our traditions, resources, and opportunities, and which respects and strengthens the role of private enterprise and competitive markets in our economy. We call our approach "promoting catalysts."

In chemistry, a catalyst is a chemical which facilitates a reaction, thereby increasing the efficiency with which resources, like heat, can be applied to a process, and sometimes making possible transformations that weren't possible before. Similarly, government policy should seek for areas of enterprise where a little public-private cooperation, a little access to credit, or a little infrastructure development can have far-reaching effects on the efficiency of our resource use, our future pattern of development and growth, and the competitiveness of our final goods industries. The examples are many. Three, which illustrate different but representative cases which the committee has examined in hearings or staff studies in the past 14 months, are semiconductors, coal, and regional high-speed passenger rail . . .

The National Transportation Study Commission reported in June 1979 that a "transportation crisis in this country is just around the corner." The commission estimated that, by the year 2000, national domestic person-miles of travel will increase between 81 and 96 percent and national domestic freight ton-miles will increase between 165 and 314 percent. It concluded that the present transportation system will be hard-pressed to handle such dramatic increases.

The U.S. highway system is rapidly deteriorating. The Federal Highway Administration projects that an expenditure of $360 billion over the next 15 years would be required merely to maintain and repair existing far-from-adequate road quality. The nation's many airports and primary air lines are also seriously congested. Many smaller communities are losing service as a result of the increasing costs, especially fuel costs, of providing service.

The nation's railway system is at the present time in no position to pick up the slack. Track and equipment are deteriorating. The increase in the price of petroleum-based fuel has made railroad travel, as air travel, increasingly expensive.

Advanced industrial nations abroad have remained dedicated to the provision of high-quality rail service. Japan inaugurated "bullet train" service almost 25 years ago. Trains between Tokyo and Shin Osaka average 100 miles per hour and attain top speeds of 130 miles per hour. One hundred twenty million passengers a year use these trains. They operate reliably, and the technologies on which they are based are being continually redesigned and improved. They also operate without government subsidies and even make a profit. In September 1981, the Tres Grande Vitesse made its debut as the French entry among bullet trains. It travels between Paris and Lyons, attaining top speeds approaching 160 miles per hour. Throughout Europe and Canada, high-speed trains are either already in operation or currently being developed.

American trains pale in comparison. The average speed of a passenger train in this country has declined from 75 miles per hour in the mid-1950s to a current average of 40 miles per hour. Amtrak today operates only 1,700 passenger cars. Despite smaller populations, the majority of the European nations operate at least five times as many passenger cars. Japan operates 26,000 cars over a rail system that covers only half the mileage of the U.S. system, in a country which is the size of the state of Montana. . . .

The committee . . . has proposed developing [high-speed passenger rail service] in 20 highly populated rail corridors.

The committee believes that such an undertaking would produce not only major direct economic benefits, but indirect ones as well, such as providing an infusion of capital into depressed industries and encouraging technology transfers throughout the economy. Now that much of the nation's highway construction is complete, the highway construction industry's talents and capabilities could be readily channeled to such purposes as grading, building bridges, pouring concrete, and building fences and stations for a new rail transportation system. Moreover, a whole new industry of rail cars, locomotives, and equipment can help reemploy our skilled manufacturing labor force and the excess capacity of our metal-working industries.

In the same way that the development of an automobile industry in the 1920s not only changed the face of America's transportation system, but also created untold new jobs and business, the development of a new high-speed rail passenger service–oriented industry would serve as the catalyst to renewed economic prosperity that the United States is so lacking today. . . .

Recommendation No. 20: Maintain Infrastructure

Perhaps the most neglected item in redeveloping the nation's industrial base is the need to maintain and restore its capital facilities. In large part, our network of highways and bridges, ports and railroads, and adequate water and utility systems are responsible for the nation's productive capacity. In recent years, however, real capital expenditures at all levels of government have declined. . . .

These declines in capital funding have resulted in a deterioration of the basic public facilities upon which our economy relies. Over 8,000 of the 42,500 miles of interstate highways and 13 percent of its bridges have now exceeded their designed service life and must be rebuilt. The costs of rehabilitating and constructing our non-urban highways necessary to maintain existing service levels will exceed $700 billion in the 1980s. The 756 urban areas with populations over 50,000 will have to spend between $75 to $110 billion just to maintain their water systems. And it will cost upward of $33 billion to replace or rehabilitate the nation's deficient bridges. Pat Choate and Susan Walker, authors of *America in Ruins*, conclude that these deteriorated facilities are a major structural barrier to the renewal of our national economy, and combined with an aging industrial plant, have contributed to the decline in American productivity.

The deterioration of the infrastructure adversely affects investment because often firms must bear the additional costs which result from infrastructure problems. According to a recent issue of *Business Week*, U.S. Steel Corporation is

losing $1.2 million per year in employee time and wasted fuel rerouting trucks around the Thompson Run Bridge, in Pennsylvania, because it is in such disrepair. Companies in Manhattan, New York, lose $166 million a year for each additional five minutes delay on the public transportation systems. Old or inadequate water and sewer systems also stifle economic development. . . . In older areas of the country, large parts of the water and sewer systems are almost 100 years old. Many of these systems, however, were designed for a maximum of 100 years of serviceable life.

Although discussions of the need to revitalize the nation's decaying infrastructure often revolve around the problems of our urban centers, similar problems which plague rural America should not be minimized. Despite growth and diversification in many rural regions during the past dozen years, nagging deficiencies in rural infrastructure persist. According to a report of the General Accounting Office (GAO) issued in March 1980, as much as one-half of the nation's substandard housing may be found in rural America . . . public transportation is used by less than 1 percent of rural people who work away from home; more than 4 million rural people have inadequate sewage disposal systems or none at all; more than 2 million do not have running water in their homes. . . .

Recommendation No. 27: Promote Energy Security

The committee continues to believe that energy conservation and the use of renewable energy alternatives are a necessary component of a comprehensive national program to improve our energy security. Substantial investment has occurred as a consequence of tax incentives for industrial and residential conservation and the installation of solar energy equipment. The continuation of these fiscal incentives is appropriate to ensure that reliance on imported sources continues to decline.

Further gains in our nation's energy security can be realized from continued research into energy conservation and the renewable energy technologies. In fiscal year 1980, federal research, development, and demonstration budget authority for these programs totaled $1.5 billion, and comprised almost 11 percent of the Department of Energy's budget. Private conservation efforts have continued to blossom and renewable energy technologies mature. Yet, administration budget requests for these programs in the current fiscal year were reduced precipitously to less than $400 million, only 3 percent of DOE's budget. Administration plans for fiscal year 1983 call for a further reduction in federal support for these programs to $22 million (conservation) and $73 million (solar).

A continued viable federal program of research on energy conservation, renewable energy, and coal technologies is a necessary component of a broad-based national program to improve our energy security. While we support efforts to eliminate waste and fraud and reduce government spending, such motives should not provide an excuse to eliminate support for conservation, renewable energy, and coal research.

Source: U.S. Congress, Joint Economic Committee, *Joint Economic Report* (Washington, D.C.: Government Printing Office, February 1982, pp. 64–155).

terms, such investments "pay off" in reduced expenses for later health and mental health care and — as the experience of many other advanced societies shows — in an economy that benefits from the productive use of its human capital.

Perhaps even more important in assessing the "costs" of the welfare state is realizing that much of its expense comes from the burden of having to mop up the consequences of the frequently preventable irrationality and mismanagement of other social institutions. In the words of the British social theorist Richard Titmuss, the modern welfare state is cumbersome and costly in part because it is a response to a larger "*dis*welfare state" that systematically creates "needs" — through joblessness, community disruption, occupational disease — which then require costly, after-the-fact attention (Titmuss, 1968). "After a corporate-dominated system destroys the economic basis of a minimally decent life in the South Bronx," writes Michael Harrington, "the victims are given a few dollars in welfare and food stamps and excoriated for not achieving a minimally decent life on their own" (1982b, p. 34). To an important extent, American social welfare policy has been (again in Titmuss' words) an "*ad hoc* appendage to economic growth" (1968, p. 164). And this is a major reason for the inefficiency and waste of human resources that often *does* characterize the social welfare system in America — as well as its pervasive stinginess.

By contrast, the vision of the welfare state implicit in a strategy of social reconstruction is a more active, less reactive, one — designed, as Norman Furniss and Timothy Tilton propose, to "not merely care for the victims of advanced industrial society," but to provide "preventive efforts to forestall unemployment, disease, waste, and urban squalor" (1977, p. 192).

Nevertheless, it remains true that there are limits to how much a society can spend for public purposes. Especially because of the new constraints on America's role in the world economy, no serious approach to social policy in

Shifting the Balance of Social Spending

the 1980s can operate under the assumption that we can endlessly accommodate both guns and butter — both soaring military spending and an effective and humane social welfare policy. The strategy of social reconstruction acknowledges that national security is a legitimate concern for any government. But it also contends that the legitimate objectives of national security can be met with considerably less cost in social resources than they are now.

As we saw in Chapter 12, the most important public policy issues surrounding military spending concern not just the sheer *size* of American defense expenditures, but also the massive *inefficiency* of much defense-related production. There is room for considerable legitimate disagreement over the optimum size and composition of American military forces and equipment, but there is no compelling argument for continuing to encourage the level of waste and inefficiency that has become the hallmark of military spending in this country. As we saw, the cost savings that may be attainable even *without* significantly shifting our military priorities are astonishing; the cost *increases* in major weapons systems alone in the course of one year amount to a sum that, if saved, could have restored *all* the Reagan administration's budget cuts in social welfare programs in 1983.

Beyond this, of course, lie deeper questions about the kinds of weapons systems we truly need — and the possibilities for significant conversion of some military production facilities to peacetime purposes. A strategy of social reconstruction must carefully reconsider what we choose to mean by "national security" (Barnet, 1981) — and whether a society can be said to be "secure" if it allows its cities, basic industries, and human resources to deteriorate in the service of boosting its capacity to wage war.

Planning for Social Reconstruction

The third strategy involves a substantial amount of economic planning in order to achieve the goals of social policy. But so, as we've seen, do the other strategies — though the first often masks this by making planning more a private, corporate function, and less a public one. The idea of public planning, especially in the United States, raises strong fears about the potential of planning: to create enormous, powerful bureaucracies; to interfere with personal freedom of choice and movement; and to concentrate too much power in the hands of a distant and unresponsive State. Most Americans have experienced (or read about) enough bureaucratic abuses, both here and abroad, to have developed a deep and understandable concern about the potential threats from an increased role for government — even a well-intentioned government — that planning seems to involve.

These are certainly legitimate worries. But, like most important social concerns, there are no easy answers. Simply opting to limit the role of *public* planning will not eliminate these dangers in a society dominated by great concentrations of *private* power. Moreover, the demand for a reduced role for government in the American economy has often been accompanied by a simultaneous demand for a greater role for government in regulating private life. Again, the realistic issue is not whether there will *be* planning in America — but *who* will do it, and in the service of what values and social ends.

Ultimately, the only effective way to diminish the potential for abuse is through the careful development of mechanisms to extend the principles of democracy and accountability to economic life. Sometimes this may mean *decentralizing* the mechanisms of economic planning to bring decision-making power closer to the communities where Americans live and the workplaces where they earn their livings (Faux, 1982). (One example — workers' participation in decisions about the introduction of new technology — is presented on pages 508 to 509.) More generally, it will require what Michael Harrington (1981, p. 326) has called the "democratization of information": ensuring that ordinary people, as workers and citizens, have access to the information that will enable them to participate effectively in the decisions that will govern the fate of their jobs, families, and communities.

Again, the questions raised for American social policy by the tensions of planning versus democracy, public decision making versus individual autonomy, are not the kind that permit simple answers. In one form or another, they are sure to be a focus of critical public debate for many years to come. For us, what's important in this book is not to try to produce a blueprint for the future, but to reaffirm the point we began with in Chapter 1: Social science, as we understand it, has an important role to play in helping to provide the tools for participation in what we hope will become an increasingly open and democratic debate over America's future.

We noted in the beginning of this book that one distinctive contribution of social science is that it teaches us about the constraints on human action. Properly understood, it also teaches us about human possibilities. It demonstrates, even in the face of confusion and cynicism, that things need not necessarily be the way they are. It does so by, among other things, demonstrating that things are done differently — and often quite effectively — in societies very much like our own, as we've seen over and over again throughout this book. And it also shows that within any given society, the effects of deliberate social action are often both tangible and significant. No abstract beneficent force, whether the "invisible hand" of the "market" or the march of historical inevitability, caused the dramatic reduction in infant deaths, the beginnings of regulation of toxic wastes, or the tripling of the number of women lawyers that we achieved during the 1970s. The limits of social action are real ones, and they can often seem overwhelming. But the possibilities are real ones, too; and it is arguable that it is when we make the most of them that we become most fully human. A thought from the late biologist and environmental activist Rene Dubos (1981, p. 9) may be an appropriate way to end a book about social problems; "We cannot escape the past," Dubos wrote, "but neither can we avoid inventing the future."

The Strategy of Social Reconstruction   **519**

Summary

This final chapter has considered some directions American social policy might take in the future, based on the analysis of earlier chapters. At least three broad approaches, or strategies, have emerged:

1. The strategy of "reprivatization" emphasizes reducing the role of government (except in defense) and relying on the forces of the market to deal with social problems. Though American society already lags behind other industrial countries in the development of social welfare measures, this approach would reduce them still further. Reprivatization accepts social inequality and environmental disruption as necessary costs of economic growth. But it's not clear that this strategy could actually deliver the long-term economic growth it promises.

2. The strategy of "revitalization" would make more explicit use of government planning to direct economic growth and improve America's competitiveness in the world economy. But such a strategy leaves many unanswered questions about its ability to generate adequate employment or to address the problems of social inequality.

3. The strategy of "social reconstruction" also argues for substantial planning — but planning that includes a basic commitment to full employment, to overcoming the inequalities of gender and race, to improving the welfare state, and to achieving a more rational balance between military and domestic spending.

For Further Reading

Bluestone, Barry, Lester Thurow, and Harley Shaiken. "Roundtable: Re-industrialization and Jobs." *Working Papers*, November-December, 1980.

Carnoy, Martin, and Derek Shearer. *Economic Democracy*. White Plains, New York: M. E. Sharpe, 1980.

Furniss, Norman, and Timothy Tilton. *The Case for the Welfare State*. Bloomington: Indiana University Press, 1977.

Harrington, Michael. "A Path for America," *Dissent*, Fall 1982.

Reich, Robert. "The Next American Frontier," *Atlantic*, April 1983.

Zwerdling, Daniel. *Workplace Democracy*. New York: Harper & Row, 1980.

Bibliography

Adams, Gordon. "The B-1: Bomber for All Seasons?" *Council on Economic Priorities Newsletter*, February 1982.

———, and Geoff Quinn. "The Iron Triangle: The Politics of Defense Contracting." *Council on Economic Priorities Newsletter*, June 1981.

Aday, LuAnn, Ronald Anderson, and Gretchen V. Fleming. *Health Care in the United States: Equitable for Whom?* Beverly Hills, Calif.: Sage, 1980.

Alexander, Tom. "A Simpler Path to a Cleaner Environment." *Fortune*, May 4, 1981.

Alperovitz, Gar. "The New Inflation." *Annals of the American Academy of Political and Social Science*, July 1981.

American Council on Life Insurance. *Women in the Labor Force*. New York: American Council on Life Insurance, 1981.

Amidei, Nancy. Testimony, U.S. Congress, House, Committee on Energy and Commerce, Subcommittee on Health and the Environment, October 1981.

Anderson, A. "Neurotoxic Follies." *Psychology Today*, July 1982.

Anderson, Bernard. "Economic Patterns in Black America." In National Urban League, *The State of Black America, 1982*. New York: National Urban League, 1982.

Anderson, Jack. "Big Spenders." *San Francisco Chronicle*, January 10, 1983.

Anderson, K. *Wartime Women: Sex Roles, Family Relations, and the Status of Women during World War II*. Westport, Conn.: Greenwood, 1981.

Anderson, Martin. *Welfare*. Stanford, Calif.: Hoover Institute, 1980.

Anton, Thomas, John Oppenheim, and Lance Morrow. "Where the Shoe Pinches: The 1983 Reagan Budget." *Economic Outlook USA*, Spring 1982.

Auletta, Ken. *The Streets Were Paved with Gold*. New York: Random House, 1979.

———. *The Underclass*. New York: Random House, 1981.

Bahr, Stephen J. "Family Determinants and Effects of Deviance." In Wesley R. Burr, et al., *Contemporary Theories about the Family*. New York: Free Press, 1979.

521

Bane, Mary Jo. *Here to Stay*. New York: Basic Books, 1976.

——, et al. "Child Care Arrangements of Working Parents." *Monthly Labor Review*, October 1979.

Barnet, Richard. *Real Security*. New York: Simon and Schuster, 1981.

——. "Ritual Dance of the Superpowers." *The Nation*, April 9, 1983.

Barrett, Nancy. "Women in the Job Market: Occupations, Earnings, and Career Opportunities." In Ralph Smith, ed., *The Subtle Revolution*. Washington, D.C.: The Urban Institute, 1979a.

——. "Women in the Job Market: Unemployment and Work Schedules." In Ralph Smith, ed., *The Subtle Revolution*. Washington, D.C.: The Urban Institute, 1979b.

Beck, E. M. "Labor Unionism and Racial Income Inequality." *American Journal of Sociology*, January 1980.

Beckett, J. O., and A. D. Smith. "Work and Family Roles: Egalitarian Marriage in Black and White Families." *Social Service Review*, June 1981.

Bell, Daniel. *The Coming of Post-Industrial Society*. New York: Basic Books, 1969.

Bendick, Marc, Jr. "Employment, Training, and Economic Development." In John L. Palmer and Isabel Sawhill, eds., *The Reagan Experiment*. Washington, D.C.: The Urban Institute, 1982.

——, and Judith R. Devine. "Workers Dislocated by Economic Change: Do They Need Federal Employment and Training Assistance?" In National Commission for Employment Policy, *7th Annual Report*. Washington, D.C.: National Commission for Employment Policy, 1981.

Beverage Industry. "Estimated Share of Market for Major Brewers." December 31, 1982.

Bianchi, Suzanne. *Household Composition and Racial Inequality*. New Brunswick, N.J.: Rutgers University Press, 1981.

Birch, David. "Who Creates Jobs?" *Public Interest*, 1982.

Bishop, John H. "Jobs, Cash Transfers, and Marital Instability: A Review and Synthesis of the Evidence." *Journal of Human Resources*, Summer 1980.

Blau, Francine D. *Equal Pay in the Office*. Lexington, Mass.: Lexington Books, 1977.

——. "The Data on Women Workers: Past, Present, and Future." In Ann H. Stromberg and Shirley Harkness, eds., *Women Working: Theories and Facts in Perspective*. Palo Alto, Calif.: Mayfield, 1978.

Blau, Judith, and Peter Blau. "The Cost of Inequality: Metropolitan Structure and Violent Crime." *American Sociological Review*, February 1982.

Blaustein, Arthur I., ed. *The American Promise: Equal Justice and Economic Opportunity*. New Brunswick, N.J.: Transaction Books, 1982.

Block, Donald. "Discussion: Violence in the Family." In A. Green, ed., *Violence and the Family*. Boulder, Colo.: Westview Press, 1980.

Block, Richard, and Carolyn Block. "Decisions and Data: The Transformation of Robbery Incidents into Official Robbery Statistics." *Journal of Criminal Law and Criminology*, Winter 1980.

Bluestone, Barry, and Bennett Harrison. *The Deindustrialization of America*. New York: Basic Books, 1982.

——, Lester Thurow, and Harley Shaiken. "Roundtable: Reindustrialization and Jobs." *Working Papers*, November-December, 1980.

Blumberg, Paul. *Inequality in an Age of Decline*. New York: Oxford University Press, 1980.

Blumstein, Alfred. "On the Racial Disproportionality of U.S. Prison Populations." *Journal of Criminal Law and Criminology*, Fall 1982.

——, Jacqueline Cohen, and Daniel Nagin, eds. *Deterrence and Incapacitation*. Washington, D.C.: National Academy of Sciences, 1978.

Bock, Betty. "How Big Are the Big Companies?" In U.S. Congress, Senate, Judiciary Committee, Subcommittee on Antitrust, Monopoly, and Business Rights, *Hearings on Mergers and Economic Concentration*, March-April 1979.

Boland, Barbara. "Incapacitation of the Dangerous Offender: The Arithmetic Is Not So Simple." *Journal of Research in Crime and Delinquency*, January 1978.

Bonacich, Edna, and John Modell. *The Economic Basis of Ethnic Solidarity: Small Business in the Japanese-American Community*. Berkeley, Calif.: University of California Press, 1981.

Borus, Michael. "Willingness to Work among Youth." *Journal of Human Resources*, Fall 1982.

Bowers, Norman. "Young and Marginal: An Overview of Youth Unemployment." *Monthly Labor Review*, October 1979.

———. "Tracking Youth Joblessness." *Monthly Labor Review*, February 1982.

Braithwaite, John, and Valerie Braithwaite. "The Effect of Income Inequality and Social Democracy on Homicide." *British Journal of Criminology*, January 1980.

———, and Gilbert Geis. "On Theory and Action for Corporate Crime Control." *Crime and Delinquency*, April 1982.

Braverman, Harry. *Labor and Monopoly Capital: The Degradation of Work in the Twentieth Century*. New York: Monthly Review Press, 1974.

Brenner, M. Harvey. "Fetal, Infant, and Maternal Mortality during Periods of Economic Instability." *International Journal of Health Services*, Summer 1973a.

———. *Mental Illness and the Economy*. Cambridge, Mass.: Harvard University Press, 1973b.

———. *Estimating the Social Costs of National Economic Policy*. U.S. Congress, Joint Economic Committee, 1976.

Brittain, John A. *Inheritance and the Inequality of Material Wealth*. Washington, D.C.: Brookings Institution, 1978.

Brock, Horace W. "Mortgaging the Future." *San Francisco Chronicle*, April 13, 1983.

Brown, Charles, Curtis Gilroy, and Andrew Cohen. "The Effect of the Minimum Wage on Employment and Unemployment." *Journal of Economic Literature*, June 20, 1982.

Brown, Michael, and Steven Erie. "Blacks and the Legacy of the Great Society." *Public Policy*, Spring 1982.

Browning, Edgar. "How Much More Equality Can We Afford?" *Public Interest*, Spring 1976.

Budd, Edward C. Prepared statement in U.S. Congress, Joint Economic Committee, Hearings on *The 1982 Joint Economic Report of the President*, Part 2, February 1982.

Budetti, Peter, John Butler, and Peggy McManus. "Federal Health Program Reforms: Implications for Child Health Care." San Francisco: Institute for Health Policy Studies, School of Medicine, University of California, 1981.

Bundy, McGeorge, et al. "Nuclear Weapons and the Atlantic Alliance." *Foreign Affairs*, Spring 1982.

Burgess, S. L. "Female Heads of Household: Their Prospects for Homeownership." *Journal of Home Economics*, Winter 1980.

Burmaster, David. "The New Pollution: Groundwater Contamination." *Environment*, March 1982.

Burnham, Walter D. *The Current Crisis in American Politics*. New York: Oxford University Press, 1983.

Burr, Wesley. In U.S. Congress, Senate, Committee on Labor and Human Resources, Hearings on *Work Ethic: Materialism and the American Family*, March 1982.

Business Week. *The Decline of U.S. Power (and What We Can Do about It)*. New York: Houghton-Mifflin, 1980a.

———. "An Oil Giant's Dilemma." August 25, 1980b.

———. Special Issue on "Reindustrialization." June 14, 1980d.

———. "Robots Join the Labor Force." June 9, 1980c.

———. "The Shrinking Standard of Living." April 8, 1980e.

———. "The Built-In Deficit." August 16, 1982a.

———. "Corporate Balance Sheet Scoreboard, 1981." March 1, 1982b.

———. "Guns vs. Butter: Special Report." November 29, 1982c.

———. "The Fallout from Whoops." July 11, 1983.

Caplow, Theodore, et al. *Middletown Families: Fifty Years of Change and Continuity*. Minneapolis: University of Minnesota Press, 1982.

Carnoy, Martin, and Derek Shearer. *Economic Democracy*. White Plains, N.Y.: M. E. Sharpe, 1980.

Carter, Luther. "The Radwaste Paradox." *Science*, January 1, 1983.

Case, John. *Understanding Inflation*. New York: Penguin, 1981.

Catalano, Ralph, and David Dooley. "Economic Predictors of Depressed Mood and Stressful Life Events in a Metropolitan Community." *Journal of Health and Social Behavior*, September 1977.

———, ———, and R. Jackson. "Economic Predictors of Admissions to Mental Health Facilities in a Non-Metropolitan Community." *Journal of Health and Social Behavior*, October 1981.

Center for Defense Information. *U.S. Military Force, 1980: An Evaluation*, Washington, D.C.: Center for Defense Information, 1980.

———. "U.S. Weapons Exports Headed for Record Level." *Defense Monitor*, no. 3, 1982.

———. "The Need for a Level Military Budget." *Defense Monitor*, no. 2, 1983.

Chapman, Stephen. "Endless Political Payoff to the Farming Interests." *San Francisco Examiner*, July 27, 1980, p. B-3.

Cherlin, Andrew. *Marriage, Divorce, Remarriage*. Cambridge, Mass.: Harvard University Press, 1981.

———, and Pamela Walters. "Trends in United States Men's and Women's Sex-Role Attitudes, 1972–1978." *American Sociological Review*, August 1981.

Chernow, Ron. "Grey Flannel Goons: The Latest in Union Busting." *Working Papers*, January-February 1981.

Chess, Stella, et al. "Early Parental Attitudes, Divorce and Separation, and Young Adult Outcomes: Findings of a Longitudinal Study." *Journal of the American Academy of Child Psychology*, January 1983.

Children's Defense Fund. Testimony, U.S. Congress, House, Subcommittee on Health, Energy, and Commerce, October 1981.

———. *Children's Defense Budget*. Washington, D.C.: Children's Defense Fund, 1982.

Choate, Pat, and Susan Walter. *America in Ruins: Beyond the Public Works Pork Barrel*. Washington, D.C.: Council of State Planning Agencies, 1981.

Clark, Kim B., and Lawrence Summers. "Unemployment Reconsidered." Harvard Business Review, November-December 1980.

Clinard, Marshall A. *Cities with Little Crime*. London: Cambridge University Press, 1978.

———, and Peter Yeager. *Corporate Crime*. New York: Free Press, 1980.

Cloward, Richard, and Lloyd Ohlin. *Delinquency and Opportunity*. New York: Free Press, 1959.

Coates, James. "Pentagon Feeling Heat from Fiscal Conservatives." *San Francisco Chronicle*, July 24, 1983.

Cobb, Sidney. "Physiological Changes in Men Whose Jobs Were Abolished." *Journal of Psychosomatic Research*, August 1974.

Cole, Robert. *Work, Mobility and Participation: A Comparative Study of American and Japanese Industry*. Berkeley: University of California Press, 1979.

Common Cause. *Gimme Shelters*. Washington, D.C.: *Common Cause*, May 1978.

———. "Throwing Money at Weapons." *Common Cause*, May-June 1983.

Commoner, Barry. *The Closing Circle*. New York: Bantam, 1971.

———. *The Politics of Energy*. New York: Knopf, 1980.

Conference Board. *The World's Multinationals: A Global Challenge*. New York: Conference Board, 1981.

Congressional Quarterly. *Environment and Health*. Washington, D.C.: Congressional Quarterly, 1981.

Conrad, John, Stephan Van Dine, and Simon Dinitz. *Restraining the Wicked: The Incapacitation of the Dangerous Offender*. Lexington, Mass.: Lexington Books, 1979.

Conservation Foundation. *Siting New Industry, An Environmental Perspective*. Washington, D.C.: Conservation Foundation, 1982a.

————. *The State of the Environment—1982.* Washington, D.C.: Conservation Foundation, 1982b.

Cook, Alice. "Collective Bargaining as a Strategy for Achieving Equal Opportunity and Equal Pay." In Ronnie Steinberg Ratner, ed., *Equal Employment Policy for Women.* Philadelphia: Temple University Press, 1980.

Cooper, David. *The Death of the Family.* New York: Vintage, 1970.

Corcoran, Mary, and Martha S. Hill. "Persistence in Unemployment among Adult Men." In Greg Duncan and James Morgan, eds., *5000 American Families, Patterns of Economic Progress,* Vol. 8. Ann Arbor: University of Michigan Institute for Social Research, 1980.

Cornelius, Wayne A. "Mexican Migration to the United States." In Jerome H. Skolnick and Elliott Currie, eds., *Crisis in American Institutions,* 5th ed. Boston: Little, Brown, 1982.

Cornell, C. P., and R. J. Gelles. "Adolescent to Parent Violence." *Urban and Social Change Review,* Winter 1982.

Council on Economic Priorities. *Jobs and Energy.* New York: Council on Economic Priorities, 1979.

————. "Occupational Safety and Health in the Chemical Industry." *Newsletter,* November 1981.

Council on Environmental Quality. *Environmental Quality, 1980.* Washington, D.C.: Government Printing Office, December 1980.

————. *Environmental Quality, 1981.* Washington, D.C.: Government Printing Office, December 1981.

————. *The Global 2000 Report to the President.* Washington, D.C.: Government Printing Office, 1982.

Crosby, Faye, et al. "Recent Unobtrusive Studies of Black and White Discrimination and Prejudice: A Literature Review." *Psychological Bulletin,* May 1980.

Currie, Elliott. "Fighting Crime." *Working Papers,* July-August 1982.

————, Robert Dunn, and David Fogarty. "The Fading American Dream: Economic Crisis and the New Inequality." In Jerome H. Skolnick and Elliott Currie, eds., *Crisis in American Institutions,* 5th ed. Boston: Little, Brown, 1982.

————, and Paul Rosenstiel. "Six Myths about Unemployment," Third Century America Project. Berkeley: University of California, 1979.

Curtin, Richard, and Thomas Neubig. "Asset Ownership," Survey of Consumer Attitudes, Working Paper No. 3. Ann Arbor: University of Michigan Survey Research Center, 1979.

Dam, Kenneth W. "Ensuring Security in the Nuclear Age." *Department of State Bulletin,* April 1983.

Danziger, Sheldon, Robert H. Havemann, and Robert Plotnick. "How Income Transfer Programs Affect Work, Savings, and the Income Distribution: A Critical Review." *Journal of Economic Literature,* September 1981.

————, and Robert Plotnick. "Demographic Change, Government Transfers, and Income Distribution." *Monthly Labor Review,* April 1977.

Darity, William. "The Human Capital Approach to Black/White Earnings Inequality: Some Unsettled Questions." *Journal of Human Resources,* Spring 1982.

Darmstadter, Joel. "Intercountry Comparisons of Energy Use: Implications for U.S. Policy." In Karen Gentemann, ed., *Social and Political Perspectives on Energy Policy.* New York: Praeger, 1981.

Datcher, Linda. "Effects of Community and Family Background on Achievement." *Review of Economics and Statistics,* February 1982.

Davis, Devra Lee. "Cancer in the Workplace: The Case for Prevention." *Environment,* July-August 1981.

Davis, J. (President of Winn-Dixie Supermarkets.) Quoted in *The Progressive,* July 1980, p. 11.

Davis, Karen, M. Gold, and Diane Makuc. "Access to Health Care for the Poor: Does the Gap Remain?" *Annual Review of Public Health,* Vol. 2, 1981.

————, and Cathy Schoen. *Health and the War on Poverty, A Ten-Year Appraisal.* Washington, D.C.: Brookings Institution, 1978.

DeGrasse, Robert. "Military Buildup Exacts Toll on Economy." *Council on Economic Priorities Newsletter*, May 1983a.

———. *Military Expansion, Economic Decline*. New York: Council on Economic Priorities, 1983b.

———, and Paul Murphy. "Impact of Reagan's Rearmament." *Council on Economic Priorities Newsletter*, May 1981.

Democratic Caucus, U.S. House of Representatives. *Rebuilding the Road to Opportunity: Turning Point for America's Economy*. Washington, D.C.: Government Printing Office, July 20, 1982.

Denton, Senator Jeremiah (D-Ala.). Statement, U.S. Congress, Senate, Committee on Labor and Human Resources, Hearings on *Work Ethic: Materialism and the American Family*, March 1982.

Derr, Patrick, et al. "Worker/Public Protection: The Double Standard." *Environment*, September 1981.

Dobash, Russel P., and R. Emerson Dobash. "Community Response to Violence Against Wives: Charivari, Abstract Justice and Patriarchy." *Social Problems*, June 1981.

Domhoff, G. William. *The Bohemian Grove: A Study in Ruling Class Cohesiveness*. New York: Harper & Row, 1974.

———. *The Higher Circles: Governing Class in America*. New York: Vintage, 1970.

Dooley, Martin, and Peter Gottschalk. "Does a Younger Male Labor Force Mean Greater Earnings Inequality?" *Monthly Labor Review*, November 1982.

DuBoff, Richard. "The New Economic Mythology." *Commonweal*, July 4, 1980.

Dubos, Rene. "The Wooing of Earth." *EPA Journal*, February 1981.

Duncan, Beverly, and Otis Dudley Duncan. *Sex Typing and Social Roles: A Research Report*. New York: Academic Press, 1978.

Duncan, Greg J. "An Overview of Family Economic Mobility." *Economic Outlook USA*, Spring 1981.

———, and Richard Coe. *The Dynamics of Welfare*. Ann Arbor: Survey Research Center, University of Michigan, 1981.

Duxbury, M. L., and S. J. Shelendick. "Contemporary Working Women on the Treadmill." In S. B. Day, ed., *Life Stress*. New York: Van Nostrand Reinhold, 1982.

Early, Steve, and Matt Witt. "How European Unions Cope with New Technology." *Monthly Labor Review*, September 1982.

Edelman, Marian Wright. "Growing Up Black in America." In National Urban League, *The State of Black America*. New York: National Urban League, 1981.

Edelstein, Michael. *The Economic Impact of Military Spending*. New York: Council on Economic Priorities, 1977.

Ehrlich, Isaac. "The Economic Approach to Crime: A Preliminary Assessment." In Sheldon L. Messinger and Egon Bittner, eds., *Criminology Review Yearbook*. Beverly Hills, Calif.: Sage, 1979.

Employment Research Associates. *The Price of the Pentagon*. Lansing, Mich.: Employment Research Associates, 1982.

Employment and Training Reporter. August 1982.

Environmental Defense Fund and Robert H. Boyle, (1979). *Malignant Neglect*, New York, Knopf.

Epstein, Samuel. *The Politics of Cancer*. New York: Doubleday, 1980.

Erez, Edna. "Planning of Crime and the Criminal Career." *Journal of Criminal Law and Criminology*, Spring 1980.

Executive Office of the President. *America's New Beginning: A Program for Economic Recovery*. Washington, D.C.: Government Printing Office, February 1981.

Fallows, James. *National Defense*. New York: Random House, 1982.

Faux, Jeff. "Who Plans?" *Working Papers*, November-December 1982.

———. "By Deficits Possessed." *The New Republic*, February 14, 1983.

Federal Bureau of Investigation. *Crime in the United States—1981*. Washington, D.C.: Government Printing Office, 1982.

Feldstein, Martin. "The Economics of the New Unemployment." *The Public Interest*, Fall 1973.

———. "The Private and Social Costs of Unemployment." *American Economic Review*, May 1978.

Fingerhut, L. A., R. W. Wilson, and J. J. Feldman. "Health and Disease in the United States." *Annual Review of Public Health, 1980*, 1981.

Forbes. "Annual Directory Issue: The *Forbes* 500's." May 9, 1983.

Forcier, Michael, and Andrew Hahn. "The Impact of Employment and Training Programs on the Work Attitudes of Disadvantaged Youth." In National Center for Research on Vocational Education, *Youth Employability: Monographs on Research and Policy Studies*. Columbus, Ohio: National Center for Research on Vocational Education, 1982.

Fortune. "The *Fortune* Directory of the 500 Largest U.S. Industrial Corporations, 1979." May 5, 1980.

———. "The Largest Industrial Companies in the World." August 23, 1982.

———. "The *Fortune* Directory of the 500 Largest U.S. Industrial Corporations, 1982." May 2, 1983.

Freedman, Marcia. "The Structure of the Labor Market and Associated Training Patterns." In National Society for the Study of Education, *Education and Work*. Chicago: University of Chicago Press, 1982.

Freeman, A. Myrick. *The Benefits of Environmental Improvement*. Baltimore: Johns Hopkins University Press, 1979.

Freeman, Richard B. *The Declining Economic Value of Higher Education and the American Social System*. New York: Aspen Institute for Humanistic Studies, 1976a.

———. *The Overeducated American*. New York: Academic, 1976b.

———. "Black Economic Progress since 1964." *Public Interest*, Summer 1978a.

———. "Discrimination in the Academic Marketplace." In Thomas Sowell, ed., *Essays and Data on American Ethnic Groups*. Washington, D.C.: Urban Institute, 1978b.

———. "Why Is There a Youth Labor Market Problem?" In American Assembly, *Youth Unemployment and Public Policy*. Englewood Cliffs, N.J.: Prentice-Hall, 1980.

———. "Troubled Workers in the Labor Market." In National Commission for Employment Policy, *7th Annual Report*. Washington, D.C.: National Commission for Employment Policy, 1981.

Friedan, Betty. *The Feminine Mystique*. New York: Norton, 1963.

———. *The Second Stage*. New York: Summit, 1981.

Friedman, Milton. *Free to Choose*. New York: Harcourt Brace Jovanovich, 1980.

Friends of the Earth et al. *Ronald Reagan and the American Environment*. San Francisco: Friends of the Earth, 1982.

Fuchs, Victor. "The Economics of Health in a Post-Industrial Society." *Public Interest*, Fall 1979.

Furniss, Norman, and Timothy Tilton. *The Case for the Welfare State*. Bloomington: Indiana University Press, 1977.

Furstenburg, Frank. "Work Experience and Family Life." In James O'Toole, ed., *Work and the Quality of Life*. Cambridge, Mass.: Harvard University Press, 1974.

Galbraith, John Kenneth. *The Affluent Society*. Boston: Houghton Mifflin, 1957.

———. *The New Industrial State*. Boston: Houghton Mifflin, 1967.

———. *Economics and the Public Purpose*. Boston: Houghton Mifflin, 1973.

Gallup Poll. Cited in *Emerging Trends*, September 1982.

Gansler, Jacques. *The Defense Industry*. Cambridge, Mass.: MIT Press, 1980.

Garbarino, James. "An Ecological Approach to Child Maltreatment." In Leroy H. Pelton, ed., *The Social Context of Child Abuse and Neglect*. New York: Human Sciences Press, 1981.

Gartner, Timothy. "Bay Area Firms Loaded with Cash." *San Francisco Chronicle*, January 16, 1981.

Gelles, R. J., and E. F. Hargreaves. "Maternal Employment and Violence Toward Children." *Journal of Family Issues*, December 1981.

Gerth, Hans H., and C. Wright Mills, eds. *From Max Weber: Essays in Sociology*. New York: Oxford University Press, 1954.

Gettys, L. D., and A. Cann. "Children's Perceptions of Occupational Sex Stereotypes." *Sex Roles*, March 1981.

Gilder, George. *Wealth and Poverty*. New York: Basic Books, 1981.

Ginzberg, Eli. "The Job Problem." *Scientific American*, November 1977.

——, and George J. Vojta. "The Service Sector of the U.S. Economy." *Scientific American*, March 1981.

Glazer, Nathan. *Affirmative Discrimination*. New York: Basic Books, 1977.

——. "Culture and Mobility." *New Republic*, July 4 and 11, 1981.

Goetting, Ann. "Divorce Outcome Research: Issues and Perspectives." In Arlene S. Skolnick and Jerome H. Skolnick, *Family in Transition*, 4th ed. Boston: Little, Brown, 1983.

Gold, David, and Geoff Quinn. "Misguided Expenditure." *Council on Economic Priorities Newsletter*, July 1981.

Goldberg, Steven. *The Inevitability of Patriarchy*. New York: Morrow, 1974.

Goodman, Paul. *Growing Up Absurd*. New York: Random House, 1958.

——. *New Reformation: Notes of a Neolithic Conservative*. New York: Random House, 1970.

Gordon, David. *The Working Poor: Towards a State Agenda*. Washington, D.C.: Council of State Planning Agencies, 1979.

Gortmaker, Steven. "Poverty and Infant Mortality in the United States." *American Sociological Review*, 44, 1979.

Gottschalk, Peter. "Have We Already Lost the War on Poverty?" In U.S. Congress, Joint Economic Committee, Hearings on *The 1982 Joint Economic Report of the President*, 1982.

Gough, Ian. *The Political Economy of the Welfare State*. London: Macmillan, 1979.

Gouldner, Alvin. "Discussion." *Social Policy*, November-December 1979.

Governor's Task Force on Civil Rights. *Report*. Sacramento, Calif.: California State Department of Fair Employment and Housing, 1982.

Green, Edward, and Russell Wakefield. "Patterns of Middle- and Upper-Class Homicide." *Journal of Criminal Law and Criminology*, Summer 1979.

Green, Mark. "Richer than All Their Tribe." *New Republic*, January 6 and 13, 1982a.

——. *Winning Back America*. New York: Bantam, 1982b.

Green, Philip. *The Pursuit of Inequality*. New York: Pantheon, 1980.

Greene, Richard. "Tracking Job Growth in Private Industry." *Monthly Labor Review*, September 1982.

Greenwood, Peter, and Allan Abrahamse. *Selective Incapacitation*. Santa Monica, Calif.: Rand Corporation, 1982.

Grier, Eunice. "Energy Pricing Policies and the Poor." In Ellis Cose, ed., *Energy and Equity*. Washington, D.C.: Joint Center for Political Studies, 1979.

Grossman, Allyson Sherman. "More than Half of All Children Have Working Mothers." *Monthly Labor Review*, February 1982.

——, and Howard M. Hayghe. "Labor Force Activity of Women Receiving Child Support or Alimony." *Monthly Labor Review*, November 1982.

Grossman, Michael. "Government and Health Outcomes." *American Economic Review*, May 1982.

Grunwald, Henry M. "American Renewal." *Fortune*, March 9, 1981.

Guzzard, Walter. "The Right Way to Strive for Equality." *Fortune*, March 9, 1981.

Hagan, John L., and Ilene H. Nagel. "White-Collar crime, White-Collar Time: The Sentencing of White-Collar Offenders in the Southern District of New York." *American Criminal Law Review*, Spring 1982.

Haggard, Merle. "Are the Good Times Really Over for Good?" (c) 1982.

Hannan, Michael, and Nancy B. Tuma. "Income and Independence Effects on Marital Dissolution: Results from the Seattle and Denver Income Maintenance Experiments." *American Journal of Sociology*, November 1978.

Hanushek, Eric. "Sources of Black-White Earnings Differences." *Social Science Research*, June 1982.

Harburg, Ernest, et al. "Socioecological Stress, Suppressed Hostility, Skin Color, and Black-White Male Blood Pressure." *Psychosomatic Medicine*, 35, 1973.

Harrington, Michael. *Decade of Decision*. New York: Simon and Schuster, 1980.

———. "A Path for America." *Dissent*, Fall 1982a.

———. "Why the Welfare State Breaks Down." In Irving Howe, ed., *Beyond the Welfare State*. New York: Schocken, 1982b.

Hartung, William. *Weapons for the World: 1982 Update*. New York: Council on Economic Priorities, 1982.

Harvey, Robert E. "Can Small Business Get More Defense Contracts?" *Iron Age*, March 10, 1982.

Hatch, John, and Tony Whitehead. "Increasing Energy Costs and the Poor: New Challenges for Community Organizations." In Karen Gentemann, ed., *Social and Political Perspectives on Energy Policy*. New York: Praeger, 1981.

Hatcher, Gordon. *Universal Free Health Care in Canada, 1947–1977*. Washington, D.C.: U.S. Department of Health and Human Services, 1981.

Hattis, Dale, Robert Goble, and Nicholas Ashford. "Airborne Lead: A Clearcut Case of Differential Protection." *Environment*, January-February 1982.

Havemann, Robert H. "Unemployment in Western Europe and the U.S." *American Economic Review*, May 1978.

———, and Gregory Christianson. "Environmental Regulations and Productivity Growth." In Henry Peskin, Paul Portney, and Allan Kneese, eds., *Environmental Regulation and the U.S. Economy*. Baltimore: Johns Hopkins University Press, 1981.

Hayes, Robert, and Robert Abernathy. "Managing Our Way to Decline." *Harvard Business Review*, September-October 1980.

Hayghe, Howard. "Husbands and Wives as Earners: An Analysis of Family Data." *Monthly Labor Review*, February 1981.

Hayward, Jack. *Trade Unions and Politics in Western Europe*. London: Frank Cass, 1980.

Hefferan, Colien. "Workload of Married Women." *Family Economics Review*, Summer 1982.

Heilbroner, Robert, and Lester Thurow. *Five Economic Challenges*. Englewood Cliffs, N.J.: Prentice-Hall, 1981.

Henle, Peter, and Paul Ryscavage. "The Distribution of Earned Income among Men and Women, 1958–77." *Monthly Labor Review*, April 1981.

Herman, Edward S. *Corporate Control, Corporate Power*. London: Cambridge University Press, 1981.

Herzog, Regula. "High School Seniors' Occupational Plans and Values: Trends in Sex Differences, 1976 through 1980." *Sociology of Education*, January 1982.

Hetherington, E. M., et al. "The Aftermath of Divorce." In J. H. Stevens and M. Mathews, eds., *Mother-Child, Father-Child Relations*. Washington, D.C.: National Association for the Education of Young Children, 1978.

Hicks, L. E., et al. "Cognitive and Health Measures Following Early Nutritional Supplementation." *American Journal of Public Health*, October 1982.

Hill, Martha S. "Authority at Work: How Men and Women Differ." In *Five Thousand American Families: Patterns of Economic Progress*, Vol. 8. Ann Arbor: Survey Research Center, University of Michigan, 1980.

———, and Mary Corcoran. "Unemployment among Family Men: A 10-Year Longitudinal Study." *Monthly Labor Review*, November 1979.

Hindelang, Michael J. "Variations in Rates of Offending." *American Sociological Review*, August 1981.

———, Travis Hirschi, and Joseph Weis. "Correlates of Delinquency: The Illusion of Discrepancy Between Self-Report and Official Measures." *American Sociological Review*, June 1979.

Hofferth, Sandra L., and Kristin Moore. "Women's Employment and Marriage." In Ralph Smith, ed., *The Subtle Revolution*. Washington, D.C.: The Urban Institute, 1979.

Hoffman, Carl, and John S. Reed. "Sex Discrimination? The XYZ Affair." *Public Interest*, Winter 1981.

Hofstadter, Richard. *Social Darwinism in American Thought*. Boston: Beacon, 1955.

Holloway, David. "War, Militarism, and the Soviet State." In E. P. Thompson and Dan Smith, eds., *Protest and Survive*. New York: Monthly Review Press, 1981.

Home Office (Great Britain). *Taking Offenders Out of Circulation*, Research Study No. 64. London: Home Office, 1980.

Horowitz, Bernard, and Isabel Wolock. "Material Deprivation, Child Maltreatment, and Agency Interventions among Poor Families." In Leroy H. Pelton, ed., *The Social Context of Child Abuse and Neglect*. New York: Human Sciences Press, 1981.

Howard, Robert. "Brave New Workplace." *Working Papers*, November-December, 1980.

Huber, J., and G. Spitze. "Wives' Employment, Household Behaviors, and Sex Role Attitudes." *Social Forces*, September 1981.

Humphrey, Melvin. "Minorities in the Energy Industries." In Ellis Cose, ed., *Energy and Equity: Some Social Concerns*. Washington, D.C.: Joint Center for Political Studies, 1979.

Illich, Ivan. *Medical Nemesis*. New York: Pantheon, 1978.

Jencks, Christopher. "Discrimination and Thomas Sowell." *New York Review of Books*, March 3, 1983.

Joe, Tom. *Profiles of Families in Poverty: Effects of the Fiscal Year 1983 Budget Proposals on the Poor*. Washington, D.C.: Center for the Study of Social Policy, February 1982.

Joel, Billy. "Allentown." (c) CBS, Inc., 1982.

Junkerman, John. "Japan-Worship." *Working Papers*, January-February 1982.

Kagan, Jerome, Richard Kearsley, and Philip R. Zelazo. *Infancy: Its Place in Human Development*. Cambridge, Mass.: Harvard University Press, 1978.

Kaldor, Mary. *Baroque Arsenal*. New York: Hill and Wang, 1981.

Kamata, Satoshi. *Japan in the Passing Lane*. New York: Pantheon, 1982.

Kamerman, Sheila B. *Parenting in an Unresponsive Society*. New York: Free Press, 1980.

Karch, Nathan, and Marvin Schneiderman. *Explaining the Urban Factor in Lung Cancer Mortality*. Washington, D.C.: National Resources Defense Council, 1981.

Kasl, Stanislav, Susan Gore, and Sidney Cobb. "The Experience of Losing a Job: Reported Changes in Health, Symptoms, and Illness Behavior." *Psychosomatic Medicine*, March-April 1975.

Kazis, Richard, and Richard Grossman. "Environmental Protection: Job-Taker or Job-Maker?" *Environment*, November 1982.

Keithan, Charles F. *The Brewing Industry*. Washington, D.C.: Bureau of Economics, Federal Trade Commission, 1979.

Kelling, George, et al. *The Kansas City Preventive Patrol Experiment*. Washington, D.C.: Police Foundation, 1974.

———, and Mark Moore. "To Serve and Protect: Learning from Police History." *Public Interest*, Winter 1983.

Kessler-Harris, Alice. *Out to Work: A History of Wage-Earning Women in the United States*. New York: Oxford University Press, 1982.

Keyserling, Leon. "The Humphrey-Hawkins Act since Its 1978 Enactment." In David C. Colander, ed., *Solutions to Unemployment*. New York: Harcourt Brace Jovanovich, 1981.

Kilson, Martin. "Black Social Classes and Intergenerational Poverty." *Public Interest*, Summer 1981.

Kinsley, Michael. "Triumph of the Will." *New Republic*, August 22 and 29, 1981.

Kirkland, Richard. "Big Steel Recasts Itself." *Fortune*, April 6, 1981.

Kneese, Allen. "Environmental Policy." In Peter Duignan and Alvin Rabushka, eds., *The United States in the 1980's*. Stanford, Calif.: Hoover Institute, 1980.

530 Bibliography

Kovar, Mary Grace. "Health Status of U.S. Children and Use of Medical Care." *Public Health Reports*, January-February 1982.

——, and Denise J. Meny. *Better Health for Our Children: A National Strategy*, Vol. 3. Washington, D.C.: U.S. Department of Health and Human Services, 1981.

Kramer, Rita. *In Defense of the Family*. New York: Basic Books, 1983.

Kristol, Irving. *Two Cheers for Capitalism*. New York: New American Library, 1979.

Laird, Melvin R. *Energy—A Crisis in Public Policy*. Washington, D.C.: American Enterprise Institute, 1977.

Lasch, Christopher. *Haven in a Heartless World: The Family Beseiged*. New York: Basic Books, 1977.

——. *The Culture of Narcissism*. New York: Warner, 1978.

Laslett, Barbara. "Family Membership, Past and Present." In Arlene S. Skolnick and Jerome H. Skolnick, eds., *Family in Transition*, 4th ed. Boston: Little, Brown, 1983.

Laws, Judith Long. *The Second X: Sex Role and Social Roles*. New York: Elsevier, 1979.

Lebowitz, Ann. "Overview: The Health of Working Women." In Diane Chapman Walsh and Richard H. Egdahl, eds., *Women, Work, and Health*. New York: Springer-Verlag, 1980.

Lein, Laura, and Mary C. Blehar. "Working Couples as Parents." In U.S. Department of Health and Human Services, *Families Today: A Research Sampler on Families and Children*, Vol. 1. Washington, D.C.: Government Printing Office, 1979.

Lekachman, Robert. *Greed Is Not Enough: Reaganomics*. New York: Pantheon, 1982.

Lens, Sidney. "Heavy Lifting." *The Progressive*, January 1982.

Leontieff, Wassily. "The Distribution of Work and Income." *Scientific American*, September 1982a.

——. "What Hope for the Economy?" *New York Review of Books*, August 12, 1982b.

Lerney, L. J., and F. H. Posey. *Comparative Effects of Energy Technologies on Employment*. Sacramento, Calif.: California Energy Commission, 1979.

Levitan, Sar A., and Richard S. Belous. *What's Happening to the American Family*. Baltimore: Johns Hopkins University Press, 1981.

——, and Clifford Johnson. "The Future of Work: Does It Belong to Us or to the Robots?" *Monthly Labor Review*, September 1982.

Lieber, James. "The American Prison: A Tinderbox." *New York Times Magazine*, March 8, 1981.

Lieberson, Stanley. *A Piece of the Pie*. Berkeley: University of California Press, 1981.

Liem, Ramsey, and Paula Rayman. "Health and Social Costs of Unemployment." *American Psychologist*, October 1982.

Liljestrom, Rita. "Integration of Family Policy and Labor Market Policy in Sweden." In Ronnie Steinberg Ratner, ed., *Equal Employment Policy for Women*. Philadelphia: Temple University Press, 1980.

Lindblom, Charles E. *Politics and Markets: The World's Political-Economic Systems*. New York: Basic Books, 1977.

Lipton, Douglas, Robert Martinson, and Judith Wilks. *The Effectiveness of Correctional Treatment*. New York: Praeger, 1975.

Livernash, E. Robert, ed. *Comparable Worth: Issues and Alternatives*. Washington, D.C.: Equal Employment Advisory Council, 1980.

Lloyd, Cynthia, and Beth Niemi. *The Economics of Sex Differentials*. New York: Columbia University Press, 1979.

Loomis, Carol J. "The Madness of Executive Compensation." *Fortune*, July 12, 1982.

Lovins, Amory B., and L. Hunter Lovins. *Energy/War: Breaking the Nuclear Link*. San Francisco: Friends of the Earth, 1980.

Lubar, Robert. "Why Unemployment Will Hang High." *Fortune*, June 14, 1982.

Lucy, William. "Can We Find Good Jobs in a Service Economy?" In C. Stewart Sheppard and Donald C. Carroll, *Working in the 21st Century*. New York: Wiley, 1980.

Lueptow, L. B. "Sex-Typing and Change in the Occupational Choices of High School Seniors." *Sociology of Education*, January 1981.

Luttwak, Edward. "How to Think about Nuclear War." *Commentary*, August 1982.

McAdoo, Harriette P., ed. *Black Families*. Beverly Hills, Calif.: Sage, 1981.

Maccoby, Eleanor, and Carol Jacklin. *The Psychology of Sex Differences*. Stanford, Calif.: Stanford University Press, 1974.

McConnell-Condry, Sandra, and Irving Lazar. "American Values and Social Policy for Children." *Annals of the American Academy of Political and Social Science*, Vol. 461, May 1982.

McFadden, Dave. "Alternate Use Planning." *Plowshare Press*, November-December 1979.

———, and Jim Wake, eds. *The Freeze Economy*. Mountain View, Calif.: Mid-Peninsula Conversion Project, 1983.

MacGraw, Onalee. Prepared statement, U.S. Congress, Senate, Committee on Labor and Human Resources, Hearings on *Work Ethic: Materialism and the American Family*, March 1982.

Magaziner, Ira, and Robert Reich. *Minding America's Business*. New York: Harcourt Brace Jovanovich, 1982.

Manpower Demonstration Research Corporation. *Summary and Findings of the National Supported Work Experiment*. Cambridge, Mass.: Ballinger, 1980.

Marcuse, Herbert. *One-Dimensional Man*. Boston: Beacon, 1964.

Mare, Robert D. "Socioeconomic Effects On Child Mortality in the United States." *American Journal of Public Health*, June 1982.

Marshall, Elliot. "The Breeder: Selling the Unsaleable?" *Science*, May 13, 1983.

Marshall, James, and Donna Funch. "Mental Illness and the Economy: A Critique and Partial Replication." *Journal of Health and Social Behavior*, September 1979.

Martin, Philip L. "Select Commission Suggests Changes in Immigration Policy." *Monthly Labor Review*, February 1982.

Maslow, Jonathan E. "Beer Wars." *Saturday Review*, July 7, 1979.

Masnick, George, and Mary Jo Bane. *The Nation's Families: 1960–1990*. Cambridge, Mass.: Harvard/MIT Joint Center for Urban Studies, 1980.

Meacham, Steve. "It's Not Just a Project, It's an Adventure." *Plowshare Press*, March-April 1983.

Mead, Lawrence M. "Social Programs and Social Obligations." *The Public Interest*, Fall 1982.

Mellor, Earl F., and George D. Stanas. "Usual Weekly Earnings: Another Look at Intergroup Differences and Basic Trends." *Monthly Labor Review*, April 1982.

Melman, Seymour. "Looting the Means of Production." *Plowshare Press*, November-December 1982.

Meltzer, Allan. "Big Government: Democracy's Deadly Creation." Smithkline Forum for a Healthier American Society, October 1980.

Menchik, Paul. "Intergenerational Transmission of Inequality: An Empirical Study of Wealth Mobility." *Economica*, November 1979.

Meyer, Herbert E. "Jobs and Want Ads: A Look Behind the Words." *Fortune*, November 1978.

———. "The Decline of Strikes." *Fortune*, November 2, 1981.

Miller, Brent. Prepared statement, U.S. Congress, Senate, Committee on Labor and Human Resources, Hearings on *Work Ethic: Materialism and the American Family*, March 1982.

Mills, C. Wright. *The Sociological Imagination*. New York: Oxford University Press, 1959.

Moore, Emily C. *Women and Health: United States, 1980*. Washington, D.C.: U.S. Public Health Service, 1980.

Morrison, Ann. "Betting the Barn at Stroh." *Fortune*, May 31, 1982.

Mott, Frank, ed. *Years for Decision: A Longitudinal Study of the Educational, Labor Market, and Family Experience of Young Women*. Columbus, Ohio: Center for Human Resources Research, Ohio State University, 1981.

———, and David Shapiro. "Pregnancy, Motherhood, and Work Activity." In Frank Mott, ed., *Women, Work, and Family*. Lexington, Mass.: Lexington Books, 1978.

Mueller, Willard F. "Conglomerates: A Non-Industry." In Walter Adams, ed., *The Structure of American Industry*, 5th ed. New York: Macmillan, 1977.

Mullen, Joan, et al. *American Prisons and Jails*, Vol. I. Washington, D.C.: National Institute of Justice, 1980.

Muller, Thomas L. "Regional Impacts." In John L. Palmer and Isabel W. Sawhill, eds., *The Reagan Experiment*. Washington, D.C.: The Urban Institute, 1982.

Myrdal, Gunnar. *Objectivity in Social Research*. New York: Pantheon, 1969.

Nathanson, Constance, and Marian Passannante. Johns Hopkins University Research. In *San Francisco Chronicle*, May 18, 1983.

National Academy of Sciences. *Women Scientists in Industry and Government: How Much Progress in the 1970's?* Washington, D.C.: National Academy of Sciences, 1980.

National Center for Education Statistics. "Women Outpaced Men In Faculty and Tenure Increases." *Bulletin*, June 1980.

———. "Does College Pay? Wage Rates Before and After Leaving School." *Bulletin*, November 1982.

National Commission for Employment Policy. *7th Annual Report*. Washington, D.C.: Government Printing Office, 1981.

———. *Hispanics and Jobs: Barriers to Progress*. Washington, D.C.: Government Printing Office, 1982.

National Commission on Employment and Unemployment Statistics. *Counting the Labor Force*. Washington, D.C.: Government Printing Office, 1979.

National Commission on Excellence in Education. *A Nation at Risk: The Imperative for Educational Reform*. Washington, D.C.: Government Printing Office, 1983.

National Research Council. *Women, Work, and Wages: Equal Pay for Jobs of Equal Value*. Washington, D.C.: National Academy Press, 1981.

National Wildlife Federation. "1983 Environmental Quality Index." *National Wildlife*, February-March 1983.

Navarro, Peter. "The Politics of Air Pollution." *Public Interest*, Spring 1980.

Newsweek. "The Battle of the Beers." September 4, 1978.

———. "The Plague of Violent Crime." March 23, 1981.

———. "Defending America." December 20, 1982a.

———. "Jobs: Putting America Back to Work." October 19, 1982b.

———. "Poverty's Bottom Line." April 26, 1982c.

Nordlund, Willis, and R. Thayne Robson. *Energy and Employment*. New York: Praeger, 1980.

Norman, Colin. "Industry Sets Conditions for Funding Clinch River." *Science*, April 1, 1983.

Norwood, Janet L. *The Female-Male Earnings Gap: A Review of Employment and Earnings Issues*. Washington, D.C.: U.S. Bureau of Labor Statistics, September 1982.

Nukazawa, Kazuo. "Now Japan Frets about Taxes and Deficit." *Wall Street Journal*, May 9, 1983.

Office of Management and Budget. *Special Analyses, Budget of the United States Government, Fiscal Year 1984*. Washington, D.C.: Government Printing Office, 1983.

Olsen, Marvin E. "Assessing the Social Impacts of Energy Conservation." In Karen Gentemann, ed., *Social and Political Perspectives on Energy Policy*. New York: Praeger, 1981.

Orsagh, Thomas, and Ann Dryden Witte. "Economic Status and Crime: Implications for Offender Rehabilitation." *Journal of Criminal Law and Criminology*, Fall 1981.

Osborne, David. "Inflation: Who Won and Who Lost." *Harper's*, January 1983.

O'Shea, William. Testimony, U.S. Congress, Senate, Judiciary Committee, Hearings on *Mergers and Economic Concentration*, May 1978.

Osterman, Paul. "Affirmative Action and Opportunity: A Study of Female Quit Rates." *Review of Economics and Statistics*, November 1982.

Ostro, Bart, and Robert Anderson. *Morbidity, Air Pollution, and Health Statistics*. Washington, D.C.: U.S. Environmental Protection Agency, Office of Policy Analysis, 1981.

Oswald, Rudolph. "Why Wages Should Not Be Blamed for the Inflation Problem." *Monthly Labor Review*, April 1982.

O'Toole, James. *Making America Work—Productivity and Responsibility*. New York: Continuum, 1981.

Paglin, Morton. "The Measurement and Trend of Inequality: A Basic Revision." *American Economic Review*, September 1975.

Parenti, Michael. "More Bucks from the Bang." *Progressive*, July 1980.

Pathirane, Leila, and Derek W. Blades. "Defining and Measuring the Public Sector: Some International Comparisons." *Review of Income and Wealth*, September 1982.

Pearce, Diana. "Women in Poverty." In Arthur I. Blaustein, ed., *The American Promise: Equal Justice and Economic Opportunity*. New Brunswick, N.J.: Transaction, 1982.

Pelton, Leroy H. "Child Abuse and Neglect: The Myth of Classlessness." In Leroy H. Pelton, ed., *The Social Context of Child Abuse and Neglect*. New York: Human Sciences, 1981.

Peltz, Rachael A. "The War at Home." Ph.D. diss., The Wright Institute, 1982.

Pertschuk, Michael. Quoted in Mark Green and Robert Massie, eds., *The Big Business Reader*. New York: Pilgrim, 1980.

Peskin, Henry, Paul Portney, and Allen Kneese. *Environmental Regulation and the U.S. Economy*. Baltimore: Johns Hopkins University Press, 1981.

Peskin, Janice. "Measuring Household Production for the GNP." *Family Economics Review*, Summer 1982.

Petersilia, Joan M., Peter W. Greenwood, and Marvin Lavin. *Criminal Careers of Habitual Felons*. Washington, D.C.: U.S. Department of Justice, Law Enforcement Assistance Administration, 1978.

Peterson, Mark, and Harriet Braiker. *Doing Crime: A Survey of California Prison Inmates*. Washington, D.C.: U.S. National Institute of Justice, 1980.

Peterson, William. "Chinese Americans and Japanese Americans." In Thomas Sowell, ed., *Essays and Data on American Ethnic Groups*. Washington, D.C.: The Urban Institute, 1978.

Piven, Frances Fox, and Richard A. Cloward. *Poor Peoples' Movements*. New York: Pantheon, 1977.

Pleck, Joseph H., Graham Staines, and Linda Lang. "Conflicts between Work and Family Life." *Monthly Labor Review*, March 1980.

Podhoretz, Norman. *The Present Danger*. New York: Simon and Schuster, 1980.

Police Foundation. *Newark Foot Patrol Experiment*. Washington, D.C.: Police Foundation, 1981.

Portney, Paul R. "The Macroeconomic Effects of Federal Environmental Legislation." In Henry Peskin, Paul Portney, and Allen Kneese, eds., *Environmental Regulation and the U.S. Economy*. Baltimore: Johns Hopkins University Press, 1981.

President's Advisory Council for Women. *Voices for Women*. Washington, D.C.: Government Printing Office, 1980.

President's Commission on Law Enforcement and Administration of Justice. *The Challenge of Crime in a Free Society*. Washington, D.C.: Government Printing Office, 1967.

Presser, Harriett B., and Wendy Baldwin. "Child Care as a Constraint on Employment." *American Journal of Sociology*, March 1980.

Public Opinion. "Opinion Roundup." January-February 1981.

Queen, Stuart A., and Delbert M. Mann. *Social Pathology*. New York: Crowell, 1925.

Rallings, E. M., and F. Ivan Nye. "Wife-Mother Employment, Family, and Society." In Wesley L. Burr, ed., *Contemporary Theories about the Family*. New York: Free Press, 1979.

Rankin, Joseph H. "The Family Context of Delinquency." *Social Problems*, April 1983.

Ratner, Ronnie S. "The Policy and Problem: Overview of Seven Countries." In Ronnie S. Ratner, ed., *Equal Employment Policy for Women*. Philadelphia: Temple University Press, 1980.

Rayman, Paula, and Barry Bluestone. *The Private and Social Response to Joblessness*, Final Report. Washington, D.C.: National Institute of Mental Health, 1982.

Reagan, Ronald. *America's New Beginning: A Program for Economic Recovery*. Washington, D.C.: Government Printing Office, February 1981.

———. "Address to the Nation." March 23, 1983. Reprinted in (*Bulletin* of the U.S. Department of State), April 1983.

Reich, Michael. *Racial Inequality*. New York: Cambridge University Press, 1981.

Reich, Robert B. "The Next American Frontier." *Atlantic*, March-April 1983.

———, and Ira C. Magaziner. *Minding America's Business*. New York: Harcourt Brace Jovanovich, 1982.

Reimers, Cordelia. "Why Are Hispanic Americans' Incomes So Low?" Cited in *Employment and Training Report of the President, 1983*, pp. 98–99, 1982.

Reubens, Beatrice G. "Review of Foreign Experience." In American Assembly, *Youth Unemployment and Public Policy*. Englewood Cliffs, N.J.: Prentice-Hall, 1980.

Reynolds, Morgan, and Eugene Smolensky. *Public Expenditures, Taxes, and the Distribution of Income*. New York: Academic, 1977.

Rhodes, Steven L., and Paulette Middleton. "Acid Rain: The Complex Challenge." *Environment*, May 1983.

Richardson, Laurel. *The Dynamics of Sex and Gender*. Boston: Houghton Mifflin, 1981.

Richman, Alvin. "Public Attitudes on Military Power, 1981." *Public Opinion*, January 1982.

Rice, Haynes, and LaRah Payne. "Health Issues for the Eighties." In National Urban League, *The State of Black America*. New York: National Urban League, 1981.

Rickover, Hyman. "Advice from Admiral Rickover." *New York Review of Books*, March 18, 1982.

Riegle, Donald. "The Psychological and Social Effects of Unemployment." *American Psychologist*, October 1982.

Riesman, David. *The Lonely Crowd*. New Haven, Conn.: Yale University Press, 1955.

Ripley, Randall, and Grace Franklin. *Private Sector Involvement in Public Employment and Training Programs*. Washington, D.C.: National Commission for Employment Policy, 1981.

Rivlin, Alice. Congressional Testimony. Quoted in *Employment and Training Reporter*, August 8, 1982.

Robinson, Clarence. "Technology Key to Strategic Advances." *Aviation Week and Space Technology*, March 14, 1983.

Rodberg, Leonard. "Energy and Jobs: The Case for CARE." In Ellis Cose, ed., *Energy and Equity: Some Social Concerns*. Washington, D.C.: Joint Center for Political Studies, 1979.

Rosen, Ellen. *Hobson's Choice: Employment and Unemployment among Women Factory Workers in New England*, Ms., Boston College. Cited in *Employment and Training Report of the President, 1983*, pp. 96–97, 1982.

Rosenfield, Carl. "Job Search of the Unemployed, May 1976." *Monthly Labor Review*, November 1977.

Rosenthal, Evelyn R. "Working in Mid-Life." In Ann H. Stromberg and Shirley Harkness, eds., *Women Working*. Palo Alto, Calif.: Mayfield, 1978.

Rossi, Peter, Richard Berk, and Kenneth Lenihan. *Money, Work, and Crime*. New York: Academic, 1980.

Rothschild, Emma. "Reagan and the Real America." *New York Review of Books*, February 5, 1981.

Rowen, Hobart. "Dr. Doom's Advice." (*New York Times* interview with investment expert Henry Kaufman.) *San Francisco Chronicle*, January 6, 1983.

Royston, Michael. "Making Pollution Prevention Pay." *Harvard Business Review*, November-December 1980.

Rumberger, Russell W. *Overeducation in the U.S. Labor Market*. New York: Praeger, 1981.

Rutledge, Gary L., and Susan L. Trevathian. "Pollution Abatement and Control Expenditure, 1972–1980." *Survey of Current Business*, February 1982.

Ruttenberg, Ruth. "Regulation Is the Mother of Invention." *Working Papers*, May-June 1981.

Rytina, Nancy F. "Occupational Segregation and Earnings Differences by Sex." *Monthly Labor Review*, January 1981.

Safilios-Rothschild, Constantina. "Women and Work: Policy Implications and Prospects for the Future." In Ann H. Stromberg and Shirley Harkness, eds., *Women Working.* Palo Alto, Calif.: Mayfield, 1979.

Sawhill, Isabel. Testimony, U.S. Congress, Senate, Committee on Labor and Human Resources, Hearings on *The Coming Decade: American Women and Human Resources Policies and Programs*, Part 1, 1979.

Sawyer, Malcolm. *Income Distribution in OECD Countries.* Paris: Organization for Economic Cooperation and Development, 1978.

Scherer, Frederick M. *Industrial Market Structure and Economic Performance*, 2nd ed. Chicago: Rand McNally, 1980.

Schipper, Lee, and A. J. Lichtenberg. "Efficient Energy and Well-Being: The Swedish Example." *Science*, December 3, 1978.

Schlozman, Kay, and Sidney Verba. "The New Unemployment: Does It Hurt?" *Public Policy*, Summer 1978.

Schnaiberg, Alan. *The Environment: From Surplus to Scarcity.* New York: Oxford University Press, 1980.

Schroeder, Steven A. "National Health Insurance: Always Just Around the Corner?" *American Journal of Public Health*, October 1981.

Sclar, Elliott D. "Community Economic Structure and Individual Well-Being." *International Journal of Health Services*, Winter 1980.

Scott, Bruce R. "Can Industry Survive the Welfare State?" *Harvard Business Review*, September-October 1982.

Shapiro, David, and Timothy J. Carr. "Work Attachment, Investments in Human Capital, and the Earnings of Young Women." In Frank L. Mott, ed., *Women, Work, and Family.* Lexington, Mass.: Lexington Books, 1978.

Shapiro, Sam, et al. "Prospects for Eliminating Racial Differences in Breast Cancer Survival Rates." *American Journal of Public Health*, October 1982.

Shaw, Lois B., ed. *Dual Careers: A Decade of Change in the Lives of Mature Women.* Columbus, Ohio: Center for Human Resources Research, Ohio State University, 1981.

Shelley, Louise I., ed. *Readings in Comparative Criminology.* Carbondale, Ill.: Southern Illinois University Press, 1981.

Shepherd, William G., and Clair Wilcox. *Public Policies toward Business*, 6th ed. Homewood, Ill.: Irwin, 1979.

Sidel, Victor W., and Ruth Sidel. *A Healthy State.* New York: Pantheon, 1977.

Siegfried, John, ed. *The Economics of Firm Size, Market Structure, and Social Performance.* Washington, D.C.: U.S. Federal Trade Commission, 1980.

Sigal, Leon V. "Warming to the Freeze." *Foreign Policy*, Fall 1982.

Skolnick, Jerome H., and Elliott Currie. *Crisis in American Institutions*, 5th ed. Boston: Little, Brown, 1982.

Smeeding, Timothy. "The Antipoverty Effects of In-Kind Transfers." *Journal of Human Resources*, Summer 1977.

Smith, James D. Testimony, U.S. Congress, House, Budget Committee, Hearings, *Data on Distribution of Wealth in the U.S.*, 1977.

————. Prepared statement, U.S. Congress, Joint Economic Committee, Hearings on *The 1982 Joint Economic Report of the President*, February 1982.

Smith, J. W., and Beninger, E. S. "Women's Nonmarket Labor: Dissolution of Marriage and Opportunity Cost." *Journal of Family Issues*, June 1982.

Smith, Ralph E. "The Movement of Women into the Labor Force." In Ralph Smith, ed., *The Subtle Revolution: Women at Work.* Washington, D.C.: The Urban Institute, 1979.

Sorrentino, Constance. "Youth Unemployment: An International Perspective." *Monthly Labor Review*, July 1981.

Sowell, Thomas. "Myths about Minorities." *Commentary*, August 1979.

————. *Markets and Minorities.* New York: Basic Books, 1981.

Stack, Carol B. *All Our Kin.* New York: Harper and Row, 1974.

Starfield, Barbara. "Child Health and Socioeconomic Status." *American Journal of Public Health*, June 1982.

Starr, Paul. *The Social Transformation of American Medicine*. New York: Basic Books, 1982.

Stegner, Wallace. "Regress and Pillage." *New Republic*, August 31, 1982.

Stein, Herbert. "Eight Questions for Conservatives." *Fortune*, January 11, 1982a.

———. "How World War III Was Lost." *Wall Street Journal*, December 3, 1982b.

Steinberg, Stephen. *The Ethnic Myth: Race, Ethnicity, and Class in America*. Boston: Atheneum, 1980.

Steinfels, Peter. *The Neoconservatives*. New York: Simon and Schuster, 1980.

Stellman, Jeanne. *Women's Work, Women's Health*. New York: Pantheon, 1979.

Steyer, Robert. "Deals of the Year." *Fortune*, January 24, 1983.

Stobaugh, Robert, and Daniel Yergin. *Energy Future*, rev. ed. New York: Vintage, 1982.

Straus, Murray A. "A Sociological Perspective on the Causes of Family Violence." In Maurice R. Green, ed., *Violence and the Family*. Boulder, Colo.: Westview, 1980.

———, Richard J. Gelles, and Suzanne Steinmetz. *Behind Closed Doors: Violence in the American Family*. New York: Doubleday, 1980.

Sutherland, Edwin. *White-Collar Crime*. New York: Holt, 1949.

Taeuber, Karl. "Racial Residential Segregation, 28 Cities, 1970–1980." Madison, Wis.: Center for Demography and Ecology, University of Wisconsin, 1983.

Thompson, E. "Hidden Bias in Utility Rates: Soaring Prices Hit Poor and Minorities the Hardest." *Power Line*, November 1980.

Thompson, James W., et al. *Employment and Crime: A Review of Theories and Research*. Washington, D.C.: Government Printing Office, 1981.

Thomson, Randall J., and Matthew T. Zingraff. "Detecting Sentencing Disparity: Some Problems and Evidence." *American Journal of Sociology*, January 1981.

Thornberry, Terence. "Sentencing Disparities in the Juvenile Justice System." *Journal of Criminal Law and Criminology*, Summer 1979.

———. *Overcrowding in American Prisons*. Athens, Ga.: University of Georgia, 1982.

Thornton, James, Richard Agnello, and Charles Lind. "Poverty and Economic Growth: Trickle Down Peters Out." *Economic Inquiry*, July 1978.

Thurow, Lester. *The Zero-Sum Society*. New York: Penguin, 1980.

———. "Death by a Thousand Cuts." *New York Review of Books*, December 17, 1981a.

———. "How to Wreck the Economy." *New York Review of Books*, May 14, 1981b.

———. "The Agenda after Reagan: The Economy." *New Republic*, March 31, 1982.

Tietze, Christopher. "Abortion Alarms." *American Journal of Public Health*, June 1982.

Time. "New Thrust in Antitrust." May 21, 1979.

———. "Can Capitalism Survive?" April 21, 1980.

Titmuss, Richard M. *Commitment to Welfare*. London: Allen and Unwin, 1968.

Tittle, Charles R. *Sanctions and Social Deviance: The Question of Deterrence*. New York: Praeger, 1980.

Tobias, Sheila, et al. *What Kinds of Guns Are they Buying for Your Butter?* New York: Morrow, 1982.

Tropin, Leonard. "New Prison Construction: Are There Alternatives?" Washington, D.C.: Conference on Alternative State and Local Policies, January-February 1983.

Tsongas, Paul. *The Road from Here: Liberalism and Realities in the 1980's*. New York: Knopf, 1981.

Tucker, William. *Progress and Privilege: America in the Age of Environmentalism*. New York: Doubleday, 1982.

Union of Concerned Scientists. *Energy Strategies: Toward a Solar Future*. Cambridge, Mass.: Ballinger, 1981.

United Nations. *The Economic Role of Women in the ECE Region*. New York: U.N. Economic Commission for Europe, 1980.

———. *Transnational Corporations in the Auto Industry*. New York: U.N. Centre on Transnational Corporations, 1983.

U.S. Bureau of the Census. *Concentration Ratios in Manufacturing, 1977 Census of Manufacturers.* Washington, D.C.: Government Printing Office, 1981.

———. *Changing Family Composition and Income Differentials.* Washington, D.C.: Government Printing Office, 1982a.

———. "Trends in Child Care Arrangements of Working Mothers." *Current Population Reports*, Series P-23, No. 117. Washington, D.C., 1982b.

———. "Characteristics of the Population Below the Poverty Level, 1981." *Current Population Reports*, Series P-60, No. 138. Washington, D.C., April 1983a.

———. "Lifetime Earnings Estimates for Men and Women in the United States: 1979." *Current Population Reports*, Series P-60, No. 139. Washington, D.C., 1983b.

———. "Money Income of Families and Households, 1981." *Current Population Reports*, Series P-60, No. 137. Washington, D.C., April 1983c.

U.S. Bureau of Labor Statistics. *Employment and Earnings,* July 1981.

———. *Linking Employment Problems to Economic Status*, Bulletin 2123. Washington, D.C.: Bureau of Labor Statistics, 1982a.

———. *One in Five Persons in Labor Force Experienced Some Unemployment in 1981.* Bulletin. Washington, D.C.: Bureau of Labor Statistics, July 20, 1982b.

U.S. Bureau of Justice Statistics. *Survey of Prisons and Prisoners, 1979.* Washington, D.C.: Bureau of Justice Statistics, January 1982.

———. *Prisoners and Alcohol.* Washington, D.C.: Bureau of Justice Statistics, 1983a.

———. *Prisoners and Drugs.* Washington, D.C.: Bureau of Justice Statistics, 1983b.

U.S. Commission on Civil Rights. *Social Indicators of Equality for Minorities and Women.* Washington, D.C.: Government Printing Office, 1978.

———. *Success of Asian-Americans: Fact or Fiction?* Washington, D.C.: Government Printing Office, 1980a.

———. *Youth Unemployment.* Washington, D.C.: Government Printing Office, 1980b.

———. *Child Care and Equal Opportunity for Women.* Washington, D.C.: Government Printing Office, 1981.

———. *Confronting Racial Isolation in Miami.* Washington, D.C.: Government Printing Office, 1982a.

———. *Unemployment and Underemployment among Blacks, Hispanics, and Women.* Washington, D.C.: Government Printing Office, 1982b.

———. *A Growing Crisis: Disadvantaged Women and Their Children.* Washington, D.C.: Government Printing Office, 1983.

U.S. Commission on Civil Rights, Illinois Advisory Committee. *Shutdown: Economic Dislocation and Equal Opportunity.* Washington, D.C.: Government Printing Office, 1981.

U.S. Congress, House Committee on Energy and Commerce, Subcommittee on Health and the Environment. *Impact of Budget Cuts on Children.* Washington, D.C.: Government Printing Office, March 1982.

U.S. Congress, House, Committee on Small Business. *Future of Small Business in America.* Washington, D.C.: Government Printing Office, August 1979.

U.S. Congress, Joint Economic Committee. *Joint Economic Report.* Washington, D.C.: Government Printing Office, January 1982a.

———. *Oil Price Decontrol and the Poor: A Social Policy Failure.* Washington, D.C.: Government Printing Office, 1982b.

U.S. Congress, Select Commission on Immigration and Refugee Policy. *U.S. Immigration Policy and the National Interest.* Washington, D.C.: Government Printing Office, 1981.

U.S. Congress, Senate, Committee on Agriculture. *Status of the Family Farm.* Washington, D.C.: Government Printing Office, 1979.

U.S. Congress, Senate, Committee on Governmental Affairs. *Interlocking Directorates among the Major U.S. Corporations.* Washington, D.C.: Government Printing Office, 1978.

U.S. Congressional Budget Office. *Federal Credit Activities: An Analysis of the President's Credit Budget for 1981.* Washington, D.C.: Government Printing Office, February 1980.

————. *CETA Training Programs: Do They Work for Adults?* Washington, D.C.: Government Printing Office, 1982a.

————. *Dislocated Workers: Issues and Federal Options.* Washington, D.C.: Government Printing Office, July 1982b.

————. *An Analysis of the President's Budgetary Proposals for Fiscal Year 1984.* Washington, D.C.: Government Printing Office, 1983a.

————. *Defense Spending and the Economy.* Washington, D.C.: Government Printing Office, 1983b.

U.S. Department of Defense. *Foreign Military Sales, Foreign Military Construction Sales, and Military Assistance as of September 1982.* Washington, D.C.: Government Printing Office, 1983.

U.S. Department of Health and Human Services. *Health—United States, 1982.* Washington, D.C.: Government Printing Office, December 1982a.

————. *National Study of the Incidence and Severity of Child Abuse and Neglect.* Executive Summary. Washington, D.C.: National Center on Child Abuse and Neglect, 1982b.

U.S. Department of Housing and Urban Development. *The President's National Urban Policy Report, 1980.* Washington, D.C.: Government Printing Office, 1980.

U.S. Department of Justice. *Attorney General's Task Force Report on Violent Crime.* Washington, D.C.: Government Printing Office, 1981.

U.S. Department of Labor. *Interim Report to Congress on Occupational Diseases.* Washington, D.C.: Government Printing Office, June 1980.

U.S. Department of Labor, Women's Bureau. *Employment Goals of the World Plan of Action: Developments and Issues in the United States.* Washington, D.C.: Government Printing Office, 1980.

————. *20 Facts on Women Workers.* Washington, D.C.: Government Printing Office, 1982.

U.S. Environmental Protection Agency. *Damages and Threats Caused by Hazardous Material Sites.* Washington, D.C.: Environmental Protection Agency, 1980.

U.S. General Accounting Office. *Income Maintenance Experiments.* Washington, D.C.: Government Printing Office, 1981.

————. *Advances in Automation Prompt Concern over Increased U.S. Unemployment.* Washington, D.C.: Government Printing Office, 1982a.

————. *CETA Programs for Disadvantaged Adults: What Do We Know about Their Enrolees, Services, and Effectiveness?* Washington, D.C.: Government Printing Office, 1982b.

————. *Implementation of the Phase-out of CETA Public Service Jobs.* Washington, D.C.: Government Printing Office, 1982c.

————. *Labor Market Problems of Teenagers.* Washington, D.C.: Government Printing Office, 1982d.

U.S. National Center for Health Statistics. *Advance Report of Final Natality Statistics 1979.* Washington, D.C.: U.S. National Center for Health Statistics, 1981a.

————. *Health—United States, 1981.* Washington, D.C.: U.S. National Center for Health Statistics, 1981b.

U.S. News and World Report. "How to Get the Country Moving Again: Advice from Six Nobel Prize Economists." January 31, 1983.

U.S. Office of Management and Budget. *Special Analyses, Budget of the United States Government, Fiscal Year 1984.* Washington, D.C.: Government Printing Office, 1983.

Urquhart, Michael, and Marilyn A. Hewson. "Unemployment Continued to Rise in 1982 as Recession Deepened." *Monthly Labor Review*, February 1983.

Van den Haag, Ernest. "Could Successful Rehabilitation Reduce the Crime Rate?" *Journal of Criminal Law and Criminology*, Fall 1982.

Vedder, Richard K. *Robotics and the Economy.* Washington, D.C.: Government Printing Office, March 1982.

Vennema, Alje. "The Status of Tuberculosis Control in New York City." *Public Health Reports*, March-April 1982.

Venture. Magazine advertisement in *Mother Jones*, September-October, 1980, p. 54.

Vera Institute of Justice. *Felony Arrests: Their Prosecution and Disposition in New York City's Courts.* New York: Longman, 1981.

Vernon, Raymond. "Gone Are the Cash Cows of Yesteryear." *Harvard Business Review*, November-December 1980.

Vickery, Claire. "Women's Economic Contribution to the Family." In Ralph Smith, ed., *The Subtle Revolution.* Washington, D.C.: The Urban Institute, 1979.

Vigderhous, Gideon, and Gideon Fishman. "The Impact of Unemployment and Familial Integration on Changing Suicide Rates in the USA." *Social Psychiatry*, Spring 1978.

Waldman, Jed M., et al. "Chemical Composition of Acid Fog." *Science*, November 12, 1982.

Wallace, Michael, and Arne L. Kalleberg. "Industrial Transformation and the Decline of Craft: The Decomposition of Skill in the Printing Industry." *American Sociological Review*, June 1982.

Waller, Willard. "Social Problems and the Mores." *American Sociological Review*, December 1936.

Wallerstein, Judith, and Joan Kelly. *Surviving the Breakup.* New York: Basic Books, 1980.

Walzer, Michael. "The Agenda after Reagan: The Community." *New Republic*, March 31, 1982.

Wanniski, Jude. *The Way the World Works.* New York: Simon and Schuster, 1979.

Ward, Barbara. *Progress for a Small Planet.* New York: Norton, 1979.

Ward, Morris A. "The Clean Air Act Controversy: Congress Confronts the Issues." *Environment*, July-August 1981.

Weichert, Barbara. "Health Care Expenditures." In U.S. Department of Health and Human Services, *Health—U.S., 1981.* Washington, D.C.: Government Printing Office, 1981.

Weinberger, Caspar. Quoted in Center for Defense Information, "The Need for a Level Military Budget." *Defense Monitor*, 1983.

Weinraub, Bernard. "Moynihan Opposes Reagan's Plan to Shift Aid for Children to States." *New York Times*, March 7, 1981.

Westcott, Diane Nilsen. "Blacks in the 1970's: Did They Scale the Job Ladder?" *Monthly Labor Review*, June 1982.

Westergaard, J. H. "Sociology: The Myth of Classlessness." In Robin Blackburn, ed., *Ideology in Social Science.* New York: Vintage, 1973.

Whelan, Elizabeth M. "Chemicals and Cancerphobia." *Society*, March-April 1981.

White, Lynn K., and David B. Brinkerhoff. "The Sexual Division of Labor: Evidence from Childhood." *Social Forces*, September 1981.

Wildavsky, Aaron. "Richer Is Safer." *The Public Interest*, Winter 1980.

Wilensky, Gail. "Government and the Financing of Health Care." *American Economic Review*, May 1982.

Will, George. "In Defense of the Welfare State." *New Republic*, May 9, 1983.

Williams, Walter. "The State Against Blacks." In Manhattan Institute for Policy Research, *Manhattan Report on Economic Policy.* New York: Manhattan Institute for Policy Research, November 1982.

Williamson, Jeffrey, and Peter Lindert. "Long-Term Trends in American Wealth Inequality." In James D. Smith, ed., *Modeling the Distribution and Intergenerational Transmission of Wealth.* Chicago: University of Chicago Press, 1980.

Wilson, James Q. *Thinking about Crime.* New York: Basic Books, 1975.

Wirtz, Willard. Testimony. In U.S. Congress, Senate, Committee on Labor and Human Resources, Hearings on *The Coming Decade: American Women and Human Resources Programs*, 1979.

Witt, Matt, and Steve Early. "The Worker as Safety Inspector." *Working Papers*, July-August 1981.

Wohl, Lisa Cronin. "Can You Protect Your Family from the Family Protection Act?" *Ms.*, April 1981.

Wolfe, Alan. *America's Impasse.* New York: Pantheon, 1981.

Wolfgang, Marvin. Testimony, U.S. Congress, Senate, Committee on the Judiciary, Hearings on *Violent Juvenile Crime*, 1981.

——, Robert Figlio, and Thorsten Sellin. *Delinquency in a Birth Cohort*. Chicago: University of Chicago Press, 1972.

Women's International League for Peace and Freedom. *Your Tax Dollars at Work*. Washington, D.C.: Women's International League for Peace and Freedom, 1983.

Working Women. *In Defense of Affirmative Action: Taking the Profit Out of Discrimination*. Cleveland: Working Women, June 1981.

Wrigley, Julia. "A Message of Marginality: Black Youth, Alienation, and Unemployment." In National Society for the Study of Education, *Education and Work*, 81st yearbook. Chicago: University of Chicago Press, 1982.

Yeager, Matthew. "Unemployment and Imprisonment." *Journal of Criminal Law and Criminology*, Winter 1979.

Yergin, Daniel. "The Agenda after Reagan: Energy." *The New Republic*, March 31, 1982.

Yudken, Joel, and Andrew Goldenkranz. "There's More than One Way to Run a Factory." *Plowshare Press*, March-April 1983.

Zacharias, Jerrold, George Rathjens, and Myles Gordon. "The Arms Race." *Bulletin of the Atomic Scientists*, January 1983.

Zimbalist, Andrew, ed. *Studies in the Labor Process*. New York: Monthly Review Press, 1979.

Zwerdling, Daniel. *Workplace Democracy*. New York: Harper and Row, 1980.

Name Index

Subject Index

Canada, health care in,
345–346
Canal system, 50
Cancer, 327
  environment and, 351
  groundwater contamination
    and, 395
  in laundry workers, 348
  lung cancer, *see* Lung cancer
  in minorities, 342
  mortality rates, 330
  occupational illness, 351–355
Capacity utilization rate, 64
Capital
  defined, 96
  gains, 101, 136–137
  intensive, defined, 96
  shortage of, 86–88
CAT scanners, 340
Catalyst, government as,
  514–516
Center for Defense
  Information, 480
Cerebrovascular disease. *See*
  Stroke
Child abuse
  death of child, 269
  Family Protection Act and,
    255
  gender inequality and,
    270–273
  poverty and, 268–269
  rate of, 267
  unemployment and, 79
Child care, 208, 262–265
  in foreign countries,
    263–264
Childbirth, 348–349
Childhood Immunization
  program, 359
Children
  divorce affecting, 251
  housework by, 260
  illegitimate, *see* Illegitimate
    children
  infant mortality, *see* Infant
    mortality
  mortality rates, 328, 329, 334
  poverty and, 115
  sex roles, 209

  and women's work
    commitment, 206–207
  see also Child abuse;
    Teenagers
Children's Defense Fund, 342
Chock-Full-O-Nuts, 32
Chrysler Corporation, 51, 52
  XM-1 tank, 477
Cirrhosis of the liver, 327
Citicorp, 229
Cities
  air quality chart, 385
  ghettos, 2
  military spending in,
    465–467
  poverty in, 112–115
Citizens for Tax Justice, 86
Civil Rights Act, 10, 143
Civil rights movement, 2
Class and race, 153–156
Clean Air Act, 361
Clean Water Act, 261
Clinch River reactor, 370–371
Coal, 369
  acid rain and, 388–389
Coal Mine Safety Act, 95
College education
  and jobs, 317–318
  women, 202–203
Community Health Centers,
  359
Compensation per
  employee-hour, 89
Competition
  defined, 96
  displaced workers, 295
  economy and international
    competition, 68–70
  and price leadership, 91
  private enterprise and, 53–54
Comprehensive Employment
  and Training Act (CETA),
  189
Concentration
  beer wars, 30–32
  defined, 96
  market concentration, *see*
    Market concentration
Conglomerate corporations, 33,
  36–37

  capital shortages, 88
  defined, 96
  and labor, 49
  mergers, 33
Congress and economic
  reconstruction, 514–517
Conservation
  as energy source, 376–379
  and jobs, 383
Conservation Foundation,
  405–406
Constant dollars, 71
  defined, 96
Consumer price index (CPI),
  73
  defined, 96
  on wages, 90
Coors beer, 30
Corporations
  capital shortages, 86–88
  concentration of power,
    25–26
  conglomerates, *see*
    Conglomerate
    corporations
  crime by, 442
  giant corporations, 25
  interlocking directorate, 37
  network, 37–38
  Top 10, chart of, 27
Cost of living, 72–73
Cost overruns in military, 475,
  480–481
Council on Economic Priorities,
  354
Courts and crime, 421–431
Credits
  for disadvantaged workers,
    319
  as welfare system, 137–140
Crime, 408–449
  bias in crime data, 437, 440
  courts and, 421–431
  determination of rate,
    410–413
  deterrence, 425–427
  family patterns and, 446–447
  in foreign countries, 435, 436
  and future policy, 447–448
  hidden crime, 440

homicide, *see* Homicide
incapacitation effect,
    427–431
increases in, 410–416
minorities and, 436–441
police, *see* Police
poverty and, 434–441
recent evidence on, 434–447
serious crime index, 414
unemployment and, 79,
    442–446
victims, *see* Victims of crimes
white collar crime, 442–445
Current dollars, 71

Death
    by child abuse, 269
    childhood death, 328, 329,
        334
    mortality rates, *see* Mortality
        rates
Decentralizing economic
    planning, 519
Decontrol of oil and gas,
    366–367
Defense. *See* Military
Defense Department contracts,
    473
Deficits, 82–84
    defined, 96
Deindustrialization, 64–65,
    294–296, 315
Demand-pull inflation,
    471–472
Democratization of
    information, 519
Demography
    and distribution of income,
        104
    and unemployment, 303–304
Denuclearization, 374, 376
Dependency ratio, 130
Depression
    defined, 96
    see also Great Depression
Deterrence from crime,
    425–427
Diabetes
    in poor persons, 333
    risk table, 335

in women, 345
Direct interlock, 37
Direct subsidies, 51, 53
Disadvantaged workers
    and minimum wage, 303
    private sector hiring, 319
Discomfort index, 67
Discouraged workers, 282–283,
    288
Discretionary income, 73
Discrimination. *See* Minorities;
    Women
Disincentives to work, 91
Displaced workers, 294–296
Disposable income, 71, 97
Distribution of income,
    101–107
    methods of measuring,
        102–103
Diswelfare state, 517
DIVAD, 477
Divorce, 242–245
    crime and, 446
    and economics of family,
        252–254
    impact of, 250–251
    rise of, 237
Domestic violence, 266–273
Downward mobility
    of minorities, 157
    of women, 220
DuPont chemical company, 354
Dual-earner families, 72
    need to work, 211

Earnings. *See* Wages
Economic concentration index,
    26–35
Economic Recovery Program,
    86, 499
    unemployment and, 284
Economy
    causes of decline, 80–95
    concentration, 25–26
    glossary of vocabulary, 96–97
    growth of, 59–60
    inequality, 100–142
    laissez-faire principles, 7
    prospects of, 4
    reconstruction of, 514–517

reprivatization and, 499–500
social impoverishment,
    269–270
and violence in family,
    268–269
Education
    and children's health, 334
    civilian labor force and, 321
    college, *see* College education
    of displaced workers, 294
    jobs and, 316–319
    of minority workers,
        170–171
    race and labor market, 320
    schools, *see* Schools
    of women, 202–205
Employment
    automation, effect of,
        310–314
    and education, 316–319
    energy and, 381–384
    environmental control and,
        402–404
    future for jobs, 315–321
    government, *see* Government
        employment
    military spending and,
        459–464
    minorities, 161–181
    public enterprises, 47
    public investment for,
        510–511
    in recession, 65
    women, *see* Women
    working versus, 284
    see also Labor;
        Underemployment;
        Unemployment
Employment-population ratio
    (EPR), 291–292
Energy, 361–384
    alternative sources, 376–381
    coal, *see* Coal
    conservation, *see*
        Conservation
    decontrol of oil and gas,
        366–367
    domestic oil reserves, 366
    foreign countries, use in,
        380–382

median family income, 183
in middle class, 156–157
minimum wage and, 302
occupational distributions of blacks, 176–177
political representation, 153
poverty, 149–152
progress and, 152–157
in South, 148
statistics on, 145
single-parent families, 247
teenage unemployment, 291–292
terminology of race, 145
underemployment, 293
unemployment, 162–166, 291–292
wages, 166–172
and welfare state, 188–190
Mixed economy, 39–40
defined, 97
Monopoly, 39
defined, 97
Morgan Guaranty Trust, 38
Mortality rates, 327
in childbirth, 348–349
of children, 328, 329, 334
infants, *see* Infant mortality
for males, 345–346
trends in, 328, 329
for women, 345
Multinational corporation, 97
Murder. *See* Homicide
MX missile, 482

Narcotics crime, 431
National Aeronautics and Space Administration (NASA), 473–474
National Crime Survey, 412
National health system, 344–346
National security. *See* Military
Native Americans, 186–187
Natural gas, 366
Necessities
cost of, 73
minimum adequacy budget, 119
New Frontier program, 10

New Mexico, Native Americans in, 186–187
New York City
military spending and, 467
tuberculosis in, 357
Nonrenewable energy sources, 365–366
Nuclear energy, 8, 369–376
breeder reactors, 370–371
costs of, 371–372
jobs and, 382
number of power plants, 375
risk estimates, 372–373
Nuclear freeze, 481–482
Nuclear family, 247
Nuclear weapons
balance of, 484–485
scaling down of, 481–482
Nursing homes, 338

Occupational crime, 442
Occupational illness, 351–355
Occupational Safety and Health Act (OSHA), 10
inspections under, 354
standards under, 354–356
Occupational segregation, 212
Office buildings, 377
Older people
distribution of income, 103
nursing homes for, 338
welfare spending, 130
OPEC, 4, 9
Overeducation, 318–319

Pabst Beer, 30
Pain index, 464–465
Paper entrepreneurship, 499
Parent abuse, 267
Parent insurance, 265
Part time work and women, 208
Particulate matter, 399
Passive deficit, 84
Permissiveness, 238–239
Philip Morris Company, 31
Photovoltaic cells, 380
Pine Ridge Reservation, 187
Planning sector, 39

Police, 431–433
determining crime rate, 410–411
Poliomyelitis, 326
Pollutant Standards Index, 386–387
Pollution. *See* Environment
Population, 42
Posttransfer poverty, 115–116, 119
Postwar period
business in, 4
women in labor force, 195
workplace in, 279–280
Poverty
and child abuse, 268–269
crime and, 434–441
diabetes and, 333
energy use and, 367–368
feminization of, 193, 222
geography of, 116
health care and, 332–338
inner-city poverty, 151
and minorities, 149–152
Native Americans, 186–187
persistence of, 112–121
redrawing line, 118–121
trends in, 113
women and, 221–227
see also Welfare
Pregnancy, 348–349
abortions, 348–350
black women, 343
Prescriptions for women, 347
Pretransfer poverty, 115–116, 119
Price-Anderson Act, 370
Price fixing, 90
Price leadership, 90–91
Primary sector, 39
Prisons, 421–431
characteristics of inmates, 438–439
crowding of, 422–423
ex-inmates, programs for, 441
Private enterprise, 23–24
dimensions of, 24–31
externalities, 54
government support, 50–54

Date Due